Discover Digital Libraries
Theory and Practice

Discover Digital Libraries
Theory and Practice

Iris Xie, PhD
University of Wisconsin-Milwaukee, Milwaukee, WI, United States

Krystyna K. Matusiak, PhD
University of Denver, Denver, CO, United States

AMSTERDAM • BOSTON • HEIDELBERG • LONDON
NEW YORK • OXFORD • PARIS • SAN DIEGO
SAN FRANCISCO • SINGAPORE • SYDNEY • TOKYO

ELSEVIER

Elsevier
Radarweg 29, PO Box 211, 1000 AE Amsterdam, Netherlands
The Boulevard, Langford Lane, Kidlington, Oxford OX5 1GB, United Kingdom
50 Hampshire Street, 5th Floor, Cambridge, MA 02139, United States

Library of Congress Cataloging-in-Publication Data
A catalog record for this book is available from the Library of Congress

British Library Cataloguing-in-Publication Data
A catalogue record for this book is available from the British Library

ISBN: 978-0-12-417112-1

For information on all Elsevier publications
visit our website at https://www.elsevier.com/

Working together
to grow libraries in
developing countries

www.elsevier.com • www.bookaid.org

Publisher: Todd Green
Editorial Project Manager: Amy Invernizzi
Production Project Manager: Mohanambal Natarajan
Designer: Greg Harris

Typeset by Thomson Digital

Contents

Biography

Dr. Xie is a Professor in the School of Information Studies at the University of Wisconsin-Milwaukee. She has been actively involved in the teaching and research of digital library design and evaluation for about 15 years. Her research interests and expertise focus on digital libraries, interactive information retrieval, human-computer interaction, as well as user needs and user studies. She has received several research grants from research grant programs for the study of digital libraries. She is the principal investigator for the Institute for Museum and Library Services National Leadership Grants "Creating Digital Library Design Guidelines on Accessibility, Usability and Utility for Blind and Visually Impaired Users" and "Designing Interactive Help Mechanisms for Novice Users of Digital Libraries". She is also the principal investigator for the Online Computer Library Center/the Association for Library and Information Science Education grant "Universal Accessibility of Digital Libraries: Design of Help Mechanisms for Blind Users." In addition, she is one of the senior personnel on the National Science Foundation Grant "The Internet Research Ethics Digital Library, Interactive Resource Center and Advisory Center." Her research projects consist of the identification of types of sighted users and blind users' help-seeking situations in interacting with digital libraries as well as implications for interface design, digital library evaluation criteria and measures from different stakeholders of digital libraries, and social media applications in digital libraries. She has a strong publishing record in the field of library and information science. This book project is a natural progression in the active focus of Dr. Xie's research, as she has conducted a series of highly cited studies on digital libraries, published numerous papers in top-ranking journals, and presented at several national and international conferences. Her book *Interactive Information Retrieval in Digital Environments* was published in 2008, and the subject of digital libraries is one of the main topics covered in the book.

Dr. Matusiak is an Assistant Professor in the Library & Information Science Program at the University of Denver. Her research interests focus on the digitization of cultural heritage materials, indexing and retrieval of digital images, information behavior, use of digital libraries, and research methods. She combines practical experience in digitization and digital collections with research interests in use and evaluation of digital libraries. She has been involved in the digitization of cultural heritage materials since 2001. Prior to accepting her position at the University of Denver, she worked as a Digital Collections Librarian at the University of Wisconsin-Milwaukee where she planned and designed over 20 distinct digital collections. She served as a coinvestigator of the digitization project, funded by the National Endowment for Humanities, "Saving and Sharing the American Geographical Society Library's Historic Nitrate Negative Images." She also served as a digitization consultant for projects funded by the Endangered Archive Programme at the British Library and assisted digital library projects at the Press Institute of Mongolia in Ulan Baatar, Mongolia and the Al-Aqsa Mosque Library in East Jerusalem. Her research projects include studies of information seeking behavior in digital collections, use of image and multimedia resources, and user interaction with large-scale digital libraries. She has published a number of articles on those topics and presented at national and international conferences. Dr. Matusiak contributes to this book her expertise in digitization, audiovisual materials, metadata, digital preservation, digital library management systems as well as her practical knowledge in building and managing digital collections.

Foreword

The time is close at hand when any student, in any part of the world, will be able to sit with his projector in his own study at his or her own convenience to examine any book, any document, in an exact replica

H.G. Wells, 1938. (p. 77).

The above quote from H. G. Wells, which also appears in the first chapter of the book, is appropriate because it foresees digital libraries, even without mentioning them by name. In addition, in 2016, when this book was published, we celebrate 150 years since Wells' birth and mourn 70 years since his death.

This book identifies the challenges, current trends, and future directions of digital library development, use, and evaluation. The coverage of the book is comprehensive, as can be easily determined by each chapter and the accompanying bibliographies.

This Foreword has a hazier aim—I am trying to examine the complex relations and connections between research and practice in the area of digital libraries:

- *Does digital library research inform digital library practice? And vice versa?*
- *To what extents are they connected now, nearly two decades after they began?*

"Digital library research" refers to various research projects funded historically by the National Science Foundation (NSF) in the United States and by European Union programs in Europe, as well as research reports presented at various digital library conferences to this day. "Digital library practice" includes working digital libraries found on the Web, reflecting any practical, operational library-oriented achievements. "Inform" refers here to a visible connection based on evidence either (1) in the sites of research projects and/or in the research literature that points to any consideration of or link to an operational digital library project, or (2) in digital library practice showing any consideration of or link to research projects found in the literature. In other words, concentration here is solely on visible or "surface" evidence.

In many fields, research and practice have a complex relationship or connection. In an ideal paradigm, (some) research, particularly toward the applied end, informs and even transforms practice and (some) practice informs research, especially in the selection of problems. In an ideal world, research and practice converge. However, in reality, it rarely works exactly that way. The links between research and practice are neither always linear nor are they often easy to discern. Their connections may be serendipitous or vague, even weak or nonexistent. Time and social context play a significant role as well. Transfer of ideas is complex. There are further considerations. Research often raises expectations, and, by definition, it neither promises nor produces predictable outcomes. Practice may advance, and in many areas has done so, without direct input of research. The area of digital libraries is not an exception to any of these points.

Historically, in the United States, the original agenda for digital library research was set and conducted through the multiagency Digital Library Initiatives (DLIs) lead by the National Science Foundation (NSF). DLI 1 (1994–98) involved six awards and $25 million; DLI 2 (1999–2003) involved 34 awards and $48 million (Griffin, 2005). It may be of interest to note that the origins of Google were acknowledged as being supported by a DLI 1 grant at Stanford University (National Science Foundation, 2004).

While the agendas for both DLIs were relatively broad, their base rested firmly in technology. Levy (2000) describes this early conclusion regarding DLI projects as reported in the research literature or at various library conferences:

> "The current digital library agenda has largely been set by the computer science community, and clearly bears the imprint of this community's interests and vision. But there are other constituencies whose voices need to be heard."

That indeed there are different viewpoints about digital libraries was also recognized half a decade later by Arms (2005). Both conclusions still hold today.

Since the end of DLI 2, NSF no longer supports research in digital libraries. All federal US support is now channelled through the Institute of Museum and Library Services (IMLS), established by law in 1996 combining the Institute of Museum Services and the Library Program Office from Department of Education. The very name (including museums) shows a shift and broadening in the coverage of the area of support. The majority of grants are for pragmatic operational projects—some involving digital libraries—as is clearly visible in the enumeration of their past grants (https://www.imls.gov/grants/awarded-grants).

Again historically, in Europe, digital library research was supported by the European Union in two programs: DELOS: Network of Excellence on Digital Libraries (2004–07, at a cost of 950,000 EUR) and DL.org: Digital Library Interoperability, Best Practices and Modelling Foundations (2008–11, at a cost of 1,200,000 EUR). Both projects involved a large number of participants and workshops across Europe. Crowning achievements for both projects were two landmark publications: The DELOS Manifesto (Candela et al., 2007) and The Digital Library Reference Model (DL.org, 2010). The Manifesto lays out basic definitions and structure of digital libraries. The Reference Model provides detailed descriptions of concepts involved, together with models of various applications and domains of digital libraries. Both documents consider digital libraries as "the meeting point of many disciplines and fields, including data management, information retrieval, library sciences, document management, information systems, the web, image processing, artificial intelligence, human-computer interaction, and digital curation." (Candela et al., 2007).

The US DLI projects were primarily oriented toward development of applications—testbed/prototype building. The European digital libraries projects were primarily oriented toward conceptual definitions and Europe-wide cooperation among researchers. However, government support for digital library research has ended in both the US and European Union.

Digital library practice is institutionally/organizationally based and oriented toward a given community, pragmatic development, and practical operations. As expected, the aims are toward the pragmatic problems at hand. Typical examples—rather than exhaustive enumerations—involve the following:

- Digitizing and providing access to specialized and historic materials by the Library of Congress through the *American Memory Project of the Library of Congress* (launched in 1990, first on CD-ROM and then in 1996 on the Web) (https://memory.loc.gov/ammem/index.html).
- Incorporating digital dimensions and providing access to electronic collections and resources, with a variety of associated services (ie, creating and managing hybrid libraries—incorporating both traditional and digital materials and services) by thousands of academic, research, public,

and special libraries, such as the *University of California Berkeley Library* (http://www.lib.
berkeley.edu/node).
- Building digital libraries by professional and other organizations, such as the subscription-based
  Association for Computing Machinery (ACM) *ACM Digital Library* (launched in 1998) (http://
  dl.acm.org/).
- Developing digital collections in specific domains, such as the *Perseus Digital Library*, covering
  digitized materials from antiquity to the Renaissance (launched on CD-ROM in 1987—four years
  before the advent of the Web; it was later established on the Web in 1995) (http://www.perseus.
  tufts.edu/hopper/).
- Developing and building huge continent- or nation-wide portals that act as an interface to many
  cultural institutions, providing millions of books, paintings, films, museum objects, archival
  records, and music and sounds that have been digitized. Examples include: (1) *Europeana*
  (launched in 2008), under a subtitle "think culture" calls to "explore 48,738,306 artworks,
  artifacts, books, videos and sounds from across Europe." (2) *Digital Public Library of America*
  (DPLA) (launched in 2013), under a subtitle "a Wealth of Knowledge" calls to "explore
  11,425,950 items from libraries, archives, and museums." (Quotes with given numbers from both
  sites are as of Jan. 2016) (http://www.europeana.eu/portal/) (http://dp.la/).

These are just a very few examples of digital and hybrid libraries. They represent only a sliver of an
explosive growth that resulted in a multitude of practical digital libraries worldwide.

Practical efforts in digital libraries share a common characteristic. Agendas were set at grassroots—
by individual libraries, academic departments, professional organizations, museums, publishers—
often driven by enthusiastic individuals. Pioneering projects from the early 1990s, such as those at
the Library of Congress mentioned above, served as examples for a great many institutions to follow.
Development of digital collections, management and preservation of digital resources, user-oriented
services, electronic publishing—with myriad issues and challenges beyond technology—are also a part
of these pragmatic efforts.

As mentioned at the beginning of this Foreword, evidence analyzed here is based either in (1) sites
of research projects that show a direct connection to practice or in (2) practical sites of digital libraries
that show a direct connection to research; in other words, it is based solely on evidence that is directly
visible or on "surface" evidence.

Here is a sample of the literature on digital libraries. *Communication of the ACM* (CACM) is the
flagship journal of the Association of Computing Machinery (ACM). CACM had three special issues
devoted to digital libraries [CACM vol. 38 (4) 1995; vol. 41 (4) 1998; and vol. 44 (5) 2001]. In the most
recent special issue on digital libraries, the article "The ACM Digital Library" stated:

> "ACM distinguished itself in its advanced planning for its digital library by paying close attention
> to three such issues: changing patterns in scholarly behavior; the functioning of copyright law in a
> networked environment; and the development of a business model" (Rous, 2001, p. 90).

No research project was mentioned or cited in the article, even though this and other two CACM special issues on digital libraries contained other articles about DLI projects that involved specific digital
libraries.

An article by Candela et al. (2007) about the Digital Library Manifesto has 17 references; none of them cite an operational digital library project. In turn, (as of Jan. 2016) the article is cited in Scopus (the largest bibliographic database covering over 22,000 titles) 31 times. A cursory examination of titles and references in those citations did not find a connection to any operational digital library project.

In contrast, the article by Bearman (2007) (among the best, if not even the best review of digital library literature up to that time) has 311 references, many of which refer to practical digital libraries. In a section devoted to practical systems, Bearman classifies them as to "Discipline- and Subject-Based Digital Libraries; Genre- and Format-Based Digital Libraries; Institutional Repositories; and Mission- and Audience-Directed Digital Libraries." The last one included children's digital libraries. This is the only article found that had descriptions of and references to practical digital libraries.

There are numerous international conferences devoted to digital libraries:

- Joint Conference on Digital Libraries (JCDL); since 2001 cosponsored by ACM and Institute of Electrical and Electronics Engineers, Computer Society (IEEE-CS), thus "joint" in the title— before 2001 they were separate.
- International Conference on Theory and Practice of Digital Libraries (TPDL); started in 1997 as the European Conference on Research and Advanced Technology on Digital Libraries (ECDL).
- International Conference on Asian Digital Libraries (ICADL).
- In addition, many other—including regional—conferences are listed in each issue of D-Lib Magazine (http://www.dlib.org/groups.html).

In other words, conferencing on digital libraries is a rich, international tradition and venue. All the major conferences publish conference proceedings, of which only two Proceedings of the Joint Conference on Digital Libraries (JCDL) are examined here in some detail: the first one that was jointly held in 2001, and the most recent one held in 2015.

Papers and presentations in JCDL 2001 are simply listed without a particular categorization. The first paper was entitled "Integrating automatic genre analysis into digital libraries," and the last was "The virtual naval hospital: the digital library as knowledge management tool for nomadic patrons." Over 80 contributions are listed; a good number are only one page long, consisting only of an abstract and references with no actual paper included.

Papers and presentations in JCDL 2015 are divided into categories labeled by sessions: "People and Their Books; Information Extraction; Big Data, Big Resources; Working the Crowd; User Issues; Ontologies and Semantics; Non-text Collections; Temporality; and Archiving, Repositories, and Content." There were 18 full and 30 short research reports. Numerous examples of applications were given, such as a papers with the title: "No More 404s: Predicting Referenced Link Rot in Scholarly Articles for Pro-Active Archiving;" or "iCrawl: Improving the Freshness of Web Collections by Integrating Social Web and Focused Web Crawling."

A random examination of papers in both JCDL conferences, particularly as to their citations, yielded no reference to a practical digital library. However, a large proportion made specific and practical suggestion how to handle digitally given objects (eg, sounds) or did research examining a process (eg, digital reading).

In sum, papers at these conferences represent an impressive diversity of efforts in digital libraries. As for authors, these conferences mainly represent efforts coming out of the computer science community and provide a minimal connection to efforts involving broader communities. While the proportion of authors outside computer science is rising, less than 20% of all authors during these years comes from outside the discipline.

Time for conclusion. A brief answer posed by questions at the outset is this:

> As it stands now, I believe that digital library research on the one hand, and digital library practice on the other, reside in parallel universes with little visible contact and intersection, as demonstrated by the diffusion channels examined here. I think that, while they are both about digital libraries, there is a digital divide between them. At present, the two communities disseminate ideas in detached formal networks of communication that are more or less self-referential. However, things and connections may change.
>
> In other words, I believe that presently, digital library research and digital library practice are conducted mostly independent of each other, minimally informing each other, and having slight or no connection.
>
> Furthermore, I also concur with David Levy's conclusion, quoted above, that the research agenda largely bears the imprint of the computer science community's interests and vision.

However, since both research and practice are in progress and the diffusion process is a function of time, we may expect changes. The approach and method adopted has obvious limitations—I took the information provided "as is" and did not pursue any deeper analysis of connections, if any, below the surface. Here are a few more limitations. It is well known that technology transfer may take place through informal as well as formal channels and records. This indeed has been common in the digital library field, a fact that cannot be ignored. Many people that are designing and developing digital libraries have attended digital library conferences and learned of research work. Likewise, a good percentage of those attending digital library conferences are practitioners who bring back to their libraries and projects what they have learned from research presentations. Further, invited talks, panel discussions, short papers, posters, and workshops are key parts of conferences where technology transfer takes place in both directions, and these have been ignored in the present analysis. Thus, conclusions here can easily be questions. Still, the subject in the leading questions should be raised.

This book covers large issues facing digital libraries. It incorporates current research perspectives on the development and evaluation of digital libraries, as well as an overview of best practices and standards for high performance. This combination of research and up-to-date practical guidelines is a unique strength of this book.

T. Saracevic

School of Communication and Information, Rutgers University, New Brunswick, New Jersey, United States

REFERENCES

Arms, W.Y., 2005. A viewpoint analysis of the digital library. D-Lib Mag. 11(7–8). Available from: http://dlib.org/dlib/july05/arms/07arms.html.

Bearman, D., 2007. Digital libraries. Ann. Rev. Inf. Sci. Technol. 41 (1), 223–272.

Candela, L., Castelli, D., Pagano, P., Thanos, C., Ioannidis, Y., Koutrika, G., Ross, S., Schek, H.-J., Schuldt, H., 2007. Setting the foundations of digital libraries: The DELOS manifesto. D-Lib Mag. 13(3–4). Available from: http://dlib.org/dlib/march07/castelli/03castelli.html.

DL.org., 2010. The Digital Library Reference Model. (Also contains the DELOS Manifesto). Available from: http://www.dlorg.eu/uploads/DL%20Reference%20Models/The%20Digital%20Library%20Reference%20Model_v1.0.pdf.

Griffin, S.M., 2005. Funding for digital libraries research: past and present. D-Lib Mag. 11(7/8). Available from: http://dlib.org/dlib/july05/griffin/07griffin.html.

Levy, D.A., 2000. Digital libraries and the problem of purpose. D-Lib Mag. 6(1). Available from: National Science Foundation. (2004). On the origins of Google. Available from: http://www.nsf.gov/discoveries/disc_summ.jsp?cntn_id=100660.

National Science Foundation (2004). On the origins of Google. Available from: http://www.nsf.gov/discoveries/disc_summ.jsp?cntn_id=100660&org=IIS.

Rous, B., 2001. The ACM Digital Library. Commun. ACM 44 (5), 90–91.

Wells, H.G., 1938. The World Brain. Doubleday, Doran & Co, Garden City, NY.

Preface

CONTEXT OF THE BOOK

The emergence of digital libraries provides an unprecedented opportunity for broader and easier access to a variety of information resources and new potential for their use. Just like there are different definitions in terms of what constitutes a digital library, different approaches have been applied to the development of the main components of digital libraries—the collection, digitalization, organization, design, preservation, retrieval, and evaluation of digital libraries. The field of digital libraries is constantly changing with the introduction of new formats, standards, technologies, best practices, and the evolving concepts of digital library design, evaluation, preservation, and digital curation. There is a strong need for a new book that addresses the changes that have taken place in the past five years in the field of digital libraries and that presents current research and developments in the world of practice.

Existing books on digital libraries contribute greatly to the research and practice of the field; however, they are often out of date and leave many unanswered questions. The limitations of current digital library-related books can be summarized as follows:

- Fail to cover all the key components of digital library development
- Focus only on either the theory component of digital library research or the practical aspects of digital library development
- Fail to include new technology development and applications in digital libraries

This book is written to address the need for updated and multifaceted scholarship and practice in the area of digital libraries.

OBJECTIVE OF THE BOOK

The objective of the book is to present a comprehensive overview of different approaches and tools for each component of digital library development, as well as to discuss the social and legal issues associated with digital libraries and the application of new technologies and standards. In particular, the authors incorporate a thorough discussion of new formats, standards, technologies, best practices, and the evolving concepts of digital library design, use, evaluation, preservation, and digital curation into the book. The book integrates current research and best practices in digitization and construction of digital collections and provides both the United States and international perspectives on the development of digital libraries.

STRUCTURE OF THE BOOK

This book consists of the following four parts:

Part I (Chapter 1) offers an overview of digital libraries and the conceptual and practical understanding of digital libraries. Chapter 1 provides an overview of the evolution of digital libraries, as well as key concepts, frameworks, major developments, and projects of digital libraries. The benefits and challenges of each period of digital library development are reviewed.

Part II (Chapters 2–7) presents approaches and tools for each component of digital library development ranging from collection development to interface design. Chapter 2 offers definitions, selection criteria, collection policies, and legal issues of digital collection development. Moreover, it also analyses the trends of collection sharing and large-scale digitization and their corresponding challenges. Chapter 3 outlines workflows, standards, and best practices of the digitization process of static media. It also reviews technical factors, imaging equipment, and minimum recommendations for preservation-quality conversion of static media including the new trend of rapid digitization. Chapter 4 identifies various standards, approaches, and challenges of sound and moving image digitization. It focuses on digitization as a reformatting strategy for preserving audiovisual collections. In addition, it includes the discussion of digitization equipment, technical factors, and formats relevant to audio and moving image conversion. Chapter 5 discusses diverse metadata schemas for knowledge representation and organization, and the metadata building process. It covers not only theoretical aspects of metadata but also the practice of designing and implementing metadata in digital collections. It further discusses user-generated tagging and linked open data in the context of describing and sharing DL resources. Chapter 6 introduces the development and selection of different types of proprietary and open access digital library content management systems. It concentrates on functionality, interoperability, and other design requirements of these content management systems. Chapter 7 shows the iterative process in the design and implementation of a user interface from the conceptual design, prototype design, and customized design to usability testing. It also discusses how to design DLs for people with disabilities.

Part III (Chapters 8–10) discusses the users, search behaviors, preservation, and evaluation of digital libraries. Chapter 8 highlights different types of user needs and their use of digital libraries. It emphasizes search tactics, search strategies, and usage patterns. Most important, factors affecting digital library use are analyzed, from the user's personal infrastructure to types of tasks and system design. Chapter 9 discusses research and practical approaches to digital preservation in the digital library context. It examines the challenges, goals, and strategies in preserving digital objects, and presents a set of practical guidelines, standards, and technical solutions for preserving digital content. Chapter 10 addresses why evaluation is important, when to evaluate, what to evaluate, how to evaluate, and factors hindering the evaluation. It includes the evaluation objectives, approaches, stages, dimensions, criteria, measurements, data collection methods, and challenges.

Part IV (Chapter 11) highlights the challenges and new developments of digital libraries. Chapter 11 emphasizes future directions and opportunities for digital library research and development. In particular, it examines the new areas of digital libraries development, such as large-scale digital libraries, social media applications in digital libraries, multilingual digital libraries, and digital curation. The challenges that researchers and practitioners face and corresponding topics for further research are also identified and proposed.

UNIQUE FEATURES OF THE BOOK

Compared to the published books on digital libraries, the unique features of this work include:

1. This book integrates both research and practice concerning digital library development, use, preservation, and evaluation. The combination of current research and practical guidelines is a unique strength of this book. The authors bring in-depth expertise on different digital library issues and synthesize theoretical and practical perspectives relevant to researchers, DL

practitioners, and students. Professor Iris Xie has conducted digital library research for more than 15 years, and has focused projects on interface design, user studies, digital library evaluation, and social media application. Professor Krystyna Matusiak who was a digital librarian for about 10 years, has built 20 distinct digital collections.

2. This book provides a comprehensive overview of the lifecycle of digital library design, use, preservation and evaluation, including collection development, digitization of multimedia resources, metadata, digital library development and interface design, digital information searching, digital preservation, and digital library evaluation. It provides up-to-date guidelines for digitization of static as well as time-based media.

3. This book reviews empirical studies of digital libraries from a variety of aspects, including many of the authors' own works: a study of blind users' help-seeking situations in interacting with digital libraries, and the implications for interface design for blind users (Chapters 7, 8); a Delphi survey of digital library evaluation criteria and measures from different stakeholders of digital libraries (Chapter 10); and a study of social media applications in digital libraries (Chapter 11.)

4. This book offers guidance regarding each component of the lifecycle of digital library development, use, preservation, and evaluation. For example, it presents detailed information regarding how to evaluate digital libraries, specifying types of evaluation dimensions, criteria, measurements, and data collection methods.

5. This book introduces new developments in the area of digital libraries, such as large-scale digital libraries, social media applications in digital libraries, multilingual digital libraries, digital curation, linked data, rapid capture, guidelines for the digitization of multimedia resources, etc.

6. This book identifies challenges and problems that are associated with the lifecycle of digital library creation, use, preservation and evaluation, along with suggestions for overcoming these challenges. In addition, further research questions in relation to these challenges are discussed in Chapter 11.

7. This book offers a comprehensive bibliography for each chapter.

TARGET AUDIENCES

This book is intended for researchers, designers, librarians, archivists, teachers, and graduate students who are interested in digitization, digital library development, management, use, and evaluation. The comprehensive literature review on theory and practice of digital libraries will provide a foundation for education, research, and practice. The implication discussion offers guidance for designers and librarians in designing and evaluating digital libraries for the general public, as well as for specific user groups. This book can also serve as a textbook for digital library education in library and information science programs as well as affiliated programs.

Members of the following associations would be the primary readers for the book: (1) Association for Information Science and Technology (ASIST), (2) Association for Computing Machinery (ACM), (3) a variety of library associations, such as the American Library Association (ALA), Special Library Association (SLA), Digital Library Federation (DLF), etc. (4) IEEE Computer Society, (5) Association for Library and Information Science Education (ALISE). The secondary audience could include researchers and practitioners from other related disciplines (e.g., computer science, engineering, health, education, etc.) who are interested in digitization, digital library design, use, and evaluation.

Acknowledgments

This book project took us about three and a half years to complete, starting from the summer of 2012—when we prepared the book proposal—to the submission of the manuscript at the end of 2015. This book is the synthesis of our research and practice in the last 15 years. More important, it highlights research and practice from researchers and practitioners in the library and information science field. At the same time, we would not be able to write this book without the support of family members, students, and colleagues.

This book would have not been possible without contributions from many researchers and practitioners in the digital library field. Iris Xie would like to thank University of Wisconsin-Milwaukee for granting her sabbatical leave, enabling her to focus on the book. She also thanks her colleagues and students for their support and inspiring conversations. Krystyna Matusiak would like to thank her colleagues and students at the University of Denver for their support and stimulating discussions. She also would like to thank her former colleagues at the University of Wisconsin-Milwaukee Libraries where she began her work in digitization.

We extend our deepest thanks to Tefko Saracevic for writing the Foreword for the book and our colleagues who reviewed the chapters and provided constructive feedback: Heather Ryan of University of Denver, Ling Meng of University of Wisconsin-Milwaukee Libraries, Benjamin Miller of Denver Public Library, Steve Miller of University of Wisconsin-Milwaukee, Doug Peterson and Peter Siegel of Digital Transitions. We would also like to acknowledge graduate students who assisted the authors with research and editing. Our sincere thanks to the doctoral students in School of Information Studies at University of Wisconsin-Milwaukee: Joel A Des Armo, Carol Sabbar, Edward Benoit, Renee Bennett Kapusniak, Hye Jung Han, Tae Hee Lee, Soohyung Joo, Sukjin You, and Yanyan Wang, and to the students in the Library and Information Science program at the University of Denver: Gina Schlesselman-Tarango, Catie Newton, and Chelsea Heinbach. Krystyna Matusiak would also like to thank Tara Kron for her editing assistance.

We would like to express our appreciation to Amy Invernizzi from Elsevier for answering our questions and supporting us at every stage of the book writing process.

Finally, we also want to express our gratitude to our family members and friends for their patience and support during the process of writing this book. Iris would like to dedicate this book to her husband, Charlie, and her daughter, Vivian, for their support, encouragement, and sacrifice as well as her parents for their support and love along the journey. Krystyna would like to dedicate the book to her sons, Alexander and Thomas, for their understanding and great hiking trips in the Rocky Mountains that provided a respite in the writing process.

I. Xie
University of Wisconsin-Milwaukee

K.K. Matusiak
University of Denver

INTRODUCTION TO DIGITAL LIBRARIES

INTRODUCTION

Digital libraries emerged in the early 1990s but were preceded by inspiring visions of innovative thinkers and several decades of intensive development within information technologies. The innovative ideas for using information technology to organize and disseminate knowledge go back to futuristic essays by H.G. Wells and the work of early information scientists Paul Otlet, Vannevar Bush, and J.C.R. Licklider (Grudin, 2011; Lynch, 2005; Rayward, 1994, 1997, 2005). Unveiling his vision of a "world brain," a universal encyclopedia, H.G. Wells wrote in 1938: "The time is close at hand when any student, in any part of the world, will be able to sit with his projector in his own study at his or her own convenience to examine *any* book, *any* document, in an exact replica" (p. 77). The ideas of H.G. Wells and Vannevar Bush captured popular imagination and inspired future information scientists and inventors, but the technology that led to the development of digital libraries turned out to be quite different from that which they envisioned.

It was progress in digital computing (rather than the analog machines proposed by Bush) and the growth of computer networks that have enabled the construction of digital libraries and remote access to digital representations of scholarly and cultural resources held in libraries, archives, and museums. Nonetheless, the futuristic visions, as reflected in H.G. Wells' quotation in the preceding paragraph became a reality to a certain extent. Nowadays, students can easily access books and other scholarly resources, including Wells' *World Brain,* from their laptops or mobile devices. Digital libraries transcend physical and technical barriers to give access to information resources and enable novel ways of examining and linking these resources together. The digitized version of Wells' book, its "exact replica," is technically available through the Google Book Project and HathiTrust Digital Library. Due to copyright restrictions, however, access to its content is limited to students and faculty whose universities are members of HathiTrust. Universal access to "*any* book, *any* document" as envisioned by Wells (1938, p. 77), is technically feasible but is currently constrained by social and legal barriers. As Michael Lesk (2012) points out, the technological obstacles that were dominant in the first phase of digital library development have been generally overcome by progress in computers and networking, but the legal and social challenges remain.

Digital libraries encompass a wide range of materials, from books to representations of three-dimensional artifacts. The content is either created digitally or converted from a variety of analog sources through digitization. Extensive digitization efforts have accompanied the construction of digital libraries to transform the wealth of traditional scholarly and cultural materials held in libraries, archives, and museums into a digital format. The conversion process is far from complete. Nonetheless, for the first time in the history of recorded knowledge, information resources can be free from physical carriers and are available in a uniform digital form, regardless of their original sources and types of presentations. David M. Levy (2003) observes, "a single medium or representational format (ones and zeros) is now capable of representing all the forms of talk we have so far managed to create: text and graphics, voice, and moving images. And a single device is capable of making all these forms manifest" (p. 36). Levy (2003) also notes that all artifacts and documents are fundamentally social, created and used in the context of human activities.

On one hand, this shift from analog to digital methods in recording, transmission, and storage offers tremendous benefits for access and new forms of interaction with text and image. On the other hand, it poses unique challenges for organizing, presenting, and preserving digital resources and serving user communities in virtual information spaces. The streams of ones and zeros don't have much value unless they can be transformed into useful and usable scholarly, educational, and personal resources. The organizational aspect became the center of attention in the early phase of digital library development as the library cataloging standards developed in the print environment did not translate well into the digital realm. The initial construction of digital libraries was accompanied by the explosion of new metadata schemas, a so-called metadata renaissance as described by Calhoun (2014). Digital libraries have emerged as complex systems that serve not only as repositories of digital objects with associated metadata but also as information systems in a networked environment providing search and retrieval mechanisms and supporting user interaction. The contributions from computer science and the advances in information search and retrieval have enhanced the functionality and technical capabilities of DL systems.

Multiple, and often competing, definitions of what is a DL have emerged in the library and computer science communities. The concept was extensively debated during the formative period in the 1990s. Researchers were trying to reconcile the mission and principles of traditional libraries with the digital format of information resources, distributed network access, and new interaction capabilities and at the same time address the uniqueness of digital libraries, especially in contrast to resources available through the open web. The debate on what constitutes a DL is very important, as it not only advances research and practice but also has broader implications for the evaluation of digital libraries and their educational and social use (Bawden and Rowlands, 1999; Borgman, 2000). Digital libraries are viewed as multidimensional phenomena consisting of multiple layers and building blocks, available in the distributed network environment, with resources and associated services developed, organized, and managed to support users' scholarly and educational activities as well as personal research. The social–technical perspective is applied to consider the complexity of digital libraries as systems of technology, documents, users, and practices existing in social contexts (Bishop et al., 2003).

The evolution of digital libraries is marked by several phases, comprising the early transitional projects and the formative decade in the 1990s, mass digitization in the 2000s, and the large-scale aggregations undertaken in the last few years. Digital libraries have evolved into complex, multilayered, distributed systems since the first digital collections were made available over the Internet in the mid-1990s. For the first two decades, digital libraries were constructed primarily as standalone entities with strong institutional ties to libraries, archives, and museums. This landscape of multiple, discrete, and dispersed collections proves to be challenging for resource discovery as it requires locating and searching individual digital libraries. The difficulties in resource discovery, however, have begun to be addressed in recent years. Large-scale digital libraries, such as the Digital Public Library of America, Europeana, or HathiTrust, aggregate content from smaller individual digital libraries and provide portals for global searching and retrieval.

The initial development of digital libraries was focused on building the technical infrastructure. At the time, they tended to be system centered and rarely incorporated research on user needs or evaluation from the user perspective. However, as digital libraries expanded, it became clear that they were difficult to use and posed usability problems (Blandford et al., 2004; Borgman, 2003). Usability became an important area of research in the digital library field, as well as becoming a form of evaluation (Buttenfield, 1999; Chowdhury et al., 2006; Jeng, 2005). Buttenfield (1999) recognized early on that digital libraries are information systems that people use to satisfy information needs not easily met in a traditional library and called for the adaptation of a wide range of usability methods. Usability has been identified by users as the most important criterion in evaluating digital libraries (Xie, 2006). The perceptions of usability and usefulness also play an important role in user adoption of digital libraries for educational use (Liu and Luo, 2011; Matusiak, 2012).

The development of digital libraries occurred concurrently with the emergence of the web. Digital libraries have adopted some Internet technical standards and have become part of the global networking infrastructure. But in this new and dramatically changing environment, libraries lost not only their primary role as information providers but also a visible and unique identity (De Rosa et al., 2005; Law, 2009, 2011; Lagoze, 2010). Digital libraries are now part of a broader information landscape, often competing for users' attention with a multitude of other information resources. Lagoze (2010) argues persuasively that digital libraries, with their institutional affiliation and traditional information models, have been less responsive to user expectations and changing information behaviors. Digital scholarly publications have become a mainstream resource in academic research, but the adoption of digital libraries in personal research and for educational use has been limited (Bearman, 2007; Liu and Luo, 2011; Matusiak, 2012; McMartin et al., 2008). Digital libraries are relatively new phenomena, and, like many new and emergent information systems, they face challenges of discovery, acceptance, and utilization. The social aspects of digital libraries and support for users' scholarly and educational activities represent areas that require further attention in research and practice.

DEFINITIONS AND FRAMEWORKS OF DIGITAL LIBRARIES

The concept of a digital library, as an entity separating from a traditional library, emerged in the mid-1990s. Prior to that, many institutions maintained collections of purchased electronic resources or even digitized materials, but did not refer to them as separate collections or libraries (Schwartz, 2000). Several different terms, including "electronic library," "virtual library," "network-accessible libraries," or "libraries without walls" were used to describe the new phenomenon in the early phase of digital library development. The term "digital library" came from the National Information Infrastructure Initiative (Bearman, 2007; Lagoze, 2010). It quickly gained acceptance despite some concerns that the combination of "digital" and "libraries" was somewhat misleading and blurred the distinction between collections of network-accessible electronic resources and libraries as institutions (Lynch, 1993). *Communications of the ACM* devoted an entire issue to digital libraries in May 1995. Fox (1995), in the introductory article, noticed a shift in terminology from "electronic library" to "digital library."

The first definitions that originated in the research community focused on the digital content and enabling technologies. The library community joined the debate in the late 1990s, emphasizing traditional library functions and services. The subsequent definitions attempted to reconcile the views of researchers and librarians and provide multifaceted perspectives emphasizing heterogeneous content, technical capabilities, and new functionality supporting diverse communities of users. The concept of digital libraries as a sociotechnical construct captures the complex nature of user interaction with these systems in the dynamic context of social practices. Digital library frameworks have emerged in response to the difficulty of describing the complexity of these systems by a single definition.

This review is limited to selected definitions illustrating the evolution of understanding of digital libraries. The proliferation of digital library definitions makes a comprehensive review very difficult. Schwartz (2000) identifies 64 formal and informal definitions. The purpose of these intensive intellectual activities has been to understand the nature of the emerging phenomenon and to provide a theoretical foundation for research and future development of digital libraries. The evolution of the concepts of digital libraries demonstrates a shift from the early focus on the traditional library model and the system-centered approach to emphasizing the complexity of these systems, their multiple dimensions, and the social context of use.

EARLY DEFINITIONS

A significant part of early digital library research efforts concentrated on defining the new phenomenon in an attempt to articulate its purpose and find answers to the fundamental question: what is a digital library? (Levy, 2000; Lyman, 1996; Marcum, 1997). Researchers not only differ in their answers and offer competing visions, but they don't even agree on whether an explicit definition is possible or necessary (Greenstein, 2000). Many researchers emphasize that the term "digital library" evokes different meanings to different people (Borgman, 1999; Fox, 1995; Schwartz, 2000). The diversity of opinions stems from the fact that the early concepts of digital libraries combined the missions, techniques, and cultures of traditional libraries with the capabilities and cultures of computing and telecommunications (Marchionini, 2000).

The early definitions of digital libraries illustrate the tension between researchers and practitioners and further focus on the networking technologies, digital format of collections, organization, and promise of universal access. The Association of Research Libraries (ARL) provided one of the early definitions of a digital library. The ARL definition is based on a book by Karen Drabenstott, *Analytical Review of the Library of the Future*, published in 1994 (Drabenstott, 1994). The definition identifies common elements of a digital library:

- The digital library is not a single entity.
- The digital library requires technology to link the resources of many.
- The linkages between the many digital libraries and information services are transparent to the end users.
- Universal access to digital libraries and information services is a goal.
- Digital library collections are not limited to document surrogates; they extend to digital artifacts that cannot be represented or distributed in printed formats (Association of Research Libraries, 1995).

The aforementioned definition focuses on the digital nature of collections, enabling network technology, and issues of access. In this respect, it reflects the early stage of thinking about digital libraries. It was, however, widely adapted in research projects (Koohang and Ondracek, 2005; Schwartz, 2000; Xie, 2006) and incorporated into other definitions.

Fox (1995) emphasizes the great potential of digital libraries in fulfilling "the age-old dream of every human being: gaining ready access to humanity's store of information" (p. 23). He embraces the computer science approach along with the traditional library perspective and sees digital libraries as networked information systems carrying out the functions of libraries in a new way, and they offer new possibilities to organize and access information resources. Fox notices that the metaphor of a traditional library is "both empowering and constraining" and points out that much of the power of digital libraries is in access to actual objects (p. 25). Lesk (1997) also highlights their new capabilities, describing them as the "powers we never had with traditional libraries" (p. 1). In his opinion, the great advantage of digital libraries lies not only in access but also in the organization of digital content enhanced by indexing and full-text retrieval. He emphasizes organization as a key element and simply defines a digital library as "a collection of information that is both digitized and organized" (p. 1).

Definitions offered by the library community shift the focus from the word "digital" to "library" and elaborate on the role and functions of libraries in the new digital environment. Digital libraries are not seen as new or unique phenomena but rather as extensions of traditional libraries delivering new types of information resources and offering new user services. The Digital Library Federation (DLF) presents a definition that de-emphasizes the digital nature of collections but stresses the functions and services offered by libraries as organizations. The DLF describes digital libraries as "organizations that provide resources, including the specialized staff, to select, structure, offer intellectual access to, interpret, distribute, preserve the integrity of, and ensure the persistence over time of collections of digital works so that they are readily and economically available for use by a defined community or set of communities" (Waters, 1998, para. 3). This definition reflects the conviction that, with time, there will be less emphasis on the digital nature of material and more on traditional roles of libraries. The DLF definition includes distinct traditional library roles—such as selection, intellectual control, providing access, and preservation—applied to digital works.

MULTIFACETED DEFINITIONS AND PERSPECTIVES

The definitions that emerged in the second decade of digital library development emphasize multiple facets of these systems and combine the technical components with services and social aspects. Borgman (1999), in her comprehensive overview of early definitions, points to the diverging views of the research and library communities. Librarians envision digital libraries as extensions or augmentations of traditional libraries with resources in digital format and new types of services, while computer scientists view digital libraries as enabling technologies and networks.

Research-oriented definitions tend to give a narrower view as they primarily concentrate on the technical aspects of digital format, information architecture, and information retrieval. Practice-oriented definitions see digital libraries in social and institutional contexts and emphasize services. Borgman proposes a definition that would bridge the two conflicting approaches. Her definition has two elements:

- Digital libraries are a set of electronic resources and associated technical capabilities for creating, searching and using information.
- Digital libraries are constructed, collected, and organized by (and for) a community of users, and their functional capabilities support the information needs and uses of that community (Borgman, 1999).

Arms (2000) also attempts to reconcile the computer science approach with the librarians' perspective. He offers a succinct definition of a digital library as a managed collection of information in a digital format, with associated services, and accessible over networks. Arms places importance on the quality of managed, curatorial collections, where digital objects are described and organized systematically and made available to the public through a searchable interface.

The concept of digital libraries as unique or complex phenomena has emerged in studies examining their actual use and in the context of constructing such systems. Marchionini (2000) stresses that digital libraries have a combination of traditional library roles as well as aspects of computing. However, in his reflections on the multiyear evaluation of the Perseus Project, he describes digital libraries as "emergent complex systems" (p. 326). Witten and Bainbridge (2003) echo earlier definitions by underscoring the principles of selection and organization. They define a digital library as "a focused collection of digital objects, including text, video, and audio, along with methods for access and retrieval, and for selection, organization, and maintenance of the collection" (p. 6). The concepts of selection, organization, and management are central to the authors' understanding of digital libraries. Although these concepts reflect traditional values of librarianship, Witten and Bainbridge do not perceive digital libraries as extensions of existing institutions, simply computerized or digitized libraries, but rather as a unique phenomenon that offers new ways of creating knowledge.

The sociotechnical perspective shifts the focus of the debate from technical aspects to the social context of digital library use and evaluation (Bishop et al., 2003). The editors of the book *Digital Library Use: Social Practice in Design and Evaluation* highlight the complexity of digital library systems, especially if viewed as part of interactions with the larger world of work, study, and collaborative activities of users and developers. Digital libraries are broadly defined as "sociotechnical systems – networks of technology, information, documents, people, and practices" (Bishop et al., 2003, p. 1). The emphasis of this perspective is on the design of digital libraries, based on an understanding of user needs and activities and on their role in the processes of knowledge construction viewed in a broader social context. The authors comment on the relationship between digital and traditional libraries, noting that some digital libraries are an outgrowth of traditional libraries, while other digital libraries only relate to traditional libraries metaphorically. The view of digital libraries as a social–technical phenomenon is espoused by several authors of chapters in the *Digital Library Use: Social Practice in Design and Evaluation* book, with Levy (2003) examining the social nature of documents and Agre (2003) commenting on digital libraries embedded in the social world.

Lagoze et al. (2005) reflect on the state of digital library development in the age of Google and argue that digital libraries should move away from the legacy of the traditional library information model built around metadata repositories. The new information model should move beyond search and access functionality and enable creating collaborative and contextual environments where information resources are "shared, aggregated, manipulated, and refined" (Lagoze et al., 2005, para. 10). The authors don't propose yet another definition but describe digital libraries in terms of desired characteristics, including

- Selection of resources according to the criteria relevant to the digital library mission
- Services to facilitate the use of resources by the target community
- Collaborative features, allowing users to contribute knowledge and reuse resources
- Contextual features enabling the relationships between the resources

Furthermore, Lagoze et al. (2005) describe their work of extending the functionality of the National Science Digital Library (NSDL), where they propose a new, resource-centric information model for managing, manipulating, and processing content and metadata.

In a recent publication, Calhoun (2014) expands the understanding of digital libraries by incorporating the architecture of digital library systems and the concepts of open access. She proposes a practical definition that combines multiple components, including systems and services, managed collections of digital content "intended to serve the needs of defined communities" (p. 18), a system architecture centered on a repository, search features, and user interfaces. This definition focuses on the technical infrastructure built with repository systems, reflecting the current state of digital library development.

Table 1.1 Selected Concepts of Digital Libraries

Author(s)	Digital Library Components	Emphasis
Single-field perspective		
Association of Research Libraries (1995)	Not a single entity = bibliographic control + digital objects + enabling network technologies	Digital nature of collections; access to full-text documents; universal access
Fox (1995)	Networked information systems = information resources + new ways to organize + new ways to access and retrieve	Distributed networks; information retrieval; extended access to information resources
Digital Library Federation (Waters, 1998)	Organizations = distributed digital resources + staff + library services	Extension of traditional libraries as organizations; traditional library roles and services
Multifaceted perspectives		
Borgman (1999)	Digital libraries = digital resources + associated technical capabilities + network distribution User-centered approach = services supporting user needs	Digital format and enabling technologies; community of users; user support
Arms (2000)	Managed collection of digital information = resources in a digital format + associated services + network access	Curatorial responsibility: selection, organization, and preservation; user services
Witten and Bainbridge (2003)	Heterogeneous systems = digital resources in multiple modes of representation + metadata + methods for access and retrieval	Selection, organization, and maintenance; new ways of creating knowledge
Bishop et al. (2003)	Sociotechnical systems = networks of technology + information + documents + people + practices	Digital technology; knowledge work; social practices; user-centered approach
Lagoze et al. (2005)	Multilayered resource-centric model = network of selected resources + structural and semantic relationships	New information model going beyond search and access; collaborative and contextual environment
Calhoun (2014)	Digital libraries = systems and services + managed collections of digital content + repository-centered architecture	Open access; support for the advancement of knowledge and culture

Unlike the earlier perspectives, Calhoun's definition calls attention to digital libraries' purpose in supporting the "advancement of knowledge and culture" (p. 18) and the availability of their content in open access. Calhoun recognizes the importance of social roles of digital libraries, noting, "social roles and communities are more likely to abide over time; collections and enabling technologies are more likely to shift" (p. 19). Table 1.1 provides a summary of selected definitions and perspectives.

Table 1.2 Digital Library Frameworks

Name/Authors	Digital Library Components	Emphasis
The DELOS Manifesto (Candela et al., 2007b)	A three-tier framework = Digital libraries as virtual organizations + DLS that users interact + DLMS providing software infrastructure	Six fundamental concepts: content, user, functionality, quality, policy, and architecture
The 5S (Fox et al., 2012)	Complex systems defined in terms of Streams Structures Spaces Scenarios Societies	Theoretical constructs capturing the essence of an information lifecycle

DIGITAL LIBRARY FRAMEWORKS

Digital library frameworks have emerged in recent years as a sign of the digital library research field becoming more mature and in response to a growing realization that the complex nature of these systems and their multiple facets are impossible to capture by a single definition or perspective (Candela et al., 2007b). The authors of the frameworks build upon the previous conceptual work and advance the understanding of digital libraries as unique, multidimensional phenomena by identifying the core concepts and outlining the relationships between them. The goals of the theoretical models are to provide a foundation for digital library research, a common vocabulary, and to further the development of information models and such systems. The two frameworks reviewed here were developed by interdisciplinary teams of researchers. Table 1.2 provides a summary of their key features.

The DELOS Manifesto is a conceptual framework developed by the members of the DELOS Network of Excellence in Digital Libraries, a research group funded by the European Union (Candela et al., 2007b). *The Manifesto* identifies key concepts, sets the foundation to facilitate the integration of research, and supports the development of improved and more flexible digital library systems. Digital libraries are understood broadly as the center of intellectual activity that enables collaboration, communication, and other forms of dynamic interaction and research activities. As demonstrated in Fig. 1.1, the digital library framework consists of three interrelated tiers:

- Digital library—represents an organization that collects, manages, and preserves the rich digital content on behalf of users.
- Digital library system (DLS)—a software system that is based on a defined architecture and provides all functionality.
- Digital library management system (DLMS)—a generic software system that provides the infrastructure to produce and administer a digital library.

Six core concepts are associated with the proposed digital library framework: content, user, functionality, quality, policy, and architecture. The three-tier framework provides a systematic approach to all levels of digital library development and use. It distinguishes between the technical infrastructure and software needed to develop and administer instances of digital libraries, the digital library systems

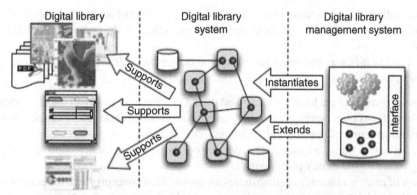

FIGURE 1.1 Digital Library, DLS, and DLMS: A Three-Tier Framework (Candela et al., 2007b)

that users interact with, and organization(s) responsible for collecting and managing digital content. The framework serves as a foundation for the Digital Library System Reference Architecture (Candela et al., 2007a). The Reference Model and DLMS are reviewed in Chapter 6. Candela et al. (2007b) also discuss the roles of actors in digital library systems: digital library end users, digital library designers, digital library system administrators, and digital library application developers. Digital library end users use the content and services via different digital library functions. Digital library designers define, customize, and maintain digital libraries based on their own expertise and knowledge. Digital library system administrators are responsible for the selection of software components, in particular the identification of the architectural configuration to construct the digital library system. Digital library application developers develop the software components of DLMS and DLS for different types of functionality.

The 5S—Societies, Scenarios, Spaces, Structures, Streams model provides a theoretical foundation for defining key constructs of digital libraries, which are viewed as complex systems of digital content, people, and technology. The authors propose a simple definition of digital libraries and define a set of abstractions representing the fundamental entities involved in the process of digital library development and use (Fox et al., 2012). This model builds on the authors' previous work in which the concepts of streams, structures, spaces, scenarios, and societies were defined (Gonçalves et al., 2004). Digital libraries are defined as complex systems that

- Help satisfy info needs of users (societies)
- Provide info services (scenarios)
- Organize info in usable ways (structures)
- Present info in usable ways (spaces)
- Communicate info with users (streams) (Fox et al., 2012, p. 6)

The focus of this definition is on the information lifecycle in which users perform tasks and interact with organized information sources in order to accomplish their goals. The theoretical elements of the framework are described as follows:

- Streams represent information flow and can be used to model content, which can be static (text, image) or dynamic (video).
- Structures support the organization of information in a usable and meaningful way.

- Spaces are collections of documents and are used in the context of access and presentation.
- Scenarios are used to describe user tasks and activities, which, in the context of digital libraries, can convey services.
- Societies refer to different communities of users; members have different roles and can undertake a range of activities.

The essential constructs are highly abstract and do not correspond directly to digital library concepts of digital objects, collections, services, etc., but can be used to define them. For example, digital objects can be described in terms of streams and structures. The *5S* framework provides a foundation for taxonomy of digital library terms and was used in developing an library and information science curriculum for educating future digital library professionals.

The review of research literature demonstrates an evolution of concepts since the emergence of digital libraries in the mid-1990s. The understanding of digital libraries has evolved from a one-dimensional perspective, seeing them as extensions of traditional libraries or network systems, to views of them as unique, multifaceted, and social phenomena that play an important role in knowledge construction. This review is based on previous work that was revised and expanded for the purpose of this chapter (Matusiak, 2010).

EVOLUTION OF DIGITAL LIBRARIES

"Digital libraries have a short yet turbulent and explosive history," remarked Tefko Saracevic in 2000 (p. 350). Although more than a decade passed, his statement is still true, especially in light of the long history of recording and organizing information resources. Despite an intensive period of development, digital libraries are a relatively new and emergent phenomenon. The history of digital libraries is divided into two decades, with some researchers placing the beginning in 1991 (Arms, 2012; Calhoun, 2014), while others point to 1994, as it was the year when systematic funding began to be available for digital library research and development (Dempsey, 2006; Lynch, 2005). The mid-1990s also coincided with the emergence of the web and the release of the first browsers. Lynch (2005), however, states that "very substantial digital library systems were developed prior to the World Wide Web" (para. 4). This section provides a brief overview of the evolution of digital libraries. It begins with highlighting the innovative ideas of early visionaries and key contributions of the pre-1990s era. Next, it traces the major phases in the development of digital libraries and reviews exemplary projects in the scientific and cultural heritage communities.

PRELUDE: EARLY VISIONARIES AND THE PRE-1990S ERA

Vannevar Bush and J.C.R. Licklider are widely recognized as digital library pioneers (Arms, 2000; Calhoun, 2014; Lesk, 2005, 2012). Lynch (2005) also points to H.G. Wells and Paul Otlet as early thinkers in the "prehistory" of digital libraries. H.G. Wells, a famous writer of science fiction, was also a utopian socialist who believed that some form of permanent world encyclopedia would bring together scattered intellectual resources and advance universal education. His idea of universal access to knowledge is formidable and some of the passages predicting the use of imaging as a duplication method to create "microscopic libraries of record" are indeed striking (Wells, 1938, p. 76). Rayward (1999) argues in his critical reassessment that Wells' vision of a "world brain," with its central control, is rather troubling. Other researchers note a collaborative nature to Wells' universal encyclopedia and see it as a precursor to Wikipedia (Reagle, 2010).

Paul Otlet was a contemporary of H.G. Wells and a strong proponent of a universal encyclopedia as well. Otlet was a Belgian bibliographer, a founder of documentation, and an innovative thinker whose contributions to knowledge organization and information science, largely forgotten, have been rediscovered thanks to the historical studies of W. Boyd Rayward (1994, 1997). As Rayward (1997) points out, Otlet was concerned with the growth of publications and believed that technological innovations would provide a solution to storage, organization, and retrieval of records of knowledge. The technologies that he had at his disposal were index cards and microphotography. He constructed systems of interlinked bibliographic records, images, and excerpts from publications. These analog databases, or "repertories" as Otlet referred to them, were standardized and used Universal Decimal Classification as a common organizational schema. Rayward (1994) describes repertories as prototypes of hypertext systems consisting of "nodes or chunks organized by a system of links and navigational devices that allowed the movement of the user from bibliographic reference to full text to image and object" (p. 240). Otlet's writings also include innovative ideas about the power of multimedia in knowledge diffusion and concepts of mechanized information retrieval. His contributions are now acknowledged and afforded him recognition as a "forefather of the Internet" (Manfroid et al., 2013, p. 312).

Vannevar Bush, an American scientist and engineer, published his essay "As We May Think" in 1945 when he was the head of the US Office of Scientific Research and Development. In his position at the Office of Scientific Research and Development, Bush oversaw the Manhattan Project and witnessed firsthand the expansion of scientific research and its unprecedented role in warfare. In his essay, he commented on the exponential growth of scientific publications and increasing specialization and argued that traditional indexing methods were inadequate to meet the demands of modern scientists. He proposed organizing resources by association, which, in his opinion, reflected the way a human mind works. Furthermore, in reviewing advancements in photography and microfilming, he predicted the use of imaging for reproduction and efficient storage, which he called the "compression" of library collections in his words. Bush envisioned automating the process of storage and retrieval and using microfilm for copies of books and other documents stored in a new kind of device that he called a memex. He described it as a "sort of mechanized private file and library" (Bush, 1945, para. 55). The memex was meant to extend researchers' memory through a trail of associations that would link documents. The physical device that Bush described resembled a desk and included screens on which material was supposed to be projected. The design of the memex was analog using the technology available at the time. As his biographer states, Bush was an expert in analog computing and code-breaking machines but never became comfortable with digital computing (Zachary, 1997). Drawings of the memex appeared in *Life* magazine, but the actual machine was never built. However, the ideas expressed in "As We May Think" inspired the new generation of information scientists and inventors.

J.C.R. Licklider was the first researcher who envisioned the use of digital technology not only to make the body of recorded knowledge available to users in a more efficient way but also to enable new forms of interactions. In 1965, when he published his book *Libraries of the Future,* digital computing was primarily conducted on large mainframe computers in research laboratories. His idea of extending the notion of libraries to computers was radical at the time. Like Bush, Licklider was concerned with the proliferation of scientific publications. He dismissed the notion of physical libraries and books as unsatisfactory forms of information storage, organization, and retrieval. His vision moves away from books and documents to transformable information, representing ideas and facts in classes of information and domains of knowledge. Licklider (1965) states: "we need to substitute for the book a device that will make it easy to transmit information without transporting material, and that will not only present the information to people but also process it for them" (p. 6). Libraries of the future, "procognitive systems" as he calls them (p. 6), are described as a meld of a structured body of knowledge and intelligent computer processing. Licklider imagined highly interactive, "question–answer" systems capable of analyzing information on behalf of users, including reading, comprehending information, and compiling abstracts. As a computer scientist and psychologist, Licklider was interested in human–computer interaction and envisioned new systems as a way of augmenting human processing.

Libraries of the Future is also known for its quite accurate prediction of the emergence of digital libraries in 1994 (Arms, 2000). Licklider (1965) indeed points to 1994 as a possible date but cautiously notes, "we expect that computers will be capable of making quite 'intelligent' contributions by 1994, [...] but we prefer not to count on it" (p. 58). Present-day digital library systems include many features predicted by Licklider, but they also fall short of his vision. Despite the digital format and more efficient storage and retrieval, digital libraries remain primarily collections of books and documents, and the level of interaction and processing is not near that which Licklider envisioned. In addition to his prescient and innovative ideas for the design of future libraries, Licklider also contributed to the development of computer networking, operating systems, and artificial intelligence. As a director of one of the agencies within the US Department of Defense's Advanced Research Projects Agency (ARPA), he was involved in developing the ARPANET, the direct predecessor to the Internet. The publication of *Libraries of the Future* in 1965 marks a transition from the visionary designs to the developments of technical infrastructure and standards that provide a foundation for constructing digital libraries (Lynch, 2005).

The period between 1965 and 1990 saw the expansion of computing beyond research labs, with a transition from mainframe systems to personal computers and the development of a globally distributed information environment. Computer networks enabled the sharing of information between interconnected sets of computers, but it was the expansion of ARPANET and the introduction of standard networking protocols that led to the emergence of the worldwide network of networks, the Internet. The advancements in networking and improvements in computer processing and storage capabilities were accompanied by research in indexing, natural language processing, and information retrieval (Calhoun, 2014; Lesk, 2005). The first commercial retrieval systems were built in the 1970s with LEXIS providing access to legal information and DIALOG serving the scientific community. As Calhoun (2014) notes "libraries were early adopters of online information systems" (p. 4) with librarians serving as intermediaries and expert searchers.

Computing was introduced in libraries in the 1960s and the library community developed their own online services and standards, such as the machine readable cataloging (MARC) format and the Z39.50 protocol. MARC was developed in the 1960s as a standardized format for exchanging cataloging records. The Library of Congress began distributing MARC records in 1969 (Arms, 2012; Calhoun, 2014; Lesk, 2012). Online library catalogs were developed in the late 1970s and became part of automated library systems. Z39.50 was one of the first protocols for distributed computing and enabled searching collections on remote systems (Arms, 2012). MARC and Z39.50 were used in some early digital projects, and although later replaced by newer standards, nonetheless, they provided a foundation in the initial phase of digital library development. Improvements in scanning technologies in the late 1980s encouraged libraries to experiment with the digitization of selected cultural heritage materials. The first digitized collections were available on CD-ROMs or through local library networks. The invention of the web by Tim Berners-Lee in 1990 changed the landscape dramatically. The early experimental projects moved to the web, and the development of digital libraries began in earnest.

THE FORMATIVE YEARS: 1991–2001

Several research findings point to 1990 as a turning point when technological advancements in computing made it possible to move from a vision and experimental project into digital library practice (Arms, 2012; Calhoun, 2014). Arms notes, "about 1990, computing reached a level where it became economically possible to mount large collections online and to access them over networks... [The] libraries of today were formed by the energy and creativity of these efforts" (2012, pp. 579–580). The first decade was a period of intensive interdisciplinary research on concepts, architectural models, metadata standards, and digitization best practices and guidelines. Digital libraries emerged as a field of scientific inquiry with research agenda focused on digital libraries as networked information systems. Research efforts were accompanied by prototype building and developing digital library technical infrastructure.

Digital Library Initiatives

Sponsored research initiatives gave considerable impetus for digital library development during the first decade. In the United States, the federal government provided systematic funding for digital library research that was formulated in a series of planning workshops sponsored by the National Science Foundation (NSF) in 1993–94 and then established as the Digital Library Initiative (Griffin, 2005; Mischo, 2005). The Digital Library Initiative consisted of two phases:

- Phase I (1994–98) involved three US federal agencies: the NSF, the National Aeronautics and Space Administration, and the Defense Advanced Research Projects Agency. The funding was awarded to six university-based projects with the focus on information technology and testbeds. Support was not provided for the creation or conversion of digital content (Griffin, 2005).
- Phase II (1998–2002) had support from NSF, the National Aeronautics and Space Administration, and the Defense Advanced Research Projects Agency as well as additional agencies, including the National Library of Medicine, the Library of Congress, the Federal Bureau of Investigation, and the National Endowment for the Humanities. The second phase of the Digital Library Initiative was envisioned as a broader program extending beyond research on information systems into content development, use, and usability. Fifty projects were awarded funding during the second phase. As Griffin (2005) notes, "the projects addressed topics spanning the entire information lifecycle—creation, access, dissemination, use, and preservation—and placed additional emphasis on measures of impact" (pp. 22).

In addition to funding through the Digital Library Initiative, support for digital projects in the United States has also been available through the Library of Congress, the Institute of Museum and Library Services, and private foundations. In the United Kingdom, government funding was provided through the Joint Information Systems Committee for the eLib program that began in 1995 (Calhoun, 2014;

Carr, 2009). The European Commission funded digital library programs through the European Union's Framework Programme.

These funded digital library projects represent the top research on different technical and social aspects of digital libraries. Among them, the Alexandria Digital Library is a typical example. It sets out to build a digital library service for spatial and geographic data. It consists of maps, remote-sensing maps, pictures, and text materials. The testbed system entails four components: a graphical user interface, a catalog component, a component for adding new items, and a storage component. The main approaches for the project are: (1) many classes of collection items, (2) user interface digital library architecture with catalog components, (3) Internet access by a variety of users, (4) interoperability with other digital library activities, (5) an iterative design by incorporating new technologies, and (6) support for traditional library functionality (Larsgaard and Carver, 1995; Smith, 1996; Smith and Frew, 1995). Fig. 1.2 presents the legacy search page of Alexandria Digital Library. This project has evolved into the current Alexandria Digital Research Library (http://alexandria.ucsb.edu/).

One unique contribution of the Alexandria Digital Library project is its iterative design process based on user feedback. A series of studies were conducted to test user interfaces of the Alexandria Digital Library. Generating data from users' interactions with the interfaces of Alexandria Digital Library, Hill et al. (2000) identify problems with the interfaces, the requirements of system functionality, and the collection of the digital library. The following implications for the design of digital library interfaces are suggested: unified and simplified search, being able to manage sessions, more options for results display, offering user workspace, offering more help functions, allowing easy data distribution, and informing users of the process status. Analyzing a 12-month time series of transaction logs from the Alexandria Digital Library, Buttenfield and Reitsma (2002) developed a model of transactions in

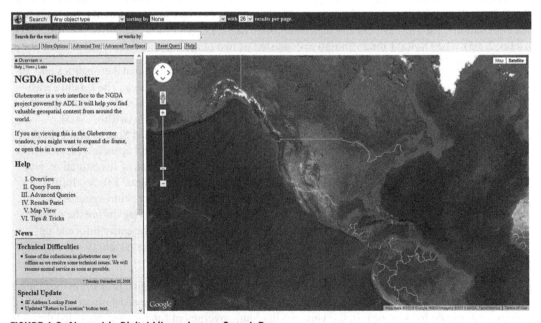

FIGURE 1.2 Alexandria Digital Library Legacy Search Page

relation to time, origin, and destination components to detect patterns of user navigation within the digital library. The findings show that user training, instead of changes to the user interface, had a significant effect on transaction patterns. Through interviews with faculty members, Borgman et al. (2005) reveal that faculty members preferred searching for locations, place names, concept, or themes and that their personal research resources were used extensively in their teaching. The findings yield implications for the creation of personal digital libraries as well as the capability to import data from different formats and standards. In addition, digital library design also needs to facilitate the sharing of resources among faculty members.

Early Digital Library Projects

The early digital library projects arose out of the traditional library environment. The Internet gave new possibilities for global information sharing. Early digital library projects gradually moved to the web environment. Examples of these transitional digital library projects include: Project Mercury sponsored by Carnegie Mellon University, the Perseus Digital Library, the Chemistry Online Retrieval Experiment (CORE), Elsevier's TULIP project, and the Envision Project. Following is a discussion of two digital library projects that represent a focus on humanities and science in this period of time: The Perseus Digital Library and the CORE project.

The Perseus Digital Library is one of the key early digital library projects. Perseus version 1.0 started as a CD-ROM of mainly Greek texts and English translations. The Perseus Digital Library went live on the web in 1995 and further expanded its collections to Greco-Roman materials. The turning point in this project was receiving funding from the Digital Library Initiative Phase 2, which enabled the Perseus Digital Library to include more digital collections in the humanities. Perseus 3.0 and the Java-based 4.0 version were released on the Internet. It moved from a teaching tool to a research tool (Crane, 2015; Preece and Zepeda, 2009). The Perseus digital library is considered as the most important resource in the study of Greece and Rome, and it is also regarded as a role model in the adoption of technology in the humanities (Dubis, 2003; Wilson, 2000). Fig. 1.3 presents the homepage of Perseus Digital Library.

Perseus is considered by researchers as a typical digital library and has been examined to generate recommendations for digital libraries in general. Several cases studies have closely analyzed the use of the Perseus project. Three years of investigation of the Perseus project in different learning environments shows that it offers information and resources for users and also requires users to apply new strategies to interact with the system (Marchionini and Crane, 1994). The Perseus Digital Library illustrates the importance of longitudinal and multifaceted evaluation of digital libraries. The subsequent recommendations for the evaluation of digital libraries are proposed: evaluation needs to consider system testing along the way; evaluation needs to adapt to changes; evaluation needs to apply both quantitative and qualitative data (Marchionini, 2000). Another case study identifies what needs to be improved in the Perseus Digital Library including the problem of implicit hyperlinks, path tools, authoring tools, etc. (Yang, 2001).

In contrast to the Perseus Digital Library, the CORE project is a digital library that mainly consists of journal articles in chemistry. The CORE project sets up a model for converting large collections of texts and graphics in a distributed network environment. The unique characteristics of this project are (1) scanning and converting a large amount of information, (2) including both text and graphical data, and (3) focusing on a specific subject area. Unlike many digital library projects, CORE consists of both a scanned image and a marked-up ASCII version for each page of the publisher's database. Each

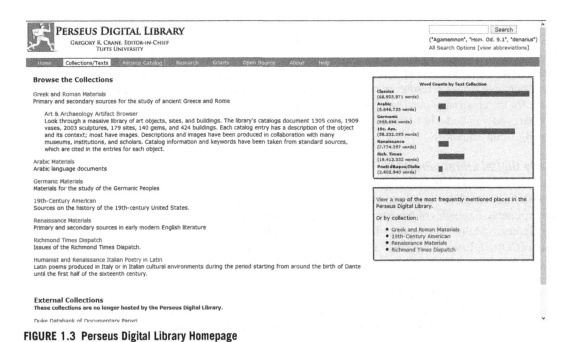

FIGURE 1.3 Perseus Digital Library Homepage

page was scanned and segmented, and graphics were separated and linked to figure references in the articles. Lack of standards for the conversion of special characters and equations was the key challenge for building CORE.

Evaluation studies were conducted to assess the CORE project. Five tasks (citation, query, browse, essay, and transform) were performed by 36 chemistry students at Cornell University, with 12 using the paper-based version, 12 using the Pixbook (a full-text search/image display system), and 12 using the Superbook (a full-text search/ASCII display system). On the query search tasks, the digital systems were better than the paper version in both performance and speed. Electronic systems performed better than the paper version on the essay task even though there was no difference in the time the task took. On the browsing task, the performance results were competitive, but the print and ASCII display were faster than the image display. For the citation task, the performance results were again the same, but the ASCII display was slower than the image display and paper version (Lesk, 1991). Based on the data collected from transaction logs, online questionnaires, online comments, interviews, and anecdotes, Entlich et al. (1996) report that the top 35% of users accounted for 80% of the usage. The analysis of users' searching, viewing, reading, and printing habits reveals that users appreciated the full-text searching capability. Among different types of searches, the author search was the most popular search, representing 32.1% of all searches. Users were still in the process of getting familiar with the digital library, and syntax and format errors accounted for 17.6% of searches. Usage data provide not only information about how users interact with digital libraries but also what affect users' interaction with digital libraries.

This period saw the first decade of digital library projects for the scientific and cultural heritage community being developed. Exemplary projects of the first decade of digital libraries in the scientific and cultural heritage community are: arXiv (pronounced AR-KIVE), a pioneering repository project; American Memory, a Library of Congress project of digitized cultural heritage collections; and JSTOR, a digital library of primarily academic journals

Launched in 1991, arXiv was created by Paul Ginsparg as an electronic bulletin board for colleagues to exchange unpublished manuscripts in the field of theoretical high-energy physics. The arXiv is also known as the "Los Alamos e-print archive." Twenty years later, the system contains about 7,000,000 full texts. It receives 75,000 new texts each year and serves close to 1 million full-text downloads to 400,000 unique users every week. ArXiv mainly covers research on physics but has extended to other related fields: mathematics, nonlinear science, computer science, statistics, etc. (Ginsparg, 2011; Luce, 2001). Further research has been conducted to investigate the effect of position in announcements of newly received articles on citation and readership in arXiv. The findings discover multiple effects in play in the digital library, ranging from the "visibility" effect for positions near the beginnings of the announcements, to the "self-promotion effect," to the "reverse-visibility" effect for positions near the ends of announcements, and a "procrastination" effect associated with submission made at the end of the day (Haque and Ginsparg, 2009, 2010). The main contribution of arXiv is the implementation of the idea of a central repository for researchers to share articles all over the world. In addition, it prompted the creation of PubMed Central by the US National Institutes of Health. Moreover, it blazed a trail for a new direction for scholarly communication. Fig. 1.4 presents the homepage of arXiv.

American Memory plays a key role in the development of digital libraries as one of the earliest large-scale projects. The Library of Congress started the American Memory as a pilot project in 1989, which became the National Digital Library Program in 1995. The American Memory project focuses on American history and culture. It was funded by congressional appropriations and private sources. The unique strength

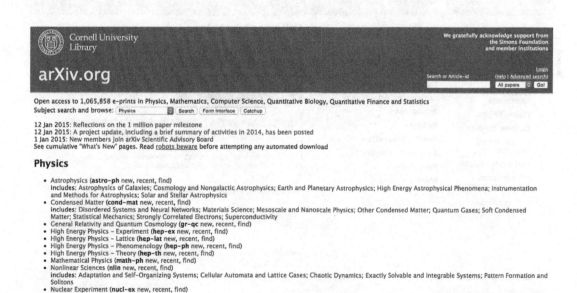

FIGURE 1.4 arXiv Homepage

of American Memory is its digital reproductions of original documents, which include texts, photographs, maps, motion pictures, and sound recordings. The selection criteria for the collections take into account the following: the uniqueness of the collection, usefulness in fulfilling other tasks including preservation, suitability for digitalization technology, and the educational value. Another strength is that it offers a standardized interface for users to navigate multiple collections. In addition to searching and browsing functions, there is an education program "Learning Page" associated with the American Memory collections. This page offers information for both teachers and students to teach and learn about not only American Memory collections but also American history (Fesenko, 2007; Lucas, 2000). Fig. 1.5 presents the homepage of American Memory.

As one of the early digital library projects, the development of American Memory provides invaluable lessons for the creation of digital libraries. Madden (2007, 2008) summarizes the contributions of the American Memory project:

- Data, in particular usage data, can help the enhancement of the digital library.
- Automation can reduce human error and stimulate standards development.
- Exceptions reduce the sustainability of data and the scalability of production.
- Interoperability is required for collaborative digitization projects.
- Flexible data model is needed to satisfy diverse needs.
- Data can be reused to accommodate lifecycle of different digital productions.

FIGURE 1.5 American Memory Homepage

JSTOR is primarily a digital library of academic journals, providing access to back issues of journal publications in social sciences, arts and humanities, and sciences. JSTOR started in 1995 as a digitization project funded by a grant from the Andrew W. Mellon Foundation. The first JSTOR collection, Arts & Sciences, became available in 1997. JSTOR contains complete back files of over 1600 core scholarly journals. Digital versions of print journals were created by scanning each page at a high resolution and searchable text was created by using optical character recognition (OCR) software plus intensive proofreading. More recently, JSTOR began adding books and primary sources. Preservation and access are the two main objectives of the JSTOR project. On the one hand, JSTOR was created to preserve digital scholarly content; on the other hand, it offers more efficient and effective access for scholarly communication. Another goal is to save a substantial amount of investment in physical library space. Fig. 1.6 presents the homepage of JSTOR.

Spinella (2007, 2008) highlights four aspects of JSTOR's success.

- First, the number of community participants gradually increased in all categories including libraries, publishers, higher education institutions, linking partners, and other types of collaborating organizations. There were more than 4300 institutions supporting JSTOR in 2007.
- Second, there is a large amount of archived journal publications. In 2007, JSTOR contained 750 journals with 25 million pages dating back to 1665. The collection spans 50 disciplines covering the humanities, social sciences, economics, education, law, and the life sciences. Moreover, JSTOR implemented standards for digitization, indexing, and metadata.

FIGURE 1.6 JSTOR Homepage

- Third, usage has increased at an average of 50% every year since 2001 and reached 500 million accesses in 2007. Large institutions are the main users of JSTOR. Disciplinary usage is affected by the number of researchers/teachers and students, as well as the number of the titles in the system. Users viewed 2–2.5 pages per article from 1997 to 2007.
- Fourth, the average cost to maintain the content and access per institution may decrease along the way. The costs for larger institutions and medium/small institutions are different. While large institutions experience declining cost per use, medium/small institutions' costs increase.

JSTOR played a significant role in facilitating the transition from print to electronic publishing in serial publications. However, creating the JSTOR repository was not an easy task. Walker et al. (2010) demonstrate the need for more resources, cohesive leadership, and open communication among all the parties in building a JSTOR repository.

It is worth noting that the development of digital libraries in this period also led to the creation and advancement of digital library architecture. In order to solve the problems of linked heterogeneous digital library services, Kahn and Wilensky (1995) created an important digital library architectural framework that defines the key entities in a digital library. It consists of four components: a digital object, a repository, a repository access protocol, and dissemination. A digital object is an instance of an abstract data type consisting of *data* and *key-metadata* in which "a handle," an identifier unique to the digital object, is a critical part. A *repository* is a storage system in which digital objects are stored for access and retrieval. The Repository Access Protocol (RAP) allows access to a stored digital object or its metadata by specifying its handle. A *dissemination* is the result of an access service request. The main contribution of this framework is the naming, identifying, and/or invoking of digital objects. Arms (1995) further enhances the key concepts in digital library architecture and identifies principles to highlight the key issues in the transition from the network services to a digital library:

- The technical framework is part of a larger legal and social context.
- The limitations of terminology hinder the understanding of digital library concepts.
- The structure and content of a digital library should be separate from each other.
- Names and identifiers are critical for a digital library.
- Digital library objects are beyond merely just data.
- Users may use a digital library object differently from the stored object.
- Repositories should be the custodian for the stored object.
- Users need useful intellectual works instead of just digital objects.

Digital library research and projects in their formative years have contributed to the development of digital library architecture, standards, iterative design, and usability studies, as well as best practices for their development. Digital library projects have contributed to the effective retrieval of multimedia objects across multiple repositories on the Internet and semantic interoperability (Schatz and Chen, 1996). After comprehensively reviewing digital library literature in terms of its content, organization, services, access, evaluation, as well as social, economic, and legal issues, Fox and Urs (2002) identify two types of challenges for digital libraries: research and practice. From the research perspective, a theory is needed that specifically accounts for different aspects of research in digital libraries; at the same time, a methodology for the design, development, and enhancement of digital libraries is also required. From the practice perspective, there is a lack of guidelines for the management of digital libraries.

BUILDING THE CONTENT AND OPENING ACCESS: 2000s

In the 2000s, digital library development rose to a new level. "By the end of the 1990s, digital libraries were no longer a novelty" (Arms, 2012, p. 583). Meanwhile, government funding ended. "As of 2005, it seems a virtual certainty that substantial programmatic US government funding of digital libraries research in terms of the construction of prototype systems is at an end" (Lynch, 2005, para. 9). In this period of time, two characteristics exemplify the development of digital libraries: Mass Digitization Projects and Open Access Repositories.

Mass Digitization Projects

Mass digitization refers to converting materials on an industrial scale without curating specific materials for digitization. OCR is used to make the full text of digitized documents searchable (Coyle, 2006). Coyle (2006) recognizes several issues in mass digitization:

- Include selection of items for digitizing, scanning, quality control, the OCR process, the creation of metadata, the creation of technical metadata, and storage
- Create book structure in a digital format
- Develop user interface for the large collection with different formats
- Develop new digitization standards for mass digitization
- Control quality of mass digitization for preservation purpose
- Define the scope of the mass digitization project

The Google Book Project represents a major mass digitization initiative undertaken by a commercial company in cooperation with the cultural heritage sector. Google initiated a massive project in 2004 to digitize millions of books and make their text searchable. The Google project is an expansion of the Early Google Print. At the beginning, five of the world's largest libraries joined the project: Harvard University, Stanford University, the University of Michigan at Ann Arbor, the University of Oxford, and the New York Public Library. Taking into consideration copyright laws, the project started digitizing works in the public domain first. To deal with copyrighted books, search engines only offer a few lines of text associated with a search term (Carlson and Young, 2005; Hanratty, 2005). The Google Book Project promotes the discussion of multiple issues and concerns. Bearman (2006) cites the five principles enumerated by the national librarians of the La Francophonie Meeting held in 2006: free access to publicly owned resources, nonexclusive agreements with content providers, preservation of standard images for long-term accessibility, protection of the integrity of the original materials, and provision of multilingual and multicultural access. However, the Google Book Project is also criticized for its image and metadata quality (Leetaru, 2008).

The Google Book Project is not the only mass digitization project although the other ones are not comparable in scale. The Internet Archive, a nonprofit group, worked with major libraries in six countries—Canada, China, Egypt, India, The Netherlands, and the United States—to incorporate their digitized books into the group's collection. They had about 77,000 books online in early 2005. These mass digitization projects are interrelated. For example, Brewster Kahle, the creator of the Open Content Alliance (OCA), is also the driving force behind the Internet Archive. Multilingual digitized text and multimedia documents are the foci of OCA. Over thirty library and cultural organizations shared their digital collections, and the content was available through the OCA web site and Yahoo (Carlson and Young, 2005; St. Clair, 2008).

Funded by the NSF, the Million Book Project is a collaborative project with international partners in China, India, and the Biblioteca Alexandrina. The main objective of the project is to advance research and development in the following areas: machine translation, massive distributed databases, storage formats, the use of digital libraries, distribution and sustainability, security, search engines, image processing, OCR, language processing, and copyright laws (St. Clair, 2008).

These mass digitization projects share similarities and differences. For example, Google Books and the Open Content Alliance represent two different approaches for mass digitized projects: one represents a proprietary model, and the other one represents an open model. After comparing the two projects, Leetaru (2008) concludes that they share many similarities even though they seem different. Google creates more powerful and intuitive interfaces for users to access the digital materials. The OCA effort ensures long-term preservation if the funding source is stable. Crane (2006) highlights the unique dimensions of a mass digitized project:

- Large scale in quantities
- Heterogeneity of content
- Granularity of objects from single catalogue entry to tagged objects
- More noise
- More audience as the result of open access
- Reduction in collections and entry points

These projects contribute to the enhancement of technology as the result of automatic processes, support for machine translation, and the improvement of information extraction. Copyright is the critical barrier for mass digitized projects, although copyright laws intend to protect new innovations. St. Clair (2008) proposes several approaches to overcome the barriers:

- Identify nonrenewed books
- Create a list of US books published between 1923 and 1963
- Obtain permission from publishers
- Digitize government publications
- Create synthetic documents, in particular in science and technology fields

The favorable rulings for HathiTrust and Google Books in *Authors Guild, Inc. v. HathiTrust* and *Authors Guild v. Google Books* have significant impact on the growth of digital libraries. Chapter 2 offers detailed discussion of the two cases, in particular how the four factors of fair use were weighted.

Open Access Repositories

An open access repository is defined as a collection of full-text documents available in online databases on the Internet that can be accessed freely and instantly. Institutional repositories are managed by research institutions to house their own authors' works (Pinfield, 2005). The creation of open access institutional repositories significantly promotes scholarly communication. Open access repositories achieved remarkable successes in this period of time. The origin of the open access repositories is associated with cost of serials. Now, a measure of high quality in repositories is whether it can also help to make research visible (Joint, 2008). Suber (2009) created and updated a timeline of the open access movement, including the development of open access repositories, such as 1991's arXiv, 1994's Perseus project, etc. Many open access repositories have been established. The Open Directory of Open Access Repositories offers a quality listing of international open access repositories. According to its

About page (OpenDOAR, 2014, para. 7), "*Open*DOAR is primarily a service to enhance and support the academic and research activities of the global community. *Open*DOAR maintains a comprehensive and authoritative list of institutional and subject-based repositories. It also encompasses archives supported by funding agencies like the National Institutes for Health in the USA or the Wellcome Trust in the UK and Europe." It had more than 2600 listings in August 2015.

On the one hand, the establishment of institutional repositories and the development of digital libraries play a critical role in the success of open access (Bailey, 2007). On the other hand, open access publishing increases the complexity and diversity of the development of digital libraries. Open access repositories can be classified as subject repository or institutional. Creaser et al. (2010) conducted an international survey and focus groups regarding awareness and attitudes toward open access repositories. The results show that in general authors support open access repositories. However, there are disciplinary differences in their preference on repositories. While authors from physical science and mathematics prefer subject-based repositories, authors from the social sciences and the humanities and arts like institutional repositories. ArXiv is a good example of a subject-based repository.

Tsakonas and Papatheodorou (2007) performed a usefulness and usability study to evaluate an open access digital library, a subject-based repository: e-prints in Library and Information Science. The findings of the study indicate that user satisfaction is influenced by usefulness and usability. Usefulness is measured by how relevant the information is, as well as the breadth of coverage. Ease of use, aesthetics, terminology, and learnability determine whether the digital library is usable. An increase in usability of a digital library is mainly owed to its open access nature and personalized features. Just as Krishnamurthy (2008) points out, the key term for open access, open access repository, and digital libraries is open.

LARGE-SCALE DIGITAL LIBRARIES: 2010–

Connecting discrete, standalone digital libraries has been a major issue since the beginning of their development. "The plurality of digital libraries is an ongoing technical challenge and major source of user frustration" (Bearman, 2007, p. 224). Major efforts have been undertaken to aggregate content from smaller individual digital libraries and to provide portals for global searching and retrieval. The large-scale digital libraries represent the next generation of discovery systems, with centralized access to a wide variety of scientific and cultural heritage materials. Characteristics of large-scale digital libraries can be summarized as follows:

- Large collection size: most of them contain more than one million items.
- Diverse formats: collection items may contain text, images, audio, video, etc.
- General and specific collection development policy: it not only contains general collection scope, quality guidelines, and selection responsibility but also depends on each participating member's policy for its specific collections.
- Copyright concern: some of them may not have copyright clearance.
- Level of access: single interface for all collection items; depending on copyright, some items have full-text access while others might have access limited to just the citation or abstract.
- Interoperability: metadata mapping is used to ensure the exchange of metadata between collections, or a single metadata schema is applied across all collections.

This section highlights the developments of four large-scale digital libraries, representing the work in building digital libraries with multiple subjects and with different ways of collaboration:

the National Science Digital Library (NSDL), HathiTrust, the Digital Public Library of America (DPLA), and Europeana.

The National Science Digital Library

The NSDL is one of the largest digital libraries constructed to advance science and math education in the so-called STEM disciplines (Science, Technology, Engineering, and Mathematics). It was funded by the US NSF initially. Most of the 64 projects focus on the development of collections in a variety of subject areas including STEM. The objective of the NSDL is to provide students and teachers a variety of interactive learning and teaching resources that are comprehensive, high quality, and authoritative. The initial effort focuses on collection building, technical infrastructure, and metadata creation (Lagoze et al., 2002; Lagoze et al., 2006; McCown et al., 2005; Zia et al., 2001). Fig. 1.7 presents the homepage of the NSDL.

The contribution of the NSDL is not just as a repository for digital collections. Lagoze et al. (2002) illustrate the core components of the NSDL architecture, which is based on previous digital library research:

- Metadata repository contains metadata.
- Search and discovery offer capabilities for users to locate and find resources in the digital library.
- Access management sets the requirements for users of the digital library and providers of intellectual property.
- User interface and portals facilitate interactions among users, collections, and services of the digital library.

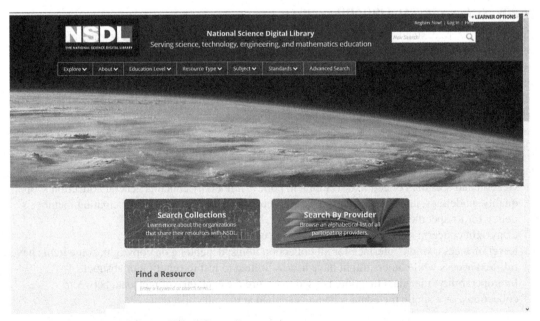

FIGURE 1.7 The National Science Digital Library Homepage

The NSDL added new standards on metadata and universal object identifiers that assist users to identify high quality resources. In addition, interoperability and reusability standards enable resources from different disciplines and different times to integrate together (Fortenberry and Powlik, 1999). Arms et al. (2003) discuss the NSDL's Metadata Repository based on the Open Archives Initiatives Protocol. It selected Dublin Core, qualified Dublin Core, IEEE Learning Technology Standards committee, Advanced Distributed Learning, MARC 21, Content Standards for Digital Geospatial Metadata, Global Information Locator Service, and Encoded Archival Description as metadata schemas. Its metadata was created at the collection level instead of item level. The Open Archives Initiative Protocol for Metadata Harvesting was considered to be used for harvesting. Lagoze et al. (2006) introduce the NSDL Data Repository, which offers a platform for new NSDL applications that promote user participation in the digital library. Its Data Repository consists of four applications: Expert Voices, a collaborative blogging system that supports Q/A discussions, recommendations and annotations, structured metadata, and the creation of relationships among resources in the NSDL; On Ramp, a distributed system that allows multiple users/groups to create, edit, and disseminate information in different formats; Instructional Architect, a system that enables users to discover, select, and design instruction materials; and the Content Alignment Tool, a system that aligns NSDL collections to state and national educational standards.

McCown et al. (2005) performed an experiment using educators to evaluate the relevance of the search results in the NSDL and Google. The results show that Google outperformed in the following areas: (1) useful educational materials, (2) retrieval precision, with Google's 38.2% compared to NSDL's 17.1%. At the same time, NSDL was found to contain higher quality resources and unique collections. One in four NSDL resources were not indexed by Google, and little overlap was identified between the two collections. NSDL has become a popular teaching and learning resources (Chen et al., 2015). A large-scale research project has been conducted nationally by a group researchers on instructors' and students' use of digital learning materials, in particular NSDL (Morgan et al., 2013, 2014; Wolf et al., 2008). The findings show that 80% of the faculty participants ranked peer review of materials as their first or second priority in relation to important digital library features. In addition, 30% of them indicated sources of pedagogical supplements as first or second priority. Students had diverse learning needs, styles, and different preferences in terms of technology and course mode. The information about students helped enhance the design of NSDL.

HathiTrust

HathiTrust represents a successful example of collaborative work on a large-scale repository/digital library. The Hathi name represents the value of the organization; Hathi in Hindi means elephant, which is well known for its memory, wisdom, and strength (Christenson, 2011). The HathiTrust started in 2006 when the University of Michigan proposed to the libraries associated with the Committee on Institutional Cooperation to build a shared digital repository to store the large files that Google digitized from the Committee on Institutional Cooperation libraries' book collections. HathiTrust, named in 2008, includes both digitized books and journal articles. This digital library contains materials in both the public domain and copyrighted works. The main issues are quality control, public search interfaces, ingestion of non-Google and nonbook content, access issues for people with disabilities, collection grouping, data mining, and academic research tools. HathiTrust is not dependent on the Google Book Project, and it has more resources from the public domain. The repository enables academic libraries to preserve collections from the last 150 years and may lead to a new direction for the future. Moreover,

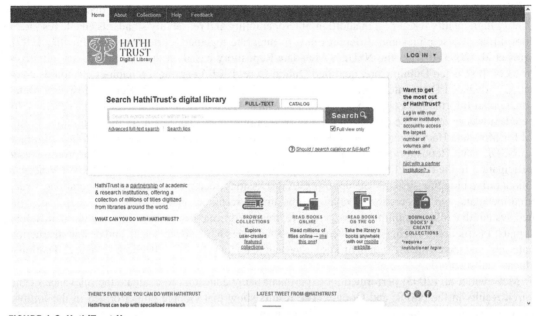

FIGURE 1.8 HathiTrust Homepage

OCLC (a global library cooperative) records the digital titles in HathiTrust in addition to printed copies in academic libraries (Pritchard, 2012). As of August 2015, the HathiTrust had more than 100 partners, and it is open to institutions all over the world. It contained more than 6 million book titles and 350,000 serial titles (HathiTrust, n.d.). Fig. 1.8 shows the homepage of HathiTrust.

The main objective of HathiTrust is to create a comprehensive digital collection of library materials owned by the participating research institutions. Simultaneously, it improves broad access to these materials, preserve important research records, coordinate shared collection management strategies to save costs, create and sustain the "public good," and develop a technical framework that enables members to build and share functionality (HathiTrust, n.d.). It is not only a digital library but also a collaborative group that works on key issues in creating and preserving a large collection of digital volumes. The wide collaboration, aggregated expertise, and integrated digital collections benefit both the participating libraries and users (Christenson, 2011). HathiTrust's metadata management system "Zephir" is a model of a metadata management system that offers the "best practical solution to organize and automate the multiple processes of metadata conversion, quality control and ingest, including making inventories and error reports" (Mallery, 2015, p. 354). Moreover, a web site was created (https://www.hathitrust.org/zephir) to provide comprehensive documentation to illustrate this multifaceted system.

The main challenge facing HathiTrust is copyright. Researchers can search for copyrighted documents but are unable to access them if their institutions are not members. Although multimedia information is included in the digital library, there is a lack of audio functionality which makes it difficult to become a digital library for special user groups, such as musicians (Downie et al., 2014). While 68% of HathiTrust's collection items are "in copyright," the other 32% are in the public domain.

The compositions of the 32% in the public domain consist of 21% in public domain worldwide including about 4% US federal government documents and 11% in US public domain (Eichenlaub, 2013).

User feedback is a key for the creation of a successful digital library. Fenlon et al. (2014) investigated user requirements for collection building in the HathiTrust Digital Library. The analysis from focus groups and interviews indicates that scholars consider collection building as a key scholarly activity and highly heterogeneous. They expect better metadata offering rich data about the documents and are willing to participate in the metadata creation and sharing process. After comparing the functionality of Google Books and HathiTrust on federal government publication use, Sare (2012) concludes that Google Books and HathiTrust each has its own strength and limitation. While Google Books has more government documents in general, HathiTrust is best for locating full-text government documents published after 1923. Google Books has an advantage in providing the added functionality of data visualization.

The Digital Public Library of America

The DPLA, a national public digital library, launched in 2013. The DPLA intends to not only serve as a center for the public to access all cultural materials free of charge but also as a platform for libraries and other cultural heritage institutions to thrive in the digital age. Its digital metadata come from large institutions, such as the National Archives and Records Administration and HathiTrust. In addition, regional service hubs contribute to metadata harvested by the DPLA. The DPLA is an aggregator of existing digital materials available in a distributed environment rather than a central repository (Cottrell, 2013; Gregory and Williams, 2014). As of 2015, the DPLA offered more than 10 million items from 1600 institutions to the public (DPLA, 2015). Fig. 1.9 presents the homepage of the DPLA.

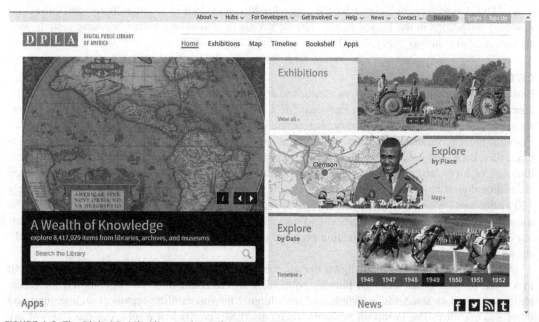

FIGURE 1.9 The Digital Public Library of America Homepage

The DPLA consists of three layers: a portal to a public web site with search functions; a platform containing the technical infrastructure, which is built using open source software; and a partnership with libraries, museums, archives, funders, universities, schools, and other institutions to promote broad access to information (Vandegrift, 2013). In addition, it is a repository for metadata. Content remains with the institutions, and only the metadata about the digital objects are harvested. Another benefit of the DPLA is that it provides APIs and open data for software developers, researchers, and others to create different types of tools for discovery, access, and communication (Eichenlaub, 2013; Ma, 2014).

The unique characteristic of the DPLA is acting as service and content hubs. According to Paulmeno (2015), DPLA partnered with different organizations and created 13 services hubs as of April 2015. These hubs collect metadata from different organizations and send them to the DPLA. At the same time, 16 content hubs had been established as of 2015. Content hubs are large institutions such as Harvard University, The New York Public Library, and The Smithsonian. Instead of collecting metadata, they each supply more than 200,000 records with their own metadata. Expanding their service and content hubs is the primary goal of the DPLA. Simultaneously, the goal of promoting DPLA usage is also vital. DPLA sponsors its annual DPLAfest in different parts of the country to encourage the involvement and use of the DPLA. With more funding, the DPLA is in the process of creating more service hubs to eventually connect online collections and serve all 50 states of United States in 2017 (DPLA, 2015). The DPLA infrastructure was also designed to be interoperable with the Europeana, which makes it possible for the creation of a worldwide network (Eichenlaub, 2013).

Just as Vandegrift (2013, p. 3) puts it, "DPLA is not a public library, a content repository, or a threat to traditional library services." The DPLA becomes the partner of, rather than a replacement for, public and academic libraries. It will greatly enhance their collections and services. The ultimate goal of DPLA is to serve as a center for the general public to explore libraries, archives, and museums' scattered collections in the United States. The DPLA also explores alternative licensing models with authors and publishers (Palfrey, 2013).

Europeana

Europeana, Europe's digital library, museum, and archive, is an across-domain and cross-cultural heritage site. Europeana means "thinks European" in Latin, and it is self-explanatory for users to understand the coverage of the digital library. Europeana was launched in 2008 and funded by the European Commission. Europeana covers Europe's cultural and scientific heritage materials and consists of pictures, files, books, photos, sounds, newspapers, manuscripts, and archival records digitized in museums, libraries, archives, and audio–visual collections (Purday, 2009). In 2014, the digital library contained 10 million digital objects from every member of the European Commission, including approximately 130 institutions (Weiss, 2014). The main objective of Europeana is to develop an open platform so that users and cultural institutions can access and manage a large collection of surrogate objects representing digital objects through an application program interface (API) (Concordia et al., 2010). Fig. 1.10 shows the homepage of Europeana.

As a large-scale and aggregate digital library, the key issues for building the digital library are split into work packages that focus on human, political, and intercommunity interoperability; interoperability of metadata standards; semantic and multilingual interoperability; technical architecture; and users and usability. The European Semantic Elements (ESE) consists of a subset of the Dublin Core and a set of 12 elements to meet its own needs (Purday, 2009). The Europeana Data Model (EDM) is

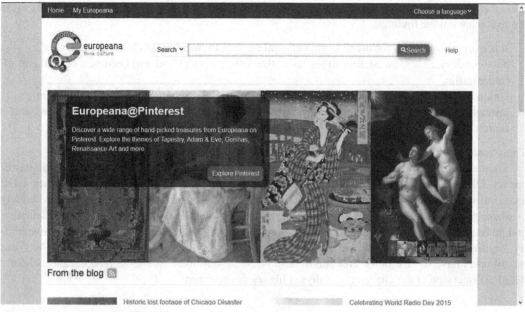

FIGURE 1.10 Europeana Homepage

replacing the European Semantic Elements to better represent millions of objects semantically across different types of Europeana's cultural heritage communities. The EDM integrates existing standards like RDF(s), Open Archive Object Reuse & Exchange, SKOS, and Dublin Core. It offers the possibility for cultural heritage institutions to move from closed information architectures to open and linked environments (Doerr et al., 2010; Haslhofer and Isaac, 2011). Peroni et al. (2013) identify some issues of EDM and suggest that content providers need to comply with the correct EDM Mapping Guideline and improve different levels of description of the objects.

Users' opinions have been solicited to enhance the design of Europeana, as has been the case with some previously discussed digital libraries. Dobreva and Chowdhury (2010) conducted a usability study of Europeana. They found that the majority of users rated the following functions highly: navigation, search functions, search results presentation, and ease of access. Users would like to have results ranked better and have higher precision results, to be able to refine their searches, to be able to overcome the language barriers, to have more help functions, to be able to use multiple ways of browsing including visualization tools, to be able to customize the interface, to have more links between items, and to be able to go back to their original searches. Nicholas and Clark (2014) analyzed log data to generate information-seeking behaviors of Europeana users. Log data analysis shows: (1) regarding site loyalty, less loyal users were found in the Europeana site than in other scholarly sites; and cultural institutions and their members were loyal users. (2) Regarding social media referrals, the overall visitors from social media referrals growth was lower (34%) than the overall visitor growth (90%) of Europeana. (3) Virtual exhibitions attracted high levels of engagement. More interestingly, from the beginning, Europeana took into consideration the design of a "lite" interface for mobile users. After analyzing log files of user interactions, in particular mobile interactions with Europeana, Nicholas et al. (2013) stress the following unique findings:

- It is extremely popular for users to use personal devices to interact with Europeana. Use of personal devices is growing four times faster than office devices and will become a critical part of future traffic.
- Unique information-seeking and use behaviors of mobile users focus on consuming content instead of creating content. They are short one-time visitors with less intensive engagement, and more visits occur during evenings and weekends.

These findings of user studies have great implications for the enhancement of Europeana.

The development of large-scale digital libraries is a necessary step in the evolution of digital libraries. On the one hand, it brings many benefits to developers to share architectures, metadata, other technical standards and guidelines, and costs. It also offers the opportunity for users to access widely available resources organized in a unified format and interface. On the other hand, it brings challenges and problems for the development of digital libraries. Copyrights, metadata harvesting, interoperability, digitizing quality, and multilanguage access are several typical challenges that researchers and practitioners have to face in the creation of large-scale digital libraries. Please read Chapter 11 for a detailed discussion of the challenges of digital library development.

REFERENCES

Agre, P.E., 2003. Information and institutional change. The case of digital libraries. In: Bishop, A.P., Van House, N.A., Buttenfield, B.P. (Eds.), Digital Library Use: Social Practice in Design and Evaluation. MIT Press, Cambridge, MA, pp. 219–240.

Arms, W.Y., 1995. Key concepts in the architecture of the digital library. D-lib Magazine 1 (1). Available from: http://www.dlib.org/dlib/July95/07arms.html.

Arms, W.Y., 2000. Digital Libraries. MIT Press, Cambridge, MA.

Arms, W.Y., 2012. The 1990s: the formative years of digital libraries. Lib. Hi Tech 30 (4), 579–591.

Arms, W.Y., Dushay, N., Fulker, D., Lagoze, C., 2003. A case study in metadata harvesting: the NSDL. Lib. Hi Tech 21 (2), 228–237.

Association of Research Libraries (ARL), 1995. Definition and purposes of a digital library. Available from: http://old.arl.org/resources/pubs/mmproceedings/126mmappen2

Bailey, C.W., 2007. Open access and libraries. Collect. Manage. 32 (3–4), 351–383.

Bawden, D., Rowlands, I., 1999. Digital libraries: assumptions and concepts. Libri 49 (4), 181–191.

Bearman, D., 2006. Jean-Noël Jeanneney's critique of Google: private sector book digitization and digital library policy. D-Lib Mag. 12 (12), 1–7.

Bearman, D., 2007. Digital libraries. Ann. Rev. Inform. Sci. Technol. 41 (1), 223–272.

Bishop, A.P., Van House, N.A., Buttenfield, B.P., 2003. Digital Library Use: Social Practice in Design and Evaluation. MIT Press, Cambridge, MA.

Blandford, A., Keith, S., Connell, I., Edwards, H., 2004. Analytical usability evaluation for digital libraries: a case study. In: Digital Libraries, Proceedings of the 2004 Joint ACM/IEEE Conference. IEEE. pp. 27–36.

Borgman, C.L., 1999. What are digital libraries? Competing visions. Inform. Process. Manage. 35 (3), 227–243.

Borgman, C.L., 2000. From Gutenberg to the Global Information Infrastructure: Access to Information in the Networked World. MIT, Cambridge, MA.

Borgman, C.L., 2003. Designing digital libraries for usability. In: Bishop, A.P., Van House, N.A., Buttenfield, B.P. (Eds.), Digital Library Use: Social Practice in Design and Evaluation. MIT Press, Cambridge, MA, pp. 85–118.

Borgman, C.L., Smart, L.J., Millwood, K.A., Finley, J.R., Champeny, L., Gilliland-Swetland, A.J., Leazer, G.L., 2005. Comparing faculty information seeking in teaching and research: implications for the design of digital libraries. J. Assoc. Inf. Sci. Technol. 56 (6), 636–657.

Bush, V., 1945a. As we may think. Atlantic Mon. 176 (1), 101–108, Available from: http://www.theatlantic.com /magazine/archive/1945/07/as-we-may-think/303881/.

Bush, V., 1945b. As we may think. Life, 19(11), 112-114, 116, 121, 123-24. [Reprinted from Bush, V. (1945). As we may think. Atlantic, 176(1), 101–108].

Buttenfield, B., 1999. Usability evaluation of digital libraries. Sci. Technol. Lib. 17 (3–4), 39–59.

Buttenfield, B.P., Reitsma, R.F., 2002. Loglinear and multidimensional scaling models of digital library navigation. Int. J. Hum-Comput. Stud. 57 (2), 101–119.

Calhoun, K., 2014. Exploring Digital Libraries: Foundations, Practice, Prospects. Neal-Schuman, Chicago.

Candela, L., Castelli, D., Pagano, P., 2007a. A reference architecture for digital library systems: principles and applications. In: Digital Libraries: Research and Development. Springer, Berlin, pp. 22–35.

Candela, L., Castelli, D., Pagano, P., Thano, C., Ioannidis, Y., Koutrika, G., Schuldt, H., 2007b. Setting the foundations of digital libraries: the DELOS manifesto. D-Lib Mag. 13 (3–4). Available from: http://www.dlib .org/dlib/march07/castelli/03castelli.html.

Carlson, S., Young, J., 2005. Google will digitize and search millions of books from 5 top research libraries. Chron. Higher Edu. 51 (18), A37–A40.

Carr, R., 2009. A history of digital library economics. In: Baker, D., Evans, W. (Eds.), Digital Library Economics: An Academic Perspective. Chandos Publishing, Oxford, UK, pp. 57–70.

Chen, H., Moore, J.L., Chen, W., 2015. Understand and analyzing learning objects: a foundation for long-term substantiality and use for elearning. Know. Manage. E-Learn. 7 (2), 280–296.

Chowdhury, S., Landoni, M., Gibb, F., 2006. Usability and impact of digital libraries: a review. Online Inform. Rev. 30 (6), 656–680.

Christenson, H., 2011. HathiTrust: a research library at web scale. Lib. Res. Tech. Serv. 55 (2), 93–102.

Concordia, C., Gradmann, S., Siebinga, S., 2010. Not just another portal, not just another digital library: a portrait of Europeana as an application program interface. IFLA J. 36 (1), 61–69.

Cottrell, M., 2013. A digital library for everybody. Am. Lib. 44 (3/4), 44–47.

Coyle, K., 2006. Mass digitization of books. J. Acad. Librar. 32 (6), 641–645.

Crane, G., 2006. What do you do with a million books? D-Lib Mag. 12 (3). Available from: http://www.dlib.org /dlib/march06/crane/03crane.html.

Crane, G. (2015). Perseus digital library. Available from: http://www.perseus.tufts.edu/hopper/

Creaser, C., Fry, J., Greenwood, H., Oppenheim, C., Probets, S., Spezi, V., White, S., 2010. Authors' awareness and attitudes toward open access repositories. New Rev. Acad. Librar. 16 (S1), 145–161.

De Rosa, C., Cantrell, J., Carlson, M., Gallagher, P., Hawk, J., Sturtz, C., 2005. Perceptions of libraries and information resources. A Report to the OCLC Membership. OCLC, Dublin, Ohio.

Dempsey, L., 2006. The (digital) library environment: ten years after. Ariadne 46. Available from: http://www .ariadne.ac.uk/issue46/dempsey.

Dobreva, M., Chowdhury, S., 2010. A user-centric evaluation of the Europeana digital library. In: Chowdhury, G., Khoo, C., Hunter, J. (Eds.), The Role of Digital Libraries in a Time of Global Change. Springer, Berlin, pp. 148–157.

Doerr, M., Gradmann, S., Hennicke, S., Isaac, A., Meghini, C., van de Sompel, H., 2010. The Europeana data model (EDM). In: World Library and Information Congress: 76th IFLA general conference and assembly pp. 10–15.

Downie, J.S., Dougan, K., Bhattacharyya, S., Fallaw, C., 2014. The HathiTrust Corpus: A Digital Library for Musicology Research? In: Proceeding of First International Digital Libraries for Musicology Workshop (DLfM 2014), ACM, New York, NY.

DPLA, 2015. Digital Public Library of America makes push to serve all 50 states by 2017 with $3.4 million from the Sloan and Knight foundations. Available from: http://dp.la/info/2015/06/26/digital-public-library-of-america -makes-push-to-serve-all-50-states-by-2017-with-3-4-million-from-the-sloan-and-knight-foundations/

Drabenstott, K., 1994. Analytical Review of the Library of the Future. Council on Library Resources, Washington, DC.

Dubis, M., 2003. Web resources for the study of New Testament backgrounds. JRTI 6 (1), 3–9.

Eichenlaub, N., 2013. Checking in with Google Books, HathiTrust, and other open access ebook collections. Comp. Lib. 33 (9), 4–9.

Entlich, R., Garson, L., Lesk, M., Normore, L., Olsen, J., Weibel, S., 1996. Testing a digital library: user response to the CORE project. Lib. Hi Tech 14 (4), 99–118.

Fenlon, K., Senseney, M., Green, H., Bhattacharyya, S., Willis, C., Downie, J.S., 2014. Scholar-built collections: a study of user requirements for research in large-scale digital libraries. Proc. Assoc. Inform. Sci. Technol. 51 (1), 1–10.

Fesenko, K., 2007. Models of digital cooperation. Slavic East Eur. Inform. Res. 8 (4), 87–97.

Fortenberry, N.L., Powlik, J.J., 1999. A national digital library for science, mathematics, engineering, and technology education. Comp. Appl. Eng. Edu. 7 (1), 45–49.

Fox, E., 1995. Digital libraries. Comm. ACM 38 (4), 23–31.

Fox, E.A., Gonçalves, M.A., Shen, R., 2012. Theoretical foundations for digital libraries: the 5S (societies, scenarios, spaces, structures, streams) approach. Synth. Lectures. Inform. Concepts Retrieval Serv. 4 (2), 1–180.

Fox, E.A., Urs, S.R., 2002. Digital libraries. Ann. Rev. Inform. Sci. Technol. 36, 503–589.

Ginsparg, P., 2011. ArXiv at 20. Nature 476 (7359), 145–147. Available from: http://www.nature.com/nature /journal/v476/n7359/full/476145a.html.

Gonçalves, M.A., Fox, E.A., Watson, L.T., Kipp, N.A., 2004. Streams, structures, spaces, scenarios, societies (5s): a formal model for digital libraries. ACM Trans. Inform. Syst. (TOIS) 22 (2), 270–312.

Greenstein, D., 2000. Digital libraries and their challenges. Lib. Trend. 49 (2), 290–303.

Gregory, L., Williams, S., 2014. On being a hub: some details behind providing metadata for the Digital Public Library of America. D-Lib Mag. 20 (7/8). Available from: http://dx.doi.org/10.1045/july2014-gregory.

Griffin, S.M., 2005. Funding for digital libraries: research past and present. D-Lib Mag. 11 (7/8). Available from: http://www.dlib.org/dlib/july05/griffin/07griffin.html.

Grudin, J., 2011. Human-computer interaction. Ann. Rev. Inform. Sci. Technol. 45 (1), 367–430.

Hanratty, E., 2005. Google Library: beyond fair use? Duke L. Tech. Rev. 2005, 10–26.

Haque, A.U., Ginsparg, P., 2009. Positional effects on citation and readership in arXiv. J. Am. Soc. Inform. Sci. Technol. 60 (11), 2203–2218.

Haque, A.U., Ginsparg, P., 2010. Last but not least: additional positional effects on citation and readership in arXiv. J. Am. Soc. Inform. Sci. Technol. 61 (12), 2381–2388.

Haslhofer, B., Isaac, A., 2011. Data. Europeana.eu: the Europeana linked open data pilot. In: International Conference on Dublin Core and Metadata Applications, pp. 94–104.

HathiTrust Digital Library, n.d. Millions of books online. Available from: http://www.hathitrust.org/.

Hill, L.L., Carver, L., Larsgaard, M., Dolin, R., Smith, T.R., Frew, J., et al., 2000. Alexandria Digital Library: user evaluation studies and system design. J. Am. Soc. Inform. Sci. 51 (3), 246–259.

Jeng, J., 2005. What is usability in the context of the digital library and how can it be measured? Inform. Technol. Lib. 24 (2), 47–56.

Joint, N., 2008. Current research information systems, open access repositories and libraries: ANTAEUS. Lib. Rev. 57 (8), 570–575.

Kahn, R., Wilensky, R., 1995. A framework for distributed digital object services. Corporation for National Research Initiatives. Available from: http://www.cnri.reston.va.us/kw.html.

Koohang, A., Ondracek, J., 2005. Users' views about the usability of digital libraries. British J. Edu. Technol. 36 (3), 407–423.

Krishnamurthy, M., 2008. Open access, open source and digital libraries: a current trend in university libraries around the world. Prog. Electron. Lib. Inform. Syst. 42 (1), 48–55.

Lagoze, C.J., 2010. Lost identity: the assimilation of digital libraries into the web. PhD dissertation, Cornell University.

Lagoze, C., Arms, W., Gan, S., Hillmann, D., Ingram, C., Krafft, D., et al., 2002. Core services in the architecture of the national science digital library (NSDL). In: Proceedings of the 2nd ACM/IEEE-CS joint conference on Digital libraries.ACM, New York, NY. pp. 201–209.

Lagoze, C., Krafft, D., Cornwell, T., Dushay, N., Eckstrom, D., & Saylor, J. (2006). Metadata aggregation and automated digital libraries: a retrospective on the NSDL experience. In: Proceedings of the 6th ACM/IEEE-CS joint conference on Digital libraries. ACM, New York, NY, pp. 230–239.

Lagoze, C., Krafft, D., Payette, S., Jesuroga, S., 2005. What is a digital library anyway, anymore? Beyond search and access in the NSDL. D-Lib Mag. 11 (11), Available from: http://dlib.org/dlib/november05/lagoze/11lagoze.html.

Larsgaard, M.L., Carver, L., 1995. Accessing spatial data online: project Alexandria. Information technology and libraries 14 (2), 93.

Law, D., 2009. Academic digital libraries of the future: an environment scan. New Rev. Acad. Librar. 15 (1), 53–67.

Law, D., 2011. Library landscapes: digital developments. In: Baker, D., Evans, W. (Eds.), Libraries and Society: Role, Responsibility and Future in an Age of Change. Chandos Publishing, Oxford, UK, pp. 361–377.

Leetaru, K., 2008. Mass book digitization: the deeper story of Google Books and the Open Content Alliance. First Monday 13 (10). Available from: http://firstmonday.org/ojs/index.php/fm/article/view/2101/2037.

Lesk, M. (1991, September). The CORE electronic chemistry library. In: Proceedings of the 14th Annual International ACM SIGIR Conference on Research and Development in Information Retrieval. ACM, New York, NY, pp. 93–112.

Lesk, M., 1997. Practical Digital Libraries: Books, Bytes & Bucks. Morgan Kaufmann Publishers, San Franciso, CA.

Lesk, M., 2005. Understanding Digital Libraries. Morgan Kaufmann, San Francisco, CA.

Lesk, M., 2012. A personal history of digital libraries. Lib. Hi Tech 30 (4), 592–603.

Levy, D.M., 2000. Digital libraries and the problem of purpose. D-Lib Mag. 6 (1). Available from: http://www.dlib.org/dlib/january00/01levy.html.

Levy, D.M., 2003. Documents and libraries: a sociotechnical perspective. In: Bishop, A.P., Van House, N.A., Buttenfield, B.P. (Eds.), Digital Library Use: Social Practice in Design and Evaluation. MIT Press, Cambridge, MA, pp. 25–42.

Licklider, J.C.R., 1965. Libraries of the Future. MIT Press, Cambridge, MA.

Liu, Z., Luo, L., 2011. A comparative study of digital library use: factors, perceived influences, and satisfaction. J. Acad. Librar. 37 (3), 230–236.

Lucas, B.E., 2000. Media review essays: learning American memories on the whole World Wide Web. Hist. Rev. 27 (1), 152–156.

Luce, R.E., 2001. E-prints intersect the digital library: inside the Los Alamos arXiv. Issues Sci. Technol. Librar. 29.

Lyman, P., 1996. What is a digital library? Technology, intellectual property and the public interest. Daedalus 125 (4), 1–33.

Lynch, C.A., 1993. Accessibility and integrity of networked information collections. Background paper no. OTA-BP-TCT-109. Washington, DC: Office of Technology Assessmnet. Available from: http://files.eric.ed.gov/fulltext/ED368360.pdf.

Lynch, C., 2005. Where do we go from here?: the next decade for digital libraries. D-Lib Mag. 11 (7/8). Available from: http://www.dlib.org/dlib/july05/lynch/07lynch.html.

Ma, H., 2014. Tech services on the Web: DPLA: Digital Public Library of America http://dp.la. Tech. Serv. Quart. 31 (1), 83–84.

Madden, L., 2007. Digital Curation at the Library of Congress: Lessons Learned From American Memory and the Archive Ingest and Handling Test. Library of Congress, Washington, DC.

Madden, L., 2008. Applying the digital curation lessons learned from American Memory. Int. J. Digital Curation 3 (2), 121–129.

Mallery, M., 2015. Zephir, the HathiTrust metadata management system; http://www. hathitrust. org/zephir. Tech. Serv. Quart. 32 (3), 354–356.

Manfroid, S., Gillen, J., Phillips-Batoma, P.M., 2013. The Archives of Paul Otlet: between appreciation and rediscovery, 1944–2013. Lib. Trend. 62 (2), 311–328.

Marchionini, G., 2000. Evaluating digital libraries: a longitudinal and multifaceted view. Lib. Trend. 49 (2), 304–333.

Marchionini, G., Crane, G., 1994. Evaluating hypermedia and learning: methods and results from the Perseus Project. ACM Trans. Inform. Sys. (TOIS) 12 (1), 5–34.

Marcum, D.B., 1997. Digital libraries: for whom? For what? J.Acad. Librar. 23. (2), 81–84.

Matusiak, K.K., 2010. Use of digital resources in an academic environment: a qualitative study of students' perceptions, experiences, and digital literacy skills. PhD dissertation, University of Wisconsin, Milwaukee.

Matusiak, K.K., 2012. Perceptions of usability and usefulness of digital libraries. Int. J. Humanities Arts Comp. 6 (1–2), 133–147.

McCown, F., Bollen, J., Nelson, M.L., 2005. Evaluation of the NSDL and Google for obtaining pedagogical resources. In: Research and Advanced Technology for Digital Libraries. Springer, Berlin, pp. 344–355.

McMartin, F., Iverson, E., Wolf, A., Morrill, J., Morgan, G., Manduca, C., 2008. The use of online digital resources and educational digital libraries in higher education. Int. J. Digital Lib. 9 (1), 65–79.

Mischo, W.H., 2005. Digital libraries: challenges and influential work. D-Lib Mag. 11 (7/8), 636–651. Available from: http://www.dlib.org/dlib/july05/mischo/07mischo.html.

Morgan, G., Dziuban, C., McMartin, F., Morrill, J., Moskal, P., Wolf, A., 2013. Evaluating Faculty and Student Use of Digital Resources for Teaching and Learning. Available from: http://hdl.handle.net/2142/55341.

Morgan, G., Dziuban, C., McMartin, F., Morrill, J., Moskal, P., Wolf, A., 2014. Technical Report: Results From the Study: Student Use of Digital Learning Materials: implications for the NSDL. Available from: https://www. ideals.illinois.edu/handle/2142/55346.

Nicholas, D., Clark, D., 2014. Information seeking behaviour and usage on a multi-media platform: case study Europeana. In: Library and Information Sciences: Trends and Research, Springer, Berlin, pp. 57–78.

Nicholas, D., Clark, D., Rowlands, I., Jamali, H.R., 2013. Information on the go: a case study of Europeana mobile users. J. Am. Soc. Inform. Sci. Technol. 64 (7), 1311–1322.

OpenDOAR, 2014. About OpenDOAR. Available from: http://www.opendoar.org/about.html.

Palfrey, J., 2013. What is the DPLA? Lib. J. 138 (7), 38–41.

Paulmeno, M., 2015. The Digital Public Library of America: building a national digital library. Mississippi Lib. 78 (2). Available from: http://epubs.library.msstate.edu/index.php/MSLib/article/view/262/303.

Peroni, S., Tomasi, F., Vitali, F., 2013. Reflecting on the Europeana data model. In: Digital Libraries and Archives. Springer, Berlin, pp. 228–240.

Pinfield, S., 2005. A mandate to self archive? The role of open access institutional repositories. Serials: J. Serials Commun. 18 (1), 30–34.

Preece, E., Zepeda, C., 2009. The Perseus Digital Library: A case study. Available from: https://repositories2.lib .utexas.edu/bitstream/handle/2152/6836/perseus_case_study.pdf?sequence=5.

Pritchard, S.M., 2012. HathiTrust libraries map a shared path: a turning point in information access. Portal Lib. Acad. 12 (1), 1–3.

Purday, J., 2009. Think culture: Europeana.eu from concept to construction. Electron. Lib. 27 (6), 919–937.

Rayward, W.B., 1994. Visions of Xanadu: Paul Otlet (1868–1944) and hypertext. J. Am. Soc. Inform. Sci. 45 (4), 235.

Rayward, W.B., 1997. The origins of information science and the International Institute of Bibliography/ International Federation for Information and Documentation (FID). J. Am. Soc. Inform. Sci. 48 (4), 299–300.

Rayward, W.B., 1999. H. G. Wells's idea of a world brain: a critical reassessment. J. Am. Soc. Inform. Sci. 50 (7), 270–312.

Rayward, W.B., 2005. The historical development of information infrastructures and the dissemination of knowledge: a personal reflection. Bull. Am. Soc. Inform. Sci. Technol. 31 (4), 19–22.

Reagle, J.M., 2010. Good Faith Collaboration: The Culture of Wikipedia. MIT Press, Cambridge, MA.

Saracevic, T., 2000. Digital library evaluation: toward an evolution of concepts. Lib. Trend. 49, 350–369.

Sare, L., 2012. A Comparison of HathiTrust and Google Books using federal publications. Pract. Acad. Librar. Int. J. SLA Acad. Div. 2 (1), 1–25.

Schatz, B., Chen, H., 1996. Building large-scale digital libraries. Computer 29 (5), 22–26.

Schwartz, C., 2000. Digital libraries: an overview. J. Acad. Librar. 26 (6), 385–393.

Smith, T.R., 1996. A digital library for geographically referenced materials. Computer 29 (5), 54–60.

Smith, T.R., Frew, J., 1995. Alexandria Digital Library. Commun. ACM 38 (4), 61–62.

Spinella, M.P., 2007. JSTOR: past, present, and future. J. Lib. Admin. 46 (2), 55–78.

Spinella, M., 2008. JSTOR and the changing digital landscape. Interlending Doc. Supply 36 (2), 79–85.

St. Clair, G., 2008. The Million Book project in relation to Google. J. Lib. Admin. 47 (1–2), 151–163.

Suber, P., 2009. Open access in 2008. J. Electron. Pub. 12 (1). Available from: http://quod.lib.umich.edu/cgi/t/text/idx/j/jep/3336451.0012.104/--open-access-in-2008?rgn=main;view=fulltext.

Tsakonas, G., Papatheodorou, C., 2007. Critical constructs of digital library interaction. In: Proceedings of the 11th Panhellenic Conference in Informatics (PCI 2007) pp. 57–66. Available from: http://eprints.rclis.org/10500/1/PCI2007_Tsakonas_Papatheodorou_eprints_.pdf.

Vandegrift, M., 2013. The Digital Public Library of America: details, the librarian response and the future. In: The Library with the Lead Pipe. Available from: http://www.inthelibrarywiththeleadpipe.org/2013/dpla/.

Walker, B., Schoonover, D., Margjoni, R., 2010. Creating a statewide JSTOR repository: initial steps taken by the Florida State University System. J. Interlib. Loan Doc. Del. Electron. Res. 20 (3), 159–172.

Waters, D.J., 1998. What are digital libraries? CLIR Issue 4, 1–6.

Weiss, A., 2014. Using Massive Digital Libraries: A LITA Guide. ALA Tech Source, Chicago.

Wells, H.G., 1938. The World Brain. Doubleday, Doran & Co, Garden City, NY.

Wilson, S., 2000. Navigating ancient worlds. Humanities 21 (5), 18–20.

Witten, I.H., Bainbridge, D., 2003. How to Build a Digital Library. Morgan Kaufmann Publishers, San Franciso, CA.

Wolf, A., Morgan, G., McMartin, F., Manduca, C., 2008. Faculty use of digital resources and the implications for digital libraries. Poster presented at 2008 Educause Annual Conference. Available from: http://d32ogoqmya1dw8.cloudfront.net/files/facultypart/faculty_use_digital_resources.pdf.

Xie, H.I., 2006. Evaluation of digital libraries: criteria and problems from users' perspectives. Lib. Inform. Sci. Res. 28 (3), 433–452.

Yang, S.C., 2001. An interpretive and situated approach to an evaluation of Perseus digital libraries. J. Am. Soc. Inform. Sci. Tech. 52 (14), 1210–1223.

Zachary, G.P., 1997. Endless Frontier: Vannevar Bush, Engineer of the American Century. Free Press, New York.

Zia, L. L., Pearce, L., Prinsen, J. G. B., Ticer, B. V., Peters, D., Pickover, M., Matylonek, J. C., et al., 2001. The NSF National Science, Technology, Engineering, and Mathematics Education Digital Library (NSDL) Program: New Projects and a Progress Report. D-lib Mag. 7(11). Available from: http://dlib.org/dlib/november01/zia/11zia.html.

DIGITAL LIBRARY COLLECTION DEVELOPMENT

COLLECTION DEVELOPMENT INTRODUCTION
HISTORY

In the book *Fundamentals of Collection Development and Management*, Johnson (2009) provides an overview of collection development history. Collection development started with the emergence of libraries, although there is no recorded information regarding collection development policy in ancient times. During that time, libraries served as storage places rather than information dissemination centers. The goal of the library was to achieve a comprehensive and complete collection. The emergence of theories of selection indicates the birth of collection development. Thaddeus M. Harris drafted the first American guide for selection in 1793. Systematic philosophies of library materials selection were only discussed around the end of the 19th century. The goal was to achieve a balance between comprehensiveness and the most relevant materials for collection development in libraries. Collection development became a specialized area in the 1970s. Starting in the late 1970s, the enormous growth of publications and rising costs challenged library budgets. The explosion of electronic resources and the corresponding legal issues raised even more challenges in the late 1990s. Digitization projects and the preservation of digital information are the main themes for libraries in the 21st century. This new trend also has led to the new collection development policies.

Nisonger (2000) points out that the complexity of collection development is caused by the emergence of new technologies and new formats for information. Corrall (2012) illustrates four phases of collection development informed by digital technology. During late 1960s–70s, automation and computer-based operations affected collection development in relation to an increase in the efficiency of the collection process. During the 1980s and early 1990s, innovation of computer-based services made it possible for users to access local and consortia collections remotely. During late 1980s–90s, digitized collections led to the birth of digital and hybrid libraries. Since the 2000s, collaborative and network-based collections have resulted in the development of digital library management systems, institutional repositories, and data curation.

Beginning in the 2000s, digital collection development has gained a fresh, new momentum. Bullis and Smith (2011) review collection management and development literature from 2004 to 2008, and identify four areas of foci: (1) the changing nature of local collections, (2) redefining collection management responsibilities and practices, (3) cooperation and collaboration, and (4) collection assessment and evaluation. With respect to changing local collections, the main characteristic is the shift from print resources to electronic resources. Open access becomes an important and unsolved issue for collection development. The emergence of a large quantity of electronic resources has required libraries to review their collection development policies and procedures and change their organizations, responsibilities, education and training, by building digital collection and appropriate selection of processes and tools. Different levels of cooperation and collaboration are implemented to deal with challenges. The influx

Discover Digital Libraries. http://dx.doi.org/10.1016/B978-0-12-417112-1.00002-8

of digital resources calls for the need for new models and tools for collection assessment and evaluation. Due to declining budgets, diverse users and the responsibility of libraries for information access, Wu (2011) also suggests that a collaborative digital collection should be the direction of libraries.

DEFINITIONS

In order to understand collection development, we first need to understand what a collection is. Gorman (2000) defines a collection as objects in the collection including tangible objects and local intangible resources owned by the library, as well as tangible objects and remote intangible resources owned by other libraries but accessible by the users of the library. According to Lee (2000, 2005), there is no standard definition of a collection. Different entities have different perspectives on a collection. The key elements of a collection from the user perspective are: a group of information resources, a defined user community, a clear collection development policy, and an integrated retrieval system. Users consider the following parameters to define a collection: instant availability, selectivity, physical collocation, catalog representation, user privilege, material stability and parameters for subcollections (Lee, 2000, 2005). Drawing perspectives from different stakeholders, Corrall and Roberts (2012) develop a collection development hierarchy for use in the digital world. At the management level, a collection is defined as a thing, and examples include prioritizing subject areas and defining the scope of the collections, collaborative collection, and preservation. At the tactics level, a collection is defined as access, and examples consist of links to web-based collections, interoperable systems and integrating libraries into nonlibrary networks. At the operations level, a collection is defined as a process, and examples include user-oriented collections, supporting collections created by communities, and linked data.

Even though there is no standard definition of collection development, the following represents the typical definition:

> Collection development is a term representing the process of systematically building library collection to serve the study, teaching, research, recreational, and other needs of library users. The process includes selection and deselection of current retrospective materials, planning of coherent strategies for continuing acquisition, and evaluation of collections to ascertain how well they serve user needs (Gabriel, 1995, p. 3).

Shaw (2012) provides a concise definition of collection development policy: "A collection development policy is a formal policy document or statement which maintains a commitment to systematic collection building and development" (p. 165).

After reviewing the relevant literature on collection development, Corrall (2012) concludes that despite the changes in the format and location of resources, the principles of selecting materials to meet the diverse needs of users are unchanged. Fieldhouse (2012) illustrates a list of collection development activities: selection and acquisition, budget management, electronic resource management, storage and preservation, weeding, collection assessment, and collaborations with different stakeholders of collections. The main characteristics of collection development can be summarized as follows:

- Satisfy user needs
- Systematically select relevant collection items
- Systematically deselect collection items
- Strategies for planning of acquisition
- Assessment of the collection

DIGITAL COLLECTION DEVELOPMENT POLICY
COLLECTION DEVELOPMENT POLICY

Based on the ALA model, Shaw (2012) specifies the main sections of a collection development policy: "introduction, purpose of the collection development policy, mission statement, clientele, content, special collections, collection depth, evaluation, cooperation, intellectual freedom and review" (p. 168). Clarity, consistency, and continuity are the requirements for effective collection development policy.

Digital library collection development policy in general consists of goals/purposes, scope/types of content, priorities, and selection criteria. Parfrey (2013) describes the collection development framework of the California Digital Library: "The California Digital Library (CDL) is a 'co-library' of the University of California (UC) whose primary collection responsibility is to develop electronic content and make it available to all faculty members and students. Some of the electronic content will be licensed and acquired from commercial sources, and some will be produced by digitizing university collections. The same three considerations used to develop library collections in the ten UC campus libraries that guide collection development for the CDL are:

- The user base
- The programs that are to be supported
- The resources available to support those users and programs" (para. 1)

In determining collection development, the main focus is on the users, associated programs, and available resources.

- Make sure collection development meets faculty's and students' information needs
- Organize digital resources and offer guidance, and include them as part of the library services
- Justify the selection of digital formats in the selection of digital resources

Balance and prioritization are the keys for digital collection development. It is important to balance different disciplines, different formats of digital resources, research and teaching, and different campuses. Priorities are given to the content that users need the most and add significant value over print materials.

Each digital collection development policy has a scope of the types of materials covered. For example, the University of Texas Libraries (2011) has different collection development policies for materials obtained or produced in different ways as follows:

- Purchased or licensed material
- Digitized materials by the University of Texas Libraries or the University
- Links and pointers of substantial scholarly value

Different types of resources have their specific collection development policies. For example, e-books in general have their own unique collection development policy. Moore (2015) offers an outline for e-book collection development policy:

- Coverage of the policy
- Selection personnel
- Collection funding
- Selection criteria
- Duplication checks

- Purchasing model preferences
- Collection access and maintenance
- Download ability
- Reading devices
- Weeding

Simultaneously, different types of digital libraries/repositories have their distinctive collection policies as well. Brown (2012) discusses the uniqueness of collection development in institutional repositories. The main point is that researchers are content suppliers as well as users. That factor changes collection policy from acquiring needed items as previously done, to requesting materials from authors without offering financial compensation (Genoni, 2004). Another uniqueness is that an enormous amount of materials will be submitted if there is an institutional mandatory submission policy, potentially posing difficulties for the institutional repository system. However, if there is no mandatory policy, promoting institutional repositories is a challenge for the collection development. Third, different stakeholders of institutional repositories have different views of institutional repository uses. It is a critical issue in terms of how to develop a coherent and coordinated approach for collection development (Ayris, 2009). Detailed discussion of selection criteria for different types of digital materials and for different types of digital libraries/repositories follows.

Collection development policy is not a one-stop task; instead, it needs to adapt and reflect the changes in the environment. Miller (2000) stresses the need for the collection development policy to evolve as technology changes and user needs change. A review of twenty years of literature indicates that collection policies need to expand to consider the change of technology; hardware and software compatibility; the perpetuity of materials, costs, training, and support; and limited access. Douglas (2011) identifies publishing trends, budgeting, and users' information needs as important elements that any modification to collection policy needs to take into consideration.

COLLECTION DEVELOPMENT CRITERIA

Collection development criteria are the central component in collection development policy. Hollman (2000) emphasizes that four basic selection criteria for library materials are still relevant for electronic materials: quality, library relevancy, aesthetic and technical aspects, and cost. Gessesse (2000) highlights three main properties of collection items: relevance, quality, and timeliness of the materials. Metz (2000) points out some new meanings of the traditional standards for electronic resources. For example, currency refers to the updating frequency. The degree to which resources may be shared refers not just to how many people can share the same information, but what also should be kept in mind is the number of the so-called information poor, those lacking technological literacy or having restricted access to digital resources. New important criteria are introduced related to cost, licensing, functionality, and archiving. Cost is difficult to estimate, as there are many contributing factors, such as the allowable number of simultaneous users, defined user communities, joining consortia, etc. Licensing is determined by the extent of resources being acquired or accessed, people who use the resources, their purposes of use and monitoring mechanisms for the licensing terms. Functionality requires the provision of clear documentation for electronic information access, an up-to-date system and network infrastructure, platform-independent information resources, compliance with the Disabilities Act, etc. Archiving is associated with solving the problem of long-term access because of technological changes, licensing resources, and lack of control of resources.

There are different types of electronic resources coming from many different disciplines. Selection criteria may vary from discipline to discipline. Case (2000) identifies four new criteria for the selection of electronic resources based on the relevant literature: price, demand and use, library infrastructure, and product interface. He also discusses the problems of applying these criteria in selecting humanities e-texts. Some of the electronic resources are very expensive; however, price should not be the main concern if users need the resources. Simultaneously, demand and usage data are not the correct indicators for selection decisions in humanities e-texts. The key is how to promote electronic resources to humanities scholars. Many libraries do not have adequate support for electronic resource use, in particular humanities e-texts. Libraries need to engage vendors, librarians, and users to enhance the support. Functionalities and ease of use are suggested by library literature as one of the key criteria for electronic resource interfaces, but user need should still be the main consideration for collection selection. In actuality, both technology and individual user's needs have to be considered in determining selection criteria. Different electronic resources also require specific selection criteria. Vasileiou et al. (2012) find that the most cited selection criteria for e-books in academic library literature are the cost of e-books and the high usage/demand, followed by licenses, business models, platform interfaces, and subject coverage. Their study is in agreement with the early studies regarding the most cited criteria: business models, licenses, price, platform interfaces, subject coverage, and reading lists. Librarians face the challenges of issues related to business models, licenses, and the pricing of e-books.

Digital collections also have their own unique selection criteria. Gertz (2011) summarizes several of the most cited digital collection selection criteria, including value and demand, copyrights, technical feasibility, infrastructure, added value, and cost:

- Does the item or collection have sufficient value to and demand from a current audience to justify digitization?
- Do we have the legal right to create a digital version?
- Do we have the legal right to disseminate it?
- Can the materials be digitized successfully?
- Do we have the infrastructure to carry out a digital project?
- Does or can digitization add something beyond simply creating a copy?
- Is the cost appropriate? (pp. 98–99)

Collaboration with other institutions became the new emerging selection criterion. Kellerman (2014) considers the following selecting criteria for digital projects: (1) project goals in relation to the institution's mission, (2) the intended audience in relation to targeted user groups, (3) the final product with valued-added features or options, (4) the requirement of collection preservation, (5) the scope of the collection to be scanned, (6) check any overlap of the digital collection on the Internet, and (7) potential collaboration with partners to share similar resources.

Of course, selection criteria might be more particular for specific types of digital libraries. For example, Kastens et al. (2005, para. 10) present seven selection criteria for an educational digital collection:

- Scientific accuracy
- Pedagogical effectiveness
- Completeness of documentation
- Ease of use for teachers and learners

- Ability to inspire or motivate learners
- Importance or significance of the content
- Robustness as a digital resource

Another example is related to collection development for the International Children's Digital Library. The primary challenge in the International Children's Digital Library project arises mainly because national libraries, publishers, and creators have different policies regarding copyrights. The other critical issue is how to deal with unsolicited books. The collection development goal is to obtain award-winning children's books, but unsolicited books were at times submitted in different languages. Advisory board members and children's literature organizations are used to determine the relevance and acceptability within a culture (Hutchinson et al., 2013).

Even though large-scale digitization projects' collection policies are commonly considered quite comprehensive and broad, they still have specific guidelines. For example, the National Science Digital Library's (NSDL) quality of selection criteria are:

- Relevant to STEM education or research
- Scientifically accurate
- Clear creator and creation information
- Functional and operational materials
- Well-documented educational resource
- Instructionally valuable
- Significant contribution to learning
- Complete documentation
- Easy to use
- Engaging learners
- Free of advertising
- Wide accessibility to users (Miller, 2007)

These selection criteria concentrate on digitizing accurate, relevant, easy-to-use, and inspiring digital items.

It is also worth noting that each institution needs to develop its strategic plan and priorities for digital collection development that correspond to its mission and goals. Different missions and goals lead to different collection development policies. These selection criteria are not just applied in one step. Collection item selection, in general, goes through several phases. Here is a typical example of three phases of collection item selection (Vogt-O'Connor, 2000):

- Identifying materials for inclusion and exclusion
- Assessing materials for digitization using selection criteria
- Prioritizing the selected materials based upon the criteria of value, use, and risk

The overall objective of going through the three phases is to make sure that the most important materials are digitized first. Kellerman (2014) offers more detailed steps for preparing resources for digital projects: (1) select materials, (2) clear rights, (3) locate and retrieve materials, (4) inventory, collate, and stabilize the materials, (5) determine digital content management platform for display and access, (6) determine file naming convention, (7) collect metadata, (8) scan, (9) collect structural metadata, (10) access and treat original materials, (11) return original materials (pp. 356–357). Each institution needs to create its own selection criteria and specific steps for the development of digital collections based on the mission and goal of the institution, the nature of materials, and targeted user needs.

COLLECTION ASSESSMENT

Collection assessment is part of collection development and is comprised of collection maintenance, assessment, and weeding (Shaw, 2012). It is critical to assess whether a collection satisfies the objectives in the collection development policy. Based on the relevant literature, Schroeder (2012) characterizes criteria to assess patron-driven collection development and acquisition: (1) cost, (2) usage data, (3) appropriateness to the collection, and (4) holdings of peer institutions. Collection data are the key data that are used in decision making and assessment in electronic collection development. Morrisey (2010) suggests using the Standardized Usage Statistics Harvesting Initiative data and electronic resource management system data. Quantitative data can help identify duplications and titles that are not accessed. In addition to quantitative data, qualitative data are also critical to make the final decision for collection assessment.

The emergence of electronic resources makes the prominence of print collections less important. Jacob et al. (2014) summarize the main reasons to weed in libraries: (1) relevance to institutional needs, (2) offering reliable and accurate information, (3) providing up-to-date information, (4) reflecting collections changes, (5) removing worn materials, (6) increasing circulation rates, (7) accessibility for staff, (8) creating space, (9) informing staff about use of the collection, (10) balancing new and old materials, (11) providing feedback for budget decisions. Tyckoson (2014) identifies the main motivations for weeding: retention policies, space, and obsolescence. The weeding of print resources focuses more on removing materials that have not been used or have been used relatively less, old editions, duplicates, and outdated resources.

Weeding in digital collections has a different meaning. Although shelf space is no longer an issue, weeding to keep currency of the collection is still important, in particular in some disciplines, such as health sciences disciplines, where outdated information is misleading and potentially dangerous (Hightower and Gantt, 2012). Many of the weeding criteria that are applied to print collections, such as currency and the quality of the content, also apply to digital collections. The difference between weeding e-books and printed books is that search results need to be populated with relevant results mainly because users access e-books via search interfaces (Waugh et al., 2015). Space is not a main concern any more; instead, it is vital to provide reliable, accurate, and current information. In addition, it is not the obsolescence of materials, rather the obsolescence of formats becomes the main concern.

LEGAL ISSUES IN COLLECTION DEVELOPMENT
COPYRIGHT PROTECTION

Copyright is a form of legal protection for the authors of original works in both published and unpublished formats. The Statute of Anne was England's first copyright law and also influenced the United States' copyright clause drafted at the Constitutional Convention of 1787. The objective of the United States' Copyright Clause was to promote the advancement of learning and public knowledge rather than to protect authors (Wu, 2011).

The three most important US copyright laws include the 1976 Copyright Act, the 1998 Copyright Term Extension Act (Sonny Bono Act), and the 1998 Digital Millennium Copyright Act (DMCA). The 1976 Copyright Act provides the basic rules for copyright protection and increases the length of protection from a 56-year maximum to the life of an author plus 50 years. In 1998, the Copyright Term Extension Act extended copyrights for another 20 years, which, in total, made authorship copyright the life of the author plus 70 years. The Copyright Term Extension Act was established to meet some specific distributors' interests. The DMCA was enacted to enforce criminal sanctions for anyone bypassing some technological protection on digital content, although it also provides some protection for nonprofit organizations.

Hirtle et al. (2009) highlight four underlying principles of copyright law: the copyright/property distinction, the "public domain," the "idea/expression dichotomy," and independent creation. Regarding the copyright/property distinction principle, it is important to note that ownership does not equal copyright. The donor, seller, or depositor of digital objects may not have the copyrights of these items. The "public domain" principle means that, when a copyright expires, the work moves to the public domain. With respect to collection development, it means that an item in the public domain can be added to a collection without obtaining permission from anyone. In addition, documents prepared by an officer or employee of the United States Government as part of his/her duties are also in the public domain. For the idea/expression dichotomy, copyright protects the expression of ideas instead of the ideas themselves. The independent creation principle requires a plaintiff to demonstrate that a copyright infringement has arisen from his/her original work. There are also prerequisites for the protected item. The item has to be in a tangible form in original works of authorship, and the authorship or publication has to be associated with the United States.

The main function of US copyright laws is to protect copyrighted works. 17 U.S.C. §106 specifies the exclusive rights in copyrighted works (Copyright Act of 1976, 2006):

- Reproduction of copyrighted works
- Preparation of derivative works, for example, reproduce art works, translations, etc.
- Distribution of copyrighted works publicly
- Performance of literary, musical, dramatic, and choreographic works, pantomimes, and motion pictures and other audiovisual works publicly
- Display of literary, musical, dramatic, and choreographic works, pantomimes, and motion pictures and other audiovisual works publicly
- Performance of sound recordings through digital audio transmission

Based on 17 U.S.C. §106, the following types of works are protected by copyright:

- Literary works
- Musical works
- Dramatic works
- Choreographic works and pantomimes
- Motion pictures and audiovisual works
- Pictorial and graphic works
- Sculptural works
- Sound recordings

Not all works are protected by copyright laws. The following three types of works are not protected by copyright laws:

- Basic facts, names, titles, basic forms, etc.
- Resources published by the US government
- Works in the public domain either because the copyright of the work expires or the copyright owner intentionally or unintentionally lets the copyright lapse

Because of the three copyright acts, it can be quite complicated for the general public to identify the length of copyright protection on a publication published at different times or under diverse conditions, often involving issues of copyright notice or renewing registration. Adapted from Hirtle et al.'s (2009) work, Table 2.1 presents the duration of copyright protection under different publication years and diverse conditions. The general principle is that copyright protects a work for life of the authors plus 70 years.

EXEMPTIONS FOR LIBRARIES AND ARCHIVES

Libraries and archives are offered exemptions on exclusive rights. 17 U.S.C. §108 illustrates the limitations on exclusive right by libraries and archives (Copyright Act of 1976, 2006). In order to be eligible for the exemption, the library or archive needs to be open to the public, and the reproduction should have no direct or indirect commercial advantage. In addition, the institution desiring the exemption must place a copyright notice on the reproduced copy or incorporate a legend stating that the work may be protected by copyright [17 U.S.C. §108(a)]. For unpublished works, up to three copies can be made for preservation and security purposes or for research use in another library or archive [17 U.S.C. §108 (b)]. For published books, up to three copies can be made for damaged, deteriorating, lost, stolen or obsolete formats if no unused replacement is available at a fair price [17 U.S.C. §108(c)]. Digital copies can be made for the preservation of unpublished works and the replacement of published works. However, the digital copy cannot be further distributed in the digital format. Most importantly, the digital copy cannot be used outside of the library or archive premises [17 U.S.C. §108 (b) (c)].

Patrons of a library or archive can also request the reproduction of either part or all of copyrighted works. The requested work should be in the collections of the library or archive. A notice needs to be provided that the copy can only be used for private study, scholarship, or research. There is also a limit of one article from within a given periodical issue [17 U.S.C. §108(d)]. If a complete work or substantial amount is requested, the same notice needs to be provided to the requester. Moreover, the library or archive needs to demonstrate that the copyrighted work cannot be obtained at a fair price [17 U.S.C. §108(e)].

One provision in 17 U.S.C. §108 (h) is closely related to digital library development. Libraries or archives, as well as nonprofit educational institutions, can reproduce, distribute, display, or perform copyrighted works including digitizing these works. The only restriction is that the published works should be within the final 20 years of the copyright term. In addition, the following conditions need to be satisfied:

- The work is subject to normal commercial exploitation.
- A copy cannot be obtained at a reasonable price.
- The copyright owner or agent has provided notice that both of the above conditions apply.

Table 2.1 Copyright Terms for Published and Unpublished Works in the United States		
Date of Publication	**Conditions**	**Copyright Term**
Before 1923	None	None: in the public domain due to copyright expiration
1923 through 1977	Published without a copyright notice	None: in the public domain due to failure to comply with required formalities
1978 to Mar. 1, 1989	Published without notice, and without subsequent registration	None: in the public domain due to failure to comply with required formalities
1978 to Mar. 1, 1989	Published without notice, but with subsequent registration	70 years after the death of author or, if work of corporate authorship, 95 years from publication
1923 through 1963	Published with notice but copyright was not renewed	None: in the public domain due to failure to comply with required formalities
1923 through 1963	Published with notice and the copyright was renewed	95 years after publication date
1964 through 1977	Published with notice	95 years after publication date
1978 to Mar. 1, 1989	Published with notice	70 years after death of author or, if work of corporate authorship, 95 years from publication
After 1977 but before 2003	Works created before 1978 that were published after 1977 but before 2003	Life of the author +70 years or 31 Dec. 2047, whichever is greater
After Dec. 31, 2002	Works created before 1978 that were published after Dec. 31, 2002	Life of the author +70 years
After Mar. 1, 1989	None	70 years after death of author or, if work of corporate authorship, 95 years from publication
Unpublished works with author(s)	None	Life of the author +70 years
Unpublished anonymous and pseudonymous works, and works made for hire (corporate authorship)	None	120 years from date of creation
Unpublished works when the death date of the author is not known	None	120 years from date of creation

Adapted from Hirtle et al. (2009), table 3.2.1 and table 3.2.2 (p. 42, p. 45).

THE DIGITAL MILLENNIUM COPYRIGHT ACT (DMCA)

In 1998, under pressure from copyright owners, Congress passed the DMCA. On the one hand, criminal sanctions are added for anyone bypassing some technological protections on digital content; on the other hand, it offers some protection for nonprofit organizations. The DMCA prohibits circumventing a technological measure that effectively controls access to a protected copyright work [17 U.S.C. §1201 (a) (1)]. Moreover, it also forbids the manufacture of hardware and software for the purpose of circumventing a technological measure that effectively controls access to a protected copyright work [17 U.S.C. §1201 (a) (2)]. At the same time, the DMCA offers the opportunity for nonprofit libraries, archives, or educational institutions to circumvent copyright to access to copyrighted works for the purposes of making decisions about whether they would like to acquire a copy of the work. However, the exemption is offered on the following conditions: (1) the work may not be retained longer than necessary to make such good faith determination; and (2) the work may not be used for any other purpose [17 U.S.C. §1201 (d) (1)]. In addition, the exemption only applies to a work when an identical copy of that work is not reasonably available in another form [17 U.S.C. §1201 (d) (2)].

Multiple challenges to the DMCA have been raised, but most of the court challenges were not successful. Gathegi (2012) summarizes three challenges:

- The DMCA is not consistent with the Constitution's intellectual property clause.
- The DMCA challenges the First Amendment.
- The DMCA prohibits access to unprotected materials.

In the DMCA provision for libraries, libraries are allowed to make digital copies of deteriorating works for preservation purposes. However, the question is whether the digital copy can only be used in the physical library or also in the digital library (Ferullo, 2004).

FAIR USE

Copyright and fair use are two sides of a coin. While authors and publishers, in general, downplay fair use, it is a powerful tool for using these works without obtaining permission. Fair use balances the requests of public access to information and the need to provide incentives for the creation and advancement of knowledge (Gathegi, 2012). The exceptions for the exclusive rights of the copyright owners is also the vital part of the copyright system. Fair use fulfills the purpose of copyright to advance science and public knowledge. Moreover, it protects free speech from otherwise being restricted by the copyright offered to the copyright owner. Although it may be complex to determine, use of a copyrighted work may be considered fair use if the use is deemed to satisfy one of these aforementioned purposes.

In the creation and development of digital libraries, the greatest challenge is to determine whether an item can be selected to be included in a digital collection for public access. Weiss (2014) puts it well: "Fair use is probably the strongest of all the exemptions to copyright, and it is the most flexible, blurred, and ultimately misunderstood of the exemptions" (p. 75). Even though 17 U.S.C. §107 defines four factors as the keys for the determination of fair use, it is still difficult for creators of digital libraries to make these judgments because interpretation of the four factors can be quite different. As Hirtle et al. (2009) point out, "Although it is possible to analyze existing case law, each fair-use case is judged on a case-by-case basis" (p. 89). Each case is determined by a judge based on his/her reasoning, as well as by legal precedents. As such, uncertainty and misunderstanding are still the main problems of applying fair use in digital library creation.

17 U.S.C. §107 defines four factors that determine fair use (Copyright Act of 1976, 2006):

- The purpose and character of the use, including whether such use is of a commercial nature or is for nonprofit educational purposes.

- The nature of the copyrighted work.
- The amount and substantiality of the portion used in relation to the copyrighted work as a whole.
- The effect of the use upon the potential market.

These factors have to be considered as a whole in determining copyright infringement or fair use.

Diaz (2013) further illustrates the four factors. In dealing with Factor 1, the more transformative a work, or the more likely the purpose of the use is different from the purpose of the original copyrighted work, the more it moves toward fair use. Regarding Factor 2, the nature of the copyrighted work is determined by how creative the works are. The use of factual works is more likely to be considered as fair use. In addition, works unavailable for purchase, such as "out of print" works, are more likely to be considered as fair use. With respect to Factor 3, the amount and substantiality are determined more on the purpose and market substitution, while also considering the quantity and quality of the use of the original copyrighted work. Factor 4 is the most important factor of fair use, although it does not automatically protect copyright owners. Courts consider reasonable markets including both traditional and potentially developed.

Lipinski (2011) points out that the first and third factors are under the control of the user while the second and fourth factors are external and cannot be changed. Even though the user cannot change the second and fourth factors, the user can control his or her use to limit the negative impact on that market or potential market or value of the work. Good purpose influences the remaining factors, often resulting in a conclusion by the court that the use is a fair use. Fair use activities include scholarship, education, use of existing works to offer illustration, example, or documentation, archiving and preservation, and social comment or critiques in art and literature, etc. Hirtle et al. (2009) highlight three characteristics of fair use:

- Fair use can be applied to all the exclusive copyrights, and it is not limited to reproductions.
- Fair use is neither an infringement of copyright nor an excuse for infringement.
- Certain uses, such as criticism, news reporting, or scholarship can be often be considered as fair use even though other uses can be found as fair use.

COPYRIGHT INFRINGEMENT AND FAIR USE CASES

Copying copyright-protected work is infringement. Infringement of copyright can be considered as direct infringement or indirect infringement. Copyright is considered directly infringed when all of the following have occurred: (1) a person is not the owner of copyright, (2) a person accesses a copyrighted work, (3) a person violates the exclusive rights in a substantial way, (4) the access is beyond the permission of the statutory exemptions, and (5) the access is without the permission of the copyright owner (Hirtle et al., 2009). Moreover, knowledge of the infringing activity is not required to assert copyright infringement. A direct infringement claim needs to be established before an institution can be charged for indirect infringement (Lipinski, 2006).

Two types of indirect infringements are identified: contributory infringement and vicarious infringement. Contributory infringement refers to inducing, causing, or contributing to the infringing act by third parties. Offering the instruments for infringing acts may lead to contributory infringement. The key concept of contributory infringement is that no intent is required. Vicarious infringement occurs when one benefits from the direct infringement without taking any precautions to stop or limit the infringement. Libraries are not liable for vicarious infringement liabilities if unsupervised reproduction equipment is used by a third party as long as copyright notice is displayed there (Gathegi, 2012).

One typical example of copyright infringement versus fair use can be found in *Authors Guild v. HathiTrust*. Members of HathiTrust allowed Google to digitize their collection items in exchange for the use of digital copies. The Authors Guild sued HathiTrust for copyright infringement for the following:

1) the mass digitization violated §108 and §106 of the Copyright Act; 2) the fair use defense was not available to libraries also invoking §108; 3) injunctive relief was necessary prevent HathiTrust libraries from making their works available to the Google Books project; 4) the planned orphan works project would lead to mass infringement and should therefore be prohibited from continuing, and 5) HathiTrust should be ordered to return all of the unauthorized digital copies within its possession (Diaz, 2013, pp. 699–700).

The district court ruled that libraries seeking §108 protection can also use the fair use defense. The court applied §107 and concluded that fair use protects the search indexing and the providing of access to print-disabled items. A district court ruled that copyright had been infringed upon in this case. Believing that they were acting according to fair use principles, HathiTrust in June 2014 appealed the decision to the Second Circuit Court of Appeals. The Appeals Court decided that providing access along with a full-text searchable database, in fact, was an instance of fair use and ordered the original district court to reevaluate whether or not the preservation of the resources is a fair use. The two parties reached an agreement regarding the lingering issue of preservation in January 2015 in which the libraries stated that they only duplicated materials that were unusable due to either a poor physical condition or the material had gone missing. Furthermore, for a period of 5 years, the libraries agreed to inform the Authors Guild in the event they did not live up to this agreement. According to Cox (2015), the implications of the victory are significant. The decision offers a compelling confirmation that mass digitization does not negate fair use. The concept of functional transformation is introduced in this case wherein a use can be judged as transformative if the purpose of the use is substantially different from its original market purpose. In addition, the court rejected the claim from the Authors Guild that §108 of the Copyright Act limits fair use (Cox, 2015). This case illustrates well how difficult determining issues of fair use can be; even judges sometimes do not agree.

Another well-known case is *Authors Guild v. Google Books*. Even though Google Books is not a digital library, the case has a huge impact on digital libraries. The key issue is whether fair use can be applied to Google's digitization of millions of books. Google started digitizing books in the early 2000s, and Google Books became searchable in 2004. The Authors Guild charged Google with copyright infringement in 2005. A settlement agreement was proposed and amended, but was rejected by courts on several grounds (Weiss, 2014). Judge Denny Chin ruled that the fair use employed by Google Books provides a significant public benefit (Chin, 2013). He discussed the case from the perspective of the four factors of fair use. As to the purpose of the use, it strongly leans toward fair use because it transforms text into a word index, like snippets, and it displays only snippets for search. Moreover, it does not supersede or supplant books. As to the nature of the copyrighted works, Google Books covers all types of books, but mainly nonfiction books, and all are published books available to the public. This also favors the finding of fair use. As to the amount of use, Google scans the full text of books, but it limits the amount of text displayed in the search result. This factor weighs slightly against fair use. As to the effects of use, Google Books promotes the use of the books, which ultimately benefits the copyright holders of these books. This factor strongly favors fair use. Overall,

Judge Chin (2013) ruled that the Google Book project "advances the progress of the arts and sciences, while maintaining respectful consideration for the rights of authors and other creative individuals, and without adversely impacting the rights of copyright holders" (p. 26). These two cases greatly encourage the development of large-scale of digital libraries and serve as perfect examples for the argument of fair use.

COLLECTION SHARING AND LARGE-SCALE DIGITAL LIBRARIES
COLLECTION DEVELOPMENT IN CONSORTIA AND LARGE-SCALE DIGITAL LIBRARIES

Burgett et al. (2004) describe the history of cooperative collection development: "Discussion of local lending arrangements has been documented as early as 1851, and formal cooperative cataloging ventures date at least to 1876" (p. 8). Electronic resources are a driving force for cooperative collection development not only for reducing cost but also for effective document access and delivery (Haar, 2003). In 2007, the American Library Association created a Cooperative Collection Development Committee to study, promote, and support cooperative collection development. Many consortia established their own collection development committees to deal with the issues of collection development. For example, in 2005, the VALE New Jersey Academic Library Consortium founded the Cooperative Collection Management Committees to address the challenge of the increase of electronic resources (Mallery and Theus, 2012).

Collaboration between libraries in building comprehensive print collections has been well established. Recently, it has evolved into collective collection development for electronic resources. Turner (2014) discusses the advantages of consortia e-resources:

- Offer wide access to content that each individual library cannot afford
- Provide more choices for full texts of journals or e-books
- Cost sharing and containment
- Value the opportunity for the consortia to negotiate with content vendors
- Promote e-resource collections

At the same time, she also specifies several challenges of consortia e-resource collection development:

- Reduce local autonomy and flexibility in collection development
- Increase workload for consortia staff and library staff
- Increase the conflict between revenue-driven publishers and the budget-limited academic institutions. One possible solution is to promote open access and scholarly communication.

Kinner and Crosetto (2009) highlight similar challenges for academic library engagement at the consortia levels. They emphasize that it is vital to maintain individual members' identity and balance individual members' and the consortium's needs in collection development. Sayed and Burnett (2014) discuss both the benefits and challenges in sharing electronic resources among three institutions. On the one hand, they can provide more coverage to users at lower cost; on the other hand, usage data for electronic resources need to be identified for different institutions. There is also a critical issue in terms of how to build collections to satisfy the unique needs of each institution.

Because of the budget demand and technology development, it is a trend for organizations to build collaborative digital projects. Eight educational institutions in Minnesota used the existing consortia to build a shared digital collection (Wagner and Gerber, 2011). The following Dickeson's (2010) criteria have been applied to assess the program:

- History, development, and expectations of the program
- External demand for the program
- Internal demand for the program
- Costs and other expenses associated with the program
- Impact, justification and overall essentiality of the program (p. 66)

While the collaboration helps relieve the cost burden, it also requires strong communication, trust, and iterative assessment of costs and user and institutional needs (Wagner and Gerber, 2011).

New technologies make it possible to digitize collections at a large scale. Beaman and Cellinese (2012) underline the key elements of infrastructure for large-scale digitization of scientific collections:

- Set priorities and identify user need
- Identify stakeholders, collaborators, and communities
- Select computational infrastructure and associated technical requirements
- Determine standards for interoperability
- Consider management, organizational structure, and sustainability issues
- Assess risks

Balke et al. (2013) propose the creation of a global natural history "meta collection" to enable access to the morphology of tens of millions of specimens now in museums worldwide.

Large-scale digitization projects are the products of collection sharing. One of the key objectives of the Digital Public Library of America is to share public resources. Moreover, several of the large-scale digitization projects also consider collaboration. For example, the Digital Public Library of America has collaborated with Europeana, the pan-Europe digital library, to create the exhibition "Leaving Europe: A New Life in America," which presents the journey of European immigrants to the United States in the 19th and early 20th centuries. It also shows related collections in the National Archives and Records Administration, Harvard University, New York Public Library, and University of Minnesota Immigration History Research Center (Palfrey, 2013). Taylor et al. (2013) examine the benefits of the creation of the Digital Library of the Caribbean (dLOC). Many of the dLOC materials are unique and have significant importance for specific research areas, but they are in remote collections/archives and with additional access restrictions. The development of dLOC removes the main barrier to access. One important step for collection development is the need for full attribution for the content creators and the partners that provide access to the content. Collection items come from partners as well as scholars. Most importantly, scholars work on academic research using dLOC materials to expand scholarship.

Although large-scale digitization projects increase the availability of cultural information and promote scholarly activities (Crane, 2006; Hawkins and Gildart, 2010), Gooding et al. (2013) outline several criticisms of mass digitization: (1) inadequate technology and implementation, such as low accuracy rates of the OCR software, (2) inaccurate metadata, such as inaccurate automatically generated metadata, and (3) cultural dominance of Anglo-American material.

LARGE-SCALE DIGITIZATION PROJECTS AND COLLECTION DEVELOPMENT POLICY

In large-scale digitization projects, multiple institutions collaborate together. Their collection development policies have not only characteristics of digital library collection policies of participating institutions but also unique characteristics of large-scale digitization projects. Here is the list of main components of the NSDL collection development policy (Miller, 2007, para.1):

- Mission of the library
- Communities served
- Resource ownership, management, and description
- Collection scope
- Quality guidelines
- Selection responsibility
- Accessioning
- Deaccessioning
- Terms of participation

This includes broad subject areas, materials from the United States and other countries, and diverse types of materials ranging from teaching and research materials to datasets and events materials. Its sources of content are also quite diverse from research and teaching institutions, to STEM publishers, STEM companies, NSDL's own productions, as well as user-suggested resources.

In large-scale digitization projects, in particular in the archival area, there is a trend to include all items without collection selection. The purpose of Greene and Meissner's (2005) proposed "More Product, Less Process" (MPLP) approach is to save costs, and it has received both praise and criticism in the field. The advantages and general principles of adopting the MPLP approach can be summarized as follows:

- Make user access paramount: get the most material available in a usable form in the briefest time possible
- Expend the greatest effort on the most deserving or needful materials
- Establish an acceptable minimum level of work, and make it the processing benchmark
- Embrace flexibility: do not assume all collections, or all collection components, will be processed to the same level
- Do not allow preservation anxieties to trump user access and higher managerial values (Greene and Meissner, 2005, pp. 175–176)

Different techniques are used to make the MPLP process efficient. Miller (2013) explores the idea of mass digitizing entire archival collections using optical character recognition software for full text searching. In that way, the archival processing would be skipped. This approach speeds up the digitization process and can provide information to users more effectively.

In developing large-scale digital libraries, sometimes referred to as large-scale digital initiatives (LSDIs), the focus is on categories instead of individual items. According to Rieger (2010), "selection decisions for LSDIs are usually made based on broad categories rather than individual assessment of titles" (p. 15). The author provides examples of the Southern Historical Collection at the University of North Carolina at Chapel Hill and the Archives of American Art, a unit of the Smithsonian Institute, in which digital collections contain every item of the collections. There is no selection of items for these projects because the selection process is completed when the special collections were created.

Recently, museums also adopted the rapid capture approach. The Free and Sackler Galleries became the first Smithsonian museum to make their entire collection of 40,000 works available in digital formats. The National Museum of Natural History also digitized its Bumbles Collection (Kutner, 2015).

The ultimate goal of developing large-scale digital libraries is to satisfy user needs. In addition to including all items in a collection, Schaffner et al. (2011) propose a user-initiated digitization approach. They stress that user need is the driving force for collection building, and scanning and delivering can efficiently distribute the requested information to users. It is an effective approach to consider user requests in selecting collections and collection items to digitize (Poole, 2007). "Mass representation" is used by Custer (2009) to characterize the relationship between selection and user-initiated digitization of special collections. His own research shows that the top 10% of requested images online attract over 50% of the users. However, different institutions, different policies, and different resources need to be analyzed for user-initiated collection item selection decisions. Mills (2015) investigates user impact on digital collection selection and development, in particular how to balance user needs and institutional interests in the digital collection development process. Chapter 3 further discusses the rapid capture approach and its potential impact on collection development.

CHALLENGES OF COLLECTION DEVELOPMENT
LEGAL CHALLENGES

The practice in digital library development has been cautious relative to copyright. Koulouris and Kapidakis (2005) analyze the access and reproduction policies of digital collections in 10 worldwide leading universities' digital libraries. They find that libraries prefer to digitize items for which they own the copyright or are in the public domain. Most of the born digital materials are obtained through licenses or are purchased from copyright owners. Libraries offer different types of access depending on the copyright of the items. If a library owns the copyright, reproduction for private use is free or with a credit to the source, but commercial use is charged a fee and written permission is required. However, librarians have not been very good at presenting copyright information in their digital collections. Schlosser (2009) surveys copyright statements in 786 digital library collections in 29 institutions. The results show that about 50% of them present copyright statements. However, these statements are vague and sometimes misleading. Moreover, there is a fuzzy line between copyright and a use statement. It is difficult to differentiate copyright statements from terms of use. The common elements for these statements are a specific ownership statement, a vague ownership statement, what users can or cannot do, and protecting the users and institutions. It is not an easy job for users to understand copyright and fair use. Many libraries hesitate to offer detailed and specific copyright statements because they do not have the information. There are still myths revolving around copyright laws.

Wu et al. (2010) report four areas of misunderstanding of copyright laws: (1) digital resources should be shared; (2) it is legitimate to download all digital resources; (3) education use equals fair use; and (4) current students are entitled to download all digital resources. It is evident that knowledge of copyright is essential for librarians. Based on the job advertisements, Kawooya et al. (2015) conclude that having a copyright librarian or someone with competence in copyright is one of the key requirements for the current and future needs of academic libraries.

It is a challenge to use copyrighted works in digitization projects, in particular to obtain permission to use a copyrighted work. George (2005) conducted a study to find the barriers to seeking copyright permission for digitizing published works. The results are quite surprising. The response rates from copyright holders to permission requests are low. Only about one-fourth of the total requests received permission to digitize. The response rate varied among different copyright holders. Associations have the best rate, followed by university presses, museums, and galleries. The commercial publishers representing the greatest copyright holders were the most reluctant to grant the permission, fearing loss of their profits. The average response time is about 3 months after sending the initial request before receiving a yes or no answer. In addition, it is quite a complicated task to prepare the request, such as searching for copyright holder contact information, creating a database, sending the requests, etc. One solution is to negotiate contracts with different vendors through an organization. For example, in order to digitize copyrighted books, the National Library of Norway negotiated a contract with an organization that represents 30 different organizations for copyrights (Vigdis, 2010).

The current legal system does not keep pace with the changes of technology nor does it define the concept of libraries (Anderson, 2001). Nolan (2011) argues that "the language of Section 108 is insufficient because it does not adequately reflect the current digital landscape" (p. 481). It is vital to consider both technology and the socio-economical cost of access to materials, specifically the digitization processes addressed by the current language of §108. In order for libraries to keep their privileges under §108, she proposed using the term "file" to replace "copy" to refer to a digital copy. Moreover, it is critical to define what does "in the library" mean precisely for libraries' digitization projects. Most importantly, fair use is still a very vague concept. It is a challenge to reach an agreement on what constitutes fair use and to come up with some solutions to demystify fair use.

The current situation of copyright laws and their application to digital library development is not satisfying. Wu (2011) well defines the problems of copyright regarding digital collection development: "In recent years, the balance of copyright appears to have tipped more toward the rights of copyright owners over the benefits to society, with legislators unable or unwilling to change that balance through new legislation. Because existing statutory language is ill-equipped to handle new technologies, wealthy and powerful copyright holders have been quick to use technology to expand protection of their works or to intimidate users" (pp. 537–538).

OTHER IMPORTANT CHALLENGES

The challenges of collection development further call for expanding collaborative digital projects. Wu (2011) identifies several challenges, including (1) the rising cost of materials, (2) the overwhelming quantity of information, (3) the interdisciplinary and international nature of scholarship, (4) insufficient library collection budgets, and (5) the need for broad and reliable access. Building a collaborative collection is an efficient approach for document delivery. Wu (2011) also introduces the proposed Taking Academic Law Libraries Online consortium. The suggested collection development policy focuses on scholarly materials not in high demand but useful for research and excludes popular items, such as textbooks. Acquired materials will be digitized, and the priority of digitization will be determined by user need.

Large-scale digitization and digital libraries challenge current practices of collection development, digitization processes, and metadata creation. Miller (2013) discusses the approach of using optical character recognition (OCR) software to mass digitize materials to avoid archival processing and creating finding aids. Sutton (2012) suggests that user-generated metadata can help minimize the metadata process and indicates that accuracy and authority issues need to be considered in the adoption of mass digitizing projects. The rapid capture approach challenges the traditional practice of collection development. It is critical to review and assess the current practice of collection development in large-scale digital libraries.

Ball (2012) summarizes the challenges and problems in relation to collection development: (1) the supply of electronic resources in terms of the package and prices is in the publishers' favor; (2) mass digitization and large-scale digitization projects will decrease the importance of traditional collection development; and (3) the open access movement exemplifies a trend to access to information not controlled by librarians and libraries. The open access movement is another trend that decreases the role of collection development. One typical product of the open access movement is institutional repositories, which consist of national, institutional, departmental, subject, and type-based institutional repositories (Brown, 2010). Nevertheless, Brown (2012) argues that collection development remains the essential component of an institutional repository.

REFERENCES

Anderson, B., 2001. Fair use, copyright law and digitized works. Behav. Soc. Sci. Librar. 20 (1), 111.

Ayris, P., 2009. New wine in old bottles: current developments in digital delivery and dissemination. Eur. Rev. 17 (1), 53–71.

Balke, M., Schmidt, S., Hausmann, A., Toussaint, E., Bergsten, J., Buffington, M., et al., 2013. Biodiversity into your hands–a call for a virtual global natural history "metacollection." Front. Zool. 10 (55), 9.

Ball, D., 2012. Managing suppliers for collection development: the UK higher education perspective. In: Fieldhouse, M., Marshall, A. (Eds.), Collection Development in the Digital Age. Facet Publishing, London, pp. 111–124.

Beaman, R.S., Cellinese, N., 2012. Mass digitization of scientific collections: new opportunities to transform the use of biological specimens and underwrite biodiversity science. ZooKeys 209, 7–17. Available from: http://doi.org/10.3897/zookeys.209.3313.

Brown, D., 2010. Repositories and journals: are they in conflict? A literature review of relevant literature. In: Aslib Proceedings. Emerald Group Publishing Limited, 62 (2), pp. 112–143.

Brown, J., 2012. Collection development and institutional repositories. In: Fieldhouse, M., Marshall, A. (Eds.), Collection Development in the Digital Age. Facet Publishing, London, pp. 149–162.

Bullis, D., Smith, L., 2011. Looking back, moving forward in the digital age: a review of the collection management and development literature, 2004–8. Lib. Res. Tech. Serv. 55 (4), 205–220.

Burgett, J., Haar, J., Phillips, L., 2004. Collaborative collection development: a practical guide for your library. American Library Association, Chicago.

Case, B.D., 2000. Love's labour's lost: the failure of traditional selection practice in the acquisition of humanities electronic texts. Lib. Trend. 48 (4), 729–747.

Chin, D. (2013). Author's Guild vs. Google Books: presiding opinion. Available from: http://www.wired.com/images_blogs/threatlevel/2013/11/chindecision.pdf.

Copyright Act of 1976. 17 U.S.C. § 106–108 (2006). Available from: http://www.copyright.gov/title17/92chap1.html.

Corrall, S., 2012. The concept of collection development in the digital world. In: Fieldhouse, M., Marshall, A. (Eds.), Collection Development in the Digital Age. Facet Publishing, London, pp. 3–25.

Corrall, S., Roberts, A., 2012. Information resource development and "collection" in the digital age: Conceptual frameworks and new definitions for the network world. In: Libraries in the Digital Age (LIDA) Proceedings, p. 12.

Cox, K., 2015. Authors Guild v. HathiTrust litigation ends in victory for fair use. Available from: http://www.arl.org/news/community-updates/3501-authors-guild-v-hathitrust-litigation-ends-in-victory-for-fair-use#.VcUhl01RGcw.

Crane, G., 2006. What do you do with a million books? D-Lib Mag. 12 (3.), Available from: http://www.dlib.org/dlib/march06/crane/03crane.html.

Custer, M. (2009). Incorporating patron requests into archival workflows and digital repository interfaces. [PowerPoint slides]. Available from: http://www2.archivists.org/search/google/custer%202009?query=custer%202009&cx=013982339786901321102%3A36mv5j9t7zm&cof=FORID%3A11&sitesearch=.

Diaz, A.S. (2013). Fair use & mass digitization: the future of copy-dependent technologies after Authors Guild v. HathiTrust. Berkeley Technol. Law J. p. 23. Available from: http://papers.ssrn.com/sol3/papers.cfm?abstract_id=2231750##.

Dickeson, R., 2010. Prioritizing academic programs and services: reallocating resources to achieve strategic balance. Jossey-Bass Publishers, San Francisco, CA.

Douglas, C.S., 2011. Revising a collection development policy in a rapidly changing environment. J. Electron. Resour. Med. Lib. 8 (1), 15–21.

Ferullo, D.L., 2004. Major copyright issues in academic libraries: legal implications of a digital environment. J. Lib. Admin. 40 (1/2), 23–40.

Fieldhouse, M., 2012. The processes of collection management. In: Fieldhouse, M., Marshall, A. (Eds.), Collection Development in the Digital Age. Facet Publishing, London, pp. 27–44.

Gabriel, M.R., 1995. Collection Development and Evaluation: A Sourcebook. Scarecrow, Lanham, MD.

Gathegi, J.I., 2012. The Digital Librarian's Legal Handbook. Neal-Schuman, New York.

Genoni, P., 2004. Content in institutional repositories: a collection management issue. Lib. Manag. 25 (6/7), 300–306.

George, C.A., 2005. Testing the barriers to digital libraries: a study seeking copyright permission to digitize published works. New Lib. World 106 (7), 332–342.

Gertz, J., 2011. Selection for preservation in the digital age. Lib. Resour. Tech. Serv. 44 (2), 97–104.

Gessesse, K., 2000. Collection development and management in the twenty-first century with special reference to academic libraries: an overview. Lib. Manag. 21 (7), 365–372.

Gooding, P., Terras, M., Warwick, C., 2013. The myth of the new: mass digitization, distant reading, and the future of the book. Lit. Ling. Comp. 28 (4), 629–639.

Gorman, G., 2000. Collection Management: International Yearbook of Library and Information Management. Library Association, London.

Greene, M., Meissner, D., 2005. More product, less process: revamping traditional archival processing. Am. Arch. 68 (2), 208–263.

Haar, J., 2003. Cooperative collection development survey responses. In: Burgett, J., Haar, J., Phillips, L. (Eds.), Collaborative Collection Development: A Practical Guide for Your Library. American Library Association, Chicago. p. 99.

Hawkins, R., Gildart, K., 2010. Promoting the digital literacy of historians at the University of Wolverhampton using nineteenth century British library newspapers online. Available from: http://www2.warwick.ac.uk/fac/cross_fac/heahistory/resources/cs_hawkins_digitalliteracy_20100426.pdf.

Hightower, B.E., Gantt, J.T., 2012. Weeding nursing e-books in an academic library. Lib. Collect. Acquisit. Tech. Serv. 36 (1–2), 53–57.

Hirtle, P.B., Hudson, E., Kenyon, A.T., 2009. Copyright and Cultural Institutions: Guidelines for Digitization for US Libraries, Archives, and Museums. Cornell University Library Press, Ithaca, NY. Available from: http://ecommons.cornell.edu/bitstream/1813/14142/2/Hirtle-Copyright_final_RGB_lowres-cover1.pdf.

Hollman, C., 2000. Are we there yet? Electronic resources: are basic criteria for the selection of materials changing? Lib. Trends 48 (4), 694–710.

Hutchinson, H.B., Rose, A., Bederson, B.B., Weeks, A.C., Druin, A., 2013. The International Children's Digital Library: a case study in designing for a multilingual, multicultural, multigenerational audience. Inf. Technol. Lib. 24 (1), 4–12.

Jacob, M., O'Brien, S., Reid, B., 2014. Weeding the collection: perspectives from three public libraries. In: Albitz, B., Avery, C., Zabel, D. (Eds.), Rethinking Collection Development and Management. Libraries Unlimited, Santa Barbara, CA, pp. 77–88.

Johnson, P., 2009. Fundamentals of Collection Development and Management, 2nd ed. American Library Association, Chicago.

Kastens, K., Devaul, H., Ginger, K., Mogk, D., DeFelice, B., DiLeonardo, C., 2005. Questions and challenges arising in building the collection of a digital library for education. D-Lib Mag. 11 (11). Available from: http://mirror.dlib.org/dlib/november05/kastens/11kastens.html.

Kawooya, D., Veverka, A., Lipinski, T., 2015. The copyright librarian: a study of advertising trends for the period 2006–2013. J. Acad. Lib. 41 (3), 341–349.

Kellerman, L.S., 2014. Digitization projects. In: Albitz, B., Avery, C., Zabel, D. (Eds.), Rethinking Collection Development and Management. Libraries Unlimited, Santa Barbara, CA, pp. 345–358.

Kinner, L., Crosetto, A., 2009. Balancing act for the future: how the academic library engages in collection development at the local and consortial levels. J. Lib. Admin. 49 (4), 419–437.

Koulouris, A., Kapidakis, S., 2005. Access and reproduction of digital production university digital collections. J. Librar. Inform. Sci. 37 (1), 25–33.

Kutner, M., 2015. Museums are now able to digitize thousands of artifacts in just hours. Available from: http://www.smithsonianmag.com/smithsonian-institution/museums-are-now-able-digitize-thousands-artifacts-just-hours-180953867/?no-ist.

Lee, H.L., 2000. What is a collection? J. Am. Soc. Inf. Sci. 51 (12), 1106–1113.

Lee, H.L., 2005. The concept of collection from the user's perspective. Lib. Quart. 75 (1), 67–85.

Lipinski, T.A., 2006. The Complete Copyright Liability Handbook for Librarians and Educators. Neal-Schuman, New York, NY.

Lipinski, T.A., 2011. Toward a functional understanding of fair use in US copyright law. Ann. Rev. Inf. Sci. Technol. 45 (1), 523–621.

Mallery, M., Theus, P., 2012. New frontiers in collaborative collection management. Tech. Serv. Quart. 29 (2), 101–112.

Metz, P., 2000. Principles of selection for electronic resources. Lib. Trend. 48 (4), 711–728.

Miller, R., 2000. Electronic resources and academic libraries, 1980–2000: a historical perspective. Lib. Trend. 48 (4), 645–670.

Miller, A., 2007. NSDL Collection Development Policy. Available from: http://nsdl.library.cornell.edu/materials/resource_contribution/NSDL_Collection_Development_Policy_2008_04_08.pdf.

Miller, L., 2013. All text considered: a perspective on mass digitizing and archival processing. Am. Arch. 76 (2), 521–541.

Mills, A., 2015. User impact on selection, digitization, and the development of digital special collections. New Rev. Acad. Librar. 21 (2), 160–169.

Moore, K.B., 2015. Are we there yet? Moving to an e-only collection development policy for books. Serials Librar. 68 (1–4), 127–136.

Morrisey, L., 2010. Data-driven decision making in electronic collection development. J. Lib. Admin. 50 (3), 283–290.

Nisonger, T., 2000. Collection development in an electronic environment. Lib. Trend. 48 (4), 639–692.

Nolan, S., 2011. Standing on the shoulders of giants: how a drastic remodeling of 17 U.S.C. § 108 could help save academia. J. Intell. Prop. Law 19 (2), 457–485.

Palfrey, J., 2013. What is the DPLA? Lib. J. 138 (7), 38.

Parfrey, W., 2013. Collection development framework. Available from: http://www.cdlib.org/services/collections/framework.html.

Poole, N., 2007. What audience? The death of mass-digitization and the rise of the market economy. The Digitaal Erfgoed Conferentie (Digital Heritage Conference), Rotterdam, The Netherlands. Retrieved from: http://www.slideshare.net/DEconferentie/k2poole.

Rieger, O.Y., 2010. Enduring access to special collections: challenges and opportunities for large-scale digitization initiatives. RBM 11 (1), 11–22.

Sayed, E., Burnett, A., 2014. Sharing electronic resources among three institutions. Qual. Quant. Method. Lib. 1, 351–359.

Schaffner, J., Snyder, F., Supple, S., 2011. Scan and Deliver!: Managing User-Initiated Digitization in Special Collections and Archives. OCLC Research, Dublin, OH. Available from: http://netweb.oclc.org/content/dam/research/publications/library/2011/2011-05.pdf.

Schlosser, M., 2009. Unless otherwise indicated: a survey of copyright statements on digital library collections. Coll. Res. Lib. 70 (4), 371–385.

Schroeder, R., 2012. When patrons call the shots: patron-driven acquisition at Brigham Young University. Collect. Build. 31 (1), 11–14.

Shaw, W., 2012. Collection development policies for the digital age. In: Fieldhouse, M., Marshall, A. (Eds.), Collection Development in the Digital Age. Facet Publishing, London, pp. 165–180.

Sutton, S.C., 2012. Balancing boutique-level quality and large-scale production: the impact of "More Product, Less Process" on digitization in archives and special collections. RBM 13 (1), 50–63.

Taylor, L.N., Vargas-Betancourt, M., Wooldridge, B., 2013. The digital library of the Caribbean (dLOC): creating a shared research foundation. Scholarly Res. Commun. 4 (3.), Retrieved from http://src/online.ca/src/index.php/src/article/view/114/246.

Turner, C.N., 2014. E-Resource acquisitions in academic library consortia. Lib. Resour. Tech. Serv. 58 (1), 33–48.

Tyckoson, D., 2014. Perspectives on weeding in academic library collections. In: Albitz, B., Avery, C., Zabel, D. (Eds.), Rethinking Collection Development and Management. Libraries Unlimited, Santa Barbara, CA, pp. 59–76.

University of Texas, 2011. Digital library collection development policy. Available from: http://www.lib.utexas.edu/admin/cird/policies/subjects/framework.html.

Vasileiou, M., Hartley, R., Rowley, J., 2012. Choosing e-books: a perspective from academic libraries. Online Inf. Rev. 36 (1), 21–39.

Vigdis, M.S., 2010. The bookshelf: digitisation and access to copyright items in Norway. Program 44 (1), 48–58.

Vogt-O'Connor, D., 2000. Selection of materials for scanning. In: Sitts, M.K. (Ed.), Handbook for Digital Projects: A Management Tool for Preservation and Access. Northeast Document Conservation Center, Andover, MA, pp. 45–72.

Wagner, D., Gerber, K., 2011. Building a shared digital collection: the experience of the cooperating libraries in consortium. Coll. Undergrad. Lib. 18 (2–3), 272–290.

Waugh, M., Donlin, M., Braunstein, S., 2015. Next-generation collection management: a case study of quality control and weeding e-books in an academic library. Collect. Manage. 40 (1), 17–26.

Weiss, A., 2014. Using Massive Digital Libraries: A LITA Guide. American Library Association, Chicago.

Wu, M.M., 2011. Building a collaborative digital collection: a necessary evolution in libraries. Law Lib. J. 103 (4), 527–551.

Wu, H., Chou, C., Ke, H., Wang, M., 2010. College students' misunderstandings about copyright laws for digital library resources. Electron. Lib. 28 (2), 197–209.

DIGITIZATION OF TEXT AND STILL IMAGES

INTRODUCTION TO DIGITIZATION

Digitization has contributed to building a critical mass of scholarly and cultural heritage resources in digital libraries. Nowadays, nearly all new information is created in digital format, and although the number of "born digital" library resources has been rapidly increasing, it still represents a small fraction of recorded knowledge. Historically, scholarly and cultural heritage resources have been recorded on a variety of analog formats, with paper being the dominant material for several centuries. Institutions within the cultural heritage community—libraries, archives, and museums—have also collected information resources recorded on other analog carriers including film and glass negatives, slides, and audio and videotapes. The inclusion of analog materials in digital libraries has required extensive conversion efforts. Since the early 1990s, digitization has been undertaken both by individual cultural heritage institutions and through collaborative initiatives. Mass digitization projects including JSTOR, the Google Book Project, and the Open Content Alliance initiative have contributed a significant body of digitized content. The process of conversion is far from complete, but digital libraries such as Europeana, the Digital Public Library of America, the Internet Archive, and HathiTrust already provide access to millions of digitized scholarly and cultural heritage objects. These large-scale digital libraries represent two decades of intensive digitization efforts undertaken by both smaller institutions and large initiatives like the Google Book Project.

Digitization is the process of creating digital representations of information resources recorded on analog carriers. In essence, digitization is "the conversion process of an analog signal or code into a digital signal or code" (Lee, 2001, p. 3). It involves sampling continuous patterns of physical media and converting them into binary streams of ones and zeros that can be processed and represented by digital devices. The term "digitization" is often used interchangeably with "scanning", but as Lee (2001) points out, there are distinct differences between the two. Scanning refers to the conversion of static textual and visual materials, and motion picture films. Digitization, on the other hand, is a broader concept that encompasses the conversion of all analog media, including sound, video, and 3D objects. Digitization, especially if undertaken for preservation purposes, aims at converting not only the informational content but also capturing unique characteristics of analog materials as much as possible. It is worth noting that digitization involves not only copying, but also transformation of the nature and functionality of information resources. While it might not always be possible to replicate all the attributes of physical objects, digitized versions facilitate new means of access and enable the use of materials that are not possible with the analog form.

Creating digital counterparts of analog scholarly and cultural heritage resources is a complex and challenging undertaking because of the variety of predigital formats and the evolving technological standards and best practices. For the purpose of digitization, analog resources are divided into static and time-based media (ALCTS, 2013; Puglia, 2011). Static media encompass textual resources such as manuscripts, printed books, newspapers, and journals as well as still images, including photographs, maps, and two-dimensional art works. Time-based or dynamic media include audio, video, and moving images. Puglia (2011) emphasizes that the complexity of the conversion process increases when we move from static to dynamic media. Static resources can be converted to digital format through an imaging process, while time-based media require playback devices in addition to conversion hardware and software. Digitization of 3D objects poses a different set of challenges. Constructing a digital representation of a three-dimensional artifact involves taking multiple still images with a digital camera from several viewpoints and stitching them together or the use of laser scanning technology that captures millions of points of measurement to represent the shape of 3D objects (Collmann, 2011; Surendran et al., 2009; Valentino and Shults, 2012).

The technological advancements of the 1990s set the stage for the digital conversion of printed materials and unique cultural heritage collections. Improvements in scanning technology, faster computer processing, and the lower cost of digital storage have enabled libraries and other cultural heritage institutions to move forward with the digitization of their analog collections. The growth of high-speed networks, especially of the World Wide Web, has allowed for the sharing of digitized collections with wider audiences. Cultural heritage institutions have primarily focused on the conversion of unique materials from their archival and special collections. The digitization of general collections of printed books and journals has required larger scale efforts and the cooperation of multiple institutions. JSTOR, a project initiated by the Andrew W. Mellon Foundation in 1995, undertook the conversion of back issues of scholarly journals. Mass digitization of books began in the mid-2000s with the Google Book Project and the Open Content Alliance taking the lead (Coyle, 2006; Leetaru, 2008).

Large-scale digitization of archives and special collections is challenging because of the unique and heterogeneous nature of the materials and the complexity of analog formats. Digitization of cultural heritage collections frequently requires attention to preservation issues and careful handling of fragile or rare items. The mass digitization of books undertaken in collaboration with commercial and nonprofit partners, however, has changed the digitization landscape and raised expectations for the digital conversion of unique cultural heritage materials (Erway, 2011; Erway and Schaffner, 2007). In recent years, there has been a growing interest in adopting rapid digitization approaches in order to increase the volume of digitized materials from unique collections in libraries, archives, and museums (Erway, 2011; Miller, 2013; Rinaldo et al., 2011; Sutton, 2012).

This chapter provides an overview of the underlying principles and technologies involved in the conversion of analog materials into digital form. The primary focus is on the digitization of cultural heritage resources. This chapter discusses the main reasons why libraries and archives engage in digital conversion and looks at strategies for undertaking digitization projects. Furthermore, it examines the steps, guidelines, technical specifications, and imaging equipment used in converting textual and photographic materials. The conversion of audio and video is discussed in Chapter 4.

RATIONALE AND STRATEGIES FOR UNDERTAKING DIGITIZATION

Libraries, archives, and museums embraced digitization relatively quickly since imaging technology became widely available in the mid-1990s. Major research and academic libraries as well as national libraries and archives led the first digitization initiatives. The 1998 survey of special collections affiliated with the Association of Research Libraries indicated that 89% of the major research libraries in the

United States were involved in digitization in 1998 (Panitch, 2001). An IFLA/UNESCO study demonstrated that as of 1999, 48% of surveyed national libraries worldwide had digitization programs (Gould and Ebdon, 1999). Two studies conducted by the Institute of Museum and Library Services (IMLS) indicated that smaller libraries, archives, and museums were initially lagging behind, but digitization activities increased in all types of cultural heritage institutions between 2001 and 2004 (IMLS, 2006). Conway (2008) notes that digitization of cultural heritage materials, especially historical photographs, has transitioned from "rarified experiments to nearly ubiquitous activity" (p. 94). Finally, a more recent OCLC survey of special collections in the United States and Canada reported that nearly all participating libraries have completed at least one digitization project and/or have an active digitization program for special collections (Dooley and Luce, 2010).

The IMLS and OCLC studies indicate a widespread adoption of digitization by cultural heritage institutions, although funding, staffing, and expertise are constant challenges. Why have libraries, archives, and museums embarked on digitization projects despite significant costs and the complexity of the conversion process? Kenney and Rieger (2000) provide an overall rationale and list two primary reasons for investing in digitization: (1) to accommodate the changing behavior of users in the digital environment and (2) to maintain the relevance of analog resources for teaching, research, and scholarship. The authors comment that "changing user behavior may jeopardize these resources and their stewardship" (Kenney and Rieger, 2000, p. 1). In examining the role of digitization and preservation a decade later, Conway (2010) observes that "in the age of Google, nondigital content does not exist, and digital content with no impact is unlikely to survive" (p. 64).

WHY DIGITIZE: ACCESS AND PRESERVATION

The question "why digitize?" has been posed since the early days of digitization projects (Smith, 1999). Cultural heritage institutions focus on special and archival collections and specific goals related to curating, access, and the new functionality of digitized materials (Besser, 2003; Conway, 2000; IMLS, 2006; Lee, 2001; Lopatin, 2006; Smith, 2001). The discussion on motivation and rationale has centered on two goals:

- Increasing access to library, archival, and museum collections
- Preserving valuable, fragile, and deteriorating materials

Institutions participating in the IMLS survey in 2006 identified additional goals. Museums gave more weight to making information about their collections accessible to artists, scholars, students, teachers, and the public, while academic and public libraries highlighted providing access to materials via the web, minimizing damage to original materials, and increasing interest in the institution. Access and preservation, however, were consistently ranked as top goals across all institutions (IMLS, 2006).

Increased access to unique cultural heritage materials has indeed been acknowledged as the major benefit of digitization (Cohen and Rosenzweig, 2006; Daigle, 2012; Smith, 1999). "Digitization is access—lots of it," emphasizes Smith (1999, p. 7). Daigle (2012) comments, "open access has been transformative to researchers who are no longer required to travel to the physical location of primary source material" (p. 252). The added value of digitization, however, goes beyond the mere convenience of remote access to surrogate copies of original documents. Researchers point to the advantages of digital image enhancement, the ability to bring together dispersed research materials, and the potential to reach audiences across social and economic boundaries (Besser, 2003; Kenney and Rieger, 2000;

Smith, 1999, 2001). The capabilities of full-text searching and cross-collection indexing afford new ways of exploring and using traditional materials (Conway, 2000; Kenney and Rieger, 2000; Lesk, 2004).

Digitization has removed physical barriers to the discovery and use of rare and fragile resources and those recorded on difficult-to-access formats. Access to rare manuscripts, photographs, maps, archival documents, and museum objects has often been limited because of their value and/or fragile nature. Digitization not only expands the reach of these materials to researchers, students, and the general public, but in many cases it enhances the visual quality of faded and illegible documents (Smith, 1999). In addition, advancements in imaging have enabled the conversion of visual materials recorded on difficult-to-access formats such as film negatives and slides. Digitization offers a new chance to shed light on unique historical collections that were previously inaccessible due to the limitations of analog formats. In fact, digitization has expanded the range of primary sources and presents students and scholars with a new body of historical evidence and even a critical mass of materials for analysis or comparison (Matusiak and Johnston, 2014).

The second main reason that libraries, archives, and museums undertake digital conversion is to facilitate the preservation of valuable analog materials. It is important to make the distinction between:

- Digitization as a means of preventive or "rescue" preservation
- Digitization as a reformatting preservation strategy

Preventive digitization is focused on creating digital copies for access and thus reducing physical use of rare or fragile originals, while digitization as a reformatting strategy has an additional goal of creating high-quality preservation copies of deteriorating analog materials. The benefits of digitization in protecting unique and valuable special collection and archival materials are widely acclaimed. Digitization can assist preservation efforts by limiting handling of original items and providing surrogate copies for immediate use (Gertz, 2007; Lee, 2001; Smith, 2001). Digital versions can also serve as backup copies if original materials are lost or damaged (Rieger, 2008).

The use of digitization as a form of preservation, however, has been more controversial. The concerns focus on the integrity and authenticity of digital data as well as on the stability of digital formats and storage mediums (Gertz, 2007; Smith, 2001). Gertz (2007) acknowledges that a digital copy can serve as a record, if an original object deteriorates or is destroyed, but maintains that digitization is a form of copying, not preservation. Digital technology, though it opens new doors for access and reformatting, has also created a set of new challenges with regard to the preservation of digitized objects. In contrast to established preservation methods such as microfilming, creating paper facsimiles, or photo duplication, digital technology is relatively new and raises questions about the access and retrieval of digitized copies due to the possible obsolescence of hardware and software. Challenges associated with the preservation of digitized objects are at the heart of the debate about using digitization as a reformatting strategy, but they are also part of a broader discussion about digital preservation that encompasses digitized as well as "born digital" materials.

The gradual acceptance of digitization as one option of many reformatting techniques reflects the progress in digital preservation and broader thinking about curating special collection and archival materials in the digital environment. The endorsement of digitization as a preservation reformatting method by the Association of Research Libraries (ARL) in 2004 represents a turning point in the debate, although its focus is primarily on print-based materials (Arthur et al., 2004). The ARL's proposal recognizes digital conversion as a viable option and points out that each preservation reformatting technique has its strengths and weaknesses. The Endangered Archive Programme (EAP) at the British

Library supports digitization as the preferred means of copying archival materials that are in danger of destruction or physical deterioration. This recommendation is particularly relevant in developing countries where other preservation methods such as microfilming may not be available. The Preservation Reformatting Division of the Library of Congress considers digital reformatting to be a preservation method for at-risk archival materials among other options, such as microfilm and paper facsimile copies. In fact, the Library of Congress uses digitization as a preservation method for the reformatting of film, sound, and video recordings (Marcum, 2007).

Digitization with new technical capabilities for capturing the content of analog materials brings renewed attention to the preservation of deteriorating historic photographs and audiovisual media. Conway (2010) emphasizes that the preservation of audiovisual collections remains a major challenge of the 21st century and points out that the efforts of the preservation community in preserving paper-based materials have not been extended to audiovisual resources. Archival photographic, audio, and video collections provide a rich and often untapped source of historical evidence, but their preservation is problematic due to complex and deteriorating formats. Ester (1996) notes that "photographic collections are deteriorating, and in many cases, much faster than monographs and periodicals" (p. 2). Still photography and time-based media with motion-picture film, audio, and video have been historically recorded on fragile and unstable carriers, including glass plates, cellulose nitrate- and acetate-based film, and magnetic audio and videotapes. The degrading analog formats lead to unrecoverable information loss. As Koelling (2004) succinctly states, "the point of digital preservation projects is to capture the information held by the original before time turns that information to dust" (p. 12). Fig. 3.1 demonstrates an example of an image scanned from a deteriorated glass plate negative from the Roman B.J. Kwasniewski Photographs at the University of Wisconsin-Milwaukee Libraries.

Digital conversion offers an opportunity to capture the visual and/or audio content of unstable media before they deteriorate even further. In addition, digitization projects restore the usefulness of visual materials as information resources by providing item-level indexing and placing them in the context

FIGURE 3.1 Image Scanned from a Deteriorated Glass Plate Negative

From the Archives Department, University of Wisconsin-Milwaukee Libraries. The image is available at: http://collections.lib.uwm
.edu/cdm/ref/collection/mke-polonia/id/31790

of other digital collections (Capell, 2010; Matusiak and Johnston, 2014). Moreover, digitization frees the recording of knowledge from physical carriers that are prone to deterioration and enables further copying without information loss.

Digitization has introduced new dimensions to the dynamic between access and preservation. While most digitization projects are undertaken to extend the reach of cultural heritage institutions and to provide online access to their collections, other initiatives connect access and preservation goals. The two complementary goals—access and preservation—can often be realized through the same digitization project. Digitization assists preservation activities by providing surrogate copies of rare and fragile materials and by offering a reformatting option for deteriorating resources. The use of digitization as a strategy for long-term preservation of analog materials is still debatable, but it is gaining recognition as a selective approach to preserving the content of deteriorating photographic materials and archival collections of time-based media. The debate surrounding digitization for preservation has recently shifted its emphasis from reformatting to the usefulness and quality of preserved items. The goal of digitization for preservation is to capture the content of deteriorating resources and to create high-quality digital assets "worthy of long-term preservation" (Conway, 2010). Detailed discussion of digital preservation can be found in Chapter 9.

DIGITIZATION STRATEGIES AND SUSTAINABILITY

The strategies for undertaking digitization tend to be closely related to the goals and mission of the parent institution. The objectives of access and preservation are commonly shared in the cultural heritage community, but individual institutions may have additional goals, such as supporting curriculum programs, engaging the local community, meeting user requests, etc. No digitization activity is the same because of the unique characteristics of the original materials and differing institutional settings. The goals of the project determine different approaches to selection, technical standards, and the level and quality of digital capture. Overall, the selection of a digitization strategy should be informed by:

- The format and characteristics of the original materials
- The goals of digitization projects/programs
- The current and potential use
- The intended audience

The projects that focus on preservation of deteriorating analog items or those that combine access and preservation goals take a more systematic and resource-intensive approach. In these cases, all items in the collection are digitized at the highest quality affordable, and preservation-quality master copies are created for long-term archiving.

Access-oriented projects may adopt lower conversion standards to increase the amount of digitized materials. This approach can be undertaken when original items are in a stable condition and the holding institutions plan to preserve analog collections. Digitization initiatives then can forgo preservation-quality conversion, opt for minimum standards, and devote the resources to creating access copies for online delivery and meeting users' requests. This strategy allows for faster conversion and a decrease in costs. As mentioned in the introductory section, the Google Book Project has had a significant impact on the digitization of archival and special collections materials, resulting in several calls for a mass approach and a number of pilot projects (Erway, 2011; Miller, 2013; Moore, 2014; Patzke and Thiel, 2009; Sutton, 2012). Rapid digitization technologies and strategies are further discussed at the end of this chapter.

Most digitization initiatives are strategic and proactive with a goal of building digital collections for online access and/or assisting preservation. In practice, some digitization activities are also initiated at user requests. Schaffner et al. (2011) focus on user-driven digitization and provide a flexible, tiered approach to digital reproduction policies and procedures to manage on-demand workflows. The proposed strategies aim at streamlining the process of conversion and adopting minimal standards in order to deliver digital images to users in an efficient and economical way. Daigle (2012) reports on a more systematic approach to fulfilling immediate user requests by scanning larger (than requested) portions of collections to maximize conversion efforts.

Digitization strategies have also evolved over time from being project-oriented to having a more systematic program approach. The early digitization initiatives were experimental in nature, often supported with external funding, and focused on selective collections or discrete uses. The project-based approach, however, poses risks to sustainability because it is limited in duration and scope, and often lacks lasting institutional support. Kenney (2000) comments that "to succeed, digital imaging programs must permeate institutional culture and daily functions" (p. 153). The shift from a project-based approach to programs is based on the premise that digitized collections are recognized as institutional assets. Smith (2001) outlines the key points of a sustainable strategy:

- Integrates digitization into the fabric of library services
- Focuses on achieving mission-related objectives
- Relies on funding from predictable streams of allocation
- Includes a plan for the long-term maintenance of its assets

Sustainable digitization programs need not only an organizational affiliation to support the conversion activities but also an institutional commitment to long-term maintenance and preservation of digital assets. Bradley (2007) emphasizes that digital sustainability is not purely a technical issue. Sustaining digital information requires organizational, socio-technical, and economic infrastructure. Digital sustainability is closely connected to digital preservation as it encompasses "the wide range of issues and concerns that contribute to the longevity of digital information" (Bradley, 2007, p. 151). The concepts of digital preservation are discussed in more detail in Chapter 9.

In the context of digitization, sustainability requires consideration of the entire digital conversion cycle to ensure the creation and management of high-quality, sustainable digital objects. The next section provides an overview of the steps in the digitization process and summarizes the general guidelines for digital conversion.

DIGITIZATION PROCESS

Digitization of static media is the process of converting analog information to a digital format through scanning or digital photography. Time-based analog media, including film, audio, and video recordings are transformed into the digital format with the use of playback devices and analog-to-digital converters. Static materials are represented in digital format by still images, while dynamic media are represented by a time-based sequence of digital audio signals or, in the case of video and moving images, digital sound synchronized with a sequence of images. Regardless of the type of analog material or equipment being used, digitization is a process that involves multiple phases. The basic digitization cycle is similar for all materials, although the complexity increases for time-based media. Digitization is more than simply scanning or converting audio or video signals. It requires processing and describing digital files so they can be presented and preserved in a meaningful way. The purpose of digitization is not only to convert analog information into a digital signal but also to make it into a functional and accessible digitized object.

DIGITIZATION STEPS

Digitization is a complex process that consists of multiple phases and a number of tasks associated with each phase. Basic digitization steps include:

- Project planning, selection, and preparation of materials for conversion
- Image capture (or conversion of audio and video signals) and creation of master files
- Digital processing of captured data and production of derivative files
- Recording of metadata
- Ingesting digitized objects and their associated metadata into digital library management systems
- Digital preservation of the objects created as a result of the conversion process

Fig. 3.2 demonstrates the multistep process of building digitized collections. Other models of the digitization cycle present similar steps but differ slightly in terminology (Chowdhury and Chowdhury, 2003; Lee, 2001; Zhang and Gourley, 2009). As discussed in the previous section, most digitization projects are undertaken in order to present digitized objects through online collections. Ad hoc digitization activities that fulfill user requests generally do not have the same level of complexity, but they also consist of several steps necessary to process files and store them properly. If items are digitized according to the established guidelines and best practices, they can be reused to meet other requests and be added to digital collections in the future.

The steps in Fig. 3.2 are presented in sequence since this step-by-step approach is often necessary to maintain proper workflows. However, the process is also dynamic, and depending on the nature of a project, some steps may overlap or occur in a different order. For example, in the digitization of published textual records, scanning and creating metadata may take place simultaneously, or metadata may be prepared ahead of digital conversion because descriptive information is readily available. On

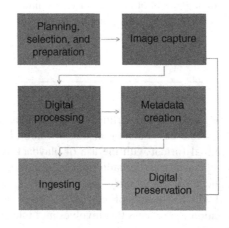

FIGURE 3.2 Digitization Steps

the other hand, in projects converting film negatives or slides, metadata creation usually takes place after scanning because high-resolution digital images provide better access to the visual content. The following section provides a brief summary of each step and associated tasks and activities.

Planning, selection, and preparation of materials is the first and the most critical step that involves defining a project's goals, scope, budget, timelines, and staff roles (Chapman, 2000). As Tanner (2001) notes, "project planning is essential to the successful implementation of any technology based project and particularly one involving digitization" (p. 329). The first phase of the project also includes selecting and assessing analog materials and preparing them for conversion, establishing technical specifications, and selecting equipment. The selection of materials for digitization requires considering multiple factors including copyright status, the format and size of originals, condition and unique characteristics, and requirements for handling fragile items. Selection criteria are discussed in more detail in Chapter 2. Damaged or deteriorating items may require some conservation efforts prior to digitization. The overall assessment of the original source collections influences the selection of digital capture equipment. Many activities in this phase are parallel to collection development, especially in rapid capture projects. Items or entire collections can be selected, processed, digitized, and rehoused as part of one project to improve efficiency of workflows and reduce material handling.

Digital capture represents the heart of the digitization process, in which analog information is sampled by capture devices (scanners, digital cameras, or analog-to-digital converters) and converted into digital signals. Depending on the availability of equipment and in-house expertise, this phase of the project can be outsourced to a digitization vendor. Dale (2007) provides a comprehensive overview of the pros and cons of outsourcing. The files produced as a result of the capture process represent information-rich digital masters, also referred to as archival master files. Digital masters represent "the best copy produced by a digitizing organization" (FADGI, n.d.). The FADGI Guidelines consider a file to be a digital master only if it meets the established technical requirements and has been quality controlled (FADGI, 2010). Master files need to be checked against quality benchmarks to ensure that they accurately represent the content of analog source materials and adhere to the established digitization guidelines. Master files serve as the source of all subsequent files to be derived. In practice, two copies of master files are usually created: one to be saved for long-term preservation, and a second one, often referred to as a service master, to serve as a source for smaller-size derivative files. The high-quality master files are important assets, so they ought to be transferred after capture to a digital repository for long-term preservation. The task of transferring digital masters for preservation is represented in the diagram by an additional arrow on the right.

Digital processing is a phase in which files created as a result of digital capture are edited and transformed to improve their quality and/or to enhance functionality. For example, copies of faded archival documents or maps can be edited to improve their contrast and legibility. In addition, artifacts introduced by the scanning process as well as scratches or dust marks can be corrected to improve the quality of the image. Noise may need to be removed from audio files, and the synchronization of audio and image might need to be improved for video files. It is recommended, however, that digital masters be saved intact, without any changes. The enhanced image should be saved as a second copy of the service master, also referred as to the production master file (FADGI, n.d.). Service master files reflect the changes introduced through digital processing and serve as a source for derivative files to be ingested into digital collections. Digital images of printed text pages can also be processed using Optical Character Recognition (OCR) software to create searchable digital documents. Textual documents can also be rekeyed to allow for encoding and/or to facilitate full-text searching. Digital processing also includes the task of quality review of service masters and derivatives.

Metadata creation involves selection of metadata schemas, customization of metadata templates, selection of controlled vocabulary tools and input guidelines, and building item-level records. Depending on the amount of information available in original collections, this process may require additional research to provide access points and contextual information. This step includes the recording of descriptive information as well as other metadata types, including administrative, structural, and technical. Quality review of metadata records is associated with this step. Chapter 5 provides more information on schemas and tools used in metadata creation.

Ingesting is a step that brings the transformation of converted items into completion, turning them into usable digitized objects. During this phase, digital content files (images, text, audio, or video) are associated with corresponding metadata records and uploaded into digital library management systems for access. After the collection building process is finalized, digitized objects are available for use. The ingesting tasks can vary depending on the content management system being used for collection building. For example, the CONTENTdm system generates derivative files for access automatically during the ingest process, while Omeka requires the preparation of derivatives in advance. The systems also vary in the level of support for metadata customization and functionality of digitized objects. Chapter 6 provides a comparative overview of six systems currently used in practice.

Digital preservation in the context of digitization refers to the maintenance of digital collections and the long-term preservation of digital master files created as a result of the digitization process. Digital master files represent valuable assets that need to be preserved over time. They serve as a source for future derivatives and as preservation copies for deteriorating analog materials. The activities associated with preserving digital masters include developing a long-term preservation policy and establishing an infrastructure and a strategy for identification, archival storage, integrity and authentication checking, regular backups, refreshing, and migration. A sustainable digitization program requires the development of an institutional approach to digital preservation and involves building a local digital repository or participating in a shared program. Digital preservation is discussed in more detail in Chapter 9.

This brief overview offers some insight into the complexity of the conversion process and necessary tasks to create high-quality usable digital objects. Quality control is an integral part of each step and encompasses procedures and techniques to verify accuracy and consistency of digitized objects (Rieger, 2000). Digitization, like many other technology-intensive projects, requires careful planning, managing multiple workflows, and proper documentation. Good project management is the key to successful digitization initiatives (Chapman, 2000; JISC Digital Media, 2014; Tanner, 2001). Over the years, members of the cultural heritage community have shared their experience and expertise in digitization through openly available tutorials and guides to best practices. The following section provides a summary of general guidelines.

GENERAL DIGITIZATION GUIDELINES

The purpose of guidelines is to ensure the creation of high-quality, sustainable digital objects that support current and intended use and are interoperable and consistent across collections and institutions. The guidelines that have emerged in the cultural heritage community, especially in the United States, are advisory rather than prescriptive in nature. They offer a range of general and technical recommendations but do not constitute a set of formal standards. The *Framework of Guidance for*

Building Good Digital Collections is described as a recommended "best practice" (NISO Framework Working Group, 2007). The most recent guidelines issued by the division of the American Library Association stress that "at this point there is no official standard for digitization, but institutions are discussing how they can collaborate and share digitized content" (ALCTS, 2013, p. 2). This approach offers individual institutions some flexibility but has also resulted in a plethora of published guides and tutorials. Conway (2008) examines 17 guides to best practices in digitizing visual resources and concludes that the lack of standardization has implications for the quality and integrity of digitized objects and may be a hindrance to wider adoption of the guidelines by small and midsize cultural institutions.

The development of best practice guides was spurred by the early adopters of digital technology, such as Cornell University Libraries, the Library of Congress, US National Archives and Records Administration (NARA), and organizations such as Digital Library Federation (DFL), International Library Federation Association (IFLA), and Research Library Group (RLG). Conway (2008) also recognizes the seminal work of imaging specialists and pioneers of digitization, including Michael Ester (1996), Anne Kenney and Steve Chapman (1996), Franziska Frey and James Reilly (1999), Steve Puglia (2000), and Steve Puglia et al. (2004). Their work on imaging concepts and specifications provided the necessary theoretical and technical foundations for developing guides to best practices. The tutorial *Moving Theory into Practice* developed at the Cornell University Libraries has contributed significantly to the training of librarians and archivists in the concepts and procedures of digitization (Kenney et al., 2000). In addition to the guidelines developed by the Library of Congress and NARA, major collaborative digitization initiatives, such as the California Digital Library (2011) and Colorado Digitization Program (BCR, 2008) issued their own sets of recommendations. Those guides to imaging best practices have in turn influenced the development of guidelines at the state and institutional levels (see Appendix A for an annotated bibliography of selected guides).

The majority of published tutorials and guides to best practice focus on static textual and visual resources, but the underlying principles can also be applied to time-based media. The guidelines emphasize digitization at the highest quality to capture informational content and attributes of analog source materials in order to create accurate and authentic digital representations. Recently released guidelines build upon foundational concepts but offer higher technical specifications that reflect the current digital environment. The approach that has emerged is to offer minimum capture recommendations for a variety of static and time-based media with an understanding that unique characteristics of source materials may require variations in the specifications. A set of accepted minimums is, however, recommended to create sustainable digitized content (ALCTS, 2013).

The following list provides a summary of the general digitization principles presented in a number of currently available guides (ALCTS, 2013; BCR, 2008; FADGI, 2010; Yale University, 2010):

- Digitize at the highest resolution appropriate to the nature of the source material
- Use standard targets for measuring and adjusting the capture metric of a scanner or digital camera. Grayscale or color targets provide an internal reference within the image for linear scale and color information.
- Create and preserve master files that can be used to produce derivative files and serve a variety of current and future use needs
- Create digital objects that are accessible and interoperable across collections and institutions
- Ensure a consistent and high-level quality of digitized objects
- Digitize at an appropriate level of quality to avoid recapture and rehandling of the source materials

- Digitize an original or first generation of the source material
- Create meaningful metadata for digitized objects
- Provide archival storage and address digital preservation of digitized objects

The general guidelines assume a use-neutral approach that has been strongly recommended since the early days of digitization projects (Besser, 2003; Ester, 1996; Kenney, 2000). It implies that a source item is digitized once and at the highest level of quality affordable to meet the needs not only of an immediate project but also of a variety of future uses. The goal of this approach is to create high-quality digital representations and to avoid redigitizing in the future. The use-neutral approach is an important component of digitization best practices, as it addresses not only the current needs but also, as Besser (2003) emphasizes, "all potential future purposes" (p. 43). It includes the notion of digital master files (sometimes referred to as archival masters) and derivatives. Ester (1996), who introduced the concepts of digital archival and derivative images, notes "an archival image has a very straightforward purpose: safeguarding the long-term value of images and the investment in acquiring them" (p. 11). In addition to the difference in purpose and use, digital masters and derivatives also differ in regard to file attributes such as size, compression, dimensions, and format.

Digital masters are created as a direct result of the digital capture process and should represent the essential attributes and information of the original material. Digital masters are supposed to be "the highest quality files available" (Besser, 2003, p. 3). They should not be edited or processed for any specific output. Because the process of creating digital masters usually results in large file sizes, digital masters are not used for online display. In fact, many archival formats such as TIFF are not supported by major web browsers. Their primary function is to serve as a long-term archival file and as a source for derivative files. Digital masters are stored in digital repositories for long-term preservation. General recommendations for digital master file creation include:

- Digitize at the highest quality affordable
- Save as an uncompressed file
- Use standard, nonproprietary file formats, such as TIFF for static media (text or still images) or WAV for audio
- Do not save any enhancements in an archival copy
- Use an established file-naming convention

Derivatives are created from digital master files for specific uses including presentation in digital collections, print reproductions, and multimedia presentations. General recommendations for derivative files include:

- Reduce the file size so it can load quickly and be transferred over networks
- Use standard formats with lossy compression such as JPEG
- Use standard formats supported by major web browsers

Table 3.1 provides a summary of formats recommended for digital masters and derivatives based on analog source type. File format is an essential component, as it provides an internal structure and a "container" for digitized content. Unlike physical objects, digital files do not exist in an independent material form. Digital data is stored in file formats and requires hardware and software to be rendered. The Sustainability of Digital Formats site at the Library of Congress provides a working definition of formats as "packages of information that can be stored as data files or sent via network as data streams (also known as bitstreams, byte streams)" (Library of Congress, 2013).

Table 3.1 Recommended File Formats for Digital Masters and Derivative Files

Analog Material	Digital Masters	Derivatives
Text	TIFF	JPEG, PDF
Photographic images (prints, negatives, slides)	TIFF	JPEG, JPEG 2000
Audio recordings	WAV/BWF	MP3
Moving image (video, film)	JPEG 2000/MXF	MPEG-4 (MP4)

File formats vary in their functionality and attributes. The master file format needs to be platform independent and have a number of attributes, such as openness, robustness, and extendibility, to support the rich data captured during the conversion and to ensure its persistence over time as technology changes (Frey, 2000a). The selection of an appropriate format has implications for access across platforms and transfer over networks as well as storage and long-term preservation. The *Framework of Guidance for Building Good Digital Collections* states as one of its principles: "a good object exists in a format that supports its intended current and future use" (NISO Framework Working Group, 2007, p. 26). The section of this chapter on technical factors provides an overview of the recommended formats for static media, including TIFF, JPEG, JPEG 2000, PDF, and PNG. Audio and moving image formats are discussed in more detail in Chapter 4.

General guidelines also include recommendations for establishing a file-naming convention. File names for digital masters and derivatives need to be determined before the digital capture process begins and preferably follow a convention adopted by the parent institution or department. Digital files should be well organized and named consistently to ensure easy identification and access. Systematic file naming helps not only to manage the project but also ensures system compatibility and interoperability. File names can be either nondescriptive or meaningful. Both approaches are valid, but each has its pros and cons (Frey, 2000a; Zhang and Gourley, 2009). Selecting a file-naming convention for digitization requires long-term thinking and a good understanding of the scope of the project and/or the size of the original collection. File-naming recommendations include:

- Assign unique and consistent names
- Use alphanumeric characters—lowercase letters and numbers 0 through 9
- Avoid special characters, spaces, and tabs
- Include institutional IDs (if available)
- Number files sequentially using leading zeros
- Use a valid file extension, such as .tif, .jpg, or .pdf
- Limit file names to 31 characters, including the three-character extension; or if possible, use 8.3 convention (8 characters plus three-character extension)—for example, aa000001.tif

DIGITIZATION OF TEXTUAL AND STATIC VISUAL RESOURCES

Static media encompasses a wide range of textual documents, from handwritten letters to printed books, and an even more complex array of photographic resources and other types of two-dimensional visuals. Photographs, archival records, postcards, rare books, manuscripts, and newspapers represent

FIGURE 3.3 Pixel Matrix of an Image Scanned from a Color Slide

the majority of digitized items in the static media category. Photographs are the most frequently digitized objects. The 2012 survey of digitization activities in Europe reports that 66% of surveyed cultural heritage institutions have digitized photographs (Stroeker and Voegels, 2012).

Textual materials and still images are converted to the digital form through scanning or digital photography. A variety of digitization equipment, from scanners to digital cameras, can be used in the conversion process. During the scanning process, an item is sampled and mapped as a grid of picture elements. A pixel is a single picture element. The captured data are represented by a series of pixels called "raster images" (also referred to as "bitmap images"). Puglia (2000) describes the structure of digitized images: "digitization converts an image into a series of picture elements of pixels, little squares that are either black or white (binary), a specific shade of gray (grayscale), or color. Each pixel is represented by a single or series of binary digits, either 1s or 0s. The pixels are arranged in a two-dimensional matrix called a bitmap" (p. 83). Fig. 3.3 demonstrates an example of a pixel matrix in an image scanned from a 35 mm color slide. The image of an Iranian woman featured in Fig. 3.3 is part of the American Geographical Society Library Digital Archive and is available at http://collections.lib. uwm.edu/cdm/ref/collection/agsphoto/id/102.

Bitmap images are characterized by a number of measures, such as resolution, pixel bit depth, and color mode, and their size and quality are affected by other technical factors including compression. The following section provides a brief overview of basic image measures, digitization equipment, and selected technical recommendations for conversion of textual and photographic resources.

TECHNICAL FACTORS

A range of technical factors play a role in the digitization process and relate to the quality and size of captured images. Paying close attention to image measures, such as resolution, bit depth, and color mode is critical during the conversion process, as these directly impact the quality of digital master files. Other factors, such as compression, need to be determined during the processing stage in the production of derivative files. Technical specifications, including resolution, bit depth, and mode of capture, have to be considered in the selection of the scanners and digital cameras.

Resolution is one of the most important factors, as it refers to the number of times an image is sampled and consequently relates to the amount of detail captured during the scanning process. Resolution specifically refers to the number of dots, or pixels (picture elements), used to represent an image. It is expressed in a number of ways, DPI (dots per inch) or PPI (pixels per inch). PPI refers to the number of pixels captured in a given inch and is used when discussing scanning resolution and on-screen display. DPI comes from the print environment in reference to the optical resolutions for images and hardware. DPI more accurately refers to output devices, or how many dots of ink per inch a printer puts on the paper or onscreen monitor display. However, the two terms are often used interchangeably. Digitization guidelines recommend scanning at the highest resolution affordable to accurately and fully capture the visual content of the original materials. Scanning resolution depends on the technical specifications of capture devices, so it is important to select a scanner or camera with sufficient optical resolution. Depending on the camera's lenses and support, the achieved resolution can sometimes be different from the optical resolution. FADGI (2010) provides helpful guidelines on sampling frequency. Items scanned at high resolution will result in large digital master files. However, there is no "one size fits all" ideal or standard resolution. The resolution should be adjusted according to the type of source item, its physical dimensions, and the amount of detail that needs to be captured. Digitization guidelines provide a range of recommended resolution measures relative to the types of sources materials and dimensions. For example, a minimum resolution for textual materials without images is 300 ppi, while a photographic 8 × 10 in. print will benefit from scanning at 600 ppi (ALCTS, 2013). Higher resolution provides more pixels and will generally render more detail, but there is also a point when increasing resolution does not yield any additional information.

Pixel bit depth influences the representation of images, rendered in a grayscale tone or a range of colors. It is a measure that "defines the number of shades that can actually be represented by the amount of information saved for each pixel" (Puglia, 2000, p. 85). Depending on the number of bits per pixel, images are represented as black or white, grayscale, or true color. One-bit images are bitonal—either black or white. Eight-bit images are necessary to represent 256 shades of gray tones in photographic images. Most color images require 24 bits per pixel to provide true representation of color. The greater the bit depth, the more information about the source is captured by the scanning device, resulting in a more accurate digital representation of the original. A bit depth of 8 can capture enough information to represent 256 colors or shades of gray. A bit depth of 24 captures over 16 million colors or shades of gray. It is worth remembering that there is a relationship between bit depth and file size. Scanning at a higher bit depth increases the overall file size. The usage of the term has evolved as institutions have moved from legacy scanning to modern raw capture. Currently, an 8-bit file means a 3-channel file with 8 bits per channel, which used to be referred to as a 24-bit image.

Color mode refers to the representation of color in images. Color images consist of three or more channels that represent color information. Several different systems are used to represent color images, with RGB being one of the most common. RGB stands for red, green, and blue, the three channels used to represent digital color images. Computer software combines the three channels for each pixel to determine the final color. An RGB color digital image file consists of three channels, each with 8 bits of data (3 channels × 8 bits = 24 bits). Many cultural heritage institutions process to 16 bits per channel to achieve subtle gradations of color.

Modes of capture refer to the way digitization equipment captures images in relation to the two measures: bit depth and color mode.

- *Bitonal* mode is appropriate for printed text materials without illustrations. Text can be scanned in bitonal mode where one bit per pixel will represent black or white values. Bitonal scanning was used in early digitization projects but now is used infrequently.
- *Grayscale* mode requires multiple bits per pixel (8 bits minimum) to represent shades of gray and is appropriate for scanning photographic black-and-white film negatives, black-and-white

photographic prints, or books and newspapers with grayscale images. Increasingly, color RGB mode is recommended for black-and-white photographic materials since it captures more information from an analog source. Generally, black-and-white prints and negatives will benefit considerably from scanning in RGB. If storage of these files is an issue, they may be converted to grayscale after scanning.

- *RGB color mode* is recommended for items with continuous tone color information. RGB mode is used for all textual and visual resources where color is present in the source item. In addition, archival textual materials or rare books are scanned in color when it is important to capture the aging nature of paper or other artifacts (handwritten notes, stamps, etc.).

Compression is the process of reducing the file size by discarding a certain amount of information. The process is, in most cases, irreversible. Compression is closely related to the quality of images and their size.

- *Lossless compression* discards redundant information and does not impact the quality of images. It allows for storing data in a more compact form. Lossless compression is supported by TIFF and JPEG 2000 formats and can be used for service masters—images created as a result of processing and image enhancement techniques. However, it should not be applied to digital master files. Digital archival masters should be saved as *uncompressed* files. *No compression* is different from lossless compression. Digital master files should retain all information captured during the conversion process.
- *Lossy compression* creates file sizes that are smaller, but it also contributes to the loss of image data and decreases quality (the amount of discarded information depends on the level of compression). It is important to remember that when a compressed image is decompressed, it is no longer identical to the original image. JPEG format applies lossy compression. JPEG file sizes can be reduced by applying compression, which makes them suitable for online access and distribution.

Formats provide a standardized method of encoding and organizing data into files. The digital conversion of textual and photographic materials results in still raster (bitmap) images, a two-dimensional grid of pixels. A variety of formats can be used for storing raster images. The distinction between digital master files and derivatives in the digitization of cultural heritage materials provides a foundation for the selection of formats. TIFF has been recommended as a master format for still images. TIFF has been widely adopted, and, as a recent study of file formats for raster still images indicates, it "has been the format of choice for the cultural heritage community" (FADGI, 2014, p. 3). JPEG and JPEG 2000 have been recommended as derivative formats for photographic images, newspapers, manuscripts, and maps. JPEG 2000 has also been considered as an archival format for master files (Buckley, 2008; Buonora and Liberati, 2008; Van der Knijff, 2011). PDF is recognized as a suitable derivative format for textual documents. PDF/A is a format recommended for archiving digital documents.

- *TIFF* (Tagged-Image File Format) is a stable and widely adopted file format for master files of raster still images. Used since the early days of digitization, TIFF has become the de facto standard for digital masters of digitized static cultural heritage materials. Fleischhauer (2014a) notes, "its endurance in time can be seen as a strength, especially considering the wide array of applications that can read it" (pp. 2–3). Highly flexible and platform-independent, it can be used for storing bitonal, grayscale, and color still images. TIFF combines raster image data with a flexible tagged field structure for metadata. TIFF supports lossy and lossless compression. It is recommended that digital masters be saved as uncompressed TIFF files, but lossless compression, such as LZW compression, can be used for service masters. Uncompressed TIFF files require a considerable amount of storage space. TIFF is an open and well-documented standard, with the specifications of TIFF Revision 6.0 maintained by the Adobe Systems. The TIFF filenames use .tif or .tiff extensions.

- *JPEG* (Joint Photographic Experts Group) is designed for compressing and thus reducing the size of grayscale and color raster still images. The JPEG standard was published in 1992 and is commonly used on the web and in digital cameras. In digitization, JPEG is used primarily for derivative images to be displayed in digital collections. JPEG applies a lossy compression method, which reduces the file size. The amount of compression can be adjusted. The typical ratio of 10:1 results in very little perceptible loss in image quality. JPEG works particularly well with photographic images of continuous tone, while images with lettering or line drawings may suffer some degradation in quality. The effective compression makes JPEG a particularly suitable format for online display and transfer over the Internet. However, because of the loss of data associated with compression, this file format should not be used for master files. The JPEG format is supported by all browsers. The JPEG file extensions are .jpg or .jpeg.

- *JPEG 2000* is an international standard for the compression of digital still images. It was proposed by the Joint Photographic Experts Group in the year 2000 as an open file format and a compression method with the goal of improving or superseding the original JPEG format. JPEG 2000 provides a new compression algorithm with progressive display, multiresolution imaging, scalable image quality, and the ability to handle large and high-dynamic range images (Buckley, 2008). The JPEG 2000 file format also offers significant improvements over earlier formats by supporting both lossless and lossy image compression. Because of its superior ability to handle large content files and dynamic display with support for zooming and panning, JPEG 2000 has been used as a derivative file format for maps, newspaper pages, and other large images (Fleischhauer, 2014b). At this point, the format cannot be viewed natively in most web browsers and requires a dedicated JPEG 2000 viewer. The potential of JPEG 2000 for storing large master files and as an alternative to uncompressed TIFFs files has also been explored due to its excellent compression performance (Buonora and Liberati, 2008; Van der Knijff, 2011). The acceptance of JPEG 2000 as a preservation format, however, has been slow and a subject of debate in the cultural heritage community (Adams, 2013; Fleischhauer, 2014b). The study conducted by Van der Knijff (2011) also identifies some preservation risks, related to the current format specification in color space and in the handling of grid resolution, which may lead to the loss of some information in future migrations. JPEG 2000 uses .jp2 and .jpx extensions.

- *PDF* (Portable Document Format) is an access format developed by Adobe Systems in 1993 to share and view digital documents. It remained a proprietary format until 2008 when it was released as an open international standard. PDF is used to represent 2D documents in a fixed-layout format. PDF documents maintain the original structure and appearance of source items and can be exchanged across many platforms. PDF is a universal format used to represent both born digital and digitized documents. A popular format in the publishing industry, PDF became a de facto standard for scholarly publications, administrative documents, and many textual documents shared over the web. In digitization, PDF is used as a derivative format to represent multipage objects, such as manuscripts, books, journals, and archival documents. Full-text searching of digitized documents can be incorporated into PDF derivatives, but it requires additional processing of source images. At a minimum level, digitized historical documents are presented in the PDF format as images—digital facsimiles. Full-text searchability is available for digitized print documents processed with Optical Character Recognition (OCR) software (Turró, 2008; Yongli, 2010). A free and widely available PDF reader can be used as a standalone program or a browser plug-in. A PDF filename has a .pdf extension.

- *PDF/A* builds upon the specifications of PDF but was developed specifically as a standard format to ensure long-term accessibility and the preservation of electronic documents. PDF/A addresses the concerns of the archival community and is recognized as a format for the digital archiving of documents (Dryden, 2008). PDF/A-1 was released in 2005, and the latest version, PDF/A-3, was made available in 2012. It provides "a mechanism for representing electronic documents in a manner that preserves their static visual appearance over time, independent of the tools and systems used for creating, storing or rendering the files" (Lazorchak, 2014). The difference between PDF and PDF/A is in the preservation function, which in PDF/A is achieved by embedding all fonts and metadata within the file so that it can be consistently rendered regardless of the hardware and software used to create or view it.
- *PNG* (Portable Network Graphics) was designed to replace the older GIF format. PNG supports raster grayscale and color image files and offers lossless compression. PNG is supported by all major web browsers and is a popular choice for transferring images over the web. The use of the PNG format in digitization projects is limited thus far. In a recent Library of Congress blog, Fleischhauer (2014b) highlights PNG support for color management and lossless compression and wonders about the potential use of PNG for master files. PNG uses a .png file extension.

The file formats used in the digitization of static media demonstrate a high degree of stability, especially in comparison to the still-evolving formats for video recordings. A comparative study of TIFF, JPEG, JPEG 2000, PNG, and PDF, conducted by the Federal Agencies Digitization Guidelines Initiative, indicates that all formats have viable sustainability, although they vary in attributes, capabilities, and cost of implementation (FADGI, 2014).

DIGITIZATION EQUIPMENT

The focus of this overview is on imaging equipment used in the digital conversion of textual and 2D visual resources recorded on a variety of analog carriers, including paper, film negatives, glass plates, or slides. The type of equipment used in the conversion process depends on the condition and format of the analog source, its physical dimensions, characteristics, rarity, and fragility. When considering the format of analog materials, it is important to make a distinction between:

- *Reflective* materials, such as paper used in creating manuscripts, books, maps, drawings or photographic prints
- *Transparent* media, such as film, slides, or glass plates

This distinction has implications for selecting an appropriate capture device and is related to the way scanners work.

A scanner is a device that analyzes the surface of an image, printed text, or transparent film and converts it into a digital image, which is a 2D pixel array. Most scanners use CCD (charge-coupled device) light-sensitive image sensors. In the case of reflective materials, such as paper-based textual resources or photographic prints, the light is reflected off the surface of the paper and read by a set of light-sensitive diodes that then convert this reading into a digital value. In the case of transparent materials, such as film negatives or slides, the light needs to pass through the material so the sensor can read the image and convert it into a digital file. Transparent materials require dedicated film scanners or flatbed scanners with a transparency adapter.

Cultural heritage institutions have collected historical materials on a variety of analog formats, and their conversion requires versatile digitization equipment. The selection of a scanner or digital camera depends on the physical dimensions and characteristics of analog sources and will greatly impact image quality. Photographic prints can be digitized using flatbed scanners. Larger film negatives such as 4×7 in., 5×7 in., or 8×10 in. can be scanned using flatbed scanners with a transparency adapter, but small negatives of 35 mm require dedicated film scanners. Textual materials on paper (reflective), if they are single-leaf documents, can be scanned using flatbed scanners or even faster sheet-fed scanners if materials are not rare. Bound materials—books and manuscripts—require overhead scanners or digital cameras. Maps and charts that are large and exceed the size of flatbed scanners will need wide-or large-format scanners. And finally, documents on microfilm, such as newspapers, require dedicated microfilm scanners. Digital cameras are increasingly being used in digitization projects, but they require a digital imaging studio with additional pieces of equipment. The price of scanners and cameras has decreased over the years, but the cost still plays a significant role in selecting equipment, especially when it comes to high-end film scanners or large-format digital cameras.

The following section provides a brief overview of types of scanners and cameras used in practice. The examples presented in the figures are meant to illustrate the types of equipment but are not intended to be an endorsement of specific models or companies.

Flatbed scanners are suitable for single-leaf text documents and most photographic prints, provided the material does not exceed the scanner's maximum imaging area. Large-format flatbed scanners and sheet-fed scanners can capture single-leaf oversized materials. Flatbed scanners are used for digitizing reflective materials. Scanning transparent materials, such as glass plates and larger film negatives, requires a transparency adapter. The major limitation of implementing scanners in a digitization program is that they are very slow and require contact of a scanned item with the glass surface of the scanning bed. Flatbed scanners are not suitable for brittle or bound materials.

Fig. 3.4 includes an example of a flatbed scanner, Epson Expression 10000, that is commonly used by archives and libraries for digitization. It provides a scanning area of 11×17 in., high optical resolution up to 2400 ppi, and high bit depth, up to 48 bit for color and 16 bit for grayscale images. A transparency adapter is optional, but it allows for the scanning of large film negatives (4×7 in., 5×7 in., or 8×10 in). The resolution 2400 ppi, however, is too low for small size film (35 mm).

Overhead scanners are used in the image capture of bound materials—books and manuscripts—as well as for fragile reflective materials, such as newspapers, prints, drawings, and small maps. The source of light is on the side, light sensors are at the top, and thus books do not need to be placed face down.

Fig. 3.5 presents an example of an overhead scanner. This scanner has a large scanning area and an integrated glass plate that allows for the flattening of uneven materials. It also includes a motorized book cradle that makes it easier when scanning bound volumes. The resolution is 400 ppi, so this type of scanner works well with books but not with smaller items that require a higher resolution.

Fig. 3.6 presents an example of DT BC100 Book Capture System, a dedicated book scanning system that offers fast, preservation-quality image capture of bound monographs and loose materials, including works on paper, serials including newspapers, loose manuscripts, photos, and drawings. The

FIGURE 3.4 Flatbed Scanner

Image courtesy of Ling Meng, Digital Collections and Initiatives, University of Wisconsin-Milwaukee Libraries.

FIGURE 3.5 Overhead Scanner

Image courtesy of Ling Meng, Digital Collections and Initiatives, University of Wisconsin-Milwaukee Libraries.

system includes a V-cradle and glass plates for flattening materials. For more fragile or rare items, the cradle can be raised so material is about to touch the glass but does not actually make contact.

Film scanners are used in the conversion of transparent media, such as 35 mm slides and film negatives. Some flatbed scanners include transparency adapters, but their resolution and dynamic range are limited in comparison to film scanners. Dedicated film scanners offer higher resolution and are

FIGURE 3.6 DT BC100 Book Capture System

Image courtesy of Digital Transitions Division of Cultural Heritage. www.dtdch.com

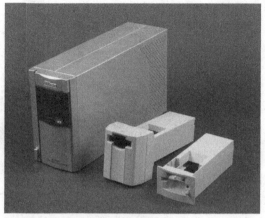

FIGURE 3.7 Nikon Film and Slide Scanner

Image courtesy of Ling Meng, Digital Collections and Initiatives, University of Wisconsin-Milwaukee Libraries.

appropriate for the small size of the original transparent material. They also enable scanning without glass. Glass attracts dust which becomes visible at high resolutions.

Fig. 3.7 includes an example of Nikon CoolScan that can create scans of 35 mm film negatives and slides at 4000 ppi. Fig. 3.8 demonstrates a high-end Hasselblad film scanner, which provides high resolution of 6000 ppi and is capable of scanning other film sizes in addition to 35 mm film. It can also scan batches of negatives in a somewhat automated fashion, but of course, high quality and scanning speed come at a price. Fig. 3.9 provides another example of a film scanner, the DTFSK scanner available

FIGURE 3.8 Hasselblad Film Scanner

Image courtesy of Ling Meng, Digital Collections and Initiatives, University of Wisconsin-Milwaukee Libraries.

FIGURE 3.9 DTFSK Film Scanner

Image courtesy of Digital Transitions Division of Cultural Heritage. www.dtdch.com

from Digital Transitions. This new generation film scanner offers not only preservation-quality image capture but also speed, being 400 times faster than legacy scanning equipment. It is capable of scanning a wide range of formats from 35 mm up to 11 × 17 in. film.

Digital camera systems provide the most versatile image capture environment, but they require setting up a more robust imaging studio. It is important to make a distinction between digital cameras and camera-based systems used in digitization. In addition to a camera unit, digital camera systems include a number of components, such as a light source, a vacuum easel for flat materials, and a cradle for books or other bound materials. Digital camera systems are designed specifically for cultural heritage applications, of which a digital camera is a very small part. There are even currently emerging technologies that incorporate all of these into a single unit. A camera unit will include a camera body, lens, and specially formatted camera back, such as those offered by PhaseOne, Leaf, and Sinar or Hasselblad. These larger format digital camera systems not only offer high resolution—they are engineered to provide the greatest dynamic tonal and color range and clarity, which can render amazing levels of image quality. Many materials of varying formats can be captured using an overhead camera, and the resulting details in the image file often show such minute details as the support composite fibers, quality of typeset or engravings, and even single bristle lines left from an artist's brushstroke. Oversize items, such as maps, can be placed on a vacuum easel or copy stand or hung on the wall for image capture, and the image quality can even facilitate multiple captures of segments of an item to be merged into a larger image with minimal quality loss rather than a single-frame capture that may not show the greatest detail of a given item.

Fig. 3.10 is an example of a camera system in place at the Denver Public Library's Imaging Services Lab, which is a division of the Western History and Genealogy Department. They have retrofitted their previous view camera system with an RCam from the Digital Transitions Division of Cultural Heritage, which utilizes a PhaseOne back and Schneider lens. It is utilized as the main tool in their digitization work as it can capture multiple format types that may have varying characteristics. These types of camera installations, however, are expensive and require substantial expertise and in-depth training. Many institutions have determined that the initial investment of high-end equipment and well-trained personnel is rewarded by superior image quality, smoother workflows, and rapid production of digital assets.

FIGURE 3.10 Large-Format Digital Camera System

Image courtesy of Benjamin Miller. Imaging Services Lab, Denver Public Library.

Less costly options include professional-grade digital SLR (single lens reflex) cameras that work well for books and other prints. Most consumer-level digital cameras are inadequate for the reproduction of special collection materials.

Many digital camera systems involve an intermediary step of working with raw files before they are processed into digital masters. The immediate result of camera-based capture is a raw proprietary file, which at the point of capture does not represent a digital master. Raw files need to be saved in the TIFF format in order to become master files. Photographic capture with its raw workflows is more complex than direct-to-TIFF scanning, but it offers more flexibility and acceleration in imaging process.

RECOMMENDATIONS FOR DIGITAL CAPTURE OF TEXT AND PHOTOGRAPHIC IMAGES

The processes for digitizing textual and photographic materials are similar to a certain extent. For both source types, the output is in the form of digital images, and masters are saved in the TIFF format. However, recommendations for resolution and bit depth vary because of the fundamentally different content, and the amount of detail that needs to be captured is greater for photographic materials. The complexity of photographic processes and formats also demands a wider range of specifications and more versatile digitization equipment. While digitized photographs remain basically as images, digitized text documents need to be further processed and transformed to make the textual content searchable.

Text digitization focuses primarily on legibility issues. Scanned pages of books, newspapers, journals, and other textual documents can be presented as images and/or as searchable text. Digitized text not only has to be legible to the human eye but also needs to be recognized and processed by software if searchable text is to be created. The size of text in original text material is an important factor when determining technical specifications. Higher resolution and bit depth are recommended for documents

Table 3.2 Minimum Digitization Recommendations for Textual Materials

Original Material	Scanning Resolution	Bit Depth	Capture Mode	Notes
Books and other text without images (nonrare)	300 ppi	8 bit	Grayscale	The resolution may be adjusted according to the detail to be represented.
Books and other text with images (nonrare)	400 ppi	8 bit or 24 bit	Grayscale or color	The resolution may be adjusted according to the detail to be represented. Capturing in color (24-bit RGB) is recommended.
Rare books	400 ppi	24 bit	Color	Increasing resolution may be necessary for less standardized fonts.
Manuscripts	400 ppi	24 bit	Color	Increasing resolution may be necessary for difficult to read handwritten documents.

with smaller typeface. Features of the original documents, such as handwritten versus print, their rare nature, or the presence of illustrations, also play a role in adjusting the specifications.

Table 3.2 is based on the most recent recommendations prepared by the Association for Library Collections and Technical Services, a division of the American Library Association (ALCTS, 2013). It is important to remember that the listed specifications represent minimum recommendations. Increasing resolution is highly recommended for rare books with ornate and irregular fonts and for manuscripts where legibility might be an issue.

Page images produced as direct output of digital conversion are not searchable. Digitized documents can be converted into fully searchable text either through manual keying or automatic processing using OCR software. A hybrid approach may combine OCR processing with a review for accuracy and manual correction. Current OCR technology can process typed or printed text with various degrees of accuracy, but is not capable of converting handwritten text. Manuscripts and other handwritten documents must be typed to become searchable. Because of a large body of digitized historical documents and manuscripts, there is a strong research interest in developing solutions for machine recognition of handwritten text (Romero et al., 2011; Sánchez et al., 2014). However, these efforts remain in an experimental stage.

In practice, most searchable text of digitized printed or typed documents is created through OCR software (Lesk, 2004; Yongli, 2010). OCR is the process that converts the text of a digitized printed page into a searchable text file. This is accomplished as the OCR software analyzes scanned page images, recognizes groups of characters (words), compares them against its dictionary, and finally translates the characters into machine-readable digital text format. Cultural heritage institutions have used a wide range of proprietary OCR software, including ABBYY FineReader, Adobe Acrobat, OmniPage, or Readiris Pro. There is also a growing interest in using open source OCR tools, such as Tesseract, that provide more customization and specifically support OCR processing of digitized historical documents (Blanke et al., 2012). OCR technology is primarily used for creating searchable text of digitized books, journals, and newspapers. Increasingly, it is also viewed as an important component in large-scale digitization of modern archival collections (Miller, 2013).

The accuracy of text produced with OCR software varies. The high rate of 99% can be reached in recognition of English-language typed or printed legal or business documents (Rice et al., 1996). However, accuracy decreases for historical documents, such as newspapers, where the rate of uncorrected OCR can be as low as 68% (Klijn, 2008). The performance of OCR software plays a role, but the accuracy of the processed text also depends on a number of other factors, including:

- Quality of the scanned images
- Legibility of the original text
  - fonts
  - contrast between printed text and page background
  - layout
- Language and script

The quality of OCR text is related to the condition of the original source materials (Klijn, 2008). The accuracy rates decrease for historical documents printed with rare and difficult-to-recognize fonts and for documents with complex layouts, such as newspapers (Holley, 2009; Tanner et al., 2009). Non-Latin language scripts, such as Arabic, pose another challenge. Digitization projects involving historic Arabic-language periodicals demonstrate relatively low accuracy of OCR text (Matusiak and Abu Harb, 2011). In addition, the artifacts present in historical documents, such as tears, speckles, poor printing, or bleeding, reduce the quality of OCR output.

Photographic images represent the most difficult materials to convert in the 2D static media category, and yet they are often the first candidates for digitization projects undertaken by cultural heritage institutions. The authors of *The Minimum Digitization Capture Recommendations* emphasize, "accurately reformatting historic photographs is among the most challenging of the static media types" (ALCTS, 2013, p. 23). This difficulty stems from the diversity of analog materials that have been used to record photographic images, from glass plates to different types of negatives. The original negatives and prints come in different sizes ranging from 35 mm to 8 × 10 in. Further, nitrate- and acetate-based film negatives used for several decades of the 20th century are chemically unstable and present preservation risks. However, as previously discussed, digitization provides a tremendous opportunity to capture the visual information of deteriorating film-based materials. The negatives may require some conservation efforts such as cleaning or straightening prior to scanning. Moreover, representing the visual content of photographs in the digital format presents a unique set of challenges related to tone and color reproduction.

The presence of original negatives along with prints in many archival photographic collections causes a dilemma in choosing which source to digitize. In general, it is recommended to digitize from the most original source (i.e., the negative). The general digitization principle, "digitize an original or first generation of the source material," is especially applicable to photographic collections. Frey (2000b) points out that "because every generation of photographic copying involves some quality loss, using intermediates immediately implies some decrease in quality" (p. 114). There are, however, some exceptions to this rule, especially in cases where there are substantial differences between the negative and the print. In some cases, photographic prints have been custom made, and scans from these derivatives will surpass a straightforward scan from an original negative. The negatives also can be in poor condition due to deterioration. In such situations, scanning from an intermediate is a better solution. In the case of artistic photography, it makes sense to scan both the negative and the print(s) if both are available.

The physical characteristics of the photographs need to be assessed in order to select the most appropriate equipment and to determine the technical specifications. The medium, format, and size are the primary factors affecting the equipment selection. Original source collections need to be evaluated with respect to:

- Number of images to capture
- Size of the original photographs
- Format and medium—reflective (photographic prints) versus transparent (film negatives, glass plates, or slides)
- Condition and unique characteristics of the original items
- Requirements for handling fragile originals

The size of original photographs is particularly important because digitization recommendations for photographic images are commonly based on the image spatial dimensions. Since film negatives and prints come in different sizes, a common practice is to use the number of pixels on the long dimension as a measure and adjust the resolution accordingly. In the early digitization projects, 4000 pixels on the long side were recommended as a minimum dimension. With improvements in the capabilities of imaging equipment and the lower cost of digital storage, 6000–8000 pixels on the long edge are currently recommended, especially for larger transparencies.

Table 3.3 provides a list of recommended technical specifications for a range of reflective and transparent photographic materials. The table does not cover all photographic types and sizes. The goal of this sample is to demonstrate that there is a significant variation in resolution that needs to be adjusted according to the size and type of the source item. This summary is based on the minimum recommendations prepared by the Association for Library Collections and Technical Services (ALCTS, 2013). The ALCTS guidelines include minimum specifications for other types of static media, such as maps, drawings, aerial photography, etc. As emphasized in the ALCTS document, these recommendations serve as a starting point, and many still images may require higher resolution and greater bit depth (16 bit for grayscale and 48 bit for color).

Table 3.3 Minimum Digitization Recommendations for Photographic Images

Original Item Dimensions	Scanning Resolution	Bit Depth	Capture Mode	Spatial Dimensions
Reflective Materials: Photographic prints				
8 × 10 in. print	400 ppi	8 bit or 24 bit	Grayscale or color	3200 × 4000 pixels
5 × 7 in. print	625 ppi	8 bit or 24 bit	Grayscale or color	3125 × 4375 pixels
4 × 5 in. print	800 ppi	8 bit or 24 bit	Grayscale or color	3200 × 4000 pixels
4 × 2.5 in. print	1200 ppi	8 bit or 24 bit	Color	4800 × 3000 pixels
Transparent Materials: Film negatives and slides				
8 × 10 in. film negative	800 ppi	8 bit or 24 bit	Grayscale or color	6400 × 8000 pixels
4 × 5 in. film negative	1200 ppi	8 bit or 24 bit	Grayscale or color	4800 × 6000 pixels
35 mm film negative or slide	4000 ppi	8 bit or 24 bit	Grayscale or color	5480 pixels on the long edge

The recommendations for digital capture of text and photographs have evolved slightly in response to changing technology, but the basic specifications have been relatively stable in the past two decades. Although there are no formal standards, the existing digitization guidelines and practices for static 2D materials have been well established. In contrast to preservation formats for time-based media that are still evolving, TIFF as an archival master format for text and images is stable and widely accepted. Digitization of textual documents and photographs is a matter of efficient practice rather than experimentation, although the conversion of versatile photographic materials is not free of unique challenges. In 2002, Lynch commented on the progress in digitization of cultural heritage materials: "we're getting pretty good at digitizing material at scale. We have a wealth of experience and a large number of successful projects" (Lynch, 2002, p. 3). In the past decade, cultural heritage institutions have built upon the early experiences and have increased digitization efforts of unique archival and special collections, although not on a massive scale.

RAPID DIGITIZATION

Rapid approaches have been proposed as an alternative to the resource-intensive, preservation-quality digitization to scale up the conversion of archives and special collections (Erway, 2011; Erway and Schaffner, 2007). Erway and Schaffner (2007) note, "as a community, we have spent more than two decades painstakingly pursuing the highest quality in our digitization of primary resources" (p. 2). The authors of this influential OCLC report recommend "shifting gears" and adopting a more flexible approach to digitizing archives and special collections. The impacts of the Google Book Project, changing user expectations, shrinking budgets, and a desire to maximize digitization efforts, are mentioned as primary reasons for shifting into rapid capture techniques and strategies.

In the archival community, the interest in mass digitization has also been spurred by the discussion about revamping the traditional processing practices and adopting the principle of More Product, Less Process (MPLP) (Greene and Meissner, 2005). Meissner and Greene (2010) address the debate surrounding MPLP in the follow-up article and articulate the general principles of MPLP:

- Make user access paramount: get the most material available in a usable form in the briefest time possible
- Expend the greatest effort on the most deserving or needful materials
- Establish an acceptable minimum level of work, and make it the processing benchmark
- Embrace flexibility: don't assume all collections, or all collection components, will be processed to the same level
- Don't allow preservation anxieties to trump user access and higher managerial values (pp. 175–176)

Although the MPLP principles were originally proposed to alter the practices in processing of physical archives, they have been also adopted in digitization to advance the large-scale conversion of archival and museum collections (Miller, 2013; Moore, 2014; Sutton, 2012).

The overall goal of rapid capture is to lower the cost of the conversion process and accelerate the rate of digitization in order to deliver more content to users. This approach has been proposed for user-initiated digitization (Schaffner et al., 2011) as well as for the mass conversion of archival and other unique cultural heritage collections (Miller, 2013; Moore, 2014; Patzke and Thiel, 2009; Rinaldo et al., 2011; Sutton, 2012). Schaffner et al. (2011) emphasize that user needs and improved access must drive all digitization efforts and add that "user requests must not be bogged down by fine-tuning images and metadata" (p. 6). In the context of archival collections, rapid imaging is seen as a solution not only to speed up the process of conversion and increase access but also to address the issue of backlogs in archival processing (Meissner and Greene, 2010; Miller, 2013; Moore, 2014).

The terms rapid capture and rapid imaging are often used interchangeably. The approaches to speeding up the conversion process and digitizing at scale, however, often go beyond the imaging phase. A number of minimalist strategies can also be applied to selection, metadata creation, and quality control to reduce the amount of time and resources devoted to each step. Those strategies focus on establishing an acceptable minimum level of work and applying it consistently across the entire project. Rapid digitization is used here as an umbrella terms that encompasses a range of techniques and strategies, including:

- *Selecting en masse* entire collections without "cherry-picking" individual items. Miller (2013) recommends digitizing archival collections in their entirety, without archival processing, at the point of accession. The focus on scanning an entire collection removes an element of selection that can slow down the digitization process.
- *Adopting minimum technical standards* during image capture and using the preset standards for resolution, color mode, and format for all items in the project. For example, access copies of archival textual documents can be created by scanning in the bitonal or grayscale mode (rather than color), at a lower resolution, and saved in the PDF or JPEG format, without creating archival TIFF files. This approach implies that preset technical specifications are applied to the entire project, which works well for collections with materials in uniform formats. However, it is problematic for collections with versatile formats where technical specifications need to be adjusted based on the size and physical characteristics of original items. Grouping items with similar characteristics and scanning them in bulk is an effective strategy for improving efficiency, while maintaining the quality of digitized items.
- *Automating image capture process* or parts of it. The use of rapid imaging equipment and techniques varies depending on the type and format of original materials. For example, loose-leaf or unbound, nonrare documents can be scanned efficiently using sheet-fed scanners (Moore, 2014). Scanning robots with a high-speed page flipping mechanism can be used to digitize books and other bound materials at extremely high volume, although they are not suitable for books with foldouts or loose pages (Rinaldo et al., 2011). Other semi-automated technologies include the use of conveyor belts to move items quickly through imaging systems. Fig. 3.11 demonstrates a rapid capture system with a conveyor belt that has been developed by Picturae, a company based in the Netherlands. The system with a conveyor has been used for digitizing at high speed the Herbarium sheets for the Naturalis Biodiversity Center in Leiden, Netherlands. The system is capable of digitizing more than 40,000 Herbarium sheets per day. The same system has been recently used at the Smithsonian Institution for digitizing a large numismatic collection from the National Museum of American History (Kutner, 2015). The collection of 250,000 historic bank notes became the Smithsonian's first full production rapid capture digitization project (Kutner, 2015).
- *Applying minimum metadata* for item and collection-level description. The reduction in the amount of resources devoted to metadata creation is one of the hallmarks of mass approaches. Generally, no new descriptive metadata is generated in large-scale projects to avoid the

FIGURE 3.11 A Rapid Capture Digitization System with a Conveyor Belt Developed by Picturae

© Picturae, Picturae's Herbarium Digistreet at Naturalis Biodiversity Center, used with permission.

https://picturae.com/uk/digitising/herbarium-sheets

resource-intensive research process that accompanies metadata creation on an item level. Only preexisting descriptive information is used for item-level metadata without additional subject headings or other access points (Moore, 2014; Sutton, 2012). For archival collections, metadata can be created on a folder or series level and supplemented by full-text searchability generated by OCR (Miller, 2013; Moore, 2014). In addition to the use of OCR technology, the proponents of the mass approach also see user-generated tags as a possible source of descriptive information (Miller, 2013; Sutton, 2012).

- *Streamlining workflows* and integrating digitization activities that can involve digitizing the same items in bulk or scanning bound volumes or a group of archival materials in a folder as single digital objects. Selecting items of the same size or in close range improves the efficiency of image capture process since the camera does not need to be refocused or recalibrated as frequently. Large-scale conversion of archival collections moves away from scanning individual items and creating item-level metadata to folder-level digitization and collective description (Miller, 2013). Streamlining also includes replicating and reusing the established standards and procedures.

The outlined strategies and techniques can be used selectively or in combination in order to facilitate faster production and large-scale digitization. Streamlining workflows is the strategy that can be used effectively in almost all projects. Erway (2011) acknowledges the difficulties of digitizing special collections at scale but also notes that "what makes a capture operation efficient is the ability to streamline workflows by setting up equipment and workflows for one set of characteristics and then capturing a mass of similar items, thereby limiting the adjustments done in between captures" (p. 17).

Rapid digitization strategies and technologies have been tested in pilot projects and in some cases integrated into regular digitization programs to increase productivity. The Smithsonian Institution has used rapid captures in a number of prototypes and in large-scale production (Crawford, n.d.; Kutner, 2015). Erway (2011) reviews a number of large-scale digitization projects in libraries, archives, and museums to see how ideas of rapid capture are being put into practice. The review focuses on equipment, throughput, and bottlenecks in the digital capture process and presents a variety of strategies and challenges due to the heterogeneous nature of special collections.

Moore (2014) reports on a case study of implementing a range of rapid capture strategies and workflows in digitizing a collection of papers at the University of Minnesota Archives. The collection of university papers and publication produced and distributed en masse, in standard document formats, and primarily with textual content made a very good candidate for routine digitization. The papers were digitized according to the preset minimum standards using a scanner with an automatic document feeder. Searchable text was generated through OCR, and only minimal descriptive metadata were added. The case of digitizing university papers at the University of Minnesota Archives demonstrates that rapid capture can be adopted successfully when materials are relatively homogenous in nature and are being digitized for access, primarily for their informational content rather than intrinsic value.

Rapid and minimalist strategies, however, can rarely be implemented in such a uniform and straightforward manner in the digitization of unique archival and special collection materials. Collections consisting of a variety of historic textual and visual resources typically require varying levels of detail in image capture and resource description. While searchable text can be generated through OCR for printed materials, manuscripts, images, and sound and video resources are difficult to discover without accompanying metadata. The minimalist approach to metadata is particularly debatable since putting large quantities of digitized materials online, without accurate description, does not guarantee that resources will be discovered, especially if users rely on keyword searching. More user studies of user information seeking and use behaviors in the context of large-scale digital projects are needed to examine if the mass approach does indeed serve user needs better. Some researchers recognize the challenges associated with the large-scale digitization initiatives, especially in digitizing unique materials, and emphasize the need to balance speed with quality and completeness (Rieger, 2010).

In practice, some projects assume a hybrid approach and attempt to balance minimalist strategies with preservation-quality, so called "boutique" digitization. Sutton (2012) presents a case study of digitizing correspondence, photographs, journals, and drawings of the John Muir Papers at the University of the Pacific Library. The project adopted rapid capture in digitizing correspondence but used high-resolution color scanning for photographs, drawings, and journals to provide greater detail and clarity. Minimum metadata were applied consistently to all digitized items, although transcripts have been created for correspondence. The author acknowledges that strictly minimalist metadata practices may be challenging for resource discovery and notes that the impact "needs to be fully assessed to ensure that this approach does not overly compromise the ability to meet user needs and expectations for discoverability in the online environment" (Sutton, 2012, p. 58).

Rapid capture techniques and strategies pose a number of challenges in regard to resource discovery and quality of digitized materials. Furthermore, the issues of digital preservation have not been discussed in the context of mass projects. A number of questions remain unanswered about the level of digital preservation for materials generated primarily for access and which quality may not be acceptable for long-term preservation. Rapid approaches, however, are an indication of a maturing digitization landscape and recognition that archival and special collections in a stable condition may require more diversified conversion standards and processes. The current practice allows for a differentiation between preservation-quality digitization, rapid capture focused on increasing access, and hybrid models with varying levels of imaging and metadata standards.

In addition to undertaking the conversion of archival and special collections on a mass scale, the digitization of audiovisual collections represents a current and challenging area of research and practice. The issues associated with the conversion of historical time-based collections are discussed in Chapter 4.

REFERENCES

Adams, C., 2013. Is JPEG-2000 a preservation risk? The Signal: Digital Preservation. Library of Congress blog, (January 28). Available from: http://blogs.loc.gov/digitalpreservation/2013/01/is-jpeg-2000-a-preservation-risk/.

ALCTS, 2013. Minimum digitization capture recommendations. Association for Library Collections & Technical Services. Division of the American Library Association. Available from: http://www.ala.org/alcts/resources/preserv/minimum-digitization-capture-recommendations.

Arthur, K., Byrne, S., Long, E., Montori, C.Q., Nadler, J., 2004. Recognizing digitization as a preservation reformatting method. Microform Imaging Rev. 33 (4), 171–180.

BCR, 2008. BCR's CDP digital imaging best practices [updated version of Western States digital imaging best practices]. Bibliographical Center for Research. Available from: http://mwdl.org/docs/digital-imaging-bp_2.0.pdf.

Besser, H., 2003. Introduction to Imaging. Getty Publications, Los Angeles, CA.

Blanke, T., Bryant, M., Hedges, M., 2012. Open source optical character recognition for historical research. J. Doc. 68 (5), 659–683.

Bradley, K., 2007. Defining digital sustainability. Lib. Trends 56 (1), 148–163.

Buckley, R., 2008. JPEG 2000: A practical digital preservation standard? Technology Watch Report 08-01. Digital Preservation Coalition.

Buonora, P., Liberati, F., 2008. A format for digital preservation of images. D-Lib. Mag. 14 (7/8), 1.

California Digital Library (CDL), 2011. CDL Guidelines for Digital Images. Version 2.0. Available from: http://www.cdlib.org/services/access_publishing/dsc/contribute/docs/cdl_gdi_v2.pdf.

Capell, L., 2010. Digitization as a preservation method for damaged acetate negatives: a case study. Am. Arch. 73 (1), 235–249.

Chapman, S., 2000. Considerations for project management. In: Sitts, M.K. (Ed.), Handbook for Digital Projects: A Management Tool for Preservation and Access. Northeast Document Conservation Center, Andover, MA, pp. 31–44.

Chowdhury, G., Chowdhury, S., 2003. Introduction to Digital Libraries. Facet Publishing, London.

Cohen, D.J., Rosenzweig, R., 2006. Digital history: A Guide to Gathering, Preserving, and Presenting the Past on the web. University of Pennsylvania Press, Philadelphia. Available from: http://chnm.gmu.edu/digitalhistory/.

Collmann, R., 2011. Developments in virtual 3D imaging of cultural artefacts. Ariadne (66), 4. Available from: http://www.ariadne.ac.uk/issue66/collmann.

Conway, P., 2000. Overview: rationale for digitization and preservation. In: Sitts, M.K. (Ed.), Handbook for Digital Projects: A Management Tool for Preservation and Access. Northeast Document Conservation Center, Andover, MA, pp. 5–20.

Conway, P., 2008. Best practices for digitizing photographs: a network analysis of influences. In: Proceedings of IS&T Archiving 2008, Imaging Science & Technology, Berne, Switzerland, June 24–27, pp. 94–102. Available from: http://deepblue.lib.umich.edu/handle/2027.42/85229.

Conway, P., 2010. Preservation in the age of Google: digitization, digital preservation, and dilemmas. Lib. Q. 80 (1), 61–79.

Coyle, K., 2006. Mass digitization of books. J. Acad. Librariansh. 32 (6), 641–645.

Crawford, K., n.d. Rapid capture open house at the Archives of American Gardens. Smithsonian Institution. Digitization Program Office blog. Available from: http://dpo.si.edu/blog/rapid-capture-open-house-archives-american-gardens.

Daigle, B.J., 2012. The digital transformation of special collections. J. Lib. Adm. 52 (3/4), 244–264.

Dale, R.L., 2007. Outsourcing and Vendor Relations. Preservation Leaflets, 6.7. Northeast Document Conservation Center, Andover, MA. Available from: http://www.nedcc.org/free-resources/preservation-leaflets/6.-reformatting/6.7-outsourcing-and-vendor-relations.

Dooley, J.M., Luce, K., 2010. Taking Our Pulse: The OCLC Research Survey of Special Collections and Archives. OCLC Research, Dublin, OH. Available from: http://www.oclc.org/content/dam/research/publications/library/2010/2010-11.pdf?urlm=162945.

Dryden, J., 2008. PDF/A-1: a ray of light in the digital dark age? J. Arch. Org. 6 (1/2), 121–124.

Erway, R., 2011. Rapid Capture: Faster Throughput in Digitization of Special Collections. OCLC Research, Dublin, OH. Available from: http://www.oclc.org/research/publications/library/2011/2011-04.pdf.

Erway, R., Schaffner, J., 2007. Shifting Gears: Gearing Up to Get Into the Flow. OCLC Programs and Research, Dublin, OH.

Ester, M., 1996. Digital Image Collections: Issues and Practice. Commission on Preservation & Access, Washington, DC.

FADGI, 2010. The Technical Guidelines for Digitizing Cultural Heritage Materials: Creation of Raster Image Master Files. Federal Agencies Digitization Guidelines Initiative. Available from: http://www.digitizationguidelines.gov/guidelines/FADGI_Still_Image-Tech_Guidelines_2010-08-24.pdf.

FADGI, 2014. Raster Still Images for Digitization: A Comparison of File Formats. Federal Agencies Digitization Guidelines Initiative. Available from: http://www.digitizationguidelines.gov/guidelines/FADGI_RasterFormatCompare_p3_20140417.pdf.

FADGI, n.d. Glossary. Federal Agencies Digitization Guidelines Initiative. Available from: http://www.digitizationguidelines.gov/glossary.php.

Fleischhauer, C., 2014a. Comparing formats for still image digitizing: Part one. The Signal: Digital Preservation. Library of Congress blog (May 14). Available from: http://blogs.loc.gov/digitalpreservation/2014/05/comparing-formats-for-still-image-digitizing-part-one/.

Fleischhauer, C., 2014b. Comparing formats for still image digitizing: Part two. The Signal: Digital Preservation. Library of Congress blog (May 15). Available from: http://blogs.loc.gov/digitalpreservation/2014/05/comparing-formats-for-still-image-digitizing-part-two/.

Frey, F., 2000a. File formats for digital masters. Guides to Quality in Visual Resource Imaging Council on Library and Information; Digital Library Federation; Research Libraries Group, Washington, DC. Available from: http://oclc.org/research/publications/library/visguides/visguide5.html.

Frey, F., 2000b. Why are photographs different? In: Sitts, M.K. (Ed.), Handbook for Digital Projects: A Management Tool for Preservation and Access. Northeast Document Conservation Center, Andover, MA, pp. 111–119.

Frey, F., Reilly, J.M., 1999. Digital Imaging for Photographic Collections: Foundations for Technical Standards. Image Permanence Institute, Rochester.

Gertz, J., 2007. Preservation and Selection for Digitization. Northeast Document Conservation Center, Andover, MA. Available from: http://www.nedcc.org/resources/leaflets/6Reformatting/06PreservationAndSelection.php.

Gould, S., Ebdon, R., 1999. IFLA/UNESCO Survey on Digitisation and Preservation. IFLA Offices for UAP and International Lending in cooperation with IFLA Programme for Preservation and Conservation, Boston, MA.

Greene, M., Meissner, D., 2005. More product, less process: revamping traditional archival processing. Am. Arch. 68 (2), 208–263.

Holley, R., 2009. How good can it get? Analysing and improving OCR accuracy in large scale historic newspaper digitisation programs. D-Lib. Mag. 15 (3/4). Available from: http://www.dlib.org/dlib/march09/holley/03holley.html.

IMLS, 2006. Status of Technology and Digitization in the Nation's Museums and Libraries. Institute of Museum and Library Services. Available from: http://www.imls.gov/assets/1/AssetManager/Technology_Digitization.pdf.

JISC Digital Media, 2014. Project management for a digitisation project. Available from: http://www.jiscdigitalmedia.ac.uk/guide/project-management-for-a-digitisation-project/.

Kenney, A.R., 2000. Projects to programs: mainstreaming digital imaging initiatives. In: Kenney, A.R., Rieger, O. (Eds.), Moving Theory into Practice: Digital Imaging for Libraries and Archives. Research Libraries Group, Mountain View, CA, pp. 153–175.

Kenney, A.R., Chapman, S., 1996. Digital Imaging for Libraries and Archives. Cornell University Libraries, Ithaca, NY.

Kenney, A.R., Rieger, O.Y., 2000. Introduction. In: Kenney, A.R., Rieger, O. (Eds.), Moving Theory into Practice: Digital Imaging for Libraries and Archives. Research Libraries Group, Mountain View, CA, pp. 1–10.

Kenney, A.R., Rieger, O.Y., Entlich, R., 2000. Moving Theory into Practice: Digital Imaging Tutorial. Cornell University Library, Ithaca, NY. Available from: https://www.library.cornell.edu/preservation/tutorial/.

Klijn, E., 2008. The current state-of-art in newspaper digitization: a market perspective. D-Lib. Mag. 14 (1). Available from: http://www.dlib.org/dlib/january08/klijn/01klijn.html.

Koelling, J.M., 2004. Digital Imaging: A Practical Approach. Altamira Press, Walnut Creek, CA.

Kutner, M., 2015. Museums are now able to digitize thousands of artifacts in just hours. Available from: http://www.smithsonianmag.com/smithsonian-institution/museums-are-now-able-digitize-thousands-artifacts-just-hours-180953867/?no-ist.

Lazorchak, B., 2014. New NDSA Report: The benefits and risks of the PDF/A-3 file format for archival institutions. The Signal: Digital Preservation. Library of Congress blog (February 20). Available from: http://blogs.loc.gov/digitalpreservation/2014/02/new-ndsa-report-the-benefits-and-risks-of-the-pdfa-3-file-format-for-archival-institutions/.

Lee, S.D., 2001. Digital Imaging: A Practical Handbook. Neal-Schuman Publishers, New York, NY.

Leetaru, K., 2008. Mass book digitization: the deeper story of Google Books and the Open Content Alliance. First Monday 13 (10).

Lesk, M., 2004. Understanding Digital Libraries. Morgan Kaufmann, Boston.

Library of Congress, 2013. Sustainability of digital formats: Planning for Library of Congress Collections. Available from: http://www.digitalpreservation.gov/formats/index.shtml.

Lopatin, L., 2006. Library digitization projects, issues and guidelines: a survey of the literature. Libr. Hi Tech 24 (2), 273–289.

Lynch, C., 2002. Digital collections, digital libraries and the digitization of cultural heritage information. First Monday 7 (5–6). Available from: http://firstmonday.org/issues/issue7_5/lynch/index.html.

Marcum, D.B., 2007. Digitizing for access and preservation: strategies of the Library of Congress. First Monday 12 (7), 1. Available from: http://firstmonday.org/ojs/index.php/fm/article/view/1924/1806.

Matusiak, K.K., Abu Harb, Q., 2011. Digitizing the historical periodical collection at the Al-Aqsa Mosque Library in East Jerusalem. In: Walravens, H. (Ed.), Newspapers: Legal Deposit and Research in the Digital Era. De Gruyter, Berlin, pp. 271–290.

Matusiak, K.K., Johnston, T., 2014. Digitization for preservation and access: restoring the usefulness of the nitrate negative collections at the American Geographical Society Library. Am. Arch. 77 (1), 241–269.

Meissner, D., Greene, M.A., 2010. More application while less appreciation: the adopters and antagonists of MPLP. J. Arch. Org. 8 (3–4), 174–226.

Miller, L.K., 2013. All text considered: a perspective on mass digitizing and archival processing. Am. Arch. 76 (2), 521–541.

Moore, E.A., 2014. Strategies for implementing a mass digitization program. Prac. Technol. Arch., 3, (November 2014). Available from: http://practicaltechnologyforarchives.org/issue3_moore/.

NISO Framework Working Group, 2007. A Framework of Guidance for Building Good Digital Collections, 3rd ed. NISO Framework Working Group. Available from: http://www.niso.org/publications/rp/framework3.pdf.

Panitch, J.M., 2001. Special collections in ARL libraries: results of the 1998 survey sponsored by the ARL Research Collections Committee. Association of Research Libraries.

Patzke, K., Thiel, S.G., 2009. Digital Imaging: Theory Joins Practice. In Ross, D.I. (Ed.), New issues in librarianship: juried papers at the ALA 2009 ALA Annual Conference, American Library Association, Chicago. Available from: http://kuscholarworks.ku.edu/dspace/bitstream/1808/11178/1/theory_practice.pdf.

Puglia, S., 2000. Technical primer. In: Sitts, M.K. (Ed.), Handbook for Digital Projects: A Management Tool for Preservation and Access. Northeast Document Conservation Center, Andover, MA, pp. 83–102.

Puglia, S., 2011. Choosing and using digitization technologies. Keynote Presentation at the Digital Commonwealth, Fifth Annual Digital Library Conference, Danvers, MA, April 26, 2011. Available from: http://www.masshist.org/pub/digicomm/digicomm_2011conf_puglia.pdf.

Puglia, S., Reed, J., Rhodes, E., 2004. Technical Guidelines for Digitizing Archival Materials for Electronic Access: Creation of Production Master Files-Raster Images. National Archives and Research Administration, Washington, DC. Available from: http://www.archives.gov/preservation/technical/guidelines.pdf.

Rice, S.V., Jenkins, F.R., Nartker, T.A., 1996. The Fifth Annual Test of OCR Accuracy. University of Nevada Las Vegas, Information Science Research Institute, Las Vegas. Available from: http://www.stephenvrice.com/images/AT-1996.pdf.

Rieger, O.Y., 2000. Establishing a quality control program. In: Kenney, A.R., Rieger, O. (Eds.), Moving Theory into Practice: Digital Imaging for Libraries and Archives. Research Libraries Group, Mountain View, CA, pp. 61–83.

Rieger, O.Y., 2008. Preservation in the Age of Large-Scale Digitization: A White Paper, CLIR Publication 141. Council on Library and Information, Washington, DC.

Rieger, O.Y., 2010. Enduring access to special collections: challenges and opportunities for large-scale digitization initiatives. RBM 11 (1), 11–22.

Rinaldo, C., Warnement, J., Baione, T., Kalfatovic, M.R., Fraser, S., 2011. Retooling special collections digitisation in the age of mass scanning. Ariadne 67. Available from: http://www.ariadne.ac.uk/issue67/rinaldo-et-al.

Romero, V., Serrano, N., Toselli, H.A., Sanchez, A.J., Vidal, E., 2011. Handwritten text recognition for historical documents. In: Proceedings of the Workshop on Language Technologies for Digital Humanities and Cultural Heritage. Available from: http://aclweb.org/anthology//W/W11/W11-4114.pdf.

Sánchez, J.A., Bosch, V., Romero, V., Depuydt, K., de Does, J., 2014. Handwritten text recognition for historical documents in the transcriptorium project. In: Proceedings of the First International Conference on Digital Access to Textual Cultural Heritage, ACM, pp. 111–117.

Schaffner, J., Snyder, F., Supple, S., 2011. Scan and Deliver! Managing User-Initiated Digitization in Special Collections and Archives. OCLC Research, Dublin, OH. Available from: http://netweb.oclc.org/content/dam/research/publications/library/2011/2011-05.pdf.

Smith, A., 1999. Why Digitize? Council on Library and Information Resources, Washington, DC. Available from: www.clir.org/pubs/reports/pub80-smith/pub80.html.

Smith, A., 2001. Strategies for Building Digitized Collections. Digital Library Federation, Council on Library and Information Resources, Washington, DC.

Stroeker, N., Voegels, R., 2012. Survey Report on Digitisation in European Cultural Heritage Institutions 2012. ENUMERATE Thematic Framework. Available from: http://www.enumerate.eu/fileadmin/ENUMERATE/documents/ENUMERATE-Digitisation-Survey-2012.pdf

Surendran, N., Xu, X., Stead, O., Silyn-Roberts, H., 2009. Contemporary technologies for 3D digitization of Maori and Pacific Island artifacts. Int. J. Imaging Syst. Technol. 19, 244–259.

Sutton, S.C., 2012. Balancing boutique-level quality and large-scale production: the Impact of "more product, less process" on digitization in archives and special collections. RBM 13 (1), 50–63.

Tanner, S., 2001. Librarians in the digital age: planning digitisation projects. Program 35 (4), 327–337.

Tanner, S., Muñoz, T., Ros, P.H., 2009. Measuring mass text digitization quality and usefulness: lessons learned from assessing the OCR accuracy of the British Library's 19th century online newspaper archive. D-Lib. Mag. 15 (7/8). Available from: http://www.dlib.org/dlib/july09/munoz/07munoz.html.

Turró, M., 2008. Are PDF documents accessible? Inform. Technol. Libr. 27 (3), 25–43.

Valentino, M., Shults, B., 2012. Creating a digital library of three-dimensional objects in CONTENTdm. OCLC Syst. Serv. 28 (4), 208–220.

Van der Knijff, J., 2011. JPEG 2000 for long-term preservation: JP2 as a preservation format. D-Lib. Mag. 17 (5/6), 1–9. Available from: http://dlib.org/dlib/may11/vanderknijff/05vanderknijff.html.

Yale University, 2010. Digitization shared practices – still images. Version 1.0. Available from: http://www.yale.edu/digitalcoffee/downloads/DigitalCoffee_SharedPractices_%5Bv1.0%5D.pdf.

Yongli, Z., 2010. Are your digital documents web friendly? Making scanned documents web accessible. Inform. Technol. and Libr. 29 (3), 151–160.

Zhang, A.B., Gourley, D., 2009. Creating Digital Collections: A Practical Guide. Chandos, Oxford.

DIGITIZATION OF AUDIO AND MOVING IMAGE COLLECTIONS

INTRODUCTION TO DIGITIZATION OF AUDIOVISUAL RESOURCES

Audio and moving image resources encompass a wide range of time-based media, from recorded sound to motion picture film and a variety of video formats. The terms "audio and moving image" and "audiovisual" are used interchangeably here. The term "audiovisual" has gained acceptance "as a convenient single word covering both moving images and recorded sounds of all kinds" (Edmondson, 2004, p. 16). In contrast to textual and photographic materials, audio and moving image resources make up a relatively small portion of digital libraries at this point, but their number is gradually increasing as analog collections are digitized and as born digital content grows rapidly. The efforts to digitize audio, video, and motion picture film resources have lagged behind the conversion of text and photographs. Cultural perceptions and copyright restrictions play a significant role in this delay. There are also several major technical factors that have hindered digitization of audiovisual materials, including proliferation of analog media types, the complexity of the conversion process, storage requirements, multiple digital formats, and the lack of clear conversion standards for video. The recommendations for preservation formats and technical specifications for the conversion of moving images are still under development. Digitization of audiovisual collections, however, has gained attention in recent years because of the preservation crisis associated with deteriorating analog formats and the obsolescence of the playback equipment (CLIR and LC, 2006, 2010, 2012; Klijn and de Lusenet, 2008; Mariner, 2014; Schüller, 2008; Wright, 2012).

Audiovisual resources are inherently different from static documents and images because of their time-based nature and the need for playback machines to access their content. Audio and moving image materials convey information through patterns and signals that are perceived for a defined period of time. Just as archival document collections are measured in linear feet, audiovisual materials can be measured in terms of hours and minutes. Audiovisual recordings provide a representation of reality in space and time and thus afford new forms of external memory. Teruggi (2004) points out that the space-time unity, especially in the case of broadcast media, has transmitted an immediate sense of reality and created the essential record of our life, history, and culture. The author states, "conveying such immediacy also meant keeping a memory of and for society, building a historical record through both trivial and historic events that have accumulated overtime and so have created a huge repository of our collective memory" (Teruggi, 2004, p. 4).

Audiovisual heritage has an enduring value for cultural memory as it provides a vivid record of historic events and lived experiences. The National Film Preservation Act in the United States recognizes "motion pictures as an art form and a record of our times" (Library of Congress, 1994, para. 2). Audio and moving images also play an important role in recording knowledge, documenting human creativity, and bringing to light events and people that have been unacknowledged in the written record. In addition to commercially produced motion pictures, music, and broadcast programming, audiovisual collections also include oral histories, speeches, lectures, performances, storytelling, poetry readings, and a record of field research in linguistics, ethnography, and many other disciplines. Schüller (2008) emphasizes that "present day knowledge of the linguistic and cultural diversity is mainly based on audiovisual documents, in their greatest part accumulated over past 50 years" (p. 4). Oral histories offer a rare opportunity "to learn about history from those who actually experienced it, in their own words" (Stevens and Latham, 2009, p. 1). Moreover, oral history narratives serve a unique role in documenting local heritage and in giving voice to underrepresented groups (Bond, 2004; Swain, 2003).

The cultural and historical significance of audiovisual heritage may not yet be fully realized. As the authors of *The State of Recorded Sound Preservation in the United States* write, "significance is too often recognized and conferred only after the passage of years" (CLIR and LC, 2010, p. 8). The educational and research potential of audiovisual resources can only be explored if the recordings are made widely available for listening and viewing and are integrated with other resources in digital libraries.

However, the majority of audio, film, and video recordings remain on analog formats that are not only difficult to access but are also prone to damage and deterioration. Based on the data from the 2005–06 TAPE survey, Wright (2012) states that about 85% of sound and moving image content is still analog. A 2012 survey of audiovisual media in European institutions of higher education places this figure at 50%, which could be an indication of the growth of digital formats in recent years (Stauder, 2013). The same study, however, indicates that half of the participating institutions had incomplete information about their audiovisual collections. The estimates could shift once inventories are completed. The lack of inventories and item-level cataloging represents a significant barrier to access and use (Mohan, 2008). Most of the surveyed institutions have digitization programs, but the amount of converted audiovisual materials is still very low (Klijn and de Lusenet, 2008; Stauder, 2013; Wright, 2012). Klijn and de Lusenet (2008) report that many institutions are involved in digitization activities and would like to do more but are holding back because of uncertainties about conversion standards and longevity of digital materials.

Digitization of audio and video collections, however, has been gaining momentum in recent years primarily because of the looming preservation crisis. The studies of audiovisual collections in Europe and the United States convey a sense of urgency, indicating that if analog audiovisual materials are not reformatted in the next few decades, their content may be lost (CLIR and LC, 2006, 2010; Klijn and de Lusenet, 2008; Schüller, 2008; Wright, 2012). In the preface to the study on preservation of sound recordings in the United States, Smith and Brylawski write: "it is alarming to realize that nearly all recorded sound is in peril of disappearing or becoming inaccessible within a few generations" (CLIR and LC, 2006, p. v). Wright (2012) echoes this statement and adds that both sound and moving image are at great risk. It is now widely accepted that digitization presents a viable, if not the only option to preserve the content of audio and video collections.

This chapter provides an overview of audiovisual collections and discusses preservation issues associated with analog formats. The focus of this chapter is on the process of converting analog audiovisual media into the digital format. Audiovisual resources are defined as "works comprising reproducible images and/or sounds embodied in a carrier" (Edmondson, 2004, p. 26). Analog audio, motion picture film, and video share their time-based nature, dependence on physical carriers, and the need for playback equipment, but they are also distinct media that use different technologies in the process of recording, reproduction, and ultimately digitization. Because of the differences in audio and moving image digitization, this chapter devotes a separate section to each medium. The general digitization guidelines and the steps in the conversion process are discussed in Chapter 3. The fundamental principles of preservation-quality digitization with the notion of archival master files and derivatives also apply to audio and moving image conversion. This chapter builds upon those concepts and focuses specifically on technical factors, conversion recommendations, and formats for audio and video.

STATE OF AUDIO AND MOVING IMAGE COLLECTIONS

Audio and moving image collections include a mix of analog and digital recordings. Analog materials still constitute the majority of archival holdings. The number of these materials, although large, is finite. The collections of analog resources can grow through donations of legacy materials, but all new audio and video materials are recorded with a digital signal. Although film is still being used in motion picture production, it is often processed with digital tools. The authors of *The Digital Dilemma 2* note, "almost all motion pictures produced today—regardless of the capture medium—reach a point of digital existence when they pass through digital image processing tools during postproduction" (STC-AMPAS, 2012, p. 12).

Analog and digital refer to fundamentally different ways of capturing, recording, and representing audio and moving image signals. Mariner (2014) makes a distinction between analog and digital signals and points out that the terms refer to the mode of recording a signal rather than a physical medium:

- Analog signals represent continuous ranges transferred to a medium as waves or pulses.
- Digital signals represent discrete values transferred to a medium as binary values (Mariner, 2014, p. 9).

Analog materials have been recorded on a variety of physical carriers, including mechanical formats, magnetic tape, and film (Coffey and Walters, 2014; Walters et al., 2014). Digital recordings can be stored on physical carriers, such as optical discs or in file-based systems.

The combination of different carriers with analog or digital modes of recording complicates the classification of audiovisual materials. From a technical point of view, sound and moving images can be divided into three groups (Wright, 2012):

- Analog recordings on cylinders, vinyl records, magnetic audio tape, VHS, U-matic videotape, and film
- Digital recordings on dedicated physical carriers, such as audio CDs, minidiscs, video DVDs, digital audio tape (DAT), and DV tape
- Digital recordings that exist as files on digital storage (file-based systems)

For the first time in the history of audiovisual recording, file-based digital recordings are independent of physical carriers. Wright (2012) emphasizes: "carrier independence is liberation: discs, tapes and films deteriorate and get damaged" (p. 3). Analog recordings require digitization in order to be converted into usable digital formats. Digital recordings on physical carriers, though already digitally formatted, need to be extracted ("ripped") and transferred into file-based systems.

The history of audio and moving image recordings is relatively brief, especially in contrast to the history of writing and printing, but is characterized by a rapid rate of technological obsolescence. The multitude of formats for sound and moving image is a result of continued innovation and the demand for durable, portable, and more effective carriers. A variety of mechanical carriers have been used for recording voice and music since the invention of the phonograph in 1877. Wax cylinders had been in use through the 1920s, at which time they were gradually replaced by flat discs. Vinyl records proved to be a durable carrier and were used in music recording for most of the 20th century, but they were eventually supplanted by digital recording on optical discs. Magnetic tape recordings with reel-to-reel and cassette tapes became popular in the second part of the 20th century (Behl, 2015; Schoenherr, 2005; Walters et al., 2014).

Motion pictures were developed in the early 1890s. Moving images were recorded primarily on film, with its own history of different film stock, from cellulose nitrate- and acetate-based to a more stable polyester film (Coffey and Walters, 2014; Gracy, 2013a; National Film Preservation Foundation, 2004). Video recording of moving images was introduced in the 1950s and became a mainstream technology in the 1970s and 1980s. Audio and moving image recording embraced digital technology quickly and by the end of the 20th century, analog formats had been replaced with digital recording on physical carriers. In addition to audio and video tapes and other analog formats, audiovisual collections now hold an assortment of CDs and DVDs, which in turn are becoming obsolete, superseded by file-based systems.

Systematic collection of audio and moving image recordings began several decades after their invention in the late 19th century. No major audiovisual archive was created before the 20th century (Wright, 2012). As Teruggi (2004) notes, "it took time before the new technological society became aware of the progressive and massive accumulation of material it was producing—and of its future importance" (Teruggi, 2004, p. 2). Currently, there are hundreds of nonprofit audiovisual archives in the United States and worldwide that collect audio, film, and video recordings from motion picture studios, independent artists, television and radio stations, as well as from scholars and private donors (STC-AMPAS, 2012). Large collections of moving image and recorded sound are held in national audiovisual archives, such as the British Film Institute, British Library Sound Archive, Cinémathèque Française, and the Audio-Visual Conservation Center at the Library of Congress. Substantial holdings of audiovisual materials are also stored in libraries, archives, and museums alongside textual and still-image collections. The TAPE survey of European audiovisual collections conducted in 2005–06 indicated that 65% of film and 40% of audio and video collections were relatively small (500 h) but still of significant value (Klijn and de Lusenet, 2008). The OCLC survey of special collections in the United States and Canada reported that 56% of participating institutions held audio collections and 51% held moving image materials (Dooley and Luce, 2010). In addition to the collections at cultural heritage institutions, audio and moving image materials are also held in corporate archives and private collections.

It is difficult to estimate the extent and the condition of audiovisual collections because of incomplete inventories and the lack of proper documentation. As the authors of *The State of Recorded Sound Preservation in the United States* state, "no comprehensive survey of recorded sound holdings in the United States, let alone the world, has ever been undertaken" (CLIR and LC, 2010, p. 10). The research conducted in Europe and in the United States in the last decade provides a glimpse at the vast and diverse holdings, located primarily within public institutions. The TAPE survey estimated European holdings as: 0.9 million hours of film, 9.4 million hours of audio, and 10.5 million hours of video, and the average increase per year expected to be 1–2% for film and audio and 6% for video (Klijn and de Lusenet, 2008). The 2005 study of the cultural heritage collections in the US public institutions estimated 46.4 million sound recordings and 40.2 million moving images (Heritage Preservation and IMLS, 2005a).

The estimates indicate an impressive amount of audiovisual content. However, only part of the holdings can be digitized and included in the open digital libraries due to copyright restrictions. Audiovisual materials, like any other works recorded in fixed form, are subject to copyright law and cannot be reproduced without the permission of the copyright owner. In the United States, published and unpublished works that are still under copyright protection can be digitized only in specific circumstances under the exemptions for libraries and archives of the US copyright law (Hirtle et al., 2009). Section 108 provisions of the Copyright Act allow libraries and archives to digitize published works in response to in-house user requests or if collection items are damaged, stolen, or recorded in an obsolete format. Digital copies cannot be used outside the library and archive premises. These exemptions do not support digitization for open access in digital libraries. Digitization is thus limited to unique materials that are either in the public domain or to which holding institutions have legal rights. The authors of the report *The State of Recorded Sound Preservation in the United States* state that "privileges extended by copyright law to libraries and archives to copy sound recordings are restrictive and anachronistic in the face of current technologies" (CLIR and LC, 2010, p. 7). The current copyright law represents a barrier to digitization in general but in the case of audiovisual collections is particularly restrictive, as it impedes conversion of materials that are in great need of preservation reformatting.

The condition of audiovisual collections cannot be fully assessed due to the scarcity of appraisal data (CLIR and LC, 2012; Klijn and de Lusenet, 2008). The existing surveys identify preservation needs and indicate a growing awareness of the preservation crisis in the audiovisual domain. The majority of institutions participating in the OCLC survey ranked the preservation needs of visual and audiovisual materials much higher than those of other materials (Dooley and Luce, 2010). The TAPE survey of European collections noted preservation risks in audio and video formats, including the presence of unstable nitrate and acetate film in many collections. The most striking finding of the TAPE survey was a large quantity of deteriorating audiocassettes in research collections (Klijn and de Lusenet, 2008). The report on the state of US cultural heritage collections emphasizes that "the condition of almost half the 86 million film reels, videos, DVDs, records, cassettes, CDs, and MP3s in public collections is unknown, leaving them in probable jeopardy" (Heritage Preservation and IMLS, 2005b, p. 5).

Audio and moving image collections at libraries and other cultural heritage institutions are comprised of unique or rare resources in archives and special collections as well as materials in general circulating collections, mostly commercially produced and available in multiple copies. A study of audiovisual media at the Indiana University Bloomington finds that 27% are unique and do not exist anywhere else, 17% are rare, and 56% are commercially issued and not considered rare (Casey et al., 2009). This study also indicates that unique audiovisual materials are at a greater preservation risk. The authors report that nearly all of the unique and rare audio recordings and half of the unique and rare video recordings need preservation attention (Casey et al., 2009). Digitization of unique and rare audio and video represents a top priority because of the risk of losing the content if original materials deteriorate beyond recovery.

PRESERVATION CRISIS: OBSOLESCENCE AND DETERIORATION

The preservation crisis in the audiovisual domain is related to two factors:

- Obsolescence of the reproduction equipment
- Deterioration of physical carriers

The obsolescence problem has been exacerbated in recent years by the rapid demise of technologies supporting audiovisual analog formats. Most playback devices for analog media are not produced anymore and are disappearing quickly. The lack of properly working reproduction equipment poses a serious threat to accessing content and to digital reformatting. Dedicated players are not only necessary to transmit and reproduce the content but are also essential in the analog-to-digital (A/D) conversion. In addition, many analog audio and video materials are recorded on unstable physical carriers that are subject to deterioration. It is the combination of these factors plus the inevitable pressure of time limitation that make the preservation crisis particularly alarming. Preservation of audiovisual content is a race against time. Schüller (2008) stresses, "the time window left to transfer contents from analog and single digital carriers to digital repositories successfully is estimated to be not more than 20 years" (p. 6).

The problem is unique to audio and moving image recordings. For the majority of paper-based textual and, to some extent, photographic materials, preservation is not a critical issue because they are recorded on stable and durable carriers or conservation efforts had been undertaken in the past (Conway, 2010). As discussed in the previous chapter, digitization as a preservation strategy is recommended as a selective approach for early photographs recorded on glass negatives or unstable cellulose nitrate- or acetate-based film. For paper-based materials, the debate "why digitize" is focused on the benefits of extended access and new functionality afforded by the digital form. For audiovisual materials, however, there is no survival without digital reformatting. As the authors of *The State of Recorded Sound Preservation in the United States* emphasize, "the discussion no longer begins with the question, Why preserve?, but with the rhetorical one, How can we not?" (CLIR and LC, 2010; p. 8).

The preservation risks associated with the obsolescence of equipment and the deterioration of physical carriers affect access to content and/or quality of reproduced signals. Casey et al. (2009) list the ways audiovisual content can be lost or degraded due to the deterioration of carriers:

- A catastrophic failure where no content is recoverable
- Partial failure where part of content is recoverable
- Diminishment where the recovered content is of lesser quality (Casey et al., 2009, p. 33)

The authors also note the catastrophic impact of the obsolescence of equipment. The lack or scarcity of properly functioning playback machines or their prohibitive cost, as well as unavailability of spare parts, repair expertise, or playback expertise can result in:

- Inability to optimally reproduce, or reproduce at all, a recording
- Inability to preserve collections (Casey et al., 2009, p. 33)

The unavailable or antiquated equipment and obsolescent formats represent the most serious threats to preservation and digitization (Schüller, 2008). The number of obsolete formats is staggering. A study of audiovisual collections at the Indiana University Bloomington found 51 different analog and physical digital (nonfile) formats (Casey et al., 2009). As Mariner (2014) points out, audiovisual information is trapped on functionally obsolete formats. Even if the content is recorded on stable carriers, it is effectively inaccessible because of the lack or limited availability of specialized equipment that can reproduce or read the formats. The risks transfer into the digital realm and affect not only the ability to digitize audiovisual materials but also the quality of digitized copies.

The preservation risks associated with deteriorating physical carriers are not uniform and vary for audio, video, and film, and their different formats. All physical resources decay with time, but the rate of deterioration depends on the type of material and the environmental conditions in which they

FIGURE 4.1 Degraded Video on Magnetic Tape

are stored. Interestingly, the older sound resources recorded on mechanical formats, such as cylinders or discs, are more stable than the more recent audio and video recordings on magnetic tape (Walters et al., 2014). Cylinders and discs are fragile and susceptible to damage and accidental breakage. Access to high-level professional playback equipment, however, is more problematic than the instability of mechanical formats.

Magnetic tape used in the recording of audio and video represents the most serious preservation risk. Like other physical carriers, tape is susceptible to mechanical damage and deformation. However, the greatest risk is related to the degradation of the tape layers, the base and binder (Walters et al., 2014). The most serious and frequent problem is related to a chemical breakdown of the binder, which causes the tape to become sticky and shed material during playback. Poor environmental conditions, including high levels of temperatures and humidity, accelerate the degradation process. The problem is severe because audio and video recordings on magnetic tape represent the largest segment of audiovisual collections held in cultural heritage institutions. The survey of moving image collections in the United States found that 78.5% of participating institutions held video on VHS tapes (Mohan, 2008). Magnetic tape was used in a variety of audio recordings, including open-reel tapes, compact cassettes, and mini cassettes as well as in recording of moving images on video using a variety of tape formats, such as VHS, U-matic, or Betacom (Behl, 2015; Coffey and Walters, 2014). Fig. 4.1 demonstrates an example of a degraded videotape. As noted by Walters et al. (2014), the preservation of these legacy media poses formidable challenges, not only because of physical deterioration of the carriers but also in light of the obsolescence and scarcity of the hardware required to access the content.

Film used in motion picture recording is the most stable carrier. Film is an analog optical format that comes in different sizes, with 35 mm, 16 mm, and 8 mm being the most common. As Coffey and Walters (2014) emphasize, "film is an excellent archival medium and will, if stored correctly, last for over a hundred years" (p. 255). The film stock of the early motion picture recordings, however, is not as stable as the polyester film introduced in the second part of the 20th century. The cellulose nitrate film had been used for over 50 years since the invention of moving images. Nitrate film is not only chemically unstable but also an extremely hazardous, flammable material (Heckman, 2010; National

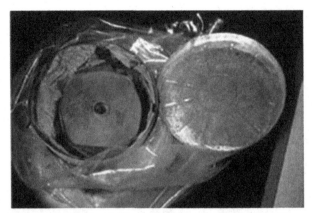

FIGURE 4.2 Decomposed Nitrate Film (National Film Preservation Foundation, 2004)

Film Preservation Foundation, 2004; Slide, 1992). Prior to the early 1950s, most 35 mm film stock had a cellulose nitrate base. Acetate film was introduced as an alternative to nitrate to address the safety risks, mostly in 8 mm and 16 mm gauges used in amateur and home productions, but proved to be prone to decay as well. Both nitrate- and acetate-based film inevitably decompose with age, leading to a significant loss of data. Fig. 4.2 demonstrates an example of decomposed nitrate film and Fig. 4.3 shows deteriorated acetate film.

The production of acetate film ceased in 1948, and nitrate film was discontinued in 1951 (Coffey and Walters, 2014). Safety and preservation challenges have remained in the forefront for film collections in library and archive settings. The TAPE study demonstrates that many institutions still have significant

FIGURE 4.3 Deteriorated Acetate Film

Courtesy of the NEH Grant Project: Saving and Sharing the AGS Library's Historic Film Collections. University of Wisconsin-Milwaukee Libraries.

holdings of nitrate- and acetate-based film (Klijn and de Lusenet, 2008). Although major preservation efforts have been undertaken to move nitrate film into cold storage, there are still collections of nitrate film that are not stored properly. Librarians and archivists often discover a stock of decaying film when they undertake digitization projects. A librarian describes a "nitrate surprise" while selecting items for digitization: "after opening a few more of the metal canisters, examining 35 mm film in varying states of decay and consulting the *Film Preservation Guide* (NFPF), I realized that these films were nitrate film, and those turning into brown dust were in the final stages of decay" (Tucker, 2013, p. 344).

To a large extent, the introduction of a stable polyester film in the 1950s helped address the preservation concerns related to moving images. Duplication of old, deteriorating film onto new, more stable and long-lasting film stock has been recommended as a preservation strategy (National Film Preservation Foundation, 2004; Slide, 1992). However, the analog approach of film-to-film preservation has come under a serious threat recently because of the "demise of celluloid" (Frick, 2014; p. 20). Eastman Kodak, the major company that produces preservation film, filed for bankruptcy in 2012. Although film is still being produced, its future is uncertain, especially because moving image production is now being done in the digital format. In response to this uncertain situation, some cultural heritage institutions are considering film digitization as a means of providing access as well as preservation (Gaustad, 2012; Morehart, 2014). The use of digital technology for preserving motion picture film, however, is new and still very controversial (FADGI, 2015). The Academy of Motion Picture Arts and Sciences maintains that there is no replacement for film as an archival medium, stating: "an archival system for digital materials that meets or exceeds the performance characteristics of traditional film archives does not yet exist" (STC-AMPAS, 2012, p. 70).

The combination of the two factors—obsolescence of the equipment and deterioration of carriers—can place some formats at a higher preservation risk than others. Although mechanical sound formats like cylinders are stable, they are often placed on the list of endangered formats because of their rarity and the lack of playback equipment (Casey et al., 2009). Likewise, film is a stable carrier, but the scarcity of projectors can put access to motion pictures in jeopardy. Coffey and Walters (2014) note that "although film projection equipment is still produced, it is, like film, an endangered species" (p. 273). Audio and video recordings on magnetic tape are assessed as high-risk preservation formats because of the degradation of tape as well as the depleting supply of audio and video players.

The goal of preservation is to protect cultural resources of long-term value, prevent further deterioration, and ensure access and usability for present and future generations (Conway, 1989, 2010). In the case of audiovisual resources, it may not be possible to prevent the deterioration of many media. Before their content is lost irretrievably, however, it can be transferred onto new technology and made available for access and use. Access and preservation goals for audiovisual collections are tightly connected. Digitization is widely accepted as an approach to providing access and ensuring long-term preservation of audiovisual materials. Wright (2012) emphasizes that "audio and video need digitization for their survival, owing to obsolescence and decay of physical items, whether analog or digital. Film on shelves can be conserved (unless it is already deteriorating) but needs digitization for access" (p. 23). The preservation concerns make digitization of audiovisual collections a more urgent and demanding undertaking than the conversion of static media. Unlike paper-based materials, many audio and video physical recordings may not be accessible in the future. Therefore, it is extremely important to create high-quality digital preservation copies since they will serve as the only representations of the original content. The following sections provide an overview of the digitization of audio and moving image, including technical factors, processes, and recommended formats and specifications.

AUDIO DIGITIZATION

"Digitize! This has to be one of the most satisfying tasks I've taken on here at the museum. […] So, one by one, I'm digitizing these old cassettes. The tape deck in the picture (Fig. 4.4) is equipped with a USB connection. A cable connects the deck to the computer, which records the sound coming out of the tape deck using a simple, free program called Audacity" (Sunshine Coast Museum & Archives blog, 2010).

The quote from the blog of the Sunshine Coast Museum & Archives in Gibsons, British Columbia, and the accompanying image in Fig. 4.4 demonstrate that audio digitization can be undertaken in-house by a dedicated staff at relatively low cost, even at a small institution. The focus of many audio conversion projects is on oral histories and other unique recordings on cassette tapes because of the one-of-a-kind nature of these materials and the preservation risks associated with deteriorating tapes (Graves, 2014; Weig et al., 2007). The staff working on an oral history digitization project at Duke University Library reports: "unfortunately, the compact cassette format hasn't aged particularly well. Due to cheap materials, poor storage conditions, and normal mechanical wear and tear, many of these tapes are already borderline unplayable a short 40 years after their first introduction" (Graves, 2014, para. 2). A survey of twenty-one archives with audiovisual holdings indicates that oral history interviews represent the most frequently digitized audio content in both access and preservation categories (STC-AMPAS, 2012).

Digitization is universally recommended as a reformatting strategy for preserving analog sound recordings (Chase, 2015; CLIR and LC, 2012; IASA, 2009; Wright, 2012). Audio digitization is well established and more advanced than the conversion of moving images. The comprehensive guidelines to reformatting, metadata, and archival storage systems for audio have been published by the International Association of Sound and Audiovisual Archives (IASA, 2009) and the Association for Recorded Sound Collections (Brylawski et al., 2015). The IASA publication addresses analog-to-digital conversion for the purposes of preservation, the transfer of digital recordings on physical carriers to storage systems, as well as the recording of original material in digital form intended for long-term archival storage. *ARSC Guide to Audio Preservation* provides an overview of audio conservation and preservation,

FIGURE 4.4 **Low-Cost Audio Digitization Equipment (Sunshine Coast Museum & Archives blog, 2010)**

including recorded sound formats and their preservation risks as well as guidelines for preservation reformatting and archival storage (Brylawski et al., 2015). In addition, several guides to best practices in audio digitization and preservation have been shared by the members of the cultural heritage community (CARLI, 2013a; Casey and Gordon, 2007; CDP, 2006).

The most recent digitization recommendations issued by the division of the American Library Association also cover time-based media and include a brief section on audio (ALCTS, 2013). The growing body of case studies and reports of pilot projects, primarily in digitization of oral histories, provides an account of methodologies, workflows, technical solutions, and cost estimates (Daniels, 2009; Durio and Grabowski, 2011; Stevens and Latham, 2009; Weig et al., 2007). Several major studies investigated the state of sound recordings (CLIR and LC, 2006, 2010; Smith et al., 2004). In the United States, the Library of Congress has launched the National Recording Preservation Plan, making audio preservation a national priority and providing a set of recommendations for implementing preservation strategies (CLIR and LC, 2012). Although some progress has been made in audio digitization, the task of reformatting audiovisual heritage is still extremely challenging for several reasons, including the sheer volume of holdings, the large number of different formats, obsolescence of playback equipment, and the range of technical factors that need to be considered in the digitization process.

TECHNICAL FACTORS

Sound is fleeting in nature. It needs to be recorded in order to be reproduced and stored in a permanent form. The invention of recording technology allowed for the capturing of the human voice, music, and sounds of the natural world and changed the relationship of sound with its temporal and ephemeral nature. Katz (2012) writes about the "magic" of recording music: "live music exists only in the moment: recordings, however, capture those fleeting sounds and preserve them on physical media. With recording technology, music could be disseminated, manipulated, and consumed in ways that had never before been possible. When recorded, music comes unmoored from its temporal origins" (p. 11).

For over a century, analog recordings had captured continuous patterns of sound. In the process of analog recording, sound waves are converted into fluctuating electric voltage, and their representation is impressed or written on a physical carrier, such as discs or tape. Digital technology has provided a new way of representing and storing sound signals as a series of binary digits (JISC Digital Media, 2014a). A digital recording can be written into a physical carrier or stored in a file-based system.

Physically, sound is a continuous pattern of pressure waves that move through the air. We perceive, or "hear" sound when the waves strike the eardrum and nerves send a signal to the brain. A sound wave can be represented graphically as a waveform with high and low pressure points. The changes of amplitude and frequency represent two principle characteristics of sound (JISC Digital Media, 2014a). Amplitude refers to a change in pressure from the peak of the waveform to the trough and is directly related to the intensity (loudness) of a sound. The frequency of the waves determines the pitch of the sound. Lower frequencies contain fewer waves in a specific amount of time while higher frequencies include more waves in the same period of time (CARLI, 2013a). Frequency is measured in cycles per second, or Hertz (Hz), often expressed in kilo Hertz (kHz).

Digitization of analog audio materials involves converting an analog sound wave into a binary stream of 1s and 0s and recording the numbers (the binary form) instead of the wave form. The analog-to-digital conversion is conducted through the process of sampling of the analog wave. During the conversion process, an analog recording is played back and processed through an analog-to-digital converter, which samples the variations of the electric current at very fast intervals. The amplitude of the original sound wave is sampled and recorded as a number at each sampling point. A continuous line of acoustic sound needs to be represented numerically in a digital system. A high number of sampling points is needed to capture the continuous line of an analog wave and to create its accurate digital representation (CARLI, 2013a). Two technical factors are critical to the quality of digitized sound: sampling rate and bit depth.

Sampling rate refers to the number of samples of a wave that are taken per second to represent sound in a digital form. The quality of the digital representation increases with the number of samples of the analog signal. The sampling rate is represented in kilohertz (kHz), thousands of samples per second. The standard sampling rate for a consumer music CD is 44.1 kHz. The recommended sampling rate for preservation-quality digitization is 96 kHz.

Bit depth describes the range of numbers used to record each measurement. In other words, bit depth refers to the number of points captured per sample. The more points captured along each wave, the higher the bit depth and the greater chance of capturing subtle changes in the sound. 16 bit, which is also a standard for commercial audio CDs, represents a minimum, while 24 bit is recommended for creating digital masters for audio preservation.

AUDIO DIGITIZATION PROCESS

The process of converting analog sound recordings into a digital format and creating sustainable digital assets consists of multiple phases, including planning and selection, digital capture, processing, metadata creation, ingesting into a digital library management system, and digital preservation. Similar to the digitization of other materials, whether static or time based, the actual conversion is one of the many steps in the cycle of preservation reformatting. The general digitization steps and principles described in Chapter 3 apply to the conversion of sound recordings. Audio digitization also makes a distinction between master files and derivatives. Master files created as a direct result of audio capture serve as preservation copies and a source of smaller derivatives for online access. Audio obviously requires different conversion equipment than static media and raises unique challenges related to its time-based nature and preservation concerns.

Each digitization project comes with its own set of unique requirements and demands individualized planning with regard to technological requirements, selection and restoration of source items, staffing, cost, and archival storage (Mariner, 2014). Time is an important factor that needs to be taken into consideration during the planning phase. Unlike a relatively fast scanning of documents, digitization of time-based media involves playing an analog recording in real time. A 60-min cassette tape actually requires 60 min to convert to a digitized copy. The condition of the analog source items needs to be assessed during the selection process to identify the best copy and/or to address the conservation needs of degraded or damaged materials. The preparation of materials for reformatting requires restorative procedures, and depending on the level of degradation, may include cleaning, flattening discs, straightening twisted tapes, or rehousing them into new shells (Graves, 2014; IASA, 2009).

Digital capture represents the most critical part of the conversion process. As IASA guidelines emphasize, "optimal signal extraction from original carriers is the indispensable starting point of each digitization process" (IASA, 2009, Section 1.4). During the capture or, using IASA terminology, extraction process, an analog source recording is played using an appropriate playback device, such as a tape or record player. An analog sound wave is sampled through an analog-to-digital converter and the digital signal is recorded, processed in audio editing software, and stored, preferably in a file-based repository system. The files created as a result of the extraction process should represent high-quality masters and should be saved uncompressed in the standard preservation format. Audio digitization guidelines recommend creating high-quality master files for preservation purposes and derivatives for access (CARLI, 2013a; IASA, 2009). The IASA guidelines cite two major reasons for digitization at the highest quality possible: "firstly, the original carrier may deteriorate, and future replay may not achieve the same quality, or may in fact become impossible, and secondly, signal extraction is such a time-consuming effort that financial considerations call for an optimization at the first attempt" (IASA, 2009, Section 5.1.1). The converted files usually require some processing in order to adjust audio quality and remove signal distortion. The enhancements are limited by the quality of original sound recording. As Weig et al. (2007) note, "regrettably, little can be done to correct analog recordings that are, for whatever reason, marred by distortion from the beginning" (p. 5).

Weig et al. (2007) describe the workflow of the audio conversion project conducted by the Louie B. Nunn Center for Oral History and University of Kentucky Libraries. The selection of oral history interviews on audiotapes and preparation of tapes were followed by analog-to-digital conversion and master file generation, quality enhancement, and the production of derivative files in the mp3 format. Master files and edited service files were archived, while derivatives with associated metadata and transcripts were uploaded to the server for online access. Metadata creation occurred at several points in the workflow.

Detailed metadata is essential for resource discovery, access, and retrieval in digital collections but is especially important in the case of sound recordings because audio content can't be browsed visually or searched by keyword. Metadata records provide the only access points to the rich content of sound recordings. Access to oral history narratives and other voice recordings can be enhanced by adding transcripts. This approach, although time-consuming if transcripts have to be generated as part of a digitization project, provides an option of presenting a textual version of the recording alongside the playable audio. Transcripts can provide full-text searchability and often include time stamps to enable the user to select parts of a recording or to follow it alongside the text. As described by Weig et al. (2007), transcript and metadata creation represented an independent step in the digitization of oral histories at the Louie B. Nunn Center for Oral History, but metadata was also recorded at other steps in the conversion cycle. Fig. 4.5 demonstrates an example of a transcript presented along with an oral history recording from the *Robert Penn Warren Civil Rights Oral History Project* created at the Louie B. Nunn Center for Oral History. The excerpt comes from an interview with Martin Luther King, Jr conducted by Robert Penn Warren on Mar. 18, 1964. The interview is available at http://nyx.uky.edu /oh/render.php?cachefile=02OH108RPWCR03_King.xml.

Access files with associated metadata are ingested into a digital library management system (DLMS) for online presentation. Online delivery of audio recordings also requires a streaming service. Many open source and proprietary DLMS, including Omeka, Collective Access, and CONTENTdm, include audio players and support standard access formats, such as mp3. Ingesting digitized audio files with associated metadata into a standard-compatible DLMS ensures interoperability and allows for integrating sound recordings with other digitized objects in digital library systems. Hosting options are available to cultural heritage institutions with limited digital library infrastructure and/or no access to streaming servers. Internet Archive provides a free platform to educational institutions and individuals and offers support for hosting and preserving audio and video files (Internet Archive, 2015). Audio and video objects represent a significant portion of the Internet Archives' collections. The Avalon Media System

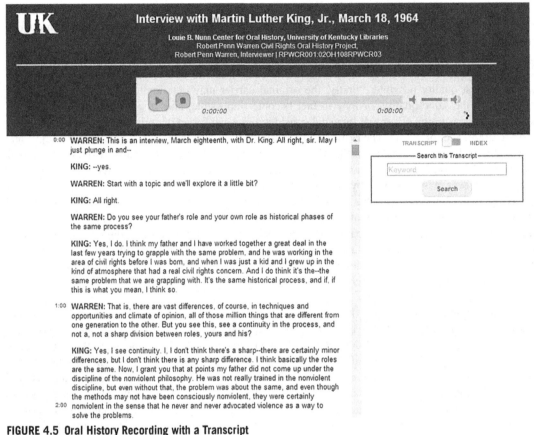

FIGURE 4.5 Oral History Recording with a Transcript

Robert Penn Warren Civil Rights Oral History Project.

is a new, open source system for managing and providing access to large collections of digital audio and video. It was developed by Indiana University Bloomington and Northwestern University with support from the National Leadership Grant from the Institute of Museum and Library Services. The Avalon Media System is freely available to libraries and archives and provides online access to their audiovisual collections for teaching, learning and research, and preservation and long-term archiving (Avalon Media System, 2015).

Digital preservation involves depositing master files into a trusted institutional or shared repository, the ongoing management of deposited audio files, and long-term preservation planning. As emphasized in the IASA guidelines, "preservation planning is the process of knowing the technical issues in the repository, identifying the future preservation direction (pathways), and determining when a preservation action, such as format migration, will need to be made" (IASA, 2009, Section 6.4.1.3). Archival storage of audio master files is a major concern because of the large size of individual files. For example, 1 h of audio digitized at 96 kHz and 24 bit with 2 channels produces a file of 1.93 GB (CDP, 2006). Digital repositories have to not only provide sufficient storage space for audio digitization but also supply capabilities for efficient transfer, management, and long-term preservation. Digital preservation is discussed in more detail in Chapter 9.

EQUIPMENT

The basic audio conversion process requires four pieces of equipment:

- An analog audio playback machine
- An analog-to-digital converter (ADC)
- A computer with audio processing software
- Digital repository to store and preserve master files

In addition to these basic components, an analog-to-digital audio workstation can also include other equipment, such as a mixing board used to adjust and enhance the audio signal. Fig. 4.6 provides an example of an audio deck used in digitization at Duke University Libraries.

The equipment used in audio conversion has a rather unique mix of antiquated playback devices, high-end computers, and analog-to-digital converters. This mix of old and new technology is characteristic of digitization of time-based media, as noticed by Mariner (2014): "while digital imaging relies on the latest hardware to faithfully reproduce digital copies of antique books and maps, much of the equipment used in the capture of audiovisual resources is decidedly antique itself and far more difficult to acquire" (p. 65). As discussed previously in this chapter, the obsolescence of playback devices represents one of the major challenges in converting and preserving time-based media. Each unique format requires a dedicated player, which in practice means that digitization labs have to acquire gramophone players for records, reel-to-reel players for recordings on open reel, and cassette tape players for audio cassettes.

FIGURE 4.6 Audio Input Deck

Image courtesy of the Digital Production Center, Duke University Libraries.

A/D converters represent the most critical technological component in the conversion process. This piece of equipment is responsible for converting analog sound waves into a binary form. It should meet the required specifications for preservation reformatting and not alter the signal or add any noise. An A/D converter can be incorporated into a computer's sound card and is also available as a standalone device. IASA (2009) recommends using standalone A/D converters and provides guidelines for their selection (Section 2.4.3). Standalone A/D converters provide a bridge between the playback devices and the computer station, and can be connected through a firewire or USB serial interface. Audio processing software is necessary to encode the converted signal and save master files in the target format. There is a wide range of audio processing software available, from the high-end Sony Sound Forge to the open source Audacity.

RECOMMENDATIONS FOR AUDIO DIGITIZATION

The audiovisual engineering and digitization communities have made significant progress in establishing consistent standards for audio reformatting. In practice, some institutions may select lower-than-optimal specifications because of the type of source material or because of concerns about processing time and archival storage demands. The adherence to standards is particularly important in light of the history of audiovisual recording, with its multiple formats and the challenges associated with transferring content onto new technologies. The established audio standards offer a level of uniformity and consistency that should alleviate some of the past risks and ensure future migrations. As IASA guidelines emphasize, "it is integral to the preservation of audio that the formats, resolutions, carrier and technology systems selected adhere to internationally agreed standards appropriate to the intended archival purposes. Non-standard formats, resolutions, and versions may not in the future be included in the preservation pathways that will enable long-term access and future format migration" (IASA, 2009, Section 2.1).

Sampling rate and bit depth represent two critical factors in determining the fidelity of digitally reformatted audio. IASA recommends a minimum sampling rate of 48 kHz for any material when producing digital copies of analog resources. For preservation quality audio digitization, 96 kHz and 24 bit are recommended as optimal specifications for master files (ALCTS, 2013; CARLI, 2013a; Chase, 2015; IASA, 2009). WAV format is recommended for encoding master files because of its wide acceptance and use in professional audio environments. Table 4.1 provides a summary of recommendations for capturing and encoding audio master files produced as a result of analog-to-digital conversion. Born digital audio should be migrated natively whenever possible (ALCTS, 2013).

Some guidelines take into consideration the type of sound recordings and list a range of audio digitization recommendations (CARLI, 2013a; CDP, 2006):

Table 4.1 Digitization Recommendations for Audio Master Files

Recommendation Level	File Format	Sample Rate	Bit Depth	Compression
Optimal	WAV/BWF	96	24	Uncompressed
Accepted	WAV/BWF	48	24	Uncompressed

- Minimum level at 44.1 kHz and 16-bit depth
- Recommended or special considerations at 48 kHz and 24-bit depth
- Optimal at 96 kHz and 24-bit depth

The guidelines prepared by the Consortium of Academic and Research Libraries in Illinois (CARLI, 2013a) note that 48 kHz and 24-bit depth are often used in the conversion of voice recordings, while the higher specifications are necessary for digitization of music and sounds from nature. The minimum recommendations at 44.1 kHz and 16-bit depth are similar to the specifications used in recording of commercial audio CDs, which are based on human ability to perceive sound. Humans "hear" sound in the range of 20–22.5 kHz and 15–17 bits per sample (CDP, 2006; Weig et al., 2007). The sampling rate of 44.1 kHz is in keeping with the Shannon-Nyquist theorem, according to which the sampling rate must be at least twice the highest analog frequency in the signal (JISC Digital Media, 2014a).

The sampling rate of 96 kHz versus 48 kHz has been a subject of ongoing debate in the digitization community (CARLI, 2013a; Casey and Gordon, 2007; CDP, 2006; Weig et al., 2007). The optimal recommendations for audio digitization in cultural heritage institutions are actually higher than those of commercial audio CDs. Some experts argue that a combination of 44.1 kHz and 16 bit used in audio CDs is considered inadequate for audio preservation of analog recordings (Casey and Gordon, 2007). Weig et al. (2007) agree that a higher sampling rate can capture subtle tones but also state that "for spoken word recordings there is little evidence to suggest such aural subtleties are relevant or warrant the significant file size increase that higher settings for their capture would incur" (p. 3). The CARLI guidelines provide a range of recommendations but also support the view that digital audio at cultural heritage institutions, especially if created for preservation purposes, should use a higher sample rate and file bit depth (CARLI, 2013a). The authors of the CARLI guide argue that there are several reasons for creating richer digital master files of archival audio materials, including:

- The accurate capture of noise like clicks, pops, and other inaudible information that resides in frequencies higher than 44.1 kHz.
- Desire to communicate inaudible harmonic information that impact perception of sound.
- Ability to record and provide content that, although not necessarily heard, helps listeners understand and hear better space, depth, and instrument location in stereo and surround sound recordings.
- The need to accommodate future user applications (CARLI, 2013a, p. 1).

The most recent guidelines issued by the division of the American Library Association acknowledge the arguments for digitizing some types of audio sources at lower quality (ALCTS, 2013). However, the ALCTS guidelines recommend 96 kHz and 24-bit depth for consistency and standardization.

Formats for master files and derivatives represent a less contentious issue. WAV, and more recently BWF, are recognized as preservation formats, while MP3 serves as a format for access files. Other formats, such as AIFF (Audio Interchange File Format) have been used in practice for archival storage as well. Master files in the WAV or BWF format should be saved uncompressed. Derivative files are saved in compressed formats for quicker transfer and streaming over the Internet. Audio processing software, such as Sony Sound Forge, Adobe Audition, or Audacity, can be used to create derivative files for access.

- *WAVE (Windows Audio File Format)*, or commonly referred as *WAV*, is uniformly recommended as a preservation format for audio files (IASA, 2009; Library of Congress, 2013). WAV was developed as a proprietary format by Microsoft and IBM and has been in use since the early 1990s. A variety of applications support WAV, and the format is compatible with Windows, Macintosh, and Linux operating systems. WAV is a PCM (Pulse Code Modulation)-type format that is widely used and accepted. IASA (2009) recommends WAV as a preservation format because of its simplicity and ubiquity. WAV files can be saved as either compressed or uncompressed. No compression is recommended for preservation master files. The file extension is .wav.

- *BWF .wav (Broadcast WAVE)* is an extension of WAV format supported by recent audio technology. The advantage of using BWF for preservation purposes is that metadata can be incorporated into the file header. BWF is increasingly recommended as a preservation target format (Chase, 2015; IASA, 2009; Wright, 2012). The WAVE file with embedded metadata (Broadcast WAVE) is listed as a preferred format in the recent publication by the Library of Congress (2015).

- *MP3* is a recognized format for audio derivatives. It is a highly compressed file that can be transferred over networks, streamed, and downloaded by users. MP3 is a widely accepted format for the distribution of digitized as well as born digital audio. Mariner (2014) comments on its widespread use: "MP3 is easily the most successful digital audio format in history. In the mid-1990s, MP3 became the de facto delivery vehicle for digital music and, for the most part, is still an accepted and usable format in almost all portable digital music players" (p. 31). Different compression algorithms are applied to reduce the file size. The amount of applied compression is expressed as bit rate, which measures the amount of information that is stored per second (JISC Digital Media, 2014a). The recommended bit rate for most audio access files in the MP3 format is 192 Kbps (CARLI, 2013a).

MP3 is currently the most widely adopted derivative format for digital audio. In addition to MP3, other access formats have been used in digital collections. Real Audio (.ra or .ram) was used in the first generation of audio digital collections. The Library of Congress provides a summary of the access formats and players used for audio recordings in the American Memory project (Library of Congress, n.d.).

MOVING IMAGE DIGITIZATION

The Norman Rockwell Museum has been awarded archival support through a generous grant from the National Endowment for the Humanities (NEH). The $85,000 grant will be used to reformat and process the Museum's collection of magnetic videotapes, which contain hundreds of hours of important oral history and documentation related to Norman Rockwell and the art of illustration. The reformatting of the tapes will be handled by George Blood Safe Sound Archive in Philadelphia, Pennsylvania, with plans to make select films freely accessible to the public through the Museum's web site. Most of these tapes have not been viewed by the public before (Norman Rockwell Museum, 2011).

This section begins with an excerpt from a blog posted by the staff at the Norman Rockwell Museum to demonstrate that cultural heritage institutions increasingly undertake digitization of moving image collections but often decide to outsource the conversion process to specialized vendors.

Analog moving image collections include motion picture film and video recordings. Film and video recordings are two distinct types of moving image, due to different technologies used for capturing moving image in the analog world. Motion picture film and video recordings are the most complex analog resources and their transfer to the digital format requires not only access to legacy playback devices and high-end conversion equipment but also a considerable amount of technical expertise.

In-house conversion of moving image collections has been conducted by audiovisual archives and national or large academic libraries (Gaustad, 2012; Peck, 2011). A few libraries, like the New York Public Library or Stanford University Libraries, have well-equipped moving image preservation labs capable of converting motion picture film and video formats. Some institutions undertake pilot projects to test their ability to digitize in-house and to establish internal procedures for meeting user requests (Gracy, 2013b; O'English and Bond, 2011).

However, when faced with the question of what to do with "a small archive of aging motion picture films without access to expensive digitization equipment or staff with specialized expertise," many small cultural heritage institutions often turn to digitization vendors (Tucker, 2013, p. 343). Even if the digitization process is outsourced, it is useful for library and archives staff to be familiar with the concepts and technical specifications of moving image digitization in order to be able to select a qualified transfer vendor and ensure that the conversion process is performed according to the recommendations established in the cultural heritage community. *Digitizing Video for Long-term Preservation* offers step-by-step guidelines and a template for preparing a Request for Proposal (RFP) to be submitted to digitization vendors (De Stefano et al., 2013). The recent Federal Agencies Digitization Guidelines Initiative (FADGI) report, *Digitizing Motion Picture Film*, includes a model statement of work for the outsourced conversion of film to video (FADGI, 2015).

In the domain of moving images, the extent of digitization activities has been limited so far, especially in comparison to the conversion of static media and audio. Despite the options of outsourcing the conversion process or conducting the transfer in-house, the percentage of digitized moving image collections is still very low. Video and motion picture film tend to be the last resources selected for digital conversion, even if institutions are committed to comprehensive digitization (Gaustad, 2012). In a study conducted with archivists and librarians working with moving image collections, Gracy (2012, 2013b) found that few of the participating institutions had digitized more than 5% of their motion picture or video collections. The participants reported that the digitization projects tended to be exploratory or aimed at creating low-resolution access copies for immediate distribution. The author notes that "few archives currently can afford to digitize moving images to a standard that may be considered preservation quality" (Gracy, 2012, p. 423). These findings are particularly disconcerting in light of the preservation issues associated with analog video formats.

The conversion of moving image collections has been marked by a slow progress, primarily due to a combination of technical challenges. Large file sizes demanding massive amounts of storage space and the lack of universally recognized preservation formats represent the major technical impediments. Gracy (2012, 2013b) identifies a number of additional barriers to digitization of archival moving image collections, including:

- Lack of financial resources
- Lack of staff with expertise in moving image conversion
- Lack of appropriate equipment
- Concern over the lack of standards and best practices for moving image digitization
- Copyright restrictions

The authors of the CARLI guidelines for moving images echo these concerns by stating, "libraries seeking to preserve and provide access to moving image content such as films, video recordings, and television broadcasts in digital format face a number of daunting obstacles. Digital video formats and specifications abound, server space to store the massive amounts of data generated must be allotted, and mature, clearly established best practices for creating preservation-worthy digital objects have yet to fully evolve" (CARLI, 2013b, p. 3). Undertaking the digitization of moving images, especially for preservation purposes, requires a major investment in digital archiving infrastructure and a commitment to ongoing digital preservation. Cultural heritage institutions are cautious about devoting their resources to the conversion of moving image collections in the environment where there is still confusion about specifications and no real consensus on preservation formats. Blood (2011) also notes that there is considerable variation in the types of video files produced by moving image archives.

Digital conversion of moving images has followed a different path than audio, although as Schüller (2009) states, "with regards to their long-term preservation, audio and video recordings are twins" (p. 5). Audio digitization is well established, with WAV/BFW recognized as a common preservation format. The IASA (2009) guidelines have helped to standardize and advance the digital conversion of sound recordings. In contrast, digitization of moving images still lacks clear guidelines on technical specifications and preservation formats. In response to the question "what is the best digital file format for video preservation?" Jimi Jones writes in the Library of Congress blog that the video realm is still "kind of the Wild West" in that there is no consensus about file formats or codecs appropriate for preservation (Jones, 2011, para. 1).

In practice, there is considerable variation between the often-compressed file formats being used for both digitized and born digital video. The study conducted by the Academy of Motion Picture Arts and Sciences brings attention to the lack of agreement on a standard format for moving image preservation. The survey of 21 nonprofit audiovisual archives found 12 different formats used for moving image preservation (STC-AMPAS, 2012). The problem is compounded by an additional array of file formats for access. Schüller (2009) points out that commercial pressure led to the widespread use of proprietary and compressed file formats. He identifies the high cost of digital storage in the 1990s as a major barrier to the development of true archival standards for digitization of moving images.

This situation, however, has been changing recently as a result of the decreasing cost of storage and an overall increase in the attention paid to digital preservation issues. There are multiple efforts underway to advance the development of common target formats and to provide guidance for the digitization of moving images. In the United States, these efforts are led by the FADGI and specifically by the Audio-Visual Working Group that published a number of documents, including *Audio-Visual Format Documentation: Background Paper* (FADGI, 2010) and most recently *Digital File Formats for Videotape Reformatting* (FADGI, 2014) and *Digitizing Motion Picture Film: Exploration of the Issues and Sample SOW* (FADGI, 2015). The PrestoCentre, a nonprofit organization located in Europe, provides a range of services in the domain of audiovisual digitization and digital preservation to its members and serves as a hub for recent research (PrestoCentre, 2015). Guides to best practices and case studies of moving image digitization are still limited. *The Minimum Digitization Capture Recommendations*, prepared by the division of the American Library Association (ALCTS, 2013), includes a brief section on video but has no recommendations for motion picture film. CARLI (2013b) guidelines review current practices and include a list of resources for the selection of hardware, software, and vendors for moving image digitization.

The following sections provide an overview of the technical factors relevant to moving image digitization and summarize the current recommendations for technical specifications and file formats. Most of the existing guidelines focus on video digitization. The conversion of motion picture film to the digital form remains a subject of significant disagreement (ALCTS, 2013). FADGI's recent guidelines for motion picture scanning projects focus on providing advice for generating high-quality output formats for current use but not on preservation reformatting. The authors of the report stress that the digitization of motion picture film is "an emergent discipline and a still-evolving set of practices" (FADGI, 2015, p. 2). Many moving image specialists argue that "more visual information is held in a film frame than could be digitally captured with their current technical capabilities" and maintain the position that preservation of analog film is best served by film duplication (STC-AMPAS, 2012, p. 52). However, some institutions undertake the digital conversion of motion picture film for access or, as discussed in the Section "Preservation Crisis," out of concern for the uncertain state of preservation film. The distinction between motion picture film and video as a source of analog materials is important in the context of digitization because they require different equipment and conversion processes.

MOVING IMAGE TYPES

Moving images are dynamic, time-based media consisting of a sequence of still images that, when projected at a rapid rate, create the illusion of continuous movement. The sequence of images may be accompanied by one or more audio channels. Different technologies and materials have been used in recording moving images and associated sound. Film, video, and born digital files are fundamentally distinct because of differences in the recording technologies associated with each medium. Broadcast television is a unique category in regard to projection since it is delivered by means of a broadcast signal, but recording has been done on a videotape or in the digital form (Coyne and Stapleton, 2008).

- *Film* was the first method used for capturing motion pictures and dominated moving image recording for over a century. Moving images captured with a film camera and recorded on a variety of film stock undergo a process of exposure and development to be ready for projection. The accompanying audio is recorded on an optical or magnetic track. Historically, moving images were created on celluloid film with an unstable chemical base. Celluloid film was later replaced with a more stable and durable polyester film. Motion picture film comes in a variety of gauges ranging from 8 mm to 16 mm to 35 mm. Footage can range from camera original to preprint or duplication materials and can contain imagery in color and black and white (FADGI, 2015).
- *Video* was originally developed for recording a broadcast television signal on tape but has been used for a wide range of applications, including direct recording. Analog video recording uses electric signal to capture images as a pattern of parallel lines. The images are organized into a series of discrete, fixed-sized frames. There is, however, some variation in the way video signal is captured and color recorded due to the limited available technology and standards used in predigital television (Coyne and Stapleton, 2008). Different standards emerged for analog video in North America (NTSC, National Television Systems Committee) and in Europe (PAL, Phase Alternating Line). Magnetic tape used for recording analog video is prone to degradation. All analog, tape-based videos present serious preservation risks and are a prime candidate for digital reformatting.

- *Born digital files* include images and soundtrack encoded as a digital signal. The frames consist of bitmapped digital images and are synchronized with an audio bit-stream. Born digital files pose a separate set of challenges, as they have been encoded in a variety of formats and may require re-encoding into a suitable preservation format. Digital files recorded on physical carriers, such as DVDs, need to be migrated into file-based systems.

There is also considerable variation of the formats and carriers within film, video, and born digital files, making analog-to-digital conversion and digital preservation extremely challenging (FADGI, 2010).

Moving images have complex structures consisting of dynamic visual and audio information. A frame, used in film and in video recording, refers to the succession of still images that capture the scene at a point in time. The sequence of images displayed at a fast rate creates the illusion of a moving image. Different types of moving images have different frame rates, film having 24 frames per second and video 30 frames per second. The synchronized audio track includes the accompanying audio information. In the case of digitized or born digital files, digital audio signal needs to be converted to an analog sound wave during transmission in order to be perceived or "heard." Frames and audio data of a digital moving image file need to be processed in order to be rendered and perceived by viewers. In addition to visual and audio streams, a moving image can include descriptive metadata and captions, which requires the processing of textual information (Coyne and Stapleton, 2008).

DIGITIZATION PROCESS AND EQUIPMENT

Digitization of analog moving image formats requires the conversion of frames consisting of still images and of associated sound recordings. The conversion process involves sampling the image portion of the frames to produce bitmapped digital images. It also requires synchronizing the audio track and translating it to a binary stream of 1s and 0s. Similarly to static media and audio conversion, digitization of moving image is a multistep process composed of several phases, including planning and assessment of analog sources, digital capture (scanning of film or sampling of video signal), production of master files and derivatives, processing and encoding of files, recording metadata, ingesting access files into a content management system for dissemination, and depositing preservation master files into a digital repository for long-term preservation. The process is complex because of the integration of visual and audio components and the differences between analog source materials. The assessment of the condition of analog materials is critical, as deteriorating film and videotapes require cleaning and repair before they can be digitized.

Different methods are used in capturing film and video in the digital capture phase. Transforming motion picture film into the digital format can be achieved using two techniques. Film as an optical medium is best converted through the imaging process and the use of a high-resolution motion picture scanner. Individual frames are scanned at high resolution ranging from 4 K to 8 K and stored as a sequence of digital images. The resulting digital files are extremely large and equipment is quite expensive. Gracy (2012) notes, "the process by which motion pictures are digitized is complex and costly enough to make transfer difficult for most archival institutions. Few institutions, aside from the largest archives, possess motion picture scanners, and the costs of sending material to digitization facilities discourage many institutions" (p. 437). The second approach is a two-step process, which involves first converting film to analog video using a telecine machine and then digitizing the resulting video.

FIGURE 4.7 Elmo TRV-16G Transfer Telecine System (O'English and Bond, 2011)

Telecine is the process of transferring motion picture film into analog video represented by an electric signal. Video can be viewed with standard video equipment and ultimately digitized with an analog-to-digital converter. Fig. 4.7 demonstrates an example of the Elmo transfer telecine system used for converting 16 mm film into video in a digitization of historic film at the Washington State University Libraries (O'English and Bond, 2011).

The conversion of video requires setting up a video digitization workstation consisting of a playback device, a high-quality analog-to-digital converter, and a dedicated computer station with a high-end processer. A video digitization lab requires an assortment of legacy video playback machines to be able to play a variety of analog video formats. Marsh (2014) describes the process of converting obsolete videotape formats at the Digital Production Center of Duke University Libraries. Fig. 4.8 demonstrates a range of input equipment used in video conversion at the Digital Production Center of Duke University. During the transfer process, while the analog video is played, its waveform amplitude is sampled (measured) at regular intervals and converted to a set of digital values by an analog-to-digital converter. This capture device, which can be an internal video conversion card or an external unit, interfaces between the playback machine and a computer, facilitating the encoding of converted data.

FIGURE 4.8 Video Input Deck

Image courtesy of the Digital Production Center, Duke University Libraries.

External analog-to-digital converters are cheaper and easier to install; however, there is a proliferation of poor-quality devices that tend to automatically compress video (Mariner, 2014). A high-quality internal video capture card is usually recommended (CARLI, 2013b; JISC Digital Media, 2014b). The video capture and processing software is required for importing and editing the resulting digital video files. Some examples of high-end video processing software include Apple's Final Cut Pro, Adobe Premiere, and Sony's Vegas Pro.

Similarly to the guidelines for static media and audio digitization, the guides to best practices for moving images emphasize creating uncompressed, high-quality archival master files (CARLI, 2013b).

The authors of the CARLI guidelines acknowledge that uncompressed files demand an enormous amount of storage but also add that "an uncompressed video is crucial to preserving the integrity of the content over the long term" (CARLI, 2013b, p. 4).

Three separate digital types of files are typically created during the digitization of moving images. These include:

- *Preservation master file* is the digital file that is saved for long-term preservation. It captures the content from the archival original at the highest possible quality and is encoded with no compression or using lossless compression. Preservation masters remain "untouched" and once ingested into a digital repository, are rarely accessed.
- *Mezzanine file* (also referred to as a service or production master) serves as a surrogate for the master file. Mezzanine files are accessed for editing and transcoding, and are used to make other duplicates and derivative files for access. Lossless or lossy compression is usually applied to mezzanine files to reduce their size.
- *Access (derivative) file* serves as a general use copy for viewing and online distribution. Access files are highly compressed (CARLI, 2013b; De Stefano et al., 2013; STC-AMPAS, 2012).

TECHNICAL FACTORS AND RECOMMENDED SPECIFICATIONS

The ultimate goal of digitization is to capture the content and properties of analog source materials and represent them faithfully in the digital form. As discussed earlier, the current guidelines provide recommendations for video digitization but not for film. The authors of *Minimum Digitization Capture Recommendations* state that "there are currently too many unknowns to make a well informed recommendation on digitizing moving image film at this time" (ALCTS, 2013, p. 37). Therefore, most of the recommendations reviewed here refer to video conversion, although many technical factors, such as resolution, aspect ratio, and frame rate also pertain to film. The complex structure of moving images requires one to consider a number of technical factors and specifications in the process of analog-to-digital conversion.

Resolution refers to the size of the image frame. Similarly to still digital images, resolution is expressed as the number of horizontal pixels (width) multiplied by the number of vertical pixels (height). The resolution of an analog source needs to be considered when converting to the digital form. For standard definition NTSC video, the resolution of 720 × 486 pixels is recommended to digitize a full frame and to create master files, whereas 640 × 480 is recommended for derivatives (ALCTS, 2013; Blood, 2011). 720 × 576 is recommended for standard definition PAL video (Blood, 2011).

Aspect ratio refers to the width of the image frame divided by its height. The aspect ratio should be maintained true to the original analog source. Most standard definition (SD) video has a 4:3 aspect ratio, while 16:9 is usually used in high-definition HD video.

Frame rate indicates the number of frames displayed per second. Thirty frames per second is the standard for digital video and television materials; film has a rate of 24 frames per second. Retaining the native frame rate is recommended for video and film digitization.

Sampling involves recording values for each pixel within a video stream. Three values are recorded: a "luma" element, corresponding to the brightness level; and two "chroma" elements, corresponding to the color levels for red and blue. A sampling schema of 4:4:4 indicates that luma and chroma elements are sampled at every pixel. This 4:4:4 sampling schema is the only true "lossless" sampling. The 4:4:4

sampling schema is recommended as best practice, while 4:2:2 is commonly used and recognized as an acceptable practice (Blood, 2011; CARLI, 2013b).

Bit depth indicates the depth of measurement. Bit depth determines the amount of data captured per image pixel and color channel and thus the accuracy with which the color information is stored. The greater the bit depth, the greater the number of gray scale or color tones that can be represented and the larger the file size. Most digital video formats use a minimum of 8 bits per color channel, while 10 bits per channel is recommended. Blood (2011) notes that the visual difference between 10-bit and smaller 8-bit files is subtle, especially in low-grade formats, such as VHS, U-matic, and Betamax. However, digitizing video using 10-bit depth is still beneficial as it allows one to capture the finer detail and subtle gradations within the range of recorded information.

Scanning in the context of video digitization refers to the way in which image frame is captured. Interlaced scanning captures the frame in two exposures, each containing one-half of the image, which may result in some image blurring. Most analog video is in interlaced format. In progressive scanning, the entire image is captured in a single exposure. Most born digital video is made using progressive scanning (CARLI, 2013b). Blood (2011) recommends retaining the native scanning format during the conversion process.

ENCODING AND FILE FORMATS

Digitized video data need to be encoded and encapsulated in a file format in order to be processed by computer software and opened by a player. Video and audio streams that contain the essence of converted video are encoded using codecs. Different codecs can be used with no compression or in combination with lossless or lossy compression. Both the selection of codec and the level of compression applied during the encoding process impact the quality of the digitized video. File formats serve as wrappers or containers for encoded video essence and for additional information, such as metadata and captions. A combination of the codec and the wrapper is used to store, transmit, and play video in the digital form. The distinction between these two concepts is helpful in understanding the complexity of video file formats.

Codec refers to the way audio and video bit streams are encoded for transmission and storage and then decoded for playback or editing. The term "codec" is constructed from the words coding/decoding. A codec is a series of algorithms and is not included in the video file itself. The playback software must include a codec or be compatible with the codec used to encode the file (CARLI, 2013b; Mariner, 2014). There is a wide range of codecs available that are used with lossy or lossless compression. Several codecs (such as FFVI, JPEG 2000, uncompressed 4:2:2, 10 bit [v210], UYVY, and YUY2) support lossless compression and are used for encoding archival master files. A recent study by FADGI provides a comparison of codecs commonly used in archival practice for encoding digitized video (FADGI, 2014). Encoding schemas with lossy compression, such as DV, MPEG-4, QuickTime, or WMV, are used for encoding born digital video and for files created for access. JPEG 2000 and FFV1 are nonproprietary codecs supporting lossless compression and are emerging as open standards for encoding archival master files (FADGI, 2014; Lorrain, 2014).

- *JPEG 2000* is an open standard developed by the Joint Photographic Expert Group. As described in Chapter 3, JPEG 2000 was developed to encode large and high-dynamic-range images. It is also used for encoding audio-visual content from video capture and film scanning. JPEG 2000 supports both lossy and lossless compression. Its adoption is still moderate. A number of large cultural heritage institutions, including the National Audiovisual Conservation Center of the Library of Congress, have selected lossless JPEG 2000 in combination with the MXF wrapper for preservation master files (FADGI, 2010, 2014; Lorrain, 2014).

- *FFV1* is a codec that is gaining significant support in the open source community. Lorrain (2014) describes it as "the most promising open source video codec for long-term preservation" (p. 8). It supports lossless compression and, in combination with an open source wrapper, Matroska provides a fully open solution for digital video preservation. Its adoption is rated low to moderate by FADGI (2014). FFVI is being used by the Austrian Mediathek, the Vancouver City Archive, and MUMOK in Vienna (Lorrain, 2014).

Wrapper is distinct from codec and plays a different role in preserving digitized and born digital video content. Wrappers serve as containers for the encoded video and audio streams and other data, such as metadata and subtitles. FADGI (2014) defines the word wrapper as a "term often used by digital content specialists to name a file format that encapsulates its constituent bitstreams and includes metadata that describes the content within" (p. 4). Wrappers determine how and by what program audiovisual streams are played. There are hundreds of wrappers available (Mariner, 2014). Some are used as containers for preservation masters files, while others are used for highly compressed access files. The Library of Congress (2013) maintains a list of moving image formats (codecs and wrappers) and provides a review of sustainability factors. FADGI (2014) has recently released a study comparing wrappers commonly used in archival practice. Table 4.2 provides a brief summary of wrappers used by cultural heritage institutions for saving preservation master files. For a more comprehensive comparison, please see *Digital File Formats for Videotape Reformatting* (FADGI, 2014).

This brief review of codecs and wrappers points to the complexity of video preservation formats and the proliferation of approaches. A compatible configuration of a codec and wrapper is necessary to make sure that the format is interoperable and can be sustained over a period of time. Additional selection criteria, such as quality, openness, adoption, transparency, durability, and functionality, need to be considered in the format selection (Lorrain, 2014). At the time of this writing, there is no file format that has been definitively recognized as the preservation standard. Cultural heritage institutions use different configurations as intermediate solutions based on the established practice and available expertise. A combination of MXF/JPEG 2000 is emerging as a desired format, but its adoption in the cultural heritage community is still low, with the exception of large national libraries.

SUMMARY OF RECOMMENDATIONS FOR VIDEO DIGITIZATION

The preservation crisis associated with the deterioration of analog moving image media and the obsolescence of playback equipment has created a sense of urgency. Cultural heritage institutions are increasingly undertaking the digitization of moving image collections despite the fact that there is no clear consensus on formats and specifications. They select options considered either best or acceptable practice knowing that there is no ideal solution and that digitized files may need to be transferred into newer formats in the future. As Lorrain (2014) points out, "uncertainty as to how formats will or will not become the future standard makes is difficult to commit to one codec and one container. However, digitization needs to take place now and it is not possible to wait for the perfect format to appear" (p. 12). Table 4.3 provides examples of recommended or acceptable practices based on the available documentation (Blood, 2011; CARLI, 2013b).

Table 4.2 Commonly Used Wrappers for Video Preservation Master Files

Wrapper	Extension	Brief Description and Usage
AVI (Audio Video Interleave)	.avi	Relatively old and well-established Windows multimedia container, developed by Microsoft. It is well documented and widely used. The US National Archives and Records Administration (NARA), Rutgers University, and Austrian Mediathek use AVI for preservation purposes.
QuickTime (MOV)	.mov	Well-established and well-documented format developed and maintained by Apple. It is widely used in both the production and cultural heritage communities. Stanford University and New York University use MOV for preservation purposes.
Matroska	.mkv	Relatively new, nonproprietary format that is beginning to be adopted in the cultural heritage and open source communities. In combination with the FFVI codec, it provides open source format for preservation of video. Its adoption is still low. The City of Vancouver Archives uses Matroska for preservation purposes.
MXF (Material eXchange Format)	.mxf	Highly flexible standard capable of wrapping complex objects with uncompressed or lossless-encoded data. Technically, it is codec agnostic, but is often used in combination with JPEG 2000. It is an open standard, but some documentation is not freely available. A draft of the AS-07 profile of the MXF application specification was released recently for review (AMWA, 2014). MXF is widely adopted in the broadcast and film industries; the use in the cultural heritage community is not yet widespread. The Library of Congress and Library and Archives Canada use MXF for preservation purposes.

Table 4.3 Summary of Recommendations for Video Digitization

Specification/Format	Source: (Blood, 2011)	Source: CARLI (2013b)
Resolution/Frame size	720 × 486	640 × 480
Aspect ratio	4:3 for SD; 16:9 for HD	4:3 for SD; 16:9 for HD
Bit depth	10 bit	10 bit
Sampling	4:2:2	4:4:4 (recommended); 4:2:2 (acceptable)
Scanning	Interlace/Progressive: Native	Progressive
Frame rate	Native, 30 or 29.97	30
Compression	Uncompressed	Uncompressed or lossless
Codec	Uncompressed 4:2:2, 10 bit; YCbCr (color space)	Uncompressed YCbCr or JPEG 2000 (recommended); MPEG-4 AVC or DV (acceptable)
Wrapper	QuickTime (MOV) or AVI	MXF (recommended); QuickTime (MOV) or AVI (acceptable)

The current guidelines vary in some specifications, as they reflect the state of intermediate practice. However, they provide recommendations that will ensure future transfer of high-quality files and uniformly stress the need to capture video uncompressed or with lossless compression. Compression is discussed in more detail in Chapter 3 with the distinction made between no compression, and lossless and lossy compression. No compression is generally recommended for master files for all media types, including text, still images, audio, and moving images. This recommendation is particularly critical in video digitization and in light of preparations for future transfer into formats such as JPEG 2000/MXF combination (Blood, 2011). Compression reduces file sizes but at the same time permanently discards a considerable amount of captured data, which can impact the accuracy of color representation. In the case of deteriorating video, there may not be another chance to digitize it and to recover the data. If digitized video is compressed, future transfers will include files of reduced quality. On the other hand, uncompressed video has a tremendous impact on processing and archival storage. Uncompressed video generates large files and demands a massive amount of storage space. An hour of uncompressed SD digital video will result in a file size of approximately 70–100 GB. In comparison, the size of the same file when lossy compression is applied is only 10–20 GB. In addition to uncompressed encoding, lossless compression of audiovisual data is considered a viable technology for long-term preservation, providing storage savings and the ability to reconstruct the same bitstream (PrestoCentre, 2014).

Compression, however, is extremely useful in reducing the size of files intended for online dissemination and other forms of access. The intermediate, mezzanine files are usually used as a source for creating smaller access files. Lossy codecs such as H.263 or MPEG-4 AVC (H.264) are used for encoding highly compressed access files. Wrappers, such as Adobe Flash (.flv) or MPEG-4 (.mp4) serve as derivative file formats (CARLI, 2013b). Other derivative video formats have been used in digital collections, such as QuickTime (.mov) or RealMedia (.rm, .ram). The Library of Congress provides a summary of access formats and players for video recordings in the American Memory project (Library of Congress, n.d.).

Access files are distributed through digital libraries or hosted video streaming platforms. Many open source and proprietary DLMS, including Omeka, Collective Access, and CONTENTdm, include video players and support standard access formats, such as mp4, WMV, or flv. Hosting options through the Internet Archive are available to cultural heritage institutions with limited digital library infrastructure and/or no access to streaming servers. Some institutions also choose to present digitized video through popular streaming platforms, such as YouTube or Vimeo.

Audio and moving image materials are media in transition, constantly upgrading carriers and methods of recording as technology evolves. Digitization is necessary not only to transfer analog audio, film, and video to a new generation of technology for access but also to preserve the content for future use. The preservation crisis caused by the deterioration of analog media and the obsolescence of playback equipment has made the conversion of audio and moving image collections an urgent issue. The guidelines for audio analog-to-digital conversion are well established, while the recommendations for moving image preservation formats are still evolving.

Digital technology provides a new method of recording and storing resources that, using file-based systems, liberates audiovisual materials from the limitations of physical carriers. However, this technology poses a new set of challenges in regard to digital preservation. These challenges are not unique to audio and moving image resources. Because of the uniform nature of the binary form, all digitized and born digital resources, whether textual or audiovisual, require preservation planning and ongoing data management. No digital format is expected to last forever and digitized, and born digital audiovisual materials will eventually have to be transferred to a new generation of formats. Adopting common standards for preservation formats will ensure that the content can be transferred properly, and will facilitate long-term digital preservation activities.

REFERENCES

ALCTS: Association for Library Collections & Technical Services. Division of the American Library Association, 2013. Minimum Digitization Capture Recommendations. Available from: http://www.ala.org/alcts/resources/preserv/minimum-digitization-capture-recommendations.

AMWA: Advanced Media Workflow Association, 2014. AS-07 MXF format for archiving and preservation. Review draft. Available from: http://www.amwa.tv/downloads/as-07/AS-07_reviewDraft_20140923.pdf.

Avalon Media System, 2015. About the project. Available from: http://www.avalonmediasystem.org/project.

Behl, H., 2015. Audio formats: Characteristics and deterioration. In: Brylawski, S., Lerman, M., Pike, R., Smith, K. (Eds.), ARSC Guide to Audio Preservation. Association for Recorded Sound Collections, Council on Library and Information Resources, and Library of Congress, pp. 14–36. Available from: http://www.clir.org/pubs/reports/pub164/pub164.pdf.

Blood, G., 2011. Refining conversion contract specifications: Determining suitable digital video formats for medium-term storage. White paper prepared for the Library of Congress Office of Strategic Initiatives. Available from: http://www.digitizationguidelines.gov/audio-visual/documents/IntrmMastVidFormatRecs_20111001.pdf.

Bond, T.B., 2004. Streaming audio from African-American oral histories. OCLC Syst. Serv. Int. Digital Lib. Persp. 25 (1), 15–23.

Brylawski, S., Lerman, M., Pike, R., and Smith, K. (Eds.), 2015. ARSC Guide to Audio Preservation. Association for Recorded Sound Collections, Council on Library and Information Resources, and Library of Congress. Available from: http://www.clir.org/pubs/reports/pub164/pub164.pdf.

CARLI: Consortium of Academic and Research Libraries in Illinois, 2009; revised 2013a. Guidelines for the Creation of Digital Collections: Digitization Best Practices for Audio. Available from: http://www.carli.illinois.edu/sites/files/digital_collections/documentation/guidelines_for_audio.pdf.

CARLI: Consortium of Academic and Research Libraries in Illinois, 2010; revised 2013b. CARLI Guidelines for the Creation of Digital Collections: Digitization Best Practices for Moving Images. Available from: http://www.carli.illinois.edu/sites/files/digital_collections/documentation/guidelines_for_video.pdf.

Casey, M., Gordon, B., 2007. Sound Directions: Best Practices for Audio Preservation. Indiana University Bloomington and Harvard University, Bloomington, Indiana/Cambridge, Massachusetts. Retrieved from http://www.dlib.indiana.edu/projects/sounddirections/papersPresent/sd_bp_07.pdf.

Casey, M., Feaster, P., Burdette, A., 2009. Media Preservation Survey: A Report. Indiana University Bloomington, Bloomington, Indiana. Retrieved from http://www.indiana.edu/~medpres/documents/iub_media_preservation_survey_FINALwww.pdf.

CDP: Collaborative Digitization Program [formerly Colorado Digitization Project]. Digital Audio Working Group, 2006. Digital Audio Best Practices. Version 2.1. Available from: https://ucblibraries.colorado.edu/systems/digitalinitiatives/docs/digital-audio-bp.pdf.

Chase, W., 2015. Preservation reformatting. In: Brylawski, S., Lerman, M., Pike, R., Smith, K. (Eds.). ARSC Guide to Audio Preservation. Association for Recorded Sound Collections, Council on Library and Information Resources, and Library of Congress pp. 110–126. Available from: http://www.clir.org/pubs/reports/pub164/pub164.pdf.

CLIR and LC: Council on Library and Information Resources and Library of Congress, 2006. Capturing Analog Sound for Digital Preservation: Report of a Roundtable Discussion of Best Practices for Transferring Analog Discs and Tapes. Commissioned and sponsored by the National Recording Preservation Board of the Library of Congress. Washington, DC: Council on Library and Information Resources and Library of Congress. Available from: http://www.clir.org/pubs/reports/pub137.

CLIR and LC: Council on Library and Information Resources and Library of Congress, 2010. The State of Recorded Sound Preservation in the United States: A National Legacy at Risk in the Digital Age. Commissioned and sponsored by the National Recording Preservation Board of the Library of Congress. Washington, DC: Council on Library and Information Resources and Library of Congress. Available from: http://www.clir.org/pubs/reports/pub148/pub148.pdf.

CLIR and LC: Council on Library and Information Resources and Library of Congress, 2012. The Library of Congress National Recording Preservation Plan. Commissioned and Sponsored by the National Recording Preservation Board of the Library of Congress. Washington, DC: Council on Library and Information Resources and Library of Congress. Available from: http://www.clir.org/pubs/reports/pub156/pub156.pdf.

Coffey, L., Walters, E., 2014. Moving image materials. In: Harvey, R., Mahard, M.R. (Eds.), The Preservation Management Handbook: A 21st-Century Guide for Libraries, Archives, and Museums. Rowman & Littlefield, Lanham, MD, pp. 255–292.

Conway, P., 1989. Archival preservation: definitions for improving education and training. Restaurator 10 (2), 47–60.

Conway, P., 2010. Preservation in the age of Google: digitization, digital preservation, and dilemmas. Lib. Q. 80 (1), 61–79.

Coyne, M., Stapleton, M., 2008. The significant properties of moving images. JISC Digital Preservation Programme. Available from: http://www.jisc.ac.uk/media/documents/programmes/preservation/spmovimages_report.pdf.

Daniels, C., 2009. Providing online access to oral histories: a case study. OCLC Syst. Serv. 25 (3), 175–185.

De Stefano, P., Tarr, K. Buchman, M., Oleksik, P., Moscoso, A., 2013. Digitizing Video for Long-Term Preservation: An RFP Guide and Template. New York: New York University. Available from: http://library.nyu.edu/preservation/VARRFP.pdf.

Dooley, J.M., Luce, K., 2010. Taking Our Pulse: The OCLC Research Survey of Special Collections and Archives. OCLC Research, Dublin, OH. Available from: http://www.oclc.org/content/dam/research/publications/library/2010/2010-11.pdf?urlm=162945.

Durio, M., Grabowski, M., 2011. The Iron Hill Museum oral history collection. Microform Digit. Rev. 40 (2), 74–76.

Edmondson, R., 2004. Audiovisual Archiving: Philosophy and Principles. UNESCO: Information Society Division, Paris.

FADGI: Federal Agencies Digitization Guidelines Initiative, 2010. Audio-Visual Format Documentation: Background Paper. Available from: http://www.digitizationguidelines.gov/guidelines/FADGI-AV_AppSpecProj_Bkgd_101007.pdf.

FADGI: Federal Agencies Digitization Guidelines Initiative, 2014. Digital file formats for videotape reformatting. Available from: http://www.digitizationguidelines.gov/guidelines/video_reformatting_compare.html.

FADGI: Federal Agencies Digitization Guidelines Initiative, 2015. Digitizing motion picture film: Exploration of the issues and sample SOW. Available from: http://www.digitizationguidelines.gov/guidelines/Motion_pic_film_scan.html.

Frick, C., 2014. "Separate but equal?": bolstering audiovisual preservation. Preserv. Digital Technol. Cult. 43 (1/2), 20–25.

Gaustad, L., 2012. Choices for preservation of moving image material. Microform Digit. Rev. 41 (3/4), 105–107.

Gracy, K.F., 2012. Distribution and consumption patterns of archival moving images in online environments. Am. Archivist 75 (2), 422–455.

Gracy, K.F., 2013a. The evolution and integration of moving image preservation work into cultural heritage institutions. Inform. Cult. 48 (3), 368–389.

Gracy, K.F., 2013b. Ambition and ambivalence: a study of professional attitudes toward digital distribution of archival moving images. Am. Archivist 76 (2), 346–373.

Graves, Z., 2014. Digitization details: re-formatting audio cassettes. Bitstreams. The digital collections blog (February 26). Duke University Libraries. Available from: http://blogs.library.duke.edu/bitstreams/2014/02/26/digitization-details-audio-cassettes/.

Heckman, H., 2010. Burn after viewing, or, fire in the vaults: nitrate decomposition and combustibility. Am. Archivist 73 (2), 483–506.

Heritage Preservation and the Institute of Museum and Library Services (IMLS), 2005a. A public trust at risk: The Heritage Health Index report on the state of America's collections. Available from: http://www .heritagepreservation.org/hhi/HHIfull.pdf.

Heritage Preservation and the Institute of Museum and Library Services (IMLS), 2005b. A public trust at risk: The Heritage Health Index summary report. Available from: http://www.heritagepreservation.org/hhi /HHIsummary.pdf.

Hirtle, P.B., Hudson, E., Kenyon, A.T., 2009. Copyright and Cultural Institutions: Guidelines for US Libraries, Archives, and Museums. Cornell University Library. Available from: http://ecommons.cornell.edu /bitstream/1813/14142/2/Hirtle-Copyright_final_RGB_lowres-cover1.pdf.

IASA: International Association of Sound and Audiovisual Archives. Technical Committee. Bradley, K. (Ed.), 2009. Guidelines on the Production and Preservation of Digital Audio Objects (web edition). (IASA-TC04). International Association of Sound and Audiovisual Archives. Available from: http://www.iasa-web.org/tc04 /audio-preservation.

Internet Archive, 2015. About the Internet Archive. Available from: https://archive.org/about/.

JISC Digital Media., 2014a. An Introduction to Digital Audio. Available from: http://www.jiscdigitalmedia.ac.uk /guide/an-introduction-to-digital-audio.

JISC Digital Media., 2014b. High Level Digitisation for Audiovisual Resources. Suggested Digitisation Workflows. Available from: http://jiscdigitalmedia.ac.uk/infokit/audiovisual-digitisation/suggested-digitisation-workflows.

Jones, J., 2011. Whither digital video preservation? The Signal: Digital Preservation. Library of Congress blog. (July 5). Available from: http://blogs.loc.gov/digitalpreservation/2011/07/whither-digital-video-preservation/.

Katz, M., 2012. Sound recording: Introduction. In: Taylor, T.D., Katz, M., Grajeda, T. (Eds.), Music, Sound, and Technology in America: A Documentary History of Early Phonograph, Cinema, and Radio. Duke University Press, Durham, NC, pp. 11–28.

Klijn, E., de Lusenet, Y., 2008. Tracking the Reel World: A Survey of Audiovisual Collections in Europe. European Commission on Preservation and Access. Available from: http://www.tape-online.net/docs/tracking_the_reel _world.pdf.

Library of Congress, 1994. Redefining Film Preservation: A National Plan. Recommendations of the Librarian of Congress in consultation with the National Film Preservation Board. Available from: https://www.loc. gov/programs/national-film-preservation-board/preservation-research/film-preservation-plan/redefining-film-preservation/.

Library of Congress, 2013. Sustainability of Digital Formats: Planning for Library of Congress Collections. Available from: http://www.digitalpreservation.gov/formats/index.shtml.

Library of Congress, n.d. American Memory Help. Available from: https://memory.loc.gov/ammem/help/view .html.

Library of Congress., 2015. Library of Congress Recommended Format Specifications 2015–2016. Available from: http://www.loc.gov/preservation/resources/rfs/TOC.html.

Lorrain, E., 2014. A Short Guide to Choosing a Digital Format for Video Archiving Masters. Available from: http://www.scart.be/?q=en/content/short-guide-choosing-digital-format-video-archiving-masters.

Mariner, M.C., 2014. Managing Digital Audiovisual Resources: A Practical Guide for Librarians. Rowman & Littlefield, Lanham, MD.

Marsh, A., 2014. Digitization details: Bringing Duke living history into your future. Bitstreams. The digital collections blog (April 9). Duke University Libraries. Available from: http://blogs.library.duke.edu /bitstreams/2014/04/09/digitization-details-bringing-duke-living-history-into-your-future/.

Mohan, J., 2008. Environmental Scan of Moving Image Collections in the United States. Digital Library Federation. Available from: http://old.diglib.org/pubs/dlf109.pdf.

Morehart, P., 2014. Saving our celluloid past. Am. Lib. 45 (3/4), 44–46.

National Film Preservation Foundation, 2004. The Film Preservation Guide: The Basic for Archives, Libraries, and Museums. San Francisco, CA. Available from: http://www.filmpreservation.org/preservation-basics/the-film-preservation-guide.

Norman Rockwell Museum., 2011. Norman Rockwell Museum receives archival support from the National Endowment for Humanities. Norman Rockwell Museum blog (April 29). Available from: http://archives-hunters.blogspot.com/2011/04/norman-rockwell-museum-receives.html.

O'English, M., Bond, T., 2011. Providing online access to historic films at the Washington State University libraries. Lib. Hi. Tech. 29 (2), 210–223.

Peck, M., 2011. Making Texas' moving image heritage accessible. Microform Digit. Rev. 40 (3), 122–126.

PrestoCentre., 2014. File formats and standards. TechWatch Report, 01. (February).

PrestoCentre, 2015. About. Available from: https://www.prestocentre.org/about-us.

Schoenherr, S., 2005. Recording technology history. Audio Engineering Society. Available from: http://www.aes.org/aeshc/docs/recording.technology.history/notes.html.

Schüller, D., 2008. Audiovisual Research Collections and Their Preservation. European Commission on Preservation and Access. Available from: http://www.tape-online.net/docs/audiovisual_research_collections.pdf.

Schüller, D., 2009. Video archiving and the dilemma of data compression. International Preservation News, 47, 5–7. Available from: http://www.ifla.org/files/assets/pac/IPN_47_web.pdf.

Slide, A., 1992. Nitrate Won't Wait: A History of Film Preservation in the United States. McFarland, Jefferson, NC.

Smith, A., Allen, D.R., Allen, K., 2004. Survey of the state of audio collections in academic libraries (No. 128). Washington, DC: Council on Library and Information Resources. Available from: http://www.clir.org/pubs/reports/reports/pub128/pub128.pdf.

Stauder, A., 2013. 2012 survey of the preservation, management, and use of audiovisual media in European higher education institutions. OCLC Syst. Serv. 29 (4), 218–234.

STC-AMPAS: The Science and Technology Council of Academy of Motion Picture Arts and Sciences, 2012. The Digital Dilemma 2: Perspectives from Independent Filmmakers, Documentarians, and Nonprofit Audiovisual Archives. Available from: http://www.oscars.org/science-technology/sci-tech-projects/digital-dilemma-2.

Stevens, K.W., Latham, B., 2009. Giving voice to the past: digitizing oral history. OCLC Syst. Serv. Int. Digital Lib. Persp. 25, 212–220.

Sunshine Coast Museum & Archives blog, 2010. Gibsons, British Columbia: Sunshine Coast Museum & Archives. Sunshine Coast Museum & Archives blog. (June 24). Available from: http://sunshinecoastmuseumandarchives.blogspot.com/2010/06/digitize.html.

Swain, E.D., 2003. Oral history in the archives: its documentary role in the twenty-first century. Am. Archivist 66 (1), 139–158.

Teruggi, D., 2004. Can we save our audio-visual heritage? Ariadne, 39 (April 30). Available from: http://www.ariadne.ac.uk/issue39/teruggi.

Tucker, B.A., 2013. A modest movie migration: digitizing and providing institutional repository access to a small archive of motion picture films at a liberal arts college. Public Serv. Q. 9 (4), 342–347.

Walters, E., Pymm, B., Davies, M., 2014. Sound materials. In: Harvey, R., Mahard, M.R. (Eds.), The Preservation Management Handbook: A 21st-Century Guide for Libraries, Archives, and Museums. Rowman & Littlefield, Lanham, MD, pp. 223–254.

Weig, E., Terry, K., Lybarger, K., 2007. Large scale digitization of oral history. D-Lib Mag. 13 (5/6), 1082–9873.

Wright, R., 2012. Preserving Moving Pictures and Sound. The DPC Technology Watch Reports. Digital Preservation Coalition.

METADATA

METADATA OVERVIEW
DEFINITIONS, STANDARDS, AND HISTORY

Metadata constitutes the foundation on which digital libraries are built. Commonly referred as to "data about data," metadata describes and organizes resources in the digital environment and enables users to discover and use the content of digital collections and repositories. Gilliland (2008) offers a broad definition of metadata as "the sum total of what one can say about any *information object* at any level of aggregation" (p. 2). Metadata can be used to capture characteristics and attributes of information resources on an item and/or collection level. The concept of metadata is used in diverse communities involved in organizing and managing information. In libraries and other cultural heritage institutions, the term is applied to the value-added information for arranging, describing, and enhancing intellectual access to information objects (Gilliland, 2008). Creation of high-quality metadata is essential to the access and preservation of digital library materials, including cultural heritage collections and scholarly publications in digital repositories.

Definitions of metadata in the library world emphasize the structured nature of metadata and the standardization of the metadata development process (NISO, 2004; Taylor and Joudrey, 2008; Zeng and Qin, 2008). NISO (2004) defines metadata as "structured information that describes, explains, locates, or otherwise makes it easier to retrieve, use, or manage an information resource" (p. 1). Zeng and Qin (2008) expand this definition by stating that metadata is "structured, encoded data that describes characteristics of information-bearing entities (including individual objects, collections, or systems) to aid in the identification, discovery, assessment, management, and preservation of the described entities" (pp. 321–322). The structure of metadata in digital libraries is governed by schemas. The concept of a metadata record grouping together all the statements about a resource is at the core of most schemas developed in digital libraries. Schemas are used in conjunction with other value and content standards, such as controlled vocabularies and input guidelines.

Libraries, archives, and museum communities have developed a range of different standards to guide the design, implementation, and exchange of structured metadata. Metadata is comprised of several building blocks including data structure standards and rules for formatting the contents of metadata records. Other standards determine how metadata is encoded and exchanged (Elings and Waibel, 2007; Miller, 2011; Mitchell, 2013a; Zeng and Qin, 2008). Thus, metadata standards are characterized by data structure (schemas), content, value, data format, and exchange:

- Schemas or metadata element sets are standards for data structures and semantics; the Dublin Core Metadata Element Set (DCMES) is an example of the most widely adopted schema in digital libraries.
- Data content standards provide the rules for metadata generation and formatting; *Anglo-American Cataloging Rules Revised,* Second Edition (AACR2), has been used in cataloging for many

Discover Digital Libraries. http://dx.doi.org/10.1016/B978-0-12-417112-1.00005-3

years and is currently being replaced by *RDA: Resource Description and Access*. Other content standards include *Describing Archives: A Content Standard* (DACS) and *Cataloging Cultural Objects* (CCO), which are used to describe archival materials and cultural objects.

- Data value standards are lists of standardized terms for recording values in metadata records. A number of authority files, subject headings, and thesauri are available from the Library of Congress and from the Getty Research Institute. The Library of Congress Subject Headings (LCSH) and the Art and Architecture Thesaurus (AAT) are examples of data value standards.
- Data format standards refer to standardized methods for encoding metadata so that computers can process data. Extensible Markup Language (XML) is a standard that is primarily used for encoding metadata in the digital library environment.
- Data exchange standards facilitate the sharing of metadata between collections and repositories. The Open Archives Initiative Protocol for Metadata Harvesting (OAI-PMH) is an interoperability standard for sharing metadata in the digital library environment. Open Archives Initiative Object Reuse and Exchange (OAI-ORE) is a standard for the description and exchange of aggregated of web resources, including compound digital objects (OAI, 2015). OAI-ORE is used in the aggregation of metadata in large-scale digital libraries and linked data projects (Mitchell, 2013c).

Elings and Waibel (2007) provide a review of the standards developed in libraries, archives, and museums and illustrate it with a grid of primary standards in use across different communities. The distinction between schemas and different standards for content and data exchange is also relevant in the linked data environment (Mitchell, 2013b).

Metadata practices in the digital library environment build on a strong tradition of cataloging and indexing in libraries, archives, and museums. In the print environment, books and other analog materials have been cataloged using MARC (MAchine-Readable Cataloging) as a structure standard and AACR2 and LCSH as data content and value standards. Many of these tools, like LCSH, have been adopted successfully for content description of digital objects. However, the application of MARC for describing complex and dynamic digital objects proved to be difficult due to its monolithic and inflexible structure. New schemas have been developed in the digital library environment to address the limitations of MARC and offer more flexibility in the means of describing and managing digital objects.

The term "metadata" can be traced back to the 1960s, but it became popular in database management literature in the 1980s (Lange and Winkler, 1997; Vellucci, 1998). Prior to the mid-1990s and the development of digital libraries, the term was used primarily by the communities engaged in the management of geospatial data and design of databases and systems (Gilliland, 2008). The early metadata initiatives in digital libraries include TEI and the Online Computer Library Center (OCLC) projects that resulted in the development of Dublin Core. The Text Encoding Initiative (TEI) published the Guidelines for Electronic Text Encoding and Interchange (TEI guidelines) in 1994; OCLC initiated the web resource cataloging project in 1994 by selecting AACR2 and the MARC format to catalog web materials. This led to the creation of the Dublin Core, which arose out of the Metadata Workshop held in 1995 (Zeng and Qin, 2008). Vellucci (1998) summarizes several metadata initiatives that surfaced in different communities in the 1990s. The library community applied traditional cataloging techniques to describe digital resources, such as MARC (Dillon and Jul, 1996). Simultaneously, scholarly, archival, and museum communities began using Standard Generalized Markup Language (SGML) or XML, such as in the TEI headers (Barbero and Trasselli, 2014; Beißwenger et al., 2012; Sperberg-McQueen, 1996; Sperberg-McQueen and Burnard, 1994).

The first decade of digital library development is marked by the explosion of metadata schemas, proposed to meet the needs of different communities and subject domains. The large number of standards, especially in the descriptive realm, demonstrates the need for individualized standards to correspond to varied contexts. The diversity of metadata standards reflects the evolving nature of information organization in digital libraries. Schema-based metadata represents two decades of intensive metadata development in the digital library environment. Linked data introduce a new data model and a significant shift in the way metadata is recorded and connected in the open web.

FUNCTIONS AND TYPES OF METADATA

Different types of metadata are needed for resource description, discovery, retrieval, use, presentation, and preservation of digital objects. The primary role of metadata is to identify, describe, and provide intellectual access to the content of a digital collection. As Miller (2011) notes, "without metadata, the collection would be virtually useless. Users would have no way to find and identify the digital objects within the collection" (p. 9). Metadata is particularly important in collections containing visual, sound, and moving image materials, which are very difficult to discover without textual description (Laursen et al., 2012).

In addition to facilitating resource discovery and use, metadata supports interoperability, organization, management, and preservation of digital objects (NISO, 2004). Lagoze et al. (1996) note the role of metadata in capturing terms and conditions of data, provenance, content rating data, linkage or relationship information, and structural data. Gilliland (2008) describes the role of metadata in maintaining the relationships between multiple versions of the same digital object and its role in retaining contextual information. The importance of recording data related to provenance, context of creation, and use is discussed in the context of digital preservation in Chapter 9.

Different types of metadata are recorded in digital libraries. The authors vary in the classification of metadata types, especially in regard to preservation and technical metadata that are often listed under administrative metadata. Gilliland-Swetland (1998) proposes a basic typology based on the functions of metadata:

- Administrative metadata that presents information associated with the management and organization of information resources
- Descriptive metadata that provides information to depict information resources
- Preservation metadata that offers information with respect to the conservation of information resources
- Technical metadata that illustrates information related to system functions and metadata behaviors

Miller (2011) classifies metadata into three categories: administrative, structural, and descriptive metadata, following a common approach adopted in library and information science literature:

- Descriptive metadata
  - elements describing or cataloging digital resources
  - information identifying the content of a digital item
  - terms required to retrieve a digital item or a group of digital items
- Administrative metadata
  - elements used for managing digital objects and collections

    - information life-cycle data from creation to dissemination
- subtypes of administrative metadata
  - technical and preservation metadata
  - rights metadata
  - use metadata
- Structural metadata
  - elements offering a structure for a complex digital object or a group of associated digital objects
  - multiple files of one digital object (e.g., pages of a book)
  - multiple views of one digital object (e.g., different views of an object).

In this framework, technical and preservation metadata are listed as subtypes of administrative metadata, and structural metadata is a separate category.

Table 5.1 provides a summary of metadata types and their functions and lists a number of corresponding schema examples. As demonstrated in the table, the relationship between metadata types and schemas is not one-to-one. In fact, certain metadata schemas, such as Dublin Core or METS, can accommodate most of the types and include elements for recording descriptive as well as administrative metadata. In addition, there are also standards dedicated exclusively to technical and preservation metadata, such as MIX, based on the NISO technical standard for still images and new standards for capturing technical specifications of audio and video (AudioMD and VideoMD). More information about the technical standards is available at the Library of Congress Standards site (Library of Congress, 2011a, b). The digital preservation standard PREMIS is discussed in Chapter 9.

Table 5.1 Summary of Metadata Types and Their Functions

Metadata Type	Metadata Functions	Schema Examples
Descriptive	Describes an object; provides access points to facilitate resource discovery; indicates relationships	Dublin Core, MODS, EAD, VRA, CDWA
Administrative	Indicates ownership/digital provenance; provides management and rights information	METS, Dublin Core, VRA, EAD
Structural	Expresses the relationships of an object (or aggregation of objects) to other related objects; describes structural characteristics of compound objects	METS
Technical	Identifies digital objects and their technical specifications; certifies integrity and authenticity	MIX—NISO Metadata for Images, AudioMD, VideoMD
Preservation	Describes properties of digital objects in archival storage; records preservation activities	PREMIS, METS

METADATA SCHEMAS

Metadata schemas provide a foundation for structuring metadata. A schema is a predefined set of elements designed for a specific purpose, such as describing and managing information resources (NISO, 2004). The term "schema" is used to denote the singular form. The plural forms of schema are "schemas" or "schemata" (Baca, 2008). Schemas specify the names of elements and define their meaning. Some schemas may also provide the rules for how content must be formulated and encoded. Defined element sets are often represented in XML. Most of the schemas developed in digital libraries have a flat structure with a linear list of elements or a hierarchical structure indicating a parent–child relationship. A record remains a central concept of schemas developed in digital libraries where all attributes and characteristics of an information resource are grouped together. The underlying data models, however, are more flexible than MARC, allowing for the refinement of elements and the development of local application profiles.

Metadata schemas represent a significant departure from the traditional bibliographic description because of their varied and flexible approaches. Duval et al. (2002) outlines the fundamental principles that inform the design and application of metadata schemas:

- *Modularity* allows the combination of elements from different schemas, as well as vocabularies and other metadata building blocks, in a syntactically and semantically interoperable way.
- *Extensibility* allows the extension of a basic element set (repeat standard elements or add new ones) to accommodate local or domain-specific needs.
- *Refinement* allows the qualification of standard elements or an increased specificity of meaning; refinement also involves the specification of value sets or defining the range of values for a given element.
- *Multilingualism* addresses metadata design in light of linguistic and cultural diversity, with metadata schemas and records available to users in their native languages and in appropriate character sets.

Multiple metadata schemas have been developed in the cultural heritage communities to address the unique characteristics of resources in diverse knowledge domains. Digital objects are complex, often comprised of multiple files, and require extensive metadata for their management, use, and preservation. The wide array of metadata schemas also corresponds to the variety of formats, greater availability of audiovisual materials in the digital form, and finally, the different needs and traditions of cultural heritage organizations. Metadata schemas differ in:

- The underlying data model: flat structure (Dublin Core) or hierarchical (MODS or CDWA)
- The number of data elements
- Granularity of description
- The use of mandatory fields
- Encoding requirements
- The application of content rules and value standards

The following section provides an overview of the most frequently used schemas in digital libraries.

DUBLIN CORE

Dublin Core is one of the most widely adopted metadata schemas. It is used to meet the needs of a variety of user communities, including libraries, archives, museums, and other information providers

(Chan et al., 2001). The Dublin Core Element Set originated from a workshop that took place in 1995 in Dublin, Ohio, and hence the name. The Dublin Core Metadata Initiative (DCMI) was established a few years later. The first workshop was held to discuss how to deal with the need to describe and organize networked resources. A variety of working groups were created to advance the development of a new schema with the DCMI guiding the process. The mission of the DCMI is to facilitate the discovery of Internet resources by developing metadata standards, defining frameworks for the interoperability of metadata schemas, and assisting the creation of community- or discipline-specific metadata schemas (Weibel and Koch, 2000).

Dublin Core includes 15 original elements: contributor, coverage, creator, date, description, format, identifier, language, publisher, relation, rights, source, subject, title, and type. In 2000, optional qualifiers were approved to enrich the schema. Beginning in 2012, the term "metadata qualifiers" was replaced by "refinements" and "encoding schemes" (DCMI, 2015a). Table 5.2 presents the basic Dublin Core Metadata Elements with associated definitions and examples. Fig. 5.1 shows an example of a customized Dublin Core record. The record example in Fig. 5.1 includes non-DC elements, such as keywords, event, and place, which have been mapped to Dublin Core. Fig. 5.1 presents a public display of a DC record. Metadata mapping is conducted by library professionals in the administrative module of the underlying software.

Table 5.2 Dublin Core (Version 1.1)

Elements	Definition
Contributor	An entity responsible for making contributions to the resource
Coverage	The spatial or temporal topic of the resource, the spatial applicability of the resource, or the jurisdiction under which the resource is relevant
Creator	An entity primarily responsible for making the resource
Date	A point or period of time associated with an event in the lifecycle of the resource
Description	An account of the resource
Format	The file format, physical medium, or dimensions of the resource
Identifier	An unambiguous reference to the resource within a given context
Language	The language of the resource
Publisher	An entity responsible for making the resource available
Relation	A related resource
Rights	Information about rights held in and over the resource
Source	A related resource from which the described resource is derived
Subject	The topic of the resource
Title	A name given to the resource
Type	The nature or genre of the resource

Dublin Core Metadata Element Set (http://dublincore.org/documents/dces/)

Title	01 - March to protest recent police action in Selma, Alabama, March 13, 1965
Date	1965-03-13
Creator	Larkey, Jay Larkey, Hinda
Description	Milwaukee civil rights demonstrators marched to protest police actions in Selma, Alabama that took place on March 7, 1965. The protest in Milwaukee was organized on March 13, 1965. About 2, 500 people marched from the headquarters of CORE to the Milwaukee County Courthouse.
Subject	African Americans--Civil rights--Wisconsin--Milwaukee Civil rights demonstrations--Wisconsin--Milwaukee
Topic	Protests
Keywords	Civil rights Connection to the national struggle Marches
Organization	Congress of Racial Equality Milwaukee Conference on Religion and Race
Event	March of March 13, 1965 to protest police action in Selma, Alabama
Place	Walnut and 3rd Streets--Wisconsin--Milwaukee
Type (DCMI)	Image
Original Collection	Jay and Hinda Larkey Papers 1963-1968 and 1987
Original Item Location	UWM Manuscript Collection 299 Box 1 Folder 4
Original Item Type	Photographs
Original Item Format	35 mm color slide
Finding Aid	http://digital.library.wisc.edu/1711.dl/wiarchives.uw-mil-uwmmss0299 ⧉
Repository	Archives / Milwaukee Area Research Center. University of Wisconsin-Milwaukee Libraries
Rights	The Board of Regents of the University of Wisconsin System
Digital Publisher	University of Wisconsin-Milwaukee Libraries
Digital Id	uwmmss0299008

FIGURE 5.1 An Example of a Customized Dublin Core Record

http://collections.lib.uwm.edu/cdm/singleitem/collection/march/id/1531/rec/1

Dublin Core can be further enhanced by element refinements and element encoding schemes (DCMI, 2015a, b; Miller, 2011). Examples of refinements to the Date element are created, valid, available, issued, and modified. Another example can be seen in refinements to the Relation element, which include Is Version Of, Has Version, Is Replaced By, Replaces, Is Required By, Requires, Is Part Of, Has Part, Is Referenced By, References, Is Format Of, and Has Format. Element encoding schemes offer either a controlled vocabulary scheme or a standard syntax encoding scheme to associate an element with an existing controlled vocabulary, formal notation, or set of rules. This helps increase the precision of information retrieval. Examples of element encoding schemes for subjects are LCSH, MeSH, TGM, or AAT. Examples of element encoding schemes for language are ISO 638-2, ISO 639-3, RFC 1766, and RFC 4646. Flexibility is one of the main characteristics of Dublin Core. There are no required elements and each element can be used multiple times. Simplicity and semantic interoperability are the two key attributes (Chan et al., 2001).

The Dublin Core schema has been widely adopted in the digital library environment. Dublin Core has been implemented not only domestically in the United States but also internationally. The two main obstacles to its adoption are the relative scarcity of elements and qualifiers and an insufficient number of guidelines for its use. Even though Dublin Core is considered easy to use, Chuttur (2014) discovered a high error rate across the groups that used best practice guidelines and definitions, though using the guidelines resulted in fewer errors. The development and adoption of updated best practice guidelines based on user needs is essential to generating useful metadata records.

Implementing Dublin Core in repositories, where content contributors are responsible for providing metadata elements, brings a new set of challenges. In one study of using this schema in DSpace, an open source institutional repository software, the results reveal different quality issues, such as incomplete records caused by skipping nonmandatory fields, a lack of authority control over subject headings, low metadata accuracy caused by unclear element definition, and metadata inconsistency due to a lack of required conventions (Kurtz, 2013).

METADATA OBJECT DESCRIPTION SCHEMA (MODS)

Metadata Object Description Schema (MODS) is a schema that has its roots in bibliographic description. The standard is maintained by the Network Development and MARC Standards Office of the Library of Congress (Library of Congress, 2015a). MODS is derived from MARC 21. As such, it is highly compatible with MARC fields. The first version of MODS was developed in 2002 and based on feedback on the first version; version 2.0 was published in 2003. Version 3.0 was made available in late 2003.

The structure of MODS is hierarchical. It contains parent elements and child elements. Attributes are used simultaneously to refine the meaning of an element. McCallum (2004) specifies several requirements and characteristics of MODS: developed for an XML environment, compatible with MARC21, simple, and having a modest amount of top-level elements. The following features correspond to the requirements and characteristics of MODS: user-oriented tags, regrouped data elements in MARC, fewer coded values, added electronic resource data, linking flexibility, recursion for related items, special attributes, round-trip transformation with MARC21, and allowance for mixed content. In addition, one characteristic of MODS is that it offers users the opportunity to use different levels of granularity. (Miller, 2011). MODS includes 20 top-level elements: titleInfo, name, typeOfResource, genre, originInfo, language, physicalDescription, abstract, tableOfContents, targetAudience, note, subject, classification, relatedItem, identifier, location, accessCondition, part, extension, and recordInfo (Library of Congress, 2014a). In addition, MODS has 47 subelements (Guenther, 2003). Table B.1 in Appendix B presents the MODS top-level elements with associated definitions.

The benefits of using MODS include its hierarchical structure allowing for granular description, detailed user guidelines, and mappings with examples. More importantly, transformation tools assisting in conversion from MODS to MARC and other metadata schemas are also available (Guenther, 2004). As Dulock (2012) describes, MODS is used for descriptive metadata in digitization projects because of its ample metadata element set. However, MODS metadata needs to be mapped to Dublin Core for harvesting purposes because of the requirements of the Open Archives Initiative Protocol for Metadata Harvesting (OAI-PMH) (Dulock, 2012).

METADATA ENCODING AND TRANSMISSION STANDARD (METS)

METS is sponsored by the Digital Library Federation, supported by the Library of Congress, and governed by the METS Editorial Board. Its first schema was made available in 2001. The development of

METS continues today (Library of Congress, 2015b). METS is defined as "an XML schema designed for the purpose of creating XML document instances that express the hierarchical structure of digital library objects, the names and locations of the files that comprise those digital objects, and the associated descriptive and administrative metadata" (Cundiff, 2004, p. 53). The main user communities of METS are university libraries, archives, and museums. In general, a METS document can have seven major subsections:

- Mets Header (metsHdr)
- Descriptive Metadata Section (dmdSec)
- Administrative Metadata Section (amdSec)
- File Section (fileSec)
- Structure Map (structMap)
- Structural Links (structLink)
- Behavior Section (behaviorSec)

Three types of metadata are identified in METS: descriptive metadata, administrative metadata, and structural metadata. METS does not offer its own vocabularies for descriptive metadata. Instead, it offers three options: (1) point to metadata in external documents; (2) point to systems using the Metadata Reference (mdRef) element; and (3) embed descriptive metadata using the Metadata Wrap (mdWrap) element. Similarly, METS does not offer its own vocabularies for administrative metadata. The administrative metadata section can be further classified into four subsections: technical metadata (techMD), rights metadata (rightsMD), source metadata (sourceMD), and digital provenance metadata (digiprovMD) (Cantara, 2005; Cundiff, 2004). The structural map is the core of a METS document, and it is the only required subsection. It represents the hierarchical structure and sequence of components of a digital object in the form of nested divisions of elements. It comprises attributes such as ID, LABEL, TYPE, and ORDER. Table B.2 in Appendix B presents the METS elements with associated definitions.

METS has been implemented in a variety of digital library projects. The METS Implementation Registry is available at the Library of Congress Standards site (Library of Congress, 2015b). METS was selected for the University of Texas' Human Rights Documentation Initiative (HRDI) because of the schema's capability in managing digital objects and metadata at several levels (Dulock, 2012). METS functions as a wrapper in which the descriptive metadata and administrative metadata sections can be connected to other parts of the METS document.

METS facilitates interoperability, but its flexibility in representing digital library objects also poses some challenges. McDonough (2006) highlights some issues with METS in terms of interoperability:

- Allows users to insert arbitrary metadata schema
- Does not control the location of metadata or the associated format
- Offers no guarantee in applying standard rules of description
- Lacks controlled vocabularies for the attributes of some elements
- Lacks structural constraints on a digital object

METS profiles enable institutions to record restrictions and requirements for the compiling of METS documents. Although METS profiles do not guarantee the interoperability, the profiles are the starting point from which to consider issues regarding sharing and exchanging complex digital objects. It is worth noting that other metadata schemas for complex digital objects share similar problems.

TEXT ENCODING INITIATIVE (TEI)

TEI, a standard for encoding textual documents, was developed as one of the first digital library metadata standards. A conference at Vassar College in Poughkeepsie, New York, in 1987 proposed the Poughkeepsie Principles, which set up the foundation of TEI. In 1990, the first edition of TEI was published, and it adopted SGML for the coding. SGML is an international standard for document markup. The most notable edition is the P3 *Guidelines for Electronic Text Encoding and Interchanges*, which was made available in 1994. It defines 600 elements for the ending of text. The P4 version was publicized in 2001 by the TEI Consortium, when TEI started to support both XML and SGML. The P5 edition is an XML-based markup for digital texts. TEI has concentrated more on functional aspects of texts (Ore and Eide, 2009; Vanhoutte, 2004). Several working groups contributed to the production of TEI P5. According to Cummings (2008), "The TEI Guidelines are not only a guide to best practice, but are also an evolving historical record of the concerns of the field of Humanities Computing" (p. 1). In that case, the TEI guidelines not only show the evolution of the recommendations but also the influences of the technical and theoretical background and development.

TEI P5 consists of 23 chapters organized from broad to specific topics. The first part (5 chapters) introduces TEI to potential users. The second part (7 chapters) focuses on each kind of specific text: verse, drama, spoken text, dictionaries, and manuscript materials. The third part (9 chapters) takes care of topics that are associated with specific applications. The fourth part (2 chapters) discusses how to encode the XML to represent the TEI scheme. The last part (1 chapter) concentrates on TEI customization and conformance. The following are the three primary functions of the TEI guidelines:

- Guide individual or local practice in text creation and data capture
- Support data interchange
- Support application-independent local processing (TEI Consortium, 2015)

The TEI encoding schema consists of a number of modules including specific XML elements and their attributes. In principle, a TEI schema may contain any combination of different modules. Among all modules, four modules are of particular importance:

- The TEI module specifies classes, macros, and data types.
- The core module comprises declarations for elements and attributes.
- The TEI header module presents declarations for the metadata elements and attributes.
- The text structure module is required for the encoding of most book-like objects (TEI Consortium, 2015).

These four modules are used in almost all the TEI schemas. TEI also defines several hundred elements and attributes. Each definition contains the following components (TEI Consortium, 2015, p. 1):

- A prose description
- A formal declaration, expressed by special-purpose XML vocabulary combined with elements extracted from the ISO schema language RELAX NG
- Usage examples

As an example, Table B.3 in Appendix B presents the TEI Header elements with associated definitions and examples.

TEI was selected to promote the exchange of data among national and international projects by exporting manuscript descriptions from a library system into TEI XML documents (Barbero and

Trasselli, 2014). TEI allows customization of elements to satisfy the needs of a variety of digital projects. Although customization is one of its design goals, that feature also creates potential problems with data sharing and exchange (Cummings, 2008). Customization is an effort to apply the TEI encoding framework to new genres and document types. Beißwenger et al. (2012) demonstrate that TEI Guidelines can be customized and applied to different types of Computer Mediated Communication (CMC) genres. TEI has mostly been applied in large projects in the humanities and social sciences. It is challenging for small institutions to implement TEI because of the detailed requirements for text encoding. The benefits of enhanced access to the digital collection may outweigh the problems in certain applications (Wisneski and Dressler, 2009).

ENCODED ARCHIVAL DESCRIPTION (EAD)

Encoded Archival Description (EAD) is an international standard for encoding finding aids for archival materials, with version 1.0 published in 1998 and revised in 2002. The standard originated from a research project at the University of California at Berkeley. Just like TEI, it was originally an application of SGML, and it became XML compatible later. EAD is maintained by the Network Development and MARC Standards Office of the Library of Congress in collaboration with the Society of American Archivists (Library of Congress, 2013). McCrory and Russell (2013) state, "EAD provides a means of structuring the language of finding aids so that they may be processed for presentation on the web and so that their descriptive elements can be exchanged with other metadata systems" (p. 99).

The EAD record structure consists of three groups of categories: <eadheader> (EAD Header), <frontmatter> (Front Matter), and <archdesc> (Archival Description). Among them, <eadheader> and <archdesc> are required elements. Multilevel description is one of the key features of EAD. The first level describes the collection; the second level presents a series of materials; the third level illustrates the individual folder. An EAD record contains elements, associated attributes, and allowed values. EAD encoders need to record the archival collections as a whole, and more importantly, they also need to provide the descriptive data for each series, box, folder, and item (Zeng and Qin, 2008). Two processes are involved in the adoption of EAD: encoding to match information in a finding aid to EAD elements and publication to make a finding aid available on the web (Yakel and Kim, 2005). EAD conforms to both SGML and XML specifications. The implementation of EAD is a complicated process because of the many options and models that need to be considered. Even though it does not necessarily reflect the exact structure of the finding aids produced, it does provide elements to represent the captured information. Table B.4 in Appendix B presents the EAD header elements with associated definitions and examples.

EAD was developed specifically to describe archival materials. Accordingly, the EAD structure adheres to the structure of an archival collection. In EAD, each level of the structure and its corresponding metadata are associated with each other (Niu, 2013). Although EAD is widely implemented in the archival field today, in a study on the diffusion and adoption of EAD in the archival community, Yakel and Kim (2005) found that the adoption rate was low, with only 42% of the respondents implementing EAD in their programs. Based on a usability study of an EAD interface, Yakel (2004) identifies several barriers for implementing EAD. The main barriers include the following: (1) Users are not familiar with EAD jargon, and (2) users do not understand the hierarchical structure of EAD. Yaco's (2008) survey findings yield similar results. After conducting a usability study on an EAD finding aid, DeRidder et al., (2012) recommend the following to enhance the usability of EAD finding aids: adding a navigational frame, adding a "search in page" feature, and modifying archival terminology.

VISUAL RESOURCES ASSOCIATION (VRA) CORE

The Visual Resources Association (VRA) Core is a metadata schema for visual resources, used primarily in art libraries and museums. According to Eustis (2013), "VRA's primary aim was to allow its members to collaborate on best practices for creating, describing, and distributing digital objects for resources such as images or cultural artifacts" (p. 441). It has also been implemented into digital library software, such as CONTENTdm. The first set of VRA Core elements was first released in 1996. The VRA 4.0 version was released in 2007. The standard is hosted by the Network Development and MARC Standards Office of the Library of Congress (LC) in partnership with the VRA (Library of Congress, 2014b). The VRA Core consists of the following 19 elements: record type (collection/work/image), agent, cultural context, date, description, inscription, location, material, measurements, relation, rights, source, stateEdition, stylePeriod, subject, technique, textref, title, and worktype. Additionally, nine global attributes are used to define each element or subelement. They include dataDate, extent, href, pref (preferred value), refid (link to internal identifiers), rules, source, vocab, and xml:lang (Visual Resources Association, 2007). Table B.5 in Appendix B presents the VRA Core 4.0 elements with associated definitions and examples.

According to a 2011 survey, 56 institutions implemented the VRA Core schema (Mixter, 2014). Van Assem et al. (2010) discuss their decision in selecting VRA Core 3.0 for the MultimediaN E-Culture project. The main reasons are that (1) VRA Core elements map well to the raw data; (2) there is clear link between the VRA Core and the Dublin Core; and (3) the VRA Core offers a coherent set of initial facets for a facet browser. There are, however, some issues in mapping richer VRA Core elements to basic Dublin Core. Even though the data elements are similar, there are semantic differences between these elements. For example, the VRA Style/Period is similar to the Dublin Core elements subject or coverage, but some loss of meaning occurs if Style/Period is reduced to either one of the Dublin Core elements (Attig et al., 2004).

CATEGORIES FOR THE DESCRIPTION OF WORKS OF ART (CDWA)

Categories for the Description of Works of Art (CDWA) is a schema that originated in the art museum community. It is designed specifically for developing a structured approach to describing works of art, architecture, and other material culture. CDWA was developed in the late 1990s by the Art Information Task Force (AITF), a group of representatives from the art library and museum communities. The work of the Task Force was partially funded by the J. Paul Getty Trust College Art Association, and the standard as well as the implementation guidelines are available at the Getty's web site (Baca and Harpring, 2009).

CDWA provides a broad framework from which existing art information can be mapped and upon which new systems can be developed or linked. It also identifies vocabulary tools and provides guidelines for their use (Baca and Harpring, 2009). CDWA allows a greater level of granularity than Dublin Core, MODS, or even VRA. For example, it defines a number of categories for Creator, such as Creator Description, Creator Identity, and Creator Role. It also includes a record for the relationship between the object and its visual and textual representation. The full set of metadata elements is quite extensive and includes 540 categories and subcategories. Within the set, a number of categories are identified as "core"—considered necessary to describe a work of art. The schema is built on a hierarchical parent–child data model with subcategories nested under the main categories. The CDWA schema is used in combination with a content standard, CCO.

CDWA Lite is a subset of the full CDWA element set. It is based on the core elements of CDWA and the guidelines included in CCO. CDWA Lite is encoded in XML. It includes 22 core elements, with several nested subelements. The purpose of CDWA Lite is to provide a structured format for sharing core records of works of art and cultural materials between museums and other repositories of visual art. CDWA Lite is compatible with the Open Archives Initiative (OAI) harvesting protocol. Woodley (2008) describes a case study of the sharing of CDWA Lite-based metadata records of images of European tapestries from the Getty Research Institute Photo Study Collection and harvesting them into ARTstor.

Several metadata schemas are described and discussed earlier. Multiple schemas have been developed for different purposes and audiences. There is no single metadata schema that could fully represent descriptive, preservation, and structural metadata. In practice, several schemas have to be used to capture different types of metadata.

INTEROPERABILITY: METADATA MAPPING AND HARVESTING

Interoperability refers to the ability of multiple systems with different hardware and software, data structures, and interfaces to exchange and share metadata (NISO, 2004). The digital library environment, with multiple schemas and content and value standards, poses many challenges for metadata exchange across collections and repositories. The goal of interoperability is to enable the exchange of data between digital library systems and to provide services that simplify discovery and increase interactions with digital library resources in a network environment (Arms et al., 2002). Metadata mapping tools and shared transfer protocols have been developed to advance interoperability and improve access to digital library resources through metadata harvesting and large-scale repositories of aggregated metadata.

Metadata mapping facilitates the exchange of metadata between collections and systems using different schemas. The terms "metadata mapping" and "metadata crosswalk" are often used interchangeably (Woodley, 2008). Woodley (2008) offers a distinction between the terms by defining mapping as "the intellectual activity of comparing and analyzing two or more metadata schemas," while crosswalks are the products of the mapping activity and can be represented as tables or charts (p. 40). Interoperability between schemas can be examined on several levels, including semantic, structural, and syntactic. Most mapping activities in digital libraries focus on semantics analyzing the definitions of the elements in two or more schemas to determine whether they have the same or similar meanings and deciding which element in one schema can be mapped to an equivalent element in the second schema. Typically, mapping is performed in preparation for the exchange of metadata between systems but can also be done during metadata design, when elements of a local application profile need to be mapped to a standardized schema. Metadata mapping ensures cross-collection searching and exposing the local metadata to a wider audience. Mapping of customized schemas to a standard element set is further discussed in the section "Designing and Implementing Metadata."

Crosswalks provide specifications for mapping one metadata schema to another and assist in converting metadata created by different communities to be included in digital libraries and shared repositories. Several crosswalks have been developed to facilitate the mapping of popular schemas. The LC provides access to a number of crosswalks for the schemas that are maintained by LC, including MARC, MODS, and EAD. These schemas are mapped to Dublin Core but also to other standards. For example, MODS is mapped to Dublin Core and MARC, and the conversion is bidirectional—a crosswalk is also available for MARC to MODS and Dublin Core to MODS (Library of Congress, 2015c).

The Getty Research Institute (2014) published a crosswalk chart for multiple schemas, including CDWA, CDWA Lite, and VRA Core.

Semantic mapping is rarely direct, due to a different number of elements and different levels of granularity among schemas. The mapping of a richer schema to a simpler set of elements usually results in some loss of information. Miller (2011) points out that "mapping from one schema to another is virtually impossible without metadata degradation" (p. 233). Fig. 5.2 provides a sample of mapped elements from MODS to Dublin Core. This example demonstrates that some refinements of elements, such as subject, will be lost when MODS is mapped to Dublin Core.

Metadata harvesting has been developed as an approach to interoperability and metadata sharing between digital collections and repositories. This method addresses the difficulties of resource discovery in the digital library environment by gathering metadata from individual digital collections and providing access through an aggregated platform. The transfer of metadata is defined by the OAI-PMH (OAI, 2015). This metadata exchange standard requires data providers to expose their metadata as a set of simple Dublin Core. If original metadata is built with other schemas, such as MODS, Qualified

MODS element	Dublin Core element	Notes
\<titleInfo>\<title>	Title	1. For multiple MODS titles use multiple instances of dc:title. 2. MODS allows \<titleInfo> subelements to be parsed: \<nonSort>, \<title>, \<subTitle>, \<partNumber>, \<partName> MODS subelements should be concatenated in Dublin Core, separated by a space or other form of punctuation.
\<name>\<namePart>	Creator Contributor	1. MODS puts all names in a repeated\<name> with type of contribution indicated in \<role>. It does not make the explicit distinction between creator and contributor in terms of primary vs. secondary roles. An application may wish to designate use of Creator or Contributor for all MODS names or use the role value to determine which DC element is used. 2. MODS allows \<name> subelements to be parsed: \<namePart>, \<displayForm>, \<affiliation>, \<role>, \<description> MODS subelements should be concatenated in Dublin Core, separated by a space or other form of punctuation.

\<subject>
    \<topic>
    \<name>
    \<occupation>
\<classification>
	Subject	

\ \<note> \<tableOfContents>	Description	
\<originInfo>\<publisher>	Publisher	
\<originInfo>\<dateIssued> \<originInfo>\<dateCreated> \<originInfo>\<dateCaptured> \<originInfo>\<dateOther>	Date	

FIGURE 5.2 Mapping of Selected MODS Elements to Dublin Core (Library of Congress, 2015b)

A full set of mapped elements is available at: http://www.loc.gov/standards/mods/mods-dcsimple.html.

Dublin Core, TEI, or VRA, mapping and transformation of metadata to simple Dublin Core need to take place prior to harvesting. The OAI-PMH standard is discussed in more detail in Chapter 6.

Interoperability is a vital issue in digital library research and practice. In Lopatin (2010), OAI-PMH emerges as the most widely adopted solution to interoperability for both academic and nonacademic libraries, although more academic libraries (77%) than nonacademic libraries (69%) selected it. The study by Park and Tosaka (2010) yields similar results. About 36.8% of the respondents exposed their metadata through OAI harvesters. Metadata interoperability is a challenge for many of the institutions because of the financial barriers, personnel requirements, and technical constraints.

DESIGNING AND IMPLEMENTING METADATA

The process of designing and implementing metadata in digital libraries is highly structured, but it also involves a significant amount of customization. The development of local, collection-specific metadata is achieved through a wide range of schemas and their modular character. As Duval et al. (2002) note, "in a modular metadata world, data elements from different schemas as well as vocabularies and other building blocks can be combined in a syntactically and semantically interoperable way" (p. 2). This flexible approach is quite different from the uniformity of bibliographic description that is found in traditional library catalogs. The use of multiple customizable metadata schemas allows one to address different user needs, unique characteristics of collections, and diverse disciplinary domains. However, the lack of a uniform metadata model, and varied metadata creation practices poses challenges to quality, interoperability, and metadata sharing and reuse (Hillmann, 2008; Park, 2009; Park and Tosaka, 2010).

The multiple roles that metadata plays in digital libraries complicate the process of designing consistent and interoperable metadata. As discussed at the beginning of this chapter, different kinds of metadata are needed for resource description, discovery, use, presentation, and preservation of digital objects. Different types are related to multiple functions of metadata that go beyond the description of digital objects. The presence of multiple goals and corresponding data types may require more than one metadata set to be associated with an object, which further complicates the process of designing, implementing, and maintaining metadata in practical digital libraries.

The role of metadata in creating and preserving digital objects is underscored in *The Framework of Guidance for Building Good Digital Collections,* an NISO guide to recommended digital library practice (NISO Framework Working Group, 2007). *The Framework* defines basic requirements for metadata and outlines six general principles for designing and implementing high-quality metadata:

1. Good metadata conforms to community standards in a way that is appropriate to the materials in the collection, users of the collection, and current and potential future uses of the collection.
2. Good metadata supports interoperability.
3. Good metadata uses authority control and content standards to describe objects and collocate related objects.
4. Good metadata includes a clear statement of the conditions and terms of use for the digital object.
5. Good metadata supports the long-term curation and preservation of objects in collections.
6. Good metadata records are objects themselves and therefore should have the qualities of good objects, including authority, authenticity, archivability, persistence, and unique identification (NISO Framework Working Group, 2007, pp. 61–62).

These principles build on the traditions of library cataloging, especially regarding the adherence to standards and use of authority control and content standards. They also highlight the new roles of metadata in supporting interoperability, rights management, and long-term preservation. The emphasis is on the standardization of the metadata creation process, which in turn supports consistent and accurate resource description, interoperability, and the preservation of digital objects. As indicated in principle no. 6, metadata records themselves are digital objects and should have the attributes of good objects in order to be maintained and preserved.

The digital library environment offers a wide range of structure and content standards to support consistent metadata creation and interoperability. The metadata design process requires a number of decisions about the selection and integration of different standards and tools. As discussed in the previous section, the digital library environment offers multiple schemas, developed by different communities that are intended to address the unique characteristics of materials in diverse knowledge domains. Schemas are used in combination with other metadata building blocks, such as authority control tools and content standards. Library, archival, and museum communities provide a range of general and discipline-specific controlled vocabulary tools to record authorized forms of names and consistent subject terms. Communities also utilize content input guidelines to ensure consistent data formatting with regard to syntax, punctuation, capitalization, etc. Many of the content tools were originally developed in the print environment and have been adopted for metadata creation in digital libraries.

Table 5.3 provides a summary of the standards used for metadata creation in digital libraries. The list was compiled based on the results of studies that surveyed metadata practices in digital collections and repositories (Lopatin, 2010; Moulaison et al., 2015; Palmer et al., 2007; Park and Tosaka, 2010). There are some discrepancies between the studies when identifying the most frequently used schemas. Palmer et al. (2007) conducted a longitudinal study of IMLS digital collections created between 2003 and 2006 and found that Dublin Core and MARC were the two top metadata schemas used during that period. Lopatin (2010) and Moulaison et al. (2015) find that Dublin Core is the most widely adopted standard in digital collections and repositories, while the results of Park and Tosaka's (2010) survey indicate that MARC is still the most frequently used standard, followed by Dublin Core. Because of the disparate results, the standards in Table 5.3 are listed alphabetically, rather than in the ranking order.

The schemas and data value standards were selected for inclusion in Table 5.3 if they were listed in at least two of the three reviewed studies. Data content standards are discussed only in the Park and Tosaka (2010) study. The list of standards and tools is not exhaustive. The schemas identified in the reviewed studies focus on descriptive metadata. Interestingly, none of the studies mentions the structural metadata standard METS, nor do they mention the preservation standard PREMIS. Lopatin (2010) and Park and Tosaka (2010) mention a significant use of home-grown schemas and locally developed

Table 5.3 Metadata Standards Used in Digital Collections and Repositories

Type of Standard	Standard Name
Metadata schemas	Dublin Core; CDWA; EAD; MARC; MODS; Qualified Dublin Core; TEI; VRA
Data value standards/controlled vocabularies	AAT; LCSH; LC NAF; LC TGM; MESH; TGN
Data content standards	AACR2; CCO; DACS; DCRM; Dublin Core guidelines; EAD guidelines; LC MODS guidelines

vocabularies and guidelines. Park and Tosaka (2010) record that 25.1% of the survey participants engaged in creating local metadata elements and home-grown content guidelines. The authors discuss the problematic nature of this approach insofar as it hinders interoperability and metadata sharing in distributed environments.

The research studies confirm that multiple schemas and content standards are indeed used in digital libraries. This multiplicity is rooted in the different traditions of describing and organizing resources in cultural heritage communities. The schemas that originated in archives and museums tend to be used with other standards and tools developed in archival and visual resources communities. For example, EAD, a finding aid standard for archival collections, is often used in conjunction with DACS, which is a content standard of archival practice. VRA Core and CDWA are two structure standards designed specifically for creating metadata for works of art. CDWA is used in conjunction with CCO, a museum data standard for describing works of art and material culture, and with controlled vocabulary tools developed by the Getty Research Institute, including the *Art and Architecture Thesaurus* (AAT) or Thesaurus of Geographic Names (TGN). The VRA schema is also used with CCO and Getty vocabularies (Elings and Waibel, 2007). Dublin Core and MODS are both cross-disciplinary and general digital library standards, and are used with a variety of controlled vocabularies, including LC Subject Headings, Thesaurus for Graphic Materials (TGM), and Getty vocabularies.

The creation of metadata in digital collections and repositories involves two distinct phases:

1. Conceptual work in metadata design
2. Resource-intensive construction of metadata records

Metadata design, which includes selecting and customizing a schema, provides a foundation for building metadata records. Schema selection and/or the development of a local application profile takes place in the beginning phase of a digital library project. Metadata design is critical to the subsequent stages of metadata implementation and interoperability. This phase involves not only selecting an appropriate metadata schema but also determining the appropriate level of description and identifying controlled vocabulary tools to be used in creating records. The decision of whether to adopt an established content standard or develop local input guidelines is also made in the planning phase. Metadata implementation involves building records for digital objects based on the standards established in the design phase, executing quality control, and producing documentation.

SELECTING A SCHEMA

Metadata schemas differ in the type and number of data elements, the designation of mandatory fields, encoding requirements, and the use of data content and value standards. Therefore, a decision about selecting a schema has implications for the quality and level of description. Several factors need to be considered in adopting a schema or developing a customized metadata profile (Kennedy, 2008; Miller, 2011; Zeng and Qin, 2008). Kennedy (2008) offers a practical guide to assist professionals in choosing a metadata schema. The guide consists of nine questions focused on (1) potential users and their needs, (2) expertise of cataloging staff, (3) time and financial resources, (4) type of access to a digital collection, (5) relationships to other collections, (6) collection scope, (7) metadata harvesting, (8) interoperability, and (9) level of maintenance and quality control. Zeng and Qin (2008) point out that the metadata creation process begins with an examination of the discipline, community, and potential users and usage and then considers a number of other criteria, including the nature of the collection and constraints in staffing and funding, as well as institutional and cooperative information systems. Miller (2011) recommends adopting an approach from information architecture that is frequently used to determine functional requirements. The triad of *context, content, and users* can be used as a framework for analyzing the organizational context in which a digital library is created, for examining the type, format, and subject content of materials, and for gathering information about users, their information-seeking behavior, and intended use.

The analysis of user needs and search behaviors provides a foundation for determining functional requirements for metadata from a user viewpoint. Metadata designed with a specific user group in mind allows for not only establishing a specific set of metadata elements but also determining the level of description and selecting appropriate vocabulary. For example, a set of metadata elements for a collection of anatomical images intended for medical students and faculty will be different from a digital collection of anatomy intended for middle school students. Children represent a special user group of digital libraries, and as Abbas (2005) demonstrates, they can benefit from metadata schemas and records developed with their unique needs in mind.

In the process of schema selection and customization, the nature of the collection, the characteristics of the resources, format and subject coverage, user needs, and anticipated use make up the major criteria for consideration. Specific types of materials may require dedicated schemas. As mentioned before, VRA Core and CDWA are schemas developed specifically for creating metadata for works of art. PBCore is often used as a dedicated schema for collections of audio recordings (Dulock and Long, 2011). General digital library schemas, such as Dublin Core and MODS, are used to create item-level descriptive records for a variety of materials, including photographs and monographs, as well as basic records for audio and video resources. Compound objects, such as monographs or newspapers, require structural metadata in addition to descriptive records. As discussed earlier in this chapter, METS is a multifunctional standard capable of providing structural metadata for compound objects as well as serving as a "wrapper" for other types of metadata, including descriptive and preservation metadata.

Digital library management systems (DLMS) are used to build digital collections and repositories. They work as a constraining factor for metadata, as they usually support only a limited number of schemas and controlled vocabulary tools. Chapter 6 reviews a current selection of open source and proprietary DLMS used for constructing digital collections of cultural heritage materials. Repository platforms that primarily serve preservation functions are discussed in Chapter 9. As indicated in the comparative review of DLMS in Chapter 6, system support for metadata schemas varies. A number of DLMS, including CollectiveAccess, CONTENTdm, and EMu provide a selection of schemas and enable customization of metadata templates, while Greenstone, Omeka, and Luna support only Dublin Core. The open source software Omeka is intended for a broad range of developers, including students, scholars, and individuals interested in building personal digital collections. The metadata template includes the basic 15 Dublin Core elements, which cannot be customized (Fig. 5.3). While this approach offers individuals with minimal technical and cataloging expertise an opportunity to build standard-compliant collections, library professionals often find the lack of template customizations limiting (Kucsma et al., 2010).

In the category of open source software, CollectiveAccess provides the strongest support for metadata creation and includes a number of schemas and controlled vocabulary tools. CollectiveAccess also allows users to import and share a variety of standards from user-contributed installation profiles and provides a forum for sharing best practices in metadata creation. Support for metadata design and customization is one of the strengths of proprietary software. CONTENTdm, managed by OCLC and widely adopted by academic and public libraries, offers a number of schemas, including Dublin Core, VRA Core, EAD, and METS. Metadata templates can be customized with local elements mapped to a standard schema.

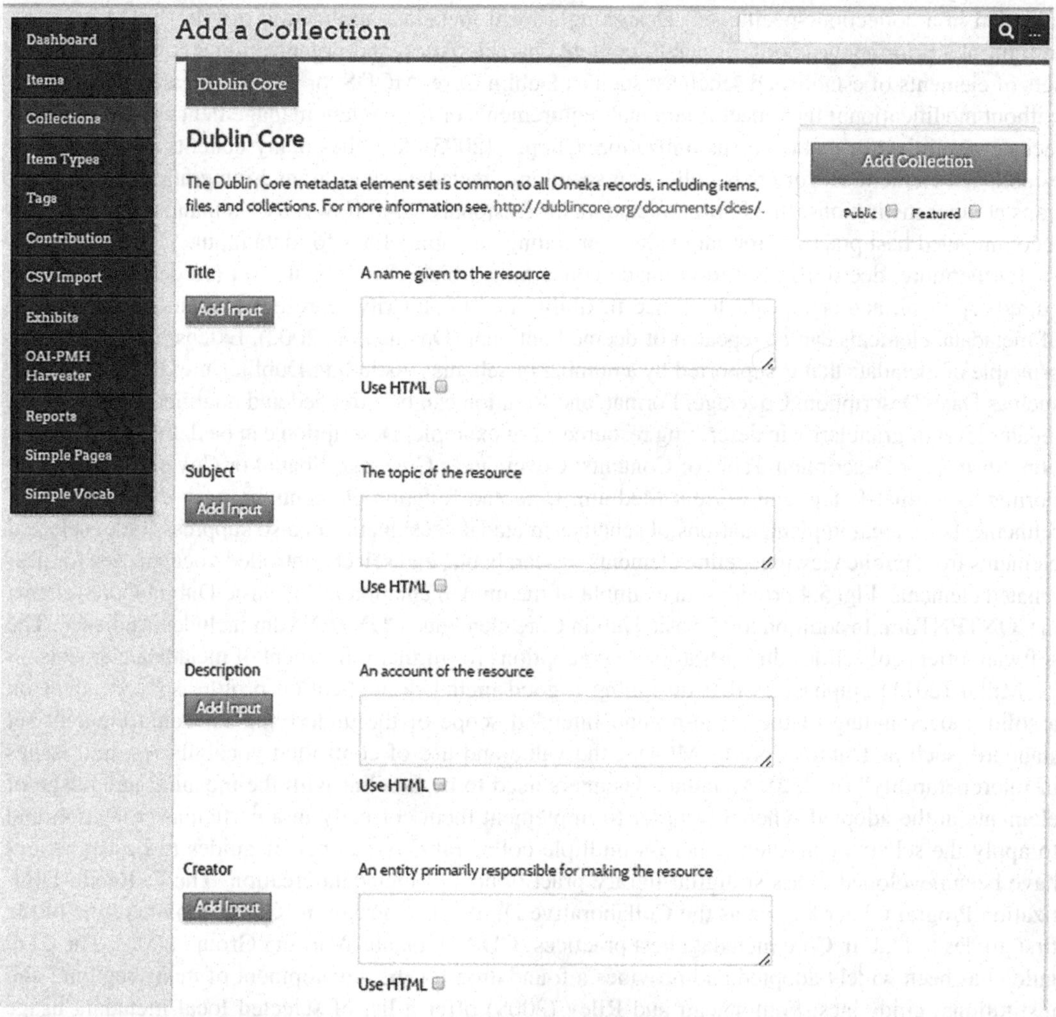

FIGURE 5.3 Selected Basic Dublin Core Elements in Omeka Metadata Template

CONTENTdm also incorporates a number of controlled vocabulary tools, including AAT, TGM, TGN, ULAN, and MeSH. The level of support for metadata creation plays an important role in choosing between an open source software or a proprietary system. Some institutions may use more than one standardized schema for different types of collections if they have access to a DLMS that offers multiple schemas. For example, Dublin Core can be used for image or text collections and EAD for finding aids.

METADATA APPLICATION PROFILES

Analyzing functional requirements and selecting a schema are the first steps in metadata design. Once a standardized schema is selected, metadata designers need to identify which elements have to be included in a collection-specific set. Designing a local metadata application profile should be made in light of a prior analysis of user needs, content characteristics, and organizational context. Standard sets of elements of established schemas, such as Dublin Core, MODS, or VRA Core are often applied without modification if they meet functional requirements or if a content management system (DLMS) lacks capabilities for metadata customization. Chopey (2005) describes many benefits of adopting an established element set for cross-collection searching, metadata sharing, and integration with collections at other institutions. In addition, metadata professionals can follow a user's manual that includes recommended best practices for data values, encoding, and guidelines for data input.

Furthermore, decisions need to be made concerning which elements in a set are designated as required, optional, and/or repeatable. Since flexibility and modularity represent fundamental principles of metadata, elements can be repeated or deemed optional (Duval et al., 2002). Extensibility is another principle of metadata that is supported by a number of schemas, including Dublin Core. Basic elements, such as Date, Description, Coverage, Format, and Relation can be extended and qualified to allow for a greater level of granularity in describing resources. For example, Description can be defined as Description-Abstract or Description-Table of Contents; Coverage as Coverage-Spatial or Coverage-Temporal; Format as Format-Extent and Format-Medium. Date and Relation elements have an extensive list of refinements. In local implementations of schemas, metadata designers can also suppress (hide) selected elements from public viewing, define elements as searchable, and select controlled vocabularies for designated elements. Fig. 5.4 provides an example of the implementation of the basic Dublin Core schema in CONTENTdm. In addition to 15 basic Dublin Core elements, CONTENTdm includes Audience. The software offers collection administrators several options for further refinement of metadata elements.

Miller (2011) emphasizes that designing a good metadata application profile is "dependent on a solid understanding of the meaning and intended scope of the underlying metadata element set standard, such as Dublin Core or MODS; the value and use of controlled vocabularies; and issues of interoperability" (p. 252). Metadata designers need to be familiar with the meaning and usage of elements in the adopted schema in order to implement them correctly in a particular collection and to apply the schema consistently across multiple collections. A number of guides to best practices have been developed to assist digital library practitioners in metadata creation. The Colorado Digitization Program, later known as the Collaborative Digitization Program (CDP), provided one of the first guides to Dublin Core metadata best practices (CDP Metadata Working Group, 2006). The CDP guide has been widely adopted and provides a foundation for the development of many regional and institutional guidelines. Foulonneau and Riley (2008) offer a list of selected local metadata usage guidelines. Chopey (2005) outlines the multiple areas of expertise required for metadata creation in digital collections and repositories, and supplies a checklist for planning and implementing a local metadata application.

Cultural heritage institutions often find the basic set of metadata elements of established schemas insufficient or too restrictive and decide to develop local application profiles (Chopey, 2005). Customized metadata profiles with local elements are usually designed to address particular user needs, disciplinary domains, and characteristics of specific collections. Customized approaches provide more robust or modular metadata structures. Local sets of metadata elements are often designed for heterogeneous digital collections that include materials from multiple source collections or a mix of resource types and formats. However, the challenge of the customized approach is to accommodate and preserve a variety of discipline- or collection-specific metadata, while maintaining consistency across collections and metadata sharing (Attig et al., 2004; Chopey, 2005).

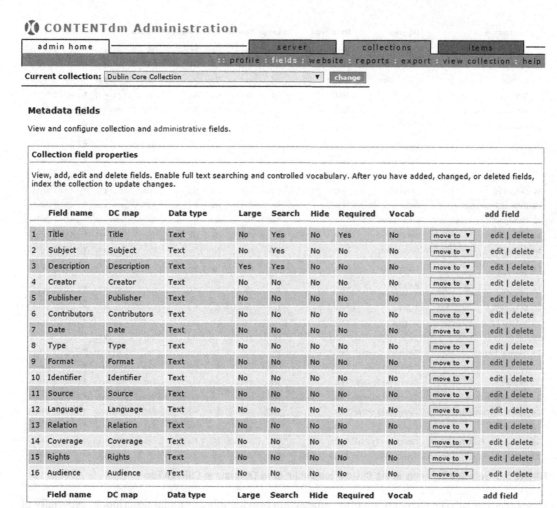

FIGURE 5.4 Basic Dublin Core Metadata Template in CONTENTdm

The process of developing a customized metadata application profile begins with adopting an existing standardized schema, such as Dublin Core, MODS, and VRA. The established schema is used as the basis for developing a local application profile where some standard elements are retained and some are extended and refined. When a new element is added, it is usually mapped to the standard schema element to enable cross-collection searching and metadata harvesting. Fig. 5.5 demonstrates an example of a customized metadata template in CONTENTdm.

Fig. 5.5 presents a portion of the customized metadata template, which in its entirety consists of 38 elements. This metadata template was designed for a large collection of digitized historic photographs at the American Geographical Society Library, where images were derived from multiple source collections (Matusiak and Johnston, 2014). A basic Dublin Core metadata in CONTENTdm is extended for this project to include a number of refined elements, such as Relation-Is Part Of and

Field name	DC map	Data type	Large	Search	Hide	Required	Vocab		add field
1 Title	Title	Text	No	Yes	No	Yes	No	move to ▼	edit | delete
2 Full Title	Title-Alternative	Text	No	Yes	No	No	No	move to ▼	edit | delete
3 Caption	Description	Text	No	Yes	No	No	No	move to ▼	edit | delete
4 Author	Creator	Text	No	Yes	No	No	Yes	move to ▼	edit | delete
5 Publication Date	None	Text	No	Yes	No	No	No	move to ▼	edit | delete
6 Part of Set	Relation-Is Part Of	Text	No	Yes	No	No	Yes	move to ▼	edit | delete
7 Notes	Description	Text	No	No	No	No	No	move to ▼	edit | delete
8 Original Publisher	Publisher	Text	No	No	No	No	No	move to ▼	edit | delete
9 Source of Publication	Source	Text	No	No	No	No	No	move to ▼	edit | delete
10 Language	Language	Text	No	Yes	No	No	Yes	move to ▼	edit | delete
11 Date of Photograph	Date	Text	No	Yes	No	No	No	move to ▼	edit | delete
12 Photographer's Note	Description	Text	Yes	No	No	No	No	move to ▼	edit | delete
13 Photographer	Creator	Text	No	Yes	No	No	Yes	move to ▼	edit | delete
14 Description	Description	Text	Yes	No	No	No	No	move to ▼	edit | delete
15 Source of Descriptive Information	Description	Text	No	No	No	No	No	move to ▼	edit | delete
16 Related Resources	Relation-References	Text	No	No	No	No	No	move to ▼	edit | delete
17 Subject TGM	Subject	Text	No	Yes	No	No	Yes	move to ▼	edit | delete
18 Subject LC	Subject	Text	No	Yes	No	No	Yes	move to ▼	edit | delete
19 Continent	Coverage-Spatial	Text	No	Yes	No	No	Yes	move to ▼	edit | delete
20 General Region	Coverage-Spatial	Text	No	Yes	No	No	Yes	move to ▼	edit | delete
21 Country	Coverage-Spatial	Text	No	Yes	No	No	Yes	move to ▼	edit | delete
22 Region	Coverage-Spatial	Text	No	Yes	No	No	Yes	move to ▼	edit | delete
23 State/Province	Coverage-Spatial	Text	No	Yes	No	No	Yes	move to ▼	edit | delete
24 County/Municipality	Coverage-Spatial	Text	No	Yes	No	No	Yes	move to ▼	edit | delete
25 City/Place	Coverage-Spatial	Text	No	Yes	No	No	Yes	move to ▼	edit | delete
26 Geographic Feature	Coverage-Spatial	Text	No	Yes	No	No	Yes	move to ▼	edit | delete
27 Type	Type	Text	No	No	No	No	No	move to ▼	edit | delete

FIGURE 5.5 Selected Elements in the Customized Dublin Core Template in CONTENTdm

Coverage-Spatial. The elements are often repeated to provide more granular description, especially of geographic coverage. The description of geographic coverage requires special attention throughout the metadata creation process because of the nature of AGS Library's photographic collections, which document geographic expeditions and scientific exploration around the world. The elements related to geographic location include Continent, Subcontinent, Country, Region, Province/State, City/Place, and Geographic Feature. Natural language labels, such as Photographer and Photographer's Note are assigned to accommodate the unique nature of the collection, but all customized elements are mapped to Dublin Core elements, as indicated in the DC column.

Metadata mapping is crucial for searching across collections within a repository and for metadata harvesting to share records in aggregated environments. Elements in local application profiles need to be mapped to semantically corresponding elements in the standard schema, in order to be exposed and shared through the harvesting process. If more than one schema is involved, then interoperability is facilitated by a crosswalk, which maps elements, semantics, and syntax from one metadata schema to those of another (NISO, 2004; Woodley, 2008). Metadata designers may decide not to map some local elements if mapping creates confusion for metadata harvesting.

Adopting an established schema and modifying it to meet collection- or domain-specific requirements are two approaches for creating local application profiles. Zeng and Qin (2008) provide an overview of other models, including profiles that assemble elements from more than one schema. Most of the customized approaches retain interoperability with the original schema base through element mapping and crosswalks. Development of a local element set without reference to an existing standard is generally not recommended, as it locks metadata into a local system without opportunities for sharing and reuse. In the cultural heritage community, it violates a fundamental principle of making metadata sharable and interoperable (NISO Framework Working Group, 2007).

Finally, it is recommended to document the metadata customization process. As Miller (2011) points out, a variety of terms are used in practice for metadata schema documentation, including metadata guidelines, data dictionaries, and metadata application profiles (MAPs). The terms are used interchangeably in the context of digital libraries and usually refer to a document that defines metadata elements for each collection, as well as guidelines for implementation. A data dictionary or metadata application profile provides a list of elements for a given collection, mapping to a standard schema, data format, information about data value tools (authority files and vocabularies), and content guidelines. Many institutions create internal documents, while others choose to share their best practices. University libraries at the University of Washington provide access to their data dictionaries, a.k.a. Schemas and Metadata Application Profiles (or MAPS), at: http://www.lib.washington.edu/msd/pubcat/mig/datadicts.

CONTROLLED VOCABULARIES

Controlled vocabularies/data value standards are essential to the process of standardized metadata creation. While schemas offer a structural framework for building records, controlled vocabularies are a source of authoritative terms to be entered for values of certain elements, such as personal, family, or corporate names, subjects, and coverage elements. The use of controlled vocabularies ensures consistent description of resources and their attributes and enables effective information retrieval and resource discovery. Controlled vocabularies allow the identification of relationships and bring together resources created by the same person or about the same topic. The selection of vocabularies is usually determined during the metadata design and customization process and may involve more than one established controlled vocabulary tool and/or the development of local controlled vocabulary lists.

The use of controlled vocabulary systems is part of a long tradition of bibliographic description in the library world. Digital libraries have adopted the fundamental principles of authority control as well as many tools from the print environment. A controlled vocabulary is defined as "a list or database of subject terms in which all terms or phrases representing a concept are brought together. Often one of the terms or phrases is designated as the preferred term or authorized phrase to be used in metadata records in a retrieval tool" (Taylor and Joudrey, 2008, p. 334). In addition to subject terms, controlled vocabularies can include names of persons, bodies, places, objects, events, and terms for resource type, genre, and format. The term covers a wide range of tools for organizing information retrieval, but at minimum, a controlled vocabulary contains a restricted list of terms. If a metadata element is designed as controlled, only terms from the designated list may be used for entry in metadata records (Hedden, 2008).

Controlled vocabularies address ambiguities and synonymous relationships of natural language at different levels of semantic control. Three types of term relationships are identified in the controlled vocabulary (Leise, 2008):

- Equivalent that includes relations between synonyms and near synonyms—for example, railroads, trains, railways
- Hierarchical that includes relations between broader and narrower concepts—for example, transportation is a broader term (BT) in the hierarchy for railroads, while Cable railroads or Electric railroads represent narrower terms (NT)
- Associative that includes relations of terms that are conceptually related—for example, railroad tracks or railroad bridges

A distinction is made among types of controlled vocabularies because of different levels of semantic relationships (ANSI/NISO, 2005; Leise, 2008):

- Simple controlled lists of terms without any semantic relationships, such as lists of language and country codes, resource type terms, etc.
- Synonym rings that list synonymous terms
- Authority files that list synonyms but also identify a single term as the preferred term, clarifying the equivalency relationship
- Taxonomies that consist of preferred terms connected through hierarchical relationships
- Thesauri that express all three semantic relationships of equivalency, hierarchy, and association

In the context of digital libraries, all five types of controlled vocabularies can be implemented. Typically, thesauri and authority files, including subject heading lists, are used in accordance with the conventions of bibliographic description established in the cultural heritage communities. Subject heading lists are types of authority files that may also include hierarchical or associative relationships. The Library of Congress Subject Headings (LCSH) represent the most widely adopted list of terms for subject description.

Many of the tools used to assign controlled vocabularies in the digital library environment have been developed in the library and museum communities. The Library of Congress offers a number of tools, including:

- *Library of Congress Name Authority File (LC NAF)* as a source of authoritative data for names of persons, organizations, events, places, and titles. Available at: http://id.loc.gov/authorities/names.html
- *Library of Congress Subject Headings (LCSH)* that provide an extensive list of authoritative terms to cover almost all domains of human knowledge. According to Lopatin (2010), LCSH were used for subject terms in digital projects by 87% of academic libraries and 69% of nonacademic libraries.
- *Library of Congress Thesaurus for Graphic Materials (LC TGM)*, which is one of the major thesauri for indexing visual materials. It serves as a source of vocabulary for topical terms in general subject areas and outlines all the semantic relationships among the terms. Available at: http://www.loc.gov/rr/print/tgm1/

The Getty Research Institute has developed a number of controlled vocabulary tools for the museum community. The Getty vocabularies contain controlled terminology for art, architecture, decorative arts, and other material culture, as well as archival materials. Two of the tools, the *Art and Architecture Thesaurus (AAT)* and the *Getty Thesaurus of Geographic Names (TGN)*, have also been adopted broadly in the digital library environment:

- *Art and Architecture Thesaurus (AAT)* includes terms, descriptions, and other information for generic concepts related to art, architecture, conservation, archaeology, and other cultural heritage. Available at: http://www.getty.edu/research/tools/vocabularies/aat/index.html

- *The Getty Thesaurus of Geographic Names (TGN)* provides controlled terms and information for current and historical geographic places and physical features. Available at: http://www.getty.edu/research/tools/vocabularies/tgn/index.html

In addition to the Library of Congress tools and Getty vocabularies, many other general and discipline-specific subject headings and thesauri can be applied in the digital library environment, including Medical Subject Headings (MeSH), UNESCO Thesaurus, National Agricultural Thesaurus, or Iconoclass (Iconographic Classification System).

Fig. 5.6 demonstrates an example of a practical implementation of a number of controlled vocabulary tools in a digital project. It depicts a metadata record from the collection at the American Geographical Society Library based on the template presented in Fig. 5.5. The controlled vocabulary for geographic coverage elements, such as Country, State/Province, and City, is selected from the *Getty Thesaurus of Geographic Names* (*TGN*). The two subject elements are designated to capture different concepts and use different controlled vocabulary tools: Subject TGM covers topical subjects and derives terms from the LC TGM, while Subject LC indicates proper names of people and objects depicted in images and uses LCSH.

BUILDING METADATA RECORDS

Creating metadata records takes place after a metadata schema has been selected, customized, and documented. Metadata records are encoded in XML, but encoding is usually facilitated by a DLMS that provides templates for building records and generates XML automatically. The process of building records is resource intensive and requires professional staff with knowledge of metadata standards, controlled vocabulary tools, and indexing guidelines. Item-level metadata records need to be constructed for all objects in a digital collection or repository. If original items have limited descriptive information, the process of metadata creation is often accompanied by extensive research to provide accurate descriptions and consistent access points. The process of metadata creation requires:

- Determining resource characteristics
- Transcribing available descriptive information
- Conducting subject analysis
- Selecting appropriate terms from a designated controlled vocabulary tool
- Following content guidelines for data entry
- Recording administrative and preservation information
- Adhering to the established standards

Content guidelines provide directions for the level of description, capitalization, and punctuation. They also specify how to handle variant titles, initial articles, abbreviations, approximate dates, and missing or incomplete information. Metadata designers can adopt an established set of guidelines or develop local guidelines for the purpose of the project or the institutional digital library program. AACR2 general content guidelines have been widely used in bibliographic description. AACR2 is currently being replaced by RDA. DACS and CCO, are domain specific guidelines that are utilized by the archives and museum communities, respectively.

The extent of indexing depends on the type of resource and the amount of descriptive information available in the original collection. As Chopey (2005) notes, creating metadata records for digital

▼ **Description**

Title	Lhasa, Potala Palace from southwest
Part of Set	1900-1901 Central Tibet
Notes	A set of 50 photographs and associated handwritten descriptive notes, acquired from the Imperial Russian Geographical Society in St. Petersburg. Tibet", are available at: http://collections.lib.uwm.edu/u?/tibet,94 ⌐
Date of Photograph	1900/1901
Photographer's Note	Potala from SSW. [Z.] This view has been taken by Ts'ibikov [Tsybikoff] during the festival he calls Ts'og Ch'od (1) [Tsog Chod] celebrated on the year (18/5 April 1901). The huge pictures hang on the palace wall beneath the Nam-gyal Ch'oide [Namgyal Ch-oide], the monastery of the palace right one) and Tara or Doma (on the left). Crowds of people cover the slope of the hill and stand at the foot of the picture. Obs. 1) Sung ch'o Rockh
Photographer	Tsybikoff, G. Ts., 1873-1930
Description	"In the first moon of the year the lamas of Potala, as well as all those from the various temples and convents of Lhasa, and those from Anterior ar myriads, assemble at the Jok'ang to read the sacred books for twenty days. In the second moon of the year there is another gathering for the sam (1). [...]) (1) This feast is called Sung ch'o (gsung ch's) in Tibetan. (p.8) Rockhill, W.W. (1890). Tibet: A geographical, ethnographical, and historical sketch derived from Chinese sources. London: Royal Asiatic Society.
Related Resources	1903 Lhasa and Central Tibet by G. Ts. Tsybikoff available at: http://collections.lib.uwm.edu/u?/tibet,66 ⌐ 1878 A-K's Plan of Lhasa available at: http://collections.lib.uwm.edu/u?/tibet,107 1891 ⌐ Rockhill's Plan of Lhasa available at: http://collections.lib.uwm.edu/u?/tibet,108 1904 ⌐ Waddell's Plan of Lhasa available at: http://collections.lib.uwm.edu/u?/tibet,110 ⌐
Subject TGM	Castles & palaces Architecture Buddhism Buddhist temples Historic sites Religious communities
Subject LC	Potala (Lhasa, China) Tibet, Plateau of
Continent	Asia
General Region	East Asia
Country	China
State/Province	Tibet (autonomous region)
City/Place	Lhasa
Geographic Feature	Qing Zang Gaoyuan (plateau)
Type	Image

FIGURE 5.6 Metadata Record from a Collection Built Using a Local Application Profile

The record is available at: http://collections.lib.uwm.edu/cdm/ref/collection/tibet/id/129.

collections requires more granular indexing than the kind of bibliographic description found in library catalogs. Archival image collections are particularly challenging because very few items will have individual annotations, and the level of consistency and accuracy of description may vary from item to item. On the other hand, monographs usually have MARC cataloging records, so the metadata process can be streamlined. In these cases, MARC-Dublin Core or MARC-MODS crosswalks can be used to automate metadata creation. An item-level metadata record details the characteristics of a digital object for the purposes of description, resource discovery, and preservation. It typically includes:

- Descriptive information
- Access points
- Contextual information
- Reference to the original item and collection
- Administrative and preservation information

Finally, metadata records need to be reviewed for quality and consistency. Ultimately, the quality of metadata and adherence to standards determine if digital objects are findable and discoverable within local digital collections, as well as in the aggregated environment of large-scale digital libraries.

USER TAGGING

The emergence of Web 2.0 technologies has challenged the traditional approaches to description and organization of digital library materials and offered new opportunities for user engagement and knowledge contribution (Alemu et al., 2012; Matusiak, 2006; Trant, 2009). Web 2.0 emerged in 2004 and transformed the web from a static platform into a dynamic, shared information space (Ding et al., 2009). In contrast to Web 1.0, the network of hyperlinked but relatively static documents, Web 2.0 introduced a participatory and interactive model where users can contribute and actively engage with web content. Web 2.0 encompasses a wide range of web applications that enable users to share their own resources and comments on the content of others.

User tagging is particularly relevant in digital libraries, as it offers an opportunity to enhance metadata created by library professionals by introducing user language and perspective to contribute additional descriptive information (Matusiak, 2006; Trant, 2009). User tagging represents an approach to organizing content in the web environment where users create their own textual descriptors using natural language terms (tags) and share them with a community of users. This new system of organization that employs users to assign keywords to their own or shared content, has been referred to by several terms, including user tagging, social tagging, collaborative tagging, folksonomy, social classification (Hammond et al., 2005), or "metadata for the masses" (Merholz, 2004).

The potential of user-generated descriptive tags for library resources has caught the attention of the researchers and practitioners, resulting in an extensive body of literature devoted to examining the benefits of tagging and comparing tags to structured metadata (Bar-Ilan et al., 2008; Kipp, 2011; Matusiak, 2006; Petek, 2012; Pirmann, 2012; Rorissa, 2010). The main benefits include a more user-centered approach to describe resources, closer connection to users and their language, user engagement, and collaborative knowledge construction. Rorissa (2010) indicates that user tags and traditional assigned index terms have different structures. Moreover, user tags reflect users' context and can be semantically richer than index terms. At the same time, professional indexers use controlled vocabularies and thoroughly evaluate a document to achieve higher precision when users are searching for a resource. In short, user-generated tagging is a double-edged sword. On one hand, tags are criticized for imprecision and inaccuracy; on the other hand, they are able to capture the breadth of user language. After analyzing tagging and controlled vocabulary studies, Thomas et al. (2009) emphasize that user tags can enhance controlled vocabularies by offering additional access points. Kipp (2011) concludes "tagging does not completely replace controlled vocabularies but provides an added dimension to subject access from the perspective of the end users" (p. 30).

Studies comparing user tags and user queries represent another area of research. After analyzing user tagging and user queries, Ransom and Rafferty (2011) confirm that user tagging can help the effectiveness of information retrieval. In particular, the authors find similarities between tags and search terms associated with people, objects, and location. Benoit (2014) further compares expert and novice user tags and investigates how these tags match with query terms. The results reveal that expert tags match query terms more than novice tags, while the combination of expert and novice tags shows the highest matching of query terms. Huang and Jörgensen (2013) investigate differences in tagging between digital collections and social sites, such as Flickr. In general, popular tags in Flickr describe more generic objects, while the popular tags identify more specific objects and time categories in the Library of Congress' photostream (LCP).

Despite the advantages of engaging users with digital library resources through tagging, the applications of user-generated tags have not been widely implemented in digital libraries. According to a 2010 survey, only 9% of the academic libraries and 25% nonacademic libraries enable user-generated metadata (Lopatin, 2010). A variety of approaches have been applied to engage users with digital libraries. For example, Bainbridge et al. (2012) designed a client-facing JavaScript browser extension that allows users to edit, merge, delete, and undo metadata elements in digital libraries.

Researchers and practitioners also identify a range of challenges with user tagging (Guy and Tonkin, 2006; Macgregor and McCulloch, 2006; Matusiak, 2006; Rorissa, 2010; Thomas et al., 2010). Some of the most common issues include:

- Misspellings or unidentifiable terms
- Imprecise and unclear tags
- Uncontrolled and inconsistent tags (e.g., variations of the same tags)
- Lack of authority control (e.g., synonyms)
- Increased recall, but low precision
- Lack of collocation

In addition, Jeong (2009) discovers that a high ratio of overlap between tags and metadata elements, such as title and description, reduces the effectiveness of tagging in information organization and retrieval. Lu et al. (2010) point out that some tags are personal and subjective rather than subject related, which hinders the integration of tags into library systems. Bar-Ilan et al. (2008) compare structured and unstructured tagging in a cultural heritage collection, and they find that different interpretations of the meaning of structured elements reduce the quality of tagging.

In addition to identifying the challenges, researchers and practitioners have also offered some suggestions for overcoming the limitations of unstructured and inconsistent tags and integrating them into standardized metadata. Thomas et al. (2010) recommend a number of solutions, including providing users with guidelines for tag creation, enabling users to edit and combine tags, and linking tags to controlled vocabularies. Since both user tags and controlled vocabularies have strengths and weaknesses, researchers propose integrating controlled vocabularies and user tags in digital library systems (Pirmann, 2012; Thomas et al., 2010).

Since their inception, Web 2.0 applications are gradually becoming integrated into DLMS. Both open source and proprietary solutions, such as Omeka, CollectiveAccess, and CONTENTdm offer technical capabilities for engaging users in the tagging of digital objects, contributing comments, and sharing resources through social media. Although many digital library systems support user tagging, in practice user-generated tags remain limited. However, the institutions that expose some of their digital library resources to the general public through social media have had more success with engaging users in tagging. Flickr: The Commons was initiated as a collaborative project between Flickr and the Library of Congress to increase the visibility of cultural heritage materials and to provide a way for the general public to contribute to the description of resources (Clark, 2008). Since the launch in 2008, many other cultural heritage institutions have decided to join Flickr: The Commons to expose their collections and take advantage of user contributions (Flickr, 2015).

LINKED DATA

The concept of linked data is associated with the Semantic Web, also referred to as the web of Data or Web 3.0. The vision of the Semantic Web goes beyond the functionality of Web 1.0 or the social interactions of Web 2.0. It aims to establish a global network of data from diverse domains, connected through semantic relationships that are not only understood by humans but can also be accessed and interpreted by computers (Berners-Lee et al., 2001; W3C, 2015a). Berners-Lee et al. (2001) envision the Semantic Web as "an extension of the current web in which information is given well-defined meaning, better enabling computers and people to work in cooperation" (p. 28). The ultimate goal is to use computing capabilities to enhance discovery of the related information, share and reuse data in the open web environment, and enrich knowledge through linking data among multiple domains. In order to make the Semantic Web a reality, data need to be open, structured, and connected through a set of standards and technologies that not only process the data but also build meaningful links among different data sets (W3C, 2015b; Yoose and Perkins, 2013). The collection of interrelated datasets on the web, referred to as linked data, is at the heart of the Semantic Web (W3C, 2015b).

Linked data rely on a stack of technologies to establish semantic relationships and publish interrelated data sets, but it is not a specific standard or technology. It is often described as a set of best practices for the publication of structured data on the web (Bizer et al., 2009; Van Hooland and Verborgh, 2014). RDF (Resource Description Framework) provides a conceptual data model for establishing relationships and representing linked information on the web. The underlying practices and technologies for developing linked data or transforming existing metadata into linked data sets are still evolving. It is an emergent field with a growing number of standards and open source tools for encoding, publishing, and retrieving linked data.

Linked data encompass all types of structured data that can be interlinked, published openly on the web, and searched through semantic queries. Increasingly, the concept is gaining attention in the library world because of its potential to address the limitations of the current metadata practices and to move library metadata from its storage silo in library systems and databases to the open web (Coyle, 2012; W3C, 2011). Singer (2009) describes problems with the quality of metadata and the isolation of library information systems in an article advocating for the adoption of linked data:

> We have silo sitting next to silo, with much duplication of data; arcane, inefficient, and sometimes completely broken methods of determining that two records are describing the same thing; and very little control over relating one resource in one system to another in a completely different application (even if these serve a similar purpose), much less data available outside the institution (p. 114).

While Singer's description may appear overly critical, it does point to a fundamental issue that remains largely unresolved despite significant efforts to improve interoperability, federated searching, and metadata harvesting. Library bibliographic and digital collection metadata, stored in separate databases, are poorly connected within the library information landscape. The separation of library systems from the open web represents an even more critical issue. The wealth of library metadata is not easily accessible to search engines requiring users to search individual catalogs, digital collections, and repositories. As the authors of *The Library Linked Data Incubator Group Final Report* note, although library databases do have searchable interfaces, library data are not integrated with web resources (W3C, 2011).

Metadata interoperability standards were developed to address the issues of resource discovery and sharing in the digital library field. The presence of multiple metadata standards and customized approaches, however, hinders interoperability and metadata harvesting in distributed environments. As Van Hooland and Verborgh (2014) point out, even if the institutions adopt metadata standards, they often implement them in a different way to accommodate the specific nature of their collections. Metadata harvesting also results in some information loss when rich metadata records are reduced to basic Dublin Core elements. The disadvantage of federated searching is the lack of granularity and the inability to support advanced queries. Lampert and Southwick (2013) note that aggregated collections "lose the richness of their original metadata when added to systems designed to enhance discovery," and cite this shortcoming as one of the reasons for embracing linked data (p. 236).

Discussions of linked data in library literature usually begin by pointing out the need for a new approach to metadata structuring and outlining the potential benefits of transforming library metadata into linked data (Alemu et al., 2012; Byrne and Goddard, 2010; Coyle, 2012; Lampert and Southwick, 2013; Mitchell, 2013a; Singer, 2009). The focus is primarily on breaking the walls surrounding library resources, exposing rich library metadata, and connecting them to related information on the web. Byrne and Goddard (2010) list a common format for all data in the linked data environment as one of the major benefits that can improve the interoperability and integration of library systems. Significant advantages of the linked data approach over current metadata practices for multiple library stakeholders are outlined in *The Library Linked Data Incubator Group Final Report* (W3C, 2011).

Exposing library metadata via the open web requires fundamental restructuring of data models and a radically different approach to recording metadata (Mitchell, 2013a; Van Hooland and Verborgh, 2014). The current metadata practices in the digital library field rely primarily on relational or XML data models with a central concept of a record governed by a schema. Metadata records, following the legacy of MARC, have a flat structure, in which all metadata statements about an object's properties (title, author, subject, etc.) are contained in a single record. Metadata schemas, such as Dublin Core or MODS, are more flexible and extensible than MARC; nonetheless they remain static, constrained by the concept of a record. Metadata sharing between different collections and domains requires the mapping of metadata elements and the adherence to a common schema. XML represents a significant step toward automatic sharing of data as it provides a standardized syntax for the exchange of structured data (Van Hooland and Verborgh, 2014). The sharing of XML-based metadata in practice, however, can be difficult because of the reliance on schema structures. RDF, the data model underlying linked data, offers greater flexibility since it moves away from a record structure and it doesn't require a schema to interpret and reuse data.

LINKED DATA MODEL AND TECHNOLOGIES

Linked data represent a radical shift in the way structured data can be created to express information about resources. Instead of a record-based model governed by a schema, it focuses on smaller chunks of meaningful metadata that can be linked and queried. In this environment, metadata statements, rather than records, represent a basic unit of metadata. This approach for structuring data is schema-neutral, but it does use a range of standardized vocabularies to define classes and properties of resources and the relationships between them (Van Hooland and Verborgh, 2014). RDF provides a data model for making simple statements and connecting them in a series. The process of developing or transforming existing metadata into linked data is based on a set of principles and relies on a number of technologies and tools. Mitchell (2013b) provides an overview of five building blocks of linked data:

1. RDF data model for structuring statements
2. Content rules
3. RDF-compatible metadata schemas and vocabularies
4. Serialization formats for encoding RDF statements
5. Technologies for publishing and exchanging linked data, including the SPARQL protocol

A full description of linked data technologies is outside of the scope of this chapter. The focus of the following section is primarily on the conceptual aspects of data modeling.

RDF provides a foundation for building linked data. It is an abstract data model used to express and interlink meaningful pieces of information and to represent them on the web. RDF offers a common framework in which information can be exchanged between applications without losing the meaning (Working Group, 2014). RDF statements are constructed as triples and consist of subjects, objects, and predicates. Any resource (subject) can have a relationship (predicate) to another resource (object). Resources can be conceptual, physical, or digital. Objects are used to express descriptions of resources (subjects), while predicates specify how the subjects and objects are related (Fig. 5.7 for a visual representation of an RDF triple). The model is flexible so that objects can become subjects in another series of statements. This simple syntax can be used to capture statements about resources. For example, for a digital image that shows a nomadic woman in Tibet (Fig. 5.8), several statements can be created, as demonstrated in Table 5.4.

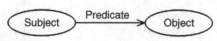

FIGURE 5.7 The Structure of an RDF Triple

FIGURE 5.8 Nomadic Tibetan Woman with Fur Hat in Tibetan Plateau

The Dublin Core metadata record available at: http://collections.lib.uwm.edu/cdm/ref/collection/tibet/id/1013.

Multiple statements, corresponding to the elements and their values in the metadata record, can be made about this image. The RDF statements also allow a more granular level of description. Another series of statements could be constructed about an original film negative to make a distinction between the analog image (physical object) and its digital representation, thus disambiguating what is being described. Moreover, the flexible nature of the RDF model allows expansion of relationships and their connections to external resources. For example, the photographer Harrison Forman is also the author of a book, *Through*

Table 5.4 Statements about a Digital Image of Nomadic Tibetan Woman, Digital ID fr203647		
Subject	**Predicate**	**Object**
Digital image fr203647	hasTitle	Nomadic Tibetan woman with fur hat in Tibetan Plateau
Digital image fr203647	hasCreator	Harrison Forman
Digital image fr203647	hasSubject	Nomads
Digital image fr203647	hasSubject	Tibet Autonomous Region (China)– Social life and customs

Table 5.5 Statements About a Book, *Through Forbidden Tibet*, LC Control Number 35025394

Subject	Predicate	Object
Book LCCN 35025394	hasTitle	*Through Forbidden Tibet: An Adventure into the Unknown*
Book LCCN 35025394	hasCreator	Harrison Forman
Book LCCN 35025394	hasSubject	Tibet Autonomous Region (China)– Social life and customs

Forbidden Tibet: An Adventure into the Unknown. Published in 1935, this book provides an account of Forman's travels through Tibet, as well as useful context for his photographic record. If a series of statements is constructed about the book *Through Forbidden Tibet,* the digital collection metadata and bibliographic data can be connected. Table 5.5 presents a sample of RDF statements about the book.

The digital image fr203647 and the book LCCN 35025394 can be linked through the RDF statements. The two resources can be further interconnected through a subject relationship: "Tibet Autonomous Region (China)—Social life and customs." RDF enables the creation of multiple statements about a resource. RDF triples are connected in a series of statements (serialization). Serialization is the process of expressing RDF triples/statements in a machine-processable syntax such as RDF-XML, Turtle, JSON-LD, etc. The RDF statements in Table 5.4 and Table 5.5 outline a few basic semantic relationships using natural language statements, but the real strength of linked data is in expressing the relationships through Uniform Resource Identifiers (URIs) so that the resources can be linked and queried on the web.

The URI identifies the name and/or location of a file or resource in a uniform format. The use of URIs for the identification of resources, their values, and relationships is part of the core principles of linked data formulated by Tim Berners-Lee (2006):

1. Use URIs as names for things
2. Use HTTP URIs so that people can look up those names
3. When someone looks up a URI, provide useful information, using the standards (RDF, SPARQL)
4. Include links to other URIs so that they can discover more things

The use of globally shared URIs is a fundamental concept of linked data. The URIs can be used to identify unambiguously any kind of object or concept. URI-based statements facilitate the building of complex relationships using external standards and vocabularies. Various linked open data vocabularies (LOVs) can be used as a source of URIs. It is recommended to reuse existing URIs available through linked data sources if possible (Bizer et al., 2009; Mitchell, 2013b; W3C, 2011). In some cases, URIs are locally assigned, for unique resources or locally controlled vocabulary terms (Lampert and Southwick, 2013; Southwick, 2015).

LOVs represent another major building block in the process of constructing and transforming existing metadata into linked data (Mitchell, 2013b). LOV is an umbrella term that encompasses a range of schemas and ontologies as well as value vocabularies. Ontologies are semantic models of the things, entities, or concepts that exist in a specific knowledge domain. The Web Ontology Language (OWL) is a full-fledged ontology language for developing ontologies and LOVs. The Resource Description Framework Schema (RDFS) is a basic level ontology language for defining relationships. Semantic Web data modeling standards such as OWL and RDFS share some similarities with traditional knowledge organization systems, but also differ from them in several fundamental respects, especially in that they are designed to allow for semantic querying and machine processing (Miller, 2015).

Schemas define classes and properties for linked data, while value vocabularies are a source of URIs for resources and their values. In the context of digital libraries many traditional metadata schemas and controlled vocabularies are being adopted for the linked data environment and transformed following the specifications provided by semantic data models, such as RDFS. A distinction can be made between:

- Metadata element sets published as RDF vocabularies. Several digital library metadata schemas have been defined as RDF vocabularies, with Dublin Core being the most frequently used. The Dublin Core Metadata Initiative (DCMI) has put significant efforts into adopting the Dublin Core Element Set for implementation in the linked data environment (DCMI, 2015b). All Dublin Core terms that conform to the DCMI Abstract Model are assigned a unique URI that provides a vocabulary for expressing relationships in RDF.
- Value vocabularies include authority files, taxonomies, subject headings, thesauri, and classification systems that have assigned unique URIs to their entries. A number of controlled vocabularies maintained by the Library of Congress and the Getty Research Institute have been made available in the linked data format (Library of Congress, 2015d; Getty Research Institute, 2015). Another example of a published linked data vocabulary is Virtual International Authority File (VIAF), developed as a collaborative project of several national libraries. DBpedia, one of the largest repositories of linked data vocabulary, was created by extracting structured information from Wikipedia (Dbpedia, 2015). Several cultural heritage institutions use Dbpedia as a source of vocabulary in their linked data projects (Pattuelli and Rubinow, 2013; Southwick, 2015).

As is the case with standard schemas and controlled vocabularies, a variety of linked open vocabularies are available, requiring the selection of appropriate tools during the implementation process. The example explored in this chapter demonstrates how several LOVs are used to assign URIs to statements. Table 5.6 shows several sets of RDF statements constructed for a digital image fr203647 and expressed as URIs, while Table 5.7 presents a set of triples for the book.

Table 5.6 Statements for a Digital Image fr203647 Expressed as URIs

Subject	Predicate	Object
http://collections.lib.uwm.edu/ ProvidedCHO/fr203647[a]	http://purl.org/dc/elements/1.1/title	Nomadic Tibetan woman with fur hat in Tibetan Plateau
http://collections.lib.uwm.edu/ ProvidedCHO/fr203647	http://purl.org/dc/elements/1.1/ creator	http://id.loc.gov/authorities/names/ n88172344
http://collections.lib.uwm.edu/ ProvidedCHO/fr203647	http://purl.org/dc/elements/1.1/ subject	http://id.loc.gov/vocabulary/ graphicMaterials/tgm007097
http://collections.lib.uwm.edu/ ProvidedCHO/fr203647	http://purl.org/dc/elements/1.1/ subject	http://id.loc.gov/authorities/subjects/ sh2008117270

[a]*The URI for the subject (digital image fr203647) is fictional since this object in the UWM Digital Collections does not have a persistent URI. The reference URL available for the object <http://collections.lib.uwm.edu/cdm/ref/collection/tibet/id/1013> is generated by CONTENTdm and is software dependent.*

Table 5.7 Statements about a Book, *Through Forbidden Tibet*, Expressed as URIs		
Subject	**Predicate**	**Object**
http://lccn.loc.gov/35025394	http://purl.org/dc/elements/1.1/title	*Through Forbidden Tibet: An Adventure into the Unknown*
http://lccn.loc.gov/35025394	http://purl.org/dc/elements/1.1/creator	http://id.loc.gov/authorities/names/n88172344
http://lccn.loc.gov/35025394	http://purl.org/dc/elements/1.1/subject	http://id.loc.gov/authorities/subjects/sh2008117270

The predicate terms (title, creator, and subject) have URIs assigned from the Dublin Core RDF-compatible vocabulary. The Library of Congress linked data sets: LC Authority File, Thesaurus for Graphic Materials, and LC Subject Headings are sources of URIs for creator and subject values. Title is the only element that has literal value because it is unique and does not belong to a controlled vocabulary.

Table 5.7 shows a sample of triples for Forman's book. The URI to represent this book uniquely (subject) is assigned by following the Library of Congress permalink. Again, title is the only element that has a literal value. The use of URIs for identifying resources uniquely, expressing relationships, and recording values, represents a significant departure from the digital library practices where so far metadata has been recorded as natural language descriptions and controlled vocabulary terms encoded as text.

The RDF data model and URIs provide a foundation for creating semantic relationships and constructing unambiguous links. An additional set of tools or "building blocks" is needed to encode and publish linked data sets so they can be processed by computers and rendered in formats usable and accessible to end users. Ultimately, linked data sets need to be presented through interfaces supporting semantic queries. RDF statements have to be encoded in a machine-readable syntax or serialization format in order to be stored and queried. It is beyond the scope of this chapter to review the rather complex stack of linked data technologies, but it is worth mentioning that several serialization formats are currently available. Mitchell (2013b) provides an overview of commonly used formats, including RDF/XML, RDF Notation-3/N3, Turtle, RDFa, and JSON-LD. Finally, a variety of tools is used to support the storage and exchange of linked data. SPARQL (SPARQL Protocol and RDF Query Language) is a W3C recommendation that provides a set of specifications to govern the query structure and a protocol for querying and exchanging data (Mitchell, 2013b).

LINKED DATA AND DIGITAL LIBRARIES

Linked data represent an emergent but rapidly growing area in digital library research and practice, with innovative and collaborative projects in the cultural heritage community. The emphasis of digital library efforts is on open data free of copyright restrictions with the term "linked open data" (LOD) frequently used in the library, archives, and museum (LAM) community. Although linked data technically do not need to be open in order to be interoperable, opening data increases the potential of linked data technology and makes data sharable and reusable (W3C, 2011). Opening data means providing the data freely, without copyright or other rights restrictions. LODLAM is an acronym for Linked Open

Data in Libraries, Archives, and Museums that refers to an informal network of scholars and practitioners engaged in the research and implementation of linked data technology in digital collections and repositories (LODLAM, 2015). The focus of digital library research and practice activities is on transforming library metadata into LOD and developing LOV.

In the context of digital libraries, adopting linked data requires a transformation of the existing schemas, controlled vocabulary tools, and record-based metadata sets into linked data formats. Although linked data represents a new approach to data modeling and recording metadata, it also builds upon the existing digital library schemas and vocabularies (Alemu et al., 2012; Yoose and Perkins, 2013). The foundational *Library Linked Data Incubator Group Final Report* (W3C, 2011) provides a set of recommendations for moving forward with the process of transforming library metadata into linked data. The key recommendations are:

- Identifying sets of data as possible candidates for early exposure as linked data and fostering a discussion about open data and rights
- Increasing library participation in Semantic Web standardization and developing library data standards that are compatible with linked data
- Creating URIs for the items in library datasets, developing policies for managing RDF vocabularies and their URIs, and expressing library data by reusing or mapping to existing linked data vocabularies
- Preserving linked data element sets and value vocabularies and applying library experience in the curating and long-term preservation of linked datasets

The authors of the Report recommend an incremental approach, noting that an effort to expose the complexity of library data as linked data all at once could be disruptive and "have limited success" (W3C, 2011, Section 4.1.1). However, some library tools, such as authority files, subject headings, and thesauri, lend themselves easily to publication as linked data. As mentioned before, several controlled vocabulary tools maintained by the Library of Congress and the Getty Research Institute have been released as LOVs in recent years (Library of Congress, 2015d; Getty Research Institute, 2015).

The transformation of metadata records in digital collections and repositories into linked data sets represents a major undertaking. Again, the process has been moving gradually from prototypes and research experiments into practical implementations. Linked data projects range from the national and large-scale digital library initiatives to smaller efforts undertaken by individual cultural heritage institutions. The number of publications and case studies documenting the process and sharing lessons in linked data development, although still limited, is growing (Hatop, 2013; Lampert and Southwick, 2013; Mitchell, 2013c; Pattuelli and Rubinow, 2013; Pattuelli et al., 2013; Southwick, 2015). Van Hooland and Verborgh (2014) provide a number of case studies in their book *Linked Data for Libraries, Archives and Museums*, while Yoose and Perkins (2013) review major LOD projects and initiatives undertaken in the library, archives, and museum communities, including SNAC (Social Networks and Archival Context Project), LOCAH (the Linked Open Copac and Archive Hub Project), and a linked data project at the Smithsonian American Art Museum. Europeana and the Digital Public Library of America (DPLA), two large-scale digital libraries and metadata aggregation platforms, are actively engaged in linked data by promoting open metadata and providing a range of linked open data resources and services (Mitchell, 2013c). Europeana and the DPLA are discussed in more detail in Chapter 1 and Chapter 11.

Several researchers stress that libraries are uniquely positioned to adopt linked data because of a strong tradition of standardization, the use of controlled vocabularies, and some experience in interoperability (Bair, 2013; Byrne and Goddard, 2010; Coyle, 2012). On the other hand, the use of library-specific standards, the disparity between the library and Semantic Web terminology, the lack of unique URIs for most library resources, and finally the complexity of linked data technology pose significant obstacles to a widespread adoption of linked data in the library world (Alemu et al., 2012; Byrne and Goddard, 2010; W3C, 2011). Byrne and Goddard (2010) note that most of the barriers are of a non-technical nature and identify the lack of awareness as a fundamental challenge for the development of linked data in libraries.

Metadata in digital libraries seems to be at a crossroads after two decades of intensive standardization and development. Linked open data offer an opportunity to integrate digital library objects with other library resources and make them more visible on the web but also requires a significant restructuring of existing metadata sets. The two models of record-based metadata and RDF-modeled linked data may coexist for a while in the digital library universe, but the current metadata practices can also be adopted in preparation for moving metadata into linked open data formats with closer attention to metadata quality, schema mapping, and a standardized assignment of unique URIs to digital library objects. As awareness in the professional community and practical experience in developing LOD increase, the body of linked metadata sets will grow, transcending the barriers between the current digital library systems and the open web.

REFERENCES

Abbas, J., 2005. Creating metadata for children's resources: issues, research, and current developments. Lib. Trends 54 (2), 303–317.

Alemu, G., Stevens, B., Ross, P., 2012. Towards a conceptual framework for user-driven semantic metadata interoperability in digital libraries: a social constructivist approach. New Lib. World 113 (112), 38–54.

Alemu, G., Stevens, B., Ross, P., Chandler, J., 2012. Linked data for libraries: benefits of a conceptual shift from library-specific record structures to RDF-based data models. New Lib. World 113 (11/12), 549–570.

ANSI/NISO, 2005. American National Standards Organization (ANSI) and National Information Standards Organization (NISO). ANSI/NISO Z39.19-2005 (R2010). Guidelines for the Construction, Format, and Management of Monolingual Controlled Vocabularies. Available from: http://www.niso.org/apps/group_public/download.php/12591/z39-19-2005r2010.pdf.

Arms, W.Y., Hillmann, D., Lagoze, C., Krafft, D., Marisa, R., Saylor, J., Van de Sompel, H., 2002. A spectrum of interoperability: the site for science prototype for the NSDL. D-Lib Magazine, 8 (1), 9. Available from: http://www.dlib.org/dlib/january02/arms/01arms.html.

Attig, J., Copeland, A., Pelikan, M., 2004. Context and meaning: the challenges of metadata for a digital image library within the university. Coll. Res. Lib. 65 (3), 251–261.

Baca, M., Harpring, P., 2009; revised 2014. Categories for the Description of Works of Art. J. Paul Getty Trust College Art Association. Available from: http://www.getty.edu/research/publications/electronic_publications/cdwa/index.html.

Baca, M., 2008. Glossary. In: Baca, M. (Ed.), Introduction to Metadata. The Getty Research Institute, Los Angeles (CA), pp. 73–78.

Bainbridge, D., Twidale, M.B., Nichols, D.M., 2012. Interactive context-aware user-driven metadata correction in digital libraries. Int. J. Digital Lib. 13 (1), 17–32.

Bair, S., 2013. Linked data—the right time? J. Lib. Metadata 13 (2–3), 75–79.

Barbero, G., Trasselli, F., 2014. Manus OnLine and the Text Encoding Initiative Schema. J. Text Encoding Init., (8-Preview). Available from: http://jtei.revues.org/1054.

Bar-Ilan, J., Shoham, S., Idan, A., Miller, Y., Shachak, A., 2008. Structured versus unstructured tagging: a case study. Online Inform. Rev. 32 (5), 635–647.

Beißwenger, M., Ermakova, M., Geyken, A., Lemnitzer, L., Storrer, A., 2012. A TEI Schema for the representation of computer-mediated communication. J. Text Encoding Init. (3). Available from: http://jtei.revues.org/476.

Benoit, E.A., 2014. MPLP: A comparison of domain novice and expert user-generated tags in a minimally processed digital archive (Doctoral dissertation). Available from: http://dc.uwm.edu/cgi/viewcontent.cgi?article=1555&context=etd.

Berners-Lee, T., 2006. Linked data. Available from: http://www.w3.org/DesignIssues/LinkedData.html.

Berners-Lee, T., Hendler, J., Lassila, O., 2001. The semantic web. Sci. Am. 284 (5), 28–37.

Bizer, C., Heath, T., Berners-Lee, T., 2009. Linked data-the story so far. Int. J. Semant. Web Inf. Syst. 5 (3), 1–22.

Byrne, G., Goddard, L., 2010. The strongest link: libraries and linked data. D-Lib Mag. 16(11/12). Available from: http://www.dlib.org/dlib/november10/byrne/11byrne.print.html.

Cantara, L., 2005. METS: the metadata encoding and transmission standard. CCQ 40 (3–4), 237–253.

CDP Metadata Working Group, 2006. Dublin Core Metadata Best Practices. Version 2.1.1. Available from: http://sustainableheritagenetwork.org/system/files/atoms/file/CDPDublinCoreBPs_0.pdf.

Chan, L.M., Childress, E., Dean, R., O'Neill, E.T., Vizine-Goetz, D., 2001. A faceted approach to subject data in the Dublin Core metadata record. J. Internet Cataloging 4 (1–2), 35–47.

Chopey, M.A., 2005. Planning and implementing a metadata-driven digital repository. CCQ 40 (3/4), 255–287.

Chuttur, M.Y., 2014. Investigating the effect of definitions and best practice guidelines on errors in Dublin Core metadata records. J. Inform. Sci. 40 (1), 28–37.

Clark, J.R., 2008. The Internet connection: Web 2.0, Flickr and endless possibilities. Behav. Soc. Sci. Librar. 27 (1), 62–64.

Coyle, K., 2012. Linked data tools: connecting on the Web. Lib. Technol. Rep. 48, 1–45.

Cummings, J., 2008. The text encoding initiative and the study of literature. A Companion to Digital Literary Studies. Blackwell, Oxford, pp. 451–476.

Cundiff, M.V., 2004. An introduction to the metadata encoding and transmission standard (METS). Lib. Hi Tech. 22 (1), 52–64.

DBpedia., 2015. About. Available from: http://wiki.dbpedia.org/.

DCMI: Dublin Core Metadata Initiative, 2015a. DCMI metadata terms. Available from: http://dublincore.org/documents/dcmi-terms/#H1.

DCMI: Dublin Core Metadata Initiative, 2015b. Metadata basics. Available from: http://dublincore.org/metadata-basics/.

DeRidder, J., Presnell, A., Walker, K., 2012. Leveraging encoded archival description for access to digital content: a cost and usability analysis. Am. Arch. 75 (1), 143–170.

Dillon, M., Jul, E., 1996. Cataloging Internet resources: the convergence of libraries and Internet resources. CCQ 22 (3–4), 197–238.

Ding, Y., Jacob, E.K., Zhang, Z., Foo, S., Yan, E., George, N.L., Guo, L., 2009. Perspectives on social tagging. J. Am. Soc. Inf. Sci. Technol. 60 (12), 2388–2401.

Dulock, M., 2012. Report of the ALCTS metadata interest group meeting, American Library Association Midwinter Meeting, Dallas, January 2012. Tech. Serv. Q. 29(4), 312–317.

Dulock, M., Long, H., 2011. The conference on world affairs archive online: digitization and metadata for a digital audio pilot. D-Lib Mag. 17(3), 3. Available from: http://www.dlib.org/dlib/march11/dulock/03dulock.html.

Duval, E., Hodgins, W., Sutton, S., Weibel, S.L., 2002. Metadata principles and practicalities. D-Lib Mag. 8(4), 16. Available from: http://www.dlib.org/dlib/april02/weibel/04weibel.html.

Elings, M.W., Waibel, G., 2007. Metadata for all: descriptive standards and metadata sharing across libraries, archives and museums. First Monday 12(3). Available from: http://firstmonday.org/article/view/1628/1543.

Eustis, J.M., 2013. Tech services on the Web. Tech. Serv. Q. 30 (4), 441–442.

Flickr: The Commons, 2015. Participating institutions. Available from: https://www.flickr.com/commons.

Foulonneau, M., Riley, J., 2008. Metadata for Digital Resources: Implementation, Systems Design and Interoperability. Chandos Publishing, Oxford.

Getty Research Institute, 2014. Metadata standards crosswalk. Available from: http://www.getty.edu/research/publications/electronic_publications/intrometadata/crosswalks.html.

Getty Research Institute, 2015. Getty vocabularies as linked open data. Available from: http://www.getty.edu/research/tools/vocabularies/lod/.

Gilliland, A., 2008. Setting the stage. In: Baca, M. (Ed.), Introduction to Metadata (1–19). The Getty Research Institute, Los Angeles (CA).

Gilliland-Swetland, A.J., 1998. An exploration of K-12 user needs for digital primary source materials. Am. Arch. 61 (1), 136–157.

Guenther, R.S., 2003. MODS: the metadata object description schema. Portal Lib. Acad. 3 (1), 137–150.

Guenther, R.S., 2004. Using the metadata object description schema (MODS) for resource description: guidelines and applications. Lib. Hi Tech. 22 (1), 89–98.

Guy, M., Tonkin, E., 2006. Tidying up tags. D-Lib Mag. 12 (1). Available from: http://webdoc.sub.gwdg.de/edoc/aw/d-lib/dlib/january06/guy/01guy.html.

Hammond, T., Hannay, T., Lund, B., Scott, J., 2005. Social bookmarking tools (I) a general review. D-Lib Mag. 2 (4). Available from: http://www.dlib.org/dlib/april05/hammond/04hammond.html.

Hatop, G., 2013. Integrating linked data into discovery. Code4Lib J. 21, 67–90. Available from: http://journal.code4lib.org/articles/8526?utm_source=rss&utm_medium=rss&utm_campaign=integrating-linked-data-into-discovery.

Hedden, H., 2008. Controlled vocabularies, thesauri, and taxonomies. Indexer 26 (1), 33–34.

Hillmann, D.I., 2008. Metadata quality: from evaluation to augmentation. CCQ 46 (1), 65–80.

Huang, H., Jörgensen, C., 2013. Characterizing user tagging and co-occurring metadata in general and specialized metadata collections. J. Am. Soc. Inf. Sci. Technol. 64 (9), 1878–1889.

Jeong, W., 2009. Is tagging effective?–overlapping ratios with other metadata fields. In: International Conference on Dublin Core and Metadata Applications, Seoul, Korea, 12–16 October, pp. 31–39.

Kennedy, M.R., 2008. Nine questions to guide you in choosing a metadata schema. J. Digital Inf. 9 (1).

Kipp, M.E., 2011. Controlled vocabularies and tags: an analysis of research methods. NASKO 3 (1), 23–32.

Kucsma, J., Reiss, K., Sidman, A., 2010. Using Omeka to build digital collections: the METRO case study. D-Lib Mag. 16 (3/4). Available from: http://www.dlib.org/dlib/march10/kucsma/03kucsma.html.

Kurtz, M., 2013. Dublin Core, DSpace, and a brief analysis of three university repositories. Inf. Technol. Lib. 29 (1), 40–46.

Lagoze, C., Lynch, C.A., Daniel Jr, R., 1996. The Warwick Framework: a container architecture for aggregating sets of metadata. Cornell University, Ithaca, NY. Available from: https://ecommons.cornell.edu/handle/1813/7248.

Lampert, C.K., Southwick, S.B., 2013. Leading to linking: introducing linked data to academic library digital collections. J. Lib. Metadata 13 (2–3), 230–253.

Lange, H.R., Winkler, B.J., 1997. Taming the Internet. Advances in Librarianship, Vol. 21. Emerald Group Publishing Limited, Bingley, UK, 21, 47–72.

Laursen, D., Christiansen, K.F., Olsen, L.L., 2012. Management of metadata for digital heritage collections. Microform Digit. Rev. 41 (3/4), 151–158.

Leise, F., 2008. Controlled vocabularies, an introduction. Indexer 26 (3), 121–126.

Library of Congress, 2011a. MIX (NISO Metadata for Images in XML). Available from: http://www.loc.gov/standards/mix//.

Library of Congress, 2011b. AudioMD and VideoMD—Technical metadata for audio and video. Available from: http://www.loc.gov/standards/amdvmd/index.html.

Library of Congress, 2013. EAD: Encoded Archival Description. Version 2002. Available from: http://www.loc.gov/ead/.

Library of Congress, 2014a. MODS User Guidelines version 3. Available from: http://www.loc.gov/standards/mods/userguide/.

Library of Congress, 2014b. VRA Core. Available from: http://www.loc.gov/standards/vracore/.

Library of Congress, 2015a. Metadata Object Description Schema (MODS). Available from: http://www.loc.gov/standards/mods/.

Library of Congress, 2015b. METS: Metadata Encoding and Transmission Standard. Available from: http://www.loc.gov/standards/mets/.

Library of Congress, 2015c. Metadata Object Description Schema (MODS). Conversion. Available from: http://www.loc.gov/standards/mods/mods-conversions.html.

Library of Congress, 2015d. LC linked data service: authorities and vocabularies. Available from: http://id.loc.gov/.

LODLAM: Linked open data in libraries, archives, and museums, 2015. About. Available from: http://lodlam.net/about/.

Lopatin, L., 2010. Metadata practices in academic and non-academic libraries for digital projects: a survey. CCQ 48 (8), 716–742.

Lu, C., Park, J.R., Hu, X., 2010. User tags versus expert-assigned subject terms: a comparison of LibraryThing tags and Library of Congress Subject Headings. J. Inf. Sci. 36 (6), 763–779.

Macgregor, G., McCulloch, E., 2006. Collaborative tagging as a knowledge organisation and resource discovery tool. Lib. Rev. 55 (5), 291–300.

Matusiak, K.K., 2006. Towards user-centered indexing in digital image collections. OCLC Syst. Serv. Int. Digital Lib. Persp. 22 (4), 283–298.

Matusiak, K.K., Johnston, T., 2014. Digitization for preservation and access: restoring the usefulness of the nitrate negative collections at the American Geographical Society Library. Am. Arch. 77 (1), 241–269.

McCallum, S.H., 2004. An introduction to the Metadata Object Description Schema (MODS). Lib. Hi Tech. 22 (1), 82–88.

McCrory, A., Russell, B.M., 2013. Crosswalking EAD: collaboration in archival description. Inf. Technol. Lib. 24 (3), 99–106.

McDonough, J.P., 2006. METS: standardized encoding for digital library objects. Int. J. Digital Lib. 6 (2), 148–158.

Merholz, P., 2004. Metadata for the masses. Available from: http://www.adaptivepath.com/ideas/e000361/.

Miller, S.J., 2011. Metadata for Digital Collections: A how-to-do-it Manual. Neal-Schuman Publishers, New York, N.Y.

Miller, S.J., 2015. Ontologies for semantic applications. In: Smiraglia, R., Lee, H.L. (Eds.), Ontology for Knowledge Organization. Ergon Verlag, Wurzburg, Germany, pp. 87–106.

Mitchell, E.T., 2013a. Metadata developments in libraries and other cultural heritage institutions. Lib. Technol. Rep. 49 (5), 5–10.

Mitchell, E.T., 2013b. Building blocks of linked open data in libraries. Lib. Technol. Rep. 49 (5), 11–25.

Mitchell, E.T., 2013c. Three case studies in linked open data. Lib. Technol. Rep. 49 (5), 26–43.

Mixter, J., 2014. Using a common model: mapping VRA Core 4.0 into an RDF ontology. J. Lib. Metadata 14 (1), 1–23.

Moulaison, H.L., Dykas, F., Gallant, K., 2015. OpenDOAR repositories and metadata practices. D-Lib Mag., 21 (3/4), 1. Available from: http://www.dlib.org/dlib/march15/moulaison/03moulaison.html.

NISO, Framework Working Group, 2007. A Framework of Guidance for Building Good Digital Collections, 3rd ed. Available from: http://www.niso.org/publications/rp/framework3.pdf.

NISO National Information Standards Organization, 2004. Understanding Metadata. http://www.niso.org/publications/press/UnderstandingMetadata.pdf.

Niu, J., 2013. Hierarchical relationships in the bibliographic universe. CCQ 51 (5), 473–490.

OAI: Open Archives Initiative, 2015. Standards for web content interoperability. Available from: https://www.openarchives.org/.

Ore, C.E., Eide, Ø., 2009. TEI and cultural heritage ontologies: exchange of information? Lit. Ling. Comp. 24 (2), 161–172.

Palmer, C.L., Zavalina, O.L., Mustafoff, M., 2007. Trends in metadata practices: a longitudinal study of collection federation. In: Proceedings of the Seventh ACM/IEEE-CS Joint Conference on Digital Libraries. ACM, pp. 386–395.

Park, J.R., 2009. Metadata quality in digital repositories: a survey of the current state of the art. CCQ 47 (3–4), 213–228.

Park, J.-R., Tosaka's, Y., 2010. Metadata creation practices in digital repositories and collections: schemata, selection criteria, and interoperability. Inf. Technol. Lib. 29 (3), 104–116.

Pattuelli, C., Rubinow, S., 2013. The knowledge organization of DBpedia: a case study. J. Document. 69 (6), 762–772.

Pattuelli, M.C., Miller, M., Lange, L., Fitzell, S., Li-Madeo, C., 2013. Crafting linked open data for cultural heritage: mapping and curation tools for the linked jazz project. Code4Lib J. 21.

Petek, M., 2012. Comparing user-generated and librarian-generated metadata on digital images. OCLC Syst. Serv. Int. Digital Lib. Persp. 28 (2), 101–111.

Pirmann, C., 2012. Tags in the catalogue: insights from a usability study of LibraryThing for libraries. Lib. Trends 61 (1), 234–247.

Ransom, N., Rafferty, P., 2011. Facets of user-assigned tags and their effectiveness in image retrieval. J. Document. 67 (6), 1038–1066.

Rorissa, A., 2010. A comparative study of Flickr tags and index terms in a general image collection. J. Am. Soc. Inf. Sci. Technol. 61 (11), 2230–2242.

Singer, R., 2009. Linked library data now! J. Electron. Res. Librar. 21 (2), 114–126.

Southwick, S.B., 2015. A guide for transforming digital collections metadata into linked data using open source technologies. J. Lib. Metadata 15 (1), 1–35.

Sperberg-McQueen, C.M., 1996. Textual criticism and the text encoding initiative. In: Finneran, R.J. (Ed.), The Literary Text in the Digital Age. University of Michigan Press, Ann Arbor, MI, pp. 37–61.

Sperberg-McQueen, C.M., Burnard, L., 1994. A gentle introduction to SGML. In: Guidelines for Electronic Text Encoding and Interchange. TEI Working Committees. University of Michigan Libraries, Chapter 2. Available from: http://quod.lib.umich.edu/t/tei/

Taylor, A.G., Joudrey, D.N., 2008. The Organization of Information. Westport, CT: Libraries Unlimited.

TEI Consortium, 2015. TEI P5: Guidelines for Electronic Text Encoding and Interchange. Available from: http://www.tei-c.org/release/doc/tei-p5-doc/en/Guidelines.pdf.

Thomas, M., Caudle, D.M., Schmitz, C., 2010. Trashy tags: problematic tags in LibraryThing. New Lib. World 111 (5/6), 223–235.

Thomas, M., Caudle, D.M., Schmitz, C.M., 2009. To tag or not to tag? Lib. Hi Tech. 27 (3), 411–434.

Trant, J., 2009. Tagging, folksonomy and art museums: early experiments and ongoing research. J. Digital Inf. 10 (1.).

Van Assem, M., Van Ossenbruggen, J., Schreiber, G., 2010. The VRA core application profile for searching and presenting cultural heritage: the MultimediaN case. In: Proceedings of the International Conference on Dublin Core and Metadata Applications, Pittsburgh, PA, USA.

Van Hooland, S., Verborgh, R., 2014. Linked Data for Libraries, Archives and Museums: How to Clean, Link and Publish Your Metadata. Neal-Schuman, Chicago.

Vanhoutte, E., 2004. An introduction to the TEI and the TEI Consortium. Lit. Ling. Comp. 19 (1), 9–16.

Vellucci, S.L., 1998. Metadata. Annual Review of Information Science and Technology (ARIST), 33, 187–222.

Visual Resources Association, 2007. VRA Core 4.0 element description. Available from: https://www.loc.gov/standards/vracore/VRA_Core4_Element_Description.pdf.

W3C RDF Working Group, 2014. RDF 1.1 Primer. Available from: http://www.w3.org/TR/rdf11-primer/.

W3C: World Wide Web Consortium, 2011. Library Linked Data Incubator Group Final Report. Available from: http://www.w3.org/2005/Incubator/lld/XGR-lld-20111025/.

W3C: World Wide Web Consortium, 2015a. Semantic Web. Available from: http://www.w3.org/standards/semanticweb/.

W3C: World Wide Web Consortium, 2015b. Linked Data. Available from: http://www.w3.org/standards/semanticweb/data.

Weibel, S.L., Koch, T., 2000. The Dublin core metadata initiative. D-Lib Mag. 6 (12), Available from: http://mirror.dlib.org/dlib/december00/weibel/12weibel.html.

Wisneski, R., Dressler, V., 2009. Implementing TEI projects and accompanying metadata for small libraries: rationale and best practices. J. Lib. Metadata 9 (3–4), 264–288.

Woodley, M.S., 2008. Crosswalks, metadata harvesting, federated searching, metasearching: using metadata to connect uses and information. In: Baca, M. (Ed.), Introduction to Metadata. The Getty Research Institute, Los Angeles (CA), pp. 38–62.

Yaco, S., 2008. It's complicated: barriers to EAD implementation. Am. Arch. 71 (2), 456–475.

Yakel, E., 2004. Encoded archival description: are finding aids boundary spanners or barriers for users? J. Arch. Org. 2 (1–2), 63–77.

Yakel, E., Kim, J., 2005. Adoption and diffusion of Encoded Archival Description. J. Am. Soc. Inf. Sci. Technol. 56 (13), 1427–1437.

Yoose, B., Perkins, J., 2013. The linked open data landscape in libraries and beyond. J. Lib. Metadata 13 (2–3), 197–211.

Zeng, M.L., Qin, J., 2008. Metadata. Neal-Schuman Publishers, New York, NY.

DIGITAL LIBRARY MANAGEMENT SYSTEMS

INTRODUCTION

The design of systems for management and delivery of digital library content is an interdisciplinary area where research on digital libraries intersects with software development, database management, information retrieval, and human-computer interaction. Digital library management systems (DLMS) share some similarities with web content management systems but are also different because of the required support for digital library standards, especially in regard to information organization and interoperability. DLMS represent a specialized category of software systems that integrate functionality for building, managing, storing, providing access to, and preserving digital objects and collections. They are part of a broader category of digital asset management systems that are used in practice for acquisition, indexing, storage, management, preservation, and delivery of digital objects. In a distributed digital library environment, DLMS also provide platforms for aggregating digital content and metadata.

The concept of DLMS is used here according to the definition proposed in the DELOS Manifesto as "a generic software system that provides the appropriate software infrastructure both to produce and administer a Digital Library System incorporating the suite of functionality considered foundational for Digital Libraries and to integrate additional software offering more refined, specialized, or advanced functionality" (Candela et al., 2007b). The DELOS Manifesto makes a distinction between a digital library system (DLS) and a DLMS. A DLS offers functionality for a particular digital library, including support for end user interactions. A DLMS provides a platform for producing and administering digital collections and services by ensuring essential functionality and incorporating additional software components for more refined and advanced features (Tramboo et al., 2012). DLMS enable an instantiation and management of digital collections and services that become part of a centralized or distributed DLS.

The design of DLMS has been an area of active development since the early days of digital libraries and has included efforts to provide conceptual models as well as platform solutions. Many of the early systems were custom-built, designed for single projects in order to meet the needs of a particular community (Suleman and Fox, 2001). The late 1990s saw the development of the first architectural models for repositories and the emergence of the dedicated content management systems for cultural heritage digital collections. Greenstone was released as open source software and has been widely adopted throughout the world. CONTENTdm became a popular choice in the category of proprietary software among the US public and academic libraries. Early 2000s marked the construction of the first digital repositories for scholarly publication with EPrints developed at the University of Southampton, UK, and DSpace and Fedora released in the United States. Currently, there are number of open source systems and commercial software packages available for building digital library systems and meeting the needs and requirements of specific communities. Many organizations, however, especially those building large-scale systems such as Europeana, HathiTrust, or National Science Digital Library (NSDL) have developed custom platforms (Concordia et al., 2010; Henry, 2012). In recent years, libraries and archives have been migrating from the first generation of open source or proprietary software, such as DSpace or CONTENTdm toward more robust and scalable open source solutions (Gilbert and Mobley, 2013; Stein and Thompson, 2015). The new generation of DLMS is comprised of several open source technologies and often integrate Fedora with other customizable platforms, such as Hydra and Islandora (Awre and Cramer, 2012; Cramer and Kott, 2010; Moses and Stapelfeldt, 2013).

The terminology of DLMS and DLS is used according to the DELOS Manifesto (Candela et al., 2007b). However, it is important to note that other terms are also used for DLMS, including digital content management systems (Han, 2004), digital collection management systems (Zhang and Gourley, 2009), repository platforms (Henry, 2012), or digital asset management systems (Breeding, 2013, 2015; Kaplan, 2009; Stein and Thompson, 2015). The term "digital asset management system" is being used widely and often interchangeably with DLMS. In practice, its usage is broad and often encompasses a wide range of software, including digital collection systems (e.g., CONTENTdm, Omeka), repositories (e.g., DSpace, Fedora, Digital Commons), digital preservation systems (e.g., Rosetta, Preservica), discovery layers (e.g., Blacklight), or even databases, such as FileMaker Pro (Stein and Thompson, 2015).

This chapter presents both theoretical and practical perspectives on developing and implementing DLMS. The focus of the review is primarily on software systems designated for building and managing digital objects and collections and on multifunctional open source repository systems. Digital repositories designed for providing long-term preservation of digital content are covered in the chapter on digital preservation (Chapter 9). This distinction is not always clear as increasingly new systems are designed to meet both preservation and access needs. The second generation of DLMS addresses the challenge of maintaining separate systems for access and preservation and offers multipurpose repository systems (Awre, 2012; Awre and Cramer, 2012; Cramer and Kott, 2010).

DESIGN AND ARCHITECTURE OF DIGITAL LIBRARY SYSTEMS

The complexity of DLS as information systems is widely acknowledged (Candela et al., 2007b; Chowdhury and Chowdhury, 2003; Concordia et al., 2010; Henry, 2012). DLS serve diverse groups of users from scientific, educational, archives, and museum communities. They provide access to scholarly publications, data sets, archival documents, and cultural heritage objects in multiple formats and languages that are described by a variety of metadata standards. Obviously, there is no single, universal software system that could meet the needs of all user communities and support the variety of data types and metadata schemas. In addition to user requirements and functionality, the design of a DLMS has to address the technical aspects of system reliability, scalability, and sustainability. Most digital libraries are created independently by content holders in research, library, archives, and museum communities using a range of standards and software solutions. Interoperability has become one of the most important issues in the development of digital libraries. The goal of interoperability is to enable the exchange of data between independent digital libraries and to provide services for easier discovery and interaction with digital library resources in the network environment (Arms et al., 2002).

The initial systems were often built "from scratch" or incorporated existing software components but offered limited modularity and interoperability. Early DLMS were standalone systems and had typical features of the system-centered design, which meant they were difficult to install, customize, or configure (Ioannidis et al., 2005). Some researchers argue that the lack of common definitions and conceptual frameworks led to such ad hoc system development and hindered interoperability (Candela et al., 2010; Gonçalves et al., 2008).

The large-scale digital libraries that have emerged in recent years pose new challenges for interoperability and system reliability, scalability, and sustainability (Henry, 2012). The aggregation of content and services can take place on consortial, regional, national, or international levels. These large-scale digital library systems are built either as centralized aggregators of content, metadata, and services or use a distributed network of content and service hubs with a service layer to facilitate access to harvested metadata and links to objects. HathiTrust is an example of a centralized model, while Europeana, the Digital Library of America, and the National Science Digital Library represent large-scale distributed systems.

The first two decades of digital library research efforts have concentrated on defining the components of digital library systems, delineating the relationships among them, and developing conceptual models that would enable interoperation between individual DLS. This section provides an overview of the research surrounding digital library architectural models, reviews functionality and other system requirements, and discusses interoperability approaches.

ARCHITECTURAL MODELS

The concept of architecture in the context of digital library systems refers to "a consistent and comprehensive set of software components necessary for a DLS and the interaction between them" (Candela et al., 2007a, p. 23). An architectural model serves as a starting point and a conceptual framework for designing flexible and interoperable systems. It is an abstract framework for identifying components and describing the relationships among them, usually independent of specific standards, technology, and implementations. The goal of an architectural model is to provide a set of common basic elements and to serve as a blueprint for an integration of subelements supporting specialized functionality (Candela et al., 2007a).

The research community has proposed several models of digital library architecture of various levels of complexity. Three core components can be identified across the frameworks, although the names of the components often vary (Candela et al., 2010; Suleman, 2012):

- Data store (also referred to as content files, data repository, or archive)
- Metadata registry (also referred to as metadata catalog, metadata store, or index)
- A set of services (e.g., index, store, manage, copy, authorize, etc.)

The separation of digital content from the structured information describing it (metadata) is a fundamental principle of digital library architectural models. A data store contains digital content files in a variety of formats and structures, such as images, audio, text files, or complex structures consisting of multiple files. A metadata registry includes associated metadata to identify stored content files and to provide information about their properties and context. The two components represent the system's repository and interact with each other through a range of services, such as submit, index, store, manage, copy, authorize, retrieve, import, export, etc. This generic model identifies only the core components and services to assure basic digital library functionality. The core components can have subcomponents that provide specialized functionality. For example, metadata store can include a selection of controlled vocabulary tools and metadata schemas. Models of open, component-based architecture provide a framework for creating and managing large distributed digital libraries.

The foundational research on architecture of digital library systems took place in the mid-1990s. In their seminal work, (Kahn and Wilensky, 2006) propose a reference model of open architecture that envisions an interoperation of multiple repositories and supports distributed digital information services. They define the concepts of digital objects, unique identifiers (handles), and repositories, and specify the method for depositing and accessing digital objects in repositories. Based on the work of Kahn and Wilensky, Arms (1995) outlines general principles and elements of digital library architecture, including the separation of the underlying architecture from the content stored in the library, names and identifiers as building blocks of digital libraries, and the concepts of digital objects and repositories.

Researchers at the Cornell Digital Library Research Group have advanced the concepts of open architecture through the development of a protocol for distributed document libraries (Dienst) and a component-based digital library architecture called CRADDL—Cornell Reference Architecture for Distributed Digital Libraries (Davis and Lagoze, 2000; Lagoze and Fielding, 1998). CRADDL identifies a set of core components of a digital library infrastructure, such as repository, index, naming, collection, and defines the interactions between them (Lagoze and Fielding, 1998). The functionality of CRADDL is defined in terms of five core services:

- The repository service that provides the mechanism for the deposit, storage, and access to digital objects
- The naming service that provides a registry of unique names for identifying digital objects
- The index service that includes information about digital objects or sets and the mechanism for their discovery via query
- The collection service that provides a method of aggregating digital objects and services into meaningful collections
- User interface services or gateways that provide entry points for collection creators and administrators to build and manage collections and for end users to search and access objects in collections

Lagoze and Fielding (1998) highlight the open architecture of this model, and note that other services can be added to enhance the core functions. The authors focus on the collection services, selection criteria, and specifications for administering collections and the dynamic nature of collections that allows for the possibility of a single object to belong to multiple collections.

The introduction of the Open Archives Initiative Protocol for Metadata Harvesting (OAI-PMH) has presented new possibilities for the interoperation among standalone digital library systems and prompted the development of new architectural models. Using OAI-PMH as a foundation, Suleman and Fox (2001) propose a framework for building open digital libraries. The model combines the capabilities of OAI-PMH as a protocol to transfer metadata with the concept of extended services and local open archives as self-contained but interoperable components. Open digital libraries are envisioned as a network of components or building blocks (open archives) with data providers sharing metadata through a union catalog and providing extended services through a common interface, such as search, browse, and recommend. The researchers provide examples of successful implementation of this model, including the Networked Digital Library Theses and Dissertations project at Virginia Tech (Suleman et al., 2003).

The component-oriented approach is proposed for large-scale digital libraries serving more than one community and whose requirements may evolve over time. The Digital Library System Reference Architecture was developed by the DELOS Network of Excellence on Digital Libraries to provide a framework for cooperative and distributed development of European digital library systems. This model presents digital library architecture as a modular and flexible structure of components and layers (Candela et al., 2007a). It identifies the core components and their subsystems; for example, the information component consists of subcomponents of data files (Archive), metadata, and controlled vocabulary tools, such as thesauri and ontology. The layers organize the components according to functionality. This model assumes easy design through component selection and replacement, sharing and reuse of components in different contexts, distributed installation and maintenance, and easy support for component modification or addition. The proposed reference model, although designed specifically for the digital library community, utilizes many concepts from computing and demonstrates that digital library system design is truly an interdisciplinary endeavor.

The design of digital library systems has been informed by architectural models in computing, especially service-oriented architecture (SOA) (Henry, 2012; Suleman, 2005, 2012). SOA is a relatively new model of software construction where tasks and services are subdivided and performed by independent components that interact with each other through standard interfaces and communication protocols (Suleman, 2005). SOA supports reusability, subtraction, and substitution of components and services and offers a potential for the development of evolving and expanding digital library systems. Suleman (2005), however, notes that, as of 2005, very few open source systems, including Greenstone, EPrints, or DSpace, applied SOA design principles.

Fedora (Flexible Extensible Digital Object Repository Architecture) represents a reference model for DLMS that is based on SOA. Fedora was originally developed by researchers at Cornell University as an architecture framework for storing, managing, and accessing digital content (Payette and Lagoze, 1998; Payette et al., 1999). Fedora's open architectural model was inspired by Kahn and Wilensky's work on digital objects. The concept of a digital object is a fundamental block of Fedora's architecture. Its object model supports many kinds of digital content including documents, images, e-books, multimedia learning objects, datasets, and other complex objects (Lagoze et al., 2006; Payette and Lagoze, 1998). In addition to defining digital objects, Fedora also provides a theoretical foundation for repository architecture focusing on extensibility and interoperability. Payette and Lagoze (1998) outline the key features of the architecture:

- Support for heterogeneous data types
- Accommodation of new types as they emerge
- Aggregation of mixed, possibly distributed, data into complex objects
- The ability to specify multiple content disseminations of these objects
- The ability to associate rights management schemes with these disseminations (Payette and Lagoze, 1998)

The Fedora reference model also identifies a set of core functions, including (1) repository services for depositing, storing, and accessing digital objects; (2) index services for discovering digital objects; (3) collection services that provide the means of aggregating sets of digital objects and services into meaningful collections; (4) naming services that register and resolve globally unique, persistent names for digital objects; and (5) user interface services that provide a human gateway into the other services

(Payette and Lagoze, 1998). Fedora offers a highly flexible architecture of relationships among digital objects and an ability to extend its components and integrate new services.

The prototype digital library system using the Fedora architecture was built in 2000 at the University of Virginia Library (Staples et al., 2003). The first version of Fedora open source software (Fedora 1.0) was released to the public in 2003. Since then, Fedora has been adopted by more than three hundred institutions worldwide (Fedora, 2015). Because of its open and flexible architecture, Fedora is used as a framework for a variety of digital library systems, including digital collections, institutional repositories, digital preservation systems, and large-scale distributed digital library networks. Fedora provides a foundation for the new generation of multifunctional platforms, including those built with Hydra or Islandora (Awre and Cramer, 2012; Cramer and Kott, 2010; Jettka and Stein, 2014; Kent, 2014; Moses and Stapelfeldt, 2013). Fedora, as an open source software, is supported by an active community of users under the stewardship of DuraSpace, a nonprofit organization (Fedora, 2015). Fedora 4.0.0 was released in 2014. The implementation of Fedora software is discussed further in the section on open source repository systems.

FUNCTIONALITY AND OTHER SYSTEM REQUIREMENTS

Designing DLMS is an extremely challenging task, as it requires the integration of architectural models, technologies, and standards. It begins with a conceptual model but also involves a range of technologies, standards, and applications. It is a combination of those elements that contributes to a flexible and usable system design and provides the required functionality for creating, managing, and using a digital library.

Functionality refers to system's capabilities in building and managing digital libraries and providing end user support. Functionality is expressed in terms of services and is often divided into fundamental and value-added services (Gonçalves et al., 2008). The set of core functions relates to object- and collection-building, managing, disseminating, and/or preservation capabilities (Gonçalves et al., 2008; Zhang and Gourley, 2009). Researchers sometimes distinguish preservation services from those focused on content creation and management (Gonçalves et al., 2008), but since many systems integrate preservation and access services, the following list includes preservation in the core functions:

- Creation of digital objects and collections, which includes ingesting and/or processing of digitally-born or digitized materials and associated metadata records; creation of collections of objects based on predefined selection criteria
- Management, which involves adding, modifying, and deleting objects; management of user rights and permissions
- Access, which includes indexing, searching, browsing, and harvesting services plus presentation of objects and collections through a web interface and tools for user interaction
- Preservation, which includes services to store and manage digital objects and archival master files

Although preservation is recognized as a core function, it needs to be noted that many systems, especially those focused on building digital heritage collections, separate access and preservation activities. In practice, preservation is often managed by an archival information system, such as a dedicated digital preservation repository, or "dark archive," that may or may not be integrated with a primary access DLMS. An example of an integrated DLMS and archival information system is OCLC CONTENTdm, where licensed users have an option of depositing their digital master files in the OCLC

Digital Archive. Many institutional repositories built with open source systems, such as DSpace or Fedora, represent hybrid, multifunctional environments with various levels of access and preservation functions. HathiTrust is an example of a custom-built system that provides both access and preservation services to its partner institutions.

In addition to core functions, DLMS can provide a wide range of advanced and/or value-added services. Some of the services, although not included in the core, are critical to building digital libraries and maintaining them over time. For example, Export service is a function of the system that provides a means of retrieving objects and/or metadata and depositing them outside of the system. Export function becomes critical when institutions decide to migrate to a different platform. There is no comprehensive list of digital library services, although some efforts have been undertaken to define services based on theoretical models. Using the 5S framework, Gonçalves et al. (2008) provide a list of services and their informal definitions, from annotating to recommending, translating, and visualizing.

Value-added services can include additional functionality, such as page turners, high-resolution image viewers, integration of thesauri, visualization tools, geo-tagging, social tagging, etc. Tools for visualization of search results are particularly useful in large-scale digital libraries. Europeana and the DPLA offer timeline and map views of their results. The expansion of functionality is enabled by modular architecture and the use of open application programming interfaces (APIs) or plug-ins. APIs provide powerful tools for integrating the components of DLMS (Zhang and Gourley, 2009). The DPLA has also opened its data and API to external software developers, researchers, and others to create novel environments for learning, tools for discovery, and engaging apps. Plug-ins are software components that add new functionality to an application. The open source Omeka system, for example, provides an array of plug-ins to expand its basic functionality in creating digital collections and exhibits.

DLMS serve two primary groups of users: (1) digital library content providers, designers, and administrators, who produce and manage digital library collections and systems, and (2) digital library end users, who search, browse, and interact with digital objects and collections. DLMS need to support complex tasks and workflows of both groups through two separate user interfaces. Fig. 6.1 demonstrates an administrative interface in the open source system, Omeka, where administrators can configure the site, add and edit items, create metadata records, group items in collections, and customize the end user interface. Fig. 6.2 provides an example of an end user interface for a digital collection created in the Omeka system. The collection of documents from the Laura Hershey Collection, a disability rights activist, was built by a group of library and information science graduate students at the University of Denver. The simple interface allows end users not only to search and browse items in the digital collection but also to share objects through a variety of social media and to contribute their own materials to the collection. As demonstrated in the Omeka example, open source software enables relatively easy development of new services to enhance the system's functionality while simultaneously leveraging the contributions of the user community.

Functionality is a key requirement of DLMS, as it supports content creation, management, and user access. In addition, there is also a range of related system features and capabilities that impact system performance, user satisfaction, maintenance, and the ability to interact with other digital library systems. The most important capabilities are outlined as:

- *Extensibility* relates to a system's capabilities of adding new components and services to accommodate the continuous expansion of digital libraries and to incorporate new technological solutions. Models of open and modular architecture that are being gradually adopted in digital library environments support system flexibility and extensibility (Suleman, 2012; Yeh et al., 2009).

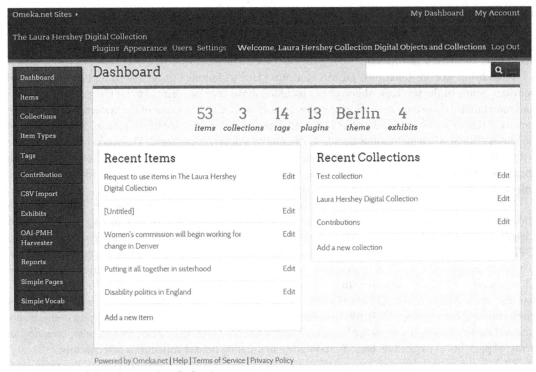

FIGURE 6.1 Administrative Interface in Omeka

- *Reliability* is a measure of system performance and relates to hardware and software failures and errors. Reliability of servers can be addressed by redundant configurations (Henry, 2012; Zhang and Gourley, 2009). Reliability decreases in a distributed large-scale digital library environment where it is more challenging to monitor systems of local content providers. Centralized large-scale digital libraries, such as HathiTrust or World Digital Library, have more control over content and the availability of the overall system.
- *Scalability* refers to a system's ability to accommodate (1) the expansion of content in the terms of the growing number and/or size of objects and collections and (2) an increasing number of users. Zhang and Gourley (2009) point out that scalability refers to the entire system: hardware, network, and software. In large-scale distributed digital library systems, scalability needs to address the growing number of content and service providers joining the network.
- *Sustainability* refers to a system's ability to provide robust management of collections and services over time. Henry (2012) notes that one needs to think of system sustainability not only in terms of hardware and software but also of the entire organization responsible for creating, managing, and maintaining the DLS over time.

Reliability, scalability, and sustainability relate to overall system performance and represent important factors influencing users' perceptions and acceptance of the system. Interoperability is a less visible but nonetheless important feature, as it offers the potential for independent digital libraries to cooperate and share content with a wider audience.

THE LAURA HERSHEY DIGITAL COLLECTION

| Browse Items | Browse Collections | Contribute an Item | Browse Exhibits | Contact Us | About Laura ▸ | About the Collection |

| Browse by Category |

ADAPT PHOTOS

PHOTOS

Photos of Laura
—General Photos
—ADAPT Photos
—Conference Photos

Laura Hershey with sign that reads:
"Disability rights or disability riots!"

Robin Stephens with sign that reads:
"AHCA – Abusive Homes Confining
Americans"

Protester with sign that reads: "I want
an attendant for my birthday"

Protesters, one with a sign that reads:
"No more pity"

FIGURE 6.2 End user Interface for a Digital Collection Built in the Omeka System

The collection is available at: http://laurahershey.omeka.net/.

INTEROPERABILITY

Interoperability refers to a system's ability to communicate with other digital library systems using standard protocols in order to exchange data. Interoperability has many aspects including uniform naming, metadata formats, document models, and access protocols (Lagoze and Van de Sompel, 2001). It has been recognized as a critical problem and a fundamental challenge since the early days of digital library development (Arms, 2000; Paepcke et al., 1998). The goal of interoperability is to build a set of services for users "from components that are technically different and managed by different organizations" (Arms et al., 2002). The challenge lies in heterogeneous content, multiple data formats, different protocols, and the variety of metadata schemas used by individual organizations. Establishing an interoperability framework is not only a technical but also organizational issue, as it requires a variety of content providers to cooperate and agree on common standards.

Three basic approaches have been identified in the "spectrum of interoperability" with different levels of engagement from content providers (Arms et al., 2002):

- *Federation* provides the strongest form of interoperability, but it also places the highest demands on the participating institutions. It requires that content providers agree that their services will conform to certain specifications. Federation is a well-established form of exchanging data in the library world. Examples of federated services include the sharing of online catalog records using Z39.50 protocol or metasearching of multiple journal databases.

- *Harvesting* represents a less rigorous approach. Participating institutions have to agree to expose and share their data, but they don't have to adopt a formal set of agreements.
- *Gathering* represents the least demanding approach for content providers. Resources openly available on the web are gathered by web crawlers, and no formal agreement may be necessary between organizations holding digital content and a digital library service provider collecting it.

Digital library service providers may select one of the approaches or a combination thereof in an effort to aggregate metadata and/or content from multiple independently operated libraries or other content providers.

Metadata harvesting with the OAI-PMH has become the most widely adopted solution to interoperability in the digital library environment. Metadata harvesting provides a model of interoperability where participating content providers agree to expose and share their metadata. The exposure of metadata allows other organizations to harvest it, aggregate it, and provide access services. Users can search across the body of aggregated metadata and link to digital objects held by original content providers. The transfer of metadata is defined by the OAI-PMH, a protocol that is easy to adopt and implement. The researchers involved in developing the OAI-PMH standard note that this low-barrier approach has contributed to its widespread adoption (Lagoze and Van de Sompel, 2003). The idea of developing a metadata harvesting standard originated in the scientific community, which was interested in a more efficient dissemination of scholarly publications (Lagoze and Van de Sompel, 2001). However, once OAI-PMH was proposed, it has been quickly accepted by digital libraries across domains and by a wide range of communities including cultural heritage organizations.

The OAI-PMH provides an interoperability framework based on metadata harvesting (Open Archives Initiative, 2002). It distinguishes between two classes of participants:

- *Data providers* adopt the OAI technical framework, and agree to open their servers for metadata harvesting.
- *Services providers* harvest metadata by employing the OAI protocol, and use the aggregated metadata as the basis for providing access services to users.

OAI-PMH uses basic Dublin Core as a common element set and requires data providers to expose metadata in that format, which poses a number of challenges for organizations using different metadata schemas. The issues of semantic interoperability and cross-walks are discussed in the chapter on Metadata (Chapter 5). From the perspective of DLMS, it is important to examine the system's support of interoperability and compliance with OAI-PMH. Most of the currently available DLMS from open source software to proprietary systems support OAI-PMH as metadata transfer protocol.

OAI-PMH was introduced in its first version in 2001. The second version, OAI-PMH 2.0, was released in 2002. Open Archives Initiative, a nonprofit organization dedicated to developing and promoting interoperability standards, is responsible for the maintenance of OAI-PMH (Open Archives Initiative, 2015). It also maintains Object Reuse and Exchange (OAI-ORE), a standard for the description and exchange of aggregations of web resources.

OAI-PMH provides a foundation for connecting independently operated digital libraries and the creation of service providers on multiple levels. The following example illustrates the multilayered interconnectivity of content and service providers. The Mountain West Digital Library, a regional aggregator, harvests metadata from multiple digital library systems in the western US and provides an interface for cross-collection searching. Moreover, a regional service provider, like the Mountain West Digital

Library, also exposes the aggregated metadata for harvesting, becoming a de facto data provider for a larger entity like the DPLA. In the decade since its release, OAI-PMH has enabled the formation of large national and international distributed digital library systems, such as the DPLA, Europeana, and NSDL, and the significance of this standard in the evolution of digital libraries cannot be overstated.

CURRENT LANDSCAPE OF DLMS

The exponential growth of digital libraries and their evolution from single, standalone projects to large-scale systems has increased the demands for developing flexible and interoperable DLMS. Two decades of research and development efforts have resulted in a diversified DLMS landscape with multiple open source solutions, proprietary software, and custom-built systems. The new generation of repositories often includes Fedora as a framework and a stack of other open source technologies. The array of choices reflects a variety of perspectives on managing and delivering digital content as well as different user requirements in regard to the functionality and technical support. Large-scale digital library systems present an impressive assemblage of records, but it is worth remembering that the actual digital content building takes place on the ground in a variety of organizations, from large research institutions to academic or public libraries, archives, historical societies, and museums. These organizations have different requirements and traditions of organizing, managing, and preserving content and provide varying levels of technical support. Large research institutions often choose to develop their own platforms, utilizing open architectural models, digital library standards, and a stack of open source technologies. However, smaller institutions that don't have the support of programmers and technical staff turn to open source or proprietary software packages that are easy to install and manage.

The diversification of DLMS is also reflected in a growing number of systems that provide specialized functionality and are developed specifically to manage certain types of digital content and/or serve different user communities. The distinctions among systems are not always clear, but a number of specialized platforms have emerged from digital repositories in academic communities to systems dedicated to managing digital heritage collections in libraries, archives, and museum settings.

Digital repositories serve primarily as platforms for preserving and providing open access to scientific papers and other forms of scholarly output, but they are also used for hosting digital heritage collections. The Open Access (OA) movement has spurred the growth of systems for open dissemination of scholarly publications including repositories and e-publishing solutions. Many digital repositories have been developed with open source software, including DSpace, EPrints, and Fedora, but there are also hosted licensed systems available in this category, such as Digital Commons, available from bepress. DigiTool provided by Ex Libris, which is an example of proprietary software used for both institutional repositories and digital collections. Open Journal Systems (OJS) represents an open source e-publishing system that provides support not only for depositing scholarly papers but also for their management through peer review and editorial processes (Public Knowledge Project, 2015).

DLMS for building digital collections of cultural heritage materials represent a distinct category because of requirements for managing and presenting heterogeneous multimedia content as well as support for digitization workflows. A wide range of options are available for cultural heritage institutions and include well-established platforms like open source Greenstone and proprietary CONTENTdm or LUNA. There is also a growing number of open source solutions including CollectiveAccess, Collection Space, and Omeka that are used by the members of the LAM (libraries, archives, and museums) community. In addition, open-source repository systems, such as DSpace, Fedora, Hydra, and Islandora are used for hosting digital collections.

The museum community has a different tradition of organizing and presenting materials from libraries or archives and requires dedicated systems to manage its unique workflows and to present digital representations of artifacts through an exhibit function. Large museum organizations often select dedicated proprietary systems that provide capabilities for managing large-scale collections and support for workflows in managing and curating objects. Museum proprietary systems include Proficio, provided by Re:discovery Software and the EMu (Electronic Museum), developed by KE Software.

The current landscape presents many alternatives and types of DLMS with new solutions continuously being added, especially in the open source category. The results of recent surveys demonstrate a wide range of systems being implemented in practice for institutional repositories and digital collections. Andro et al. (2012) compared the features and functionality of ten DLMS used in France and internationally. The authors identified Invenio, Greenstone, DSpace, Omeka, EPrints, and ORI-OAI in the open source category and, for proprietary software, DigitTool, CONTENTdm, and two products used primarily in France: Mnesys and Yoolib (Andro et al., 2012). Moulaison et al. (2015) conducted a nationwide survey among US-based repositories registered with the Directory of Open Access Repositories (OpenDOAR) and found that DSpace was the most common system used for open repositories, followed by Digital Commons (bepress), Fedora, ExLibris DigiTool, Hydra, Islandora, Omeka, and CONTENTdm. Stein and Thompson (2015) surveyed institutions migrating from old digital asset management systems to new platforms. Since the category of digital asset management systems is broad, the list of software identified in this study was more varied. Among the top currently used systems that the survey participants considered abandoning were two proprietary systems, ExLibris DigiTool and CONTENTdm, and one open source system, DSpace. Stein and Thompson (2015) noticed a trend in the migration pattern where institutions were more often than not moving away from proprietary systems towards open source solutions. A desire for more local control was cited by respondents as a primary reason for this migration. Islandora and Hydra were identified as the top choices that institutions were selecting as their new open source platforms.

It is impossible to review all available options within the limits of this chapter. There is also the risk of the information becoming outdated quickly, a risk inherent in any type of discussion about digital technology. The following section compares the benefits and limitations of open source versus proprietary software, and provides a brief review of selected systems. The focus of this review is on software systems used for building and managing digital collections and on multipurpose systems that are used for institutional repositories and digital collections. Platforms in the category of digital repositories that serve primarily preservation functions are discussed in the chapter on digital preservation (Chapter 9). Finally, this chapter concludes with a brief overview of approaches to the selection of DLMS.

OPEN SOURCE VERSUS PROPRIETARY SOFTWARE

Open source software refers to any software that provides free distribution and redistribution as well as access to source code. The Open Source Initiative defines open source software as "software that can be freely used, changed, and shared (in modified or unmodified form) by anyone" (Open Source Initiative, 2015, para. 4). The code source is available under a GNU public license, which allows developers to modify and redistribute it. As Goh et al. (2006) note, open source is different from freeware in that it is freely released but without licenses for modification and redistribution. Shareware, on the other hand, is free only for a limited period of time. The availability of the source code represents a great potential for modifications, improvements, and further software development. Sustainability of open source software, however, requires an active developer community.

Researchers point out a natural affiliation between the open source movement and the library world because of libraries' long history dealing with licensed content, a tradition of sharing and collaboration, and positive perceptions of open source software (Krishnamurthy, 2008; Palmer and Choi, 2014; Payne and Singh, 2010; Rafiq, 2009). Librarians not only select open source software for library applications but also are becoming active participants in its development (Fox, 2006; Payne and Singh, 2010; Samuels and Griffy, 2012). Some of the benefits of open source software for DL applications include:

- Low cost of implementation, which is particularly important because of shrinking library budgets
- Ability to modify software and adapt to meet specific user needs
- Ability to improve functionality of the software
- Institutional autonomy and freedom of commercial licensure
- Support of a large user community

However, open source software has its limitations. A recent study identified some challenges for adopting open source software in libraries, including:

- The need for highly skilled staff that could provide support for the open source system
- Poor documentation
- The need for additional training or expertise
- Substandard development practices (Thacker and Knutson, 2015)

Open source solutions lack the formal technical support and training offered by commercial vendors. Adopting open source software requires a commitment to invest time and resources in learning the software and maintaining it, which can slow down the actual digital library project. Samuels and Griffy (2012) state that the economic benefits of low initial costs can be canceled out by expenses involved in trouble-shooting and learning cumbersome workflows. The authors recommend considering "total cost of ownership," which includes not only the initial investment but also direct and indirect costs throughout the entire software lifecycle. The study, examining the cost of operating institutional repositories, found almost no difference between annual operating expenses for institutions that use open source software and institutions that use proprietary solutions (Burns et al., 2013).

Proprietary software packages offer relatively easy solutions for building and managing digital collections, but this ease-of-use often has a price tag to match. Proprietary DLMS are sold or licensed without access to the software code and with restrictions on how the system may be modified. The license may have provisions for the number of software instances, the size of collections, and/or the number of collections. In addition to the license cost, institutions are also required to pay an annual maintenance fee, which guarantees access to upgrades and documentation. Ease of installation and use, documentation, technical support, system stability, and integrated functionality represent clear benefits of proprietary digital library software. The cost and limited opportunity for customization are the obvious disadvantages.

The decision to adopt open source software or purchase proprietary software for building and managing digital collections is quite complex and requires the consideration of multiple factors. Institutions need to weigh the benefits and costs, evaluate and test potential candidates, and select the solution that meets the organizational needs and user requirements. As mentioned before, there is a general trend for libraries to select open source solutions, but there are also some institutions that choose to migrate to proprietary systems after using open source for several years (Corbett et al., 2016).

The following section provides a brief overview of currently available open source and proprietary DLMS and compares some of their features. The focus of the review is primarily on software used for building digital collections. Open source repository software, including DSpace, Fedora, Hydra, and Islandora are presented separately. It is difficult to compare these systems to the "out-of-the-box" software because of their unique structure, the requirements for additional development of the interface layer, and the integration of other open source solutions on top of the repository platform. The DLMS reviewed below are in the "turnkey" category of systems that are relatively easy to install and manage. In addition, several of the programs like CONTENTdm, LUNA, and Omeka offer hosted solutions, making collection building possible for small institutions with limited access to servers. The selected systems are well established and widely adopted by their designated user communities. The selection criteria for systems included in this section are: (1) a minimum of five years of development and use, and (2) a user base with a minimum of 100 active institutional users. Obviously, there are more than six DLMS that meet these criteria, but the limitations of this chapter dictate reducing the number. In addition, an attempt was made to present DLMS used in a variety of cultural heritage institutions, including archives and museums. The review of the systems is by no means comprehensive, nor is it meant to serve as a recommendation or evaluation. The goal of the review is purely informative and meant to provide a description of a sample of DLMS in open source and proprietary categories.

OPEN SOURCE SYSTEMS

CollectiveAccess (http://www.collectiveaccess.org/) is an open source content management system designed for cataloging, managing, and publishing museum and archival collections. It is also increasingly used by libraries, nonprofit organizations, private collectors, artist studios, and performing arts organizations (CollectiveAccess, 2015). The software was created in 2006 by Whirl-i-gig, a software development and consulting company, and was released to the public under the open source GNU Public License in 2007. It has been adopted by a variety of cultural institutions including archives, historical societies, libraries, and museums. CollectiveAccess provides users with highly configurable features including integrated metadata standards and controlled vocabularies, batch uploading of a variety of file formats, and customizable interfaces. The range of supported audio, video, and multimedia formats is impressive and probably one of the reasons why this software has been adopted by several film archives. The system includes two modules: *Providence*, the backend cataloging application and *Pawtucket*, the public-access interface. Both modules can be customized to obtain additional functionality. CollectiveAccess takes a flexible, cooperative approach to metadata standards, allowing users to import and share a variety of standards from user-contributed installation profiles (CollectiveAccess, 2015). It supports Dublin Core, PBCore, and VRA Core, as well as several archival and museum metadata standards including CDWA, CCO, DACS, and DarwinCore. The software also provides multilingual support in seven languages. Fig. 6.3 demonstrates an example of a bilingual German/English collection of photographs and videos of the fall of the Berlin Wall and German reunification. This software is highly configurable, but does require some customization and programming knowledge. Support is provided through a user forum and a wiki available to all institutional users.

Greenstone (http://www.greenstone.org/) represents the first generation of digital library software, but it has been upgraded several times and is actively used throughout the world. It was developed at

FIGURE 6.3 *Wir waren so frei*—Built in CollectiveAccess by the Deutsche Kinemathek

The collection is available at: http://www.wir-waren-so-frei.de.

the University of Waikato, New Zealand, in 1997, and became available as open source software under the GNU General Public License in 1998 (Witten and Bainbridge, 2003). It has been distributed in cooperation with UNESCO and the Human Info NGO in Belgium. Greenstone provides capabilities to create fully searchable collections of documents, books, photographs, newspapers, audio (mp3 files), and video. It supports the Dublin Core metadata standard (both unqualified and qualified). In addition, plug-ins can be used to ingest externally prepared metadata in different formats. Most collections are distributed on the web, but several collections of documents with humanitarian information have been produced on CD-ROM for distribution in developing countries (Witten, 2008).

Greenstone has a strong international and humanitarian focus and has been used as a platform for building digital collections representing indigenous cultures and social and environmental issues such as community development, poverty, sustainability, globalization, etc. (see Fig. 6.4 for a collection of UNESCO documents built in Greenstone). Multilingual support is one of Greenstone's strengths. For many years, Greenstone was the only digital library software providing Unicode support and the capability to process and display documents in non-Latin characters (Matusiak and Myagmar, 2009). Greenstone is one of the most widely adopted DLMS worldwide, with collections in more than 50 languages.

Omeka (http://omeka.org/) (hosted version: http://www.omeka.net/) provides a lightweight solution to building digital projects for cultural institutions and individuals. Omeka was created by the Center

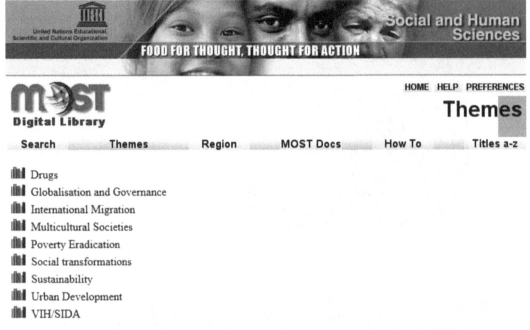

FIGURE 6.4 UNESCO Collection of Documents Documenting Social Science Research of the MOST Programme Built with Greenstone Software

UNESCO MOST Digital Library is available at: http://digital-library.unesco.org/shs/most/gsdl/cgi-bin/library?c=most&a=p&p=about.

for History and New Media at George Mason University in 2008. It is designed with non-IT specialists in mind to offer the opportunity to create digital collections and exhibits to those with limited infrastructure and/or technical skills (Omeka, 2015a). Omeka offers an easy-to-use platform to small archives and museums as well as to scholars and students in digital humanities and education. Fig. 6.5 provides an example of a digital history project created in Omeka by the Center for History and New Media in partnership with the Gulag Museum in Perm and the International Memorial Society in Russia. Users can choose to install an Omeka instance on their own servers from omeka.org, or they can use a hosted account with omeka.net. The installed version can be enhanced with the addition of plug-ins and has fewer customization restrictions than the omeka.net version. Omeka.net, however, provides an option of building digital collections to institutions and individuals who do not have access to the servers. As the documentation on the Omeka site indicates, the software has been adopted to teaching digital history, English, and library science courses (Omeka, 2015b). Fig. 6.2 provides an example of a digital collection built by graduate students.

Omeka accepts most formats for text, image, audio, and video files including jpg, jp2, PDF, mp3, mp4, and tif. The file size in the hosted version is restricted to 64 MB. The support of metadata standards is limited to basic Dublin Core. Some digital collection builders feel restricted by the limited fields in unqualified Dublin Core and the lack of the metadata template customizations (Kucsma et al., 2010). The "out-of-the-box" software provides very basic functionality, which can be expanded by the use

FIGURE 6.5 Gulag: Many Days, Many Lives

The project is available at: http://gulaghistory.org/.

of plug-ins. A selection of plug-ins is available for downloading to expand collection-building functions and to incorporate Web 2.0 tools. In addition to building objects and collections, Omeka offers capabilities for designing exhibits. The exhibit plug-in is one of the strengths of Omeka. The software is used sometimes as the digital exhibition platform in conjunction with other DLMS (Gilbert and Mobley, 2013).

PROPRIETARY SYSTEMS

CONTENTdm (http://www.oclc.org/en-US/contentdm.html) represents one of the first proprietary content management systems dedicated to building digital collections. This Windows-based software package was developed at the University of Washington in the late 1990s, and eventually acquired by OCLC (Zick, 2009). It was originally designed as an image management system, but through subsequent upgrades, the software has offered support for compound objects, PDFs, and streaming of audio

FIGURE 6.6 A Video Clip of Martin Luther King, Jr., Speech

The collection was built at the University of Wisconsin-Milwaukee Libraries with CONTENTdm software. The record is available at: http://collections.lib.uwm.edu/cdm/ref/collection/wtmj/id/49.

and video (see Fig. 6.6 for an example of a video collection). The software is licensed to participating institutions with a variety of license options and levels that depend on the size of collections. A hosted version is available for an additional fee (OCLC, 2015). CONTENTdm is intended to be scalable, enabling institutions to upgrade license levels as they increase capacity. CONTENTdm has been adopted by a wide range of cultural heritage institutions, from large academic libraries to smaller public libraries and archives. OCLC provides an entry-level hosted version to OCLC FirstSearch subscribers at no additional charge. OCLC members can take advantage of CONTENTdm's integration with Connexion cataloging tool and harvesting services through WorldCat Digital Collection Gateway. The software provides a wide range of services for streamlined digital collection building with metadata template customization, batch upload of content files and metadata, and automated creation of derivatives. Interface customization is limited, although users can make some changes through the CONTENTdm API.

KE EMu (http://www.kesoftware.com/) is an electronic museum content management system developed by the KE company based in Melbourne, Australia. The software is designed primarily for the museum market to manage internal workflows and to provide a platform for building and presenting digital collections online. The software has a diverse user base from small to large museums including American Museum of Natural History, National Museum of Australia, and National Museum of the American Indian (see Fig. 6.7 for an example of the implementation of EMu). EMu is designed to

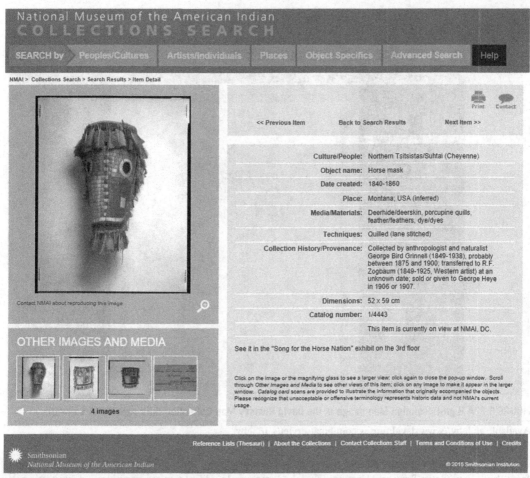

National Museum of the American Indian
COLLECTIONS SEARCH

| SEARCH by | Peoples/Cultures | Artists/Individuals | Places | Object Specifics | Advanced Search | Help |

NMAI > Collections Search > Search Results > Item Detail

Print   Contact

<< Previous Item   Back to Search Results   Next Item >>

Culture/People:	Northern Tsitsistas/Suhtai (Cheyenne)
Object name:	Horse mask
Date created:	1840-1860
Place:	Montana; USA (inferred)
Media/Materials:	Deerhide/deerskin, porcupine quills, feather/feathers, dye/dyes
Techniques:	Quilled (lane stitched)
Collection History/Provenance:	Collected by anthropologist and naturalist George Bird Grinnell (1849-1938), probably between 1875 and 1900; transferred to R.F. Zogbaum (1849-1925, Western artist) at an unknown date; sold or given to George Heye in 1906 or 1907.
Dimensions:	52 x 59 cm
Catalog number:	1/4443
	This item is currently on view at NMAI, DC.

See it in the "Song for the Horse Nation" exhibit on the 3rd floor

Contact NMAI about reproducing this image

OTHER IMAGES AND MEDIA

◄   4 images   ►

Click on the image or the magnifying glass to see a larger view; click again to close the pop-up window. Scroll through *Other Images and Media* to see other views of this item; click on any image to make it appear in the larger window. *Catalog card* scans are provided to illustrate the information that originally accompanied the objects. Please recognize that unacceptable or offensive terminology represents historic data and not NMAI's current usage.

Reference Lists (Thesauri) | About the Collections | Contact Collections Staff | Terms and Conditions of Use | Credits

Smithsonian
National Museum of the American Indian   © 2015 Smithsonian Institution

FIGURE 6.7 The National Museum of the American Indian Use of EMu Software

The record is available at: http://www.nmai.si.edu/searchcollections/item.aspx?irn=15330&hl=443.

facilitate multiple functionalities with modules for collection management, cataloging, interpretation, and online publishing. The collection management module is designated to record object details and to track activities, such as exhibitions, loans, and acquisitions. The module is compliant with SPECTRUM, a guide to good practice for museum documentation. The software supports Dublin Core and Darwin Core and integrates a number of controlled vocabulary tools. EMu allows for the customization of metadata fields so that the fields match the discipline and attributes of the object (KE Software, 2015). EMu also provides an interpretation module for capturing experts' knowledge and presenting a collection within a cultural, historical, or scientific context. Digital objects and their online publication are managed with a digital asset management module. With a highly modular structure, strong support of multiple media formats, and several metadata standards, EMu provides a powerful tool for managing unique museum workflows and building online collections. The licensing structure depends on the number of concurrent users, types, and sizes of legacy databases that need to be converted, and training required.

FIGURE 6.8 A High-Resolution Map Image in the David Rumsey Map Collection Built with LUNA Software

Available at: http://www.davidrumsey.com/luna/servlet/s/163gby.

LUNA software is produced and licensed by Luna Imaging, Inc., a company formed with support from the J. Paul Getty Trust and Eastman Kodak Company. In addition to maintaining and supporting the software, Luna Imaging, Inc., also provides imaging and consulting services to cultural heritage institutions. LUNA software is primarily used for managing and presenting visual collections, although it is capable of managing other types of content as well, including text, audio, and video. However, its powerful image viewer with zoom and pan capabilities makes is particularly suitable for presenting high-resolution visuals, such as art images, maps, or medical and scientific imagery (see Fig. 6.8 for an example of a map from the David Rumsey Collection). The software provides additional tools to annotate images, export to PowerPoint, and create dynamic presentations and slide shows. Because of its strong capabilities in presenting high-resolution images and integrating with presentations software, LUNA has been adopted by museums and academic libraries with visual collections. As of November 2015, Luna Imaging offered a site license for installing the software on the local server and a hosted version, Luna Solo, for smaller institutions and individuals. The hosted option requires an annual fee and allows 100 GB of data (Luna Imaging, 2015). The software provides some Web 2.0 tools, including integration with Flickr images.

Table 6.1 provides a summary of selected features of the reviewed DLMS based on openly available documentation. The review was conducted in 2014 and updated in 2015; it captures the features of

Table 6.1 Comparison of Selected Features of Open Source and Proprietary DLMS

Features	Open Source			Proprietary		
	Collective Access	Greenstone	Omeka	CONTENTdm	EMu	LUNA
File formats	jpg, jp2, PDF, mp3, mp4, tiff, plus many audio and video formats[a]	jpeg, PDF, gif, jif, tiff, mp3, mpeg, midi, and others	jpg, jp2, PDF, mp3, mp4, tiff, and others	jpg, jp2, PDF, mp3, mp4, tiff,	jpg, PDF, avi, wav, mpeg, and others	jpg, PDF, png, gif, bmp,mp3, tiff, flv
File conversion	√	U	N/A	√	√	√
Batch upload of files	√	√	√	√	√	√
Batch upload of metadata	√	√	√	√	√	√
Metadata schemas	Dublin Core, Darwin Core, and archival and museum standards[b]	Dublin Core	Dublin Core	Dublin Core, VRA Core, EAD, METS	Dublin Core, Darwin Core, XMP, IPTC	Dublin Core
Metadata template customization	√	√	N/A	√	√	√
Controlled vocabulary	AAT, TGN, GeoNames, LCSH, your own vocabulary	N/A	LCSH, your own vocabulary	AAT, TGM, TGN, ULAN, CSH, your own vocabulary, and more	AAT, LCSH, TGN, ULAN, many others, your own vocabulary	Your own vocabulary
Persistent object identifier	N/A	N/A	N/A	√	U	√
Allow multiple collections	√	√	√	√	√	√
Global update of metadata	√	U	N/A	√	√	√
Multilingual support	√	√	√	√	√	√
High-resolution Image Viewer	√	N/A	N/A	√	√	√
Interoperability	OAI-PMH	OAI-PMH, Z39.50	OAI-PMH	OAI-PMH, Z39.50	OAI-PMH, Z39.50	OAI-PMH
Platform	Windows, Unix/Linux, Mac OS-X	Windows, Unix/Linux, Mac OS-X, FreeBSD	Windows, Unix/Linux, Mac OS-X	Windows, Unix/Linux	Windows, Unix/Linux, Mac OS-X	Windows Unix/Linux, Solaris
Hosted platform	N/A	N/A	√	√	N/A	√

U, unknown; NA, not available/applicable.
[a]*For a complete list of formats, see: http://docs.collectiveaccess.org/wiki/Supported_Media_File_Formats.*
[b]*For a complete list of supported metadata standards, see: http://docs.collectiveaccess.org/wiki/Metadata_Standards.*

Table 6.2 Web 2.0 Features and Visualization Tools of Selected Open Source and Proprietary DLMS

Features	Open Source			Proprietary		
	Collective Access	Greenstone	Omeka	CONTENTdm	EMu	LUNA
Web 2.0 Features and Visualization Tools						
Geo-referencing	√	N/A	√	N/A	√	√
Visualization tools	√	N/A	√	N/A	√	√
Social media sharing	√	N/A	√	√	N/A	√
User tagging	√	N/A	N/A (only those logged in can tag, public users cannot)	√	N/A	N/A
User contribution	√	N/A	√	N/A	N/A	√
NA, not available/applicable.						

the systems at that time. It is very likely that the systems will evolve and add new functionality in the future. The comparison in Table 6.1 focuses on a small number of core functionality related to content creation.

Table 6.2 examines a handful of Web 2.0 features and visualization tools. It is by no means a comprehensive comparison, as it does not address the functionality related to content management, discovery, presentation, user interface, or administration. Nonetheless, the tables provide a snapshot of differences and similarities between currently available open source and proprietary DLMS, and to a certain extent between early systems like Greenstone or CONTENTdm and the next generation of DLMS, such as CollectiveAccess or Omeka.

As Tables 6.1 and 6.2 demonstrate, there is no single system that will provide all features (even if the list is narrowed to one category, such as content creation and ingest). In fact, this small-scale comparison reveals considerable differences between the systems in both open source and proprietary categories. All systems support Dublin Core and OAI-PMH, but beyond basic Dublin Core, options for selecting other schemas and customizing metadata templates vary. CollectiveAccess offers the largest selection of metadata standards, but at the same time it requires more technical skills in configuring the system. Open source DLMS, like CollectiveAccess or Omeka, provide support for the widest range of file formats, especially in audio, video, and multimedia, but all reviewed systems support at least one standard audio and video file format. The biggest difference between newer open source systems and proprietary software is in the integration of Web 2.0 tools for sharing objects through social media, user tagging, and user contribution. The generation of DLMS developed in the open source culture of collaboration and sharing, such as CollectiveAccess or Omeka, are much better at integrating Web 2.0 features into their systems.

The systems reviewed in this section focus primarily on providing access to digital cultural heritage content from libraries, archives, and museums. The functionality is centered on managing and ingesting digital objects, their discovery, and online delivery. Long-term preservation of digital assets, especially of master files, is typically not supported in digital collection software. Thus, institutions need to purchase or build separate digital preservation systems, and integrate them with digital collection platforms. In addition, institutions may need to maintain digital repositories to provide access and preservation of open access scholarly publications and research data. The multitude of systems creates a complex environment with challenges in streamlining operations and providing integrated services and discovery experiences.

OPEN SOURCE REPOSITORY SYSTEMS

Digital repositories are multifunctional information systems that support a wide range of digital curation activities, including content management, submission, ingesting, storing, discovery, access, and preservation (Rieger, 2007). The first digital repository systems were developed in the early 2000s to enable open access to scholarly publications. In support of scholarly communication and open access, repositories were designed to provide an infrastructure and services for capturing and managing open access scholarly publications and electronic dissertations and theses. Digital repositories are a key component of the Open Access (OA) movement (Swan, 2012). Repositories provide access to intellectual output of an institution or in a specific discipline. Institutional repositories represent the most common type (OpenDOAR, 2015). Lynch (2003) defines institutional digital repositories as "a set of services that a university offers to the members of its community for the management and dissemination of digital materials created by the institution and its community members" (p. 328). Early repository software, such as DSpace and EPrints were developed to support self-deposits of open access scholarly publications and to enable resource discovery and retrieval in the open web environment. The first generation of open-source repository systems was designed primarily as open access publication databases with limited support for other types of digital objects and services (Fay, 2010).

The content and roles of digital repositories, however, have become more diversified with time. In addition to providing open access to scholarly articles and dissertations and theses, repositories began to host diverse content of digitized archival and special collections, geospatial data, research data, audiovisual materials, and complex multimedia objects. In the case of institutions participating in the Google Book Project, institutional repositories also serve as preservation systems for master copies of digitized books (Cramer and Kott, 2010). Rieger (2007) outlines a long list of repository roles. The top purposes include:

- Enable digital asset management
- Offer preservation services
- Provide institutional visibility
- Support learning, teaching, and research
- Facilitate discovery of content
- Enable reuse and repurposing of content

Increasingly, repositories are also seen as platforms for curating faculty's digital scholarship and supporting access, preservation, and reuse of digital assets created or collected by faculty as part of their research and teaching activities. Digital repositories that aggregate diverse content are especially valuable for research and instruction (Kutay, 2014).

Digital preservation has emerged as an equally important goal as access for repository systems. The challenges, strategies, and technologies for preserving born digital and digitized objects are described in more detail in chapter on digital preservation (Chapter 9). Digital repositories are discussed there in terms of providing preservation services. As mentioned before, the early repository systems, such as EPrints and DSpace, offer limited support for digital preservation. The need for more robust preservation services is cited as one of the reasons for migrating from the early generation repository software toward newer and more versatile systems (Cramer and Kott, 2010).

The new generation of open source repository systems addresses the limitations of the early repositories by offering stronger support for features essential to digital preservation. The emerging open source solutions also address the challenge of maintaining more than one system in support of institutional curatorial processes. The new systems serve multiple purposes and offer multiple functions with user interface for deposit, description, discovery, and retrieval of digital content as well as a range of specialized functions to make deposited assets available over the long term. Adherence to digital preservation standards and integration of tools, such as checksums and format validation applications, ensure integrity, authenticity, and reusability of digital objects (Awre and Cramer, 2012; Cramer and Kott, 2010; Kent, 2014). Fig. 6.9 demonstrates a multipurpose model of the Stanford Digital Repository (SDR) with three distinct yet integrated areas: (1) management, (2) discovery and delivery, and (3) preservation.

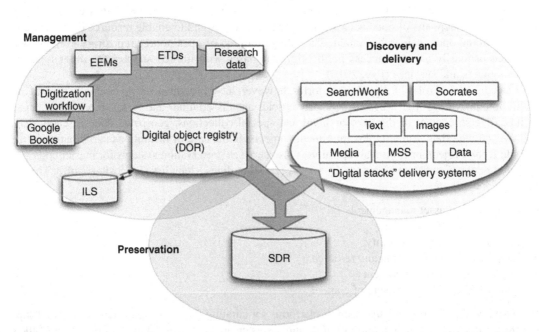

FIGURE 6.9 Model of the Stanford University Digital Repository System with Three Main Spheres: Management, Preservation, and Access (Cramer and Kott, 2010)

The new repository serving the Stanford University community is designed to accommodate diverse content and serve multiple functions. It is based on modular architecture and constructed with multiple open source technologies, including Fedora as an object management framework (Cramer and Kott, 2010). More recently, Stanford joined the Hydra Project and incorporated Hydra into a suite of the repository technologies (Awre and Cramer, 2012).

The emerging generation of multipurpose repository systems adopts modular architecture and integrates a suite of open source applications. As outlined by Fay (2010), modular architecture allows:

- Independence of functional components
- A separation of digital objects from particular software installations
- An iterative approach to developing capacity in different functional areas
- Flexible design according to evolving demands and requirements

Modular architecture and the integration of several open source components enable customization and ensure flexibility and extensibility.

The following section reviews four open source repository systems: DSpace, Fedora, Hydra, and Islandora. DSpace and Fedora are listed in the survey research as widely used repository systems (Moulaison et al., 2015; Stein and Thompson, 2015). DSpace is an example of the early repository software. Fedora is central to the digital library development not only as an architectural model but also as a software used in many operational repositories, and a foundation for the new repository systems. Hydra and Islandora represent the new generation of DLMS.

DSpace (http://www.dspace.org/) is one of the first open source repository solutions supporting not only the dissemination of scholarly publications but also the access to digital collections. It was developed under the leadership of the Massachusetts Institute of Technology (MIT) and in collaboration with the Hewlett Packard Corporation. Since its release in 2002, DSpace has been widely adopted and is used by over 1000 institutions worldwide (DSpace, 2015; OpenDOAR, 2015). Its usage accounts for 43% repositories registered with the Directory of Open Access Repositories (OpenDOAR, 2015). Currently, DSpace is supported by a community of users and maintained through DuraSpace (DSpace, 2015).

DSpace supports Dublin Core metadata standard but does not include other metadata schemas. It is compliant with the OAI-PMH interoperability standard (Smith et al., 2003). Metadata may be entered by end users as they submit content, or it might be derived from other metadata as part of an ingest process (Tramboo et al., 2012). It uses a handle system for identifiers. The software is relatively easy to install and customizable. However, some limitations of its early architecture are noticed especially in comparison to Fedora. Fay (2010) compared DSpace, EPrints, and Fedora. The author identified a number of DSpace disadvantages, including its monolithic and restrictive data model, limited support for complex objects and digitized collections, lack of support for identifier schemas, and the lack of attention to preservation storage. The limited support of DSpace for preservation services was also found in another comparative study (Madalli et al., 2012).

Fedora (http://fedorarepository.org/) has emerged as one of the most versatile solutions among open source digital repositories. Built on the Fedora flexible and extensible architecture, the repository software supports a wide range of applications including institutional repositories, electronic records archives, e-publishing, trusted repositories for digital preservation, digital collections, and distributed digital libraries (Lagoze et al., 2006). In comparison to DSpace and EPrints, Fedora supports a wider range of objects and multiple metadata schemas and can be customized to local requirements (Fay, 2010). Fedora offers a flexible data model and a robust repository but requires additional tools to build an interface layer. Fedora requires significant local development in order to achieve any useful functionality (Fay, 2010). The user and web services interfaces need to be developed with other open source applications. Fedora provides a very flexible environment, but it requires substantial technical skills to implement—thus it is often adopted by larger institutions with sufficient programming and technical staff.

Fedora serves as a foundation for major scientific digital libraries, including the Public Library of Science (PLoS ONE), the National Library of Medicine (NLM), and the National Science Digital Library (NSDL). The NSDL served as a testing environment for Fedora repository structure and additional open source development (Krafft et al., 2008). NLM selected Fedora after extensive testing and comparing it to ten other open source and proprietary systems (Marill and Luczak, 2009). Fedora also provides a repository platform for cultural heritage collections, including Open Vault, a moving image archives project of the WGBH Media Library and Archives (WGBH Educational Foundation, 2015). Like DSpace, Fedora is supported by a community of users and maintained through DuraSpace (Fedora, 2015). Increasingly, Fedora is integrated with the new generation of front-end applications, such as Islandora and Hydra. As of Nov. 30, 2015, the Fedora user registry listed 73 Islandora/Fedora and 35 Hydra/Fedora registered repositories (DuraSpace, 2015a).

Hydra (http://projecthydra.org/) is a multipurpose open source repository solution that has been developed as a collaborative project by several organizations (Hydra Project, 2015). The Hydra Project started in 2008 with the University of Hull in the UK, Stanford University, University of Virginia, and Fedora Commons (now DuraSpace) as foundational partners (Awre, 2012; Awre and Cramer, 2012; Green and Awre, 2009). Since then other institutions have joined the Hydra Project as partners and have formally committed themselves to supporting Hydra's open source development (Hydra Project, 2015).

The collaborative Hydra Project was initiated in light of the recognition that no single system can provide the full range of repository-based solutions and that no single institution can support such large-scale development (Awre, 2012; Awre and Cramer, 2012). Thus, the goal of the Hydra Project participants was to develop jointly a common repository framework upon which flexible solutions can be built and shared. An African proverb, "If you want to go fast, go alone, if you want to go far, go together" became the project's motto. Multiinstitutional collaboration has become a vital aspect of the project.

Building on Fedora, Hydra is designed as a flexible application framework that can support the development of multiple systems tailored to local needs. As Awre and Cramer (2012) point out, the use of the term "Hydra" deliberately indicates one body and many heads. Hydra provides a common and reusable framework, which can be adopted, extended, and modified. Each instance of Hydra adoption can become its own Hydra head. Hydra developers and adopters also contribute to the wider Hydra community (DuraSpace, 2015b). Hydra software is released as open source under the Apache 2.0 license.

As a technical framework, Hydra provides a set of reusable open source components that can be combined and configured to meet different needs. The major components include:

- Fedora as a repository layer to support object management
- Apache Solr, indexing software to provide access to indexed objects
- Blacklight: a next-generation discovery interface that provides faceted search and customized views
- Hydra plugin, a collection of components that facilitate workflow in managing digital content
- Solrizer, a component that indexes Fedora-held content into a Solr index (Awre, 2012)

Several of the components use Ruby on Rails as the coding language. Hydra software or its components have been implemented by a number of large research institutions worldwide. In addition to the initial Hydra partners, the software has been adopted by Northwestern University, Indiana University, Columbia University, London School of Economics, and many others (Hydra Project, 2015). The list of Hydra partners and adopters is growing steadily. Hydra offers a multipurpose, multifunctional DLMS by combining the flexibility of the repository structure with versatile functionality and rich applications. However, it requires substantial development work and expertise in the Ruby on Rails programming language.

Islandora (http://islandora.ca/) is an open source software framework designed to help institutions collaboratively manage and discover digital assets. It was originally developed by the University of Prince Edward Island's Robertson Library but is now adopted by an international community of users (Islandora, 2015). Since its initial release in 2006, Islandora has been upgraded to support diverse content and extend its functionality (Moses and Stapelfeldt, 2013). Islandora has evolved into a multipurpose repository system serving as a platform for open access publishing as well as a digital asset management system for cultural heritage collections (Jettka and Stein, 2014; Kent, 2014; Moses and Stapelfeldt, 2013). Islandora is released as an open source software under a GNU license.

Islandora's technical framework is built using a modular architecture approach. It is based on Fedora and integrates additional open source applications. The core components include:

- Fedora as a repository framework to support data storage, RDF relationships, and metadata harvesting
- Drupal as a front-end content management application to provide user interface and extend Islandora elements
- Solr for indexing services

Islandora's functionality can be further extended by incorporating other open source applications (Moses and Stapelfeldt, 2013). Islandora uses Drupal module to create solution packs for different content types and formats, such as audio and video or PDFs. Each solution pack has its own set of tools to support automatic processing during ingest. For example, while a batch of master files in the TIFF format is uploaded for archival storage, JPEG or JPEG 2000 derivatives are created automatically for access (Kent, 2014). Islandora supports the MODS schema but accepts other metadata standards at ingest, which are then mapped to MODS. It offers support for digital preservation standards and tools, including PREMIS metadata standard and checksums.

Islandora has been implemented as an open access scholarly repository with a suite of unique services supporting digital scholarship (Moses and Stapelfeldt, 2013). It has also been used as a solution for presenting diverse scholarly and cultural heritage content in digital collections and digital humanities projects. University of Hamburg adopted Islandora to construct a repository for a multilingual collection of spoken language resources (Jettka and Stein, 2014). A consortium of academic libraries in Minnesota selected Islandora as a platform for providing access and supporting preservation of digital collections (Kent, 2014). Islandora is supported collaboratively by a community of users who interact through Islandora Camps and Google Groups (Islandora, 2015).

The reviewed open source repository systems accommodate diverse content and formats, and seek to serve multiple repository purposes. In contrast to DSpace, the new generation of systems offers more flexible platforms and stronger support for complex objects and digital preservation. The new systems are constructed using a stack of open source technologies. While Fedora provides a core repository framework, the systems also incorporate other open source components. They can be modified and extended by integrating additional applications to meet new requirements. Collaborative, multiinstitutional development is a distinct feature of the new generation of open source repository systems. Shared development contributes to the system functionality and sustainability, but can also help in sharing other digital library standards and best practices.

SELECTION OF DLMS

The design of DLMS has evolved in the past decade with the introduction of low-barrier systems, robust and flexible open source repository systems, and more specialized options available to specific user communities like archives and museums. Selection of an appropriate system among so many alternatives, however, is not easy. The variety of DLMS and their features makes the selection and evaluation process challenging. In addition to the "out-of-the-box" solutions, institutions have the option of customizing available open source software or building their own custom systems. The choice really depends on institutional needs and requirements, types of resources, scale of collections, technical infrastructure and expertise, long-term goals, and budget. As discussed above, the selection between open source and proprietary systems needs to be considered not only in terms of initial cost but also in light of total cost of ownership (Samuels and Griffy, 2012). Selecting a well-established proprietary system can make perfect sense for an institution with limited technical and programming staff, especially if the system meets other functionality requirements. Selecting the right system requires a considerable amount of research, evaluation of options, and testing the performance of selected candidates. Zhang and Gourley (2009) identify four steps in the selection process:

- Identifying organizational requirements and resources
- Developing selection criteria
- Researching available systems
- Evaluating candidates

Organizational requirements depend on the types and characteristics of resources, needs of intended users, traditions of information organization and resource sharing, strategic goals, consortia agreements, and the technical infrastructure of individual institutions. Selection criteria need to be developed in light of organizational requirements. Developing a list of selection criteria and system requirements can be an overwhelming task. There is no single checklist that would include all the requirements for content creation and management, online presentation and access, user interface, preservation, user and system administration, etc. The lack of evaluation tools has been noted by the researchers examining open source DLMS (Goh et al., 2006; Samuels and Griffy, 2012) and is further discussed in Chapter 10.

Several case studies focus on the process of selecting and evaluating open source DLMS and report their methodology and findings. Although these studies concentrate exclusively on open source software, their approaches and selection criteria can be useful for evaluating proprietary systems as well. In search of a suitable DLMS, the researchers at the University of Arizona Library adopted the systems analysis process (Han, 2004). They identified four major areas of functional requirements: information organization focusing on content and its associated metadata, presentation, access including interfaces for both internal and external users, and preservation. For the purpose of their study, the researchers developed detailed criteria within those categories and conducted a comparative study of three DLMS: Greenstone, Fedora, and DSpace.

Goh et al. (2006) conducted a study in order to develop a standardized checklist for evaluating open source DLMS. The researchers identified 12 categories and developed a weighted list of criteria within those categories. The checklist categories include content management, content acquisition, metadata, search support, access control and privacy, report and inquiry capabilities, preservation, interoperability, user interfaces, standard compliance, automatic tools, system support, and maintenance. The evaluation checklist generated as a result of this research was used in evaluating four DLMS CERN CDSware, Greenstone, Fedora, and EPrints. Greenstone emerged as a system that consistently fulfilled the majority of the criteria and obtained full scores in five of the 12 categories.

Based on the case studies of Han (2004) and Goh et al. (2006) as well as their own experiences, Zhang and Gourley (2009) proposed a model called "FITS to Organizations" or "FITS to O" to be used in selecting and evaluating DLMS. This model groups the core requirements into four categories, functionality, interface, technology, and support, and then identifies subcategories within each group. The categories along with suggested weights are compiled into a relatively comprehensive yet flexible checklist. As the authors point out, the checklist can be adopted to individual institutional needs or used in evaluating selected DLMS components like functionality or interface (Zhang and Gourley, 2009).

A number of studies discuss the selection of open source repository software and provide criteria for their evaluation (Fay, 2010; Marill and Luczak, 2009; Rieger, 2007). Rieger (2007) discusses the selection process in light of multiple purposes of repositories and presents an evaluation model that involves several steps, including stakeholder analysis, needs assessment, service definition, and identification of use cases and governance-related matters. Marill and Luczak (2009) report on the process of selecting a repository system for NLM. In this case, ten repository systems were evaluated according to the established functional and nonfunctional evaluation criteria. Three systems that ranked high, DigiTool, DSpace, and Fedora, were tested further. Fedora achieved the highest rank in this rigorous evaluation process and was recommended for implementation at NLM. Likewise, Fedora emerged as the most flexible repository in a comparative study conducted by Fay (2010). The NLM case study includes a useful list of evaluation criteria that can be applied in other settings (Marill and Luczak, 2009). DLMS evaluation categories and criteria are also part of larger digital library evaluation studies that are discussed in Chapter 10.

The landscape of DLMS has evolved from the early standalone systems to flexible, open models and collaborative, multipurpose systems. The development of open source software and the competing systems from commercial vendors provide digital library developers with many options to create and manage digital content. The development of lightweight solutions like Omeka has dramatically changed the DLMS landscape, and opened the participation in digital content creation to smaller institutions and individuals. Building digital collections no longer has to be tied to the institutions and large-scale DLMS. The range of specialized DLMS offers differing features that can be tailored to the needs of user communities and different types of content. The selection process, although still not easy, is informed by a growing body of research on evaluation models and criteria.

The increasing diversity of DLMS does not mean that the currently available systems meet all user requirements. While there has been significant progress in interoperability and building flexible systems, user-level functionality still leaves much to be desired. DLMS function for the most part as databases of objects and associated metadata with limited capabilities for building layers to present contextual information. Further, they are limited in their ability to provide workspaces for end users to manipulate digital objects, contribute their own materials, or collaborate with others. Ioannidis et al. (2005) describe a number of hypothetical scenarios for advanced digital library functionality to support users in cultural heritage and scientific communities. Many concepts proposed in those scenarios, such as real-time construction of collections, personal annotations, or collaborative spaces, are still not supported by most standard DLMS. The design of DLMS is still a work in progress.

REFERENCES

Andro, M., Asselin, E., Maisonneuve, M., 2012. Digital libraries: comparison of 10 software. Lib. Collect., Acquisit. Tech. Serv. 36 (3), 79–83.

Arms, W.Y., 1995. Key concepts in the architecture of the digital library. D-Lib Mag. 1 (1).

Arms, W.Y., 2000. Digital Libraries. MIT Press, Cambridge, MA.

Arms, W.Y., Hillmann, D., Lagoze, C., Krafft, D., Marisa, R., Saylor, J., Van de Sompel, H., 2002. A spectrum of interoperability: the site for science prototype for the NSDL. D-Lib Mag. 8 (1), 9. Available from: http://www.dlib.org/dlib/january02/arms/01arms.html.

Awre, C., 2012. Hydra UK: flexible repository solutions to meet varied needs. Ariadne 70. Available from: http://www.ariadne.ac.uk/issue70/hydra-2012-11-rpt.

Awre, C., Cramer, T., 2012. Building the Hydra together: enhancing repository provision through multi-institution collaboration. J. Digital Inf. 13 (1), 1–11.

Breeding, M., 2013. Technology alternatives for special collections. Comp. Lib. 33 (9), 19–22.

Breeding, M., 2015. The Future of Library Resource Discovery. A White Paper Commissioned by the NISO Discovery to Delivery (D2D) Topic Committee. NISO. Available from: http://www.niso.org/apps/group_public/download.php/14487/future_library_resource_discovery.pdf.

Burns, C.S., Lana, A., Budd, J.M., 2013. Institutional repositories: exploration of costs and value. D-Lib Mag. 19 (1–2). Available from: http://www.dlib.org/dlib/january13/burns/01burns.html.

Candela, L., Castelli, D., Pagano, P., 2007a. A reference architecture for digital library systems: principles and applications. In: Digital Libraries: Research and Development, pp. 22–35. Berlin: Springer.

Candela, L., Castelli, D., Pagano, P., Thano, C., Ioannidis, Y., Koutrika, G., Schuldt, H., 2007b. Setting the foundations of digital libraries: the DELOS manifesto. D-Lib Mag. 13 (3), 4. Available from: http://www.dlib.org/dlib/march07/castelli/03castelli.html.

Candela, L., Castelli, D., Fox, E.A., Ioannidis, Y., 2010. On digital library foundations. Int. J. Digital Lib. 11 (1), 37–39.

Chowdhury, G., Chowdhury, S., 2003. Introduction to Digital Libraries. Facet Publishing, London.

CollectiveAccess, 2015. About CollectiveAccess. Available from: http://www.collectiveaccess.org/support/library.

Concordia, C., Gradmann, S., Siebinga, S., 2010. Not just another portal, not just another digital library: a portrait of Europeana as an application program interface. IFLA J. 36 (1), 61–69.

Corbett, H., Ghaphery, J., Work, L., Byrd, S., 2016 forthcoming. Choosing a repository platform: open source vs. hosted solutions. In: Burton, B., Callicott, D.S., Wesolek, A. (Eds.), Making Institutional Repositories Work. Charleston Insights in Library, Archival, and Information Sciences. Purdue University Press. Available from: http://scholarscompass.vcu.edu/cgi/viewcontent.cgi?article=1036&context=libraries_pubs.

Cramer, T., Kott, K., 2010. Designing and implementing second generation digital preservation services: a scalable model for the Stanford digital repository. D-Lib Mag. 16 (9), 1. Available from: http://www.dlib.org/dlib/september10/cramer/09cramer.html.

Davis, J.R., Lagoze, C., 2000. NCSTRL: design and deployment of a globally distributed digital library. J. Am. Soc. Inf. Sci. 51 (3), 273.

DSpace 2015, DSpace Home. Available from: http://www.dspace.org/.

DuraSpace, 2015a. Fedora user registry. Available from: http://www.duraspace.org/registry/fedora.

DuraSpace, 2015b. Hydra community framework. Available from: https://wiki.duraspace.org/display/hydra/Hydra+Community+Framework.

Fay, E., 2010. Repository software comparison: building digital library infrastructure at LSE. Ariadne 64. Available from: http://www.ariadne.ac.uk/issue64/fay.

Fedora, 2015. Fedora Repository Home. Available from: http://fedorarepository.org/.

Fox, R., 2006. The digital library in the bazaar. OCLC Syst. Serv. Int. Digital Lib. Persp. 22 (2), 100–106.

Gilbert, H., Mobley, T., 2013. Breaking up with CONTENTdm: why and how one institution took the leap to open source. Code4lib J. 20 (4). Available from: http://journal.code4lib.org/articles/8327.

Goh, D.H.-L., Chua, A., Khoo, D.A., Khoo, E.B.-H., Mak, E.B.-T., Ng, M.W.-M., 2006. A checklist for evaluating open source digital library software. Online Inf. Rev. 30 (4), 360–379.

Gonçalves, M.A., Fox, E.A., Watson, L.T., 2008. Towards a digital library theory: a formal digital library ontology. Int. J. Digital Lib. 8 (2), 91–114.

Green, R., Awre, C., 2009. Towards a repository-enabled scholar's workbench. D-Lib Mag. 15 (5/6). Available from: http://www.dlib.org/dlib/may09/green/05green.html.

Han, Y., 2004. Digital content management: the search for a content management system. Lib. Hi Tech. 22 (4), 355–365.

Henry, G., 2012. Core Infrastructure Considerations for Large Digital Libraries. Council on Library and Information Resources, Digital Library Federation, Washington, DC.

Hydra Project, 2015. About Hydra. Available from: http://projecthydra.org/.

Ioannidis, Y., Maier, D., Abiteboul, S., Buneman, P., Davidson, S., Fox, E., Weikum, G., 2005. Digital library information-technology infrastructures. Int. J. Digital Lib. 5 (4), 266–274.

Islandora, 2015. About. Available from: http://islandora.ca/about.

Jettka, D., Stein, D., 2014. The HZSK repository: implementation, features, and use cases of a repository for spoken language corpora. D-Lib Mag. 20 (9/10). Available from: http://www.dlib.org/dlib/september14/jettka/09jettka.html.

Kahn, R., Wilensky, R., 2006. A framework for distributed digital object services. Int. J. Digital Lib. 6 (2), 115–123.

Kaplan, D., 2009. Choosing a digital asset management system that's right for you. J. Archival Org. 7 (1/2), 33–40.

KE Software, 2015. Research. Available from: http://emu.kesoftware.com/about-emu/overview/research.

Kent, A., 2014. Islandora. Comp. Lib. 34 (9), 12–32.

Krafft, D.B., Birkland, A., Cramer, E.J., 2008. NCore: architecture and implementation of a flexible, collaborative digital library. In: Proceedings of the Eighth ACM/IEEE-CS Joint Conference on Digital Libraries, pp. 313–322. ACM.

Krishnamurthy, M.M., 2008. Open access, open source and digital libraries: a current trend in university libraries around the world. Prog. Electron. Lib. Inf. Syst. 42 (1), 48–55.

Kucsma, J., Reiss, K., Sidman, A., 2010. Using Omeka to build digital collections: the METRO case study. D-Lib Mag. 16 (3/4). Available from: http://www.dlib.org/dlib/march10/kucsma/03kucsma.html.

Kutay, S., 2014. Advancing digital repository services for faculty primary research assets: an exploratory study. J. Acad. Librar. 40 (6), 642–649.

Lagoze, C., Fielding, D., 1998. Defining collections in distributed digital libraries. D-Lib Mag. 4 (11).

Lagoze, C., Van de Sompel, H., 2001. The open archives initiative: building a low-barrier interoperability framework. In: Proceedings of the First ACM/IEEE-CS Joint Conference on Digital Libraries, pp. 54–62.

Lagoze, C., Van de Sompel, H., 2003. The making of the open archives initiative protocol for metadata harvesting. Lib. Hi Tech. 21 (2), 118–128.

Lagoze, C., Payette, S., Shin, E., Wilper, C., 2006. Fedora: an architecture for complex objects and their relationships. Int. J. Digital Lib. 6 (2), 124–138.

Luna Imaging, 2015. Luna Solo. Available from: http://www.lunaimaging.com/solo.

Lynch, C.A., 2003. Institutional repositories: essential infrastructure for scholarship in the digital age. Portal Lib. Acad. 3 (2), 327–336.

Madalli, D.P., Barve, S., Amin, S., 2012. Digital preservation in open-source digital library software. J. Acad. Librar. 38 (3), 161–164.

Marill, J.L., Luczak, E.C., 2009. Evaluation of digital repository software at the National Library of Medicine. D-Lib Mag. 15 (5–6). Available from: http://www.dlib.org/dlib/may09/marill/05marill.html.

Matusiak, K.K., Myagmar, M., 2009. Newspaper digitization project in Mongolia: creating a digital archive of Mongolian rare periodicals. Ser. Librar. 57 (1), 118–127.

Moses, D., Stapelfeldt, K., 2013. Renewing UPEI's institutional repository: new features for an Islandora-based environment. Code4lib J. 21 (9). Available from: http://journal.code4lib.org/articles/8763.

Moulaison, H.L., Dykas, F., Gallant, K., 2015. OpenDOAR repositories and metadata practices. D-Lib. Mag. 21 (3/4), 1. Available from: http://www.dlib.org/dlib/march15/moulaison/03moulaison.htm..

OCLC, 2015. CONTENTdm. Available from: http://www.oclc.org/en-US/contentdm.html.

Omeka, 2015a. Omeka: Project. Available from: http://omeka.org/about/.

Omeka, 2015b.Teaching with Omeka. Available from: http://omeka.org/codex/Teach_with_Omeka.

Open Archives Initiative 2002. The open archives initiative protocol for metadata harvesting. Available from: http://www.openarchives.org/OAI/2.0/openarchivesprotocol.htm.

Open Archives Initiative (OAI), 2015. Home. Available from: https://www.openarchives.org/.

Open Source Initiative, 2015. Open Source Definition. Available from: http://opensource.org/.

OpenDOAR: Directory of Open Access Repositories, 2015. Usage of open access repository software—worldwide. University of Nottingham, UK. Avaialble from: http://www.opendoar.org/find.php?format=charts.

Paepcke, A., Chang, C.C.K., Winograd, T., García-Molina, H., 1998. Interoperability for digital libraries worldwide. Commun. ACM 41 (4), 33–42.

Palmer, A., Choi, N., 2014. The current state of library open source software research: a descriptive literature review and classification. Lib. Hi Tech 32 (1), 11–27.

Payette, S., Lagoze, C., 1998. Flexible and extensible digital object and repository architecture (FEDORA). Second European Conference on Research and Advanced Technology for Digital Libraries, Heraklion, Crete, Greece, September 21–23. Available from: http://arxiv.org/abs/1312.1258.

Payette, S., Blanchi, C., Lagoze, C., Overly, E., 1999. Interoperability for digital objects and repositories. D-Lib Mag. 5 (5). Available from: http://www.dlib.org/dlib/may99/payette/05payette.html.

Payne, A., Singh, V., 2010. Open source software use in libraries. Lib. Rev. 59 (9), 708–717.

Public Knowledge Project, 2015. Open Journal Systems. Available from: http://pkp.sfu.ca/ojs/.

Rafiq, M., 2009. LIS community's perceptions towards open source software adoption in libraries. Int. Inf. Lib. Rev. 41 (3), 137–145.

Rieger, O.Y., 2007. Select for success: key principles in assessing repository models. D-Lib Mag. 13 (7–8). Available from: http://www.dlib.org/dlib/july07/rieger/07rieger.html.

Samuels, R.G., Griffy, H., 2012. Evaluating open source software for use in library initiatives: a case study involving electronic publishing. Portal Lib. Acad. 12 (1), 41–62.

Smith, M., Barton, M., Bass, M., Branschofsky, M., McClellan, G., Stuve, D., Walker, J. H., 2003. DSpace: An open source dynamic digital repository. D-Lib Mag. 9(1). Available from: http://www.dlib.org/dlib/january03/smith/01smith.html.

Staples, T., Wayland, R., Payette, S., 2003. The Fedora Project: an open-source digital object repository management system. D-Lib Mag. 9 (4). Available from: http://www.dlib.org/dlib/april03/staples/04staples.html.

Stein, A., Thompson, S., 2015. Taking control: identifying motivations for migrating library digital asset management systems. D-Lib Mag. 21 (9). Available from: http://www.dlib.org/dlib/september15/stein/09stein.html.

Suleman, H., 2005. Analysis and evaluation of service oriented architectures for digital libraries. In: Peer-to-Peer, Grid, and Service-Orientation in Digital Library Architectures, Springer, Berlin and Heidelberg, pp. 130–146.

Suleman, H., 2012. The design and architecture of digital libraries. In: Chowdhury, G.G., Foo, S. (Eds.), Digital Libraries and Information Access: Research Perspectives. Neal-Schuman, Chicago, IL, pp. 13–28.

Suleman, H., Fox, E.A., 2001. A framework for building open digital libraries. D-Lib Mag. 7 (12). Available from: http://www.dlib.org/dlib/december01/suleman/12suleman.html.

Suleman, H., Fox, E.A., Kelapure, R., Krowne, A., Luo, M., 2003. Building digital libraries from simple building blocks. Online Inf. Rev. 27 (5), 301–310.

Swan, A., 2012. Policy Guidelines for the Development and Promotion of Open Access. UNESCO, Paris.

Thacker, C., Knutson, C., 2015. Barriers to initiation of open source software projects in libraries. Code4Lib J. 29. Available from: http://journal.code4lib.org/articles/10665.

Tramboo, S., Shafi, S.M., Gul, S., 2012. A study on the open source digital library softwares: special reference to DSpace, EPrints and Greenstone. Int. J. Comp. App. 59 (16), 1–9.

WGBH Educational Foundation, 2015. Open Vault. Available from: http://openvault.wgbh.org/.

Witten, I.H., 2008. The development and usage of the Greenstone digital library software. Bull. Am. Soc. Inf. Sci. Technol. 35 (2), 31–38.

Witten, I.H., Bainbridge, D., 2003. How to Build a Digital Library. Morgan Kaufmann, San Francisco.

Yeh, J.H., Sie, S.H., Chen, C.C., 2009. Extensible digital library service platform. In: Theng, Y.-L., Foo, S., Goh, D., Na, J.-C. (Eds.), Handbook of Research on Digital Libraries: Design, Development, and Impact. Information Science Reference, Hershey, NY, pp. 27–40.

Zhang, A.B., Gourley, D., 2009. Creating Digital Collections: a Practical Guide. Oxford, England, Chandos.

Zick, G., 2009. Digital collections: history and perspectives. J. Lib. Adm. 49 (7), 687–693.

INTERFACE DESIGN AND EVALUATION

FOUNDATIONS FOR INTERFACE DESIGN AND DESIGN PRINCIPLES
FOUNDATIONS FOR INTERFACE DESIGN

The information retrieval (IR) process is an interaction process between users and IR systems. In a digital library environment, interface design needs to facilitate the interactions between users and digital libraries. Saracevic's (1996, 1997) stratified interaction model highlights the interface (the platform for exchange) in which the interactions between users and systems take place. According to Ingwersen and Jarvelin's (2005) integrated IS&R Research Framework, the interaction process can be further considered as the interactions among cognitive actors of all the stakeholders in the information retrieval and seeking process, which consist of the following human groups in the information creation, organization, dissemination, use process as well as interface design and retrieval engine design:

- Creators of information objects
- Indexers constructing representations of information objects to facilitate retrieval of information objects
- Designers creating interfaces to facilitate users' interaction with systems
- Designers building retrieval engines and algorithms to facilitate users' effective information retrieval
- Gatekeepers determining the availability of information objects into a collection
- Information seekers or searchers looking for information to accomplish their tasks
- Dommunities representing a variety of groups in different organizational, social, and cultural contexts

The critical challenge for interface design is how to offer an interface platform for users to interact with all the cognitive actors involved in the process. To be more specific, in Belkin's (1996) episode model of interaction with text, he proposes an approach that shows how interface design can support different types of interactions by supporting various types of information-seeking strategies.

DESIGN PRINCIPLES

General interface design principles also apply to digital library interface design. Nielsen (1995) proposes 10 detailed user-interface heuristics: visibility of system status; match between system and real work; user control and freedom; consistency and standards; error prevention; recognition rather than recall; flexibility and efficiency of use; aesthetic and minimalist design; help users recognize, diagnose, and recover from errors; and help and documentation. Shneiderman's (1998) eight golden rules of interface design are similar to Nielsen's interface heuristics. He does point out some unique design rules, such as offering informative feedback and permitting easy reversal of actions. Norman (2002) presents two principles of good design: (1) a conceptual model and (2) visibility. He specifies the following guidance for a good design:

- Visibility—Extremely important aspect of interface design; features should be obvious to aid users' awareness of their purpose.
- Mappings—Features should correspond to the perceived use.
- Affordances—The interface promotes understanding of how to use features.
- Constraints—Design should take into account the limitations of features.
- Conceptual model—Mental idea of a design element should be based on mappings, affordances, and constraints.
- Mental model—Users' actions interactions with features should relate to conceptual metaphors by which the users are already familiar.
- Feedback—Interface should make users aware of their use of features and the results of such use.

These guidelines can serve as general design principles for digital library interface design. More importantly, digital library interface design needs to have its own unique characteristics.

ITERATIVE DESIGN

Digital library interface design cannot be done in one step. It is an iterative design process that moves from design to evaluation, to redesign and reevaluation, back to redesign again, and so on. The most important step in developing a digital library is to identify the audience and its information needs as well as to understand the iterative design process (Norberg et al., 2005). Somerville and Brar (2009) discuss the methodologies for studying user needs in a user-centered approach: interviews, focus groups, ethnographic studies, and observation. They place an emphasis on iterative design from prototyping to evaluation, modification, and implementation. Nielsen (1993) recommends at least three rounds of iteratively designing an interface based on user testing.

The iterative design process is an effective approach for digital library design. Norberg et al. (2005) discuss their redesign process of a digital library based on usability testing and focus groups. Prototypes of redesigns were presented to each focus group for its feedback. The feedback was incorporated into each successive redesign of the digital library. The redesign process was an iterative and participatory process involving the key stakeholders of the digital library. They conclude that users' interactions with digital libraries are task oriented and context dependent. Based mainly on the direct observation and interviews, Ferreira and Pithan (2005) report on the usability study integrating HCI principles and information search processes revealing issues in the design. Further improvements of the digital library are suggested.

Iterative design is closely associated with iterative user-centered evaluation. Bertot et al. (2006) focus on the functionality, usability, and accessibility of iterative digital library assessment. Functionality assesses whether a digital library enables users to perform desired operations. Suggested criteria include the ability to refine searches and the ability to apply a variety of search options. Usability assesses whether a digital library enables users to use different features of the digital library, which include navigation, content presentation, labels, and search process. Accessibility assesses whether a digital library enables users with disabilities to access the digital library, dealing with factors such as alternative forms of content, color independent, clear navigation mechanisms, and table transformation.

DESIGN AND CUSTOMIZATION OF USER INTERFACE

The process of designing and implementing a user interface consists of the following steps.

CONCEPTUAL DESIGN: IDENTIFICATION OF USERS' UNIQUE NEEDS

The design of a user interface first needs to consider what users want. Phillips (2012) proposes to address the following questions:

- Who will use the interface?
- What can be done with the interface, and what are its limitations?
- Where will the interface be used?
- Why will users use the interface?
- How will the interface be used?

In order to characterize the user behavior, here are the main questions that need to be answered:

- How does the interface encourage or discourage users' tasks?
- How are information search features designed to facilitate user tasks?
- How do users employ information relative to the larger information setting?
- How do users search tactics promote task completion, and do these tactics remain constant throughout the task?
- How do users understand, save, and use data, and what features are they using to do so?
- How do users determine success?

Different types of users have different requirements. Chapter 8 discusses in detail the needs of different types of users. Digital library interface design needs to tailor to specific user needs. Children are one specific type of user group. Here is one example of how to convert children's needs into an interface design. Kaplan et al. (2004) include children as partners to prototype, test, and develop digital libraries. The following questions were examined:

- What do the concepts reading and library mean to children in this age group?
- How do American tweens and teens read in their everyday lives? What are its uses and rewards for them?
- How do their knowledge about digital technologies and their experiences with computers and the Internet shape their expectations of online texts? (pp. 90–91).

In addition to the six children on the design team, they also solicited opinions from 40 children for contextual inquiry. Observation, note-taking, and interview methods were used to collect data when children engaged in the following tasks: locating reading materials in public libraries, reading for pleasure at home, working on reading assignments at home, and working on reading assignments as part of the class work in a public library. A sticky notes session, brainstorming, and prototyping were applied to develop the user interface for children.

Simultaneously, the design of interface also has been taken into consideration for the types of digital libraries. Users exhibit different types of strategies in searching musical and video digital libraries. Based on an ethnographic study consisting of interviews, focus groups, and observations, Cunningham et al. (2003)

identify the following music information-seeking strategies for the design of a music digital library: known item, significant browsing activity, collaborative music shopping, useful journal run strategy, keeping up to date, visual music shopping, and reluctance to ask for help. These behaviors are not well supported by the current musical digital libraries. The following suggestions for interface design are made: (1) serendipitous browsing by offering CD covers accompanied by snippets of songs from each album; and (2) genre browsing supported by similarities of sound or rhythm.

Let us examine three examples of digital libraries development: a digital musical library, a children's digital library, and a video digital library. In establishing a digital musical library test bed system, the main user interface components were first proposed, consisting of search window, audio player, playlist, timeliner, score viewer, and bookmark editor. Associated functionality was also defined. For example, the functionality of a search window was specified as "using a metadata model designed specifically for cataloging and finding classical and popular music. The search window lets user input such music-specific criteria as composer, performer, work, and key. The search results present, for example, all the performances of a particular work, along with information about performers so that users can pick out the performance of interest" (Notess et al., 2005, p. 302).

In building an international children's digital library, Druin (2005) reports a more intensive design study with children. Children from age 7–11 were selected to participate. On average, they stayed with the project for two years. Adult and children researchers worked together twice a week during the school year and intensive weeks over the summer. The International Children's Digital Library interface was developed based on the following methods: children interviewing other children, writing one thing a child likes and dislikes, group discussion sessions, and prototypes to sketch new ideas. The associated features that were implemented are search categories, feelings, colors, customizable good reader colors, and spiral book reader.

Focusing on the video content, Albertson (2013) proposes an interaction and interface design framework for video digital libraries. The key for the conceptual design is associating user requirements with the interface design. The uniqueness of the framework is that it maps the conceptual understanding of the users' interaction with video digital libraries to the design of user interfaces. He created two figures to illustrate the conversion. While Fig. 7.1 specifies user interaction components of the framework, Fig. 7.2 suggests interface design components of the framework. In both figures, the user and situation are the main dimensions of the interactive video retrieval process. User factors represent different levels of experience, knowledge, and domain affiliation, which are presented vertically from a low level (bottom of the figure) to a high level (top of the figure). Situational factors represent system support and/or barriers, which are presented horizontally from high situational support (left) to low levels of support (right). The third dimension is related to the user interaction and its associated interface designs/features. Undoubtedly, user interaction and interface design are dependent on the user and situational factors. Interface design closely corresponds to user interaction. The size variation distinguishes the differences from broad to specific concepts, and the center section highlights the core of the framework. The main contribution of this framework is that it connects user interaction to system supportive features.

PROTOTYPE DESIGN

As part of the iterative design, prototype design is a quick and flexible approach for the developers to solicit feedback from users and stakeholders. It simulates part or all of a user interface by drawing it

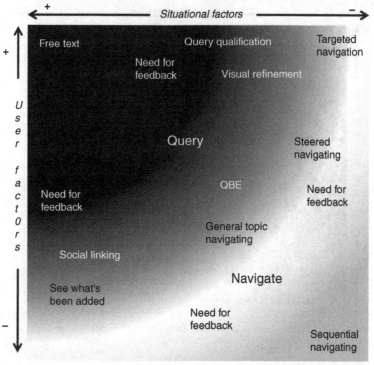

FIGURE 7.1 User Interaction Component of Framework (Albertson, 2013, p. 677)

out using paper and pen or a different tool. Hackos and Redish (1998) provide main components to include in prototypes:

- The overall architecture of the interface
- Visual depiction of main screen layout
- Visual depictions of secondary screens
- Visual depictions of the primary features
- Alternate design concepts

Wagner (1990) discusses the advantages of how a prototype enables designers to present design ideas more efficiently and can easily modify their designs based on the feedback. Most prototype design ideas are sketched on paper. There are also tools used to facilitate prototype design. Electronic tools can recognize widgets and widget behaviors, unlike paper prototypes' static images. For example, researchers developed the electronic Sketching Interfaces Like Krazy (SILK) to allow designers more flexibility in creating and evaluating design prototypes. SILK shows interface elements or widgets' behaviors and supports the creation of storyboards (Landay and Myers, 2001).

A good digital library design takes several rounds of prototype design and assessment. Norberg et al. (2005) report their development and testing of prototypes of user interfaces in a digital library via a series of focus groups. The focus groups were presented with the original site and prototype redesigns.

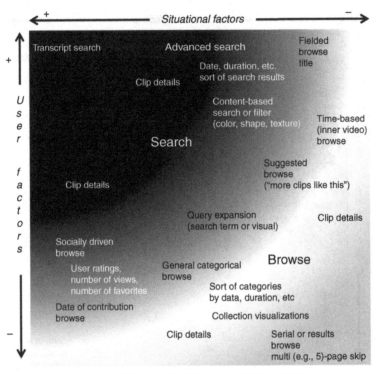

FIGURE 7.2 Interface Design Component of Framework (Albertson, 2013, p. 677)

Open-ended questions were asked to solicit feedback for different ideas of prototype designs. Several rounds of prototype design took place ranging from changing the color scheme to fonts or position of elements. During the prototype tests, users participated in the iterative design process. Somerville and Brar (2009) describe another example of user-centered design for digital library projects. Students were involved in investigating their peers' information-seeking needs. Their findings led to the creation of paper prototypes and usability tests. Positive user experiences are important to incorporate into the digital library projects.

Prototype design is also a great approach for the design of children's digital libraries. Prototype design allows children to view examples of designs in different formats. Children were shown a web-based mock-up of the three interface designs of a children's digital library. After dividing children into several groups, they were give a paper-based version of the three interface designs for more careful examination. They were instructed to write down three things they liked and three they desired for the digital library interfaces. The results show that they prefer the use of bright colors, good graphics, and audio (Theng et al., 2000). Prototype design is also employed for visualization design for digital libraries. Using paper-based prototyping, users worked in pairs to sketch design ideas in visualization form for the given scenario. After presenting the initial ideas, the group collaborated to develop the final prototypes. The study demonstrates that it is beneficial to include users and other stakeholders in the design of digital libraries (Zaphiris, 2004).

INTERFACE DESIGN: CONFIGURATIONS

Digital library interface design has to consider both the needs of users and characteristics of digital collections. Among all the interface components, features to support collection selection, query formulation, results manipulation and evaluation, and help use are vital for digital library interface design. Chowdhury (2004) summarizes the design components of digital libraries:

- Interface features:
  - types of interface including simple and advanced search interface
  - languages of the interface
  - navigation options, shortcuts, and system information
  - screen features including colors, typography, layout, and graphics
  - personalization of the interface
- Resource selection
- Query formulation
- Results manipulation
- Help

There are multiple digital library content management systems available to design these interfaces. Detailed discussion of these systems are shown in Chapter 6. Each content management system has its own tutorials for its interface design. As CONTENTdm is one of the most popularly used systems, Table 7.1 presents the configuration options of the interface for a collection built with CONTENTdm.

Not all digital library systems apply the same approach to interface configuration. Omeka uses themes to customize the look and feel of the public Omeka site. Themes are a collection of template files and help functions that use data in each specific Omeka archive and display those data to end users. From the administration side, designers can control some of that display through configurations. In versions 1.3 and above, all themes are configurable in the Settings > Themes admin screen.

Configurations are unique for each theme and will be saved with the theme. Each theme must be configured when changing designs. Upon returning to the original theme, all of the initial configurations will be saved. The configuration includes the look of the digital library site, navigation, featured elements, homepage text, and metadata displayed (Omeka, 2015).

- Choose a logo file. Designers can use their own logo file. Recommended maximum width is also suggested.
- Custom Header Navigation. Designers are allowed to create their own theme header with corresponding text.
- Display Featured Item. Designers can show a featured item on the homepage.
- Display Featured Collection. Designers can show a link featuring a collection on the homepage.
- Display Featured Exhibit. Designers can show a link featuring an exhibit on the homepage.
- Homepage Recent Items. Designers can choose the number of recent items to be displayed on the homepage.
- Homepage Text. Designers can add brief text to be displayed on the homepage.
- Footer Text. Designers can add text to be displayed in a theme's footer. This can be a good place to add credits or links to funders, such as credits information.
- Display Copyright in Footer. Designers can display copyright information in the footer (para. 5).

Table 7.1 Configuration Options Offered by CONTENTdm (Configuring, n.d., p. 3)	
Quick Config[a]	An optional way to set up some initial global configurations that help establish the site identity.
Appearance	Use the Appearance configurations to tailor the look and feel of your Web site or collections by modifying the header and setting fonts and colors to reflect your branding.
Searching and Browsing	Use the Searching and Browsing options to configure the default search mode and advanced search scope and to configure the results page display, default sorting, and more.
UI Widgets	Use the UI Widgets configurations to enable and define features that can help users explore and experience items in your collections. For example, create Suggested Topics, which guide end users in their research, and tailor the QuickView display, which helps users quickly scan items with some additional detail.
Image Viewer	Use the Image Viewer configurations to tailor toolbar options and other features to best showcase items in your collections.
Navigation	Use the Navigation configurations to edit or add to the header and footer navigation links.
Items	Use the Items configurations to set various options that are available when end users view items in your collections. For example, manage user-generated content, enable and configure the Share and Reference URL features, choose whether to display the full text for items with transcripts, and configure metadata display settings.
Page Types	Use the Page Types configurations to edit the contents and set representative item display options for key pages of your Web site, optionally replace key pages with custom pages, enable your site for RSS, and define the display of compound objects and PDF files.
Tools	Use the Tools option to configure the localized version of your Web site interface text, including the default language, uploading a custom language file, and enabling users to select from multiple languages. You also can configure a CONTENTdm Log In/Out link on your Web site, and configure the credentials used by a custom form for end-user content submission.
Custom Pages/ Scripts	Use the Custom Pages/Scripts options to add additional pages to your Web site and use your own JavaScript scripts and CSS to modify the Web site behavior and appearance.

[a]*For this class you should not see the Quick Config option. If you can, please do not use it as it will alter the settings for the entire class website.*

The earlier two examples illustrate interface configurations from a commercial digital library content management system and an open source system. Both CONTENTdm and Omeka have rather limited options for interface configuration. Each content management system has its own options and instructions. Chapter 6 offers more detailed discussions on the main digital library content management systems.

CUSTOMIZED DESIGN AND VISUAL TOOLS

Each digital library has its own unique content and unique user groups. It is essential for the interface to reflect the uniqueness of the theme of the digital library or collection. Content management systems in general allow customization of digital library interface. Here is one example from UWM Libraries' Digital Collections (http://collections.lib.uwm.edu/). UWM Digital Collections are built using CONTENTdm, which provides an open application programming interface (API). CONTENTdm APIs enable developers to customize the layout and integrate various features into a digital library interface. In particular, it is possible to integrate different features into an interface by connecting collections through APIs provided by the digital library system, although the customization is limited, and integrating applications requires quite a bit of programming.

The timeline view collection application was successfully added to the UWM digital library site (Fig. 7.3), and the application accessed the metadata organized in a JSON file to display the content of the selected collections. The Web page in Fig. 7.3 displays a collection of items related to March On Milwaukee. The items are organized into sections arranged chronologically. Each section header describes an historical event and its timeline, followed by a short description of the event, and a link to a file presenting the event in detail. There are various resources including images, video, and audio. The timeline application was also implemented in other digital library software, such as Omeka (omeka.org) (Fig. 7.4). The image was created by Sukjin You by using and revising the following timeline open source code to the Omeka system: https://timeline.knightlab.com/; https://github.com/NUKnightLab/TimelineJS. It proved that the timeline application can be implemented in different digital library platforms that provide an option for embedding customized pages or allow access to the content.

Visualization is an approach applied quite popularly in digital libraries. Developers can design their own visual tools to facilitate users' effective interaction with digital libraries. Many digital libraries have incorporated visual tools into the interface design. Fig. 7.5 shows the map from the Digital Public Library of America. Users can select digital objects from different states. When a circle on the map is clicked, the titles of digital objects and thumbnails are displayed. Visualizing query and search results is the most applied application of visual tools. Linn et al. (2007) introduce the SearchGraph that enables users to view abstract visualization of search results. Moreover, users can manipulate the display, and use sort and filter options to view the search results from different perspectives. Seifert (2011)

Timeline

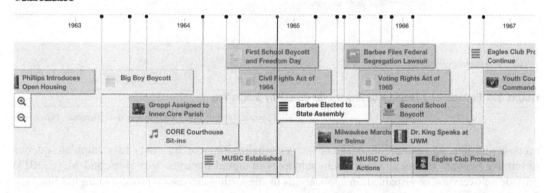

November 4, 1964

Barbee Elected to State Assembly

In 1964 attorney Lloyd Barbee was elected to the Wisconsin State Assembly, where he served until 1977. Even before his election, he had dedicated his life to civil rights by participating in the NAACP, coordinating protests, and

FIGURE 7.3 Implementation of the Timeline Application in the University of Wisconsin-Milwaukee Digital Collection "March on Milwaukee" Built in CONTENTdm

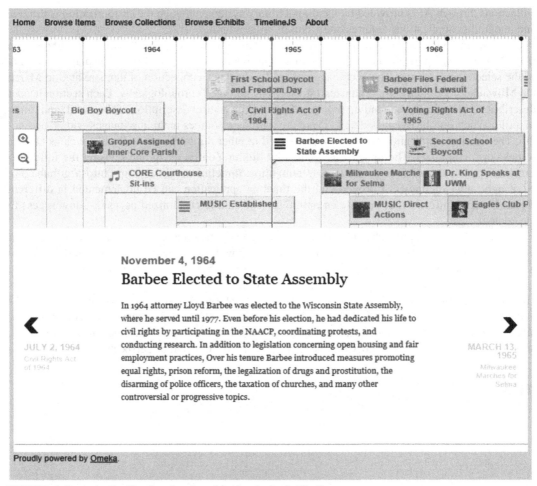

FIGURE 7.4 Example of a Timeline Developed for Omeka by Sukjin You

With permission from Sukjin You (University of Wisconsin–Milwaukee).

proposes an interactive multidimensional query visualization tool for users to manipulate queries to retrieve relevant results under different subtopics in digital libraries. Van Hoek and Mayr (2013) provide an overview of visualization applications in supporting the search process in digital libraries. Examples include VQuery that visualizes the query and assists users to specify queries using Boolean operators; INVISQUE system that integrates the division between query specification and results; Info-Syk that contains a hierarchical tree browser and a star map providing a good overview of documents; The Cat-A-Cone system that is an early 3-dimensional system that uses cone trees to display category hierarchies; and the 3-dimensional search interface NIRVE system that connects user query terms to concepts.

In contrast to searching, browsing is a unique component for digital libraries. Rajkumar (2006) designed a visual browsing interface that offered users the opportunity to navigate through the records of a digital library with multidimensional, hierarchical, and categorical data. The visual interface was

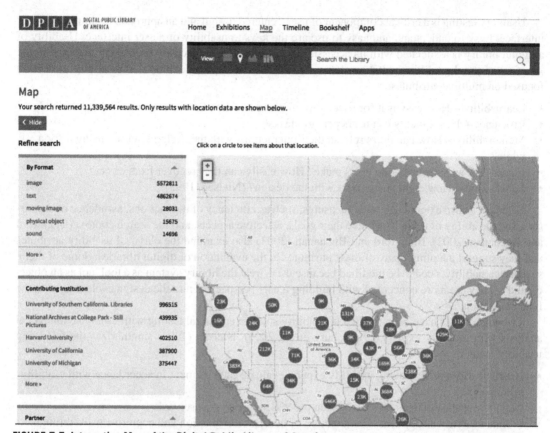

FIGURE 7.5 Interactive Map of the Digital Public Library of America

designed following three principles: consider browsing structure as the primary data, display all possible browsable dimensions, and treat dimensions uniformly.

Metadata has been used to improve the design of visual interfaces in digital libraries. Shiri (2008) examined 21 metadata-enhanced digital library visual interfaces, in particular their visualization techniques and metaphors. Types of metaphors implemented include treemaps, timelines, scatter plots, Venn diagrams, charts, sematic-spatial maps, and association networks metadata. He points out that visualization techniques and metaphors become an effective approach to support users exploring information in digital libraries. In addition, ActiveGraph is a visualization tool that enables users to view and customize content of a digital library by adding or editing metadata (Marks et al., 2005).

USABILITY TESTING

The objective of digital library evaluation is to assess to what extent it meets its objectives and offer suggestions for enhancements. Citing human computer interaction research, Shneiderman (1998) discusses human computer interaction/interface evaluation criteria: usability, functionality, effort, as well as task appropriateness and failures.

Usability testing is a critical component of user-centered design and an approach for improving user interface. Easy to understand and easy to use are the keys to usability of a user interface. Usability of a digital library is associated with its accessibility, in particular how easily users can interact with the interface of the digital library (Chowdhury et al., 2006). Accepted definitions of usability have been focused on multiple attributes:

- Learnability—How easy is it for users to perform tasks when first interacting with the design?
- Efficiency—How quickly can users perform tasks?
- Memorability—How can users refresh their interactions with the design after not using it for a while?
- Errors—How many errors do users make? How easily can they recover from errors?
- Satisfaction—How content are users with the design? (Nielsen, 1993).

Usability is also extended to other measures, such as efficiency of interactions, avoidance of user errors, and the ability of users to achieve their goals, affective aspects, and the search context (Blandford and Buchanan, 2002). Blandford and Buchanan (2003) also examine the classical usability attributes and they suggest adopting many of these attributes to the evaluation of digital libraries. Some of them, such as learnability, need to be modified because users treat the library system as a tool, not as an object of study. They are more concerned with building a user perspective into the design cycle than with the final evaluation.

Two approaches have been applied to usability studies: empirical testing with users and analytical analysis with usability experts (Chowdhury et al., 2006). Nielsen (1994) summarizes the following usability methods:

- Heuristic evaluation: Having usability experts evaluate each element in accordance with usability principles.
- Cognitive walk-throughs: A step-by-step process simulating a user task.
- Formal usability inspections: Combination of heuristics evaluation and cognitive walk-through.
- Pluralistic walk-throughs: Similar to cognitive walk-through, but conducted in a group setting with users, developers, and usability experts discussing the steps of the walk-through together.
- Feature inspection: Assessing a proposed feature set to see whether it is natural for users to use and does not require extensive knowledge/skills to use the set.
- Consistency inspection: External designers checking an interface to see whether the new design operates in a similar fashion to other designs.
- Standards inspection: Inspecting the interface for compliance with standards by an expert.

In the context of digital libraries, Bertot et al. (2006) suggest some important questions for the usability testing that help the enhancement of the digital libraries:

- Were the basic navigation identification tasks intuitive?
- Were data presented within each interface logical, clear, and easy to understand?
- Did each interface perform as users expected it would?
- Could the data obtained from the testing be useful?
- What are some specific recommendations to make each interface more useful?
- What are some specific recommendations to improve each interface? (pp. 22–23).

A pilot study is essential for usability testing. Notess et al. (2005) identify several issues that a pilot study can help resolve, including the design of test tasks, system bugs, rewording of the tasks, etc.

USABILITY TESTING: CRITERIA AND APPROACHES

According to Liew's (2009) review article on organizational and people issues in digital library research, use/usability issues account for the majority of the work. Among the use/usability category, most of the papers focus on usability. Jeng (2005a, b) concludes that usability is a multidimensional construct. She further proposes an evaluation model for the assessment of the usability of digital libraries by examining their effectiveness, efficiency, satisfaction, and learnability. User satisfaction is a complicated construct that covers ease of use, organization of information, labeling, visual appearance, content, and error correction. The evaluation model was tested, and the results revealed that effectiveness, efficiency, and satisfaction are interrelated. Dillon (1999) develops a qualitative framework (termed TIME) for designers and implementers to evaluate the usability of digital libraries which focuses on user task (T), information model (I), manipulation facilities (M), and the ergonomic variables (E). Buttenfield (1999) suggests two evaluation strategies for usability studies of digital libraries: the convergent method paradigm that applies the system lifecycle into the evaluation process and the double-loop paradigm that enables evaluators to identify the value of a particular evaluation method under different situations. Even though usability is widely discussed, it is important to characterize the uniqueness of usability attributes for the assessment of digital libraries.

Before conducting usability testing, researchers have to make decisions regarding the selection of appropriate usability criteria. Design elements are one of the popular components of usability studies, which is essential for interface enhancement. Van House et al. (1996) focus on query form, fields, instructions, results displays, and formats of images and texts in the iterative design process for the University of California Berkeley Electronic Environmental Library Project. After reviewing literature on digital library user interface, Hariri and Norouzi (2011) identify the top 10 evaluation criteria for digital library interface: navigation, searching, design, guidance, error management, presentation, learnability, user control, consistency, and language. These criteria match pretty well with Nielsen's (1995) 10 interface heuristics.

Comparison of two user interfaces is a popular approach for conducting usability studies and offer useful design recommendations for digital library designers. Miller et al. (2012) compare the usability of the interfaces of the Open Library, Google Books, and HathiTrust on aesthetics, usability, and main interface components. Subjects first evaluated the aesthetics of the interfaces based on Lavie and Tractinsky's (2004) measures on aesthetic, being pleasant, clear, and clean. Next, subjects were instructed to evaluate the usability of three interfaces by adopting McGee et al. (2004) and Flanagin and Metzger's (2003) 10 items: "the extent to which interfaces were consistent and efficient, organized, easy and intuitive, effective, useful, controllable, complete and sophisticated, professional, trustworthy, and reliable" (p. 367). In addition, the following interface components were assessed: "collection browse, collection search, viewer navigation, viewer options, output options, accessibility, and help features" (p. 367). The findings indicate that most of the subjects preferred the Open Library for its aesthetic and large elements within its interface, as well as for presenting elements in a similar fashion to their counterparts in the physical library. Users like the familiarity of Google Books' Google-based interface. Interestingly, too many options are not welcomed by users. For that reason, the interface of HathiTrust is considered too complicated.

Some usability studies examine specific designs or features for interfaces, such as the organization approaches of digital libraries. Meyyappan et al. (2004) measure the effectiveness and usefulness of the alphabetic, subject category, and task-based organization approaches in a digital library, and the results show that the task-based approach takes the least time in locating information resources. By applying usability and affordance strength questionnaires, interviews, think-alouds, and observations, Shiri et al. (2013) examine the main elements of two user interfaces consisting of multilingual features, thesaurus and search functions, and visualization and visual appeal. Users prefer an integrated interface that connects thesaurus, query, and document spaces together. Ease of use of multilingual features, thesaurus, and search functions are the main reasons for users' liking of one of the interfaces.

Usability studies of digital libraries are often performed as a collection of studies across time. In Cherry and Duff's (2002) longitudinal study of a digital library collection, they focus on how the digital library is used and the level of user satisfaction with response time, browse capabilities, the comprehensiveness of the collection, print function, search capabilities, and the display of document pages. Hill et al. (2000) tested user interfaces of the Alexandria Digital Library (ADL) through a series of studies. The following usability requirements were derived from user evaluations: a unified and simplified search, being able to manage sessions, more options for results display, offering user workspace, holdings visualization, offering more Help functions, allowing easy data distribution, and informing users of the process status. Bertot et al. (2006) adopt a broad understanding of usability, including satisfaction, in addition to ease of use, efficiency, and memorability in the iterative evaluation of the Florida Electronic Library. They also bring in functionality and accessibility as major digital library evaluation criteria.

Interaction between users and digital libraries is also an important component for usability testing. Budhu and Coleman (2002) highlight the key attributes of interactivities: reciprocity, feedback, immediacy, relevancy, synchronicity, choice, immersion, play, flow, multidimensionality, and control. They evaluate interactivities in a digital library with regard to multiple aspects including interactivities in interface. Thong et al. (2002) identify the determinants of user acceptance of digital libraries, and among them, perceived usefulness and ease of use are the major factors that can be predicted by the interface characteristics (terminology clarity, screen design, and navigation clarity), organizational context (relevance and system visibility), and individual differences (computer self-efficacy, computer experience, and domain knowledge).

USABILITY TESTING: SPECIFIC DIGITAL LIBRARIES AND SPECIFIC USERS

Some researchers concentrate on specific digital libraries and specific users, in particular, educational digital libraries and learners. Focusing on digital libraries for teaching and learning, Borgman et al. (2000) conducted formative evaluation in formulating design requirements and summative evaluation in judging learning outcomes. Yang (2001) examined learners' problem solving process in using the Perseus digital library by adopting an interpretive and situated approach. The findings of the study help designers develop and refine better intellectual tools to facilitate learners' performance. Kassim and Kochtanek (2003) performed usability studies of an educational digital library in order to understand the user needs, find problems, identify desired features, and assess overall user satisfaction.

Children have very unique interaction characteristics as users of digital libraries. As design partners, children show preference to a simple interface with unique characteristics, such as bright colors and images, and audio (Theng et al., 2000). Bilal and Bachir (2007a, b) investigated the interaction of 10 Arabic-speaking children with the ICDL to find Arabic books resulting from four tasks. Individual interviews, group interviews, and log analysis were employed to collect data. The findings offer suggestions for the improvement of ICDL. Younger children have difficulty understanding all the representations of the ICDL. A simple visual interface with meaningful icons and audio capabilities assists international children in effectively seeking information in ICDL. Well-designed icons for the text-based browse and search functions are essential for the children without much knowledge of English. An Arabic version of the ICDL that supports keyword searching in Arabic is also requested. A drawing and coloring feature for children to express feelings, thoughts, and perceptions is also desired.

Based on children's interaction with IR systems at home, Druin et al. (2010) identify seven search roles that children play: developing searcher, domain-specific searcher, power searcher, nonmotivated searcher, distracted searcher, visual searchers, and rule-bound searcher. Even though this study is not designed specifically in a digital library environment, their findings are applicable for improving the digital library interface design. They further offer interface design implications for children:

- Support multiple search roles
- Learn from power searchers to support other searcher roles
- Overcome known barriers
- Design interface to attract children to search
- Use the interface to have positive impact

Martens (2012) stresses that four areas need to be taken into consideration when designing interfaces for children:

- Children's unique developing cognitive and motor skills
- Children with different ages requiring different designs
- Classification, hierarchies, and metadata need to be age appropriate
- Social components, such as graphics and interactive and personalization features, need to be attractive to children.

Another specific group of users is people with disabilities. The discussion of how to design for people with disabilities is in the latter section of this chapter. The detailed discussion of different types of user groups and their needs and behaviors in interacting with digital libraries can be found in Chapter 8.

USER PERSPECTIVE AND ORGANIZATIONAL USABILITY

Some researchers solicit user perceptions regarding some of the digital library evaluation criteria. In Jeng's (2005a, b) study, the evaluation is designed to detect users' perceptions of ease of use, organization of information, terminology, attractiveness, and mistake recovery. For example, ease of use is considered "simple," "straightforward," "logical," "easy to look up things," and "placing common tasks upfront." Very few researchers have conducted digital library evaluation criteria studies from users' perspectives. Xie (2006) investigated digital library evaluation criteria based on users' input. Users developed and justified a set of essential criteria for the evaluation of digital libraries. At the same time, they were requested to evaluate digital libraries of their own selection by applying the criteria that they developed. After comparing evaluation criteria identified by the users and researchers, and criteria applied in previous studies, the author found that there was a commonality in the overall categories of the evaluation criteria. However, users place more emphasis on their own perspectives and less on the perspectives of developers and administrators. Users value the ease of use of the interface. Xie (2008) further examined users' evaluation of digital libraries based on their uses. The results show that users' evaluation of digital libraries is largely based on their own experience of using them. To be specific, digital library use affects its evaluation in two folds. First, the problems users encountered in their use of digital libraries lead to their negative evaluation. Second, the availability of new features or design sets up a higher standard for digital library evaluation. The design of digital libraries has to take into consideration users' preference, experience, and knowledge structure. It seems impossible to design a one-size-fits-all digital library to satisfy all types of user needs. The findings of this study reveal some dilemmas, such as simplistic versus attractive interfaces, default versus customized interfaces, general help versus specific help, etc.

Interestingly, another study also reveals the same difference on digital library evaluation criteria between users and experts. Lai et al. (2014) investigate important criteria for digital library interface evaluation among students, teachers, and experts. For example, ease of use is ranked 1st for students, 5th for teachers, and 7th for experts respectively. Teachers care the most about presentation while experts consider design as the most important. Although the rankings are different, the findings show that seven criteria are deemed as important by all three groups: ease of use, searching, language, design, presentation, customization, and interaction. After reviewing relevant literature, Heradio et al. (2012) conclude that the standard definition of digital library usability, criteria, and measurements pose challenges for further research. Chapter 10 offers a more in-depth discussion of digital library evaluation criteria from different stakeholders' perspectives.

Usability research goes beyond just interface usability. Content usability, organizational usability, and interorganizational usability are also studied (Lamb, 1995). Among them, organizational usability is considered as one of the most important aspects for the development of digital libraries and associated interfaces. Elliott and Kling (1997) specify three levels of organization usability: individual, organizational, and environmental. All of these levels have an impact on interface design. Davies (1997) develops a model showing the roles played by different groups of stakeholders in the development of digital libraries. Following Davies' (1997) model, Xie and Wolfram (2002) illustrate three types of interactions among the players of a state digital library: influenced-based interactions, activities-based interactions, and communication-based interactions. These interactions in turn influence the enhancement of digital library interfaces.

Cultural issues, such as colors, symbols, metaphors, and language, also affect the usability of a digital library, indicating that the design of digital libraries needs to take into consideration cultural issues as well (Duncker et al., 2000; Liew, 2005, 2009). Even though the cultural aspect of usability has not been widely studied, some researchers have explored the area. Smith (2006) addresses the usability-culture connection by applying cognitive theory to the usability of digital libraries in a multiple culture, multiple intelligence context. In an empirical study, Arabic-speaking younger children show difficulty understanding all the representations of the ICDL (Bilal and Bachir, 2007a, b). Suggestions for how to consider cultural issues are discussed in Section "Usability Testing: Specific Digital Libraries and Specific Users."

HELP DESIGN

For the time being, digital libraries have no standard design. Users have to learn how to interact with each digital library. According to Nahl (1999), novice searchers are the main users of help features, and these users require different types of assistance, including help in learning about new IR systems. Novice users encounter many types of help-seeking situations in new searching environments. A help-seeking situation is characterized by a user engaged in information seeking within a digital library in order to achieve his/her tasks/goals and needing some form of help in the process (Xie and Cool, 2009). The situation of novice users working within a new search environment creates more challenges for help seekers and for the design of effective help functionalities. However, users do not use help features because they are often not helpful to users. Monopoli et al. (2002) report only 34.6% of 246 respondents used the online help feature of a digital library, and 20% of those preferred human help.

Help features can be classified into explicit and implicit help features. Explicit help features refer to features that are labeled as "Help" or "?" while implicit help features refer to any features that facilitate users to solve their help-seeking situations even though they are not labeled as Help features. In their analysis of 120 information retrieval episodes, Xie and Joo (2010) also observe that searchers rarely use explicit help, especially help page views in their search processes. In their transaction log analysis of a digital library, Han et al. (2013a, b, 2014) confirm that users rarely visit help pages provided by the these system. Instead, searchers are more likely to use implicit help. Othman and Halim (2004) suggest that users prefer context-sensitive, implicit help features such as relevance feedback, term weighting, synonyms linked to terms in the thesaurus, and extensive search examples. Xie (2007) examines explicit and implicit help features in selected digital libraries. Explicit Help features are self-explanatory, with Help as part of the name. Implicit Help consists of a variety of features, such as FAQs, Contact Us, Advanced Search, About, Collection Descriptions, Site Map, Glossary, My Digital, How to View, etc. Some of the features can be under both explicit and implicit Help. For example, FAQs itself is an implicit Help feature. If FAQs is under the name of Help, then it is part of the explicit Help. For example, In American Memory Help, the explicit Help consists of implicit Help features, such as How to View, Search Help, FAQs, and Contact Us. These explicit and implicit Help features analyzed from the selected digital libraries can be classified into the following categories: general Help, search-related Help, collection-related Help, navigation Help, terminology Help, personalized and customized Help, and view-and-use-related Help. Six types of problems of help feature designs in digital libraries are identified: lack of standards, tradeoff between using explicit Help and implicit Help, tradeoff between using general Help versus specific Help, lack of interactive Help features, lack of dynamic presentation styles, and lack of Help features for advanced users and users who do not understand English.

Based on a series of user studies on the user interfaces of a digital library, Hill et al. (2000) notice that users prefer the following help features: (1) presenting search examples to assist users in formulating queries, (2) offering context-sensitive help, and (3) providing tutorials and FAQs. Frumkin (2004) suggests that a useful approach might be to make user interfaces complement to digital libraries. To conduct a usability evaluation of an automated help mechanism in a digital library, it is important to understand the searching behaviors of novice users and the help-seeking situations that arise while using it (Borgman and Rasmussen, 2005).

Xie and her associates have conducted a series of studies to identify help-seeking situations in information retrieval, evaluate help features, and inquire about users' perspectives to those help features. Xie and Cool (2006) discover that users acknowledge the importance of help mechanisms in using IR systems, but at the same time, express the ineffectiveness of existing help mechanisms and consequently tend to use those help features infrequently in their search process. Xie and Cool (2009) explore different help-seeking situations in using digital libraries. To be more specific, they identify fifteen unique help-seeking situations in searching digital libraries. Those situations are classified into seven categories of situations that users are unable to complete without a certain type or types of help: (1) inability to get started, (2) inability to identify relevant digital collections, (3) inability to browse for information, (4) inability to construct search statements, (5) inability to refine searches, (6) inability to monitor searches, and (7) inability to evaluate search results. Factors from users, tasks, digital libraries, and interaction

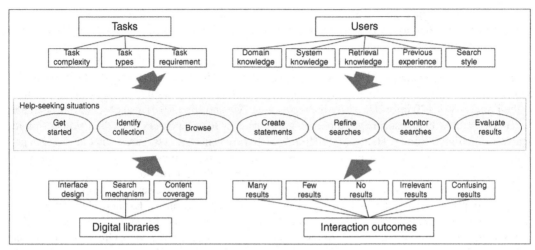

FIGURE 7.6 Factors Affecting Types of Help-Seeking Situations

Adapted from Xie and Cool, 2009, p. 490.

outcomes that affect help-seeking situations are also recognized. Fig. 7.6 presents the types of factors affecting help-seeking situations. Xie et al. (2013) comprehensively examine user engagement and different types of system support in interactive IR processes including applying help tactics. The challenge is to understand how users can convey their problems to the systems and how the systems can understand users' problems and offer appropriate help features to assist users to solve these problems. Compared to normal users, people with disabilities encounter unique help-seeking situations. The identification of help-seeking situations for blind users and the implications for digital library interface design is discussed in the next section.

To summarize, different types of explicit and implicit help features need to be offered in digital libraries. Here are some suggestions for the design of help mechanisms of digital libraries to solve different types of help-seeking situations:

- Overview of the digital library structure
- Intuitive interface design
- Context-sensitive knowledge assistance
- Interactive dialog protocol
- Search mechanism for identifying specific collection(s)
- Examples of how to create search statements
- Templates of searches based on task type and complexity
- Integrating the help page into actual browsing and searching page
- Demo of browsing options and structure
- Explicit and implicit feedback mechanisms
- Search history and search path options
- Different evaluation mechanisms for different types of tasks
- Examples for dealing with unsatisfied interaction outcomes
- FAQs

INTERFACE DESIGN FOR PEOPLE WITH DISABILITIES

Tim Berners-Lee, the founder of the World Wide Web, was quoted by the W3C saying, "The power of the Web is in its universality. Access by everyone regardless of disability is an essential aspect" (as cited in W3C, 1997, para. 1). Web Accessibility Initiative (http://www.w3.org/WAI/) widely develops guidelines that are regarded as the international standard for Web accessibility. Web Content Accessibility Guidelines (WCAG) 2.0 extends to all types of virtual communication including interactive multimedia content and is more usability oriented, including a navigable, meaningful sequence, and consistent navigation guidelines. It also covers several types of disabilities, such as cognitive, language, learning, and physical disabilities (Riberta et al., 2009). Snead et al. (2005) discuss functionality, usability, and accessibility in the digital library context. Accessibility is to assess how well systems allow users with disabilities to have equal use of information and services. The measures are associated with the World Wide Web Consortium or section 508 of the Rehabilitation Act.

Developers of digital libraries need to know that making them accessible for users with disabilities is a legal necessity as per the Americans with Disabilities Act (ADA). ADA mandates that all digital content available for public consumption be accessible to users with disabilities. For users with disabilities, this means the digital library interface and its constituent content and features should be accessible with screen-readers. Compliance with accessible Web design principles as those forwarded by the Web Content Accessibility Guidelines and Section 508 of the U.S. Rehabilitation Act are necessary. Blansett (2008) found that libraries were not yet fully in compliance at the time of the study. Southwell and Slater (2012) surveyed 69 US academic library Web sites and found that 58% of the sampled digital collection items were not screen-readable. After examining 64 academic and public libraries in Ontario, Oud (2012) identifies an average of 14.75 accessibility problems per library consisting of poor color contrast, lacking text alternatives for images, and tables that are not readable by screen readers. Yoon et al. (2013) suggest the integration of a high-level information architecture for users who use screen readers based on the analysis of accessibility barriers for visually impaired users.

People with disabilities require special assistance to access information items. The Digital Accessible Information System is a standard for Digital Talking Book. The standard makes it possible to organize the text within a structure and specify headings, subheadings, and pages numbers (Kerscher, 2002; Morgan, 2003). ALI is a project that creates a digital archive of DAISY books produced by the Swedish universities for students with reading disabilities consisting of journal articles, book chapters, and materials presented by teachers (Forsberg, 2007).

People with different types of disabilities have different requirements. The review of 20 Web design guidelines yielded the top recommendations for interface design for people with cognitive disabilities: use pictures, graphics, icons, and symbols with text; use clear and simple text; use consistent navigation and design on every page; and use headings, titles, and prompts (Friedman and Bryen, 2007). Borg et al. (2014) conclude that people with cognitive disabilities have different accessibility needs, requirements, and preferences, and these need to be further investigated and incorporated into the accessibility guidelines. Deo et al. (2004) describe the process of how to create a digital library for illiterate users:

- The first step is to conduct a user study to obtain user requirements via questionnaire and observing how subjects interact with a digital library interface. User requirements consist of ease of learning and ease of remembrance, no textual requirements, icons and visual display, internationalization, localization, simple, easy to navigate, ease to use and tolerant of errors, useful content and robust design, providing contextual information, and supporting simple browsing strategy.

- The second step is to create paper prototype designs evaluated by subjects. Two interface design guidelines are preferred: an interface with a side menu of the collection to avoid the use of the navigation buttons and to go back to the Home page, and incorporation of audio support into the digital library interface.
- The third step is to test the usability of standard digital library interfaces and an interface designed for illiterate users. It is essential to reduce collection size and browsing structure complexity to minimize human memory overload.

In this section, blind users are used as an example to illustrate how to study their needs and design digital libraries to help users with disabilities. The global blind population exceeds 45 million (Pascolini and Mariotti, 2012), two million of which reside in the United States (American Foundation for the Blind, 2012). The blind comprise a significant user group that interacts with information retrieval systems, including digital libraries, in entirely different ways from sighted users. A "blind user" refers to an individual who lacks the functional sight to see information presented on a computer screen. For these users, interacting with an IR system is a listening activity. They predominantly rely on text-to-speech software called screen-reader (SR) to interact with computers and the Internet (Lazar et al., 2007). An SR identifies and interprets textual content on the screen and presents the screen information through a synthetic voice (Di Blas et al., 2004). In order to design digital libraries to be effectively used by blind users, developers and researchers need to understand the unique needs of blind users. The great promise of digital libraries becoming the gateway to the universal access to information cannot be realized if not all groups of users can use them effectively. Digital libraries represent one type of information retrieval system that as of yet is not commonly utilized by blind users.

Previous literature shows that the help needs of blind users have not been examined and considered. There are few studies directly investigating their help needs. Related research has identified multiple cognitive and physical constraints of the blind in information use on the Internet: (1) avoidance of pages containing severe accessibility problems, such as dynamic content (Bigham et al., 2007; Craven, 2003); (2) structural problems when browsing as well as difficulties with the serialized-monolithic presentation of SRs (Salampasis et al., 2005); (3) the sequential nature of interaction, meaning at any given point a blind user perceives only a snippet of the content and loses all contextual information (Lazar et al., 2007); (4) mere translation of text content with a synthetic speech and not a complete narration of information presented (Babu, 2011); important cues embedded in color, images and videos that aid in navigation and interpretation are lost (Leuthold et al., 2008); (5) cognitive overload from spending cognitive resources in trying to understand the browser, the Web site, and the SR simultaneously (Chandrashekar, 2010; Theofanos and Redish, 2003); and (6) improper labeling causing significant confusion, frustration, and disorientation, particularly for interface objects (Lazar et al., 2007).

Xie et al. (2015) performed a study with 15 blind users to explore types of help-seeking situations during their interactions with digital libraries. The blind participants were asked to conduct three search tasks, including known-item search, specific information search, and exploratory search, using American Memory Digital Collections. Findings of this study identify some unique help-seeking situations that blind users encountered at both the physical and cognitive levels. Nine main help-seeking situations at the physical level emerged from the data. They can be further classified into three subcategories:

(1) difficulty in accessing information, (2) difficulty in identifying current status and path, and (3) difficulty in efficiently evaluating information. Eight main help-seeking situations at the cognitive level were derived from the data. They can be further classified into four subcategories: (1) confusion about multiple programs and structures, (2) difficulty in understanding information, (3) difficulty in understanding and using digital library features, and (4) avoidance of a specific type of format or approach.

Corresponding design implications are suggested to overcome help-seeking situations at both physical and cognitive levels. For example, in order to help blind users understand the file name of an image, digital libraries should provide clear labels for alternative text, and most importantly, the alternative text has to be meaningful for blind users. In order to assist blind users to make sense of digital library structure, header information needs to offer an overview of a page, and it is essential for the screen reader to continuously inform blind users of the current section in a page. Moreover, standardization of home and resource page layouts in collections would greatly reduce user confusion and facilitate them to decipher the overall structure of the digital library or a page. See also Chapter 8 for a related discussion of information needs of people with disabilities and their use of digital libraries.

The research for supporting universal accessibility of digital libraries is still in its infancy. While most of the research has focused on the accessibility issues for people with disabilities, there is still a long way to go to make digital libraries universally accessible. Moreover, accessibility of digital libraries is only the basic requirement, since blind users first need to access digital libraries and their associated pages. Usability of digital libraries is the second requirement because ease of understanding and ease of using are vital for blind users to interact effectively with digital libraries. More importantly, the ultimate goal for IR is to assist users to achieve their tasks (Saracevic, 2007a, b, 2015). Utility, or the usefulness of digital libraries in helping users to accomplish their information needs and tasks, is the third requirement, and is the most difficult one to fulfill, as distinct disabilities lead to distinctly complicated physical and cognitive help-seeking situations. The main challenge is whether we can design one digital library to satisfy all users' needs, including users with and without disabilities.

REFERENCES

Albertson, D., 2013. An interaction and interface design framework for video digital libraries. J. Doc. 69 (5), 667–692.

American Foundation for the Blind, 2012. Facts and figures on Americans with vision loss. Available from: http://www.afb.org/info/blindness-statistics/adults/facts-and-figures/235.

Babu, R., 2011. Developing an understanding of the accessibility and usability problems blind students face in web-enhanced instruction environments (Doctoral Dissertation). Available from: ProQuest Dissertations and Theses. (Accession Order No. AAT 3473492).

Belkin, N., 1996. Intelligent information retrieval: whose intelligence? In: Krause, J., Herfurth, M., Marx, J., (Eds.), Herausforderungen an die Informationswirtschaft. Informationsverdichtung, Informationsbetwertung und Datenvisualisierung. In: Proceedings of the Fifth International Symposium for Information Science (ISI'96). Konstanz: Universitatsverlag, Konstanz, pp. 25–31.

Bertot, J., Snead, J., Jaeger, P., McClure, C., 2006. Functionality, usability, and accessibility: iterative user-centered evaluation strategies for digital libraries. Perform. Meas. Metrics 7 (1), 17–28.

Bigham, J.P., Cavender, A.C., Brudvik, J.T., Wobbrock, J.O., Lander, R.E., 2007. WebinSitu: A comparative analysis of blind and sighted browsing behavior. In: Proceedings of the Ninth International ACM SIGACCESS Conference on Computers and Accessibility. New York, NY: ACM, pp. 51–58.

Bilal, D., Bachir, I., 2007a. Children's interaction with cross-cultural and multilingual digital libraries: I. understanding interface design representations. Inform. Process. Manag. 43 (1), 47–64.

Bilal, D., Bachir, I., 2007b. Children's interaction with cross-cultural and multilingual digital libraries: II. information seeking, success, and affective experience. Inform. Process. Manag. 43 (1), 65–80.

Blandford, A., Buchanan, G., 2002. Workshop report: Usability of digital libraries @JCDL'02. In: Blandford, A., Buchanan, G., (Eds.). JCDL'02 Workshop on Usability of Digital Libraries. Available from: http://www.uclic.ucl.ac.uk/annb/docs/SIGIR.pdf.

Blandford, A., Buchanan, G., 2003. Usability of digital libraries: a source of creative tensions with technical developments. IEEE Tech. Comm. Digital Lib. Bull. 1 (1). Retrieved from http://discovery.ucl.ac.uk/16648/1/16648.pdf.

Blansett, J., 2008. Digital discrimination. Lib. J. 133 (13), 26.

Borg, J., Lantz, A., Gulliksen, J., 2014. Accessibility to electronic communication for people with cognitive disabilities: a systematic search and review of empirical evidence. Univers. Access Inform. Soc. 4 (4), 547–562.

Borgman, C., Rasmussen, E., 2005. Usability of digital libraries in a multicultural environment. Design and Usability of Digital Libraries: Case Studies in the Asia Pacific, 270–284.

Borgman, C., Gilliland-Swetland, A., Leazer, G., Mayer, R., Gwynn, D., Gazan, R., Mautone, P., 2000. Evaluating digital libraries for teaching and learning in undergraduate education: a case study of the Alexandria Digital Earth ProtoType (ADEPT). Lib. Trends 49 (2), 229–249.

Budhu, M., Coleman, A., 2002. The design and evaluation of interactivities in a digital library. D-Lib Mag. 8 (11). Retrieved from http://webdoc.sub.gwdg.de/edoc/aw/d-lib/dlib/november02/coleman/11coleman.html.

Buttenfield, B., 1999. Usability evaluation of digital libraries. Sci. Tech. Lib. 17 (3–4), 39–59.

Chandrashekar, S., 2010. Is hearing believing? Perception of online information credibility by screen reader users who are blind or visually impaired. Doctoral dissertation, University of Toronto.

Cherry, J.M., Duff, W.M., 2002. Studying digital library users over time: a follow-up survey of Early Canadiana Online. Inf. Res. 7 (2). Retrieved from http://www.informationr.net/ir/7-2/paper123.html.

Chowdhury, G., 2004. Access and usability issues of scholarly electronic publications. In: Gorman, G.E., Rowland, F. (Eds.), Scholarly Publishing in an Electronic Era. International Yearbook of Library and Information Management. Facet Publishing, UK, pp. 77–98.

Chowdhury, S., Landoni, M., Gibb, F., 2006. Usability and impact of digital libraries: a review. Online Inf. Rev. 30 (6), 656–680.

Configuring the CONTENTdm Interface Tutorial Part I, n.d. Available from: http://dltre.sois.uwm.edu/files/Configuring%20the%20CONTENTdm%20Interface%20Tutorial%20Part%201.pdf.

Craven, J., 2003. Access to electronic resources by visually impaired people. Inf. Res. 8 (4). Retrieved from http://www.informationr.net/ir/8-4/paper156.html.

Cunningham, S.J., Reeves, N., Britland, M., 2003. An ethnographic study of music information seeking: Implications for the design of a music digital library. In: Proceedings of the Third ACM/IEEE-CS Joint Conference on Digital Libraries. IEEE Computer Society, pp. 5–16.

Davies, C., 1997. Organizational influences on the university electronic library. Inf. Process. Manag. 33 (3), 377–392.

Deo, S., Nichols, D.M., Cunningham, S.J., Witten, I.H., Trujillo, M.F., 2004. Digital library access for illiterate users. In: Proceedings of the International Research Conference on Innovations in Information Technology (IIT 2004). Dubai, UAE, pp. 506–516.

Di Blas, N., Paolini, P., Speroni, M., 2004. "Usable accessibility" to the Web for blind users. Proceedings of Eighth ERCIM Workshop: User Interfaces for All, Vienna. Available from: http://ui4all.ics.forth.gr/workshop2004/files/ui4all_proceedings/adjunct/accessibility/109.pdf.

Dillon, A., 1999. TIME–a multi-leveled framework for evaluating and designing digital libraries. Int. J. Digital Lib. 2 (2–3), 170–177.

Druin, A., 2005. What children can teach us: developing digital libraries for children with children. Library 75 (1), 20–41.

Druin, A., Foss, E., Hutchinson, H., Golub, E., Hatley, L., 2010. Children's roles using keyword search interfaces at home. In: Proceedings from the Twenty Eighth International Conference on Human Factors in Computing Systems (CHI '10). New York, NY: ACM, pp. 413–422.

Duncker, E., Theng, Y.L., Mohd-Nasir, N., 2000. Cultural usability in digital libraries. Bull. Am. Soc. Inf. Sci. Technol. 26 (4), 21–22.

Elliott, M., Kling, R., 1997. Organizational usability of digital libraries: case study of legal research in civil and criminal court. J. Am. Soc. Inf. Sci. 48 (11), 1023–1035.

Ferreira, S.M., Pithan, D.N., 2005. Usability of digital libraries: a study based on the areas of information science and human-computer-interaction. OCLC Syst. Serv. 21 (4), 311–323.

Flanagin, A.J., Metzger, M.J., 2003. The perceived credibility of personal Web page information as influenced by the sex of the source. Comput Hum. Behav. 19 (6), 683–701.

Forsberg, A., 2007. Ali—a digital archive of daisy books. J. Access Serv. 5 (1/2), 85–92.

Friedman, M.G., Bryen, D.N., 2007. Web accessibility design recommendations for people with cognitive disabilities. Technol. Disabil. 19 (4), 205–212.

Frumkin, J., 2004. Defining digital libraries. OCLC Syst. Serv. 20 (4), 155–156.

Hackos, J., Redish, J., 1998. User and Task Analysis for Interface Design. John Wiley and Sons, New York.

Han, H.J., Joo, S., Wolfram, D., 2013a. Tales from transaction logs: user search session patterns in an image-based digital library. In: Hodges, K., Meyers, E., O'Brien, H. (Eds.), Tales from the Edge: Narrative Voices in Information Research and Practice. Proceedings of the 35th Annual Conference of the Canadian Association for Information Science. Available from: http://www.cais-acsi.ca/proceedings/2013/HanJooWolfram_submission_23.pdf

Han, H.J., Joo, S., Wolfram, D., 2013b. Tales from transaction logs: user search session patterns in an image-based digital library. In: Proceedings of the 41st CAIS Conference. Retrieved from: http://www.cais-acsi.ca/ojs/index.php/cais/article/viewFile/829/751

Han, H.J., Joo, S., Wolfram, D., 2014. Using transaction logs to better understand user search session patterns in an image-based digital library. J. Korea Biblia Soc. Lib. Inf. Sci. 25 (1), 19–37.

Hariri, N., Norouzi, Y., 2011. Determining evaluation criteria for digital libraries' user interface: a review. Electron. Lib. 29 (5), 698–722.

Heradio, R., Fernández-Amorós, D., Cabrerizo, F.J., Herrera-Viedma, E., 2012. A review of quality evaluation of digital libraries based on users' perceptions. J. Inf. Sci. 38 (3), 269–283.

Hill, L.L., Carver, L., Larsgaard, M., Dolin, R., Smith, T.R., Frew, J., Rae, M.-A., 2000. Alexandria digital library: user evaluation studies and system design. J. Am. Soc. Inf. Sci. 51 (3), 246–259.

Ingwersen, P., Jarvelin, K., 2005. The Turn: Integration of Information Seeking and Retrieval in Context. Springer, Dortecht, the Netherlands.

Jeng, J., 2005a. Usability assessment of academic digital libraries: effectiveness, efficiency, satisfaction, and learnability. Libri 55 (2–3), 96–121.

Jeng, J., 2005b. What is usability in the context of the digital library and how can it be measured? Inf. Technol. Lib. 24 (2), 3–12.

Kaplan, N., Chisik, Y., Knudtzon, K., Kulkarni, R., Moulthrop, S., Summers, K., Weeks, H., 2004. Supporting sociable literacy in the international children's digital library. Proceedings of the 2004 Conference on Interaction Design and Children: Building a Community. New York, NY: ACM, pp. 89–96.

Kassim, A.R.C., Kochtanek, T.R., 2003. Designing, implementing, and evaluating an educational digital library resource. Online Inf. Rev. 27 (3), 160–168.

Kerscher, G., 2002. Structured access to documents, digital talking books, and beyond: The DAISY consortium. In: Computers Helping People with Special Needs. Berlin Heidelberg: Springer, pp. 1–2.

Lai, C., Chiu, P., Huang, Y., Chen, T., Huang, T., 2014. An evaluation model for digital libraries' user interfaces using fuzzy AHP. Electron. Lib. 32 (1), 83–95.

Lamb, R., 1995. Using online resources: reaching for the *.*s. In: Shipman, F.M., Furuta, R., Levy, D.M. (Eds.), Digital Libraries '95. Department of Computer Science, Texas A&M University, Austin, TX, pp. 137–146.

Landay, J.A., Myers, B.A., 2001. Sketching interfaces: toward more human interface design. Computer 34 (3), 56–64.

Lavie, T., Tractinsky, N., 2004. Assessing dimensions of perceived visual aesthetics of web sites. Int. J. Hum. Comput. Stud. 60 (3), 269–298.

Lazar, J., Allen, A., Kleinman, J., Malarkey, C., 2007. What frustrates screen reader users on the web: a study of 100 blind users. Int. J. Hum. Comput. Int. 22 (3), 247–269.

Leuthold, S., Bargas-Avila, J.A., Opwis, K., 2008. Beyond web content accessibility guidelines: design of enhanced text user interfaces for blind internet users. Int. J. Hum. Comput. Stud. 66 (4), 257–270.

Liew, C.L., 2005. Cross-cultural design and usability of a digital library supporting access to Maori cultural heritage resources. In: Ng, Y.-L., Foo, S. (Eds.), Design and Usability of Digital Libraries: Case Studies in the Asia-Pacific. Idea Group Pub, Hershey, PA, pp. 284–297.

Liew, C.L., 2009. Digital library research 1997-2007: organisational and people issues. J. Doc. 65 (2), 245–266.

Linn, M.C., Hussell, J.A.T., Hettinga, R.K., Powell, J.E., Mane, K.K., Martinez, M.L.B., 2007. Information visualization and large-scale repositories. Lib. Hi Tech 25 (3), 366–378.

Marks, L., Hussell, J.A., McMahon, T.M., Luce, R.E., 2005. ActiveGraph: a digital library visualization tool. Int. J. Digital Lib. 5 (1), 57–69.

Martens, M.m., 2012. Issues of access and usability in designing digital resources for children. Lib. Inf. Sci. Res. 34 (3), 159–168.

McGee, M., Rich, A., Dumas, J., 2004. Understanding the usability construct: User-perceived usability. In: Proceedings of the Human Factors and Ergonomics Society Annual Meeting, vol. 48, No. 5. SAGE Publications, pp. 907–911.

Meyyappan, N., Foo, S., Chowdhury, G., 2004. Design and evaluation of a task-based digital library for the academic community. J. Doc. 60 (4), 449–475.

Miller, M., Choi, G., Chell, L., 2012. Comparison of three digital library interfaces: open library, Google books, and Hathi Trust. Proceedings of the 12th ACM/IEEE-CS joint conference on Digital Libraries. ACM, New York, pp. 367–368.

Monopoli, M., Nicholas, D., Georgiou, P., Korfiati, M., 2002. A user-oriented evaluation of digital libraries: Case study the "electronic journals" service of the library and information service of the University of Patras, Greece. In: Aslib Proceedings, vol. 54, No. 2. UK: Emerald Group, pp. 103–117.

Morgan, G., 2003. A word in your ear: library services for print disabled readers in the digital age. Electron. Lib. 21 (3), 234–239.

Nahl, D., 1999. Creating user-centered instructions for novice end-users. Ref. Serv. Rev. 27 (3), 280–286.

Nielsen, J., 1993. Iterative user-interface design. Computer 26 (11), 32–41.

Nielsen, J., 1994. Usability inspection methods. In: Conference Companion on Human Factors in Computing Systems. Boston, MA: ACM, pp. 413–414.

Nielsen, J., 1995. 10 Usability heuristics for user interface design. Available from: http://www.nngroup.com/articles/ten-usability-heuristics/.

Norberg, L., Vassiliadis, K., Ferguson, J., Smith, N., 2005. Sustainable design for multiple audiences: the usability study and iterative redesign of the documenting the American South digital library. OCLC Syst. Serv. 21 (4), 285–299.

Norman, D.A., 2002. The Design of Everyday Things. Doubleday, New York.

Notess, M., Kouper, I., Swan, M., 2005. Designing effective tasks for digital library user tests: lessons learned. OCLC Syst. Serv. 21 (4), 300–310.

Omeka, 2015. Managing themes 2.0. Available from: https://omeka.org/codex/Managing_Themes_2.0.

Othman, R., Halim, N.S., 2004. Retrieval features for online databases: common, unique, and expected. Online Inf. Rev. 28 (3), 200–210.

Oud, J., 2012. How well do Ontario library web sites meet new accessibility requirements? Partnership Can. J. Lib. Inf. Prac. Res. 7 (1), Retrieved from https://journal.lib.uoguelph.ca/index.php/perj/article/view/1613/2520#.VneMOZMrLMU.

Pascolini, D., Mariotti, S.P., 2012. Global estimates of visual impairment: 2010. Br. J. Ophthalmol. 96 (5), 614–618.

Phillips, D., 2012. How to develop a user interface that your real users will love. Comput. Lib. 32 (7), 6–15.

Rajkumar, J.L.S., 2006. ETANA-CMV: a coordinated multiple view visual browsing interface for ETANA-DL. Doctoral dissertation, University Libraries, Virginia Polytechnic Institute and State University.

Riberta, M., Porras, M., Boldu, M., Termens, M., Sule, A., 2009. Web content accessibility guidelines 2.0: a further step towards accessible digital information. Prog. Electron. Lib. Inf. Syst. 43 (4), 392–406.

Salampasis, M., Kouroupetroglou, C., Manitsaris, A., 2005. Semantically enhanced browsing for blind people in the WWW. In: Proceedings of the Sixteenth ACM conference on Hypertext and hypermedia. New York, NY: ACM, pp. 32–34.

Saracevic, T., 1996. Modeling interaction in information retrieval (IR): a review and proposal. Proc. Am. Soc. Inf. Sci. 33, 3–9.

Saracevic, T., 1997. The stratified model of information retrieval interaction: extension and applications. Proc. Am. Soc. Inf. Sci. 34, 313–327.

Saracevic, T., 2007a. Relevance: a review of the literature and a framework for thinking on the notion in information science. Part II: nature and manifestations of relevance. J. Am. Soc. Inf. Sci. Technol. 58 (3), 1915–1933.

Saracevic, T., 2007b. Relevance: a review of the literature and a framework for thinking on the notion in information science. Part III: behavior and effects of relevance. J. Am. Soc. Inf. Sci. Technol. 58 (13), 2126–2144.

Saracevic, T., 2015. Why is relevance still the basic notion in information science? (Despite great advances in information technology). International Symposium on Information Science (ISI 2015). Zadar, Croatia. May 18–21, 2015.

Seifert, I., 2011. A pool of queries: interactive multidimensional query visualization for information seeking in digital libraries. Inf. Vis. 10 (2), 97–106.

Shiri, A., 2008. Metadata enhanced visual interfaces to digital libraries. J. Inf. Sci. 34 (6), 763–775.

Shiri, A., Ruecker, S., Bouchard, M., Doll, L., Fiorentino, C., 2013. User evaluation of searchling and T-saurus: multilingual thesaurus-enhanced visual interfaces for digital libraries/Évaluation par les usagers de Searchling et de T-saurus: Les interfaces visuelles à thesaurus multilingue pour les bibliothèques numériques. Can. J. Inf. Lib. Sci. 37 (2), 137–160.

Shneiderman, B., 1998. Designing the User Interface. Addison-Wesley, Reading, MA.

Smith, C., 2006. Multiple cultures, multiple intelligence: applying cognitive theory to usability of digital libraries. Libri 56 (4), 227–238.

Snead, J.T., Bertot, J.C., Jaeger, P.T., McClure, C.R., 2005. Developing multi-method, iterative, and user-centered evaluation strategies for digital libraries: functionality, usability, and accessibility. Proc. Am. Soc. Inf. Sci. Technol. 42 (1), doi: 10.1002/meet.14504201161.

Somerville, M., Brar, N., 2009. A user-centered and evidence-based approach for digital library projects. Electron. Lib. 27 (3), 409–425.

Southwell, K.L., Slater, J., 2012. Accessibility of digital special collections using screen readers. Lib. Hi Tech 30 (3), 457–471.

Theng, Y.L., Nasir, N.M., Thimbleby, H., Buchanan, G., Jones, M., Bainbridge, D., Cassidy, N., 2000. Children as design partners and testers for a children's digital library. In: Research and Advanced Technology for Digital Libraries. Springer Berlin Heidelberg, pp. 249–258.

Theofanos, M.F., Redish, J.G., 2003. Bridging the gap: between accessibility and usability. Interactions 10 (6), 36–51.

Thong, J.Y., Hong, W., Tam, K.Y., 2002. Understanding user acceptance of digital libraries: what are the roles of interface characteristics, organizational context, and individual differences? Int. J. Hum. Comp. Stud. 57 (3), 215–242.

Van Hoek, W., Mayr, P., 2013. Assessing visualization techniques for the search process in digital libraries. arXiv preprint arXiv:1304.4119.

Van House, N.A., Butler, M.H., Ogle, V., Schiff, L., 1996. User-centered iterative design for digital libraries. D-Lib Mag. 2 (3). Retrieved from http://webdoc.sub.gwdg.de/edoc/aw/d-lib/dlib/february96/02vanhouse.html.

W3C., 1997. World Wide Web Consortium launches International Program Office for Web Accessibility Initiative [press release]. Available from: http://www.w3.org/Press/IPO-announce.

Wagner, A., 1990. Prototyping: A day in the life of an interface designer. In: Laurel, B., Mountford, S.J. (Eds.), The Art of Human-Computer Interface Design. Addison-Wesley Pub. Co, Reading, MA, pp. 79–84.

Xie, H., 2006. Understanding human-work domain interaction: implications for the design of a corporate digital library. J. Am. Soc. Inf. Sci. Technol. 57 (1), 128–143.

Xie, H., 2007. Help features in digital libraries: types, formats, presentation styles, and problems. Online Inf. Rev. 31 (6), 861–880.

Xie, I., 2008. Interactive Information Retrieval in Digital Environments. IGI Publishing, Hershey, PA.

Xie, H., Cool, C., 2006. Toward a better understanding of help seeking behavior: An evaluation of help mechanisms in two IR systems. In: Dillon, A., Grove, A., (Eds.), Proceedings of the Sixty Ninth American Society of Information Science and Technology, vol. 43, No.1, pp. 1–16. Available from: http://eprints.rclis.org/archive/00008279/01/Xie_ Toward.pdf.

Xie, I., Cool, C., 2009. Understanding Help-Seeking within the context of searching digital libraries. J. Am. Soc. Inf. Sci. Technol. 60 (3), 477–494.

Xie, I., Joo, S., 2010. Tales from the field: search strategies applied in Web searching. Future Internet 2 (3), 259–281.

Xie, H., Wolfram, D., 2002. State digital library usability: contributing organizational factors. J. Am. Soc. Inf. Sci. Technol. 53 (13), 1085–1097.

Xie, I., Joo, S., Bennett-Kapusniak, R., 2013. User engagement and system support in the search process: user dominated, system dominated and balanced search tactics. Proc. Am. Soc. Inf. Sci. Technol. 50 (1), 1–4.

Xie, I., Babu, R., Joo, S., Fuller, P., 2015. Using digital libraries non-visually: understanding the help seeking situations of blind users. Inf. Res. 20, 2.

Yang, S.C., 2001. An interpretive and situated approach to an evaluation of Perseus digital libraries. J Am. Soc. Inf. Sci. Technol. 52 (14), 1210–1223.

Yoon, K., Newberry, T., Hulscher, L., Dols, R., 2013. Call for library websites with a separate information architecture for visually impaired users. Proc. Am. Soc. Inf. Sci. Technol. 50 (1), 1–3.

Zaphiris, P., 2004. Exploring the use of information visualization for digital libraries. New Rev. Inf. Network. 10 (1), 51–69.

USER NEEDS AND SEARCH BEHAVIORS

8

TYPES OF USERS AND THEIR USE OF DIGITAL LIBRARIES

Users are the main stakeholders of digital libraries. In order to design digital libraries for diverse types of users, we must first understand their needs, their search behaviors, and associated factors. Users of digital libraries have not been evenly investigated. While most of the studies focus on the children and college students, less research has been done on other types of users such as elderly people and people with disabilities.

CHILDREN AND DIGITAL LIBRARIES

By studying children's information-searching behaviors, researchers have identified tactics that children apply and roles they assume in the digital library searching process. With respect to the steps involved with searching, Bilal et al., (2008) studied the information-seeking behaviors of Arabic-speaking children interacting with the International Children's Digital Library (ICDL). Children's information search tactics consist of seven modes: Start, Recognize (scanning and selecting), Browse (viewing, verifying, and examining), Differentiate (viewing and sweeping), Read (viewing and flipping), Explore (navigation and backtracking), and Finish (ending a task or stopping). Foss and Druin (Foss, 2014; Foss and Druin, 2014) conducted a longitudinal study of 50 children from 2008–13 focusing on the roles children play in their interactions with digital libraries. At the outset of the study in 2008, researchers identified seven types of roles exhibited by the children, which emerged from the data: Developing, Domain specific, Power, Nonmotivated, Distracted, Visual, and Rule bound. In 2013, follow-up analysis of the same 50 participants revealed that the major change in children as they aged was the occurrence of a new Social role. The developing role and the domain-specific role were the most frequently observed roles in both the beginning and end of the study, in 2008 and 2013, respectively. However, over the course of the study as time progressed, the greatest percentage of change was in children moving from domain-specific searchers to power searchers, the most skilled type of role. Another interesting finding is that the study participants embodied multiple roles over the course of the longitudinal study.

Unique characteristics of children influence the design of digital libraries. In particular, children's special cognitive and physical abilities are an essential consideration for digital library design. Based on a review of the literature regarding how children's cognitive states influence their interactions with digital interfaces, Martens (2012) identifies children's developmental restrictions, which include underdeveloped motor skills, difficulty with spelling, and difficulty in understanding hierarchies and metadata. Children's diversity in age, race, background, and developmental skills poses a challenge for the development of digital libraries for children. Theng et al. (2000) worked with children as design partners and testers for the development of a children's digital library. They found that children like a

231

simple interface design with bright colors, graphics, and audio, and they enjoy having links to other relevant sources. In order to design digital libraries to satisfy children's needs, multilingual, multicultural, and multigenerational issues also need to be considered (Hutchinson et al., 2005). After comparing children's searching behaviors using different types of category browsers (tools for navigating categories) in the ICDL, Hutchinson et al., (2007) conclude that a flat interface is better than a hierarchically structured interface for children to perform both Boolean searching and casual browsing searches.

In addition to characteristics of children, the types of tasks that children perform also influence their interactions with digital libraries. After studying children's searching for entertainment-related information versus problem-solving information, Wu (2015) discovers that children prefer to use a digital library more for entertainment, rather than to satisfy a particular information need or solve a problem. Moreover, they are more comfortable with uncertainty and demonstrate greater user control of the discovery process when searching for entertainment information than problem-solving information. The results also indicate that a gamelike interface is a great tool for learning.

Of course, not all children exhibit the same information-searching behaviors in digital libraries. After investigating children's information-searching behaviors in the ICDL, Reuter and Druin (2004) conclude that first-grade children prefer browsing strategies while fifth-grade children apply more query searches. At the same time, girls love to search by colors while boys gravitate to character searching. In addition, older boys are more inclined to search by genre. In another study, Druin et al. (2010) point out that the developing searchers often need search tools with helpful features, such as auto-complete text or spelling correction, whereas children personifying the nonmotivated role usually do not ask for help when confronted with difficulties in searching information. The research of Druin et al. (2010) shows that factors, such as age, gender, and types of searcher, contribute to different information-searching behaviors in children.

International children have their own unique issues in searching digital libraries. After investigating the searching behavior of Arabic-speaking children using the ICDL, Bilal and Bachir (2007) notice that Arabic-speaking children do not recognize the representations embedded in the interfaces of the ICDL. This phenomenon was found to be mainly caused by three factors: lack of enough experience in using the Internet, lack of cognitive preparation, and lack of language ability. The researchers propose a simple visual interface with meaningful and noticeable icons along with an audio option to facilitate use among a variety of children representing culturally diverse groups. According to Jochmann-Mannak et al. (2008), most of the problems children experience with searching and browsing are caused by the interface design being designed by adults based on an understanding of adults' needs. Adults generally have not considered children's low motor skills nor their different approaches to searching and browsing. More research should investigate children's search behaviors, and prototypes of digital library interfaces need to be designed and tested with children.

COLLEGE STUDENTS AND DIGITAL LIBRARIES

Compared to children, college students have a different set of unique characteristics in using digital libraries. A large amount of money has been invested in online library resources, in particular digital libraries. However, college students do not frequently use these sources; instead, they choose less credible but easy to access Internet-based electronic resources (Booker et al., 2012; Gross and Latham, 2011). According to Booker et al. (2012), information literacy instruction is beneficial only at the early stages of students' digital library use; however, a positive outcome has also been found through continued use of digital libraries after receiving information literacy instruction. In that case, the design of digital libraries needs to guide users, in particular expert users, to make good use of digital libraries.

Research has indicated that both undergraduate and graduate students use digital libraries because of ease of access, but interestingly, there is a difference among the two groups in the factors leading to not using digital libraries. Liu and Luo (2011) compared the digital library use of both undergraduate and graduate students. Research projects and papers are the main motivations for both groups to use digital libraries. For both groups, digital library use has saved considerable time in locating materials and resulted in reduced visits to physical libraries. They find that the factors affecting digital library use are similar between the two groups. Both groups consider "remote access," "24 h access," and "faster access" as the most important factors in deciding to use digital libraries. However, the factors influencing students who are not using digital libraries are quite different. While 52.0% of undergraduates selected "digital libraries are difficult to use" as the major factor, only 28.7% of graduate students chose the same reason. In contrast to undergraduate students, graduate students cited the lack of the availability of relevant materials and no access to archival and older publications as the main reasons for not opting to use digital libraries. After investigating the relationship between resistance to change and the perceived ease of use of a university digital library, Nov and Ye (2008) identify personalities that are resistant to change as a significant factor that determines the perceived ease of use, and further influences digital library use in a university setting.

Integrating different system acceptance models, Cheng (2014) proposes a model to explain users' intentions to continue to use a digital library based on questionnaires distributed in a Taiwan university. Among the factors, the most vital ones accounting for users' continuance intention for using digital libraries were found to be those of information relevance, system accessibility, and technical support. In another study, also based on questionnaires, Hu et al. (2014) analyze the factors affecting users' perceptions of university digital libraries in China. Within all the service factors, information-providing services, information-retrieval services, and individual services play direct roles in influencing users' perceptions of digital libraries, while the information-organizing services have an indirect role. In a qualitative study of undergraduate students' use of digital resources, Matusiak (2012) finds that user perceptions of usefulness and usability, especially perceived ease of use, play an important role in user intentions to adopt and use digital collections for academic learning and teaching. The limited use of digital libraries is related to the following perceptions: (1) Library systems are not viewed as user friendly, which in turn discourages potential users from trying digital libraries provided by academic libraries; (2) Academic libraries are perceived as places of primarily textual resources; perceptions of usefulness, especially in regard to relevance of content, coverage, and currency, seem to have a negative effect on user intention to use digital libraries, especially when searching for visual materials.

College students apply a variety of specific information search tactics and strategies in interacting with digital libraries. Joo (2013) investigated how college students exercised different types of search tactics and how digital libraries supported these tactics. Users performed a known-item search task, a specific information search task, and an exploratory search task. The findings indicate there are differences in terms of the frequency and time of search tactics applied for different types of search tasks. The shifts between a series of search tactics form search strategies, which arise in their interactions in digital libraries. The data uncover four types of search strategies: result evaluation strategy, browsing strategy, iterative browsing strategies, and iterative search results evaluation strategies. Students' perceptions of system support, difficulty, and satisfaction for each type of tactic were measured and were found to influence aspectual recall and users' satisfaction with search results. In addition, system support for the evaluation of search results and the modification of search statements are considered less important than other types of tactics. With a different focus from Joo's tactic study, Huang (2014) focuses on how learning styles affect college students' help-seeking behaviors in digital libraries. This study explores how four dimensions—processing (active/reflective), input (visual/verbal), perceiving (sensing/intuitive), and understanding (sequential/global)—of learning styles affect users' help-seeking behaviors, as well as help feature uses in their digital library searching process. Qualitative data analysis presents eight types of help features that are used by users with different learning styles. Active learners preferred interactive help features while reflective learners chose reflective help features; visual learners used visual help features, and verbal learners made use of both verbal and exploring help features; sensitive learners selected scaffolding help features, and intuitive learners preferred channeling help features; sequential learners liked the help features that include the sequential order, and the global learners did not use specific help features. Quantitative data confirm that three dimensions of learning styles—processing, input, and perceiving—influence subjects' use of different types of help features when interacting with digital libraries.

Not all college students share the same search behaviors in digital libraries. Nicholas et al. (2009) compared students' information-seeking behaviors with that of other academic communities in a digital scholarly environment. The results reveal that among students and other academic communities, students are the biggest users in terms of sessions and pages viewed. Undergraduate students are more likely to use the search features in one system but use the alphabetical or subject menu in another system. Undergraduate students are more frustrated than graduate students by searches not yielding enough results and by an overwhelming number of results with not enough details (Dougan, 2012).

Researchers have also compared college students and other types of users in their usage and evaluation of digital libraries. Matusiak (2006) uncovers a substantial difference between college students' and community users' information-seeking behaviors in searching digital libraries. In their first encounter with the collections, most students performed keyword searches. Simple one-word or one-phrase queries were entered by most of the students. They rarely used Advanced Search features. In contrast, community users applied more browsing searches, explored more features, and were more successful in finding relevant results. The main reason for the difference lies in the different mental models that students and community users have. While students treat the collection as another dynamic searchable web site that they are used to searching, the community users consider the site as an online exhibit. They take advantage of visual cues and browse the digital collections. Interestingly, Górny et al. (2015) observe that even though students and academics are not different from nonacademic users in their evaluation of digital libraries, nonacademic users rate the quantity of resources, reliability of digital library, and information searching higher than students and academics. On the other hand, expectations of nonacademic users are lower than the students and academics, who expect full-text searching, mainly because they are unexperienced users.

In summary, college students are an important demographic group for digital libraries. Nonetheless, it is a challenge to attract the Google generation of college students. Digital libraries must consider the unique characteristics and search behaviors of this group in order to attract these users and facilitate the effective use of digital libraries for them.

ELDERLY PEOPLE, PEOPLE WITH DISABILITIES, AND DIGITAL LIBRARIES

Elderly people have special needs as part of the natural aging process. Although no research has been conducted specifically on elderly people's interaction with digital libraries, it is beneficial for us to review some of the relevant research on elderly people's information searching. Fiske et al. (2009) specify the changes that aging brings to elderly people, including sensation (color, vision, auditory), perception (awareness of the environment), cognition (reasoning and memory), and movement (control to coordination). Older people have more difficulty accomplishing different computer tasks, which could lead to frustration (Decker, 2010; Smith et al., 1999). Elderly people in general have low self-efficacy and higher anxiety in using computers (Czaja et al., 2006). They have a tendency not to look for information beyond their comfort and ability level (Martyn and Gallant, 2012). Butcher and Street (2009) suggest that keeping instructions simple helps elderly users. On the contrary, Nasmith and Parkinson (2008) present different findings based on their study on senior blind users' use of a digital talking book player in New Zealand. They find that seniors do have a positive attitude to change and are not afraid of technology if they are well supported.

In terms of using IR systems, compared to younger adults, older users, and in particular the ones who do not have computer experience, do not understand the search features and operations, and are not able to complete all the tasks and show more errors (Mead et al., 2000). Moreover, Stronge et al. (2006) notice that elderly people do not effectively apply search strategies. It is a challenge for some elderly people to understand IR systems and features (Mates, 2004). New technologies, such as mobile devices, bring both opportunity and challenge to elderly people. E-books and other digital materials are becoming more prevalent online. According to Kapusiak (2015), most of the Baby Boomers are unaware that public libraries offer e-books and other digital materials. Few were found to have accessed their public library web site from their mobile devices. Kapusiak further developed the Baby Boomer Mobile Device Searching Model based on her research findings that incorporated Predisposing, Intermediary, and Transactional Factors, which affected their use of mobile devices and their interactions with the mobile system. These factors include the perceptions of the user; knowledge infrastructures; digital literacy skills; self-efficacy/confidence; comfort level/uncertainty; physical ability; the information need and search task; mobile device; environmental, social, and cultural context consisting of the stability of the Internet connection; and social ageism. These interrelated factors influence the Baby Boomers' tendency to initiate and perform a search on a mobile device. Not surprisingly, nonmobile device usage is still important and is still utilizied on a regular basis by most of the Baby Boomer participants.

While universal accessibility is a goal for digital libraries, few studies concentrated on people with disabilities. Bell and Peters (2005) report on four representative examples for using digital information technology to improve the accessibility and usability of digital libraries for all users: *Online Programming for All Libraries (OPAL), Mid-Illinois Digital Talking Book (MI-DTB), Project: Audible E-Books, OverDrive: Unabridged Digital Audio Books,* and *InfoEyes* (a virtual reference service for the visually impaired). Zhang et al. (2012) illustrate that accessibility technologies applied in the China Digital Library for the Visual Impairment web site can be beneficial. These technologies include accessibility of web site design, content presentation accessibility, and accessibility of auxiliary technology compatibility. Bertot et al. (2006) highlight accessibility as an important factor in digital library evaluation in addition to the functionality and usability. Accessibility refers to the ability for users with disabilities to access a digital library and focuses on the issues related to alternative forms of content, color independent, clear navigation mechanisms, and table transformation.

As one of the few researchers who have investigated blind users' interaction with digital libraries, Xie et al. (2014, 2015) conducted a study with blind users to explore types of help-seeking situations that occurred in their search processes. Three tasks representing typical search activities were selected for blind participants to perform in the Library of Congress Digital Collections: (1) a known-item search (find the letter written by Alexander Graham Bell to Helen Keller dated Mar. 23, 1907); (2) a specific information search (find when and how Presidents Lincoln and Garfield were assassinated); and (3) an exploratory search (identify some US immigration policy issues using multiple sources). A laptop with Internet Explorer 10, JAWS 12, and Morae 3.1 was used for this study. Multiple data collection methods were employed: prequestionnaires, presearch interviews, think-aloud protocols, transaction logs, and postsearch interviews. The main contribution of this study is the identification of nine types of unique help-seeking situations at the physical level and eight types of help-seeking situations at the cognitive level.

Help-seeking situations at the physical level are mainly related to the difficulty in accessing information, difficulty in identifying current status and paths, and difficulty in efficiently evaluating information. In particular, there are nine types of help-seeking situations: (1) difficulty in identifying the format of an item, (2) difficulty in finding the alternative text for an image, (3) difficulty in recognizing preexisting text in the input box, (4) difficulty in identifying the current location, (5) difficulty in returning to home, (6) difficulty in recognizing the page-loading status, (7) difficulty in finding a specific word or phrase in the digital library pages, (8) difficulty in finding heading information, and (9) difficulty in efficiently evaluating information (Xie et al., 2015).

Simultaneously, help-seeking situations at the cognitive level can be characterized as confusion about multiple programs and structures, difficulty in understanding information, difficulty in understanding and using digital library features, and avoidance of a specific type of format or approach. In particular, there are eight types of help-seeking situations that arise: (1) confusion about multiple programs, (2) confusion about digital library structure, (3) difficulty in recognizing a label, (4) difficulty in understanding help information, (5) difficulty in understanding how to use a specific function, (6) difficulty in making sense of organizational criteria, (7) avoidance of visual items, and (8) avoidance of the browsing approach (Xie et al., 2015).

Marcus (2003) introduces the universal design movement, which started in the United States. This movement presents a challenge for user-centered design for the disabled and elderly. Universal design anticipates diversity of ability and needs, thereby facilitating the development of sensible, useful, and doable designs. While the movement began over a decade ago, there is still a long way to go to create universal design for different user groups with diverse needs. Higgins and King (2013) point out that universal access to digital libraries is still in its infancy. It will take time and effort for the creation of digital libraries for the "disadvantaged," which not only covers traditional minorities, such as African Americans, Hispanics, and Native Americans, but also persons with lower income and education, those living in rural areas, the physically disabled, as well as those in developing countries. Different challenges exist for different types of groups. These challenges include the tension among low-income users, publishers, and public libraries; varying standards for people with disabilities; cost issues; and technology infrastructure for people living in rural and developing countries.

For a related discussion of people with disabilities and digital libraries, see Chapter 7.

CHARACTERISTICS OF INFORMATION SEARCH BEHAVIORS

Convenience is identified as one of the key characteristics of information search behavior in a digital library environment. Convenience consists of users' preference for information sources, satisfaction with the sources, and their ease of use, as well as their time spent in the information search process.

Research has shown that convenience is one of the main criterion used in the information search process. Users may sacrifice content for convenience (Connaway et al., 2011). The convenience principles affect how users learn and use digital libraries. Information search behaviors are characterized by information search tactics and information search strategies. They are the foci of user studies.

INFORMATION SEARCH TACTICS

Search tactics and moves are the elements of information search strategies. Researchers have applied different definitions of tactics and moves in their papers. In some cases, tactics and moves are used interchangeably. Incorporating Bates' (1979, 1990, 1992) and Marchionini's (1995) definitions, Xie and Joo (2010) further define the meaning of the terms moves and search tactics. According to them, moves are basic thoughts or actions in the information search process, while search tactics refer to a series of moves, including search choices and actions, that users apply to advance their searches in the information search process.

Tactic research has focused on query formulation and reformulation. Fidel's (1985) operational moves are characterized by reducing or enlarging the size of search results, and conceptual moves are exemplified by intersecting, narrowing, or expanding the meaning of queries. Other researchers discovered the following tactics: broadening, narrowing, searching for an author, term checks, changing topics, error, and repeat (Shute and Smith, 1993; Vakkari et al., 2003; Wildemuth, 2004).

In addition to query formulation and reformulation tactics, tactics have been identified for different aspects of the search process. Bates (1979) organizes 29 tactics into monitoring (e.g., check, correct, etc.), file structure (e.g., select survey, etc.), search formulation (specify, exhaust, etc.), and term tactics (e.g., super, related, etc.). Extending Bates' work on the Internet, Smith (2012) incorporates new dimensions—evaluation tactics and new tactics, such as context evaluating, crosschecking, etc. Search tactics are further analyzed with respect to the search process. Yue et al. (2012) associate the search tactics Query, View, Save, Workspace, Topic, and Chat with a search process, such as defining a problem, selection of sources, and examining results. Children's information search tactics in digital environments are classified into seven modes: Start, Recognize (scanning and selecting), Browse (viewing, verifying, and examining), Differentiate (viewing and sweeping), Read (viewing and flipping), Explore (navigation and backtracking), and Finish (ending a task or stopping) (Bilal et al., 2008).

Previous research on moves and tactics sets up a foundation for researchers to further investigate patterns of search tactics in the digital library environment. Very few studies have explored the application of search tactics in digital libraries. Joo (2013) examined how users incorporated search tactics in terms of frequency, time, changes in a session, and transition patterns in their interactions with digital libraries. Adopting the tactics identified by Xie (2008) and Xie and Joo (2010), Joo (2013) analyzed the application of nine types of tactics: create search statements, explore information, modify search statements, organization of search results, access forward, access backward, evaluation of results, and evaluation of individual documents. The results show that users apply different search tactics for different types of search tasks. The accessing forward, browsing information, and evaluating results tactics are the top search tactics used in accomplishing a known-item search. Evaluating results, accessing forward, accessing backward, and evaluating individual documents are the top search tactics chosen in achieving a specific information search task. In fulfilling an exploratory task, evaluation of individual documents, accessing forward, accessing backward, and evaluating results are the top search tactics employed. Interestingly, the exploring tactic takes the longest for a known-item search; the evaluation of result tactics takes the longest for a specific task; and the evaluation of an individual document tactic takes the most time to complete for an exploratory task. The findings of tactics applications in digital libraries offer significant implications for system design to support different types of search tactics in the search process.

INFORMATION SEARCH STRATEGIES

Search strategies consist of combinations of tactics or moves and can be characterized by types and dimensions. Research has indicated that there are unique qualities in terms of information search strategies as applied in the online database environment. Building blocks, pearl growing, successive fractions, most specific facet first, and lowest postings facet first are the top strategies cited by researchers (Markey and Atherton, 1978). The known-item instantiation strategy, the search-option heuristic strategy, the thesaurus-browsing strategy, and the screen-browsing strategy represent strategies associated with system features (Chen and Dhar, 1991). Plan strategies occurring before the first move are comprised of author, title, concepts, external support, system features, etc. Reactive strategies are exercised based on the previous move including focus shifts, search-term relationships, error recovery, etc. (Soloman, 1993).

Search strategies in web search engines have similarities as well as differences from other digital environments. Search strategies inferred from log analysis show similarities and differences compared to an OPAC environment. The similar strategies include specified, generalized, and building blocks, etc., while the following different strategies have been found: dynamic, multitasking, and recurrent (Bruza and Dennis, 1997; Lau and Horvitz, 1999; Rieh and Xie, 2006). The novel design and features of the web and web searching environment have also spurred the identification of new strategies. Wang et al. (2000) highlight 10 problem-solving strategies in web searching: surveying, double checking, exploring, link following, back and forward going, shortcut seeking, engine using, loyal engine using, engine seeking, and metasearching.

Information search strategies in digital library environments also have their uniqueness. The design of digital libraries is rooted in the associated search strategies: query searching and browsing. Reuter and Druin (2004) discuss the differences in using query search and browsing strategies in children's interactions with digital libraries. Marchionini and Geisler (2002) specify three types of search strategies in video digital libraries: searching, browsing, and contributing. Matusiak (2006) studied how university students and community members interact with digital libraries and found that users started either with browsing or keyword searching, and applied both strategies as they continued their interactions with the system. Albertson (2015) reviews research conducted on visual information searching. Search and browse are the two common strategies in information searching. Although searching occurs throughout the information search process, it is the most common starting point for users. Search can also be the product of exploratory browsing. Search for visual items in general starts from broad and moves to narrow searches. Browsing plays a more important role in visual systems, including digital libraries, because these systems' browsing mechanisms facilitate users' navigation through their collections, and can serve as an exploratory action. Compared to searching, browsing is still considered as a secondary strategy.

Joo (2013) further looked into search strategies based on the order of a series of tactics. In a known-item search, users implemented a search result evaluation strategy and a browsing strategy. A specific task search was found to be similar to a known-item search, in that users selected the same search strategies, with the difference being that search result evaluation strategies were more frequently used with iterative loops. In an exploratory search, iterative browsing and iterative search result evaluation strategies were most frequently chosen. Search strategies consisting of various tactics need to be further scrutinized to identify search patterns. A deeper understanding of the patterns arising out of search tactics and strategies could be translated into design implications for more effective interaction with digital libraries.

USAGE PATTERNS

Log analysis is an effective approach to illustrate usage patterns, in particular how users interact with digital libraries. Digital libraries were not frequently used compared with other types of online resources, especially in the early age of digital library development. In a study in 1996, 35% of users accounted for 80% of the usage (Entlich et al., 1996). Fifteen years later, many college students still do not use digital libraries (Booker et al., 2012; Gross and Latham, 2011).

Query analysis is one research area that log analysis has focused on. Research has shown that short queries and a lack of the use of advanced searches typify digital library searches. A single search term was used in 81.5% search operations, and only 18.49% searches used Boolean operators, with a 0.1% subset of the Boolean searches incorporating previous result sets (Sfakakis and Kapidakis, 2002). According to Lowe's (2013) search log analysis of the ARTstor Cultural Heritage Digital Library, the average number of terms per query is 1.88 terms. Nearly 80% of the queries contain two or less terms, with half of the queries as one-term queries (49.70%) and 30.07% as two-term queries. The unique queries, nonunique queries, and queries with refiners comprise 54.89%, 21.39%, and 23.73%, respectively. Remarkably, queries become more generalized, simplified, and shortened across time. The findings are echoed by another log analysis study of digital libraries reporting an average 1.96 terms per query (Han et al., 2014). In searching for folktales, searchers on average entered 1.4 terms in a single query when conducting simple searches, but most of the queries (75%) consist of only a single term. In advanced searches, the queries are composed of 1.95 terms per query. The most noteworthy finding is that 3.4 result pages are viewed on average (Trieschnigg et al., 2013).

The special focus of a digital collection determines whether users search for mostly names of events, people, places, and actions. Choi and Rasmussen (2003) discover that the most popular searches generated by college faculty and students in searching the American History Digital Collection are the names of an event, action, or condition; individual names; and place names, consisting of 64.87% generic terms and 26.49% specific terms. In searching the ARTstor Digital Library, people, locations, and objects account for approximately 30% of the submitted queries (Lowe, 2013). A recent study (Han et al., 2014) yields similar results. Query analysis of digital collection usage shows that personal names and geographical locations are the main foci of searches. Of course, the top type of query is related to the nature of the digital collection. For example, art historical information and local information represent the top queries in the above two studies, respectively. Trieschnigg et al. (2013) notice that simple searches and advanced searches are used for different purposes. In their study of the Dutch Folktale Database, these researchers indicate that searching for subgenres and main characters are more often satisfied by simple searches. Advanced searches concentrate on particular stories or collections, subgenres, and story types. Duffy (2013) performed a study on historians' searches in HathiTrust. The findings show that historians use more open book repositories to search for relevant information, but searching full text is a big challenge for them. In addition to primary sources for historians, HathiTrust offers Library of Congress Subject Headings (LCSH), which enable historians to increase the precision of their searches. It is important to teach researchers and students alike to learn how to incorporate LCSH in their searches.

Among all the features in the digital libraries, search features, organizational features, and viewing features are the most frequently utilized. For example, the search function was found to be the most used based on the transaction logs of a Korean digital library (Zhang et al., 2001). In particular, the author search was the most popular search, accounting for 32.1% of all searches. Research also reveals that syntax and format errors occurred in 17.6% of searches (Entlich et al., 1996). In a similar finding to that of the investigation of the Korean digital library, Lowe (2013) concludes that the most frequently used type of search in the ARTstor Cultural Heritage Image Database is an artist name search. An artist name search and an author search can both be considered searches for the creator. Organizational feature scaffolds were the most utilized in the context of finding science information among high school students (Lumpe and Butler, 2002). In another study, "search" and "present" corresponded to more than 80% of the operation usage. Few users employed the "browse" operation (4%) or the "search history" operation (1%) to refine their search results (Sfakakis and Kapidakis, 2002). Users' viewing behaviors and content viewing also have been investigated (Nicholas et al., 2005, 2006).

Usage pattern research has also extended to mobile users' interaction with digital libraries. After analyzing log data of Europeana mobile users, Nicholas and his associates (Nicholas et al., 2013; Nicholas and Clark, 2014) find that mobile users are the fastest-growing user groups, and they exhibit unique interaction behaviors compared to nonmobile users. They prefer to use personal mobile devices to interact with Europeana rather than their office desktop or laptop devices. They are less interactive and view less content. In addition, they do not spend a long time on the site, and they normally visit on evenings and weekends. Cultural institutions and their members are loyal users. Interestingly, Europeana user growth from the site itself is higher than the overall visitors from social media referrals.

Moreover, usage patterns have been analyzed to identify the impact of digital libraries, which includes research trends, the value of digital libraries, and a deep understanding of users' information-seeking behaviors. Bollen et al. (2003) compared digital library usage patterns to the Institute for Scientific Indexing (ISI) Impact Factor values during the same years to identify local research trends in the institution. Similarly, Górny et al. (2015) uncover the impact of digital library use on users' interest based on survey results of Polish digital library use from nonacademic users. They discover the emergence of digital libraries in Poland leads to great interest in genealogical or local historical research because of the content coverage of digital libraries. Kurtz et al. (2005) introduce the concept of utility to assess the value of digital libraries. By integrating usage logs, membership statistics, and gross domestic product (GDP) data, the impact of the NASA Astrophysics data system digital library is assessed. They also assign specific values for digital library evaluation. To be more specific, the value of the digital library in 2002 equaled 736 full-time researchers, or $250 million. Employing deep log methods of analysis of a million users' request to a digital library, researchers (Nicholas et al., 2005, 2006) explore users' view behaviors, especially what a user is viewing, to understand their degree of penetration of a system.

Notably, usage patterns do not show much difference in different environments. Most of the users apply their mental model of web search engines to digital libraries. Short queries, short sessions, minimum view of search results, and similar unique queries are shown in web search engine, OPACs, and digital library environments (Xie, 2008). More queries contain Boolean operators in digital library environments than in web search engine environments (Jones et al., 2000; Wang et al., 2003). Wolfram and Xie (2002) define the context of digital libraries as representing a hybrid of both "traditional" IR, using primarily bibliographic resources provided by database vendors, and "popular" IR, exemplified by public search systems available on the World Wide Web. Users' search topics are suited to online databases, but their search behaviors are more similar to searching web search engines. After analyzing log data from two large-scale digital libraries, the National Science Digital Library and Opening History, Zavalina and Vassilieva (2014) conclude that users prefer a basic keyword search rather than an advanced search, which is consistent with users searching online catalogs and other information retrieval systems. However, users opt for more advanced searching in both large-scale digital libraries than when searching on the web or in online databases. This is mainly attributed to the case that there might be a large number of domain expert users in digital-scale domain-specific digital libraries. Contrary to other research findings, this study also reports that the average search query length in digital libraries is shorter than in most transaction log analysis studies of online catalogs and web search engines. It seems the results of usage patterns from log data vary among different types of digital libraries. More research is needed to better understand the commonalities that do exist from one digital library to another. Design library designers should be extremely mindful of the specific usage patterns of their target user groups.

USER INVOLVEMENT AND SYSTEM SUPPORT
PREVIOUS RESEARCH

While users take leading roles in applying some search tactics, systems play dominant roles in other tactics. Users need to be intellectually engaged while the system assists them by providing different system features. According to Xie et al. (in press), user involvement is defined as users' behavioral and cognitive activities in applying different types of search tactics during the search process. System support refers to types of functions that IR systems provide to users to facilitate the effective completion of users' search processes. Researchers have long investigated the extent of user control and system support for handling different types of search tactics (Bates, 1990; Beaulieu and Jones, 1998; White and Ruthven, 2006; Xie and Cool, 2000; Xie, 2003; Xie et al., 2013, in press). In IR processes, users are requested to be an active participant rather than a passive recipient of, and reactor to, output from the system (Belkin, 1993).

Since Bates (1990) initiated the issue of balancing user involvement and system support in terms of IR system design, it has become an ongoing research topic (Bates, 2002; Hendry and Harper, 1997; Savage-Knepshield and Belkin, 1999; White and Ruthven, 2006; Xie, 2003; Xie et al., in press). In particular, two studies specifically have investigated the issue of ease of use and user control. Xie (2003) directly compared users' perceptions of ease of use versus user control in fulfilling their search activities. The major finding of her study is that the extent of system support and user control differed by various search activities. The proposed model of optimal support for ease of use and user control highlights different roles that systems and users play in achieving various IR subtasks. Focusing on user control, White and Ruthven (2006) find that users prefer more control during search result evaluation, but expect system assistance in query reformulation and making search decisions.

Researchers have recognized the importance of offering different options to support both basic and advanced interfaces (Vilar and Zumar, 2005). Matching user behaviors and system support is another area for research. Marki et al. (2008) identify different types of information behaviors and associated system supports. More specifically, different types of supportive techniques are proposed for different types of users' involvement in search processes (Yuan and Belkin, 2007, 2010). Faceted interfaces for effective browsing are suggested to support users with poorly defined goals (Wilson et al., 2009).

Accordingly, new measurements have been proposed to judge user engagement and system support. With respect to user engagement, four elements have been identified, including the point of engagement, the period of sustained engagement, disengagement, and reengagement (O'Brien and Toms, 2008). Turning to system support, how the usefulness of system features is measured depends on how users' search tactics, search strategies, and goals are supported (Belkin et al., 2009; Wilson, 2009). The main contribution of these studies in IR system evaluation is that they not only focus on interaction outcomes but also interaction processes.

AN IN-DEPTH LOOK AT USER INVOLVEMENT AND SYSTEM SUPPORT IN DIGITAL LIBRARIES

Recently, Xie et al. (2013; in press) explored various types of user involvement and system support relative to different types of search tactics occurring during interactions with four type of IR systems: web search engines, OPACs, online databases, and digital libraries. In this section, the report of the findings concentrates on user involvement and system support in digital libraries. Information-searching diaries and questionnaires serve as data collection instruments to study 61 subjects. Three categories of search tactics are derived from quantitative analysis: user dominated, system dominated, and balanced tactics. User-dominated tactics consist of selecting databases/collections, creating search statements, exploring, and evaluating tactics. System-dominated tactics include monitoring, organizing, accessing, and recording. Balanced tactics consist of learning and reformulating tactics. While users and the system have to play dominant roles in accomplishing user- and system- dominated tactics respectively, users and systems are equally engaged in applying balanced tactics. The authors propose a model that illustrates user involvement and system support in applying user-dominated tactics, system-dominated tactics, and balanced tactics.

Some examples may help shed light on user-dominated, system-dominated, and balanced tactics in the digital library environment. Considering user-dominated tactics, participants had to make intellectual decisions by applying their domain knowledge, system knowledge, and information-retrieval knowledge and skills to the Select, Create, Explore, and Evaluation tactics. Participants clearly knew what they wanted and hoped digital libraries could enhance their knowledge to make quick decisions. In order to effectively explore information, participants had to have some knowledge on the organization of the browsing mechanism. A typical quote sums it up, "When exploring information I would like the IR system to organize the topics into headings or subcategories. American Memory does this a little with photos and prints, and then once the user's clicks on that topic, it breaks into subcategories about what types of pictures." In the process of evaluation, participants also needed to understand how the results are organized so they could effectively select the relevant item. As one participant put it, "For the IR system that I dislike the most in terms of organization is American Memory. American Memory organizes in terms of relevance but was not clear to me at first of how it might be relevant without further exploration."

Moving to system-dominated tactics, systems play a major role, while users are the originators of these tactics. Participants decided when and what to monitor, organize, access, and record, and they expected the system to implement their decisions. Participants delegated execution of system-dominated tactics to the system. To this end, they needed more features capable of achieving these tasks. Without these features, participants had to spend more time and effort to get the work done. Monitoring is essential in the search process for users to know their current status and their paths, and participants relied on system features, such as search history, to lead them. One participant complained, "The National Science Digital Library does not have a way for me to view search history or to return to previous search screens. This makes it difficult for me to return to other search results I find helpful or to return to the original search after I've modified the results." Again, another complaint regarding the lack of a zoom feature when accessing individual documents, "I was most disappointed by American Memory's access to written documents. When I was looking at some of Lincoln's letter, I could not view the larger image along with the transcription. I was also not able to zoom in on a particular word that I might have trouble reading."

Balanced tactics require that both users and systems collaborate together. For example, in the process of learning how to use a digital library, users have to interact with the help mechanism. Users need to identify the problem and select appropriate help features while systems need to provide understandable explicit and implicit help features regarding how to solve the problem. It was difficult for participants to find the help they needed. One participant revealed a problem with a lack of context-sensitive help, "The search help page on the American Memory was ambiguous, and if the direct question was not listed under FAQ's, then one must attempt to browse more collections by 'trial and error.' This particular feature was not one I felt was easily explained through the help section."

In order to support user-dominated tactics, it is important for digital libraries to adapt to users in their search process. One approach is to offer knowledge support based on user profiles, search patterns, and click-through data. Social media, in particular social tagging, can be also beneficial to users to extend their topic knowledge by allowing users to see how others provide relevant terms for an item. In support of system-dominated tactics, digital libraries need to offer more options for users to monitor their search process, organize their search results, access individual documents, and record different formats of documents. It is also essential to remove all unnecessary paths and provide one-click solutions for users to effectively apply system-dominated tactics. To assist users with balanced search tactics, it is vital to promote interactions between users and digital libraries. Offering relevant feedback is an implicit way for digital libraries to interact with users to assist them in modifying their search statements. Context-sensitive help is one good example of initiating effective interactions from the digital library side for users to acquire system, domain, and information-retrieval knowledge.

FACTORS AFFECTING DIGITAL LIBRARY USE

Fig. 8.1 summarizes and illustrates the factors—user personal infrastructure, tasks, digital libraries—that affect information search tactics, strategies, and digital library use.

USER PERSONAL INFRASTRUCTURE

User personal infrastructure, consisting of domain knowledge, system knowledge, information retrieval-knowledge learning/cognitive styles, and self-efficacy, has been demonstrated as one of the key factors affecting IR system use. Among the three types of knowledge, domain knowledge has influenced

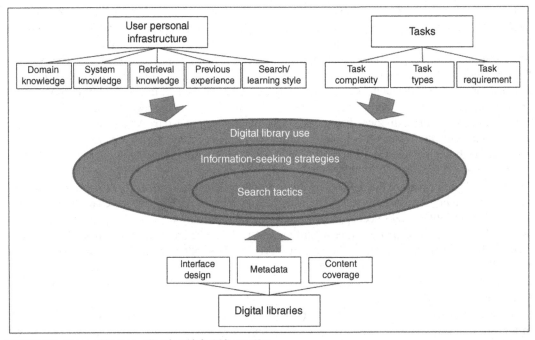

FIGURE 8.1 Types of Factors Affecting Digital Library Use

information search tactics, information search success, and information-seeking behavior (Bilal, 2001; Hirsh, 1997, 2004; Hsieh-Yee, 2001; Marchionini, 1995). In particular, domain knowledge affects the selection of search tactics, change of search tactics, the creation of complex queries versus ineffective search strategies, and making physical moves (Hembrooke et al., 2005; Hsieh-Yee, 1993; Shiri and Revie, 2003; Wildemuth, 2004). Kelly and Cool (2002) state that as users' familiarity with a topic increases, their searching efficacy increases and their reading time decreases.

Research has shown that domain knowledge has a particular impact on children's information searching and their outcome. Hirsh (1997, 2004) finds that children with high domain knowledge perform better in information searching than children with low domain knowledge. Hirsh (2004) notices that children with high domain knowledge are able to modify their search queries based on the retrieved results. These same children prefer keyword searching, while children with low domain knowledge favor using the browsing strategy. One plausible explanation is that the limited domain knowledge of children causes difficulties in formulating queries via keyword search (Gossen et al., 2013). Despite the work of some, not all researchers generate the same results. Bilal (2001) emphasizes that the influences of children's domain knowledge are not significant based on her research results, but "this finding was mainly due to the unequal distribution in the number of children who had high ratings on these variables and those who had low ratings" (p. 130).

In the digital library environment, user studies yield similar results regarding the impact of domain knowledge. Albertson (2010) investigated how users' familiarity with visual search topics influenced their interactions with interactive video digital libraries. The variables associated with user interactions consist of the keyword, title browse, color, shape, texture, all visuals, textual promote, and details.

The results show that topic familiarity affects users' use of details, use of promotes, use of color, and use of textual promote. Information-retrieval knowledge and search experience also influence users' search behaviors. The number of pages, task solution time, and types of items accessed are different between novice and expert users (Saito and Miwa, 2007). Just as those with domain knowledge, expert users are better at searching than novice users, whereas the novice users tend to browse (Lazonder, 2000). Users who have advanced digital library knowledge create advanced queries (Trieschnigg et al., 2013).

In most of the cases, different types of user knowledge codetermine users' behaviors in searching a digital library. Users, who have better knowledge in searching digital libraries and their topics, use more complex structures, and more specialized and informative access points. Moreover, user behavior changes over time. Users decrease the number of operations in their sessions, as they get more experienced with digital libraries (Sfakakis and Kapidakis, 2002). Collecting data from 120 subjects, Xie and Cool (2009) identify 15 types of help situations which can be further characterized into seven categories: (1) inability to get started, (2) inability to identify relevant digital collections, (3) inability to browse for information, (4) inability to construct search statements, (5) inability to refine searches, (6) inability to monitor searches, and (7) inability to evaluate results. Sixteen factors lead to the 15 types of help situations that subjects encounter in their interactions with digital libraries. These 16 factors represent four categories: personal knowledge structure, task dimensions, system design, and interaction outcome. Personal knowledge structure is composed of knowledge related to the digital library that users interact with, retrieval knowledge related to how to search for information, users' past experience in searching for information in different types of IR systems, as well as their preference in searching for information. Each type of knowledge either determines or codetermines different types of help-seeking situations. Based on the data collected from 60 subjects constituting different academic disciplines, Huang (2014) explored how learning styles affected novice users' help-seeking behaviors in searching digital libraries. The results indicate that novice users with different learning styles select different types of help features. Quantitative data supports the finding that learning styles have an effect on help-seeking interactions. Fifteen help-seeking approaches occurring in users' interactions with digital libraries are identified. Self-efficacy is another factor that plays a role in users' interactions with digital libraries. Tang and Tseng (2013) investigated the relationships between distance learners' self-efficacy and their information literacy skills in using digital libraries. The results show that learners with high self-efficacy in information searching in digital libraries demonstrate higher self-efficacy in online learning. In addition, learners with high self-efficacy show better skills in selecting digital resources than learners with low self-efficacy.

TYPES OF INFORMATION-SEARCH TASKS

Just like user personal infrastructure, the task is another crucial factor that affects information search behaviors. Both work tasks and search tasks have an impact on information search behaviors (Byström and Järvelin, 1995; Li, 2009; Xie, 2009). Xie (2009) identifies nature, stages, and time frame as dimensions of work task; and origination, types, and flexibility as dimensions of search task. She finds that information-seeking processes, such as planning, search strategy selection, and shifts in tactics, vary in different work and search tasks. In addition, task complexity has been demonstrated to have a direct impact on information-seeking activities and search performance (Byström, 2002; Byström and Järvelin, 1995; Li, 2010).

The relationships between types of search tasks and tactics have been investigated, although there is discrepancy in the results. According to Hsieh-Yee (1998), there is no significant differences among search tactics (tactics for starting, tactics for too many items retrieved, and tactics for no relevant items retrieved) enacted for known-item searches and subject searches. In contrast, search task types of known-item searching and subject searching have been found to significantly affect search tactics, such as web site views and search tool use (Kim and Allen, 2002). Children select more natural language queries in addition to looping and backtracking more on fact-based tasks, and browse more on self-generated tasks. They also apply more analytic searches on these two tasks than on research tasks (Bilal and Kirby, 2002).

Meyyappan et al. (2004) created a task-based digital library in which three different information organization approaches (alphabetical, subject category, and task based) are used to organize heterogeneous resources. The results of the comparison of three approaches indicate that the task-based approach is the most effective in organizing information in the digital library. Xie (2006) investigated human-work interaction in a corporate setting for the development of a digital library. In her study, the first type of interaction activity consists of task activities. The author identifies three dimensions of work tasks:

- The nature of task (routine, typical, or new)
- The type of task (updating information or looking for specific information, a known item, or items with common characteristics)
- The time frame of the task (extremely urgent, urgent, or nonurgent)

The three dimensions of task activities greatly affect three types of interaction activities: decision, collaboration, and in particular, strategy activities. "Updating information corresponds to a 'browsing strategy,' in which a user scans to find a match with his or her information need. Looking for specific information is associated with an 'analytical search' whereby a user analyzes his or her needs and compares relevant aspects of information resources. Looking for items with common characteristics corresponds to an 'analytical search' and 'search by analogy' wherein a user finds items that are similar to a known item. Looking for known items is related to a 'bibliographical search' in which a user knows some information regarding an item, such as author, title, etc." (p. 134). It is important to investigate the multiple dimensions of tasks and how they influence users' information-searching behaviors.

In digital library environments, different types of tasks have been demonstrated as one of the key determining factors affecting users' information-searching behaviors. In a help-seeking situation study (Xie and Cool, 2009), three types of task dimensions represent a task: task requirement, task type, and task complexity. Task requirement refers to a special condition for a task, such as time, identifying different approaches, etc. Task type refers to different types of tasks, such as looking for specific information, items with common characteristics, and different aspects of a topic. Task complexity refers to the level of difficulty of a task. The findings of the study show that task requirement, although codetermined with other factors, influences the help situations related to browsing and refining searches; task type affects the help situations related to creating search statements, refining searches, and evaluating results; and task complexity determines the help situations related to creating search statements and refining searches.

SYSTEM DESIGN

User personal infrastructure, tasks, and system design are the three parallel factors having an impact on information-searching behaviors and search performance. The interface design of IR systems has a huge impact on children's search behaviors (Jochmann-Mannak et al., 2008). Complex interfaces, in particular, have affected children's information-seeking behavior (Bilal, 2004). Hutchinson et al. (2006) investigated whether the flat and the hierarchical interfaces influenced children's search performance. Children were able to perform searches faster on the flat interface than on the hierarchical interface. Likewise, it was easier for them to use the flat interface than the hierarchical one.

In digital library environments, interface design, collections, and metadata are all part of a digital library. After examining the usage data of different access points, Sfakakis and Kapidakis (2002) conclude that the type of content in a collection and the detail of the existing metadata play a role in how users choose different access points. Focusing on museum practitioners, Chen's (2007) study suggests that both the context of the collection and the system itself, including cataloging practices, have an impact on the information-seeking behaviors of the user. The organization of search results also leads to unusual viewing behaviors. While users view far fewer result pages in other types of IR systems, on average they viewed 3.4 result pages in a digital library. One explanation for the large number of result pages viewed might be the fact that the results are not ranked by relevance, but by ID number (Trieschnigg et al., 2013). In a log analysis study of two large-scale digital libraries, users engaged in more advanced searches in the National Science Digital Library (NSDL) than Opening History (OH) because NSDL offered more search limit options than OH. In addition, the coverage of the digital libraries also impacts the content that users search for. While NSDL users searched more for concepts and objects, OH users searched more for place, person, corporate body, ethnic group, event, and class of persons (Zavalina and Vassilieva, 2014).

Joo (2013) examined how users applied different search tactics in conjunction with the associated system support in the digital library environment. In this study, system support refers to "the representation of system features to assist users' behavioral activities or cognitive intention to facilitate user-system interactions during an IR process" (p. 14). His results show that system support significantly affects users' satisfaction with the search process, their satisfaction with the search results, and aspectual recall. Adapting Skov's nested diagram model, Joo (2013) adds contextual factors into the diagram to illustrate the features that influence the information-retrieval process.

The diverse needs of different user groups, consisting of children, college students, scholars, elderly people, and people with disabilities, and their unique information-searching behaviors pose a challenge for the development of digital libraries with diverse collections built in different content management systems. The questions are: Should we design a one-size-fits-all digital library for everyone? How can we design digital libraries to satisfy diverse user needs and behaviors? Moreover, the Google generation is used to web search engines. The impact of web search engines on digital library use is obvious. A related question is: Is it possible to keep the unique design (e.g., browsing features) of digital libraries and also adopt simple interface design? Therefore, user needs and behavior studies should take system design implications into consideration and offer recommendations to promote and facilitate the interactions between users and systems.

REFERENCES

Albertson, D., 2010. Influences of users' familiarity with visual search topics on interactive video digital libraries. J. Am. Soc. Inf. Sci. Technol. 61 (12), 2490–2502.

Albertson, D., 2015. Visual information seeking. J. Assoc. Inf. Sci. Technol. 66 (6), 1091–1105.

Bates, M.J., 1979. Information search tactics. J. Am. Soc. Inf. Sci. 30 (4), 205–214.

Bates, M.J., 1990. Where should the person stop and the information search interface start? Inf. Process. Manag. 26 (5), 575–591.

Bates, M.J., 1992. Search and idea tactics. For information specialists: interpretations of reference and bibliographic work (183–200). Norwood, NJ: Ablex.

Bates, M.J., 2002. The cascade of interactions in the digital library interface. Inf. Process. Manag. 38 (3), 381–400.

Beaulieu, M., Jones, S., 1998. Interactive searching and interface issues in the Okapi best match probabilistic retrieval system. Interact. Comput. 10 (3), 237–248.

Belkin, N.J., 1993. Interaction with texts: information retrieval as information seeking behavior. Inf. Retr. 93, 55–66.

Belkin, N.J., Cole, M., Liu, J., 2009. A model for evaluation of interactive information retrieval. In: Proceedings of SIGIR Workshop on the Future of IR Evaluation. Boston, pp. 7–8.

Bell, L., Peters, T., 2005. Digital library services for all: innovative technology opens doors to print-impaired patrons. Am. Lib. 36 (8), 46–49.

Bertot, J., Snead, J.T., Jaeger, P.T., McClure, C.R., 2006. Functionality, usability, and accessibility: iterative user-centered evaluation strategies for digital libraries. Perform. Meas. Metrics 7 (1), 17–28.

Bilal, D., 2001. Children's use of the Yahooligans! Web search engine: II. Cognitive and physical behaviors on research tasks. J. Am. Soc. Inf. Sci. Technol. 52 (2), 118–136.

Bilal, D., 2004. Research on children's information seeking on the Web. In: Chelton, M.K., Cool, C. (Eds.), Youth Information-Seeking Behavior: Theories, Models, and Issues, vol. 1, Scarecrow Press, Lanham, MD, pp. 271–291.

Bilal, D., Bachir, I., 2007. Children's interaction with cross-cultural and multilingual digital libraries. II. Information seeking, success, and affective experience. Inf. Process. Manag. 43 (1), 65–80.

Bilal, D., Kirby, J., 2002. Differences and similarities in information seeking: children and adults as Web users. Inf. Process. Manag. 38 (5), 649–670.

Bilal, D., Sarangthem, S., Bachir, I., 2008. Toward a model of children's information seeking behavior in using digital libraries. In: Proceedings of the Second International Symposium on Information Interaction in Context. ACM, New York, pp. 145–151.

Bollen, J., Luce, R., Vemulapalli, S.S., Xu, W., 2003. Usage analysis for the identification of research trends in digital libraries. D-Lib Mag., 9 (5). Available from: http://www.dlib.org/dlib/may03/bollen/05bollen.html.

Booker, L.D., Detlor, B., Serenko, A., 2012. Factors affecting the adoption of online library resources by business students. J. Am. Soc. Inf. Sci. Technol. 63 (12), 2503–2520.

Bruza, P., Dennis, S., 1997. Query reformulation on the Internet: empirical data and the Hyperindex search engine. In: Proceedings of the RIAO'97 Conference on Computer-Assisted Information Searching on Internet. ACM Press, Montreal, pp. 488–499.

Butcher, W., Street, P.A., 2009. Lifelong learning with older adults. APLIS 22 (2), 64–70.

Byström, K., Järvelin, K., 1995. Task complexity affects information-seeking and use. Inf. Process. Manag. 31 (2), 191–213.

Byström, K., 2002. Information and information sources in tasks of varying complexity. J. Am. Soc. Inf. Sci. Technol. 53 (7), 581–591.

Chen, H., Dhar, V., 1991. Cognitive process as a basis for intelligent retrieval systems design. Inf. Process. Manag. 27 (5), 405–432.

Chen, H.L., 2007. A socio-technical perspective of museum practitioners' image-using behaviors. Electron. Lib. 25 (1), 18–35.

Cheng, Y.M., 2014. Why do users intend to continue using the digital library? An integrated perspective. Aslib J. Inf. Manag. 66 (6), 640–662.

Choi, Y., Rasmussen, E.M., 2003. Searching for images: the analysis of users' queries for image retrieval in American history. J. Am. Soc. Inf. Sci. Technol. 54 (6), 497–510.

Connaway, L.S., Dickey, T.J., Radford, M.L., 2011. "If it is too inconvenient I'm not going after it": convenience as a critical factor in information-seeking behaviors. Lib. Inf. Sci. Res. 33 (3), 179–190.

Czaja, S.J., Charness, N., Fisk, A.D., Hertzog, C., Nair, S.N., Rogers, W.A., Sharit, J., 2006. Factors predicting the use of technology: findings from the Center for Research and Education on Aging and Technology Enhancement (CREATE). Psychol. Aging 21 (2), 333–352.

Decker, E.N., 2010. Baby boomers and the United States public library system. Lib. Hi Tech 28 (4), 605–616.

Dougan, K., 2012. Information seeking behaviors of music students. Ref. Serv. Rev. 40 (4), 558–573.

Druin, A., Foss, E., Hutchinson, H., Golub, E., Hatley, L., 2010. Children's roles using keyword search interfaces at home. In: Proceedings of the SIGCHI Conference on Human Factors in Computing Systems. ACM, New York, pp. 413–422.

Duffy, E.E., 2013. Searching HathiTrust: old concepts in a new context. partnership. Can. J. Lib. Inf. Prac. Res. 8 (1), 1–13.

Entlich, R., Garson, L., Lesk, M., Normore, L., Olsen, J., Weibel, S., 1996. Testing a digital library: user response to the CORE project. Lib. Hi Tech 14 (4), 99–118.

Fidel, R., 1985. Moves in online searching. Online Inf. Rev. 9 (1), 61–74.

Fiske, A., Wetherell, J.L., Gatz, M., 2009. Depression in older adults. Ann. Rev. Clin. Psychol. 5, 363–389.

Foss, E., 2014. Internet searching in children and adolescents: a longitudinal framework of youth search roles (Doctoral dissertation). University of Maryland.

Foss, E., Druin, A., 2014. Roles of reaction: developing and non-motivated searchers. In: Marchionini, G. (Eds.), Children's Internet Search: Using Roles to Understand Children's Search Behavior: Synthesis Lectures on Information Concepts, Retrieval, and Services #34. Chapel Hill: Morgan & Claypool, pp. 37–44.

Gross, M., Latham, D., 2011. Experiences with and perceptions of information: a phenomenographic study of first-year college students. Library 81 (2), 161–186.

Górny, M., Catlow, J., Mazurek, J., 2015. Evaluating Polish digital libraries from the perspective of non-academic users. Electron. Lib. 33 (4), 714–729.

Gossen, T., Hempel, J., Nürnberger, A., 2013. Find it if you can: usability case study of search engines for young users. Pers. Ubiquit. Comput. 17 (8), 1593–1603.

Han, H.J., Joo, S., Wolfram, D., 2014. Tales from transaction logs: user search session patterns in an image-based digital library. In: Proceedings of the Annual Conference of CAIS/Actes du congrès annuel de l'ACSI.

Hembrooke, H.A., Granka, L.A., Gay, G.K., Liddy, E.D., 2005. The effects of expertise and feedback on search term selection and subsequent learning. J. Am. Soc. Inf. Sci. Technol. 56 (8), 861–871.

Hendry, D.G., Harper, D.J., 1997. An informal information-seeking environment. J. Am. Soc. Inf. Sci. 48 (11), 1036–1048.

Higgins, S., 2013. Access to digital libraries for disadvantaged users. Lib. Philos. Pract. (e-journal), p. 916. Retrieved from: http://digitalcommons.unl.edu/cgi/viewcontent.cgi?article=2280&context=libphilprac.

Hirsh, S.G., 1997. How do children find information on different types of tasks? Children's use of the Science Library Catalog. Lib. Trends 45 (4), 725–745.

Hirsh, S.G., 2004. Domain knowledge and children's search behavior. In: Chelton, M.K., Cool, C. (Eds.), Youth Information-Seeking Behavior: Theories, Models, and Issues. Scarecrow Press, Lanham, MD, pp. 241–270.

Hsieh-Yee, I., 1993. Effects of search experience and subject knowledge on the search tactics of novice and experienced searchers. J. Am. Soc. Inf. Sci. 44 (3), 161–174.

Hsieh-Yee, I., 1998. Search tactics of Web users in searching for texts, graphics, known items and subjects: a search simulation study. Ref. Lib. 28 (60), 61–85.

Hsieh-Yee, I., 2001. Research on Web search behavior. Lib. Inf. Sci. Res. 23 (2), 167–185.

Hu, C., Hu, Y.h., Yan, W., 2014. An empirical study of factors influencing user perception of university digital libraries in China. Lib. Inf. Sci. Res. 36 (3/4), 225–233.

Huang, C., 2014. Understanding Novice Users' Help-seeking Behavior in Getting Started with Digital Libraries: Influence of Learning Styles (Doctoral dissertation). University of Wisconsin-Milwaukee.

Hutchinson, H.B., Bederson, B.B., Druin, A., 2006. The evolution of the International Children's Digital Library searching and browsing interface. In: Proceedings of the 2006 Conference on Interaction Design and Children. ACM, New York, pp. 105–112.

Hutchinson, H.B., Druin, A., Bederson, B.B., 2007. Supporting elementary-age children's searching and browsing: design and evaluation using the international children's digital library. J. Am. Soc. Inf. Sci. Technol. 58 (11), 1618–1630.

Hutchinson, H.B., Rose, A., Bederson, B.B., Weeks, A.C., Druin, A., 2005. The international children's digital library: a case study in designing for a multilingual, multicultural, multigenerational audience. Inf. Technol. Lib. 24 (1), 4–12.

Jochmann-Mannak, H.E., Huibers, T.W.C., Sanders, T.J.M., 2008. Children's information retrieval: beyond examining search strategies and interfaces. In: The Second BCS-IRSG Symposium: Future Directions in Information Access. British Computer Society: London, pp. 64–72.

Jones, S., Cunningham, S.J., McNab, R., Boddie, S., 2000. A transaction log analysis of a digital library. Int. J. Digital Lib. 3 (2), 152–169.

Joo, S., 2013. Investigating User Search Tactic Patterns and System Support in Using Digital Libraries (Doctoral dissertation). University of Wisconsin-Milwaukee.

Kapusiak, R.B., 2015. Baby Boomers and Technology: Factor and Challenges in Utilizing Mobile Devices (Doctoral dissertation). University of Wisconsin-Milwaukee.

Kelly, D., Cool, C., 2002. The effects of topic familiarity on information search behavior. In: Proceedings of the Second ACM/IEEE-CS Joint Conference on Digital Libraries, ACM, New York, pp. 74–75.

Kim, K.S., Allen, B., 2002. Cognitive and task influences on Web searching behavior. J. Am. Soc. Inf. Sci. Technol. 53 (2), 109–119.

Kurtz, M.J., Eichhorn, G., Accomazzi, A., Grant, C., Demleitner, M., Murray, S.S., 2005. Worldwide use and impact of the NASA astrophysics data system digital library. J. Am. Soc. Inf. Sci. Technol. 56 (1), 36–45.

Lau, T., Horvitz, E., 1999. Patterns of search: analyzing and modeling Web query refinement. In: Proceedings of the Seventh International Conference on User Modeling, Banff, Canada, June 1999, Springer, New York, pp. 119–128.

Lazonder, A.W., 2000. Exploring novice users' training needs in searching information on the WWW. J. Comput. Assist. Lear. 16 (4), 326–335.

Li, Y., 2009. Exploring the relationships between work task and search task in information search. J. Am. Soc. Inf. Sci. Technol. 60 (2), 275–291.

Li, Y., 2010. An exploration of the relationships between work task and interactive information search behavior. J. Am. Soc. Inf. Sci. Technol. 61 (9), 1771–1789.

Liu, Z., Luo, L., 2011. A comparative study of digital library use: factors, perceived influences, and satisfaction. J. Acad. Librar. 37 (3), 230–236.

Lowe, H.A., 2013. Search Log Analysis of the ARTstor Cultural Heritage Image Database. University of California, Los Angeles (Doctoral dissertation).

Lumpe, A.T., Butler, K., 2002. The information seeking strategies of high school science students. Res. Sci. Ed. 32 (4), 549–566.

Makri, S., Blandford, A., Cox, A.L., 2008. Using information behaviors to evaluate the functionality and usability of electronic resources: from Ellis's model to evaluation. J. Am. Soc. Inf. Sci. Technol. 59 (14), 2244–2267.

Marchionini, G., 1995. Information Seeking in Electronic Environments. Cambridge University Press, Cambridge.

Marchionini, G., Geisler, G., 2002. The open video digital library. D-Lib Mag. 8 (12), 1082–9873.

Marcus, A., 2003. Universal, ubiquitous, user-interface design for the disabled and elderly. Interactions 10 (2), 23–27.

Markey, K., Atherton, P., 1978. ONTAP: On-Line Training and Practice Manual for ERIC Database Searchers. ERIC Clearinghouse on Information Resources, Syracuse University, Syracuse, NY.

Martens, M.M., 2012. Issues of access and usability in designing digital resources for children. Lib. Inf. Sci. Res. 34 (3), 159–168.

Martyn, H., Gallant, L.M., 2012. Over 50 and wired: Web-based stakeholder communication. First Monday, 17 (6) Available from: http://firstmonday.org/ojs/index.php/fm/article/view/3449/3262.

Mates, B., 2004. Who aren't you serving digitally? Lib. Technol. Rep. 40 (3), 6–9.

Matusiak, K.K., 2006. Information seeking behavior in digital image collections: a cognitive approach. J. Acad. Librar. 32 (5), 479–488.

Matusiak, K.K., 2012. Perceptions of usability and usefulness of digital libraries. Int. J. Humanit. Arts Comput. 6 (1–2), 133–147.

Mead, S., Sit, R., Rogers, W., Jamieson, B., Rousseau, G., 2000. Influences of general computer experience and age on library database search performance. Behav. Inf. Technol. 19 (2), 107–123.

Meyyappan, N., Foo, S., Chowdhury, G.G., 2004. Design and evaluation of a task-based digital library for the academic community. J. Doc. 60 (4), 449–475.

Nasmith, W., Parkinson, M., 2008. Senior citizens embrace change and make a new technology work for them. Electron. Lib. 26 (5), 673–682.

Nicholas, D., Clark, D., 2014. Information seeking behaviour and usage on a multi-media platform: Case study Europeana. In: Library and Information Sciences: Trends and research. Springer: Berlin, Heidelberg, pp. 57–78.

Nicholas, D., Clark, D., Rowlands, I., Jamali, H.R., 2013. Information on the go: a case study of Europeana mobile users. J. Am. Soc. Inf. Sci. Technol. 64 (7), 1311–1322.

Nicholas, D., Huntington, P., Watkinson, A., 2005. Scholarly journal usage: the results of deep log analysis. J. Doc. 61 (2), 248–280.

Nicholas, D., Huntington, P., Monopoli, M., Watkinson, A., 2006. Engaging with scholarly digital libraries (publisher platforms): the extent to which "added-value" functions are used. Inf. Process. Manag. 42 (3), 826–842.

Nicholas, D., Huntington, P., Jamali, H.R., Rowlands, I., Fieldhouse, M., 2009. Student digital information-seeking behaviour in context. J. Doc. 65 (1), 106–132.

Nov, O., Ye, C., 2008. Users' personality and perceived ease of use of digital libraries: the case for resistance to change. J. Am. Soc. Inf. Sci. Technol. 59 (5), 845–851.

O'Brien, H.L., Toms, E.G., 2008. What is user engagement? A conceptual framework for defining user engagement with technology. J. Am. Soc. Inf. Sci. Technol. 59 (6), 938–955.

Reuter, K., Druin, A., 2004. Bringing together children and books: An initial descriptive study of children's book searching and selection behavior in a digital library. In: Proceedings of the 67th Annual Meeting of the American Society for Information Science and Technology, Medford, NJ: Information Today, pp. 339–348.

Rieh, S.Y., Xie, H.I., 2006. Analysis of multiple query reformulations on the web: the interactive information retrieval context. Inf. Process. Manag. 42 (3), 751–768.

Saito, H., Miwa, K., 2007. Construction of a learning environment supporting learners' reflection: a case of information seeking on the Web. Comput. Ed. 49 (2), 214–229.

Savage-Knepshield, P.A., Belkin, N.J., 1999. Interaction in information retrieval: trends over time. J. Am. Soc. Inf. Sci. Technol. 50 (12), 1067–1082.

Sfakakis, M., Kapidakis, S., 2002. User behavior tendencies on data collections in a digital library. In: Research and Advanced Technology for Digital Libraries. Springer: Berlin, Heidelberg, pp. 550–559.

Shiri, A.A., Revie, C., 2003. The effects of topic complexity and familiarity on cognitive and physical moves in a thesaurus-enhanced search environment. J. Inf. Sci. 29 (6), 517–526.

Shute, S.J., Smith, P.J., 1993. Knowledge-based search tactics. Inf. Process. Manag. 29 (1), 29–45.

Smith, A.G., 2012. Internet search tactics. Online Inf. Rev. 36 (1), 7–20.

Smith, M.W., Sharit, J., Czaja, S.J., 1999. Aging, motor control, and the performance of computer mouse tasks. Hum. Factors 41 (3), 389–396.

Soloman, P., 1993. Children's information retrieval behavior: a case analysis of an OPAC. J. Am. Soc. Inf. Sci. 44 (5), 245–264.

Stronge, A.J., Rogers, W.A., Fisk, A.D., 2006. Web-based information search and retrieval: effects of strategy use and age on search success. Hum. Factors 48 (3), 434–446.

Tang, Y., Tseng, H.W., 2013. Distance learners' self-efficacy and information literacy skills. J. Acad. Librar. 39 (6), 517–521.

Theng, Y.L., Mohd-Nasir, N., Thimbleby, H., 2000. Purpose and usability of digital libraries. In: Proceedings of the Fifth ACM Conference on Digital Libraries. ACM, New York, pp. 238–239.

Trieschnigg, D., Nguyen, D., Meder, T., 2013. In search of Cinderella: A transaction log analysis of folktale searchers. In: The Proceedings of the First Workshop on the Exploration, Navigation and Retrieval of Information in Cultural Heritage, Thirty Sixth Annual ACM SIGIR Conference, SIGIR 2013: Dublin.

Vakkari, P., Pennanen, M., Serola, S., 2003. Changes of search terms and tactics while writing a research proposal: a longitudinal case study. Inf. Process. Manag. 39 (3), 445–463.

Vilar, P., Zumar, M., 2005. Comparison and evaluation of the user interfaces of e-journals. J. Doc. 61 (2), 203–227.

Wang, P., Berry, M.W., Yang, Y., 2003. Mining longitudinal Web queries: trends and patterns. J. Am. Soc. Inf. Sci. Technol. 54 (8), 743–758.

Wang, P., Hawk, W.B., Tenopir, C., 2000. Users' interaction with World Wide Web resources: an exploratory study using a holistic approach. Inf. Process. Manag. 36 (2), 229–251.

White, R.W., Ruthven, I., 2006. A study of interface support mechanisms for interactive information retrieval. J. Am. Soc. Inf. Sci. Technol. 57 (7), 933–948.

Wildemuth, B.M., 2004. The effects of domain knowledge on search tactic formulation. J. Am. Soc. Inf. Sci. Technol. 55 (3), 246–258.

Wilson, M.L., 2009. An analytical inspection framework for evaluating the search tactics and user profiles supported by information seeking interfaces. (Doctoral dissertation, University of Southampton).

Wilson, M.L., Schraefel, M.C., White, R.W., 2009. Evaluating advanced search interfaces using established information-seeking models. J. Am. Soc. Inf. Sci. Technol. 60 (7), 1407–1422.

Wolfram, D., Xie, H., 2002. Traditional IR for web users: a context for general audience digital libraries. Inf. Process. Manag. 38 (5), 627–648.

Wu, K.K., 2015. Affective surfing in the visualized interface of a digital library for children. Inf. Process. Manag. 51 (4), 373–390.

Xie, H., 2006. Understanding human-work domain interaction: implications for the design of a corporate digital library. J. Am. Soc. Inf. Sci. Technol. 57 (1), 128–143.

Xie, I., 2003. Supporting ease-of-use and user control: desired features and structure of Web-based online IR systems. Inf. Process. Manag. 39 (6), 899–922.

Xie, I., 2008. Interactive Information Retrieval in Digital Environments. IGI Global Inc., Hershey, Pennsylvania.

Xie, I., 2009. Dimensions of tasks: influences on information-seeking and retrieving process. J. Doc. 65 (3), 339–366.

Xie, I., Babu, R., Jeong, W., Joo, S., Fuller, P., 2014. Blind users searching digital libraries: types of help-seeking situations at the cognitive level. In: iConference 2014 Proceedings. pp. 853–857.

Xie, I., Babu, R., Joo, S., Fuller, P., 2015. Using digital libraries non-visually: understanding the help seeking situations of blind users. Inform. Res., 20 (2), Paper 673. Available from: http://InformationR.net/ir/20-2/paper673.html.

Xie, I., Cool, C., 2000. Ease of use versus user control: an evaluation of Web and non-Web interfaces of online databases. Online Inform. Rev. 24 (2), 102–115.

Xie, I., Cool, C., 2009. Understanding help seeking within the context of searching digital libraries. J. Am. Soc. Inform. Sci. Technol. 60 (3), 477–494.

Xie, I., Joo, S., 2010. Transitions in search tactics during the Web-based search process. J. Am. Soc. Inform. Sci. Technol. 61 (11), 2188–2205.

Xie, I., Joo, S., Bennett-Kapusniak, R., 2013. User engagement and system support in the search process: user dominated, system dominated and balanced search tactics. In: Proceedings of Seventy Sixth ASIS&T Annual Meeting. Montreal, Canada, November, 2013.

Xie, I., Joo, S., Bennett-Kapusniak, R., in press. User involvement and system support in applying search tactics. J. Am. Soc. Inform. Sci. Technol.

Yuan, X., Belkin, N.J., 2007. Supporting multiple information strategies in a single system framework. In: Proceedings of the Thirtieth Annual International ACM SIGIR Conference on Research and Development in Information Retrieval. SIGIR 2007. ACM Press, New York, pp. 247–254.

Yuan, X., Belkin, N.J., 2010. Investigating information retrieval support techniques for different information-seeking strategies. J. Am. Soc. Inform. Sci. Technol. 61 (8), 1543–1563.

Yue, Z., Han, S., He, D., 2012. A comparison of action transitions in individual and collaborative exploratory Web search. In: Information Retrieval Technology. Springer: Berlin, Heidelberg, pp. 52–63.

Zhang, Y., Lee, K., You, B.J., 2001. Usage patterns of an electronic theses and dissertations system. Online Inform. Rev. 25 (6), 370–377.

Zhang, W., Song, L., Li, C., 2012. An analysis of the development of China digital library for visual impairment website. Electron. Lib. 30 (6), 756–763.

Zavalina, O., Vassilieva, E.V., 2014. Understanding the information needs of large-scale digital library users. Lib. Res. Tech. Serv. 58 (2), 84–99.

DIGITAL PRESERVATION

INTRODUCTION

Digital preservation represents an emergent area of digital library research and practice. It focuses on the policies, technologies, and strategies to ensure that digital library objects and collections are available and usable now and in the future. Digital preservation encompasses materials born in the digital format as well as those converted from the analog format through the digitization process. Concerns about preserving digital content are not unique to digital libraries. All resources in the digital format are fragile and susceptible to information loss. Multiple risks stem from the unstable nature of digital formats, degradation of storage media, and technological obsolescence. As the members of the Blue Ribbon Task Force on Sustainable Digital Preservation and Access note, digital preservation is a universal and "urgent societal problem" (Berman et al., 2010, p. 9).

In the context of digital libraries, the challenge of digital preservation is compounded by the structural complexity of digital objects and the interrelatedness of objects, collections, and repositories (Ross, 2012). The models and solutions for preserving content in present-day digital libraries will have an impact on future access to cultural heritage and scientific information. As Seadle (2008) emphasizes, "the digital libraries in 100 years will face problems that stem from the choices that we as librarians make today" (p. 5). Long-term preservation of digital content is recognized as a core function of digital libraries in the DELOS Manifesto (Candela et al., 2007), but it does not feature prominently in other definitions and frameworks. The practice of preserving digital objects has evolved since the first digital libraries were developed in the mid-1990s, but research in the area of digital preservation is relatively new (Chowdhury, 2010; Ross, 2012).

The concept and principles of preserving analog materials are well established in the library and archival community, although, as Cloonan (2007) points out, the institutional, custodial model is somewhat paradoxical in the modern world. Preservation is understood as an act of responsible custody aimed at preventing the deterioration of cultural heritage materials and restoring their usefulness and information value (Conway, 2007, 2010). Conway argues that the fundamental principles of digital preservation are the same as those of the analog world and define the priorities for ensuring the longevity and the useful life of information resources. The core concepts of preserving analog materials in regard to longevity, choice, quality, integrity, and access carry over to the digital environment, but the methods and practice are fundamentally transformed.

A comparison of analog and digital preservation approaches points to a continuum in principles but also highlights the distinct nature of preservation activities in the digital realm. In contrast to traditional practices, digital preservation is an urgent and ubiquitous issue. All digital objects, rather than selected items, are subject to preservation, although the level of activities performed on the object can differ. Digital objects are inherently more vulnerable than analog materials and require immediate attention

Discover Digital Libraries. http://dx.doi.org/10.1016/B978-0-12-417112-1.00009-0

from the point of creation. The standards and formats selected for encoding have implications for the quality and long-term maintenance of digital content. As Walters and Skinner (2010) stress, "the ways that objects are created, curated, and stored matter immensely in how preservation-ready they ultimately are" (p. 264).

Digital preservation needs to be ongoing with activities integrated into all phases of creating, managing, and storing information. Cloonan (2015) emphasizes the dynamic nature of the digital preservation cycle—that it is not linear and requires multiple actions. Lavoie and Dempsey (2004) point out that digital preservation is not an isolated activity but rather a set of practices diffused throughout the information lifecycle. In the analog world, conservation activities tend to occur toward the end of a resource's lifecycle. Once physical items receive conservation treatment and are stored properly, no additional attention may be required. In contrast, this type of "benign neglect" can be catastrophic for digital materials (Corrado and Moulaison, 2014; Ross, 2012; Walters and Skinner, 2010). Ross (2012) notes, "as a result of the constant evolution of technology, the degradation of storage media and the ever-increasing pace of 'semantic drift,' digital objects do not, in contrast to many of their analog counterparts, respond well to benign neglect" (p. 46). Digital preservation involves not only an active and continuous management of digital content but also monitoring of the evolving technological environment and preservation methods.

Digital preservation is a complex technical, social, economic, and organizational issue. Its complexity in digital libraries stems from the fact that it is interwoven into the process of creating, using, and maintaining a wide array of digital materials and collections. The sustainability of digital content depends on the careful management of preservation risks, organizational policies, institutional commitment, and technical infrastructure (Bradley, 2007; Corrado and Moulaison, 2014). Technical aspects have received a considerable amount of attention in the preservation community because of the immediate need of keeping intact files and protecting them from storage media failure and obsolescence. Increasingly, the researchers in the digital library field recognize that contextual information needs to be preserved along with the bitstream to render the bits as useful and meaningful objects (Beaudoin, 2012a; Chowdhury, 2010; Ross, 2012). Lesk (2014) captures the broader aspects of digital preservation by observing, "the greatest danger to digital materials is that we forget the meaning of them. Preservation depends on our knowledge: we may have bits but be unable to interpret them" (p. xvi).

The field of digital preservation is still evolving, but significant progress has been made in building technological infrastructure and in developing policies, recommendations, and standards. The Task Force on Archiving Digital Information was established in 1994. The work of the Task Force resulted in a foundational report, which not only identified the critical challenges to preserving digital content but also provided a set of far-reaching recommendations (Waters and Garrett, 1996). The National Digital Information Infrastructure Preservation Program (NDIIPP) was formed by the Library of Congress in 2000. The National Digital Stewardship Alliance continues the work of NDIIPP, setting the agenda for national digital preservation and contributing to the development of standards and tools. Similar collaborative initiatives have been established in other countries with exemplary programs in the Netherlands and New Zealand (Library of Congress, n.d.). A number of research projects undertaken in Europe, including DELOS, Open Planets Foundation (currently Open Preservation Foundation), and DigitalPreservationEurope, have had a significant impact on advancing the field of digital preservation (Ashenfelder, 2011; Brown, 2013; Library of Congress, n.d.). The last two decades of preservation research and practice resulted in developing more stable formats, preservation metadata standards, and trusted repositories.

DEFINING DIGITAL PRESERVATION

Several definitions and conceptual models of digital preservation emerged in the cultural heritage community. They tend to focus on general policies, strategies, and activities to ensure access to any cultural or scientific information encoded in digital form. The context of digital libraries and their complex structures are rarely addressed as a separate issue. Conway (2007) notes, "preservation remains an ill-defined concept when applied to the development of digital library projects and collections" (para. 1). digital libraries not only share goals and approaches for preserving digital content with other scientific and cultural heritage domains, but also face unique challenges in regard to maintaining the relationships between digital objects and collections. The evolving terminology and theoretical models in digital preservation and associated disciplines impact the understanding of preservation in the context of digital libraries.

TERMINOLOGY: DIGITAL CURATION, DIGITAL STEWARDSHIP, AND DIGITAL PRESERVATION

The plethora of terms that are used to describe activities associated with managing and maintaining digital assets complicates an attempt to understand and define digital preservation. Many authors note that digital preservation is a young discipline and precise vocabulary has yet to mature (Brown, 2013; Jones and Beagrie, 2008). A number of alternative terms have been used for the same or similar concepts, reflecting different origins or the evolving understanding of the concept. Terms, such as digital curation, digital stewardship, and digital preservation, are often used interchangeably. Caplan (2008) points out the differences in usage between the United States and the United Kingdom (UK). In the United States, the use of the term digital preservation tends to be broader and encompasses all activities in managing digital assets from the point of creation. In the UK, the term digital curation is used for lifecycle management, while digital preservation is reserved for those activities specifically geared toward future accessibility (Caplan, 2008). Lazorchak (2011) attempts to discern "what's in (some) names" by looking at their different origins and context of use. He notes that preservation has a long-standing tradition in the cultural heritage community and is a core component of broader concepts, such as digital curation and digital stewardship.

Digital curation originated in the scientific and e-science community with a focus on research data and the entire information lifecycle. The term is relatively new. The Digital Curation Centre (DCC), a UK-based consortium that was launched in 2004, has contributed to promote the concept (Higgins, 2011). Digital curation, as defined by DCC, involves maintaining, preserving, and adding value to digital research data throughout its lifecycle (DCC, 2004–15). The digital curation cycle includes the whole range of actions from creation, through access and use, to transformation. Preservation is one of the actions undertaken throughout the curation lifecycle to ensure the long-term maintenance and retention of digital objects (Higgins, 2008). Harvey (2010) expands on this definition by emphasizing active management of data and the goals of digital curation in "supporting reproducibility, reuse of, and adding value to that data, managing it from its point of creation until it is determined not be useful, and ensuring its long-term accessibility, preservation, authenticity, and integrity" (p. 8).

Digital stewardship has its roots in the cultural heritage community. It is promoted as a broader concept, encompassing both cultural heritage materials and research data. Lazorchak (2011), in the Library of Congress blog, notes, "digital stewardship satisfyingly brings preservation and curation together in one big, happy package, pulling in the lifecycle approach of curation along with research in digital libraries and electronic records archiving, broadening the emphasis from the e-science community on scientific data to address all digital materials" (para. 11). The term has been adopted by the National Digital Stewardship Alliance (NDSA), a consortium of US research, government, and cultural heritage institutions committed to the long-term preservation of digital information. The definition of digital stewardship included in the *2014 National Agenda for Digital Stewardship* (NDSA, 2014) echoes earlier definitions of digital preservation, but the shift in the vocabulary indicates a broader approach. The adoption of the term, however, is still limited.

Digital preservation is an integral part of digital curation and digital stewardship frameworks and thus applies to activities focused on managing and preserving a wide range of materials from scientific data to cultural heritage resources. The term digital preservation has been used the longest (Cloonan, 2015). It makes a connection to the principles of analog preservation and places the new activities of curating digital content in the long tradition of preserving cultural heritage materials. Digital preservation is at the center of several definitions adopted in practice and is used in the context of digital libraries.

DEFINITIONS OF DIGITAL PRESERVATION IN THE PRACTICE COMMUNITY

The early definitions and models of digital preservation were developed in the practice community, often as part of training efforts to prepare library professionals for the emerging discipline. The Digital Preservation Management (DPM) Tutorial, launched by the digital preservation team at Cornell University Library in 2003 and maintained since by the DPM workshop faculty, offers a working definition of digital preservation as "a broad range of activities designed to extend the usable life of machine-readable computer files and protect them from media failure, physical loss, and obsolescence" (DPM Tutorial, 2003–15, para. 1). The DPM Tutorial makes an important distinction between preservation activities that promote the long-term maintenance of bitstream and those that provide continued and meaningful access to its content. The Tutorial also cites the DPM model, an early example, showing the multiple dimensions of digital preservation with three core components:

- Organizational infrastructure with policies, procedures, practices, and people
- Technological infrastructure consisting of the required equipment, software, hardware, a secure environment, and skills
- Resources framework that addresses the necessary funding for starting, continuing, and sustaining the digital preservation program

The authors use the metaphor of a three-legged stool (see Fig. 9.1) to demonstrate that digital preservation is not just a technical issue. Fully implemented and viable preservation programs require balancing of technological infrastructure, organizational aspects, and funding resources.

The Association for Library Collections and Technical Services, a division of the American Library Association (ALA), developed a range of definitions to promote an understanding of digital preservation within the library community. The core concepts are presented in short, medium, and long versions to accommodate a variety of needs. The medium definition states:

Digital preservation combines policies, strategies, and actions to ensure access to reformatted and born digital content regardless of the challenges of media failure and technological change. The goal of digital preservation is the accurate rendering of authenticated content over time (ALA ALCTS, 2007, para. 8).

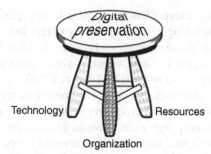

Technology   Resources

Organization

FIGURE 9.1 Three-Legged Stool Representing Three Aspects of Digital Preservation (Kenney and McGovern, 2003)

This definition has been widely adopted and incorporated into more recent statements. The definition of digital stewardship articulated in the *2014 National Agenda for Digital Stewardship* emphasizes "policies, strategies, and actions that ensure that digital content of vital importance to the nation is acquired, managed, organized, preserved, and accessible for as long as necessary" (NDSA, 2014, p. 6).

Digital Preservation Coalition (DPC), a UK-based organization, defined digital preservation broadly as the series of managed activities necessary to ensure continued access to digital materials, but also distinguished different levels of preservation activities:

- Long-term preservation that ensures continued access to digital materials, or at least to the information contained in them, indefinitely
- Medium-term preservation that provides continued access to digital materials beyond changes in technology for a defined period of time but duration is not indefinite
- Short-term preservation that provides access to digital materials either for a defined period of time, but it doesn't extend beyond changes in technology (Jones and Beagrie, 2008, p. 25)

The levels of preservation help to establish institutional goals for preservation programs and specify the requirements for repositories. This approach also reflects a realistic assessment of the digital landscape where not all resources will or should be preserved indefinitely.

Recent discussions of digital preservation are built on the early foundational concepts but shift the attention from the challenges of technology to management issues. Corrado and Moulaison (2014) analyze the key aspects of the DPC definition in terms of policy implications. Those key aspects include managed activities; necessary, continued access; and digital materials. The authors acknowledge the importance of technological infrastructure and technical skills but stress that digital preservation is mostly a management issue. Corrado and Moulaison (2014) propose a modified model of the three core components of digital preservation. The Digital Preservation Triad is presented in a form of Celtic knot with three interconnected parts: technology, content, and management. The emphasis of this model is on planning and policy development.

UNDERSTANDING DIGITAL PRESERVATION IN THE CONTEXT OF DIGITAL LIBRARIES

Research on theoretical models of digital preservation in the context of digital libraries has been limited. The fields of digital preservation and digital libraries have existed side by side for over two decades, but the emphasis of digital library research has been primarily on expanding access to cultural heritage and scientific resources rather than long-term sustainability (Chowdhury, 2010; Ross, 2012). The early discussions of digital preservation make a distinction between digital archives and repositories intended for long-term preservation and digital libraries, which provide access to digital information, but may not be committed to its long-term preservation (DPM Tutorial, 2003–15; Waters and Garrett, 1996). In practice, this distinction has prevailed with content management systems specifically for building digital collections for access and a separate suite of repository systems. In the research domain, however, this situation has been changing gradually, with more attention given to the issues of digital preservation in digital libraries and calls for conceptual models and frameworks for capturing contextual information. Both technological and semantic aspects of digital preservation are discussed in research literature.

In practice, analog and digital preservation goals coexist in many digitization projects and are a source of some confusion between the concepts. Digital libraries contain a significant number of resources converted from analog formats, including fragile and deteriorating materials digitized for preservation purposes. In this context, and in light of broader discussions about preserving cultural heritage with digital technologies, it is necessary to make a clear distinction between digital preservation and digitization for preservation (Caplan, 2008; Conway, 2010). Digitization as a preservation strategy undertakes the conversion of deteriorating analog materials to create high-quality copies for preservation purposes, while digital preservation activities focus on the preservation of the digital assets created as a result of digitization as well as born digital materials. As Conway (2010) points out, "digitization for preservation creates valuable new digital products, whereas digital preservation protects the value of those products, regardless of whether the original source is a tangible artifact or data that were born and live digitally" (p. 64). Digital preservation represents an important component of all digitization projects, as digital master files created as a result of the conversion process require long-term preservation activities. Digitization as a preservation method and a debate surrounding this approach are discussed in more detail in Chapters 3 and 4.

A distinction between bitstream preservation and semantic aspects of preserving digital content is particularly relevant in the digital library context. Bitstream preservation focuses on the technical aspects to ensure that bits are accessible and usable, while semantic preservation is concerned with maintaining the means of interpreting informational content of preserved bits. Technical level of bitstream maintenance is critical, but as Ross (2012) stresses, digital preservation is more than preserving the streams of 0s and 1s. Digital preservation is about "maintaining the semantic meaning of the digital object and its content, about maintaining its provenance and authenticity, about retaining its 'interrelatedness,' and about securing information about the context of its creation and use" (Ross, 2012, p. 45). Contextual information needs to be preserved along with the bitstream to render the bits as useful and meaningful information objects. Furthermore, Ross (2012) notes that the approach to preservation in the digital library environment needs to vary with different levels of preserving the content and context, including:

- Retaining the content of some materials held in digital libraries
- Retaining the environment and context of creation and use for other materials
- Reproducing the experience of use for other materials to ensure the right semantic representation and information is passed to the future

In his paper, Ross (2012) also argues for more research on preservation issues in digital libraries and for the development of theoretical models and a knowledge base. He proposes adopting the framework of archival science with the core principles of authenticity, uniqueness, provenance, arrangement, and description as a theoretical foundation for digital preservation in digital libraries.

The contextual dimension of digital preservation emerges as a new area of research. Chowdhury (2010) examines the research on digital preservation from the user perspective and concludes that context, especially information about the time and place where digital objects were created, is particularly important to facilitate understanding, interpreting, and future use of digital content. Time and place also appear as important categories in a framework for contextual information in digital collections (Lee, 2011). The framework proposed by Lee focuses on the contextual categories required for the comprehensive documentation of the "life history" of digital objects. The proposed contextual information framework identifies nine classes, including object, agent, occurrence, purpose, time, place, form of expression, concept, and relationship. Lee (2011) notes, "relationships to other digital objects can dramatically affect the ways in which digital objects have been perceived and experienced" (p. 6). The relationship class allows for capturing contextual information about the relations of the object as well as the collection level. Although the framework does not focus specifically on preservation, the proposed classes of contextual information are intended to support the curation of digital objects and collections.

Beaudoin (2012a) emphasize the role of context in the digital preservation of cultural objects and argues that knowledge about the context of digital objects is critical to making sense of them—their use, care, and preservation. The current approaches to recording contextual information in descriptive metadata are insufficient to ensure meaningful preservation and use of digital objects. Beaudoin (2012a) stresses that "context is especially important in discussions of digital preservation since in most instances the digital materials have been separated from their original format and context in the process of digitization and preservation" (p. 3). She proposes a framework for the use of contextual metadata in the digital preservation of cultural objects with a focus on multiple dimensions, including technical, intangible, utilization, curatorial, authentication, authorization, and intellectual (Beaudoin, 2012a, b).

A comprehensive approach to digital preservation that includes both technological and semantic aspects is particularly important in the context of digital libraries. Digital objects that represent the content of deteriorating analog materials serve as preservation copies, and contextual information is critical to their understanding, future use, and long-term management. The recent research on the contextual dimensions of digital preservation provides a foundation for the undertaking of broad preservation activities on digitally born as well as digitized objects. Digital preservation in the context of digital libraries concentrates on policies and technologies to ensure the long-term maintenance and rendering of digital files as well as the retention of the contextual information that enables interpretation of digital objects and collections.

PRESERVING DIGITAL CONTENT

Digital preservation is challenging due to the vulnerable nature of digital objects and the constantly changing technological environment. Information encoded in digital form can be easily altered and corrupted, which is a source of distrust and concerns about the authenticity and integrity of digital objects. In addition, turning digital objects into meaningful and usable information requires multiple layers of technology. As Lynch (2000) states, "bits are not directly apprehended by the human sensory apparatus—they are never truly artifacts. Instead, they are rendered, executed, performed, and presented to people by hardware and software systems that interpret them" (p.4). The reliance on software and hardware poses risks to access because this technology is susceptible to technological failure and obsolescence. A number of strategies as well as practical guidelines in the digital library field have been developed to address the challenges in maintaining integrity of digital objects and ensuring long-term accessibility. Authenticity remains a challenge because of the very nature of digital information and the connection to broader issues of trust and organizational management.

DIGITAL PRESERVATION CHALLENGES

Digital objects break. Digital materials occur in a rich array of types and representations. They are bound to varying degrees to the specific application packages (or hardware) that were used to create or manage them. They are prone to corruption. They are easily misidentified. They are generally poorly described or annotated (Ross, 2012, p. 44).

The list of challenges to preserving digital content can go on, but, as the above quote indicates, it starts with the fragile and complex nature of information in digital form. Unlike resources in analog form where content and carrier are inseparable, digital objects are not affixed to any permanent medium. Instead, informational content encoded as streams of 0s and 1s is copied from one storage medium to another and transmitted over networks. On one hand, this separation from physical carriers offers tremendous benefits for access and even for preservation as multiple digital copies can be stored in several different locations. On the other hand, the lack of permanence poses risks to the authenticity and integrity of information encoded in digital form. Information unattached to a permanent medium can be easily altered, damaged, or even destroyed. The lack of fixity and the separation of descriptive metadata from content files also make it harder to determine the authorship and provenance.

In addition, digital objects may exist in multiple copies, in several manifestations, and may have associated representation information. This phenomenon is evident in digitization projects where multiple copies of master files are created for preservation purposes. A master file is then a source for several derivatives, which tend to be smaller and have a different configuration of bits. Yet, all these different objects are representations of the same informational content, ideally described by consistent and linked metadata. A useful distinction between data objects and information objects is made in the Open Archival Information System (OAIS) reference model, described later in this chapter in the Digital Preservation Technology section. Brown (2013) expands on this concept and notes, "each conceptual information object can be manifested through one or more different data objects, which can in turn exist in multiple identical copies" (p. 201). He recognizes two primary threats to preservation in light of this distinction:

- Loss of data objects, referring to the physical loss of 1s and 0s that encode information
- Loss of the information object, referring to the loss of means to interpret those 1s and 0s as meaningful and authentic information (Brown, 2013, p. 202)

Another preservation challenge lies in determining what objects need to be preserved long-term, distinguishing between multiple manifestations and their copies, and maintaining the relationships between them.

Thibodeau (2012) recognizes the complexity and fluidity of digital information as a major challenge in preserving digital memory, depicting it as "a shape shifter that takes on very different forms" (p. 15). He relates the challenges in preserving cultural heritage in digital form to the characteristics of digital information itself and the rapid rate of technological change. Digital information is fluid, variable, and, as Thibodeau describes it, "polymorphous." This polymorphism results from several key factors, including:

- The transmission from one storage medium to another.
- The difficulty of determining the boundaries of digital objects, which in many cases are dynamic and dependent on external applications; the dynamic and transitory nature of those objects makes it difficult to define what content needs to be captured and preserved.
- The complex relationship between data objects stored in computer systems and objects presented to users through the online delivery systems.
- The necessity to process data objects with computer technology in order to be used; the process of transmission and rendition can involve changes in the object structure and even lead to alteration or corruption.

Thibodeau (2012) views the lack of permanence of digital objects as a source of tension between fluid digital information and digital preservation, which seeks to keep things unchanged.

The unstable and mutable nature of digital information poses risks to its authenticity and integrity. Ross (2002) indicates, "digital objects that lack authenticity and integrity have limited value as evidence or as information resource" (p. 7). The concepts of authenticity and integrity have been debated in the field of digital preservation in an attempt to determine the essential properties of digital objects that need to be preserved. They relate to the basic questions in digital preservation: (1) How do we know that digital objects are complete and have not been altered or corrupted? and (2) Are preserved digital objects reliable and genuine representations of what they claim to be? In an exploratory paper, Lynch (2000) provides working definitions of these fundamental, yet elusive concepts:

- *Integrity* means that a digital object has not been corrupted over time or in transit; in other words, that we have in hand the same set of sequences of bits that came into existence when the object was created (p. 5).
- *Authenticity* entails verifying claims that are associated with an object—in effect, verifying that an object is indeed what it claims to be (p. 6).

The integrity of files can be checked through technical measures such as checksums or digital signatures, but as Lynch (2000) comments, verifying authenticity is more challenging, as it requires judgment and an inquiry into an object's nature, provenance, and chain of custody. He relates the process of verifying authenticity and integrity to the broader concepts of trust and identity. One of the factors users employ to determine the authenticity or integrity of digital information is the level of trust attributed to the infrastructure or the organization responsible for preservation activities. Ross (2002) expands on the concepts underpinning authenticity and integrity. In addition to the trust, he lists fixity, stabilization, and the requirements of custodians and users. Furthermore, user needs and requirements can vary and may depend on the types of objects.

In a more recent article, Seadle (2011) reexamines the concepts of authenticity and integrity in light of the criteria used in the evaluation of analog materials. He acknowledges the difficulty of defining and assessing digital authenticity and states, "in the digital world, there are not originals, only copies, and the mutability of digital objects makes authenticity especially challenging" (Seadle, 2011, p. 548). While digital integrity can be measured through checksums, there are no clear measures for authenticity. In his comparative analysis, however, he notices that the concepts of authenticity and integrity in the digital environment are more closely related. He suggests using some of the technical measures to verify authenticity. Seadle (2011) concludes that analog and digital environments are different, and new means of assessing authenticity need to be developed for digital content.

In addition to the inherent properties of digital information, the technological environment in which digital objects are created and maintained represents a second area of challenge. This environment encompasses equipment and formats for generating and encoding digital information as well as any hardware and software platforms necessary for processing, storing, rendering, and transmitting it. There is a wide range of risks associated with digital technology, from hardware failures where a loss is sudden and catastrophic, to the obsolescence of formats or software, which can go unnoticed until a file cannot be rendered. Overall, technological threats can be grouped into those that result in:

- *Physical loss*, damage, or decay of digital objects
- *Inability to access* digital objects due to technological obsolescence

Brown (2013) outlines a number of threats and the ways they endanger the integrity, reliability, and usability of preserved objects (pp. 202–206). A long list of risks to integrity ranges from accidental deletion to software failures.

Technological failures as preservation challenges in the context of digital libraries are presented in a case study of Chronicling America (Littman, 2007). Chronicling America, part of the National Digital Newspaper Program (NDNP), was a collaborative initiative aimed at digitizing American historic newspapers. Littman (2007) reports on the actual preservation threats encountered in the process of constructing a repository to provide for the long-term preservation of the digital objects generated as a result of this large-scale digitization project. The project team, building a repository for both access and preservation, experienced a number of challenges, including:

- Media failures, particularly problems with portable hard drives that were used to transfer files between the partner institutions; fixity checks performed on the files readily caught the problems.
- Hardware failures—a number of hard drive failures were encountered in the storage system; this issue was addressed by having an array of hard drives in the storage system.
- Software failures were experienced at different stages of ingesting digital objects into the repository.
- Operator errors, which represented the most serious threat as it resulted in the deletion of some files from the repository system.

This case study demonstrates that technological failures and human errors represent very real and serious threats to preserving digital content. The risks can be mitigated by careful planning and the implementation of a number of preservation strategies, such as fixity checking and using multiple storage media.

Technological obsolescence has been recognized as a major challenge since the early days of digital preservation (DPM Tutorial, 2003–15; Jones and Beagrie, 2008; Rothenberg, 1995; Waters and Garrett, 1996). Physical storage media, data formats, hardware, and software all become obsolete over time, posing significant technical challenges to preserving digital objects. Technological progress introduces innovations and improvements in formats and computer platforms but simultaneously deems older versions obsolete. Digital objects created with the older generation of technology may be intact but inaccessible because of the lack of functioning software to render them. Technological obsolescence poses threats to long-term access to digital objects. It impacts several components of the technological environment:

- *Storage media obsolescence* is a serious concern because of rapid changes in the storage technology. As Brown (2013) comments, "no computer storage medium can be considered archival, irrespective of its physical longevity—technological obsolescence is inevitable" (p, 222). Physical degradation of hard disks and magnetic tape used for storage poses a threat as well, but obsolescence often occurs long before deterioration of media becomes a problem (Jones and Beagrie, 2008). Newer technology offer increases in storage capacity but at the same time requires copying digital objects into new media.
- *Hardware and software obsolescence* is an inevitable result of technological advancement, part of the environment of ongoing change (Thibodeau, 2012). Constant upgrades to hardware, operating systems, and software applications bring improved speed and functionality, but also cause incompatibility and the inability to render objects created with older platforms. Software and hardware obsolescence are interrelated. New computers may not support older versions of the software necessary for executing files. New software may not run on legacy hardware.
- *File format obsolescence* has been recognized as one of the major threats to preservation (Abrams, 2004; DPM Tutorial, 2003–2015; Jones and Beagrie, 2008). Formats provide structures for encoding and decoding bistreams but can be superseded by newer specifications. The threat of format obsolescence has been addressed by the development of tools for format identification (DROID) and validation (JHOVE). Format registries, such as PRONOM, identify access tools and migration pathways for converting legacy formats. Rosenthal (2010) argues that format obsolescence is not as a significant threat as it was previously assumed because of more mature technology and the availability of open source formats. As discussed in Chapters 3 and 4, the guidelines in the digital library field recommend selecting nonproprietary, well-documented, and standardized formats. Wide adoption of the guidelines in digital library practice contributes to minimizing the risks of format obsolescence. The Library of Congress (2013) maintains a list of formats and provides a review of sustainability factors.

DIGITAL PRESERVATION GOALS

The ultimate goal of digital preservation is to ensure long-term access to digital content, but it needs to be considered in light of the challenges related to the unique characteristics of digital objects as well as the risks of technological failures and obsolescence. Furthermore, as the research in the digital library field indicates, the objectives of digital preservation should also encompass contextual and semantic aspects related to provenance, context of creation, and use in order to render preserved objects as authentic, meaningful, and useful information (Beaudoin, 2012a; Ross, 2012). Thus, the goals for digital preservation are twofold: (1) focusing on bit preservation and ensuring the integrity of digital objects, and (2) maintaining sources of representation information and ensuring the authenticity of preserved objects. Brown (2013) recognizes the dual nature of preservation activities and identifies a number goals related to maintaining the integrity of data objects as well as those that focus on dimensions of authenticity, specifically the reliability and usability of preserved information. This list is expanded by the goals identified in the digital library contextual research and includes:

- Maintaining integrity of digital objects by protecting them from alteration and corruption
- Protecting digital objects from media failure, physical loss, and technological obsolescence
- Ensuring that digital content can be uniquely and persistently identified
- Maintaining the semantic meaning of objects and the relationships between objects and collections

- Maintaining documentation on provenance and curatorial process
- Providing context of creation and use

Meeting preservation goals requires careful planning, developing a preservation policy, establishing a robust technological infrastructure, and practicing active management of digital assets.

DIGITAL PRESERVATION STRATEGIES

The active approach to digital preservation means not only an ongoing attention to the integrity and authenticity of digital information, but also constant monitoring of the technological environment to ensure that the digital objects can be accessed and reused in the future. Digital preservation practitioners should emphasize prevention rather than recovery. Although techniques to recover inaccessible files are being developed in digital archaeology and digital forensics, those approaches, as Brown (2013) points out, should be used as a last resort or an emergency measure. Digital forensics tools and techniques are useful in an archival practice that deals with the acquisition of born digital legacy materials. In digital library practice, digital forensics can assist with the recovery of born digital or digitized objects stored on removable media, and can help with the process of transferring them into more sustainable preservation environments (Lee et al., 2012). Again, forensics techniques should be used as an exception rather than a norm. Digital forensics tools are also very useful in determining and establishing authenticity and provenance.

A number of preservation strategies have been developed as preemptive measures to mitigate the risks and challenges associated with digital technology. There is no single approach that would provide a universal solution; rather, an appropriate strategy or a combination of them need to be selected depending on the changes in the technological environment and the types of objects that need to be preserved. The preservation strategies that address risks associated with technological failures and obsolescence include:

- *Bitstream copying*, known as "backing up your data," refers to making multiple exact copies of digital objects. Bitstream copying is not a long-term preservation strategy; rather it serves as a preventive measure, protecting data from media failures and physical loss (DPM Tutorial, 2003–15).
- *Refreshing* mitigates the risk of media storage obsolescence. It involves copying files from one storage device to another. There should be no detectable change in the bitstream configuration during the refreshing process.
- *Migration* is undertaken in response to technological obsolescence, either format or hardware and software obsolescence. It involves the periodic transfer of files from one hardware/software configuration to a newer platform. Objects encoded in formats that are at risk of becoming obsolete need to be transformed into new target specifications. Brown (2013) emphasizes that the migration process might result in some information loss, as not all properties of the original object may be transformed or supported by the target format.
- *Normalization* is a form of format migration undertaken at the point of capturing or ingesting into a repository. The goal of normalization is to transform data into open and consistent formats or to minimize the number of managed formats in a repository. In the context of digital collections, normalization often takes place when images captured with digital cameras are transformed from proprietary raw formats into a standard TIFF format.

- *Emulation* represents a different strategy to combat technological obsolescence. Rather than transforming digital objects into new formats, emulation keeps digital objects in their original form, but reconstructs the functionality of an obsolete platform, usually through the use of emulation software. Emulation is often used in the preservation of games but can also be applied to the preservation of complex multimedia objects in digital libraries.

DIGITAL PRESERVATION IN DIGITAL LIBRARY PRACTICE

Digital libraries share access and preservation goals. Digital libraries collect, manage, and provide access to cultural and scientific resources to the current community of users, but an equally important part of their mission is the preservation of valuable digital content for the long-term (Candela et al., 2007). In practice, the balance is often tipped toward access and building online collections, with digital preservation activities often delegated to an IT department or outsourced to a service provider. Many stakeholders, including library administrators, do understand and support building digital collections as a form of expanding access, meeting user expectations, and increasing the online visibility of their institutions. Gaining full support for digital preservation as an equal component of digital library programs, however, is more difficult, especially at institutions with limited resources.

Brown (2013) argues that awareness of digital preservation is growing in the professional community. A lack of financial support and a lack of technical expertise are cited as major obstacles for establishing and implementing digital preservation programs. A study of 72 research libraries, members of the Association of Research Libraries (ARL), found that 39.3% of the surveyed institutions had no digital preservation system in place (Banach and Li, 2011). A case study conducted at CUNY Queens College demonstrates that small cultural heritage institutions not only lack an infrastructure for preserving digital content created as a result of digital projects, but don't even have preservation plans (Dolan-Mescal et al., 2014). However, it needs to be noted here that the state of digital preservation practice in the digital library field varies. While smaller institutions still struggle with developing preservation plans, national libraries and large research libraries have well-established and robust programs.

A sustainable digital library program requires developing an institutional approach to digital preservation and establishing a policy of commitment to the long-term maintenance of digital objects and collections. Developing a long-term preservation policy is a broader organizational issue, as a policy needs to encompass not only digital content created and collected as part of digital library programs, but also born digital archival acquisitions and other institutional digital assets. Preservation policies define how to manage digital assets to prevent the risk of content loss or damage. The process of developing an institutional digital preservation policy involves multiple steps, which includes stating the objectives, appraising and selecting content, assessing risks, outlining the scope of preservation actions, identifying resources and responsibilities, and establishing the requirements for building a technical infrastructure. A number of recent publications on digital preservation offer useful guidance on developing a policy (Brown, 2013; Corrado and Moulaison, 2014; Harvey, 2010). *Digital Preservation Policies Study* provides a model for developing institutional policies and a range of exemplars from the cultural heritage and research institutions (Beagrie et al., 2008). A recent case study presents the process of developing an organizational policy for digital preservation at the Ohio State University Libraries (Noonan, 2014).

A digital preservation plan in the context of digital libraries needs to be prepared at the very beginning of a project, ideally as part of a broader institutional policy. The plan can rely on the institutional infrastructure but may also call for new resources and solutions. Preservation of digital library content requires:

- Creating an institutional digital repository, or participating in a shared preservation repository, or using a reliable preservation service
- Conducting an inventory of the existing digital assets and verifying their integrity
- Defining the levels of preservation (long-term, medium-term, and short-term)
- Establishing a policy for data transfer, backup, refreshment, and migration
- Recording preservation metadata using standards, such as PREMIS and METS
- Maintaining project documentation and preservation metadata to support identification, access, and preservation process
- Maintaining the relationships between archival master files, access files, and metadata

Digital projects, if undertaken according to best practices and guidelines, produce valuable digital assets. The *Framework of Guidance for Building Good Digital Collections* states as one of its principles: "a good object is preservable" and provides a series of guidelines for creating digital objects with digital preservation in mind (NISO, 2007, p. 48). In addition to digital master files that are the primary focus of digital preservation actions, digital projects also generate a considerable amount of descriptive metadata and contextual information. In practice, the relationships between those various components are not always well maintained and preserved. The current digital library environment does not integrate access and preservation requirements. Most content management systems used for building digital collections present access files and metadata, but do not provide preservation functions. In a best-case scenario, digital preservation is managed by a separate repository system or outsourced to service providers. A study of open source repository systems conducted in 2012 found that the support for metadata standards and preservation functions varies between systems and is particularly limited for digital library multimedia objects (Madalli et al., 2012). Maintaining the relationships between multiple versions of digital objects, metadata, and curatorial documentation in this complex environment remains one of the major challenges for preserving digital content.

PRACTICAL GUIDELINES

This section provides practical recommendations for preserving master files on bit-level, but does not address the issues of maintaining associated metadata and preserving the relationships between the various entities in the digital library environment. This is an area that requires more attention and research, and hopefully useful guidelines and best practices will emerge in the near future. Bit preservation is a useful starting point but represents only a subset of preservation activities (Johnston, 2010). The technical guidelines for creating high-quality digital assets are discussed in more detail in Chapters 3 and 4. In light of discussions on technological obsolescence, it is worth reiterating that master files should be created with a use-neutral approach and saved in open, standard, and widely accepted formats. They should be saved uncompressed and follow an established file-naming convention.

Master files need to be stored in a reliable and secure preservation system. A decision about selecting a dedicated repository system needs to be made prior to undertaking a digital project in light of project goals and the established preservation plan. A number of factors have to be considered in selecting an appropriate solution, including the size of the project, the infrastructure available in-house, staff technical expertise and skills, and cost. The solutions range from institutional or shared repositories to hosted preservation services. The section on Digital Preservation Technology provides an overview of the options currently available. In practice, an organization may select a repository and a combination of a networked drive and/or removable media for backup. If a repository system is implemented, some tasks, such as integrity checking or format validation and normalization, can be automated.

The following guidelines for bit-level preservation of digital master files are based on the recommendations included in the digital preservation handbooks and practical guides (Brown, 2013; DPM Tutorial, 2003–15; Harvey, 2010; Jones and Beagrie, 2008).

- Create multiple copies (minimum three) of master files
- Calculate checksums on the file level and use them for integrity checking
- Store checksum data separate from master files
- Ensure that sufficient identification and representation information is stored with files
- Store at least one copy in a separate geographical location
- Ensure that all objects are stored on a minimum of two different reliable storage media
- Create an inventory of all files before moving them into a repository/storage system
- Copy or migrate digital objects to new media at regular intervals
- Practice active preservation by checking and verifying archival files regularly.

DIGITAL PRESERVATION TECHNOLOGY: STANDARDS AND REPOSITORIES

"Technology advances, while sure to present new challenges will also provide new solutions for preserving digital content" (Arms, 2000, para. 36). Arms discusses the challenges in preserving digital content at the National Digital Library Program (NDLP) of the Library of Congress in the early phase of digital preservation. Her quote indicates a great amount of uncertainty about the future of digital preservation but also some hope that technology will offer new solutions. Fifteen years later, we can definitely talk about some progress in preserving digital resources with more stable digital formats, preservation metadata standards, and trusted repositories in place. McGovern (2007) analyzed the first decade of digital preservation activities in terms of balancing the fundamental components of digital preservation (organization, resources, and technology), represented in the three-legged stool metaphor (see Fig. 9.1). She notices considerable progress in all three areas, but especially in organization, with a strong development of preservation policies.

The first decade, marked by the publication of the influential report, *Preserving Digital Information* (Waters and Garrett, 1996), established a basis for building standardized preservation systems and services. The concept of trusted repositories and two fundamental standards, OAIS reference model and PREMIS preservation metadata, were all introduced in the early 2000s. The first repository platforms, DSpace and Fedora, were also developed around that time and have been widely adopted. Format registries, such as PRONOM, and a range of tools for integrity checking, an automatic file format identification tool (DROID—Digital Object Record Identification), and an object characterization tool (JHOVE—JSTOR/Harvard Object Validation Environment) were also introduced during the first decade.

The most recent period is characterized by the widespread development of operational digital preservation services. The new generation repository software incorporates the relevant standards and tools, enabling the building of more reliable preservation systems. In addition, the current environment offers a number of options for selecting preservation approaches, from institutional repositories to shared or hosted solutions. The models with cloud-based services, such as DuraCloud or Preservica, make digital preservation more affordable and accessible to smaller cultural heritage institutions.

STANDARDS

The development and adoption of open standards proved to be critical to progress in digital preservation. Conceptual frameworks and metadata standards provide a theoretical foundation for developing reliable preservation systems and services. Two standards that have been recognized as particularly influential are the OAIS reference model and PREMIS metadata standard.

OAIS reference model is a high-level standard that provides a conceptual framework and consistent terminology for developing and maintaining archival information systems (Lee, 2010). The major purpose of the model is "to facilitate a much wider understanding of what is required to preserve and access information for the long term" (CCSDS, 2012, p. 2.1). It was developed by the researchers at the Consultative Committee for Space Data Systems (CCSDS) in 2001 and became an ISO standard in 2002. The model identifies the key players in the information environment, including Producers, Managers, and Consumers. In defining Information Object, it makes a distinction between Data Object (sequence of bits) and Representation Information. Data Object is interpreted with the associated Representation Information, yielding a useful and meaningful Information Object. This distinction is important in the context of archival information systems that need to support preservation of bits as well as the maintenance of Representation Information.

In addition to defining informational concepts, the Reference Model provides a functional layout of an archival system, identifying six main entities (Preservation Planning, Administration, Ingest, Data Management, Archival Storage, and Access), and the way that information flows between them (see Fig. 9.2). It addresses both the access and preservation aspects of ingesting digital objects and associated descriptive information into a repository for long-term storage. Lee (2010) notes that many aspects of the model rest on the distinction between the Submission Information Packages (SIP) received from Producers, the Archival Information Package (AIP) generated from SIPs upon ingest and managed by archives, and the Dissemination Archival Package (DIP) accessed by Consumers. The OAIS model provides a foundation for building and implementing standard and interoperable repository systems.

PREMIS (Preservation Metadata: Implementation Strategies) is the international standard for metadata to support the preservation of digital objects and ensure their long-term usability (Library of Congress, 2015). It specifies the metadata units that a repository needs to maintain core preservation functions. The standard was developed by the OCLC/RLG working group in 2005. Its current development is managed by the Library of Congress in conjunction with the PREMIS Editorial Committee. The standard consists of a Data Model and Data Dictionary. An XML schema is also available to support the implementation of the data dictionary in digital repository systems. Version 2.2 of the PREMIS Data Dictionary is currently available though the Library of Congress (PREMIS Editorial Committee, 2012).

The Data Dictionary defines preservation metadata as "the information a repository uses to support the digital preservation process" (PREMIS Editorial Committee, 2012, p. 3). Preservation metadata spans a number of metadata types, including descriptive, structural, technical, and administrative. The Data Dictionary places a strong emphasis on the documentation of digital provenance (the history of an object) and the documentation of relationships, especially relationships among different objects within the preservation repository.

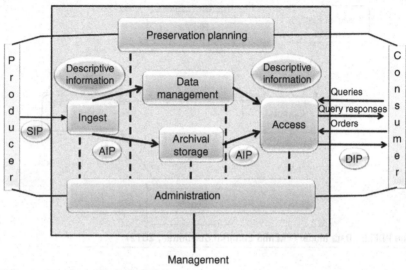

FIGURE 9.2 OAIS Functional Entities (CCSDS, 2012)

PREMIS standard provides a simple data model to organize the semantic units defined in the Data Dictionary and to encourage a shared way to organize preservation metadata (Dappert and Enders, 2010). The following entities are defined in the Data Model:

- Intellectual Entity: a set of content that is considered a single intellectual unit for purposes of management and description, for example, a particular book, map, photograph, or database.
- Object (or Digital Object): a discrete unit of information in digital form.
- Event: an action that involves or impacts at least one Object or Agent associated with or known by the preservation repository.
- Agent: person, organization, or software program/system associated with Events in the life of an Object or with Rights attached to an Object.
- Rights: assertions of one or more rights or permissions pertaining to an Object and/or Agent (PREMIS Editorial Committee, 2012, p. 6).

Fig. 9.3 demonstrates the entities in the PREMIS data model and the relationships between them.

The PREMIS Data Dictionary defines semantic units, not metadata elements. As Caplan (2009) explains, PREMIS does not specify how metadata should be represented or implemented in a repository system; it only defines what the system needs to know and should be able to export to other systems. Semantic units describe properties of digital objects and their contexts or the relationships between them. Each semantic unit defined in the Data Dictionary is mapped to one of the entities in the Data Model. For example, the Object entity is described by a number of semantic units, such as objectIdentifierType or objectIdentifierValue, defined as mandatory (M) and nonrepeatable (NR). Semantic units are presented in a hierarchical structure.

PREMIS may be implemented in a variety of ways, which offers the potential of broad application across a wide range of preservation contexts. Guenther (2010) explores using PREMIS within a METS

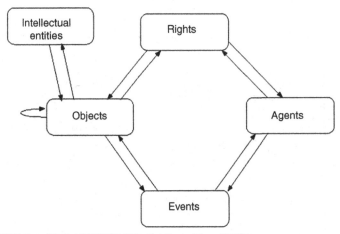

FIGURE 9.3 The PREMIS Data Model (PREMIS Editorial Committee, 2012)

container and points to the benefits of using the two metadata standards together. A number of research studies investigate implementation of PREMIS in practical digital library settings. Alemneh (2009) examined the barriers to adopt PREMIS in cultural heritage institutions. Donaldson and Conway (2010) present a case study in which PREMIS is implemented in the Florida Digital Archive. Findings point to the iterative nature of the implementation process and to the necessity of adopting the standard in the local repository. Donaldson and Yakel (2013) investigated the adoption of PREMIS by several organizations registered with the Library of Congress PREMIS Implementers Group. The researchers confirm the findings of the earlier studies, indicating that many institutions have made the decision to adopt PREMIS, but few have fully implemented it.

DIGITAL REPOSITORIES

Digital repositories are information systems that ingest, store, manage, preserve, and provide access to digital content. The OAIS model provides a conceptual foundation for designing standard-compliant repositories. Digital repositories are a relatively new phenomenon that emerged in the early 2000s. A concept of trusted digital repositories has been advanced to ensure high-level preservation services for all types of repositories. There are several repositories types, including institutional, disciplinary, government, and centralized repositories, which aggregate content from several subsidiary repositories. According to the Directory of Open Access Repositories, most of the content in open access (83.2%) is available through institutional repositories (OpenDOAR, 2015). As Lynch (2003) observes, institutional repositories offer an essential infrastructure for scholarship in the digital age and a potential to revolutionize scholarly communication. He also notes that a key part of the service is to manage technological change and the migration of digital content from one set of technologies to the next.

Institutional digital repositories serve multiple purposes. Their primary goal is to support scholarly communication and provide open access to articles, dissertations, and research data. In addition, they provide platforms for storing and preserving the digital master files created as a result of digitization projects. The boundaries between a repository and digital libraries are sometimes blurred, as repositories also host digital collections for access. The combination of access and preservation functions poses significant challenges. McGovern and McKay (2008) investigated the juncture of institutional repository implementation and digital preservation programs and provided a set of recommendations for leveraging the benefits of institutional repositories to strengthen long-term preservation. A number of research studies examine the current practices of digital preservation in the institutional repository environment (Banach and Li, 2011; Kunda and Anderson-Wilk, 2011; Neatrour et al., 2014; Oehlerts and Liu, 2013).

Trusted digital repositories perform preservation functions. This notion was first introduced in the seminal report, *Preserving Digital Information* (Waters and Garrett, 1996). The authors emphasize the role of trust in managing the identity, integrity, and quality of digital information in archival systems and recommend developing a process of certification. The concept of a trusted digital repository was fully articulated in another foundational report, *Trusted Digital Repositories: Attributes and Responsibilities*, prepared by a RLG/OCLC working group (Beagrie et al., 2002). A trusted digital repository is defined as one "whose mission is to provide reliable, long-term access to managed digital resources to its designated community, now and in the future" (Beagrie et al., 2002, p. 5). In order to gain recognition as "trusted," a repository has to have certain attributes that ensure the reliability and authenticity of stored information. The RLG/OCLC group outlines the following characteristics of sustainable digital repositories:

- Accept responsibility for the long-term maintenance of digital resources on behalf of its depositors and for the benefit of current and future users
- Have an organizational system that supports not only long-term viability of the repository but also the digital information for which it has responsibility
- Demonstrate fiscal responsibility and sustainability
- Design its system(s) in accordance with commonly accepted conventions and standards to ensure the ongoing management, access, and security of materials deposited within it
- Establish methodologies for system evaluation that meet community expectations of trustworthiness
- Be depended upon to carry out its long-term responsibilities to depositors and users openly and explicitly
- Have policies, practices, and performance that can be audited and measured (Beagrie et al., 2002, p. 5)

In addition, the RLG/OCL report discusses methods and strategies for the certification of trusted digital repositories. A regular cycle of certification and audit is recommended for digital repositories to remain trustworthy. The process of certification has gained considerable attention in the last decade, and a number of standards and checklists have emerged, such as TRAC (The Trustworthy Repositories Audit & Certification Checklist), superseded by the ISO 16363:2012—Audit and Certification of Trustworthy Digital Repositories international standard. A range of tools have been developed in Europe, including nestor, DRAMBORA, Platter, and Data Seal of Approval. The recent publications on digital preservation provide an overview of these tools (Brown, 2013; Corrado and Moulaison, 2014).

PRESERVATION REPOSITORY SOFTWARE

Building operational digital repositories requires a technical infrastructure and dedicated software to support the functions of ingesting, storing, managing, preserving, and providing access to digital content. Digital repository software is an area of active development, with several open source and proprietary solutions emerging. The benefits and limitations of open source versus proprietary software are discussed in Chapter 6 in the context of digital library management systems (DLMS).

Many early open source solutions, including DSpace (http://www.dspace.org/), EPrints (http://www.eprints.org/), and Fedora (http://fedorarepository.org/) were developed as part of the Open Access (OA) movement to provide platforms for the open dissemination of scholarly publications. Comparative studies of the early generation of open source repository software that focused on DSpace, EPrints, and Fedora found varying levels of support for preservation functions. In the examined group, Fedora demonstrates the strongest support for features essential to digital preservation (Fay, 2010; Madalli et al., 2012). Fedora is one of the most versatile solutions among open source software, as it provides support for building digital collections for access and performs digital preservation functions. It is often integrated with the new generation of open source systems, such as Hydra and Islandora. DSpace, Fedora, Hydra, and Islandora as multipurpose digital library management systems, are described in more detail in Chapter 6. The new generation of open source preservation repository software, including such software as Archivematica and DAITSS, is built in compliance with the OAIS functional model and implements active preservation strategies.

The following list provides a brief overview of selected open source and proprietary solutions. The review of the software is by no means comprehensive, nor is it meant to serve as a recommendation or evaluation. There are many other options available, especially in the open source category. Archivematica represents a more recent development in the open source category. Rosetta is an example of a proprietary software that is often used in conjunction with digital library management systems.

- *Archivematica* (https://ww.archivematica.org/en/) is an open source, standards-based, integrated suite of software tools designed to process digital objects from ingest to access. Archivematica version 0.10 was released in 2013; as of Nov. 2015, version 1.4 was available. Its functionality is based on the OAIS reference model. It supports a range of preservation standards, including Dublin Core, METS, and PREMIS metadata standards and incorporates the Library of Congress BagIt file packaging format and other task-specific applications. Archivematica can be integrated with digital library management or preservation systems, including AtoM, DSpace, CONTENTdm, Islandora, LOCKSS, and DuraCloud.
- *Rosetta* (http://www.exlibrisgroup.com/category/RosettaOverview) is a proprietary software developed by Ex Libris in collaboration with the National Library of New Zealand. It is intended for managing and preserving digital library resources as well as research data. Rosetta is compliant with the OAIS reference model. It serves as an integrated solution with one central repository, which can be synchronized with many other applications. It is used by a number of libraries in Europe, the United States, and New Zealand. University of Utah's J. Willard Marriott Library uses Rosetta as a preservation system alongside CONTENTdm, which is used for building digital collections (Neatrour et al., 2014).

PARTNERSHIPS AND HOSTED SERVICES

Operational digital repositories can be developed in house with a custom-built approach or by using an open source and proprietary software. Developing and managing an institutional repository requires a significant investment of resources and expertise, and some institutions decide to share the burden and participate in cooperative programs or outsource the preservation functions to a hosted preservation service.

Shared repositories are preservation repositories created through the membership or partnerships of libraries and archives to store and share their digital collections. They represent collaborative efforts to advance digital preservation by reducing cost and sharing expertise. Two models of collaborative initiatives have emerged: (1) centralized infrastructure and services supported by membership fees, and (2) infrastructure and services distributed geographically and shared among participating members. HathiTrust and Portico are two well-known examples of the centralized model, while MetaArchive represents a successful case of collaboration in a distributed environment. Walters and Skinner (2010) argue that interinstitutional repositories provide a sustainable approach to digital preservation. Participating members not only distribute costs but also have an opportunity to leverage expertise across a diverse body of institutions.

- *HathiTrust* (http://www.hathitrust.org/) was launched in 2008 as a collaborative initiative of major research libraries to ensure that the cultural record is preserved and accessible long into the future. Initially, HathiTrust was created to provide a preservation platform for storing a large volume of items digitized through mass digitization projects, such as the Google Book Project and Open Content Alliance (OCA). HathiTrust is also a large-scale digital library, and as such is described in more detail in Chapter 1. As Christenson (2011) emphasizes "at the heart of HathiTrust is a shared secure digital repository owned and operated by a partnership of major research libraries" (p. 95). Currently, there are more than 60 partners in HathiTrust, and membership is open to institutions worldwide. The HathiTrust repository now contains the largest collection of digital volumes outside of Google Books. It represents an example of a "light archive," meaning that the repository also functions as a digital library and provides access to some of their collections. Access is restricted to items under copyright.
- *MetaArchive* (http://www.metaarchive.org/) was established in 2003 as a "community-owned and community-operated distributed digital preservation network" (Walters and Skinner, 2010, p. 264). MetaArchive works as a cooperative, with members paying membership fees but also contributing in-kind with staff, technology, and space. As Walters and Skinner (2010) note, these in-kind contributions keep preservation costs low. The cooperative includes members from over 50 institutions in 13 states and 3 countries. The distributed model relies on the open source software, LOCKSS (Lots of Copies Keep Stuff Safe), developed at Stanford University. Member institutions host servers within their own organizational infrastructures, while LOCKSS software enables connecting the servers in a secure network and replicating the content for preservation purposes. Servers are selected and assigned to content on the basis of their widespread geographical distribution (MetaArchive, 2015). MetaArchive is an example of a dark archive, meaning there is no public access to it.

Hosted preservation services, sometimes referred as "preservation-as-a-service," are digital repositories maintained by nonprofit organizations that provide archiving services for a fee. The pricing structure is usually based on the number of digital objects and/or size in terabytes of the collection(s). There are a number of hosted services available on the market. OCLC DigitalArchive and DuraCloud serve primarily cultural heritage institutions.

- *OCLC DigitalArchive* (http://www.oclc.org/digital-archive.en.html) is an archiving solution for institutions that prefer to outsource the preservation of their digitized assets to a nonprofit organization. OCLC DigitalArchive provides a hosted preservation option to institutions involved in digitization that decide not to build their own repository or participate in collaborative initiatives. OCLC can securely store digital master files for a fee. OCLC DigitalArchive is convenient for institutions using CONTENTdm software, as the ingest of digital master files is integrated with CONTENTdm functionality. There is an additional fee for archiving on top of a CONTENTdm subscription. Like MetaArchive, OCLC DigitalArchive is also a dark archive.

- *DuraCloud* (http://www.duracloud.org/) is a hosted, cloud-based preservation service offered by DuraSpace, a not-for-profit organization founded in 2009 by the stakeholders of DSpace Foundation and Fedora Commons. DuraCloud is one of several open source services supported by DuraSpace. It is focused on providing preservation support and access services for academic libraries and other cultural heritage organizations. In addition to cloud storage, DuraCloud provides services that enable digital preservation, data access, transformation, and data sharing.

Digital technology presents a paradox in the realm of digital preservation. On one hand, it poses a number of challenges and risks for preserving digital content because of technological failures and obsolescence. On the other hand, technological progress offers improved solutions and tools for maintaining digital objects in the long-term in reliable and trusted repository systems. Measurable progress has been made in establishing a conceptual framework for repository systems, developing validation tools, and building a technical infrastructure. Digital libraries are part of this active development, but in practice, insufficient attention and resources are allocated to digital preservation priorities, especially at smaller institutions. Digital preservation practice in the digital library field is still in the early stages of development. While practical guidelines are available for bit-level preservation, more research is needed on capturing and maintaining representation and contextual information. National libraries and large research libraries have taken a lead in establishing preservation programs and developing new solutions and best practices. Hopefully, with an increasing awareness of the importance of digital preservation and the diffusion of best practices and tools, sustainable models will be adopted in the mainstream digital library practice in the near future.

REFERENCES

Abrams, S.L., 2004. The role of format in digital preservation. Vine 34 (2), 49–55.

ALA ALCTS: Association for Library Collections & Technical Services. Division of the American Library Association, 2007. Definitions of digital preservation. Available from: http://www.ala.org/alcts/resources/preserv/defdigpres0408.

Alemneh, D.G., 2009. Barriers to adopting PREMIS in cultural heritage institutions: an exploratory study. In: Archiving Conference, Vol. 2009, No. 1. Society for Imaging Science and Technology, pp. 113–118.

Arms, C.R., 2000. Keeping memory alive: practices for pressing digital content at the National Digital Library Program of the Library of Congress. RLG DigiNews, 4 (3). Available from: http://webdoc.gwdg.de/edoc/aw/rlgdn/preserv/diginews/diginews4-3.html.

Ashenfelder, M., 2011. DigitalPreservationEurope. The Signal: Digital Preservation. Library of Congress blog. (October, 14). Available from: http://blogs.loc.gov/digitalpreservation/2011/10/digitalpreservationeurope/.

Banach, M., Li, Y., 2011. Institutional repositories and digital preservation: assessing current practices at research libraries. D-Lib Mag. 17 (5), 1.

Beagrie, N., Bellinger, M., Dale, R., Doerr, M., Hedstrom, M., Jones, M., Woodyard, D., 2002. Trusted digital repositories: attributes and responsibilities. Research Libraries Group (RLG) & Online Computer Library Center (OCLC) Report. Available from: http://www.oclc.org/content/dam/research/activities/trustedrep/repositories.pdf.

Beagrie, N., Semple, N., Williams, P., Wright, R., 2008. Digital preservation policies study. Joint Information Systems Committee (JISC). Available from: http://citeseerx.ist.psu.edu/viewdoc/download?doi=10.1.1.214. 9056&rep=rep1&type=pdf.

Beaudoin, J.E., 2012a. Context and its role in the digital preservation of cultural objects. D-Lib Mag., 18 (11), 1. Available from: http://www.dlib.org/dlib/november12/beaudoin/11beaudoin1.html.

Beaudoin, J.E., 2012b. A framework for contextual metadata used in the digital preservation of cultural objects. D-Lib Mag., 18 (11/12), 3. Available from: http://dlib.org/dlib/november12/beaudoin/11beaudoin1.print.html.

Berman, F., Lavoie, B., Ayris, P., Choudhury, G.S., Cohen, E., Courant, P., Dirks, L., Friedlander, A., Gurbaxani, V., Jones, A., Kerr, A.U., Lynch, C.A., Rubinfeld, D., Rusbridge, C., Schonfeld, R., Smith-Rumsey, A., Van Camp, A., 2010. Sustainable economics for a digital planet: ensuring long-term access to digital information. Final report of the Blue Ribbon Task Force on Sustainable Digital Preservation and Access. Available from: http://brtf.sdsc.edu/biblio/BRTF_Final_Report.pdf.

Bradley, K., 2007. Defining digital sustainability. Lib. Trends 56 (1), 148–163.

Brown, A., 2013. Practical Digital Preservation: A How-To Guide for Organizations of Any Size. Neal-Schuman, Chicago.

Candela, L., Castelli, D., Pagano, P., Thano, C., Ioannidis, Y., Koutrika, G., and Schuldt, H., 2007. Setting the foundations of digital libraries: the DELOS manifesto. D-Lib Mag., 13 (3), 4. Available from: http://www.dlib.org/dlib/march07/castelli/03castelli.html.

Caplan, P., 2008. The preservation of digital materials. Lib. Technol. Rep. 44 (2), 1–38.

Caplan, P., 2009. Understanding PREMIS. Library of Congress. Available from: http://www.loc.gov/standards/premis/understanding-premis.pdf.

CCSDS: Consultative Committee for Space Data Systems, 2012. Reference Model for an Open Archival Information System (OAIS). Washington, DC: CCSDS. Available from: http://public.ccsds.org/publications/archive/650x0m2.pdf.

Chowdhury, G., 2010. From digital libraries to preservation research: the importance of users and context. J. Doc. 66 (2), 207–223.

Christenson, H., 2011. HathiTrust: a research library at web scale. Lib. Res. Tech. Serv. 55 (2), 93–102.

Cloonan, M.V., 2015. Preserving Our Heritage: Perspectives From Antiquity to the Digital Age. Neal-Schuman, Chicago.

Cloonan, M.V., 2007. The paradox of preservation. Lib. Trends 56 (1), 133–147.

Conway, P., 2007. The relevance of preservation in a digital world. Northeast Document Conservation Center (NDCC). Available from: https://www.nedcc.org/free-resources/preservation-leaflets/6.-reformatting/6.4-the-relevance-of-preservation-in-a-digital-world.

Conway, P., 2010. Preservation in the age of Google: digitization, digital preservation, and dilemmas. Lib. Q. 80 (1), 61–79.

Corrado, E.M., Moulaison, H.L., 2014. Digital Preservation for Libraries, Archives, and Museums. Rowman & Littlefield, Lanham, MA.

Dappert, A., Enders, M., 2010. Digital preservation metadata standards. Inf. Stand. Q. 22 (2), 156–166.

DCC: Digital Curation Centre, 2004–15. What is digital curation? Available from: http://www.dcc.ac.uk/digital-curation/what-digital-curation.

Dolan-Mescal, A., Farwell, M., Howard, S., Rozler, J., Smith, M., 2014. A digital file inventory of the Queens College Special Collections and Archives. OCLC Syst. Serv. 30 (2), 78–90.

Donaldson, D., Conway, P., 2010. Implementing PREMIS: a case study of the Florida Digital Archive. Lib. Hi Tech. 28 (2), 273–289.

Donaldson, D., Yakel, E., 2013. Secondary adoption of technology standards: the case of PREMIS. Arch. Sci. 13 (1), 55–83.

DPM Tutorial, 2003–15. Digital Preservation Management. Cornell University Library. Available from: http://www.dpworkshop.org/.

Fay E., 2010. Repository software comparison: building digital library infrastructure at LSE. Ariadne, 64. Available from: http://www.ariadne.ac.uk/issue64/fay.

Guenther, R., 2010. Metadata to support long-term preservation of digital assets: PREMIS and its use with METS. In: Proceedings of the 2010 Roadmap for Digital Preservation Interoperability Framework Workshop. Association for Computing Machinery, ACM, New York, p. 14.

Harvey, R., 2010. Digital Curation: A How-To-Do-It Manual. Neal-Schuman, New York.

Higgins, S., 2008. The DCC curation lifecycle model. IJDC 3 (1), 134–140.

Higgins, S., 2011. Digital curation: the emergence of a new discipline. IJDC 6 (2), 78–88.

Johnston, L., 2010. Developing bit preservation services at the Library of Congress. In: Proceedings of the 2010 Roadmap for Digital Preservation Interoperability Framework Workshop. Association for Computing Machinery, ACM, New York, p. 12.

Jones, M., Beagrie, N., 2008. Preservation Management of Digital Materials: A Handbook. Digital Preservation Coalition (DCP). Available from: http://www.dpconline.org/advice/preservationhandbook.

Kenney, A.R., McGovern, N.Y., 2003. The five organizational stages of digital preservation. In: Hodges, P., Bonn, M., Sandler, M., Wilkin, J.P. (Eds.), Digital Libraries: A Vision for the Twenty-First Century, A Festschrift to Honor Wendy Lougee. The University of Michigan Scholarly Monograph Series. Available from: http://quod.lib.umich.edu/s/spobooks/bbv9812.0001.001/--digital-libraries-a-vision-for-the-21st-century.

Kunda, S., Anderson-Wilk, M., 2011. Community stories and institutional stewardship: digital curation's dual roles of story creation and resource preservation. Portal Lib. Acad. 11 (4), 895–914.

Lavoie, B., Dempsey, L., 2004. Thirteen ways of looking at digital preservation. D-Lib Mag. 10 (7/8), 1082–9873.

Lazorchak, B., 2011. Digital preservation, digital curation, digital stewardship: What's in (some) names? The Signal: Digital Preservation. Library of Congress blog. (August 2). Available from: http://blogs.loc.gov/digitalpreservation/2011/08/digital-preservation-digital-curation-digital-stewardship-what%E2%80%99s-in-some-names/.

Lee, C.A., 2011. A framework for contextual information in digital collections. J. Doc. 67 (1), 95–143.

Lee, C.A., Kirschenbaum, M.G., Chassanoff, A., Olsen, P., Woods, K., 2012. BitCurator: tools and techniques for digital forensics in collecting institutions. D-Lib Mag. 18 (5), 3.

Lee, C.A., 2010. Open archival information system (OAIS) reference model. Encyclopedia of Library and Information Science 4020–4030. 3rd ed. Taylor & Francis, Abingdon, UK.

Lesk, M., 2014. Foreword. In: Corrado, E.M., Moulaison, H.L. (Eds.), Digital Preservation for Libraries, Archives, and Museums. Rowman & Littlefield, Lanham, MA, pp. xv–xvi.

Library of Congress, 2013. Sustainability of digital formats: planning for Library of Congress Collections. Available from: http://www.digitalpreservation.gov/formats/index.shtml.

Library of Congress, 2015. PREMIS: preservation metadata maintenance activity. Available from: http://www.loc.gov/standards/premis/.

Library of Congress, n.d. On the leading edge. Available from: http://www.digitalpreservation.gov/series/edge/index.html.

Littman, J., 2007. Actualized preservation threats: practical lessons from Chronicling America. D-Lib Mag. 13 (7), 5.

Lynch, C., 2000. Authenticity and integrity in the digital environment: an exploratory analysis of the central role of trust. Washington, DC: Council on Library and Information Resources. Available from: http://www.clir.org/pubs/reports/pub92/lynch.html.

Lynch, C.A., 2003. Institutional repositories: essential infrastructure for scholarship in the digital age. Portal Lib. Acad. 3 (2), 327–336.

Madalli, D.P., Barve, S., Amin, S., 2012. Digital preservation in open-source digital library software. J. Acad. Librar. 38 (3), 161–164.

McGovern, N., 2007. A digital decade: where have we been and where are we going in digital preservation? RLG DigiNews 11 (1), 1.

McGovern, N.Y., McKay, A.C., 2008. Leveraging short-term opportunities to address long-term obligations: a perspective on institutional repositories and digital preservation programs. Lib. Trends 57 (2), 262–279.

MetaArchive, 2015. Methodology. Available from: http://www.metaarchive.org/methodology.

NDSA: National Digital Stewardship Alliance, 2014. 2014 National Agenda for Digital Stewardship. Available from: http://www.digitalpreservation.gov/ndsa/documents/2014NationalAgenda.pdf.

Neatrour, A., Brunsvik, M., Buckner, S., McBride, B., Myntti, J., 2014. The SIMP Tool: facilitating digital library, metadata, and preservation workflow at the University of Utah's J. Willard Marriott Library. D-Lib Mag., 20 (7), 2.

NISO Framework Working Group, 2007. A framework of guidance for building good digital collections. 3rd ed. Available from: http://www.niso.org/publications/rp/framework3.pdf.

Noonan, D., 2014. Digital preservation policy framework: a case study. EDUCAUSEreview, (July 28). Available from: http://www.educause.edu/ero/article/digital-preservation-policy-framework-case-study.

Oehlerts, B., Liu, S., 2013. Digital preservation strategies at Colorado State University libraries. Lib. Manag. 34 (1/2), 83–95.

OpenDOAR: Directory of Open Access Repositories, 2015. Open Access repository types—worldwide. University of Nottingham, UK. Available from: http://www.opendoar.org/index.html.

PREMIS Editorial Committee, 2012. PREMIS Data Dictionary for preservation metadata, version 2.2. Available from: http://www.loc.gov/standards/premis/v2/premis-2-2.pdf.

Rosenthal, D.S., 2010. Format obsolescence: assessing the threat and the defenses. Lib. Hi Tech. 28 (2), 195–210.

Ross, S., 2002. Position paper on integrity and authenticity of digital cultural objects. DigiCULT: Integrity and Authenticity of Digital Cultural Heritage Objects, 1 (August).

Ross, S., 2012. Digital preservation, archival science and methodological foundations for digital libraries. New Rev. Inf. Network. 17 (1), 43–68.

Rothenberg, J., 1995. Ensuring the longevity of digital documents. Sci. Am. 272 (1), 42–47.

Seadle, M., 2008. The digital library in 100 years: damage control. Lib. Hi Tech. 26 (1), 5–10.

Seadle, M., 2011. Archiving in the networked world: by the numbers. Lib. Hi Tech. 29 (1), 189–197.

Thibodeau, K., 2012. Wrestling with shaper-shifters: perspectives on preserving memory in the digital age. In: Proceedings of the Memory of the World in the Digital Age: Digitization and Preservation, pp. 15–23. Available from: http://www.ciscra.org/docs/UNESCO_MOW2012_Proceedings_FINAL_ENG_Compressed.pdf.

Walters, T.O., Skinner, K., 2010. Economics, sustainability, and the cooperative model in digital preservation. Lib. Hi Tech. 28 (2), 259–272.

Waters, D., Garrett, J., 1996. Preserving digital information. Report of the Task Force on Archiving of Digital Information. Washington, DC: The Commission on Preservation and Access. Available from: http://files.eric.ed.gov/fulltext/ED395602.pdf.

EVALUATION OF DIGITAL LIBRARIES

10

THE NEED FOR DIGITAL LIBRARY EVALUATION

Digital library evaluation entails a systematic assessment of value and significance. The objective of digital library evaluation is to determine to what extent it meets its objectives and offer suggestions for its improvement (Chowdhury and Chowdhury, 2003). Digital library evaluation includes every aspect of its development and operation (Tsakonas et al., 2013). Recommendations for undertaking periodic evaluations are part of the guidelines for "building good digital collections" (NINCH, 2002; NISO, 2007). However, the exponential growth of digital libraries has not been accompanied by extensive evaluation studies (Saracevic, 2004). Moreover, there is no agreement on the key concepts, assumptions, parameters, and criteria related to digital library evaluation (Fuhr et al., 2007). Just as Tsakonas and Papatheodorou (2011) state, "Digital library evaluation is a complex field, as complex as the phenomena it studies…. However, the community has still to reach a consensus on what evaluation is and how it can effectively be planned" (p. 1577). As digital libraries are also under constant development change, it is important to evaluate digital libraries to ensure the right direction for future development and the acceptance by users and other stakeholders. Since digital libraries are new, complex, and multifaceted entities, researchers and practitioners need a set of guidelines pertaining to why it is important to evaluate, when to undertake evaluation, what to evaluate, how to evaluate, and how to incorporate the results into the development process.

The objectives of evaluation provide a rationale for why we evaluate. The purposes of digital library evaluations can be understood from the constructs, the relationships, and the evaluation (Fuhr et al., 2007). There are a variety of purposes for digital library evaluation including identifying user needs and problems, enhancing the interface design, planning, making budget decisions, etc. Determining the objective(s) sets the foundation for digital library evaluation.

The next question is when to evaluate. Digital library development and management go through a series of phases: planning, prototyping, building, testing, launching, operating, and upgrading. At different phases of digital library development, the objective of its evaluation might be different. Accordingly, different evaluation criteria and measurements might be applied. In addition, phases of digital library development also affect research methods and approaches (Buttenfield, 1999).

Evaluation criteria and measures are associated with what to evaluate. Although those used in assessing library print collections are applicable to a certain extent, they are insufficient for the new dimensions that emerged with digital libraries, such as interface design, system performance, sustainability, effects on users, and user engagement. As Van House et al. (1990) point out and as remains true today, there is no single, best way to do an evaluation; furthermore, the digital library environment, accompanied by rapid changes in users' expectations and behaviors, calls for evaluation from multiple viewpoints with an emphasis on the user's perspective (Carr, 2006; Kani-Zabihi et al., 2006; Nicholson, 2004). Evaluation involves comprehensive activities that compare "what is" to "what ought to be" (Van House et al., 1990). To measure "what is," evaluation frameworks should include well-defined evaluation criteria and corresponding reliable and valid measures. The key concepts in evaluation consist of criteria and measures. Criteria refer to a standard or set of standards by which something can be judged or decided (Saracevic, 2004). Buchanan and Salako (2009) point out that what to measure and how to measure are the key challenges for digital library evaluation.

The final question focuses on how to evaluate. Since a digital library is a complex and dynamic system, digital library evaluation requires multifaceted approaches (Marchionini, 2000; Marchionini et al., 2003). Digital library evaluation employs multiple data collection methods ranging from online surveys to think-aloud protocols and log analyses. Moreover, it integrates both qualitative and quantitative methods. Most important, user-centered digital library evaluation is drawing more attention. Researchers emphasize the importance of incorporating digital library evaluation criteria and collection instruments to solicit users' perspectives and feedback (Heradio et al., 2012; Xie, 2008; Zhang, 2010).

Researchers and practitioners have expanded their digital library evaluation efforts from evaluation criteria, measurements, and methods to objectives and phases. However, it remains one of the most confusing areas in the library and information science field (Saracevic, 2004; Tsakonas et al., 2013; Zhang, 2010). Several limitations exist in digital library evaluation research and practices. First, there are few comprehensive frameworks and models available for digital library evaluation. Several researchers note that holistic evaluation studies are conspicuously absent from the digital library field and discuss the potential benefits of comprehensive approaches (Chowdhury et al., 2006; Saracevic, 2000; Xie, 2006; Zhang, 2010). Most of the current evaluation practices have focused narrowly on particular aspects or services. Second, there are still huge gaps between researchers and practitioners. Various digital library evaluation models have been suggested by researchers. However, those models are still mostly conceptual and theoretical, as they have not been tested in digital library practice. Researchers have not provided specific, feasible measures. As a result, digital library practitioners have adopted few of the models suggested by researchers. Third, few evaluation frameworks or models have been validated empirically from the perspectives of stakeholders. These limitations call for further investigation of issues related to digital library evaluation.

The remainder of this chapter provides an overview of the current research on evaluation frameworks as well as evaluation criteria and measures. In addition, it presents the authors' recent study as a detailed example of digital library evaluation within ten dimensions incorporating multiple digital library stakeholders' perspectives.

EVALUATION FRAMEWORKS

Several researchers and research groups developed digital library evaluation frameworks and models to identify the main constructs of such libraries and illustrate their relationships in their assessment. Tsakonas and Papatheodorou (2011) illustrate the ontology development of digital library evaluation at two layers: the upper strategic layer and the lower procedural layer. Although the strategic layer specifies the purpose of the evaluation consisting of classes that define the scope of the evaluation and its relationship to other evaluation studies, the procedural layer focuses on the evaluation activities including their classes describing exact processes, constraints, and requirements.

Saracevic's (2000; 2004) digital library evaluation framework is one of the most widely cited models. His framework comprehensively covers multiple aspects of digital libraries, including content, technology, interface, process/service, user, and context. His framework is the first attempt to measure context, such as institutional fit, sustainability, and community impact. Additionally, Saracevic (2004) suggests a list of measures for different criteria. Zhang (2010) further investigated and validated Saracevic's evaluation framework. Zhang studied the importance of multiple constructs of Saracevic's six dimensions using survey data from heterogeneous stakeholders. She further developed a holistic model for digital library evaluation that presents specific criteria that can be selected and "tailored for multifaceted and multilevel digital library evaluations" (p. 107).

In Europe, DELOS is a collaborative digital library project that represents joint research activities involving major European teams in this area. The DELOS Network of Excellence has conducted a series of evaluation studies. Fuhr et al. (2001) proposed a digital library evaluation scheme containing four dimensions: data/collection, system/technology, users, and usage. Tsakonas et al. (2004) further examined the interactions of digital library components and suggested key evaluation foci in digital libraries, such as usability, usefulness, and system performance. Fuhr et al. (2007) also developed a digital library evaluation framework by integrating Saracevic's (2004) four dimensions of evaluation activities (construct, context, criteria, and methodology) and key questions in relation to why, what, and how to evaluate. As part of DELOS project results, Candela et al. (2007) established a three-tier digital library model, named the DELOS Manifesto. Even though the DELOS Manifesto is not an evaluation framework, it is a conceptual model that provides useful concepts for digital library evaluation. The DELOS model (Fig. 10.1) posits six core concepts: Content, User, Functionality, Quality, Policy, and Architecture (Candela et al., 2007).

Another frequently cited digital library evaluation model is the quality model developed by Gonçalves et al. (2007). Derived from the previous 5S (streams, structures, spaces, scenarios, and societies) digital library model (Gonçalves, Fox, Watson, and Kipp, 2004), Gonçalves et al. (2007) proposed a quality model, consisting of dimensions and measurements of quality. Seventeen types of

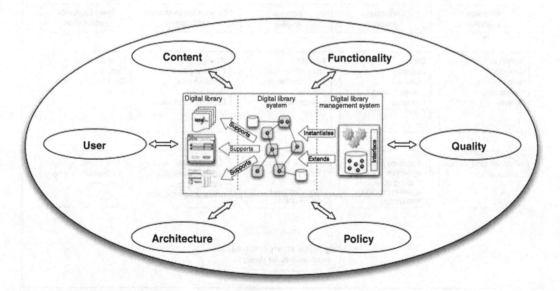

FIGURE 10.1 DELOS Model (Candela et al., 2007)

quality dimensions are identified: accessibility, accuracy, completeness, composability, conformance, consistency, effectiveness, efficiency, extensibility, pertinence, preservability, relevance, reliability, reusability, significance, similarity, and timeliness. The timeliness dimension includes three associated characteristics of response time corresponding to efficiency, cost of migration associated with preservability, and number of service failures linking to assess reliability. Moreover, this model is also connected to different phases of information lifecycle in order to assess, identify, and solve quality problems.

Xie's (2006, 2008) research focuses more onto users and suggests a user-driven evaluation model (Fig. 10.2). She points out that little has been done on the identification of evaluation criteria from the perspectives of users. Her model was derived from her empirical study investigating users' perceptions through diaries and questionnaires. Based on the study, she identifies five dimensions of digital library evaluation and specific criteria consisting of usability, collection quality, service quality, system performance efficiency, and user feedback solicitation. Focusing on a specific type of digital library, Albertson (2015) created a user-centered visual digital library evaluation framework after synthesizing the relevant literature on the topic. This framework is constructed with the following components: user, interaction, system, user–interaction, user–system, interaction–system, user–interaction–system, and domain and topics. The visual context requires more user–system interactions occurring in visual digital libraries.

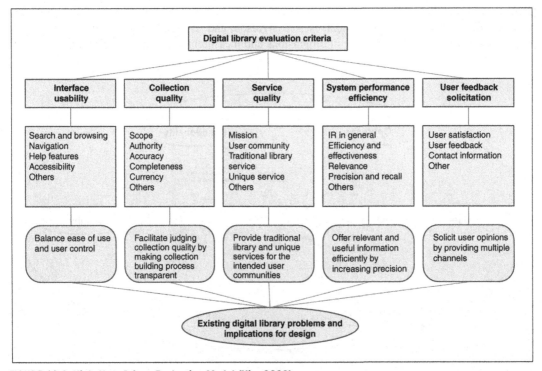

FIGURE 10.2 Xie's User-Driven Evaluation Model (Xie, 2008)

Resulting from comprehensive digital library evaluation research, Vullo (2010) developed an integrated LIS-oriented evaluation framework from both the user and system perspectives. Four entities constitute the model: organization, content, services, and users. Although the user perspective starts from users, the system perspective begins with organizations. Based on expert interviews, Lagzian et al. (2013) built a model for the identification of successful factors in a digital library. Six dimensions emerged from the data: motivation, resource, people, process, location, and time. Accordingly, 36 criteria are classified into six dimensions.

At the same time, evaluation models also emphasize different aspects of digital library dimensions. For example, Dillon (1999) created a multileveled framework for evaluating the usability of digital libraries ranging from physical to social-cultural. He identifies four key factors affecting usability with the acronym TIME. Specifically, T refers to tasks that reveal users' needs and uses for the materials; I refers to an information model that represents users' mental models to organize the information space; M refers to manipulation skills, in particular the design of manipulation facilities to support the users' use of documents; and E refers to the visual ergonomics that assists reading electronic text effectively. In accomplishing different tasks, the sequence of TIME might be different. Kim and Kim (2008) developed an evaluation framework tailored to digital collections, which covers four dimensions and 18 criteria. Those four dimensions are as follows: content; management and policy; system and network; and use, user, and submitter. Their model was built empirically from interviews with digital collection managers. More important, they suggest specific measures to numerically represent the evaluation criteria.

In the area of operational libraries, several practical tools have been proposed to expand evaluation efforts, including DigiQUAL, eMetrics, and EQUINOX, but they are often limited to specific elements or services. DigiQUAL was created as a tool for assessing service quality (Kyrillidou and Giersch, 2005). Based on the analysis of focus group data, the DigiQUAL research team identifies 250 items related to digital library service evaluation. These items are further classified into the following dimensions: accessibility/navigability, interoperability, community for users, developers and reviewers, collection building, federations' role, copyright, resource use, collection evaluation, and digital library sustainability (Kyrillidou, Cook, and Lincoln, 2009). The ARL's e-metrics project and the COUNTER and SUSHI protocols were devised for the purpose of assessing the outputs of digital libraries using the usage statistics, but they focus more on vendor-provided data.

EVALUATION METHODS
DIGITAL LIBRARY EVALUATION METHODS

Evaluation is not just product testing; instead, it can be viewed as a research process. Collecting multiple data and triangulating the results are essential for digital library evaluation (Marchionini, 2000).

After reviewing evaluation studies, Saracevic (2004) summarizes data collection methods: questionnaires, surveys, interviews, focus groups, observations, task accomplishment, think aloud, case studies, transaction log analyses, experimentation, records analysis, usage analysis, document analysis, and economic analysis. He concludes that almost all evaluation methods have been used for digital library evaluation except the historical method. Ethnography is also proposed as an approach to evaluating digital libraries (Crabtree et al., 1997). Bollen and Luce (2002) analyzed usage patterns to evaluate the impact of a digital library and to determine the structure of a given user community. In addition, focus groups and online surveys have been used to evaluate digital library services (Choudhury et al., 2002). Albertson (2015) suggests mixed data collection methods for user-centered visual digital library evaluation. Survey, log, observation, interview, and results analysis are the suggested data collection methods to assess user, system, and interactions between them.

Multifaceted approaches are also applied to digital library evaluation at various stages of its development. Marchionini et al. (2003) used three case studies to assess user needs in order to design a prototype of the interface for the Library of Congress National Digital Library Program. Multiple types of data collection methods were used to collect data: reading room visits and interviewing staff, questionnaires of prospective users, and document analysis of reading room handouts and brochures, user study reports and email correspondences between users and librarians. Adams et al. (2005) also applied case studies to assess how social context and system design influence the empowerment of users' use of digital libraries. In-depth interviews and focus groups were used to collect data. Multifaceted approaches help researchers and practitioners have a better understanding of the digital library.

For usability testing, questionnaire, interview, focus groups, think aloud, and logs are the most applied data collection methods (Jeng, 2005a, b; Kengeri et al. 1999; Park, 2000). For example, Ferreira and Pithan (2005) used interviews, think alouds, observations, and logs to conduct a usability study. Blandford et al. (2004) highlight two usability approaches: empirical and analytical. Although the empirical approach involves users in the testing, an analytical approach only involves usability experts in the testing by applying established theories and methods. They employ four analytical techniques to evaluate the usability of digital libraries: heuristic evaluation, cognitive walkthrough, claims analysis, and concept-based analysis of surface and structural misfits. In addition, they discuss strengths and limitations of each technique. Buttenfield (1999) identifies different methods for usability evaluation at different stages. In the system design phase, the method of ethnographic evaluation is the most frequently applied for user needs and requirements. Task analysis is another type of evaluation method. Heuristic evaluation is the third method applied at the design and the development phases. At the system development phase, cognitive walkthroughs and interviews are frequently employed to solicit information about interface design. At the system deployment phase, usability testing and usability inspection are performed, in particular the application of transaction log analysis and think-aloud protocols, and pre- and postsurveys. Van House (2003) also emphasizes the reliance on an ethnographic method to study users' behaviors in natural settings. Hilary et al. (2007) performed comparative studies with children searching and browsing using two types of category browsers in the International Children's Digital Library. Their results suggest that a flat, simultaneous interface provides advantages over a hierarchical and sequential interface for children in both Boolean searching and casual browsing. According to Khoo et al. (2012), "the usability and design literature already recognizes that ambiguity and misunderstanding can occur in user studies" (p. 1623). Based on a comparison of usability studies conducted between users and evaluators, they propose support for users to perform digital library evaluation and use their own terms to collect evaluation data. In this way, evaluation data are not lost in translation between researchers' analysis and the presentation of usability data.

After analyzing conference presentations at the Joint Conference on Digital Libraries (JCDL) and the European Conference on Digital Libraries (ECDL), Tsakonas et al. (2013) find that instruments mainly consist of test collections, prototypes, and algorithms. These evaluation studies are commonly conducted in laboratories. Survey and comparison studies are other preferred methods for evaluation. Experiments are employed to compare different digital libraries, different interface designs, and different organization approaches. For example, Meyyappan et al. (2004) designed an experiment to compare different information organization approaches—alphabetical, subject category, and task-based—by performing a series of task scenarios. The effectiveness and usefulness of digital libraries' information organization approaches were compared. Both quantitative and qualitative data were collected and analyzed. A task-based information organization approach was considered more useful than the traditional approaches.

MULTIFACETED EVALUATION OF DIGITAL LIBRARIES (MEDaL): STUDY METHODOLOGY

This chapter is written based on a review of the previous research as well as our own research on digital library evaluation. The authors conducted a comprehensive study on digital library evaluation, titled "Multifaceted Evaluation of Digital Libraries (MEDaL)." The study employed document analysis and Delphi surveys. Detailed discussion of our study methodology is presented later including sampling, data collection, and data analysis.

In order to identify digital library evaluation dimensions and associated criteria, Joo and Xie (2013) first conducted document analysis focusing on keywords "digital library," "evaluation," "criteria," "assessment," and other associated terms in different combinations. Google Scholar and digital library-related online databases offered by EBSCO were selected to search for relevant documents published primarily between 2000 and 2010. Two criteria were used to make relevance judgments: (1) whether the paper covers any evaluation theories, frameworks, criteria, indicators, or measures or (2) whether the paper consists of actual evaluation studies or pilot tests. Finally, 85 relevant documents and five digital library evaluation project web sites (EQUINOX, DigiQUAL, LibQUAL+, eVALUEd, DELOS) were chosen and further analyzed for digital library evaluation dimensions and corresponding evaluation criteria.

Strauss and Corbin's (1990) open coding technique was selected for data analysis, which is the process of breaking down, examining, comparing, conceptualizing, and categorizing. Ten dimensions emerged from the analysis of the selected literature and the websites, including collection, information organization, interface design, system performance, effects on users, user engagement, services, preservation, sustainability/administration, and context of use. In addition, associated criteria identified in previous works were also incorporated into the next stage of the Delphi survey.

In the empirical phase of the MEDaL study, two-round Delphi surveys were conducted to identify the importance of evaluation criteria and the appropriateness of measures from different stakeholders of digital libraries. We partnered with five academic libraries in the data collection stage. Ninety subjects were recruited with 30 subjects for each of the three groups. The scholar group includes international researchers who have conducted digital library research with high citations or professors who have taught digital library courses. Scholars were identified based on search results from Web of Knowledge or Google Scholar, as well as from web sites of library and information science schools. Digital librarians were randomly selected from the top 200 US colleges (according to US News Rank: www.usnews.com/rankings) that have operating digital libraries, as well as librarians from the partner libraries. User group subjects, which consisted of faculty members and graduate and undergraduate students, were recruited from five partner academic libraries across the country.

The scholar subjects had well-balanced proportions in professor rank and gender. Digital libraries were their major research areas, and other related research areas include the following: information retrieval, metadata, HCI, and preservation. On average, the digital librarian subjects have had about 8.48 years of experience in digital library-related services. Their official titles contained digital librarian, digital initiative librarian, digital collection librarian, etc. User subjects, consisting of 20 students with 8 undergraduate students and 12 graduate students, as well as 10 faculty members, participated in the survey. This group contained more female subjects than male subjects. Students and faculty members came from different majors/disciplines.

Two rounds of Delphi surveys were administered to different groups of stakeholders of digital libraries including scholars, digital librarians, and users. In the first round, the importance of evaluation criteria was investigated by using a seven-point Likert scale in which 7 is rated as extremely important and 1 as not at all important. The objective of the first round is to determine which evaluation criteria would be important from the perspectives of different stakeholders. To help subjects understand the meaning of evaluation criteria, researchers presented definitions of each criterion to the subjects. Also, the first-round survey instructed subjects to enter additional dimensions and criteria they perceived to be important that were not included as part of the list. Moreover, subjects were also instructed to indicate at which stages of digital library development and operation that each criterion should be applied for evaluation. Seven phases were identified: planning, prototyping, building, testing, launching, operating, and upgrading. Finally, the survey solicits information in relation to purposes of digital library evaluation and the factors that hinder this process. Fig. 10.3 shows an example of the first-round survey.

The results from the first-round survey were incorporated into the design of the second round. The second-round survey concentrated on the examination of the appropriateness of measures to their corresponding criterion. For the second round, 198 measures were identified and presented to the subjects.

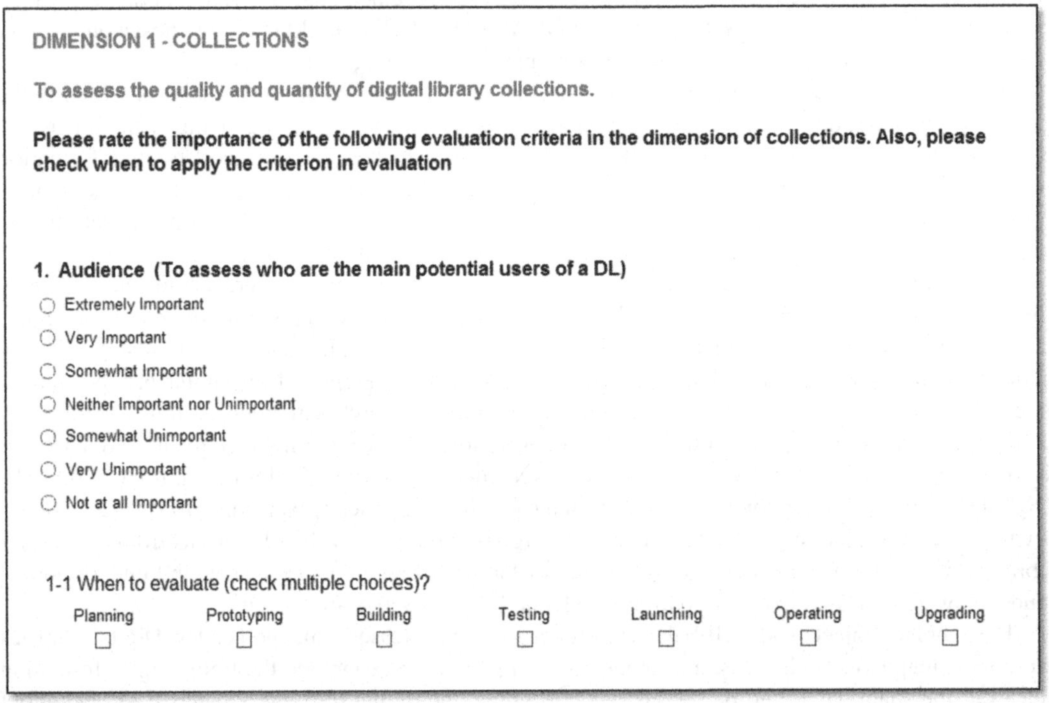

DIMENSION 1 - COLLECTIONS

To assess the quality and quantity of digital library collections.

Please rate the importance of the following evaluation criteria in the dimension of collections. Also, please check when to apply the criterion in evaluation

1. Audience (To assess who are the main potential users of a DL)

○ Extremely Important

○ Very Important

○ Somewhat Important

○ Neither Important nor Unimportant

○ Somewhat Unimportant

○ Very Unimportant

○ Not at all Important

1-1 When to evaluate (check multiple choices)?

Planning	Prototyping	Building	Testing	Launching	Operating	Upgrading
☐	☐	☐	☐	☐	☐	☐

FIGURE 10.3 An Example Question from the MEDaL Study About the Importance of a Digital Library Evaluation Criterion

Using a seven-point Likert scale, this study attempted to confirm the appropriateness of measurements for each criterion. Also, the subjects were given the opportunity to modify the measures provided or to suggest new measures.

Since most of the data collected through the Delphi surveys contained numerical ratings, quantitative analysis was applied. For the first-round survey, descriptive statistical analysis was performed, such as average and standard deviation, to show the importance of evaluation criteria. Based on the mean average ratings, evaluation criteria from the most important to the least were ranked. In addition, ratings of digital library evaluation criteria of stakeholders were compared in order to better understand different perspectives and needs of stakeholders. Inferential statistical tests, such as ANOVA and t-tests, were conducted to compare the similarities and differences among stakeholders. Similarly, descriptive statistics were used to check the appropriateness of measures to each corresponding criterion. In this chapter, only the descriptive analysis results are reported.

EVALUATION OBJECTIVES AND PHASES
EVALUATION OBJECTIVES

Identification of evaluation objectives is the first step for digital library evaluation because different purposes require different criteria and measurements. This evaluation may serve multiple purposes. Most of the research focuses on users' use of digital libraries and usability evaluation in order to identify user needs and weaknesses of digital libraries, in particular for interface enhancement. Chapters 7 and 8 offered detailed discussion related to usability and user need studies. Some evaluation studies try to compare different designs of the digital library interfaces and help select one design interface over another one (Hilary et al., 2007). Digital library evaluation is conducted for library administrations to understand users' experiences and reactions to their interactions with digital library interface (Mansor and Ripin, 2013). Digital library evaluation is also done to interpret its values based on the perceptions and uses of targeted users (Waugh et al., 2015). In addition, digital library evaluation is used to check the status of its development in a country (Alipour-Hafezi and Nick, 2015). Sometimes, digital library evaluation is performed for multiple purposes. For example, the effectiveness of its services is assessed for making budget decisions as well as to improve the quality of services (Stejskal and Hajek, 2015).

MEDaL investigates digital library evaluation purposes from the three groups of participants. Eleven types of digital library purposes were derived from the document analysis. Based on the average rating from three groups of stakeholders on a seven-point Likert scale (Fig. 10.4), the Delphi surveys reveal that the top three most important purposes are (1) understanding user needs (6.59), (2) identifying problems and weaknesses (6.54), and (3) evidence-based future planning (6.38). Interestingly, users rated "understanding user needs" the highest, 6.83, compared with the other groups (scholars: 6.61, librarians: 6.35). Both scholars (6.69) and librarians (6.48) selected "identifying problems and weaknesses" as the most important purpose of digital library. The least important purposes are (1) promotion/marketing (5.66), (2) benchmarking (5.54), and fundraising and grant writing (5.48).

EVALUATION PHASES

Digital library creation and management go through several phases: planning, prototyping, building, testing, launching, operating, and upgrading. During each phase, the focus of the assessment is different. Each phase requires its own evaluation dimensions, criteria, and methods. At some phases, multiple dimensions

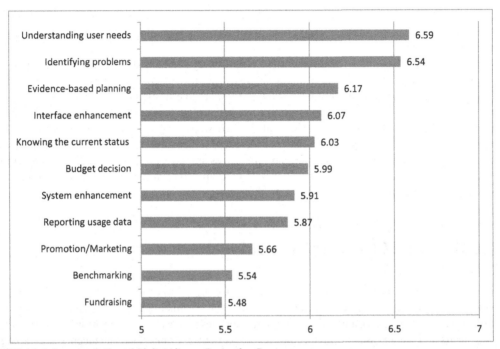

FIGURE 10.4 Average Rating of Digital Library Evaluation Purposes

of the assessment are required; at other phases, a specific evaluative dimension is needed. For example, in the prototyping phase, interface design assessment is the key; in the operating phase, most of the evaluation dimensions need to be considered. Of course, that also depends on the purpose of digital library evaluation. During the operating phase, usability evaluation places an emphasis on the interface and its corresponding criteria (Hilary et al., 2007); digital library value evaluation focuses on user engagement and the effects on user dimensions and related criteria (Waugh et al., 2015); the evaluation of the effectiveness of digital library services concentrates on the service dimension and associated criteria (Stejskal and Hajek, 2015).

Buttenfield (1999) discusses digital library evaluation, in particular usability evaluation during system design, system development, and system deployment. At different stages of digital library evaluation, researchers apply different evaluation methods. Buttenfield further specifies the methods used at different phases. For example, surveys and cognitive walkthroughs are applied at the initial design phase; online user surveys and focus groups are employed at the development phase; and transaction logs are initiated at the deployment phase.

EVALUATION DIMENSIONS AND THEIR IMPORTANCE
EVALUATION DIMENSIONS

Tsakonas and Papatheodorou (2011) define dimensions as a consideration of the scope of evaluation activities and describing evaluation purposes and outcomes. They further identify the following dimensions: effectiveness, performance measurement, service quality, outcome assessment, and technical excellence. Dimensions are the main constructs of digital library evaluation frameworks and models (refer to the Evaluation Framework section for a discussion of frameworks with associated dimensions). Among the dimensions, Tsakonas et al. (2013) find that effectiveness, performance measurement, and technical excellence are the main research interests in digital library evaluation, which reflect the system-centered digital library evaluation approach, based on the analysis of conference presentations at the JCDL and the ECDL.

Saracevic's (2000, 2004) digital library evaluation framework specifies six dimensions: content, technology, interface, process/service, user, and context. Moreover, Zhang (2010) investigated and validated the importance of Saracevic's six dimensions from different stakeholders of digital libraries. Hu et al. (2014) further examined how the six dimensions influence users' perceptions of university digital libraries. The results yield two types of influences. On the one hand, information-providing services, information retrieval services, and individual services have a direct influence on user perception of university digital libraries. On the other hand, information organization services have an indirect influence on user perception of university digital libraries through information retrieval services and individual services. Cheng (2014) concludes that information relevance, system accessibility, and technical support are the main reasons that users continue using digital libraries.

IMPORTANCE OF DIGITAL LIBRARY EVALUATION DIMENSIONS IN THE MEDaL STUDY

Ten dimensions are identified in the MEDaL study based on document analysis, in particular, of documents regarding digital library evaluation theoretical frameworks, models, and other related literature. The MEDaL study not only discovers the key dimensions but also further reveals the importance of these dimensions from the perceptions of different digital library stakeholders. Table 10.1 presents the ten dimensions, definitions, and the average importance ratings by scholars, digital librarians, and users. Interestingly, interface design (6.38), collections (6.36), and information organization (6.31) were ranked as the most important dimensions. In contrast, administration (5.82), context (5.74), and service (5.65) were rated as the least important dimensions. Curiously, service is deemed as one of the important dimensions for library evaluation but was considered less important in the digital library environment in this study. It needs further examination.

EVALUATION CRITERIA AND THEIR IMPORTANCE
EVALUATION CRITERIA

In the area of LIS research, a number of evaluation criteria have been suggested corresponding to various dimensions of digital libraries. Fuhr et al. (2001) select the following criteria for the four key dimensions: data/collection (content, meta-content, and management), technology (user technology, information access, system structure technology, and document technology), and users/uses (user, domain, information seeking, purpose, and distribution). Saracevic (2004) identifies six classes of criteria, representing content, technology, interface, process/service, user, and context. He summarizes the digital library evaluation criteria applied by related studies consisting of:

- Usability: content (accessibly, availability, clarity, complexity, informativeness, transparency, understanding, effort to understand, adequacy, coverage, overlap, quality, accuracy, validity, reliability, and authority), process (learnability, effort/time, convenience, ease of use, lostness,

Table 10.1 MEDaL: Importance of Ten Digital Library Evaluation Dimensions		
Dimension	**Definition**	**Importance**
Interface design	Assess the usability of digital library interfaces and the extent these interfaces support users' interaction with digital libraries	6.38
Collections	Assess the quality and quantity of digital library collections	6.36
Information organization	Assess the representation, grouping, and presentation of digital information	6.31
Effects on users	Assess the impact and value of digital libraries on users' accomplishing their tasks	6.26
System and technology	Assess the efficiency, accessibility, and reliability of digital libraries as well as their retrieval performance	6.22
Preservation	Assess the extent and ways of digital library support for preservation	5.87
User engagement	Assess the extent and ways of usage of digital libraries and user involvement in their development	5.85
Services	Assess the quality and quantity of the offered digital library services	5.82
Context	Assess the extent of digital libraries fitting into, responding to, following larger context—institutional, economic, legal, social, cultural, and others	5.74
Administration	Assess administrative-related factors that affect the development of digital libraries; assess whether they can be sustained and enhanced	5.65

support, completion, interpretation difficulty, sureness in results, and error rate), format (attractiveness, sustaining efforts, consistency, representation of labels, and communicativeness of messages), overall assessment (satisfaction, success, relevance, usefulness of results, impact, value, quality of experience, barriers, irritability, preferences, and learning).

- System features consisting of technology performance (response time, processing time, speed, capacity, and load), process/algorithm performance (relevance, clustering similarity, functionality, flexibility, comparison with human performance, error rate, optimization, logical decisions, path length, clickthroughs, and retrieval time), and overall system (maintainability, scalability, interoperability, sharability, and costs).
- Usage consisting of usage patterns, use of materials, usage statistics, who uses what and when and for what reasons/decisions.

Gonçalves et al. (2007) propose a quality model for digital library evaluation, which consists of quality dimensions and associated criteria: digital object (accessibility, pertinence, preservability, relevance, similarity, significance, and timeliness), metadata specification (accuracy, completeness, and conformance), collection (completeness), catalog (completeness and consistency), repository (completeness and consistency), and services (composability, efficiency, effectiveness, extensibility, reusability, and reliability). Xie's (2006, 2008) evaluation framework posits the following criteria associated with five dimensions: collection quality (collection quality in general, scope, authority, accuracy, completeness, currency, and copyright), service quality (mission, user community, traditional library service, and unique services), system performance (system performance in general, efficiency and effectiveness, relevance precision and recall, and usefulness), and user satisfaction (user satisfaction, user feedback, and contact information).

Zhang (2010) identifies the top digital library evaluation criteria that are agreed upon by five groups of stakeholders including administrators, developers, librarians, researchers, and users. These agreed criteria consist of content (accessibility, accuracy, and usefulness), technology (ease of use and reliability), interface (ease of use, effectiveness, and consistency), service (accessibility, integrity, reliability, responsiveness, and usefulness), user (successfulness, satisfaction, and efficiency of task completion), and context (sustainability, collaboration/sharing, and managerial support). Vullo (2010) offers some examples of digital library criteria for the four core dimensions: organization (management and policies), content (quality of data, metadata, and digital collections), service (quality of technologies and quality of design), and user (quality of interactions between users and the digital library).

In addition to comprehensive evaluation criteria, some researchers focus on the usability aspect of digital library and its associated criteria. Kengeri et al. (1999) applied ease of use ratings (easiest to read, easiest to learn, easiest to browse, easiest to search, and easiest overall), search time, and search errors as usability evaluation criteria to compare four digital libraries. Evans et al.'s (2002) usability framework proposes the following criteria: visibility of system status, match between system and the real world, user control and freedom, consistency and standards, error prevention, recognition rather than recall, flexibility and efficiency of use, aesthetic and minimalist design, recovery from errors, and help. Jeng (2005a, b) suggests an evaluation framework for usability of academic digital libraries concentrating on four criteria: effectiveness, efficiency, satisfaction (ease of use, organization of information, labeling, visual appearance, contents, and error correction), and learnability. Tsakonas and Papatheodorou (2008) select the following criteria to evaluate the usefulness (relevance, format, reliability, level, and coverage) and usability (ease of use, aesthetic, navigation, terminology, and learnability) of open access digital libraries. Similarly, Buchanan and Salako (2009) come up with the following digital library usability and usefulness criteria: effectiveness, efficiency, aesthetic appearance, terminology, navigation, learnability, relevance, reliability, and currency.

Hariri and Norouzi (2011) synthesize relevant literature on digital library user interface and usability and recommend the following 22 digital library interface evaluation criteria: navigation, searching, design, guidance, error management, presentation, learnability, user control, consistency, language, feedback, ease of use, match between system and the real world, customization, user support, user workload, interaction, compatibility, visibility of system status, user experience, flexibility, and accessibility. Following Hariri and Norouzi's research, Lai et al. (2014) rank the top five digital library evaluation criteria on user interface: ease of use, searching, language, presentation and design by applying fuzzy analytic hierarchy process (AHP) to obtain weights of evaluation criteria.

Special attention is also paid to digital reference services. Lankes et al. (2003) suggest six criteria as quality standards to assess digital reference services: courtesy, accuracy, satisfaction, repeat users, awareness, and cost. Researchers have also examined relationships among digital library evaluation criteria. According to Jeng (2005a, b), interrelated relationships are found among effectiveness, efficiency, and satisfaction.

Other aspects of digital library evaluation criteria have also been explored. For example, Lagzian et al. (2013) identify corresponding criteria for dimensions that affect motivation (e.g., top management commitment and support, middle management commitment and support, and clear digital library policies and standards), resources (e.g., content production, structural and descriptive metadata, harvesting of resources, and metadata), people (e.g., managing overall digital library, training and education, and personnel competency), process (e.g., accuracy and reliability of service, rights statement, and digital preservation), location/network (knowledge sharing and scholarly communication), and time (provision of access and fast access to the digital library). Additional digital library evaluation criteria are also identified such as suitability, accuracy, costs, informativeness, timeliness, usefulness, use environment, and others (Kenney et al., 1998; Larsen, 2002; Kim and Kim, 2008).

IMPORTANCE OF DIGITAL LIBRARY EVALUATION CRITERIA IN THE MEDaL STUDY

The results of the Delphi surveys employed in our MEDaL study indicate the importance of digital library evaluation criteria based on the average rating from the three groups of stakeholders for each of the 10 dimensions.

Dimension 1—collections

Overall, digitization standards, authority, and cost turned out to be the three most important evaluation criteria in the dimension of collections, whereas completeness, diversity, and size were the least important. Ratings of importance vary by different groups. Authority, which is related to the reliability of collection quality, was considered the most important by users. Scholars perceived audience as the most important, whereas librarians rated digitization standards the highest. Interestingly, completeness, diversity, and size were considered less important by all three groups of subjects. Table 10.2 presents the importance of evaluation criteria in the dimension of a collection.

Table 10.2 Importance of Evaluation Criteria in the Dimension of Collections

Criterion	Definition	Importance
Digitization standards	To assess the types and methods of digitization practices conducted, as well as identify best practices to build a digital library	6.26
Authority	To assess whether the information provided by a digital library comes from trustworthy sources	6.24
Cost	To assess costs to build collections in a digital library	6.15
Item quality	To assess the quality of a digitized item provided by a digital library within its format	6.13
Format compatibility	To assess whether the format of collections in a digital library are compatible with a variety of software and systems for different purposes	6.08
Audience	To assess who are the main potential users of a digital library	6.05
Scope/Coverage	To assess the range of topics that are covered by a digital library	5.62
Contextual information	To assess what type of additional, related information, such as bibliographies, biographies, encyclopedia entries, timelines, and interpretive essays, are available to users in a digital library	5.51
Completeness	To assess whether a digital library covers all documents in each topic area	5.29
Diversity	To assess whether a digital library deals with a variety of issues in relation to a topic of interest	5.16
Size	To assess the amount of collection items provided by a digital library	5.10

Table 10.3 Importance of Evaluation Criteria in the Dimension of Information Organization

Criterion	Definition	Importance
Appropriateness	To assess whether the organizational structure and associated categories adequately organize items in a digital library	6.21
Accessibility to metadata	To assess how easily a user can obtain the metadata information of each item	6.19
Metadata accuracy	To assess how accurately metadata elements are assigned for each item	6.16
Metadata standards	To assess whether metadata elements follow predefined standard and guides	6.04
Consistency	To assess whether metadata are consistent across collections in a digital library	5.93
Comprehensiveness	To assess whether the organization structure covers all the access points of a digital library	5.88
Depth of metadata	To assess the levels of the metadata scheme used for a digital library	5.83
Metadata interoperability	To assess whether metadata elements of a digital library are compatible to different digital libraries	5.67
Controlled vocabulary	To assess the types and numbers of controlled vocabularies used in a digital library	5.56

Dimension 2—information organization

For the dimension of information organization, appropriateness, accessibility to metadata, and metadata accuracy were ranked first, second, and third, respectively, whereas depth of metadata, metadata interoperability, and controlled vocabulary were perceived the least important. Scholars rated appropriateness the most important, whereas librarians chose accessibility to metadata. Users selected metadata accuracy, the most important with regard to information organization in digital libraries. Table 10.3 presents the importance of evaluation criteria in the dimension of information organization.

Dimension 3—interface design

In terms of interface design, all three groups regarded search function and browsing function as the most important criteria in evaluating digital libraries. Searching and browsing are the two main approaches in the information search process, and subjects rated search and browsing functions as the top two criteria. Navigation and intuitive operation were chosen as relatively important evaluation criteria across the three groups. Visual appeal, user control, and personalized page were rated least important in the dimension of interface design. Table 10.4 presents the importance of evaluation criteria in the dimension of interface design.

Dimension 4—system and technology

In the dimension of system and technology, retrieval effectiveness, reliability, and server performance were identified in the MEDaL as the most important criteria. As digital libraries are considered as a type of information retrieval system, subjects thought retrieval effectiveness, such as precision and recall, was important in evaluating them. Simultaneously, reliability and server performance were the

Table 10.4 Importance of Evaluation Criteria in the Dimension of Interface Design		
Criterion	**Definition**	**Importance**
Search function	To assess what types of search functions are offered by a digital library and how easy it is to use them	6.54
Browsing function	To assess in what ways and to what extent the interface supports a user's ability to surf related items in a digital library	6.34
Navigation	To assess in what ways and to what extent the interface supports a user's exploration in a digital library	6.26
Intuitive operation	To assess how straightforward a digital library interface is for a user to understand its operation and how easily a user can learn to operate the interface	6.25
Search results presentation	To assess how the types of formats/options of search results are presented to users in a digital library	6.18
Consistency	To assess whether the design and layout are coherent across a digital library interface	6.12
Reliability	To assess the ability of a digital library to perform and maintain its functions under different circumstances	6.11
Help function	To assess what types of help functions are offered and how effectively they support users in their help-seeking process	5.64
Visual appeal	To assess to what extent the interface of a digital library is visually attractive to users	5.61
User control	To assess to what extent a digital library allows users to manipulate its interface	4.95
Personalized page	To assess whether a digital library offers personalized pages based on user profile	4.25

criteria that were needed to provide stable services in digital library. Less important criteria were error rate/error correction, flexibility, and linkage with other digital library. Table 10.5 presents the importance of evaluation criteria in the dimension of system and technology.

Dimension 5—effects on users

In the ratings of effects on users, research productivity and learning effects were chosen as the most important criteria. This is not surprising because this survey was conducted in an academic setting. Perceptions of digital libraries and information literacy/skill change were regarded less important. It seems that the subjects considered real effects more important than perceptions. The difficulty of conducting longitudinal studies to identify the change might have contributed to the lower rating of information literacy/skill change. Table 10.6 presents the importance of evaluation criteria in the dimension of effects on users.

Dimension 6—services

In the dimension of services, subjects chose service quality, usefulness, and user satisfaction as the three most important criteria. Service quality, usefulness, and user satisfaction are commonly applied

Table 10.5 Importance of Evaluation Criteria in the Dimension of System and Technology

Criterion	Definition	Importance
Retrieval effectiveness	To assess how effective the search algorithm is in a digital library	6.31
Reliability	To assess how stable a digital library performance is over time	6.18
Server performance	To assess the ability of a server to run a digital library	6.17
Response time	To assess how quickly a digital library responds to a user's request	6.13
Fit-to-task	To assess to what extent a digital library is adequate to perform tasks that a user requests	6.04
Connectivity	To assess how stable a digital library system is when connected to other information systems	5.99
Page loading speed	To assess how quickly a digital library presents a user-requested page	5.97
Integrated search	To assess whether a digital library offers an integrated search environment for different collections within a digital library	5.95
Error rate/ error correction	To assess the degree of errors encountered during the use of the content management system and the ability to fix the errors	5.93
Flexibility	To assess whether a digital library responds to potential internal or external changes in a timely manner	5.66
Linkage with other digital libraries	To assess the identification of and in what ways a digital library is linked to other related digital libraries	5.29

Table 10.6 Importance of Evaluation Criteria in the Dimension of Effects on Users

Criterion	Definition	Importance
Research productivity	To assess in what ways and to what extent a digital library affects a user's research outputs	5.46
Learning effects	To assess in what ways and to what extent a digital library influences a user's learning outcome	5.30
Knowledge change	To assess in what ways and to what extent a digital library influences a user's knowledge structure	5.04
Instructional efficiency	To assess in what ways and to what extent a digital library enhances a user's teaching effectiveness	4.91
Perception of digital libraries	To assess in what ways and to what extent a digital library influences a user's view of digital libraries	4.84
Information literacy/Skill change	To assess to what extent a digital library enhances a user's literacy skills	4.64

criteria for service evaluation in general. The evaluation criterion for services for users with disabilities was rated fourth. On the other hand, user education, types of unique services, and customized services were ranked as the least important criteria. It seems that subjects cared more for the quality and usefulness of the digital library services and less for the unique services offered to users. Table 10.7 presents the importance of evaluation criteria in the dimension of services.

Dimension 7—preservation

In the dimension of preservation, completeness, ability to migrate, and preservation policy were ranked first, second, and third, respectively. Institutional support, types of archiving methods, and cost per

Table 10.7 Importance of Evaluation Criteria in the Dimension of Services

Criterion	Definition	Importance
Service quality	To assess in what ways and to what extent digital library services satisfy users' needs	6.24
Usefulness	To assess in what ways and to what extent digital library services are useful for users to achieve their tasks	6.23
User satisfaction	To assess in what ways and to what extent users are satisfied with services provided by a digital library	6.18
Types of services for users with disabilities	To assess the types of services offered to users with disabilities	6.12
Reliability	To assess how users of a digital library perceive the trustworthiness of services provided	6.01
Responsiveness	To assess the reaction time to a user's request for a digital library service	5.97
Timeliness	To assess in what ways and to what extent services are offered to users in a timely manner	5.94
Types of services	To assess the types of services provided by a digital library	5.62
Availability of digital library staff	To assess in what ways and to what extent a user can easily contact staff of a digital library for questions, feedback, and comments	5.61
Confidence	To assess in what ways and to what extent users have a positive attitude toward services offered by a digital library	5.55
Follow-up services	To assess in what ways and to what extent adequate and timely continuing services are provided to users by a digital library when necessary	5.21
FAQ/Q&A	To assess whether and how many FAQs or Q&As a digital library provides to help users in using it	5.13
User education	To assess the types of user education offered by a digital library	5.10
Types of unique services	To assess the unique types of services provided by a digital library compared to other related digital libraries	4.79
Customized services	To assess whether a digital library offers personalized services based on user profile information or user requests	4.75

Table 10.8 Importance of Evaluation Criteria in the Dimension of Preservation

Criterion	Definition	Importance
Completeness	To assess to what extent the archiving process to preserve archived materials is complete and comprehensive	6.22
Ability to migrate	To assess the ability of data migration for preservation.	6.19
Preservation policy	To assess whether a policy regarding preservation is developed and what is covered by the policy	6.00
Preservation infrastructure	To assess the types of archiving equipment and facilities a digital library uses for digital preservation	5.85
Institutional support	To assess how many staff members or resources are dedicated to the preservation tasks of a digital library	5.76
Types of archiving methods	To assess the archiving methods/approaches a digital library staff member has to apply in order to preserve information	5.73
Cost per record	To assess the average cost for archiving one record	5.44

record were less important according to the survey. Overall, librarians assigned a higher score of the importance of evaluation criteria to the dimension of preservation. This reveals that librarians emphasize preservation more than the other two groups. Table 10.8 presents the importance of evaluation criteria in the dimension of preservation.

Dimension 8—administration

Since users do not have sufficient knowledge of digital library, they were excluded from the survey in this dimension. Based on the responses from scholars and librarians, budget, planning, and staffing turned out to be the most important criteria in the dimension of administration. Management policy, fundraising/sponsor, and incentive were considered less important by the two groups. Table 10.9 presents the importance of evaluation criteria in the dimension of administration.

Dimension 9—user engagement

In the dimension of user engagement, resource use, user feedback, and site visit were the three highly rated evaluation criteria by three groups. Resource use is one of the fundamental criteria in the evaluation of libraries, and it is also perceived as an important evaluation criterion in the context of a digital library. Moreover, all three groups perceived user feedback as the important criterion to judge user engagement. On the other hand, user participation channels, user knowledge contribution, and e-commerce support were perceived as less important. Table 10.10 presents the importance of evaluation criteria in the dimension of user engagement.

Dimension 10—context

Finally, subjects selected copyright, information ethics compliance, and organizational mission as the most important evaluation criteria in this dimension. Again, the groups from the academic library setting expressed their view on the importance of information ethics compliance. On the other hand, content sharing, collaboration, and social impact were considered less important. Table 10.11 presents the importance of evaluation criteria in the dimension of context.

Table 10.9 Importance of Evaluation Criteria in the Dimension of Administration

Criterion	Definition	Importance
Budget	To assess the amount and arrangement of monetary resources to efficiently manage a digital library	6.18
Planning	To assess whether strategic plans are established to create, manage, maintain, and enhance a digital library	6.10
Staffing	To assess the quantity and arrangement of human resources to efficiently manage a digital library	6.02
Staff training	To assess the types, frequency, and efficiency of training programs offered to digital library staff	5.79
Marketing	To assess the publicity efforts of a digital library to attract potential users and inform related communities	5.67
Regular assessment	To assess whether regular, continuous evaluation is performed to maintain and enhance a digital library	5.59
Management policy	To assess whether a well-defined policy for administration is offered by a digital library	5.40
Fundraising/sponsor	To assess the effort of fundraising to support a digital library financially	5.28
Incentive	To assess the types of incentives provided to digital library staff	4.32

Table 10.10 Importance of Evaluation Criteria in the Dimension of User Engagement

Criterion	Definition	Importance
Resource use	To assess in what ways and to what extent users use resources in a digital library	6.04
User feedback	To assess the types of user comments and suggestions received by a digital library and in what ways and to what extent these comments and suggestions are incorporated into the enhancement of the digital library	5.97
Site visit	To assess how frequently users visit a digital library web site and the duration for each visit	5.74
Integration with external applications	To assess in what ways users can export digital objects and integrate with external applications, such as slide presentation software	5.51
Help feature use	To assess which help features are offered to users, how frequently, and in what context users try to use help-related features in a digital library	5.43
User participation channels	To assess the types of channels available to users to communicate with the staff of a digital library	5.39
User knowledge contribution	To assess the ways users can contribute to digital library content and organization through tagging, commenting, and adding their own objects	5.26
E-commerce support	To assess the capabilities of ordering digital objects online	4.61

Table 10.11 Importance of Evaluation Criteria in the Dimension of Context

Criterion	Definition	Importance
Copyright	To assess whether a digital library identifies and conforms to copyright issues	6.26
Information ethics compliance	To assess whether a digital library identifies and conforms to ethical issues related to its creation and use	6.23
Organizational mission	To assess in what ways and to what extent digital library creation and use conform to organizational objectives	5.79
Targeted user community	To assess in what ways and to what extent a digital library engages in targeted user groups	5.77
Content sharing	To assess in what ways and to what extent stakeholders of a digital library are willing to share their content	5.69
Collaboration	To assess in what ways and to what extent stakeholders of a digital library work together; to assess in what ways and to what extent stakeholders of a digital library cooperate with stakeholders of another one	5.30
Social impact	To assess in what ways and to what extent the use of a digital library influences society	4.97

EVALUATION MEASUREMENTS
DIGITAL LIBRARY EVALUATION MEASUREMENTS

In order to effectively perform digital library evaluations, not only the criteria but also measurements are essential. Compared to the evaluation, it is more difficult to validate its measurements. Marchionini (2000) makes two suggestions for digital library evaluation measurements. First, it is important to integrate as many specific measures instead of depending on one single measure. Second, it is vital to integrate statistical data and qualitative data. Albertson (2015) also stresses the importance of having both quantitative and qualitative measures for user-centered visual digital library evaluation. Just as Heradio et al. (2012) states, "there is an increasing trend to blend quantitative and qualitative data within a study to provide a broader and deeper perspective" (p. 277).

Researchers have proposed different types of measurements for either overall digital library evaluation or its specific aspects. Gonçalves et al. (2007) suggest mostly quantitative measurements for the quality evaluation of digital libraries—for example, accurate attributes, number of attributes in the record for accuracy of and missing attributes, schema size for completeness of and conformant attributes, and schema size for conformance of metadata specification. Heradio et al. (2012) review the quality digital library evaluation from users' perceptions, in particular related to utility, usability, and their costs. Specifically, they introduce two alternative measurements: Likert scales and fuzzy linguistic information. They conclude that Likert scales have the advantage of measuring user's opinion distribution although "the assumption of interval for Likert data in the digital library context has to be justified" (p. 280) whereas fuzzy linguistic modeling generates better results. Buchanan and Salako (2009) recommend measures for each of the digital library usability and usefulness criteria. For example, tasks completed for effectiveness, time to complete for efficiency, attractiveness for aesthetic, appropriateness for appearance, comprehension and consistency for terminology, steps to complete for navigation, repetition of failed commands for learnability, relevant results and utility for relevance, credibility for reliability, and creation date and last citation for currency.

Electronic resource evaluation accounts for a large part of digital library evaluation. Noh (2010) identifies multiple sectors and their corresponding evaluation indices for electronic resource development and uses. Based on three rounds of the Delphi survey, Noh presents evaluation measurements for evaluation criteria in relation to e-resource acquisition, e-resource use, and environment for e-resource use. For example, annual number of sessions to web database (DB) per service recipient, and the annual number of DB hits per service recipient, and annual number of Web DB downloads per service recipient are the measurements of use of Web DB. Blixrud (2002, 2003) and Shim (2002) report the project conducted by members of the Association of Research Libraries (ARL). They developed measures for the assessment of electronic resources in terms of resources, expenditures, and usage. Among the measures, library digitization activities are assessed by size of library digital collection, use of library digital collection, and cost of digital collection construction and management.

Evaluation of services offered by digital libraries is an area of keen interest to researchers and practitioners. Brophy (2001) summarizes digital library performance indicators based on the opinions from the professional community as part of the EQUINOX project: percentage of the population reached; number of sessions on each digital library service per member of the target population; number of remote sessions on these services per member of the population to be served; number of documents and entries viewed per session for each service; cost per session for each service; cost per document or entry viewed for each service; percentage of information requests submitted electronically; library computer workstation use rate; number of library computer workstation hours available per member of the population to be served; rejected sessions as a percentage of total attempted sessions; percentage of total acquisitions of expenditure spent on acquisition of services; number of attendees at formal service training sessions per member of the population to be served; number of library staff developing, managing, and providing digital libraries and user training as a percentage of total library staff; and user satisfaction with digital library services. Lankes et al. (2003) propose five types of performance measures to assess digital reference services: descriptive statistics and measures, log analysis, user satisfaction measures, cost, and staff time expended.

- *Descriptive measures:* the number of digital reference questions received, number of digital reference responses, number of digital reference answers, total reference activities, percentage of digital reference questions to total reference questions, digital reference fill rate, digital reference completion rate, number of unanswered digital reference questions, types of digital reference questions received, saturation rate, sources used per question, and repeat users.
- *Examples of log measures:* the number of digital reference sessions, usage of digital reference services by day of the week.
- *User measures:* awareness of service, accessibility of service, expectation for service, etc.
- *Cost measures:* cost of digital reference service, cost of digital reference service as a percentage of total reference budget, etc.
- *Staff measures:* percentage of staff time spent overseeing technology and assisting users with technology.

Even though specific measures have been suggested for different aspects of digital library evaluation, there is a lack of measure for all the dimensions. Moreover, there is no systematic analysis and discussion about measures for each criterion under each dimension. Our MEDaLstudy presented, as follows, fills in the gap.

APPROPRIATENESS OF MEASUREMENTS IN THE MEDaL STUDY

Measures are the foci of the second part of the MEDaL study presented in this chapter. In the second round, we suggested specific measures and operational definitions for evaluation criteria. In this round, the user group was excluded from the survey because they do not have in-depth knowledge of measurements. Fifty-five subjects out of 61 participated in the second-round survey, which is a 90.1% participation rate. They were asked to rate the appropriateness of measures based on the seven-item Likert scale (7 as the most appropriate and 1 as not at all appropriate). This section summarizes the survey results. Different measurements for each criterion are listed based on their rated appropriateness from high to low in the following tables.

Dimension 1—collections

Twenty-one measures in this dimension were suggested in this study, and scholar and librarian subjects were instructed to rate the appropriateness of each measure to its corresponding criterion. Subjects gave a rating over 6 for compliance with digitization standards (6.327), quality specification (6.164), and presence of resource reference information (6.036). However, level of domain knowledge (4.985), presence of diverse perspectives (4.945), and potential user demographic data (4.873) were rated the least appropriate to explain their criteria, respectively. Table 10.12 presents the appropriateness of evaluation measurements in the dimension of collections.

Dimension 2—information organization

In the second dimension—information organization—total 17 measures for 9 criteria were presented to the subjects. All measures were rated over 5 in terms of their appropriateness. There were three measures that are rated over 6: compliance to the metadata standards (6.164), compliance to interoperability standards (6.109), and incorrect data value (6.091). The least three appropriate measures were metadata elements used (5.127), subject analysis (5.036), and depth of description (5.036). Table 10.13 presents the appropriateness of evaluation measures in the dimension of information organization.

Dimension 3—interface design

In the interface design dimension, 32 measures were identified for 10 criteria. Eight measures were rated over 6 for their appropriateness, which indicates at least "very appropriate." These 8 measures are as follows: search function usefulness (6.327), types of search features (6.309), search function ease of use (6.291), overall ease of use (6.200), design consistency (6.164), browsing function usefulness (6.036), navigation usefulness (6.036), and browsing function ease of use (6.018). However, 2 measures suggested for the criterion of user participatory design were perceived less appropriate: extent of user participation (5.055) and types of user participation in interface design (5.018). Also, use of help features was considered least appropriate among 32 measures in this dimension. Table 10.14 presents the appropriateness of evaluation measures in the dimension of interface design.

Dimension 4—system and technology

In Dimension 4, 21 measures for 15 criteria were shown to the subjects. These measures are mostly adopted from evaluation research on information retrieval evaluation or system evaluation. Six measures

Table 10.12 Appropriateness of Evaluation Measures in the Dimension of Collections

Criterion	Measure and Definition
Digitization standards	*Compliance with digitization standards:* Whether a digital library adheres to the established digitization standards
Authority	*Presence of resource reference information:* Whether resource reference information for each item is available
Item quality	*Quality specification:* Technical specification for creating digitized objects
Cost	*Cost of metadata:* Average cost for creating metadata per record
	Cost for building a digital collection: Average cost for building a collection
	Cost of conversion: Average cost for converting to a digitized item
Format compatibility	*Types of access files:* Types of access files used in the collection
	Data type: Types of data used in the collection
Audience	*User demographic data:* Whether user information data are collected
	Potential user demographic data: Types of potential users and their demographic characteristics
Scope/Coverage	*Time span of coverage:* Time period covered in the collections
	Subject coverage: Number of topics in a digital library
Contextual information	*Presence of contextual information for collection:* Whether there are secondary resources for digital collections to provide contextual information
Completeness	*Item size in specific topic:* Number of items per topic
Diversity	*Presence of diverse perspectives:* Whether a digital library contains diverse perspectives on a topic
Size	*Collection size:* Number of digitized objects
Collection development policy	*Presence of collection development policy:* Whether a digital library has a documented policy about collection development
	Components of policy: Types of components of collection development policy
Currency	*Currency of collections:* Proportions of newly archived collections in recent years
Re-use	*Re-use of digital objects:* Types of digital objects that can be reused
Collection developer knowledge	*Level of domain knowledge:* To what extent collection developers have domain knowledge

were perceived "very appropriate," which scored over 6 on average on a seven-point scale: precision (6.273), system failure (6.218), response time to search results (6.200), recall (6.055), system response time (6.036), and search across collections (6.000). On the contrary, replacement and update of equipment (5.109), use of emerging technologies (5.018), and presence of open source (4.909) were rated relatively lower in this dimension. Table 10.15 presents the appropriateness of evaluation measures in the dimension of system and technology.

Table 10.13 Appropriateness of Evaluation Measures in the Dimension of Information Organization

Criterion	Measure and Definition
Appropriateness	*Domain appropriateness:* Metadata appropriateness as judged by domain experts
	User-perceived appropriateness: Metadata appropriateness as judged by users
Accessibility of metadata	*Ease of access to metadata:* Users' perceived accessibility of metadata
Metadata accuracy	*Incorrect data value:* Percentage of incorrect data values
	Inaccurate data entry: Percentage of inaccurate data entry
Metadata standards	*Compliance to the metadata standards:* Proportion of accurately mapped elements compared to the selected metadata schema
	Types of metadata standards: Whether a digital library adheres to the selected metadata standard
Consistency	*Metadata element consistency:* The extent to which the selected metadata elements are used for data input across collections in a digital library
	Metadata schema consistency: The extent to which the selected metadata schema is used for data input across collections in a digital library
Comprehensiveness	*Completed metadata:* Average number of metadata fields populated per record
	Metadata elements used: Percentage of metadata elements used compared to the selected metadata schema
Depth of metadata	*Subject analysis:* Average number of subject terms per record
	Depth of description: Length of item description
Metadata interoperability	*Compliance to interoperability standards:* Whether a digital library complies with interoperability standards
Controlled vocabulary	*Presence of controlled vocabularies:* Whether a digital library uses controlled vocabularies in organizing objects
	Ease of access to controlled vocabularies: Users' perceived access to controlled vocabularies
	Presence of controlled vocabularies: Whether a digital library offers controlled vocabularies

Dimension 5—effects on users

In the effects on users dimension, 11 measures were identified for 5 evaluation criteria. In this dimension, no measure scored over 6. This dimension contains many criteria that are related to change, and it is hard to measure them by a simple study. The top three ranked measures in terms of appropriateness are willingness to continue use of the digital library (5.982), in teaching (5.691), and for research (5.636). On the contrary, two measures were rated less than 5: attitude change after digital library uses (4.982) and perceived information literacy/skill (4.982). Table 10.16 presents the appropriateness of evaluation measures in the dimension of effects on users.

Table 10.14 Appropriateness of Evaluation Measures in the Dimension of Interface Design

Criterion	Measure and Definition
Search function	*Usefulness:* Users' perceived usefulness of the search function
	Types of search features: Types of search features available
	Ease of use: Users' perceived ease of use
	Use of search features: Average frequency of and time spent on search feature use in a session
Browsing function	*Usefulness:* Users' perceived usefulness of the browsing function
	Ease of use: Users' perceived ease of use
	Browsing access points and paths: Types of browsing access points and paths available
	Organization of browsing structure: Experts' assessment of logic and quality of the browsing structure
	Use of browsing features: Average frequency of and time spent on browsing feature use in a session
Navigation	*Usefulness:* Users' perceived usefulness of the navigation features
	Ease of use: Users' perceived ease of use
	Navigation features: Types of navigation features available
	Use of navigation features: Average frequency of and time spent using the navigation features in a session
Intuitive operation	*Overall ease of use:* Users' perceived ease of use to operate the interface of a digital library
Consistency	*Design consistency:* Consistency in fonts, layout, menus, colors, etc
	Consistency from user perspective: Users' perceived consistency of the interface
Help function	*Ease of use:* Users' perceived ease of use of the help function
	Usefulness: Users' perceived usefulness of the help function
	Help use situations: Under what situations users use help features
	Types of help features: Types of help features available
	Use of help features: Average frequency of and time spent on help feature use in a session
Visual appeal	*Visual aesthetics:* Users' perception of the interface aesthetics
User control	*Usefulness:* Users' perceived usefulness of user control features
	Ease of use: Users' perceived ease of use
	Types of user control features: Types of user control features available
	Use of user control feature: Average frequency of and time spent on using each type of user control feature in a session
Personalization feature	*Ease of use:* Users' perceived ease of use
	Usefulness: Users' perceived usefulness of personalization features
	Types of personalization features: Types of personalization features provided
	Use of personalization features: Average frequency of and time spent on personalization feature use in a session
User participatory design	*Extent of user participation:* To what extent users participate in interface design
	Types of user participation in interface design: Types of user participation in the process of interface design

Table 10.15 Appropriateness of Evaluation Measures in the Dimension of System and Technology

Criterion	Measure and Definition
Retrieval effectiveness	*Precision:* Precision = Number of relevant items retrieved/number of retrieved items
	Recall: Recall = Number of relevant items retrieved/number of relevant items in the digital library collection
	Aspectual recall: Ratio of aspects of the search topic identified in the documents saved by the subject to the total number of aspects of the topic
Retrieval efficiency	*Response time to search results:* Response time to present search results after a search request is submitted
Server performance	*Bandwidth:* Bandwidth speed
	Traffic: The volume of total traffic accessing a digital library site
Reliability	*System failure:* Number of system failures occurring in a specific period of time
Response time	*System response time:* End-to-end response time after a page request is made
Fit to task	*Perceived fit to task:* The extent to which a user perceives the appropriateness of a digital library to carry out his/her search task
Speed of page loading	*Page loading speed:* Average downloading speed per page
System connectivity	*Compatibility with other types of systems:* Technical ability to connect to other types of systems
	Ease of connection: Experts' assessment of ease of connection to other systems
Error rate and correction	*Error rate:* Ratio of number of error occurrences over number of page attempts
	Error correction rate: Ratio of corrected errors compared with errors encountered
Integrated search	*Search across collections:* Whether a digital library provides an integrated search function across multiple collections
Customizability	*Capability to adopt system features:* To what extent a digital library is able to add or customize new features
	Availability of API: Whether a digital library provides APIs to developers or users
Open source	*Presence of open source:* Whether a digital library provides a platform for open source
Emerging technologies	*Use of emerging technologies:* Types of emerging technologies incorporated in a digital library
Lifecycle of equipment	*Replacement and update of equipment:* Frequency of replacement and upgrade of equipment
Technical support	*Technical support from the IT team:* Types of technical support from institution's IT team

Table 10.16 Appropriateness of Evaluation Measures in the Dimension of Effects on Users	
Criterion	**Measure and Definition**
Research productivity	*Digital library uses for research:* Frequency of digital library use for research purposes
	Effects of digital library uses on research: In what ways a digital library enhances a user's research productivity
	Research productivity change: To what extent a digital library enhances a user's research productivity
Domain knowledge change	*Perceived domain knowledge change:* Perceived increase of domain knowledge after using a digital library
	Domain knowledge change after digital library uses: Domain knowledge change between the pretest and posttest after digital library use study
Instructional effectiveness	*Digital library uses in teaching:* Frequency of digital library uses in teaching
	Effects of digital library uses on teaching effectiveness: In what ways a digital library improves users' teaching effectiveness
Perception of digital libraries	*Attitude change after digital library uses:* To what extent users change attitude toward digital libraries in general
	Willingness to continue use of a digital library: Perceived willingness to continue use of a digital library
Information literacy/skill change	*Perceived information literacy/skill change:* Perceived improvement of information literacy skill after using a digital library
	Change of information literacy/skill: Change between the pretest and posttest after using a digital library

Dimension 6—services

In the services dimension, 26 measures were identified for 10 criteria. There were two measures rated over 6: overall usefulness (6.145) and overall satisfaction (6.091). These two measures are frequently used in service evaluation, and they were also selected as highly appropriate measures in the context of digital libraries. However, ratings for types of services—uniqueness (4.945), number of reference services provided (4.909), and staff accessible hours (4.873) were comparatively lower. Table 10.17 presents the appropriateness of evaluation measures in the dimension of services.

Dimension 7—preservation

In the preservation dimension, 11 measures were identified for 6 criteria. Among them, exporting capability (6.309), presence of preservation policy (6.164), and migratable data type (6.036) were rated highly appropriate. On the other hand, components of preservation policy (5.618), refresh frequency (5.473), and preservation cost per record (5.400) were rated less appropriate to account for associated evaluation criteria. Table 10.18 presents the appropriateness of evaluation measures in the dimension of preservation.

Dimension 8—administration

Regarding the administration dimension, 25 measures were identified for 11 evaluation criteria. Among them, presence of copyright policy (6.309), presence of sustainability plans (6.091), and presence of strategic plans (5.782) were determined to be the three most appropriate measures for their associated

Table 10.17 Appropriateness of Evaluation Measures in the Dimension of Services

Criterion	Measure and Definition
Overall usefulness	*Perceived overall usefulness:* Users' perceived usefulness of overall services provided in a digital library
	Ways of usefulness: In what ways digital library services are useful to users
Overall satisfaction	*Perceived overall satisfaction:* Users' perceived satisfaction to overall services provided in a digital library
Services for users with disabilities	*Types of services:* Types of services for people with disabilities offered in a digital library
	Usefulness: Disabled users' perceived usefulness
	Ease of use: Disabled users' perceived ease of use of digital library services
	Frequency of service uses by people with disabilities: Frequency of each type of service used by people with disabilities in a specific time period
Overall reliability	*Reliability of services:* Users' perceived reliability
Overall responsiveness	*Perceived responsiveness:* Service responsiveness rated by users
Update	*Update frequency:* Frequency of and types of services updated in a specific time period
Types of services	*Types of user services:* Types of user services offered in a digital library
	Usefulness: Users' perceived usefulness for each type of service
	Ease of use: Users' perceived ease of use for each type of service
	Uniqueness: Number of unique services offered in a digital library compared to library services or other digital library services
	Frequency of service uses: Frequency of each type of service used in a specific time period
Accessibility to managerial staff	*Perceived availability of staff:* User perception of the availability of digital library management staff
	Staff accessible hours: Number of hours users can access digital library management staff
Reference services	*Types of reference services:* Types of reference services offered in a digital library
	Usefulness: Users' perceived usefulness of reference services offered in a digital library
	Ease of use: Users' perceived ease of use of reference services
	Number of reference services provided: Number of times/instances that reference services are provided to users in a specific period of time
	Response time to digital library reference requests: Average response time to a reference request regarding digital library resources
Customized services	*Types of customized services:* Types of customized services offered by a digital library
	Usefulness: Users' perceived usefulness of customized services
	Ease of use: Users' perceived ease of use of customized services
	Use of customized services: Frequency of each type of customized service used in a specific period of time

Table 10.18 Appropriateness of Evaluation Measures in the Dimension of Preservation

Criterion	Measure and Definition
Ability to migrate	*Migratable data type:* Types of data that can be migrated to a digital library
	Exporting capability: Whether a digital library has a function to export data in different formats for preservation
Preservation policy	*Presence of preservation policy:* Whether a digital library has a documented policy regarding preservation practices
	Components of preservation policy: Types of components in the preservation policy
	Strategies of preservation: Types of strategies presented in the preservation policy
Preservation infrastructure	*Types of preservation tools:* Types of preservation tools offered
Institutional support	*Types of support:* Types of support offered by the institution
	Level of support: The extent of support offered from the institution
Cost per record	*Preservation cost per record:* Average cost for preserving a record
Ability to refresh	*Refreshable data type:* Types of data that can be refreshed
	Refresh frequency: How frequently data are refreshed

criteria. On the contrary, the three least appropriate measures were as follows: frequency of marketing/promotion activities (4.982), student hours on digital library (4.800), and number/amount of grant/fundraising attempts (4.673), each of which was given less than five points in the survey. Table 10.19 presents the appropriateness of evaluation measures in the dimension of administration.

Dimension 9—user engagement

In the user engagement dimension, 18 measures were identified for 7 criteria. In particular, 5 measures were suggested for the criterion of site visits, such as frequency, session length, and unique visits. In this dimension, most of the measures were related to measuring resource usage in digital library. As to the most appropriate measures, item viewed (6.000), item downloading (6.000), and frequency of site visits (5.982) were highly rated. Also, the top seven most appropriate measures are related to resource uses in digital library. On the contrary, quantity of user feedback (5.473), ease of purchasing (5.091), and number of orders (4.909) were rated less appropriate. Table 10.20 presents the appropriateness of evaluation measures in the dimension of user engagement.

Dimension 10—context

Finally, 16 measures were suggested for 9 criteria in the context dimension. Interestingly, there was no measure rated over 6 on average, and overall the ratings were relatively lower compared to measures in other dimensions. This implies that they are more difficult to measure. Most of the measures in this dimension are qualitative, which are more prone to subjectivity. The three most appropriate measures were deemed to be user community engagement (5.727), organizational mission—ways of support (5.691), and level of user community engagement (5.691). On the contrary, types of collaborations (5.182), number of collaborations (5.127), and components of guidelines for ethics (5.073) were rated least appropriate. Table 10.21 presents the appropriateness of evaluation measures in the dimension of context.

Table 10.19 Appropriateness of Evaluation Measures in the Dimension of Administration

Criterion	Measure and Definition
Copyright	*Presence of copyright policy:* Whether a digital library has a documented policy regarding copyright management
	Components of copyright policy: Types of components in the copyright policy
Budget	*Budget amount:* Total amount of budget for a digital library
	Proportion of digital library budget: Proportion of digital library budget over total library budget
	Distribution of digital library budget: Distribution of budget for different components of a digital library
Planning	*Presence of strategic plans:* Whether there are documented strategic plans for a digital library
	Components of plans: Components of strategic plans
Staffing	*Number of staff:* Number of staff dedicated to a digital library
	Staff hours on digital library: Number of professional staff hours dedicated to a digital library
	Student hours on digital library: Number of student worker hours dedicated to a digital library
Staff training	*Types of training for digital library staff:* Types of training offered to digital library staff for a specific period of time
	Resources: Amount of resources for training allocated to a digital library
Marketing/ Promotion	*Marketing/promotion methods:* Types of marketing/promotion methods used for promoting a digital library
	Frequency of marketing/promotion activities: Frequency of each type of marketing activity taking place for a digital library in a specific period of time
	Recognition of digital libraries: Number of people aware of a digital library based on survey
Assessment	*Frequency of assessment:* Frequency of digital library assessment in a specific period of time
	Dimensions of assessment: Dimensions of a digital library included in the assessment
Management policy	*Presence of management policy:* Whether there is a documented management policy on a digital library
	Components of management policy: Types of components in the management policy related to a digital library
Grant/Fundraising	*Number/Amount of grant/fundraising:* Total number/amount of grants/fundraising for digital libraries in a specific period of time
	Number/Amount of grant/fundraising attempts: Number/amount of grants/fundraising attempted on digital libraries in a specific period of time
	Number/Amount of grant/fundraising received: Number/amount of grants/fundraising received in a specific period of time
Cost effectiveness	*Cost effectiveness:* The ratio of total digital library uses to the cost
Sustainability plan	*Presence of sustainability plans:* Whether there are documented sustainability plans for a digital library
	Components of plans: Components of sustainability plans for a digital library

Table 10.20 Appropriateness of Evaluation Measures in the Dimension of User Engagement	
Criterion	**Measure and Definition**
Digital object use	*Items viewed:* Number of items viewed
	Time spent on an item: Average time spent on viewing an individual item
	Item downloading: Number of items downloaded.
User feedback	*User feedback channels:* Types of user feedback channels offered in a digital library
	Quantity of user feedback: Amount of user feedback submitted for a digital library
Site visit	*Frequency of site visits:* Number of site visits within a specific period of time
	Session length: Average time spent on a digital library from the beginning to the end of a session
	Frequency of page visits: Number of page visits within a specific period of time
	Unique site visits: Number of unique (site) visits within a specific period of time
	Unique page visits: Number of unique (page) visits within a specific period of time
Integration with external applications	*Compatibility with external applications:* Types of external applications that are compatible with a digital library
	Ease of integration: Degree of ease to integrate a digital library to external application as assessed by an expert
User/community knowledge contribution	*Types of user/community knowledge contributions:* Types of user/community knowledge contribution channels available in a digital library
E-commerce support	*Number of orders:* Number of orders placed for items in a digital library within a specific period of time
	Ease of purchasing: Users' perceived ease of purchasing digital objects
Search pattern	*Queries entered:* Number of queries entered per session
	Categories viewed: Number of category pages viewed per session
	Search result evaluation: Number of search result pages viewed per session

FACTORS HINDERING DIGITAL LIBRARY EVALUATION

Although there are more studies on digital library evaluation criteria and measures, fewer studies concentrate on factors. Multiple factors affect digital library evaluation. Our study explored what factors negatively influence digital library evaluation research and practices. Twelve factors hindering the evaluation of digital libraries were specified. Among them, the three most influential factors were as follows: limited evaluation tools directly applicable to practices (5.82), insufficient experience in evaluation (5.76), and limited awareness of the importance of digital library evaluation (5.59). It seems that the lack of evaluation tools and experience contributed the most to the impediment of digital library evaluation. On the contrary, the three least influential factors were selected as lack of user participation (5.21), limited application of evaluation results (5.18), and lack of incentive for evaluation (5.16). Fig. 10.5 presents the hindering factors affecting digital library evaluation.

Table 10.21 Appropriateness of Evaluation Measures in the Dimension of Context

Criterion	Measure and Definition
Information ethics	*Presence of ethics guidelines:* Whether a digital library has guidelines for ethical issues
	Components of guidelines for ethics: Types of components in the guidelines for ethics
Organizational mission	*Conformity to organizational mission:* The extent to which a digital library conforms to organizational mission
	Ways of support: In what ways a digital library supports the organizational mission
Targeted user community	*User community engagement:* Types of user community engagements (e.g., outreach, collaboration, participation in collection development, etc.)
	Level of user community engagement: To what extent a digital library engages in user communities
Content sharing	*Types of content sharing:* Types of digital library content sharing partners
	Types of resources shared: Types of digital library items shared with partners
	Number of items shared: Number of items shared with partners
Collaboration	*Types of collaboration:* Types of digital library collaboration partners or stakeholders
	Number of collaborations: Number of digital library collaborations in a specific period of time
Social impact	*Types of social impacts:* Types of social impacts of a digital library on community and society
	Level of social impact: To what extent a digital library influences society
Knowledge change in communities	*Ways of knowledge change:* In what ways a digital library supports knowledge change in communities or societies
Multilingual access	*Types of languages:* Types of languages supported by a digital library
Multicultural audiences	*Types of multicultural audiences:* To what extent a digital library engages in multicultural audiences

EVALUATION CHALLENGES

Even though researchers and practitioners realize the importance of digital library evaluation, there are still challenges and problems for performing successful evaluation. First, definitions of digital library evaluation criteria need clarification and to be agreed upon. Heradio et al. (2012) point out that the lack of a standard definition for usability and usefulness is one of the main digital library evaluation challenges from user perspectives. Researchers and practitioners use different terms for the same concept, or they use the same terms but with differing meanings. It is critical to develop standard definitions of digital library evaluation criteria that are agreed upon and adopted as a standard by researchers and practitioners.

Second, digital library evaluation is complex because digital libraries mean different things to different groups (Van House, 2003; Zhang, 2010). Scholars, librarians, and users are the three main stakeholders of digital libraries. However, they do have differing opinions regarding the important criteria for digital library evaluation because they play different roles in its research, creation, management, and use. Although researchers and users consider the ideal situations in digital library evaluation, librarians

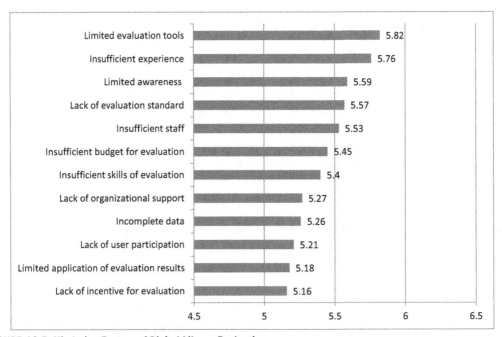

FIGURE 10.5 Hindering Factors of Digital Library Evaluation

have to consider the practical side of its management. It is beneficial to engage scholars, librarians, and users in digital library evaluation in order to have a more comprehensive picture.

Third, evaluation objectives or purposes are the leading forces for digital library evaluation. It is a challenge to match digital library evaluation criteria and measurements with diverse evaluation objectives or purposes. Future research needs to identify the relationships between evaluation objectives and associated criteria and measurements and further offer a set of specific evaluation criteria with associated measures for each specific evaluation objective so practitioners and researchers can mix and match different digital library criteria and measurements for their specific objectives.

Fourth, challenges related to measurements mainly focus on the identification of types of data used for measurements. There are disagreements on the acceptance of different types of measurements, such as the interval status for Likert scales and Likert scales versus fuzzy linguistic modeling (Heradio et al., 2012). It requires further research to identify the most appropriate measurements for different types of evaluation criteria.

Fifth, existing research has suggested that both qualitative and quantitative methods, as well as multiple data collection methods and multiple measurements, are needed for digital library evaluation. As such, the challenge is to find a research team or person who can integrate all the research methods into the assessment of digital libraries. Digital library evaluation requires the involvement of multiple personnel who have expertise in different data collection and data analysis methods.

Sixth, in order to create a comprehensive digital library evaluation framework and associated criteria and measurement, it is beneficial to create a community for evaluation research and to provide data repositories to share research findings and reach consensus (Fuhr et al., 2007). The challenge is how to build this type of community and repositories, in particular internationally. The other related issues are data reuse and data protection.

Seventh, this challenge is related to how to evaluate digital libraries as emergent systems. Digital libraries are dynamic and complex systems (Marchionini, 2000; Saracevic, 2004). Can we evaluate digital libraries while taking into consideration their dynamic changes librarys and all the factors affecting them? Longitudinality and flexibility in evaluation might help overcome this challenge (Marchionini, 2000).

Eighth, the final challenge is related to the diverse types of digital libraries. Digital libraries can be classified based on content, audience, formats, and sponsors, as well as languages. The challenges for building these digital libraries vary, and so do the challenges for evaluating them. For example, Diekema (2012) enumerates the challenges that multilingual digital libraries encounter: cross language barrier, data management, representation in relation to standardization of encoding schemes, development considering cultural differences, and interoperability. Albertson (2015) emphasizes the uniqueness of evaluating visual digital libraries, which demands more user–system interaction. These challenges have to be considered for digital library evaluation. Different types of digital libraries may bring distinctive challenges for digital library evaluation.

REFERENCES

Adams, A., Blandford, A., Lunt, P., 2005. Social empowerment and exclusion: a case study on digital libraries. ACM Trans. Comput.-Hum. Interact. (TOCHI) 12 (2), 174–200.

Albertson, D., 2015. Synthesizing visual digital library research to formulate a user-centered evaluation framework. New Lib. World 116 (3/4), 122–135.

Alipour-Hafezi, M., Amanollahi Nick, H., 2015. Evaluation of digital libraries of Iranian research institutions based on the DigiQUAL protocol. Electron. Lib. 33 (4), 824–841.

Bishop, A.P., Mehra, B., Bazzell, I., Smith, C., 2003. Participatory action research and digital libraries: reframing evaluation. In: Bishop, A.P., Van House, N.A., Buttenfield, B.P. (Eds.), Digital Library Use: Social Practice in Design and Evaluation. The MIT Press, Cambridge, MA, pp. 161–189.

Blandford, A., Keith, S., Connell, I., Edwards, H., 2004. Analytical usability evaluation for digital libraries: a case study. In: Proceedings of the 2004 Joint ACM/IEEE Conference on Digital Libraries. ACM, New York, NY, pp. 27–36.

Blixrud, J.C., 2002. Issues in research library measurement. J. Lib. Admin. 35 (4), 3–5.

Blixrud, J.C., 2003. Measures for electronic use: the ARL E-Metrics project. Statistics in Practice—Measuring and Managing, 73–84. Available from: http://www.lboro.ac.uk/microsites/infosci/lisu/downloads/statsinpractice-pdfs/blixrud.pdf.

Bollen, J., Luce, R., 2002. Evaluation of digital library impact and user communities by analysis of usage patterns. D-Lib Mag. 8 (6), 1–13.

Borgman, C.L., Leazer, G.H., Gilliland-Swetland, A.J., Gazan, R., 2001. Iterative design and evaluation of a geographic digital library for university students: a case study of the Alexandria Digital Earth Prototype (ADEPT). Research and Advanced Technology for Digital Libraries (EBT). Springer, Berlin, Heidelberg, pp. 390–401.

Brophy, P., 2001. Electronic Library Performance Indicators: the EQUINOX project. Serials 14 (1), 5–9.

Buchanan, S., Salako, A., 2009. Evaluating the usability and usefulness of a digital library. Lib. Rev. 58 (9), 638–651.

Buttenfield, B., 1999. Usability evaluation of digital libraries. Sci. Technol. Lib. 17 (3–4), 39–59.

Candela, L., Castelli, D., Pagano, P., Thanos, C., Ioannidis, Y., Koutrika, G., Ross, S., Schek, H., Schuldt, H., 2007. Setting the foundations of digital libraries: the DELOS Manifesto. D-Lib Mag. 13 (3/4.), Available from: http://www.dlib.org/dlib/march07/castelli/03castelli.html.

Carr, R., 2006. What users want: an academic "hybrid" library perspective. Ariadne 46. Available from: http://www.ariadne.ac.uk/issue46/carr/.

Chowdhury, G., Chowdhury, S., 2003. Introduction to Digital Libraries. Facet, London.

Chowdhury, G., Poulter, A., McMenemy, D., 2006. Public library 2.0: towards a new mission for public libraries as a "network of community knowledge." Online Inform. Rev. 30 (4), 454–460.

Choudhury, S., Hobbs, B., Lorie, M., Flores, N., 2002. A framework for evaluating digital library services. D-Lib Mag. 8 (7/8), 1082–9873.

Crabtree, A., Twidale, M.B., O'Brien, J., Nichols, D.M., 1997. Talking in the library: implications for the design of digital libraries. In: Proceedings of the Second ACM International Conference on Digital Libraries. ACM, New York, NY, pp. 221–228.

Diekema, A.R., 2012. Multilinguality in the digital library: a review. The Electron. Lib. 30 (2), 165–181.

Dillon, A., 1999. TIME—A multi-level framework for the design and evaluation of digital libraries. Int. J. Digit. Lib. 2 (2/3), 170–177.

Evans, J., O'Dwyer, A., Schneider, S., 2002. Usability evaluation in the context of digital video archives. In: Fourth DELOS Workshop. Evaluation of Digital Libraries: Testbeds, Measurements, and Metrics, pp. 79–86. Available from: http://wwwold.sztaki.hu/conferences/deval/presentations/DELOSWorkshop4OnEval_report .pdf#page=79.

Ferreira, S.M., Pithan, D.N., 2005. Usability of digital libraries: a study based on the areas of information science and human-computer-interaction. OCLC Syst. Serv. 21 (4), 311–323.

Fuhr, N., Hansen, P., Mabe, M., Micsik, A., Sølvberg, I., 2001. Digital libraries: a generic classification and evaluation scheme. Research, Advanced Technology for Digital Libraries, 5th European Conference. Springer, Berlin, Heidelberg, pp. 187–199.

Fuhr, N., Tsakonas, G., Aalberg, T., Agosti, M., Hansen, P., Kapidakis, S., Sølvberg, I., 2007. Evaluation of digital libraries. Int. J. Digit. Lib. 8 (1), 21–38.

Gonçalves, M.A., Moreira, B.L., Fox, E.A., Watson, L.T., 2007. What is a good digital library? A quality model for digital libraries. Inform. Process. Manag. 43 (5), 1416–1437.

Gonçalves, M.A., Fox, E.A., Watson, L.T., Kipp, N., 2004. Streams, structures, spaces, scenarios, societies (5S): a formal model for digital libraries. ACM Trans. Inform. Syst. 22 (2), 270–312.

Hariri, N., Norouzi, Y., 2011. Determining evaluation criteria for digital libraries' user interface: a review. The Electron. Lib. 29 (5), 698–722.

Heradio, R., Fernández-Amorós, D., Cabrerizo, F.J., Herrera-Viedma, E., 2012. A review of quality evaluation of digital libraries based on users' perceptions. J. Inform. Sci. 38 (3), 269–283.

Hilary, B.H., Druin, A., Bederson, B.B., 2007. Supporting elementary-age children's searching and browsing: design and evaluation using the International Children's Digital Library. J. Am. Soc. Inform. Sci. Technol. 58 (11), 1618. Available from: https://ezproxy.lib.uwm.edu/login?url=http://search.proquest.com/docview/23141 7597?accountid=15078.

Hu, C., Hu, Y., Yan, W., 2014. An empirical study of factors influencing user perception of university digital libraries in China. Lib. Inform. Sci. Res. 36 (3/4), 225–233.

Jeng, J., 2005a. Usability assessment of academic digital libraries: effectiveness, efficiency, satisfaction, and learnability. Libri 55 (2–3), 96–121.

Jeng, J., 2005b. What is usability in the context of the digital library and how can it be measured. Inform. Technol. Lib. 24 (2), 47–56.

Joo, S., Xie, I., 2013. Evaluation constructs and criteria for digital libraries: a document analysis. In: Cool, C., Ng, K.B. (Eds.), Recent Developments in the Design, Construction and Evaluation of Digital Libraries. IGI Global, Hershey, PA, pp. 126–140.

Kani-Zabihi, E., Ghinea, G., Chen, S.Y., 2006. Digital libraries: what do users want? Online Inform. Rev. 30 (4), 396–412.

Kengeri, R., Seals, C.D., Harley, H.D., Reddy, H.P., Fox, E.A., 1999. Usability study of digital libraries: ACM, IEEE-CS, NCSTRL, NDLTD. Int. J. Digit. Lib. 2 (2–3), 157–169.

Kenney, A.R., Sharpe, L.H., Berger, B., 1998. Illustrated book study: digital conversion requirements of printed illustration. In: Nikolaou, C., Stephanidis, C. (Eds.), Research and Advanced Technology for Digital Libraries: Proceedings of the Second European Conference. Springer, Berlin, pp. 279–293.

Khoo, M., Kusunoki, D., MacDonald, C., 2012. Finding problems: when digital library users act as usability evaluators. In: System Science (HICSS), 2012 45th Hawaii International Conference, pp. 1615–1624.

Kim, Y.H., Kim, H.H., 2008. Development and validation of evaluation indicators for a consortium of institutional repositories: a case study of dCollection. J. Am. Soc. Inform. Sci. Technol. 59 (8), 1282–1294.

Kyrillidou, M., Cook, C., Lincoln, Y., 2009. Digital library service quality: what does it look like? In: Tsakonas, G., Papatheodorou, C. (Eds.), Evaluation of Digital Libraries: An Insight into Useful Applications and Methods. Chandos Publishing, Oxford, pp. 187–214.

Kyrillidou, M., Giersch, S., 2005. Developing the DigiQUAL protocol for digital library evaluation. In: Digital Libraries, 2005. Proceedings of the Fifth ACM/IEEE-CS Joint Conference on JCDL'05, pp. 172–173. Available from: http://citeseerx.ist.psu.edu/viewdoc/download?doi=10.1.1.107.9245&rep=rep1&type=pdf.

Lagzian, F., Abrizah, A., Wee, M.C., 2013. An identification of a model for digital library critical success factors. The Electron. Lib. 31 (1), 5–23.

Lai, C.F., Chiu, P.S., Huang, Y.M., Chen, T.S., Huang, T.C., 2014. An evaluation model for digital libraries' user interfaces using fuzzy AHP. Electr. Lib. 32 (1), 83–95.

Lankes, R.D., Gross, M., McClure, C., 2003. Cost, statistics, measures, and standards for digital reference services: a preliminary view. Lib. Trend 51 (3), 401–413.

Larsen, L., 2002. The DLib Test Suite and Metrics Working Group: Harvesting the Experience from the Digital Library Initiative. D-Lib Working Group on Digital Library Metrics Website. Available from: http://www.dlib.org/metrics/public/papers/The_Dlib_Test_Suite_and_Metrics.pdf.

Mansor, Y., Ripin, F.M., 2013. Usability evaluation of online digital manuscript interface. Lib. Phil. Prac. 986, 1–12.

Marchionini, G., 2000. Evaluating digital libraries: a longitudinal and multifaceted view. Lib. Trends 49 (2), 304–333.

Marchionini, G., Plaisant, C., Komlodi, A., 2003. The people in digital libraries: multifaceted approaches to assessing needs and impact. In: Bishop, A.P., Van House, N.A., Buttenfield, B.P. (Eds.), Digital Library Use: Social Practice in Design and Evaluation. The MIT Press, Cambridge, MA, pp. 119–160.

Meyyappan, N., Foo, S., Chowdhury, G.G., 2004. Design and evaluation of a task-based digital library for the academic community. J. Document. 60 (4), 449–475.

Nicholson, S., 2004. A conceptual framework for the holistic measurement and cumulative evaluation of library services. J. Document. 60 (2), 164–182. Available from: http://arizona.openrepository.com/arizona/bitstream/10150/106172/1/holistic.pdf.

The National Initiative for a Networked Cultural Heritage (NINCH), Humanities Advanced Technology and Information Institute (HATII) (2002). The NINCH Guide to Good Practice in the Digital Representation and Management of Cultural Heritage Materials. Available from: http://www.nyu.edu/its/humanities/ninchguide/.

NISO, 2007. A Framework of Guidance for Building Good Digital Collections, 3rd ed. Available from: http://www.niso.org/publications/rp/framework3.pdf.

Noh, Y., 2010. A study on developing evaluation criteria for electronic resources in evaluation indicators of libraries. J. Acad. Librar. 36 (1), 41–52.

Park, S., 2000. Usability, user preferences, effectiveness, and user behaviors when searching individual and integrated full-text databases: implications for digital libraries. J. Am. Soc. Inform. Sci. 51 (5), 456–468.

Saracevic, T., 2000. Digital library evaluation: toward evolution of concepts. Lib. Trends 49 (2), 350–369.

Saracevic, T., 2004. Evaluation of digital libraries: an overview. In: Notes of the DELOS WP7 Workshop on the Evaluation of Digital Libraries, pp. 13–30. Available from: http://comminfo.rutgers.edu/~tefko/DL_evaluation_Delos.pdf.

Shim, W., 2002. Measuring services, resources, users and use in the networked environment. J. Lib. Admin. 35 (4), 71–84.

Strauss, A.L., Corbin, J., 1990. Basics of Qualitative Research. Sage Publications, Newbury Park, CA.

Stejskal, J., Hajek, P., 2015. Effectiveness of digital library services as a basis for decision-making in public organizations. Lib. Inform. Sci. Res. 37 (4), 346–352.

Tsakonas, G., Kapidakis, S., Papatheodorou, C., 2004. Evaluation of user interaction in digital libraries. In: Notes of the DELOS WP7 Workshop on the Evaluation of Digital Libraries, pp. 45–60. Available from: http://citeseerx.ist.psu.edu/viewdoc/download?doi=10.1.1.101.9642&rep=rep1&type=pdf.

Tsakonas, G., Mitrelis, A., Papachristopoulos, L., Papatheodorou, C., 2013. An exploration of the digital library evaluation literature based on an ontological representation. J. Am. Soc. Inform. Sci. Technol. 64 (9), 1914–1926.

Tsakonas, G., Papatheodorou, C., 2008. Exploring usefulness and usability in the evaluation of open acess digital libraries. Inform. Process. Manag. 44 (3), 1234–1250.

Tsakonas, G., Papatheodorou, C., 2011. An ontological representation of the digital library evaluation domain. J. Am. Soc. Inform. Sci. Technol. 62 (8), 1577–1593.

Van House, N.A., 2003. Digital libraries and collaborative knowledge construction. In: Bishop, A.P., Van House, N.A., Buttenfield, B.P. (Eds.), Digital Library Use: Social Practice in Design and Evaluation. The MIT Press, Cambridge, MA, pp. 271–295.

Van House, N., Weil, B., McClure, C., 1990. Measuring Academic Library Performance: A Practical Approach. American Library Association, Chicago.

Vullo, G., 2010. A global approach to digital library evaluation. Liber Quart. 20 (2), 169–178.

Waugh, L., Hamner, J., Klein, J., Brannon, S., 2015. Evaluating the University of North Texas' Digital Collections and Institutional Repository: an exploratory assessment of stakeholder perceptions and use. J. Acad. Librar. 41 (6), 744–750.

Xie, H., 2006. Evaluation of digital libraries: criteria and problems from users' perspectives. Lib. Inform. Sci. Res. 28 (3), 433–452.

Xie, H.I., 2008. Users' evaluation of digital libraries (DLs): their uses, their criteria, and their assessment. Inform. Process. Manag. 44 (3), 1346–1373.

Cheng, Y.M., 2014. Why do users intend to continue using the digital library? An integrated perspective. Aslib J. Inform. Manag. 66 (6), 640–662.

Zhang, Y., 2010. Developing a holistic model for digital library evaluation. J. Am. Soc. Inform. Sci. Technol. 61 (1), 88–110.

NEW DEVELOPMENTS AND CHALLENGES

Since the emergence of digital libraries in the 1990s, the development of digital libraries has entered a new era. The new directions of digital libraries include social media applications, large-scale digital libraries, multilingual digital libraries, and digital curation. Simultaneously, researchers and practitioners face challenges and problems brought by these new developments as well as problems inherited from the initial development of digital libraries.

SOCIAL MEDIA APPLICATIONS AND THE IMPACT ON DIGITAL LIBRARIES
DEFINITIONS OF SOCIAL MEDIA TOOLS

The most popularly applied social media in digital libraries include blogs, microblogs, photo sharing, podcasts, RSS feeds, and social networks, such as Facebook and Twitter. There is some cross-classification as a few social media applications have more than one function. Table 11.1 offers definitions of different types of social media presented in one of the author's recent work (Xie and Stevenson, 2014).

SOCIAL MEDIA APPLICATIONS IN DIGITAL LIBRARIES

The evolution of web technologies has allowed social media tools to become a part of digital libraries. Users of digital library are no longer passive receivers of information (Mitropoulos et al., 2014); now they can respond and contribute to the digital library landscape. Social media tools have been applied in libraries and digital libraries but have not been fully investigated. According to Emery and Schifeling (2015), academic libraries have a long history of adopting new technologies including social media tools. There are no specific data regarding the application of Twitter in digital libraries. We know, however, that the application of social media in digital libraries has been gradually increasing. The increased development of digital libraries has resulted in many institutions treating them as an extension of their institution, as is the case with the University of California and the California Digital Library. However, it is important for digital librarians to know their users in order to provide appropriate digital outreach services. As many institutions have already implemented social media into other facets of services, it seems natural to begin to add social media to digital library interfaces.

Digital libraries either have their own unique social media pages or use their institution's social media pages to disseminate information to users and followers. For example, Twitter, Facebook, and social bookmarking sites were incorporated into the California Digital Library, opening more opportunities for the organization to communicate with the existing and potential user communities (Starr, 2010). Figs. 11.1 and 11.2 present examples of the applications of social media tools in digital libraries.

Table 11.1 Definitions of Different Types of Social Media

Types	Definitions	Examples
Blogs	Opinion or information-based web sites consisting of discrete entries or "posts"; readers can comment on and engage in ongoing discussions with the blogger and/or other readers of the blog.	Blog
Microblogs	Allows users to communicate with followers by writing short messages, typically 140 characters, or sharing images or links to web pages. Content is frequently tagged by users with a hashtag, which is a method of categorizing posts across multiple users.	Twitter, Tumblr
Photosharing	Online image and video hosting sites that allow users to share, comment, and connect through posted images.	Facebook, Flickr, Pinterest, Twitter, Instagram
Podcasts	Multimedia digital file, typically an audio file, that is stored on the Internet and is available to download, and is similar to a radio broadcast that is available freely online.	Podcast
RSS feeds	Rich Site Summary or Really Simple Syndication is a frequently updated web feed that indicates news, events, and blog entries that a user can subscribe to and follow. RSS takes current headlines from different web sites and pushes those headlines down to your computer for quick scanning.	RSS feeds
Social networks	Online platform for users to connect and communicate with friends, professional associates, and others with shared backgrounds, interests, and activities.	Facebook, Twitter, Reddit

Adapted from Xie and Stevenson (2014), Table 1. (p. 504)

Researchers and practitioners have called to incorporate social media tools into libraries (Bhatt and Kumar, 2014; Cho, 2013; Paul, 2014) and digital libraries to promote communication with users (Gu and Widén-Wulff, 2011). More specifically, librarians need to find better approaches to communicate with users through social media (Gu and Widén-Wulff, 2011). It is a challenge to examine the interplay between information activities within two important spaces: the social web and the library (Kronquist-Berg, 2014). In particular, it is even more of a challenge to investigate users' and librarians' activities in the social web and digital libraries. Buigues-García and Giménez-Chornet (2012) identify the most implemented social media tools in libraries as Facebook, Twitter, user information services such as RSS, the publication of bulletins, and blogs. The survey results indicate that the majority prefer that libraries use social media tools to provide services to them (Bhatt and Kumar, 2014).

Schrier (2011) suggests that social media tools can promote digital collections, and recommends principles including listening, participation, transparency, policy, and strategy for digital librarians to integrate social media into a digital library development strategic plan. Griffin and Taylor (2013) assess social media's impact on special collections and conclude that only moderate success is achieved. It seems that the incorporation of digital collections into an existing social site has more impact than introducing social media tools to digital libraries. For example, posting images to Flickr results in a 200% increase in accessing the associated digital collection (Michel and Tzoc, 2010). In another study,

FIGURE 11.1 California Digital Library Twitter Page

FIGURE 11.2 Library of Congress Podcast Page

the results show that objects from digital collections uploaded to Historypin are accessed three times more than on their original platform. Interestingly, not all collections are the same in terms of their access. One of the six collections tested uncover more access in its library web site than in Historypin. It is determined that the nature of the collection contributes to the difference. Another revealing finding is that Historypin and Pinterest direct only less than 1% of the traffic back to the original digital library sites (Baggett and Gibbs, 2014).

In one of the author's own studies, Xie and Stevenson (2014) explored social media application in digital libraries. In order to represent a variety of digital libraries developed or sponsored by different types of organizations, 10 institutions were selected from the following cultural institutional types for inclusion in the study: public libraries, academic libraries, museums, government agencies, and international organizations. Each institution's digital library has its own social media application, and these social media applications are well maintained and updated. Among all the social media tools, Facebook and Twitter are the most heavily utilized in these institutions overall, whereas blogs and Flickr are the most popular choices to convey or promote digital library–related information. While eight of the ten institutions use blogs to communicate digital library information, the Denver Public Library's Digital Library is the only one offering a digital library–specific blog, entitled "Western History and Genealogy."

Furthermore, in the same study, Xie and Stevenson (2014) find that while social media tools are mostly available on the institution homepage, users can also engage in social media activities on the digital library's collection level specifically in about 50% of the selected institutions. Because few institutions have dedicated social media tools for digital libraries, it is difficult to identify the patterns or frequency of updates for these tools. The interaction between librarians and users is the key to applying social media to digital libraries; in the study, different levels of interactions were observed, including very strong, strong, and weak.

FUNCTIONS OF SOCIAL MEDIA IN DIGITAL LIBRARIES

Previous research suggests that the inclusion of social media within a digital library brings benefits to users' utilization of digital libraries. According to McDonnell and Shiri (2011), integration of social media into a digital library leads to more successful search results because users are more comfortable using the digital library. Paul (2014) recommends three activities that library and information services can engage in to take advantage of social media tools: information communication, knowledge organization, and knowledge distribution. These functions are echoed by the author's own study results. The findings of Xie and Stevenson's study (2014) show that providing information, marketing/promotion, peer-to-peer connections, and information sharing are the main functions that social media plays in a digital library environment. All institutions in the study use social media, in particular Facebook and Twitter, to convey information related to their library or digital library activities or status, such as when digital library maintenance is scheduled. Many institutions employ social media as marketing/promotion tools to promote their upcoming digital collections and events. Some institutions actively engage their user group on Flickr by asking users to unveil the mystery of a specific image. Facebook and Twitter are the two most popular tools for peer-to-peer connections between librarians/institutions and users as well as between the users themselves. The results indicate that the item level of the digital collection allows the best opportunity for connection between the digital library and users through social media. Information sharing occurs when institutions link their digital collections with other digital or physical collections through different social media tools. Blogs, Facebook, Twitter, Flickr, RSS feeds, and YouTube are the most common tools to share information with users.

The main function of social media, as used by libraries, is the promotion of collections and services. Khan and Bhatti (2012) conducted a study that explored how different types of social media applications could be utilized to market library services; they conclude that social media tools such as Facebook, wikis, LinkedIn, blogs, and YouTube are considered positive for the promotion of library services. However, it should be noted that the findings of this study are based on perspectives from librarians and library and information science school academics. It is equally important to survey users in order to make decisions regarding the selection of social media applications for libraries and digital libraries. Taranto (2009) notices that the integration of social media has become part of library outreach programs. Twitter is deemed an effective tool to attract new audiences to the California Digital Library (Calisphere), as well as to promote its collections (Starr, 2010). However, very little research has been conducted to investigate the functions of social media in digital libraries.

In another of the author's research projects (Xie and Stevenson, 2015, unpublished data), 15,713 tweets were analyzed from the Twitter pages of 15 digital libraries. The number of tweets per digital library varied from 18 to 1272. The number of followers for each of these Twitter accounts ranges between 92 and 9138, and they had a following range of 37–2088. Five types of functions were identified from the data: information, promotion, related sources, social connection, and social identity; each type has its own subcategories. The functions that social media plays with respect to digital libraries based on the gathered Twitter data are the following:

- Information
  - information-digital library
  - information-digital library-problem
  - information-digital library-reference question
  - information-digital library-staff
  - information-institutional
- Promotion
  - promotion-digital library-collection
  - promotion-digital library-connection
  - promotion-digital library-event
- Related resources
  - related resources-digital library
  - related resources-institutional
- Social connection
  - social connection-digital library-interaction
- Social identity
  - social identity-digital library-collection
  - social identity-digital library-institutional
  - social identity-digital library-interaction
  - social identity-digital library-social media

The data reveal that the majority of tweets focus on offering information rather than on interaction. Since social media tools are created to facilitate interactions, the use of social media in digital libraries has therefore not reached its full potential. More research is needed to identify the reasons for this phenomenon in an effort to better understand how to promote interaction in the application of social media in digital libraries.

Social media has inherent problems that have been recognized by researchers in the LIS field including information divides, digital divides, information overload, and poor information literacy skills. Moreover, challenges exist related to the dynamic nature of the information presented in social media and how to organize social media information that is by nature disorganized (Bawden and Robinson, 2009; Kronquist-Berg, 2014; Serantes, 2009). Most important, social media application in digital libraries is just at its infancy. The return on investment is not yet evident, and there is an urgent need to promote user engagement. Providing prompt responses to user interactions and providing relevant information are the keys to engaging users (Lamont and Nielsen, 2015; Webb and Laing, 2015).

LARGE-SCALE DIGITAL LIBRARIES
CHARACTERISTICS OF LARGE-SCALE DIGITAL LIBRARIES

The development of large-scale digital libraries is rooted in years of research. Early digital library concepts emerged from visionary thinkers in the 1930s and 1940s (Bush, 1945; Wells, 1938) even before the birth of modern computers. The first digital libraries began to take shape in the 1990s, funded by several agencies of the US government (Griffin, 2005), with projects developing metadata standards, architectures, and digitization best practices. One of the earliest large-scale digital libraries, the American Memory Project, is an extension of the largest physical library in the world—the Library of Congress. The project focuses on American history and culture and includes digitized copies of original primary sources. The project lays the groundwork for future large-scale digital libraries. "While many of these large-scale digital libraries have been created for the general public, some serve more specific audiences of scholars and educators in different disciplines or domains" (Zavalina and Vassilieva, 2014).

More recent large-scale digital libraries have several characteristics in common. Most obvious is that they incorporate large collections. American Memory was considered a large project when it was created and contained more than 135 collections. HathiTrust, a more recent large-scale digital library, contains 13,000,000 volumes with 4.5 billion pages of text (Hinze et al., 2015). Another feature common to large-scale digital libraries is that many organizations must collaborate in support of the project; a single institution cannot do it alone. HathiTrust, Smithsonian Institute, National Archives and Records Administration, New York Public Library, etc. are the partners of the Digital Public Library of America (DPLA). It is worth noting that the open invitation to join enables DPLA to build its own contributor community (Vandegrift, 2013). The need to integrate a variety of metadata is also a common aspect of large-scale digital libraries. It is imperative for large-scale digital libraries involving multiple partners to find ways to allow their resources—particularly the metadata associated with the digital resources—to be combined together into a unified collection. One of the core operational services is creating a central metadata repository to organize collection items in the National Science Digital Library (NSDL). The NSDL architecture consists of a common core metadata vocabulary, core metadata with different domain specific metadata, and harvesting of the metadata and its use (Lagoze and Van de Sompel, 2001; Zia, 2001). At the same time, based on a user study of potential user groups of the HathiTrust Digital Library (Fenlon et al., 2014), metadata enrichment that advances the traditional bibliographic record is highly needed. It includes incorporating scholar-enriched metadata, tracking the origin of enriched metadata, and enabling interoperability of metadata across different domains.

A final characteristic of many large-scale digital libraries is the need for multilingual support. Europeana was created as Europe's digital library with 4.5 million digital items drawn from every member of the European Commission (Purday, 2009). Understandably, it is vital that projects such as this embrace and support multiple languages. Thus, common functions of large-scale digital libraries must include the assimilation of objects and metadata schemas from multiple contributing partners, often with diverse languages, into cohesive large collections.

CHALLENGES AND PROBLEMS

Large-scale digital libraries can offer users access to a wealth of high-quality resources, but they also face challenges. Although successful, HathiTrust presents an example of the challenge of copyright issues facing many large-scale digital libraries. Due to legal restrictions, the collection is not always able to provide access to the desired content. Another challenge associated with HathiTrust and other large-scale digital libraries is that it is not easy for users to find relevant and useful documents from large-scale digital libraries, which apply traditional lexically based retrieval techniques. A semantic search approach is suggested to overcome the lexical search approach (Hinze et al., 2015). The DPLA is a large-scale digital library functioning as a portal, aggregating digital resources from disparate collections; it exemplifies another challenge facing large-scale digital libraries: sustainability. Initially funded by a private foundation as well as the National Endowment for the Humanities, funding is limited, and the project will eventually have to seek further options to sustain itself. A fourth challenge of large-scale digital libraries can be found in Europeana. Considering that this digital library has digital objects from 1000 collections throughout Europe (Purday, 2009), it is evident that integrating metadata schemas from a variety of institutions is difficult. Although large-scale digital libraries have come a long way from the imagination of futurist thinkers, issues regarding copyright, search functions, sustainability, and metadata interoperability still require more thought, more attention, and more research. The last but not the least significant challenge is that users apply different information-searching strategies in the large-scale digital libraries, in particular in distinct domain areas. However, there has been no systematic investigation of information searching in domain-specific large-scale digital libraries. The comparison of user searching in NSDL and Opening History (OH) shows that the domain and interface design both contribute to the differences in searching in different domain-specific large-scale digital libraries. From a domain perspective, concepts and objects are the most frequently searched queries in NSDL whereas place, person, corporate body, ethnic group, event, and class of persons are the most common queries in OH. This suggests that different-faceted searches are required for different domains. From an interface design perspective, a digital library with more advanced options attracts more users to engage in more sophisticated searches. There is hence a need for creating advanced search options in large-scale digital libraries (Zavalina and Vassilieva, 2014).

MULTILINGUAL DIGITAL LIBRARIES
THE NEED FOR MULTILINGUAL DIGITAL LIBRARIES

Researchers have agreed that the internationalization of the user interface is important (Agosti et al., 2009a). Multilingual digital libraries offer valuable information resources for diverse user groups that speak different languages. They further reinforce individual cultures, promoting diversity and improving a global information infrastructure (Budzise-Weaver et al., 2012; Nichols et al., 2005). There is a rapid growth in research on multilingual digital libraries "since the need to support retrieval across languages becomes even more urgent given the increasing interaction between different cultures" (Vassilakaki and Garoufallou, 2013). Relevant literature can be classified into two areas: the "system oriented" and the "users oriented." System-oriented research focuses on offering solutions for effective multilingual information retrieval from a technical perspective, whereas users-oriented research concentrates on examining users' behaviors and expectations in interacting with multilingual digital libraries (Vassilakaki and Garoufallou, 2013).

Language is an essential part of a user's cultural identity. According to Gäde (2014), two steps are essential for the creation of multilingual user interfaces: internalization and localization. First, with respect to internationalization, flexible source code is needed to satisfy linguistic or culture-specific requirements. Second, regarding localization, the customization of date formats, symbols, icons, and other culture-specific elements needs to be done for each supported language. Some of these customizations are language and culture dependent such as date formats. Large and Moukdad (2000) bring to light the challenge for languages that use non-Roman script. Adoption of multiple language interfaces is the key for multilingualism in digital libraries. Two typical solutions involve an active interface language and passive interface language change options. An active interface language option allows users to change the interface language via drop-down menus, and a passive interface language option automatically chooses users' languages based on their data, such as IP address and language settings (Gäde, 2014). Focusing on the strategies of building multilingual digital libraries, Budzise-Weaver et al. (2012) conducted a case study of American multilingual digital libraries. They found that collaboration and crowdsourcing were the most important strategies for creating multilingual digital libraries.

After surveying 358 subjects from 19 different countries, Wu et al. (2012) report their findings on multilingual services, multilingual search functions, and interfaces. Their findings indicate the need for the following multilingual services: translation functions for terminologies, having materials organized by subjects, search functions for multilingual information, and full text translation. Specific to multilingual functions and interfaces, the most desirable capabilities are translations for less commonly used languages, organizing search results by languages, search interfaces for multilingual information, having a multilingual translation toolbar, and offering multilingual translation dictionaries. User needs and expectations for multilingual access features are affected by the user's own language; in particular, non-English users experienced strong multilingual needs for multilingual information access. According to Petrelli et al. (2002), search assistance and interactive information retrieval functions are even more important when users have to deal with content in multiple languages. Performing various tasks using an interactive multilingual prototype, study participants expressed the need to choose the language they wanted to conduct a search in based on the individual's skills and the information-seeking task. Based on their findings, the authors suggest that user-assisted query translation should be offered as an advanced search option if the initial query translation fails or does not satisfy the user's information need. A survey focusing on multilingual access to Europeana found that the majority of users (80%) were willing to control the query translation process themselves (Agosti et al., 2009b).

MULTILINGUAL DIGITAL LIBRARIES: USER STUDIES

User studies are essential for the development and enhancement of multilingual digital libraries. Multilingual digital libraries need to investigate their target users' needs and preferences. Bilal and Bachir (2007b) point out that lack of language skills is one of the contributing reasons that Arabic-speaking children do not recognize the representations embedded in the interfaces of the International Children's Digital Library (ICDL). Arabic-speaking children have search behaviors in ICDL unique to that demographic. As expected, and highlighting the importance of a multilingual interface, they clicked on "Arabic" from the pull-down menu to browse Arabic books. Intuitive design across different cultures and backgrounds is essential for the development of multilingual digital libraries (Bilal and Bachir, 2007a,b).

Agosti and her associates (2009a) performed user studies on the use of Europeana utilizing user surveys on multilingual information access. Browsing and searching were the main activities for users to interact with multilingual content. While 88% of the users at least sometimes browsed multilingual content, 84% of them at least sometimes searched for multilingual content. It seems that participants of the study show different preferences in interacting with query formulation and expansion functions. More than half of them (52%) never or seldom specified their desired language for the results. The majority of them wanted to have the results displayed in multiple target languages. Another interesting finding is that 80% of them preferred to interact with the query translation process and to iteratively refine it. Preferences of the study participants were equally distributed among the following ways of presenting multilingual results: in relevance order with results in different languages, organized by languages and then relevance, and highlighting results in different languages in different colors. The complexity of the user interface may contribute to user preferences in regard to language; 44% of participants indicated they did not like or were unsure about the multilingual results filtering function. Only 28% of them showed an interest in having a multilingual results translation function, mainly because of the advanced language skills of the participants. The majority of the participants preferred a multilingual user interface in their native language. Interestingly, the majority of them also liked to switch the user interface into their native language manually rather than have it automatically switched by the system. In another user study of the European Library Web portal, Agosti et al. (2010) found that switching the interface language automatically does not assist users in navigating the web portal, with poor translation quality further contributing to the problem. Marlow et al. (2008) explored users' needs and the design implications for the Multimatch Project, which offers multilingual/multimedia access to cultural heritage artifacts on the web. Automatic query translation was found to be the option for users conducting searches in unknown languages. Thesauri could be used to cover variations of words across languages. Users also needed assistance in browsing documents in foreign languages, the solution for which is to provide an interface that automatically translates summaries and/or documents into alternate languages.

Keegan and Cunningham (2005) examined 4 weeks of usage logs from the New Zealand Digital Library (NZDL) while switching the default language settings between English and Maori every week. They found that users performed more searches during the English weeks. During the Maori weeks, 74% of the users changed the language setting back to English. Moreover, users exhibited different searching and browsing behaviors during the English weeks in contrast to the Maori weeks. Users in Maori sessions preferred browsing, whereas users in English sessions were more likely to search. In a different setting, Gäde and Petras (2014) analyzed usage log data of the Europeana digital library. They discovered that the majority of users selected their native language in their browser (69%) and when using Google (91%), but only 31% of them selected their native language in Europeana. It suggests that users of Europeana accept the default English version, which contradicts the results regarding their language selection behavior with Google and browsers. The proposed explanation is that users do not change the language in Europeana because it requires greater effort, infrequent use of the system, a perceived lack of benefit, or lack of comprehension of the default language. Further analysis of query language, usage of language facets, and language of viewed objects can shed more light on the issue.

MULTILINGUAL DIGITAL LIBRARY LANGUAGE SEARCH FUNCTIONS

A survey was conducted by the authors to examine the functions associated with language of several key multilingual digital libraries including Europeana, European Library, International Children's Digital Library, Meeting of Frontiers, The Perseus Digital Library, and Project Gutenberg. Table 11.2 presents these digital libraries, their sponsors, content coverage, targeted audience, default language, and types of language-selection functions. The number of available languages is presented in parentheses immediately following each language function. The results show that users can set the language to search or browse using one of three main approaches: (1) select a language option from the main page (or sometimes any page) of a digital library; (2) select a language option from advanced search options; (3) select a language option when they refine their searches.

Oard (1997) points out that challenges for multilingual digital library development focus on query formulation and document selection. Another challenge is the delivery of high-quality documents selected by users. Moreover, he raises many of the nontechnical issues with digital libraries related to the diverse needs of users and the social impact and availability of technology. Recently, upon reviewing the relevant literature on multilingualism in digital library, Diekema (2012) identifies several following challenges that multilingual digital libraries face:

- *Cross-language barrier*: the key for multilingual digital libraries is to enable users to search across different languages. The first challenge is the availability of digital information objects in various languages.
- *Data management*: this challenge is associated with translating metadata, instructions, and the interface in a way that makes sense to users. Internationalization and localization are the key. Indexing multilingual documents and using OCR documents are the related challenges.
- *Representation*: this challenge corresponds to the selection and standardization of encoding schemes and the fact that not all languages are included in encoding schemes.
- *Development*: the challenge here is to create international software by considering subtle and sensitive cultural differences. Cross-cultural collaboration is the solution. Another challenge is related to representing cultural materials to ensure accuracy of the information.
- *Interoperability*: this challenge is to build a system architecture and data-sharing method that allow digital libraries to translate one query into all of the applicable languages and present relevant items from all of the languages represented in the digital library.

For interoperability, digital libraries must be able to establish common strategies, data models, processes, and structures in order to build and support multilingual collections (Vassilakaki and Garoufallou, 2013). After analyzing four multilingual digital libraries, Budzise-Weaver et al. (2012) conclude that machine translation and cross-language information retrieval techniques have not been applied and implemented into the development of digital libraries. While some information scientists focus on system-side technical challenges of digital libraries such as automatic translation, other researchers believe the challenge for multilingual digital library research is largely associated with their users and the countries and cultures they represent. Clough and Eleta (2012) emphasize the importance of understanding users, their profiles, and the context of digital library use in order to effectively design multilingual digital libraries. Gäde (2014) focuses on several issues regarding user studies of multilingual digital libraries, including small sample sizes on the basis of the target population and recruiting users who speak different languages. Very few studies analyze digital library usage data from the perspective

Table 11.2 Multilingual Digital Libraries and Their Search Functions

Name	Sponsors	Coverage	Targeted Audience	Default Language	Language Selection Functions
Europeana	Cofunded by the European Union—museums, archives, libraries, etc.	Cultural heritage—books and manuscripts, photos and paintings, television and film, sculpture and crafts, diaries and maps, sheet music, recordings, drawings, newspapers, letters, and newsreels	General	English	Drop-down menu (web page—any pages including main page) (30) Search: refine by language (30) Translate into (52) any web page
European Library	CENL (The Conference of European National Librarians), LIBER (Ligue des Bibliothèques Européennes de Recherche—Association of European Research Libraries) and CERL (Consortium of European Research Libraries)	Digital items and bibliographic records: humanities, social sciences, natural sciences and mathematics, biomedical sciences, and technological sciences	Research community worldwide	English	Drop-down menu (web page—any pages including main page) (36) Search: refine by language (45) Advanced: refine by language (400+) 36 (any web pages)
International Children's Digital Library	International Children's Digital Library Foundation National Science Foundation (NSF) and the Institute for Museum and Library Services (IMLS), a collaborative project between the University of Maryland and the Internet Archive	Books: a collection of books that represents outstanding historical and contemporary books from the world	Children	English	Main page (5), search by language link Search: refine by language and location (20) Book search by language and advanced search (79) Keyword search (79) Book summary depends on available language (drop-down menu)
Meeting of Frontiers	US and Russian libraries: The Library of Congress, Russian State Library (RSL), etc.	Manuscripts, maps, films, photographs, sound recordings, printed material, and sheet music	For use in US and Russian schools and libraries and by the general public in both countries	Both support (2) English and Russian	Web page (2) Russian is not supported in search page
The Perseus Digital Library	Annenberg/CPB Projects, Digital Library Initiative, etc.	Mainly the history, literature, and culture of the Greco-Roman world and other disciplines	Not specified	English	Language support depends on works Search by language (6)

The number of available languages are presented in parentheses immediately following each language function.

of users from different countries with different languages. Most important, Vassilakaki and Garoufal-lou (2013) stress the need for user studies to generate tangible and usable findings that can apply to the enhancement of the user interface design for multilingual digital libraries.

DIGITAL/DATA CURATION
DIGITAL/DATA CURATION DEFINITIONS

Digital libraries not only contain digital objects but also digital data. Digital data curation is a new area for digital library researchers and practitioners to explore. According to Walters (2009), digital libraries and archives set the foundation for digital curation and associated programs. Citing the DELOS Digital Library Reference Model Foundations for Digital Libraries, Chowdhury (2010) identifies the shifts in the field of digital libraries as signified by moving from a content-centric to a person-centric system and focusing on communication, collaboration, and interaction instead of just accessing information in the digital library. Weber et al. (2012) point out that "digital research data have introduced a new set of collection, preservation, and service demands into the tradition of digital librarianship" (p. 305). Digital curation is a collaborative activity starting with research planning and ending with data reuse.

According to the Digital Curation Center (DCC) (n.d.), "digital curation is maintaining and adding value to a trusted body of digital research data for current and future use; it encompasses the active management of data throughout the research lifecycle." Lord and Macdonald (2003) define digital curation as "the activity of managing and promoting the use of data from its point of creation, to ensure it is fit for contemporary purpose, and available for discovery and re-use. For dynamic datasets this may mean continuous enrichment or updating to keep it fit for purpose. Higher levels of curation will also involve maintaining links with annotation and with other published materials" (p.12). Data curation is a comparatively older concept; however, in many contexts, "data" and "digital objects" are treated the same. Therefore, digital curation and data curation have been considered as synonyms in recent publications (Ball, 2010; Giaretta, 2007). Digital curation is an interdisciplinary field, embracing archival, information, library, and computer science (Dobreva and Duff, 2015).

DIGITAL/DATA CURATION PROCESS AND ISSUES

The lifecycle of data curation has been the focus of research. (Cervone, 2010; Higgins, 2009, 2011; Lynch 2008). Yakel (2007) further highlights the key areas of data curation: the lifecycle of data from record creation; the involvement of records creators and digital curators; the appraisal and selection of materials; access development and provision; and ensuring preservation, usability, and accessibility of the objects. In addition to the above areas, Ramírez (2011) also emphasizes the importance of creating metadata for descriptions, proving the authenticity and reliability of the data, and complying with data requirement standards. Citing other researchers' works (Brandt, 2007; Macdonald and Martinez-Uribe, 2010), Harris-Pierce and Quan Liu (2012) identify several issues in data curation: storage capacity, data sharing, data description and organization, confidentiality, intellectual property rights, complexity, and developing new approaches to managing data.

Walters (2009) proposes a model for data curation program development in a university setting. The four main components of the model consist of: (1) the assessment of how faculty create, store, manage, share, and use data; (2) the selection, design, and development of the technology platforms to support lifecycle process of data; (3) the selection and creation of service models addressing methods of importing large data sets, metadata creation, cost model for data storage use and reuse, as well as data transfer; and (4) the development of data curation policy. The Curation Lifecycle Model as proposed by the DCC is shown in Fig. 11.3. Digital data, consisting of digital objects and databases, are at the center of the model. The full lifecycle of the digital curation includes the following four levels:

- *Description and representation information*: create appropriate and standard metadata to ensure data can be used and reused
- *Preservation planning*: plan for preservation through the digital curation lifecycle
- *Community watch and participation*: monitor community data and engage in the development of standards, tools, and software
- *Curate and preserve*: pursue planned management and administrative actions

On the basis of a comprehensive literature review, Poole (2015) discovers that sharing data, open access, and the reuse of science data are the key issues in research on digital curation. Not all scholars are willing to share. For researchers who see the benefits of sharing data, only a minority of them actually do,

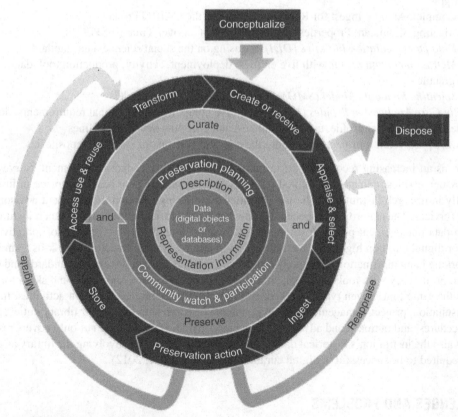

FIGURE 11.3 DCC Curation Lifecycle Model

(http://www.dcc.ac.uk/resources/curation-lifecycle-model)

because of various reasons including standards, time, intellectual property, potentially revealing errors, and funding (Borgman, 2010; Scaramozzino et al., 2012; Schofield et al., 2009; Tenopir et al., 2011). After conducting focus groups with faculty and other researchers, McLure et al. (2014) reveal the needs of researchers in relation to data curation. There is a definite need for data curation as researchers are involved in data collection, especially as their file sizes increase moving into the future. They consider the key stages in accomplishing projects as the planning, creating, producing and transferring stages. For library support, they expect to have opportunities for training regarding data management, but most importantly, they would like to have a central system that collects, stores, and disseminates data for them. Peer and Green (2012) report how an open data repository, including experimental data, metadata, and files, is created for a specific research community. The feedback from the community shows the success of the repository, which enables researchers to play out their data management plan as part of the study. Alerts regarding newly available data promote further research on this subject.

Ball (2010) summarizes a variety of standards and tools for data curation. For example, the following are used for the preservation of metadata:

- *The PREMIS Data Dictionary* containing five entities: intellectual entities, objects, events, agents, and rights
- The Complex Archive Ingest for Repository Objects (the CAIRO Project)
- Investigating Significant Properties of Electronic Content over Time (InSPECT)
- *The Data Documentation Initiative (DDI)*: focusing on the social science data standard
- *The MOLES metadata profile* with five entities: deployment, activity, production tool, data, and data granule
- *The Scientific Metadata Model (SMDM)* with several associated models
- *Dublin Core Application Profiles (DCAP)* with five components: functional requirements, domain model, description set profile, usage guidelines, and encoding syntax guidelines
- *Software preservation project*: examining the cost and benefits for software repositories

There is an increasing recognition of the importance of research data management. Survey data from UK universities indicate that limited research on data management has taken place in libraries, especially in research institutions. The top priorities are offering research management advisory and training services. The majority of respondents state that their libraries have engaged in their institution's research data management policy development (Cox and Pinfield, 2014). Analysis of job advertisements for digital curation highlights the following top five required knowledge and skills: familiarity with working in an information technology–intensive environment, knowledge of standards and specifications, proficiency with tools and applications, project management, and functional skills for curation. At the same time, seven types of responsibilities are also identified: curation activities, training and consultation, project management, professional and research activities, other library duties, policy and procedures, and outreach and advocacy (Kim et al., 2013). Data curation not only covers research data but also the institution's historical data. Collaboration, in particular involving the library as a partner, is required to be successful in digital curation (Latham and Poe, 2012).

CHALLENGES AND PROBLEMS

Challenges can be associated with different aspects and perspectives on digital curation. The Cornell University Library (CUL) Data Working Group (DaWG) (2008) raises challenges from organizations' perspectives: financial sustainability, appraisal and selection, digital preservation, intellectual property, confidentiality and privacy, and participation by data owners. Harris-Pierce and Quan Liu (2012) discover that there is a gap in LIS education on data curation. The LIS curriculum is not able to keep pace with the need for information professionals who are able to manage data curation. In addition, standardizing course objectives and learning outcomes is essential for adequate data curation education. Peer and Green (2012) specify the following challenges in creating an open data repository: policy, technology, sustainability, extensibility and scalability, and interoperability. In surveying current activities, Cox and Pinfield (2014) discover that respondents believe that library staff do not have adequate skills needed for research data management and that resources and funding issues are additional challenges for digital curation.

Generated from the two data curation summits, Weber et al. (2012) propose that future research on data curation should focus on different approaches of educational training, interoperability issues between publishing workflow and academic research data archiving, and finding a commonly agreed upon vocabulary. On the basis of a review of the literature, Poole (2015) effectively summarizes the challenges and future research on digital curation as follows:

- *Sustainability*: the challenges are connected to the technical, social and economic infrastructure, funding models, plans, and policies.
- *Costing*: the challenges correspond to costs required for the lifecycle of the data and metrics for the cost model.
- *Planning and policy*: the challenges focus on the development of local, national, and international policies, in particular policies on legal issues.
- *Training and education*: the challenges concentrate on the role of library and information science, a balanced curriculum, and training for researchers and professionals.
- *Researcher practice*: the challenges are relevant to the understanding of the data practices of researchers in different domains.
- *Raising awareness*: the challenges are in regard to the awareness of data sharing, data reuse, and advocating for the significance of digital curation.

Most important, digital curation is a complicated activity mainly because of the increasing complexity of digital objects and the evolution of the contexts of using these objects (Dobreva and Duff, 2015).

CHALLENGES AND PROBLEMS OF DIGITAL LIBRARIES

Despite the successful development of digital libraries and extensive research on different aspects of digital libraries, researchers and practitioners still face a variety of challenges and problems. The following is a summary of critical issues digital libraries face, including the key challenges as well as associated research questions for future study.

- *Diverse user needs and information behaviors*: children, students, elderly, and disabled users differ in domain knowledge, system knowledge, information-retrieval knowledge, interaction styles, and physical and cognitive development. In particular, people with disabilities encounter physical, cognitive, and affective challenges when interacting with multimedia materials in digital libraries. In addition, multilingual digital libraries are essential for global access. Related questions for further research include the following:

- How can we design digital libraries to support diverse user needs and user behaviors?
- How can digital libraries best be designed to support people with disabilities?
- What are the preferred features for multilingual digital library searching and browsing?
- Can one-size-fits-all digital libraries be developed?
- *The gap between research and practice*: it is important to promote the communication between research and practice. Practice benefits from research outcomes, while at the same time, research also needs to investigate issues that are relevant to practitioners. Related questions for further research include the following:
  - How to facilitate communication between researchers and practitioners?
  - How to promote collaboration between researchers and practitioners?
  - How to promote the application of digital library research into practice?
- *Interoperability, standards, and aggregation of digital libraries*: major efforts have been undertaken to aggregate content from individual digital libraries and to provide portals for global searching and retrieval. A lack of interoperability and standards associated with data conversion, metadata, interface design, etc. has been recognized as a critical problem and a fundamental challenge since the early days of digital library development, arising from the fact that digital libraries are designed and developed by different organizations. It is not only a technical challenge but also a source of user frustration. Related questions for further research include the following:
  - What are the key issues of interoperability in creating large-scale digital libraries?
  - What are the standards critical to the development of digital libraries?
  - How to ensure interoperability and the application of standards among digital libraries?
- *Ensure sustainability*: digital library sustainability is a complicated topic with related issues ranging from the longevity of digital information—including the stability of digital formats and storage medium and flexibility to incorporate new items—to funding for digital libraries. Related questions for further research include the following:
  - How to ensure the stability of digital formats and storage media and solve associated obsolescence issues?
  - How to ensure a digital library has the flexibility to add new digital objects after its initial development?
  - How to ensure the funding for digital libraries after the initial development?
- *Copyright protection and fair use*: copyright is an ongoing concern for digital library developers and users. The concept of fair use must be fully considered in the development of digital libraries while do not overstep and infringe on copyright. There is no clear and comprehensive guidance on copyright and fair use in digital libraries. Related questions for further research include the following:
  - What are the main concerns of copyright issues in digital library development?
  - What are the best approaches to provide clear copyright information?
  - What are the best solutions to solve copyright problems in digital libraries?
  - What are the challenges in protecting copyright in global digital library environments and at the same time support fair use?
- *Complexity of digital library evaluation*: the dynamic and complicated nature of digital libraries greatly impacts the complexity of digital library evaluation including evaluation dimensions, evaluation criteria, and measurements. Different stakeholders of digital libraries have diverse

perceptions in terms of the importance of digital library evaluation criteria. Related questions for further research include:

- What are the main components of digital library evaluation models/framework?
- What are the key digital library evaluation dimensions, criteria, and associated measurements?
- How can digital library evaluation criteria and measurements be matched with diverse evaluation objectives or purposes?
- How to apply both qualitative and quantitative approaches to evaluate digital libraries?
- What are the similarities and differences in evaluation criteria and measurements from digital library researchers, designers, and users?

- *New web technologies applied to digital libraries*: various social media tools have been applied to promote the use of digital libraries. However, the use of social media in digital libraries has not reached its full potential to enhance interactivity between librarians and their users. The dynamic, ephemeral nature of the information provided through social media also poses a challenge. As new technologies emerge, it is important to consider how they might be applied to digital libraries, as well as their corresponding benefits and problems. Related questions for further research include the following:

- How to promote interactions between librarians and users of digital libraries?
- How to organize and manage the dynamic information created and distributed through social media?
- How to deal with the inherent problems of social media in relation to digital divides, information overload, and poor information literacy skills?
- What is the role of linked data in making digital library resources visible and discoverable on the open web?
- What are the new developments in technologies that can be applied to digital libraries, and what are their benefits and problems?

- *Mobility of digital libraries*: a trend of digital library use is its mobile access. Page views in Europeana from personal mobile devices increased at a rate four times higher than that of office devices between 2010 and 2011 (Nicholas et al., 2013). Mitropoulos et al. (2014) also confirm that mobile access to digital libraries increases along with the rise in the use of mobile phones. This trend of mobile access suggests the overall trend for future digital library use. As such, it has significant impact on digital library interface design. Related questions for further research include the following:

- What are the unique behaviors of mobile users in their interactions with digital libraries?
- How to design digital library interfaces to facilitate the use of different mobile devices and different browsers to effectively interact with digital libraries?

REFERENCES

Agosti, M., Crivellari, F., Deambrosis, G., Ferro, N., Gäde, M., Petras, V., et al., 2009a. D2.1.1: report on user preferences and information retrieval scenarios for multilingual access in Europeana—EuropeanaConnect Project. Available from: http://www.europeanaconnect.eu/documents/D2.1.1_eConnect_Report_User_Preference_MLIA_v1.0_20091222.zip.

Agosti, M., Crivellari, F., Di Nunzio, G.M., Ioannidis, Y.E., Stamatogiannakis, E., Triantafyllidi, M.L., Vayanou, M., 2009b. Searching and browsing digital library catalogues: a combined log analysis for the European Library. In: Agosti, M., Esposito, F., Thanos, C. (Eds.), Proceedings from IRCDL '09, Padova, Italy. pp. 120–135.

Agosti, M., Ferro, N., Peters, C., de Rijke, M., Smeaton, A., 2010. Multilingual and multimodal information access evaluation. International Conference of the Cross-Language Evaluation Forum, vol. 6360, CLEF 2010, Padua, Italy, September 20–23, 2010.

Baggett, M., Gibbs, R., 2014. Historypin and Pinterest for digital collections: measuring the impact of image-based social tools on discovery and access. J. Lib. Admin. 54 (1), 11–22.

Ball, A., 2010. Review of data management lifecycle models. Project Report. University of Bath, Bath, UK. Available from: http://opus.bath.ac.uk/28587/1/redm1rep120110ab10.pdf.

Bawden, D., Robinson, L., 2009. The dark side of information: overload, anxiety and other paradoxes and pathologies. J. Inform. Sci. 35 (2), 180–191.

Bhatt, R.K., Kumar, A., 2014. Student opinion on the use of social networking tools by libraries: a case study of Jawaharlal Nehru University, New Delhi. Electr. Lib. 32 (5), 594–602.

Bilal, D., Bachir, I., 2007a. Children's interaction with cross-cultural and multilingual digital libraries. II. Information seeking, success, and affective experience. Inform. Process. Manage. 43 (1), 65–80.

Bilal, D., Bachir, I., 2007b. Children's interaction with cross-cultural and multilingual digital libraries: I. Understanding interface design representations. Inform. Process. Manage. 43 (1), 47–64.

Borgman, C.L., 2010. Who will share what, with whom, when, and why? Fifth China—North America Library Conference, September 8–12, 2010, Beijing, China. Available from: http://works.bepress.com/cgi/viewcontent.cgi?article=1237&context=borgman.

Brandt, E., 2007. How tangible mock-ups support design collaboration. Knowledge Technol. Policy 20 (3), 179–192.

Budzise-Weaver, T., Chen, J., Mitchell, M., 2012. Collaboration and crowdsourcing: the cases of multilingual digital libraries. Electr. Lib. 30 (2), 220–232.

Buigues-García, M., Giménez-Chornet, V., 2012. Impact of Web 2.0 on national libraries. Int. J. Inform. Manage. 32 (1), 3–10.

Bush, V., 1945. As we may think. The Atlantic Monthly 176 (1), 101–108.

Cervone, H.F., 2010. An overview of virtual and cloud computing. OCLC Syst. Services 26 (3), 162–165.

Cho, A., 2013. YouTube and academic libraries: building a digital collection. J. Electr. Resources Lib. 25 (1), 39–50.

Chowdhury, G., 2010. From digital libraries to digital preservation research: the importance of users and context. J. Doc. 66 (2), 207–223.

Clough, P., Eleta, I., 2012. Investigating language skills and field of knowledge on multilingual information access in digital libraries. In: Wei, C., Li, Y., Gwo, C. (Eds.), Multimedia Storage and Retrieval Innovations for Digital Library Systems. IGI Global, Hershey, PA, pp. 85–100.

Cox, A.M., Pinfield, S., 2014. Research data management and libraries: current activities and future priorities. J. Lib. Inform. Sci. 46 (4), 299–316.

Diekema, A.R., 2012. Multilinguality in the digital library: a review. Electr. Lib. 30 (2), 165–181.

Digital Curation Center (DCC). (n.d.). DCC Charter and Statement of Principles. Available from: http://www.dcc.ac.uk/about-us/dcc-charter/dcc-charter-and-statement-principles.

Dobreva, M., Duff, W., 2015. The ever changing face of digital curation: introduction to the special issue on digital curation. Arch. Sci. 15 (2), 97–100.

Emery, K., Schifeling, T., 2015. Libraries using Twitter better: insights on engagement from food trucks. Proceedings of ACRL 2015. Available from: http://www.ala.org/acrl/sites/ala.org.acrl/files/content/conferences/confsandpreconfs/2015/Emery_Schifeling.pdf.

Fenlon, K., Senseney, M., Green, H., Bhattacharyya, S., Willis, C., Downie, J.S., 2014. Scholar built collections: a study of user requirements for research in large scale digital libraries. Proceedings of the American Society for Information Science and Technology, 51 (1), 1–10.

Gäde, M., 2014. Country and language level differences in multilingual digital libraries (Doctoral dissertation, Humboldt-Universität zu Berlin, Philosophische Fakultät I). Available from: http://edoc.hu-berlin.de /dissertationen/gaede-maria-2014-02-05/PDF/gaede.pdf.

Gäde, M., Petras, V., 2014. Multilingual interface preferences. Proceedings of the 5th Information Interaction in Context Symposium. ACM, New York, pp. 231–234.

Giaretta, D., 2007. The CASPAR approach to digital preservation. Int. J. Digital Curation 2 (1), 112–121.

Griffin, S.M., 2005. Funding for digital libraries research past and present. D-Lib Magazine, 11 (7/8). Available from: http://dlib.org/dlib/july05/griffin/07griffin.html.

Griffin, M., Taylor, T.I., 2013. Of fans, friends, and followers: methods for assessing social media outreach in special collections repositories. J. Web Lib. 7 (3), 255–271.

Gu, F., Widén-Wulff, G., 2011. Scholarly communication and possible changes in the context of social media: a Finnish case study. Electr. Lib. 29 (6), 762–776.

Harris-Pierce, R.L., Quan Liu, Y., 2012. Is data curation education at library and information science schools in North America adequate? New Lib. World 113 (11/12), 598–613.

Higgins, S., 2009. Information security management: the ISO 27000 (ISO 27K) series. Available from: http://www.dcc.ac.uk/resources/briefing-papers/standards-watch-papers/information-security-management-iso-27000-iso-27k-s#1.

Higgins, S., 2011. Digital curation: the emergence of a new discipline. Int. J. Digital Curation 6 (2), 78–88.

Hinze, A., Taube-Schock, C., Bainbridge, D., Matamua, R., Downie, J.S., 2015. Improving access to large-scale digital libraries through semantic-enhanced search and disambiguation. Proceedings of the 15th ACM/IEEE-CE on Joint Conference on Digital Libraries. ACM, New York, pp. 147–156.

Keegan, T.T., Cunningham, S.J., 2005. Language preference in a bi-language digital library. In: Marlino, M., Sumner, T., Shipman, F. (Eds.), Proceedings of the 5th ACM/IEEE-CS Joint Conference on Digital Libraries. ACM, New York, pp. 174–175.

Khan, S.A., Bhatti, R., 2012. Application of social media in marketing of library and information services: a case study from Pakistan. Webology 9 (1), 1–8.

Kim, J., Warga, E., Moen, W., 2013. Competencies required for digital curation: an analysis of job advertisements. Int. J. Digital Curation 8 (1), 66–83.

Kronquist-Berg, M., 2014. Social media and public libraries: exploring information activities of library professionals and users. PhD thesis, Åbo Akademi University, Finland. Available from: http://www.doria.fi /handle/10024/94661.

Lagoze, C., Van de Sompel, H., 2001. The Open Archives Initiative: building a low-barrier interoperability framework. Proceedings of the 1st ACM/IEEE-CS Joint Conference on Digital Libraries. ACM, New York, pp. 54–62.

Lamont, L., Nielsen, J., 2015. Calculating value: a digital library's social media campaign. Bottom Line 28 (4), 106–111.

Large, A., Moukdad, H., 2000. Multilingual access to web resources: an overview. Program 34 (1), 43–58.

Latham, B., Poe, J.W., 2012. The library as partner in university data curation: a case study in collaboration. J. Web Lib. 6 (4), 288–304.

Lord, P., Macdonald, A., 2003. E-Science curation report: data curation for e-Science in the UK: an audit to establish requirements for future curation and provision. Digital Archiving Consultancy Limited.

Lynch, C., 2008. Big data: how do your data grow? Nature 455 (7209), 28–29.

Macdonald, S., Martinez-Uribe, L., 2010. Collaboration to data curation: harnessing institutional expertise. New Rev. Acad. Lib. 16 (S1), 4–16.

Marlow, J., Clough, P., Ireson, N., Cigarrán Recuero, J., Artiles, J., Debole, F., 2008. The MultiMatch project: multilingual/multimedia access to cultural heritage on the web. In: J., Trant, D., Bearman, (Eds.), Museums on the Web Conference (MW2008): Proceedings, Toronto: Archives & Museum Informatics. Available from: http://www.museumsandtheweb.com/mw2008/papers/marlow/marlow.html.

McDonnell, M., Shiri, A., 2011. Social search: a taxonomy of, and a user-centred approach to, social web search. Program 45 (1), 6–28.

McLure, M., Level, A.V., Cranston, C.L., Oehlerts, B., Culbertson, M., 2014. Data curation: a study of researcher practices and needs. Portal 14 (2), 139–164.

Michel, J.P., Tzoc, E., 2010. Automated bulk uploading of images and metadata to Flickr. J. Web Lib. 4 (4), 435–448.

Mitropoulos, S.S., Baltasis, G.D., Rodios, M., Douligeris, C., 2014. SociaLib: a collaborative digital library model platform using Web 2.0. Electr. Lib. 32 (5), 622–641.

Nicholas, D., Clark, D., Rowlands, I., Jamali, H.R., 2013. Information on the go: a case study of Europeana mobile users. J. Am. Soc. Inform. Sci. Technol. 64 (7), 1311–1322.

Nichols, D.M., Witten, I.H., Keegan, T.T., Bainbridge, D., Dewsnip, M., 2005. Digital libraries and minority languages. New Rev. Hypermedia Multimedia 11 (2), 139–155.

Oard, D., 1997. Serving users in many languages: cross-language information retrieval for digital libraries. D-Lib Magazine. Available from: http://dlib.org/dlib/december97/oard/12oard.html.

Paul, K., 2014. Social networking: a powerful tool for the LIS professionals in digital era. Asian Journal of Multidisciplinary Studies, 2 (6). Available from: http://www.ajms.co.in/sites/ajms/index.php/ajms/article/view/366.

Peer, L., Green, A., 2012. Building an open data repository for a specialized research community: process, challenges and lessons. Int. J. Digital Curation 7 (1), 151–162.

Petrelli, D., Beaulieu, M., Sanderson, M., Hansen, P., 2002. User requirement elicitation for cross-language information retrieval. New Rev. Inform. Behav. Res. 3, 17–35.

Poole, A.H., 2015. How has your science data grown? Digital curation and the human factor: a critical literature review. Arch. Sci. 15 (2), 101–139.

Purday, J., 2009. Think culture: Europeana. EU from concept to construction. Electr. Lib. 27 (6), 919–937.

Ramírez, M.L., 2011. Opinion: Whose role is it anyway?: a library practitioner's appraisal of the digital data deluge. Bull. Am. Soc. Inform. Sci. Technol. 37 (5), 21–23.

Scaramozzino, J.M., Ramírez, M.L., McGaughey, K.J., 2012. A study of faculty data curation behaviors and attitudes at a teaching-centered university. Coll. Res. Lib. 73 (4), 349–365.

Schofield, P.N., Bubela, T., Weaver, T., Portilla, L., Brown, S.D., Hancock, J.M., Rosenthal, N., 2009. Post-publication sharing of data and tools. Nature 461 (7261), 171–173.

Schrier, R.A., 2011. Digital librarianship & social media: the digital library as conversation facilitator. D-Lib Magazine, 17 (7/8). Available from: http://dlib.org/dlib/july11/schrier/07schrier.html.

Serantes, L.C., 2009. Untangling the relationship between libraries, young adults and Web 2.0: the necessity of a critical perspective. Lib. Rev. 58 (3), 237–251.

Starr, J., 2010. California digital library in Twitter land. Comput. Lib. 30 (7), 23–27.

Taranto, B., 2009. It's not just about curators anymore: special collections in the digital age. RBM 10 (1), 30–36.

Tenopir, C., Allard, S., Douglass, K., Aydinoglu, A.U., Wu, L., Read, E., Frame, M., 2011. Data sharing by scientists: practices and perceptions. PloS one 6 (6), e21101.

Vandegrift, M., 2013. The Digital Public Library of America: details, the librarian response and the future. In the Library with the Lead Pipe. Available from: http://www.inthelibrarywiththeleadpipe.org/2013/dpla/.

Vassilakaki, E.E., Garoufallou, E.G., 2013. Multilingual digital libraries: a review of issues in system-centered and user-centered studies, information retrieval and user behavior. Int. Inform. Lib. Rev. 45 (1/2), 3–19.

Walters, T.O., 2009. Data curation program development in US universities: The Georgia Institute of Technology example. Int. J. Digital Curation 4 (3), 83–92.

Webb, H., Laing, K., 2015. Engaging with social media: The Emily Carr University of Art and Design Library Experience. Art Doc. 34 (1), 137–151.

Weber, N.M., Palmer, C.L., Chao, T.C., 2012. Current trends and future directions in data curation research and education. J. Web Lib. 6 (4), 305–320.

Wells, H.G., 1938. World Brain. Methuen & Co., Ltd, London.

Wu, D., He, D., Luo, B., 2012. Multilingual needs and expectations in digital libraries: a survey of academic users with different languages. Electr. Lib. 30 (2), 182–197.

Xie, I., Stevenson, J., 2014. Social media application in digital libraries. Online Inform. Rev. 38 (4), 502–523.

Yakel, E., 2007. Digital curation. OCLC Syst. Services 23 (4), 335–340.

Zavalina, O., Vassilieva, E.V., 2014. Understanding the information needs of large-scale digital library users. Lib. Resources Tech. Services 58 (2), 84–99.

Zia, L.L., 2001. The NSF national science, technology, engineering, and mathematics education digital library (NSDL) program: new projects and a progress report. D-Lib Magazine, 10 (3). Available from: http://dlib.org/dlib/march04/zia/03zia.html.

DIGITIZATION GUIDES, STANDARDS, AND BEST PRACTICES

ASSOCIATION FOR LIBRARY COLLECTIONS & TECHNICAL SERVICES (ALCTS). (2013): MINIMUM DIGITIZATION CAPTURE RECOMMENDATIONS (http://www.ala.org/alcts/resources/preserv/minimum-digitization-capture-recommendations)

Creator: The Association for Library Collections & Technical Services Preservation and Reformatting Section

Date released: June 2013

Intended for libraries, these digitization recommendations focus on technical specifications for both static and time-based media. Although preservation is not addressed, it is suggested that following these guidelines will prevent the need for re-digitization. File naming, metadata, and storage are also covered.

FEDERAL AGENCIES DIGITIZATION GUIDELINES INITIATIVE (FADGI). (2010): THE TECHNICAL GUIDELINES FOR DIGITIZING CULTURAL HERITAGE MATERIALS: CREATION OF RASTER IMAGE MASTER FILES (http://www.digitizationguidelines.gov/guidelines/FADGI_Still_Image-Tech_Guidelines_2010-08-24.pdf)

Creator: Federal Agencies Digitization Initiative (FADGI) – Still Image Working Group

Date released: 2009, Revised August 2010

Meant for those working with still images, these guidelines outline best practices for digitization of cultural heritage materials. The document focuses on the creation of digital raster (master) files to allow for online access and hard copy reproduction and may not be appropriate for preservation efforts. Image capture, color encoding, digital image performance, workflows, metadata, file formats, file naming, storage, and quality management are addressed.

A FRAMEWORK OF GUIDANCE FOR BUILDING GOOD DIGITAL COLLECTIONS. 3RD EDITION (2007): NISO FRAMEWORK ADVISORY GROUP (http://www.niso.org/publications/rp/framework3.pdf)

Creator: National Information Standards Organization (NISO) Framework Working Group

Date released: December 2007 (3rd edition)

Meant for cultural heritage and funding organizations, this framework reviews the creation of digital collections, identifies resources that support the creation of local digitization practices, and encourages community involvement in the development of digitization best practices. Principles and resources related to collections, objects, metadata, and initiatives are addressed.

THE NINCH GUIDE TO GOOD PRACTICE IN THE DIGITAL REPRESENTATION AND MANAGEMENT OF CULTURAL HERITAGE MATERIALS. (2002): THE NATIONAL INITIATIVE FOR A NETWORKED CULTURAL HERITAGE (NINCH) (http://www.nyu.edu/its/humanities/ninchguide/)

Creators: Humanities Advanced Technology and Information Institute (HATII), University of Glasgow, National Initiative for a Networked Cultural Heritage (NINCH)

Date released: October 2002

With the aim of illustrating the importance of adopting good practice, this guide presents recommendations for digital representation and management of cultural heritage materials. Meant for a variety of audiences, it covers project planning, selection of materials, rights management, digitization, text encoding, image capture and management, audio/video capture and management, quality control and assurance, distribution, sustainability, assessment, digital asset management, preservation, equipment, metadata, and sampling. Includes helpful checklists and other resources.

INSTITUTIONAL GUIDELINES

BCR: BIBLIOGRAPHICAL CENTER FOR RESEARCH (2008). BCR'S CDP DIGITAL IMAGING BEST PRACTICES. (2008): UPDATED VERSION OF WESTERN STATES DIGITAL IMAGING BEST PRACTICES (http://mwdl.org/docs/digital-imaging-bp_2.0.pdf)

Creator: Bibliographical Center for Research's Collaborative Digitization Program Digital Imaging Best Practices Working Group

Date released: June 2008 (2nd version)

Intended for libraries and cultural heritage organizations in the western United States, this document presents best practices for digital imaging of text, photographs, maps, and graphic materials. General principles, digitization, hardware, software, workspace, quality control, description/metadata, and storage are addressed. This document is not meant for those working with audio, video, moving images, oversized materials, bound materials, or materials with nonstandard formats or sizes.

CALIFORNIA DIGITAL LIBRARY (CDL). (2011): CDL GUIDELINES FOR DIGITAL IMAGES. VERSION 2.0 (http://www.cdlib.org/services/access_publishing/dsc/contribute/docs/cdl_gdi_v2.pdf)

Creator: California Digital Library (CDL) Digital Object Working Group

Date released: January 2011 (2nd version)

Meant for institutions working with CDL, these guidelines address the preparation of digital master image files for reprocessing. File formats, compression, watermarking, cameras, and thumbnails are outlined, though the document does not cover resolution, pixel array, bit depth, workflow, or quality control. Preservation is not explicitly addressed.

CARLI: CONSORTIUM OF ACADEMIC AND RESEARCH LIBRARIES IN ILLINOIS. (2009; 2013): CARLI GUIDELINES FOR THE CREATION OF DIGITAL COLLECTIONS: DIGITIZATION BEST PRACTICES FOR IMAGES (http://www.carli.illinois.edu/sites/files/digital_collections/documentation/guidelines_for_images.pdf)

Creator: Consortium of Academic and Research Libraries in Illinois (CARLI) Digital Collection Users' Group (DCUG)

Date released: March 2013

This document describes best practices for the digitization of images, or two-dimensional, non-textual materials such as photographs, maps, and paintings. Recommendations for image quality, file formats, storage, access, monitor calibration, and technical metadata are included.

CARLI: CONSORTIUM OF ACADEMIC AND RESEARCH LIBRARIES IN ILLINOIS. (2009; 2013): CARLI GUIDELINES FOR THE CREATION OF DIGITAL COLLECTIONS: DIGITIZATION BEST PRACTICES FOR TEXT (http://www.carli.illinois.edu/sites/files/digital_collections/documentation/guidelines_for_text.pdf)

Creator: Consortium of Academic and Research Libraries in Illinois (CARLI) Digital Collection Users' Group (DCUG)

Date released: March 2013

These guidelines address best practices for digitizing text, including image quality, file formats, OCR, text encoding, storage, and access. Intended for libraries, it outlines digital imaging, scanning, derivative and access images, file naming, machine-readable text, software, transcription, digital object creation, and more.

CARLI: CONSORTIUM OF ACADEMIC AND RESEARCH LIBRARIES IN ILLINOIS. (2009; REVISED 2013): CARLI GUIDELINES FOR THE CREATION OF DIGITAL COLLECTIONS: DIGITIZATION BEST PRACTICES FOR AUDIO (http://www.carli.illinois.edu/sites/files/digital_collections/documentation/guidelines_for_audio.pdf)

Creator: Consortium of Academic and Research Libraries in Illinois (CARLI) Digital Collection Users' Group (DCUG)

Date released: March 2013

Meant for those working with CARLI digital collections, this document provides recommendations for digitizing audio such as oral history and natural sounds. Sample rates, bit depths, file formats, software, hardware, and workflow are addressed. Background information on digital audio is also included.

CARLI: CONSORTIUM OF ACADEMIC AND RESEARCH LIBRARIES IN ILLINOIS. (2010; REVISED 2013): CARLI GUIDELINES FOR THE CREATION OF DIGITAL COLLECTIONS: DIGITIZATION BEST PRACTICES FOR MOVING IMAGES (http://www.carli.illinois.edu/sites/files/digital_collections/documentation/guidelines_for_video.pdf)

Creator: Consortium of Academic and Research Libraries in Illinois (CARLI) Digital Collection Users' Group (DCUG) Digital Collections Users' Group, Standards Subcommittee.

Date released: March 2013

A lengthier CARLI document, these recommendations review best practices for digitizing analog and born digital moving images for both preservation and web access. Suggestions for technical specifications, metadata, file formats, web delivery, workflow, hardware, and software are outlined. A primer on digital video is also included.

YALE UNIVERSITY. (2010): DIGITIZATION SHARED PRACTICES—STILL IMAGES VERSION 1.0 (http://www.yale.edu/digitalcoffee/downloads/DigitalCoffee_SharedPractices_%5Bv1.0%5D.pdf)

Creator: Yale Digital Coffee Group

Date released: August 2010

Meant for institutions that are involved with in-house digitization, this document provides a variety of recommendations for image capture, storage, and preservation. Specifically, suggestions for working with text, photographs, maps, 3D objects, and graphic materials are presented, including hardware, software, metadata, quality control, file naming, storage, recording, and verification. Recommendations for audio, video, 3D modeling, born digital materials, prepress matters, staffing, workflow, selection, and system/network architecture are not addressed.

EXAMPLES OF METADATA SCHEMAS REVIEWED IN CHAPTER 5

B

Table B.1 MODS (Version 3)

Types of Elements	Definition
TitleInfo	A word, phrase, character, or group of characters, normally appearing in a resource, that names it or the work contained in it
Name	The name of a person, organization, or event (conference, meeting, etc.) associated in some way with the resource
TypesofResource	A term that specifies the characteristics and general type of content of the resource
Genre	A term or terms that designate a category characterizing a particular style, form, or content, such as artistic, musical, literary composition, etc.
OriginInfo	Information about the origin of the resource, including place of origin or publication, publisher/originator, and dates associated with the resource
Language	A designation of the language in which the content of a resource is expressed
PhysicalDescription	Describes the physical attributes of the information resource
Abstract	A summary of the content of the resource
TableofContents	A description of the contents of a resource
TargetAudience	A description of the intellectual level of the audience for which the resource is intended
Note	General textual information relating to a resource
Subject	A term or phrase representing the primary topic(s) on which a work is focused
Classification	A designation applied to a resource that indicates the subject by applying a formal system of coding and organizing resources according to subject areas
RelatedItem	Information that identifies other resources related to the one being described
Identifier	Contains a unique standard number or code that distinctively identifies a resource
Location	Identifies the institution or repository holding the resource, or the electronic location in the form of a URL where it is available
AccessCondition	Information about restrictions imposed on access to a resource
Part	The designation of physical parts of a resource in a detailed form
Extension	Provides additional information not covered by MODS
RecordInfo	Information about the metadata record

Top-level Elements in MODS (http://www.loc.gov/standards/mods/userguide/generalapp.html)

Discover Digital Libraries. http://dx.doi.org/10.1016/B978-0-12-417112-1.00013-2

Table B.2 METS (Version 1.9)	
Types of Elements	**Definition**
Element <mets>	The root element <mets> establishes the container for the information being stored and/or transmitted by the standard.
Element <metsHdr>	The METS header element <metsHdr> captures metadata about the METS document itself, not the digital object the METS document encodes. Although it records a more limited set of metadata, it is very similar in function and purpose to the headers employed in other schema, such as the Text Encoding Initiative (TEI) or the Encoded Archival Description (EAD).
Element <agent>	The agent element <agent> provides for various parties and their roles with respect to the METS record to be documented.
Element <name>	The element <name> can be used to record the full name of the document agent.
Element <note>	The <note> element can be used to record any additional information regarding the agent's activities with respect to the METS document.
Element <altRecordID>	The alternative record identifier element <altRecordID> allows one to use alternative record identifier values for the digital object represented by the METS document; the primary record identifier is stored in the OBJID attribute in the root <mets> element.
Element <metsDocumentID>	The metsDocument identifier element <metsDocumentID> allows a unique identifier to be assigned to the METS document itself. This may be different from the OBJID attribute value in the root <mets> element, which uniquely identifies the entire digital object represented by the METS document.
Element <dmdSec>	A descriptive metadata section <dmdSec> records descriptive metadata pertaining to the METS object as a whole or one of its components. The <dmdSec> element conforms to same generic datatype as the <techMD>, <rightsMD>, <sourceMD>, and <digiprovMD> elements and supports the same subelements and attributes. A descriptive metadata element can either wrap the metadata (mdWrap) or reference it in an external location (mdRef) or both. METS allows multiple <dmdSec> elements, and descriptive metadata can be associated with any METS element that supports a DMDID attribute. Descriptive metadata can be expressed according to many current description standards (i.e., MARC, MODS, Dublin Core, TEI Header, EAD, VRA, FGDC, DDI) or a locally produced XML schema.
Element <amdSec>	The administrative metadata section <amdSec> contains the administrative metadata pertaining to the digital object, its components, and any original source material from which the digital object is derived. The <amdSec> is separated into four subsections that accommodate technical metadata (techMD), intellectual property rights (rightsMD), analog/digital source metadata (sourceMD), and digital provenance metadata (digiprovMD). Each of these subsections can either wrap the metadata (mdWrap) or reference it in an external location (mdRef) or both.
Element <fileSec>	The overall purpose of the content file section element <fileSec> is to provide an inventory of and the location for the content files that comprise the digital object being described in the METS document.
Element <fileGrp>	A sequence of file group elements <fileGrp> can be used to group the digital files comprising the content of a METS object either into a flat arrangement or, because each file group element can itself contain one or more file group elements, into a nested (hierarchical) arrangement.

Table B.2   METS (Version 1.9) *(cont.)*

Types of Elements	Definition
Element <structMap>	The structural map section <structMap> is the heart of a METS document. It provides a means for organizing the digital content represented by the <file> elements in the <fileSec> of the METS document into a coherent hierarchical structure. Such a hierarchical structure can be presented to users to facilitate their comprehension and navigation of the digital content. It can further be applied to any purpose requiring an understanding of the structural relationship of the content files or parts of the content files. The organization may be specified to any level of granularity (intellectual and or physical) that is desired. Since the <structMap> element is repeatable, more than one organization can be applied to the digital content represented by the METS document.
Element <structLink>	The structural link section element <structLink> allows for the specification of hyperlinks among the different components of a METS structure that are delineated in a structural map. This element is a container for a single, repeatable element, <smLink>, which indicates a hyperlink between two nodes in the structural map. The <structLink> section in the METS document is identified using its XML ID attributes.
Element <behaviorSec>	A behavior section element <behaviorSec> associates executable behaviors with content in the METS document by means of a repeatable behavior <behavior> element. This element has an interface definition <interfaceDef> element that represents an abstract definition of the set of behaviors represented by a particular behavior section. A <behavior> element also has a <mechanism> element, which is used to point to a module of executable code that implements and runs the behavior defined by the interface definition. The <behaviorSec> element, which is repeatable as well as nestable, can be used to group individual behaviors within the structure of the METS document.
Element <techMD>	A technical metadata element <techMD> records technical metadata about a component of the METS object, such as a digital content file. The <techMD> element conforms to the same generic datatype as the <dmdSec>, <rightsMD>, <sourceMD>, and <digiprovMD> elements and supports the same subelements and attributes. A technical metadata element can either wrap the metadata (mdWrap) or reference it in an external location (mdRef) or both. METS allows multiple <techMD> elements, and technical metadata can be associated with any METS element that supports an ADMID attribute.
Element <rightsMD>	An intellectual property rights metadata element <rightsMD> records information about copyright and licensing pertaining to a component of the METS object. The <rightsMD> element conforms to same generic datatype as the <dmdSec>, <techMD>, <sourceMD>, and <digiprovMD> elements and supports the same subelements and attributes. A rights metadata element can either wrap the metadata (mdWrap) or reference it in an external location (mdRef) or both. METS allows multiple <rightsMD> elements, and rights metadata can be associated with any METS element that supports an ADMID attribute.
Element <sourceMD>	A source metadata element <sourceMD> records descriptive and administrative metadata about the source format or media of a component of the METS object such as a digital content file. It is often used for discovery, data administration, or preservation of the digital object. The <sourceMD> element conforms to same generic datatype as the <dmdSec>, <techMD>, <rightsMD>, and <digiprovMD> elements and supports the same subelements and attributes. A source metadata element can either wrap the metadata (mdWrap) or reference it in an external location (mdRef) or both. METS allows multiple <sourceMD> elements, and source metadata can be associated with any METS element that supports an ADMID attribute.

(Continued)

Table B.2   METS (Version 1.9) (*cont.*)

Types of Elements	Definition
Element <digiprovMD>	A digital provenance metadata element <digiprovMD> can be used to record any preservation-related actions taken on the various files that comprise a digital object (e.g., those subsequent to the initial digitization of the files such as transformation or migrations) or, in the case of born digital materials, the files' creation. In short, digital provenance should be used to record information that allows both archival/library staff and scholars to understand what modifications have been made to a digital object and/or its constituent parts during its lifecycle. This information can then be used to judge how those processes might have altered or corrupted the object's ability to accurately represent the original item. One might, for example, record master derivative relationships and the process by which those derivations have been created.
Element <file>	The file element <file> provides access to the content files for the digital object being described by the METS document. A <file> element may contain one or more <FLocat> elements that provide pointers to a content file and/or an <FContent> element that wraps an encoded version of the file. Embedding files using <FContent> can be a valuable feature for exchanging digital objects among repositories or for archiving versions of digital objects for off-site storage. All <FLocat> and <FContent> elements should identify and/or contain identical copies of a single file. The <file> element is recursive, thus allowing subfiles or component files of a larger file to be listed in the inventory.
Element <div>	The structural divisions of the hierarchical organization provided by a <structMap> are represented by division <div> elements, which can be nested to any depth. Each <div> element can represent either an intellectual (logical) division or a physical division. Every <div> node in the structural map hierarchy may be connected (via subsidiary <mptr> or <fptr> elements) to content files that represent that div's portion of the whole document.
Element <mptr>	Like the <fptr> element, the METS pointer element <mptr> represents digital content that manifests its parent <div> element. Unlike the <fptr >, which either directly or indirectly points to content represented in the <fileSec> of the parent METS document, the <mptr> element points to content represented by an external METS document. Thus, this element allows multiple discrete and separate METS documents to be organized at a higher level by a separate METS document.
Element <fptr>	The <fptr> or file pointer element represents digital content that manifests its parent <div> element. The content represented by an <fptr> element must consist of integral files or parts of files that are represented by <file> elements in the <fileSec>. Via its FILEID attribute, an <fptr> may point directly to a single integral <file> element that manifests a structural division. However, an <fptr> element may also govern an <area> element, a <par>, or a <seq>, which in turn would point to the relevant file or files. A child <area> element can point to part of a <file> that manifests a division, while the <par> and <seq> elements can point to multiple files or parts of files that together manifest a division.
Element <par>	The <par> or parallel files element aggregates pointers to files, parts of files, and/or sequences of files or parts of files that must be played or displayed simultaneously to manifest a block of digital content represented by an <fptr> element.
Element <smLink>	The Structural Map Link element <smLink> identifies a hyperlink between two nodes in the structural map. You would use <smLink>, for instance, to note the existence of hypertext links between web pages, if you wished to record those links within METS. NOTE: <smLink> is an empty element. The location of the <smLink> element to which the <smLink> element is pointing MUST be stored in the xlink:href attribute.

Table B.2   METS (Version 1.9) *(cont.)*

Types of Elements	Definition
Element <seq>	The sequence of files element <seq> aggregates pointers to files, parts of files and/or parallel sets of files, or parts of files that must be played or displayed sequentially to manifest a block of digital content.
Element <area>	The area element <area> typically points to content consisting of just a portion or area of a file represented by a <file> element in the <fileSec>.
Element <smLinkGrp>	The structMap link group element <smLinkGrp> provides an implementation of xlink:extendLink and provides xlink compliant mechanisms for establishing xlink:arcLink type links between two or more <div> elements in <structMap> element(s) occurring within the same METS document or different METS documents.
Element <smLocatorLink>	The structMap locator link element <smLocatorLink> is of xlink:type "locator." It provides a means of identifying a <div> element that will participate in one or more of the links specified by means of <smArcLink> elements within the same <smLinkGrp>.
Element <smArcLink>	Element <smArcLink> contained within <smLinkGrp>
Element <behavior>	A behavior element <behavior> can be used to associate executable behaviors with content in the METS document. This element has an interface definition <interfaceDef> element that represents an abstract definition of a set of behaviors represented by a particular behavior. A <behavior> element also has a behavior mechanism <mechanism> element, a module of executable code that implements and runs the behavior defined abstractly by the interface definition.
Element <interfaceDef>	The interface definition <interfaceDef> element contains a pointer to an abstract definition of a single behavior or a set of related behaviors that are associated with the content of a METS object.
Element <mechanism>	A mechanism element <mechanism> contains a pointer to an executable code module that implements a set of behaviors defined by an interface definition.
Element <mdRef>	The metadata reference element <mdRef> element is a generic element used throughout the METS schema to provide a pointer to metadata that resides outside the METS document.
Element <mdWrap>	A metadata wrapper element <mdWrap> provides a wrapper around metadata embedded within a METS document.
Element <binData>	The binary data wrapper element <binData> is used to contain Base64 encoded metadata.
Element <xmlData>	The xml data wrapper element <xmlData> is used to contain XML encoded metadata.
Element <FLocat>	The file location element <FLocat> provides a pointer to the location of a content file. It uses the XLink reference syntax to provide linking information indicating the actual location of the content file, along with other attributes specifying additional linking information. NOTE: <FLocat> is an empty element. The location of the resource pointed to MUST be stored in the xlink:href attribute.
Element <FContent>	The file content element <FContent> is used to identify a content file contained internally within a METS document. The content file must be either Base64 encoded and contained within the subsidiary <binData> wrapper element or consist of XML information and be contained within the subsidiary <xmlData> wrapper element.
Element <binData>	A binary data wrapper element <binData> is used to contain a Base64 encoded file.

(Continued)

Table B.2   METS (Version 1.9) (cont.)

Types of Elements	Definition
Element <xmlData>	An xml data wrapper element <xmlData> is used to contain an XML encoded file. The content of an <xmlData> element can be in any namespace or in no namespace. As permitted by the XML Schema Standard, the processContents attribute value for the metadata in an <xmlData> element is set to "lax." Therefore, if the source schema and its location are identified by means of an xsi:schemaLocation attribute and then an XML processor will validate the elements for which it can find declarations.
Element <stream>	A component byte stream element <stream> may be composed of one or more subsidiary streams. An MPEG4 file, for example, might contain separate audio and video streams, each of which is associated with technical metadata. The repeatable <stream> element provides a mechanism to record the existence of separate data streams within a particular file, and the opportunity to associate <dmdSec> and <amdSec> with those subsidiary data streams if desired.
Element <transformFile>	The transform file element <transformFile> provides a means to access any subsidiary files listed below a <file> element by indicating the steps required to "unpack" or transform the subsidiary files. This element is repeatable and might provide a link to a <behavior> in the <behaviorSec> that performs the transformation.

http://www.loc.gov/standards/mets/docs/mets.v1-9.html

Table B.3   TEI Header (Version 2.8.0)

Types of Elements	Definition	Example
titleStmt	(title statement) Groups information about the title of a work and those responsible for its content	
editionStmt	(edition statement) Groups information relating to one edition of a text	
extent	(extent) Describes the approximate size of a text stored on some carrier medium or of some other object, digital or nondigital, specified in any convenient units	
publicationStmt	(publication statement) Groups information concerning the publication or distribution of an electronic or other text	A publisher or distributor; licensing conditions; identifying numbers
seriesStmt	(series statement) Groups information about the series, if any, to which a publication belongs	
notesStmt	(notes statement) Collects together any notes providing information about a text additional to that recorded in other parts of the bibliographic description	Note; annotation
sourceDesc	(source description) Describes the source from which an electronic text was derived or generated, typically a bibliographic description in the case of a digitized text, or a phrase such as "born digital" for a text that has no previous existence	

Table B.3   TEI Header (Version 2.8.0) *(cont.)*

Types of Elements	Definition	Example
encodingDesc	(encoding description) Documents the relationship between an electronic text and the source or sources from which it was derived	
profileDesc	(text-profile description) Provides a detailed description of non-bibliographic aspects of a text, specifically the languages and sublanguages used, the situation in which it was produced and the participants and their setting	
revisionDesc	(revision description) Summarizes the revision history for a file	

TEI Header (http://www.tei-c.org/release/doc/tei-p5-doc/en/html/HD.html#HD21)

Table B.4   EAD Header Elements (Version 2002)

Types of Elements	Definition
<eadheader> EAD Header	A wrapper element for bibliographic and descriptive information about the finding aid document rather than the archival materials being described. The <eadheader> is modeled on the Text Encoding Initiative (TEI) header element to encourage uniformity in the provision of metadata across document types.
<eadid> EAD Identifier	A required subelement of <eadheader> that designates a unique code for a particular EAD finding aid document
<filedesc> File Description	A required subelement of the <eadheader> that bundles much of the bibliographic information about the finding aid, including its author, title, subtitle, and sponsor (all in the <titlestmt>), as well as the edition, publisher, publishing series, and related notes (encoded separately)
<profiledesc> Profile Description	An optional subelement of the <eadheader> that bundles information about the creation of the encoded version of the finding aid, including the name of the agent, place, and date of encoding. The <profiledesc> element also designates the predominant and minor languages used in the finding aid.
<revisiondesc> Revision Description	An optional subelement of the <eadheader> for information about changes or alterations that have been made to the encoded finding aid. The revisions may be recorded as part of a <list> or as a series of <change> elements. Like much of the <eadheader >, the <revisiondesc> element is modeled on an element found in the Text Encoding Initiative (TEI) DTD. The TEI recommends that revisions be numbered and appear in reverse chronological order, with the most recent <change> first.

For more EAD Elements: http://www.loc.gov/ead/tglib/element_index.html

EAD Elements: <eadheader> EAD Header (http://www.loc.gov/ead/tglib/elements/eadheader.html)

Table B.5   VRA Core (Version 4.0)

Types of Elements	Definition	Example
work, collection, or image	A choice of one of three elements, work, collection, or image, defines a VRA 4.0 record as describing a work (a built or created object), a collection (an aggregate of such objects), or an image (a visual surrogate of such objects)	
agent	The names, appellations, or other identifiers assigned to an individual, group, or corporate body that has contributed to the design, creation, production, manufacture, or alteration of the work or image	
cultural context	The name of the culture, people (ethnonym), or adjectival form of a country name from which a work, collection, or image originates, or the cultural context with which the work, collection, or image has been associated	
date	Date or range of dates associated with the creation, design, production, presentation, performance, construction, or alteration, etc. of the work or image. Dates may be expressed as free text or numerical.	
description	A free-text note about the work, collection, or image, including comments, description, or interpretation, that gives additional information not recorded in other categories	
inscription	All marks or written words added to the object at the time of production or in its subsequent history, including signatures, dates, dedications, texts, and colophons, as well as marks, such as the stamps of silversmiths, publishers, or printers	
location	The geographic location and/or name of the repository, building, site, or other entity whose boundaries include the work or image	Repository locations; creation locations; discovery locations
material	The substance of which a work or an image is composed	
measurements	The physical size, shape, scale, dimensions, or format of the work or image	
relation	Terms or phrases describing the identity of the related work and the relationship between the work being cataloged and the related work or image. Use this element to relate work records to other work or collection records or image records to work or collection records	
rights	Information about the copyright status and the rights holder for a work, collection, or image	
source	A reference to the source of the information recorded about the work or the image	
stateEdition	The identifying number and/or name assigned to the state or edition of a work that exists in more than one form and the placement of that work in the context of prior or later issuances of multiples of the same work	

Table B.5   VRA Core (Version 4.0) *(cont.)*

Types of Elements	Definition	Example
stylePeriod	A defined style, historical period, group, school, dynasty, movement, etc. whose characteristics are represented in the work or image	
subject	Terms or phrases that describe, identify, or interpret the work or image and what it depicts or expresses	
technique	The production or manufacturing processes, techniques, and methods incorporated in the fabrication or alteration of the work or image	
textref	Contains the name of a related textual reference and any type of unique identifier that text assigns to a work or collection that is independent of any repository	
title	The title or identifying phrase given to a work or an image	
worktype	Identifies the specific type of work, collection, or image being described in the record	

VRA Core 4.0 Element Description (http://www.loc.gov/standards/vracore/VRA_Core4_Element_Description.pdf)

Subject Index

Printed in the United States
By Bookmasters